Polish Law
Throughout the Ages

EDITED BY

Wenceslas J. Wagner

HOOVER INSTITUTION PRESS

Stanford University • Stanford, California

Hoover Institution Publications 91
Standard Book Number 8179-1911-2
Library of Congress Card Number 76-115759
Printed in the United States of America

HOOVER INSTITUTION PUBLICATIONS

Polish Law Throughout the Ages

Contents

Acknowledgments

Sincere thanks are due to all those who offered their knowledge, time, and effort to render this publication possible. In most cases, it meant much sacrifice, as most Polish jurists living abroad do not work in the field of Polish law any longer.

Clearly, it would have been much easier to write such a book in Poland, with access to available materials. The general editor is very pleased to state that he was able to secure the cooperation of excellent legal minds for his project: all the contributors are scholars of high standing and achievement. He is also much obliged to Elizabeth A. Palewski-Wellington, a New York lawyer, for volunteering to revise one of the chapters, to the great advantage of its style.

It was a very friendly gesture on the part of the Hoover Institution on War, Revolution and Peace to agree to publish the present volume in connection with the Polish Congress of Contemporary Science and Culture in Exile. I wish particularly to thank Professor Witold S. Sworakowski, Associate Director of the Hoover Institution, who was so prompt to lend complete understanding and support when this publishing venture was first proposed. The book will be of interest to anyone for whom developments in Poland, and more generally in Eastern and Central Europe, are not matters of indifference. For the law of a nation is a reflection of the spirit of that nation, its traditions, its beliefs and its entire cultural heritage. This volume deals with the history of the Polish law—but its contributors are not only lawyers; some are political scientists and economists. While a few chapters are more technical than others, all of them will be readily understood by a historian or a sociologist—or even by a scientist or a person not specializing in any field of knowledge. It may be hoped that for many participants in the Congress the book will be a cherished souvenir to which they will return from time to time.

When I submitted to the Polish Institute of Arts and Sciences in America a proposal to organize a congress similar in concept but limited to the New Continent, I dared not hope that the event would be so successful. That Congress took place in 1966 at Columbia University, with nearly six hundred participants in attendance. One hundred twenty-seven papers were read; fifteen sections were in session. Many scholars unable to come expressed their regrets. Besides the scholarly advantages they gained from the meeting, professors of Polish extraction meeting or hearing about one another came to realize the great extent of their contribution to the development of knowledge in the United States and Canada. The Congress also facilitated another project I submitted to the Institute—the publication of a list of scholars of Polish descent in North America.

I sincerely wish all possible success to the London Congress. My heartiest congratulations to the Organizing Committee, and warmest greetings to all participants.

Wenceslas J. Wagner

Contributors

VINCENT C. CHRYPIŃSKI is Professor of Political Science at the University of Windsor in Canada. For five years prior to World War II he was engaged in governmental service in Poland, where he also served two years of apprenticeship in the Polish Courts (*Aplikacja Sądowa*). He has published various articles dealing with Eastern Europe and several on Poland.

ARTHUR P. COLEMAN, now retired, has taught and lectured in modern and Slavic languages, primarily at Columbia University. He served for twelve years as president of Alliance College and is a past president of both the National Federation of Modern Languages Teachers Associations and the American Association of Teachers of Slavic and East European Languages. He is a foreign laureate of the Polish Academy of Literature and has written extensively on Polish and East European literatures and languages.

JURIJ FEDYNSKYJ was educated at Lwów University, Innsbruck University, Columbia University, and Indiana University. Before being appointed to his present position of Associate Professor of Law at Indiana University, he taught law of Slavic countries at the universities of Lwów, Innsbruck, and Graz. At Indiana University he is also Associate Law Librarian. For many years he was Secretary of the Ukrainian Shevchenko Scientific Society in New York. Among his publications are articles on Polish civil law.

CHARLES S. HAIGHT received a Doctor of Law degree from Harvard University after completing his undergraduate studies at Yale University. Until his death in 1968 he practiced law with the New York firm of Haight, Gardner, Poor & Havens.

BRONISŁAW HEŁCZYŃSKI is Professor at the Polish University Abroad in London. Formerly a Professor at Cracow University, he was also a member of the Polish Codification Commission and in this latter capacity he co-authored the Polish Commercial Code of 1934. From 1934 to 1939 he was the First President of the Supreme Administrative Tribunal of Poland. His Polish publications include: *Ubezpieczenie na cudzy rachunek* ("Insurance on Behalf of Another Person") and *Komercjalizacja przedsiębiorstw państwowych* ("Commercialization of the State Enterprises"). Some of his English works are: *The Underlying Principles of Polish Commercial Law*, *The Polish Scholar and Society*, and *The Polish Code of Administrative Procedure*.

LUDWIK KOS-RABCEWICZ-ZUBKOWSKI is Advocate of the Bar of Montreal, Vice President of the Canadian Inter-American Research Institute, and Professor of Criminal Law at the University of Ottawa. He was formerly Professor of Slavic Institutions and Civilizations at the University of Montreal as well as Associate of the Russian Research Center, Harvard University, and a Simon Senior Research Fellow at the University of Manchester in England. His many published works include *Le Règlement des différends internationaux relatifs à la navigation aérienne civile* (1948) and *East European Rules on the Validity of International Commercial Arbitration Agreements* (1969), as well as articles written in English, French and Spanish.

GEORGES S. LANGROD is Professor of Law at the Polish University Abroad, London, and Professor Emeritus of the Law Faculty of the University of Saarbrücken. In addition he serves as Research Director of the French Governmental Center for Scientific Research and as Vice Chairman, Section for Juridical and Political Sciences, of the French National Committee for Scientific Research. A former member of the Juridical Commission of the Polish Academy of Arts and Sciences in Cracow, he is currently a member of the International Institute of Political Philosophy in Paris. He has published a number of articles in both French and English journals.

JAROSŁAW A. PIEKAŁKIEWICZ is Associate Professor of Political Science and Slavic and Soviet Area Studies at the University of Kansas. He was educated at Trinity College, University of Dublin, and at Indiana University. Between 1961 and 1963 he was a Ford Foundation Fellow and spent a year in Poland studying Polish local administration. In the 1968-1969 academic year he engaged in research under a senior fellowship of the Inter-University Committee on Travel Grants. He is the author of the forthcoming book, *Communism Viewed from Below: A Study of*

Polish Local Government, as well as of articles on Polish administration and politics of East Central Europe.

WACŁAW W. SOROKA, a graduate of the Catholic University in Lublin, Louvain University, and Indiana University, is Professor of History at Wisconsin State University, Stevens Point. He attended the Preparatory Session of the European College in Bruges and has conducted research at the Jagiellonian University in Cracow under the direction of Professor Stanislaw Kutrzeba. His publications include numerous articles on recent Eastern and Central European history.

RICHARD SZAWŁOWSKI, Associate Professor of Political Science at the University of Calgary in Canada, received his Doctor of Law degree from Warsaw University and a Diplôme supérieur de droit comparé from the International University of Comparative Studies in Luxembourg. He held a Senior Research Fellowship at the Alexander-von-Humboldt Foundation in West Germany, was a Research Scholar at the University of Glasgow Institute of Soviet and East European Studies, and later was Senior Research Officer of the German Federal Institute of Sovietology in Cologne. He has written many articles on state control and public finance and a book, *Les finances et le droit financier d'une organization internationale intergouvernementale,* is forthcoming.

WACŁAW SZYSZKOWSKI is Professor of Constitutional Law at Copernicus University in Toruń, Poland, where he has been Dean of the Faculty of Law since 1969. Among his publications are a number of articles on the history of law and the book, *International Agreements and Municipal Law* (1964).

MICHALINA VAUGHAN received her Doctor of Law degree from the University of Paris and is presently Lecturer in Sociology at the London School of Economics. She has contributed several articles on law and social order to British periodicals.

WOJCIECH WASIUTYŃSKI received a Doctor of Law degree from Warsaw University and is currently Deputy Chief of the Polish Desk for Radio Free Europe in New York. He is a member of the Polish Arts and Sciences Institute in America. In addition to being a reviewer of books on Polish medieval law for the Polish emigré press, he has written several books on cultural and political topics. He is the author of *Regal młynny w średniowiecznym prawie polskim* ("The King's Share of the Mills in Polish Medieval Law") and, more recently, of *Nowy Świat* (Essays on Contemporary American Life).

W. J. WAGNER is Professor of Law at Indiana University and is a member of the Indiana Bar. Before going to Indiana University he taught at Fordham and Northwestern Universities, the University of Notre Dame, and as visiting professor at Cornell University and the Universities of Paris and Rennes. He now serves as Vice President of the American Foreign Law Association, as Director of the American Association for the Comparative Study of Law, and as a member of the Board of Editors of the American Journal of Comparative Law. He has made more than 100 contributions to legal literature, including two books: *Les libertés de l'air* (1947) and *The Federal States and Their Judiciary* (1959).

WENCESLAS J. WAGNER

Introduction

In 1966, Poland celebrated her millennium: one thousand years of Christianity. Although her history is much longer, and some of her earliest citizens had been baptized previously, 966 marked a turning point in her development: it was then that the ruler of the country, Mieczysław I, decided to accept the new faith for himself and the whole nation, proclaimed Christianity as the official Polish religion, and invited foreign missionaries to spread the new doctrine. He exemplified his fervor by personally destroying some statues of Slavic gods.

Wedged between powerful enemies, Poland found progress and development difficult; repeatedly she was forced to defend her independence and territorial integrity against foreign attacks and interference. However, her baptism stabilized her status as a member of the community of Western nations and at the same time deprived German chieftains of the pretext that their invasions were prompted by the desire to convert their eastern neighbor.

Celebrations of the Polish millennium began as early as 1960 and came to a climax in 1966. They were exemplified by hundreds of projects undertaken all over the world by the Poles, by foreign citizens of Polish descent, by non-Polish groups, and even by foreign governments. Such projects ranged from the issuance of a commemorative stamp in the United States to the publication of many books and articles, to speeches, meetings, conventions, festivals, and congresses. Unfortunately, and against the wishes of the nation's people, the communist government of Poland did everything possible to minimize the occasion, fearing that it might indirectly strengthen the position of the Church, Poland's staunchest opponent of communism and the greatest exponent of the Polish Western heritage. The long-planned visit of the Polish Primate, Cardinal Wyszyński, to the United States, which was to have been a highlight of the celebrations on this side of the ocean, was rendered

1

impossible by the refusal of the Polish government to grant him a passport. Similarly, another project was cancelled: the pilgrimage of the Pope himself to the famous Black Madonna of Czestochowa — a visit which would have made history as the first trip of the Holy Father to a communist country. Polish visas were also refused to thousands of persons, of both Polish and non-Polish origin, including cardinals and bishops. Celebrations of the millennium organized by the Polish government disregarded its most salient aspect: a thousand years of Polish association with the West; indeed, since 966 Poland has become the eastern outpost of Western culture, and her eastern frontier is the border between two worlds. In the centuries following her conversion, Poland became the most Latinized country in Europe, and the Jagiellonian University in Cracow, established in 1364 (and thus much older than any German or Russian university), spread Christian learning in many Central and East European countries.

The present volume has been designed as commemoration of the millennium by the legal profession. Despite the enormous interest of the Western world in Slavic nations, and despite the fact that Polish history is often both unique and thrilling and that her legal development often progressive and instructive, is well worth studying, there has been no previous publication in English covering the history of Polish law. This book is intended to fill this important gap in legal literature.

The idea of publishing such a work occurred to the general editor as early as 1959. The period of its preparation lasted longer than expected. Some legal scholars asked to contribute were for various reasons unable to accept the invitation. Others, unable to prepare their studies, were replaced, but in a few cases the originally planned topics had to be abandoned. A few studies took longer than anticipated. But at last the book is here, and the authors are glad to submit it to the general public.

The contributors were given freedom regarding the length of their contributions, their approach, and the format which they wished to use. The use of standard terms was not sought, nor have bibliographies been requested for the use of legal comparatists. It is common knowledge that most foreign law terms defy accurate translation, and it was thought best to give the reader a selection of terms from which he might draw his own conclusions. The general editor felt that his central duty was to provide coverage for all the important areas. Some overlapping of subject matter has been permitted, so that the reader will find comments of more than one author on a few points. Each chapter has been written to stand by itself.

Aside from their technical interest, the legal and constitutional developments of such a country as Poland are of general cutural and historical importance. To people who know little of the Polish heritage, the present volume will be revealing. They may be surprised to learn that Poland was a pioneer in the development of modern democratic institutions and that in many respects she was more progressive than any other nation. Thus as early as 1430 the Privilege of Jedlna, known as *Neminem captivabimus*, guaranteed to the Polish nobility freedom from arbitrary arrest and confiscation of property, while the celebrated English *Habeas Corpus* Act was not enacted until 1689, and similar protection was not proclaimed in other countries until much later — in some, only in the twentieth century. Thus in France, until the end of the *ancien régime*, the king could deliver *lettres de cachet* — blank arrest warrants to his favorites for their use against personal enemies.

In the fifteenth century, the Polish parliamentary system was also developed. While in other nations such as France, Germany, and Spain — not to mention Russia — the power of the rulers remained absolute for centuries, the authority of the monarchs in Poland had been limited in some ways from the very beginning of her history. By the Privilege of Kosice, in 1374, the imposition of taxes by the king without the consent of the nobles was prohibited. The Statute of Nieszawa in 1454 imposed further restrictions on the individual power of the king, and that of Piotrków in 1496 finally established a parliamentary system of government. The constitution *Nihil novi* of 1505 proclaimed that the king would enact no new laws without the consent of the parliament: an achievement without parallel in this early period. The constitutional character of Poland's monarchy, in which the power of the king was strictly limited, was further reinforced at the end of the sixteenth century by the *Pacta Conventa*, by virtue of which the kings had to reaffirm all existing laws and privileges and promise to respect them. Should a king fail to fulfill this obligation, the nation could denounce him and refuse to recognize his authority.

While most other countries held the belief that a monarch's power was bestowed upon him by the Almighty alone, so that a royal title was usually preceded with the words, "By the grace of God," the Poles, always deeply religious, supplemented the phrase with "and the will of the nation." Indeed, the principle that the national sovereignty belongs to the whole nation, not to one individual, was put into practice at the end of the fourteenth century, when kingship became elective. For two centuries, members of the Jagiellonian dynasty were always elected to the position, but when the dynasty became extinct, all nobles became eligible. Indeed, a few of the later monarchs were of rather modest descent. The Polish monarchy was called a Republic of the Nobles; it was unique in the history of mankind. The general belief was that this system was the best safeguard for the famous Polish *złota wolność* ("golden freedom") and that the highest office in the state should be held by a person who had proven his qualities and capacities. Thus, the position of the king in the constitutional monarchy of Poland was comparable to that of a state president elected for life.

Coexistent with political democracy was the deeply embedded tradition of religious tolerance. Poland has been a predominantly Catholic nation during the whole course of her history. But she permitted non-Christians, such as the Moslems and the Jews, to settle freely in the country. The great influx of Jews began in the fourteenth century during the reign of Casimir the Great, who granted them special privileges and guaranteed freedom of worship at a time when they were terribly persecuted in other countries, including England, where in many instances they were buried alive in their synagogues. It is not surprising that for many years, until Hitler exterminated the Polish Jewry, the percentage of Jews in Poland was higher than that in any other country in the world.

Another striking result of the Polish spirit of religious freedom was the fact that, while religious disputes and wars raged in all the great European nations from the time of the Reformation on, such struggles were unknown in Poland. The principle that no one could be prosecuted for his religious beliefs (not articulated in France, for instance, until 1791) had always been recognized in Poland. Said the great Catholic statesman, Jan Zamoyski, Chancellor of the Crown in the sixteenth century: "I would give half of my life if those who have abandoned the Roman Catholic church would voluntarily return to its pale; but I would prefer giving all my life than to suffer anybody to be constrained to do it, for I would rather die than witness such an oppression."[1]

A further outstanding feature of Polish history is the fact that for centuries she did not wage aggressive wars. She knew how to defend herself and how to deal with aggression; her armies would not only repel invasion but pursue the enemy deep into its own territory. The Polish army was at times in Moscow, in Prague, and in various German towns, but her presence was always the consequence of foreign aggression and not of Polish lust for foreign possessions.

True, for a long time Poland was the biggest and most powerful country in Europe (especially in the sixteenth century), and the kingdom included territories not inhabited by Poles. However, the extension of the state was brought about, curiously enough, by peaceful means, through voluntary unions with other nations. The most famous of these was the union with Lithuania, brought about by the *Unja Krewska* ("Union of Krewo") in 1387, and reinforced in Horodło in 1413. By the Union of Lublin in 1569, the two nations decided to establish a state in which each maintained a high degree of autonomy

---

[1]Lednicki, *Life and Culture of Poland as Reflected in Polish Literature* (1944), p. 47.

4

while delegating common problems to a central authority. It appears that the Polish-Lithuanian union constituted the first federal state in the world. It existed until Poland was partitioned at the end of the eighteenth century.

The Polish Commonwealth fought against aggression and defended freedom and independence not only for herself, but also for those who needed her help. For centuries Polish armies struggled with barbaric hoards of infidels, Turks and Tartars, throughout central Europe and the Balkans. Many times they saved the continent from Asiatic invaders. Not only did thousands of ordinary Polish soldiers give their lives for the defense of Christian nations, but also scores of military leaders, such as the famous Commander-in-Chief Zółkiewski in 1620. Even kings, who often personally led their armies to the fight, perished on the field of glory. Thus, Henryk Pobożny (Henry the Pious) was killed at the battle of Lignica in 1241, and Władysław Warneńczyk at the battle of Warna, in distant Bulgaria, in 1444. Probably the most famous of the Polish struggles against the infidels was the defense of Vienna by the King John III Sobieski in 1683, when the power of Turkey was checked and her army forced to retreat. The role that Poland played in these battles merited her the honorable name of the "Bulwark of Christianity."

Poland was one of those rare countries where there were no devastating civil wars and where not a single king was killed by his own nation – a considerable contrast with Italy, for instance, where few princes escaped the threat of poison, and Russia, where in the two centuries before the Revolution nearly all the tsars were murdered.

It must be observed, of course, that during most of her history the Polish "golden freedom" and democratic institutions could be fully enjoyed only by a minority of the population: the nobles. Until very recent times, this was true in all European countries. The percentage of nobles in Poland was, however, very high in comparison with that in other nations. It was estimated that the nobility constituted from 10 to 14 percent of the entire Polish population, while in France, for example, the nobles made up only one-tenth of 1 percent, and in early ninteenth century England the electors formed less than 2 percent of the population.

As for Polish peasants, their situation was generally better than in other European countries. Although their obligations increased over the centuries, such duties were still lighter than those imposed in Germany, and the scope of their liberties was broader than in England. Instances of foreign peasants who took refuge in Poland were not uncommon. Even before the Constitution of May 3, 1791, granted to the peasants freedom and the full protection of the law, a number of landlords voluntarily had emancipated their subjects.

The downfall of Poland — the country was partitioned between her powerful neighbors, Russia, Prussia, and Austria at the end of the eighteenth century — occurred during a spectacular renaissance of her moral and intellectual strength. The external causes were evident: she was overpowered by the three militaristic, well-organized, and absolutist nations.

Historians, however, have in the past asserted that internal factors contributed to the tragedy: that the excesses and abuses of democracy had brought about Poland's weakness, and that at the time of crisis it was too late to restore her old might and ability to resist. In particular, it is often said that the constitutional principle of *liberum veto*, which required unanimity for adopting resolutions of the parliament, was a factor in preventing the country from keeping abreast of her neighbors. That such a principle was unreasonable can hardly be gainsaid. For a long time, however, it did not bring about any disastrous results; while it was in force, the country lived through its "Golden Age" of cultural development and became a leading power in Europe. The idealistic philosophy of the age was that the laws of the nation should not be changed lightly and that the minority should be protected against the wishes of the majority. The rules established by past generations were to remain in force unless their impracticality was recognized by everyone. In practice, the minority did not generally take advantage of its veto power until the middle of the seventeenth century. In the centuries preceding, it was traditional for the minority to yield.

By way of comparison, it is interesting to note the custom of some of the ancient Greek city-states, in which the proponent of a new law was supposed to bring to the town meeting a rope with which to hang himself if his motion were defeated.

The rule of unanimity may, nevertheless, seem absurd to us, but there are modern parallels. How can one defend the American practice of the filibuster, by which a recalcitrant legislator is permitted to frustrate the expectations of the entire nation and render impossible orderly proceedings in Congress by speaking or reading irrelevant material for hours in order to prevent a bill from being passed? On the international scene, the requirement of unanimity in the League of Nations, and now the veto power of the great countries in the United Nations, present other examples of legal practice which will be condemned by future generations as unreasonable and retrogressive.

By surveying the Polish constitutional and legal system during the period of her grandeur, the reader will learn of the plight of the Poles under oppressive laws by the foreign powers during the century and a half of her subjugation. With the suppression of every national uprising, further oppressive rules were enacted by her conquerors, but the Polish nation did not lose her indomitable spirit of liberty and her craving for independence. In ancient times the Poles had repelled Asiatic invaders to save other Christian nations; now they were struggling against absolutist tyranny over their own nation. Throughout their history, the Poles could say: "We are fighting for our freedom – and yours."

A short period of independence between the two world wars was followed by the delivery of Poland to her eastern neighbor, who imposed on her a communist system of government against the desires of the vast majority of the population. Poland, the first nation among the Allies to succumb to invasion, by Germany and Soviet Russia, gained at the beginning of World War II the nickname of the "Inspiration of Nations," but was abandoned by her opportunist friends.[2] The constitutional and legal rules enacted under the new regime are contrary to Polish traditions and beliefs and will be discarded at the first opportunity. The official doctrine of class struggle and hatred will be replaced by that of love and mutual understanding, in the internal relations of Poland as well as in her attitude toward other nations. Such humanistic beliefs are characteristic of the Polish heritage and are well exemplified by the following excerpt (translated here from Latin) from the Polish-Lithuanian Union of Horodło (1413) – a truly remarkable document:

> It is known to all that the grace of redemption will not be bestowed on those who are not moved by the secrets of love – love which does not act haphazardly, but emanates rays of charity, settles controversies, unites adversaries, abolishes hatred, cancels anger, and gives peace to all; it assembles that which is scattered, comforts the discouraged, evens the bumpy, straightens out what is slanted, supports all virtues and does not harm any one; it cherishes everything, and if someone takes refuge under its wings, will find security and will not fear any attack from anywhere. Owing to it, laws are established, kingdoms governed, towns organized, and the Polish Commonwealth achieves her highest goals: it excellently inspires all virtues, and he who should repudiate it, will lose everything.

[2] See Arthur Bliss Lane (former American Ambassador to Poland), *I Saw Poland Betrayed* (1948).

WACŁAW W. SOROKA

Historical Studies of Polish Law

The historical evolution of Polish law has scarcely been noticed in the English-speaking countries.[1] It surely deserves more attention, since scholarly interests and daily experience are now extending far beyond the Germanic-Latin family of nations. What little is known on the subject of Polish law stems from general historical treatises or from publications in

[1] A general, up-to-date treatment in English of Slavic law, including Polish law, can be found in an article by Stanisław Kutrzeba, in the *Encyclopaedia of Social Science*, s. v. "Law, Slavic." Feodor F. Zigel's *Lectures on Slavonic Law, Being the Ilchester Lectures for the Year 1900* (London: H. Frowde, and New York: Oxford University Press, 1902) contains a chapter on Polish Law (p. 100-36). Although the book is antiquated and now of small value, it remains the only monograph in English in the field. John Henry Wigmore's *A Panorama of the World's Legal Systems*, 3 vols. (Saint Paul: West Publishing Company, 1928) includes in Vol. II a chapter on Slavic legal systems (Bohemia, Poland, Yugoslavia, and Russia). *Studies in Polish and Comparative Law; a Symposium*, published by the Polish Lawyers' Association in the United Kingdom (London: Stevens & Sons, 1945), and *Polamerican Law Journal*, a periodical published from June 1938 to August 1941, in Chicago by the National Association of Polish American Bar, both include some articles dealing wholly or in part with the history of Polish law. Occasionally, one can find interesting articles on particular problems in legal periodicals.

In the *Cambridge History of Poland*, 2 vols. (Cambridge: University Press, 1941-50) two chapters – "Constitutional Conditions in the Fifteenth and Sixteenth Centuries," by J. Siemieński (I, 416-40); and "The Constitution of Poland Before Partitions," by Paweł Skwarczyński (II, 49-71) present some information about Polish law. The last contains a paragraph on "The Judicial Organization" directly related to the topic of this paper.

In recent times, Polish monographic as well as periodical publications have often been supplied with English summaries along with Russian, French, or German ones. A monthly, *Państwo i Prawo* (Warsaw), which occasionally treats historical problems, inserts English, French, and Russian summaries in the form of separate

other Western languages, mainly French and German, devoted to political history of Poland.[2] As a result, the history of Polish political, social, and administrative institutions is better known than the history of Polish private or criminal law.[3]

However, there exists in Poland a library of sophisticated historical studies of Polish law in all its aspects as well as of other Slavic, European, and non-European laws. Many factors are responsible for this development. One has been the inclusion of Polish and foreign legal history in law school curricula and the study of certain legal elements in Polish university history departments. Among such elements have been the political, social, and administrative organization of the state; parlamentarianism; the position of the king; the organization of the judiciary; and other constitutional matters.

The Polish law schools have taught legal history as an element of professional training as well as of general historical education and culture. Courses required of a Polish law student include: History of Political and Social Institutions of Poland, as well as the History of Polish Private Law—a course which embraces Polish and other private law in force in the territory of Poland, criminal law, and civil and criminal procedures. All these fields are now treated jointly as an interrelated process of legal evolution.[4] The required program also includes a survey of corresponding

supplements. Summaries in Western and Russian languages are included in *Czasopismo Prawno-Historyczne* ("Legal Historical Review") (Poznań).

There is no comparison between the number of studies on the history of Western European law available in English, and those on Polish, Slavic, or other Central and East European legal history, including Russian, although the last has aroused more interest, particularly in recent times. A series called *The Continental Legal History* (Boston: Little, Brown, 1918) devoted separate volumes to French, Italian, and German law but no chapter on Polish law can be found there. It also might be worthwhile to mention that neither the *Encyclopedia Americana* nor the *Britannica* includes any entry on these subjects, although they provide their readers with articles on French, German, and other laws.

[2]Concerning historical studies, see: Oskar Halecki, "Problems of Polish Historiography," *The Slavonic and East European Review,* American series, II (1942-43), 223-39; and Piotr Wandycz, "The Treatment of East Central Europe in History Textbooks," *The American Slavic and East European Review,* XVI (1957), 515-23.

[3]Oswald P. Backus III, in his "The Problem of Feudalism in Lithuania, 1506-1548," *Slavic Review,* XXI (1962), 639-59, emphasizes the need for thorough knowledge of the history of law in historical studies on Lithuania and Russia. The same point is raised in relation to the Polish-Lithuanian Union in his "The Problem of Unity in the Polish-Lithuanian State," *Slavic Review,* XXII (1963), 411-31 and 450-55.

[4]The treatise, *Historia państwa i prawa Polski* ("History of the State and Law of Poland"), being published by the Polish Academy of Sciences under the general

10

historical sources and literature as they appear in the course of institutional evolution. In addition, courses in such subjects as Roman law, Church law (since 1948-49 called Denominational Laws of the State), and the history of law in Western Europe (now called Universal History of State and Law) form a part of every law student's required historical studies.[5]

A strong trend toward the consideration of legal studies as merely professional training rather than academic education was evident from editorship of Juliusz Bardach (in cooperation with Z. Kaczmarczyk, B. Leśnodorski, J. Banaszkiewicz, T. Cieślak, K. Grzybowski, K. Koranyi, K. Pośpieszalski, J. Sawicki, W. Sobociński, and Z. Zdrójkowski) (Warsaw: Państwowe Wydawnictwo Naukowe, 1957-62), includes all the fields of Polish law in their development throughout Polish history. It is considered a standard work applying the Marxist method in an historical study of the Polish state and law. By now volumes I and II, and part I of volume V have appeared; the last discusses the period 1918-39. The publication is to be in five volumes. The second edition began to appear in 1964. An excellent bibliography, brought up to date, is included, although without publishers mentioned.

[5]Historical law studies at the Polish law schools have constituted a considerable portion of their curricula in all four branches: History of Roman Law, Polish Law, European Law, and Church Law. Wiktor Hahn's *Kronika Uniwersytetu Lwowskiego* ("Chronicle of Lwów University") (Lwów, 1912), II, 304-46, lists such courses as Roman Law, History of Western European Law, Histories of Polish and German Law, Polish Law, and Polish Constitutional Law. Between two world wars, they were taught the History of Roman Law (Institutions, Family Law, Property Law, Inheritance: 180 hours), and the History of Polish Law (State Organization, Polish Private Law, Judicial Procedure, Lithuanian Law, Commonors' Law: 180 hours). The History of West-European Law included the History of State, the Organization of Roman Countries, and the History of West-European Law. Church history covered universal and particular laws as well as the sources. See: *Program wykładów oraz skład Uniwersytetu w roku akad., 1932-33* ("Program of Courses and Index of the University") (Lwów: Uniwersytet Jana Kazimierza, 1932), p. 8. At Cracow University, specific additions were: History of State Organization of Polish Land after the Partitions, Polish Private Law, and Old Polish Judicial Law (criminal law and procedures). Courses on the History of Law in Western Europe conducted historical comparative studies of the beginnings of Western states and of their criminal and private law. The history of the sources of Polish law received heavy stress. (See: *Spis wykładów na rok 1923-24 a 1935-36,* ("Index of Lectures for the Year 1923-24 and 1935-36"), issued by Cracow University.)

A thorough although extremely concise description of historical studies in Poland was given by Professor Adam Vetulani in his *Dzieje historii prawa w Polsce* ("A History of the History of Law in Poland"), a publication issued by the Polish Academy of Arts and Sciences (PAU), as Vol. XVII-a in its series, *Historia Nauki Polskiej w Monografiach* ("Monographic History of Polish Learning"). Also see Michał Sczaniecki, "Nauczanie historii prawa w Polsce," *Czasopismo Prawno-Historyczne,* IX (1957), 399-402.

11

1945 to 1954. Separate training schools under the authority of the Ministry of Justice were created to produce candidates for state attorneyship and judgeship after six months' training.[6] This lowering of standards did not prevail. The university law schools in Poland maintain their traditional curricula, slightly adapted to the new situation and needs.[7] A broad liberal arts education and basic training in all disciplines of law are required from the whole legal profession in Poland. There is no doubt, however, that lawyers must submit to the uniform socialistic concepts of state and law, as well as to the all-embracing Marxist outlook on law.[8]

[6] Jerzy Jodłowski, "Akcja szkolenia kadr wymiaru sprawiedliwości," *Demokratyczny Przegląd Prawniczy,* II, No. 7 (July 1946) (special issue), 28-36. He quotes a decree of January 22, 1946 [*Dziennik Ustaw Rzeczypospolitej Polskiej,* ("Official Journal of Laws of the Polish Republic"), No. 4, Item 33, 1946]. The first session of such schools started on April 1, 1946. The project proved to be a failure.

The question of professional training was reflected in changes of law school curricula in Poland and the creation of three branches of legal study: civil law, criminal law, and administrative law, based however on a common background which included the history of state and law, Polish and universal. By 1954-55, the Cracow University Catalog, *Spis wykładów* (Cracow: Uniwersytet Jagielloński, 1955), had abandoned the changes and stated that "legal studies are uniform studies that last four years. There is no division into special curricula at the law schools." All the law students had to be prepared professionally for all three branches of the legal profession as well as for independent research. In 1957-58, examinations on history and geography were introduced to the candidates in the law schools. Some concern about this problem was reflected in the article "Teaching in the Polish Law School," by J. Wróblewski, *Northwestern Law Review,* LVII (Mar.-Apr. 1962), 54. Also see: "Dyskusja w Komitecie Nauk Prawnych *PAN* poświęcona sytuacji w nauce prawa" ("Discussion in the Committee of Legal Sciences of the *PAN* on the Situation in Teaching Law"), *Państwo i Prawo,* XI, No. 8-9 (Sept. 1956), 385-91.

[7] In the course, Universal History of State and Law, careful attention is given to the history and systems of law in the United States and in the Anglo-Saxon countries. For example, a textbook written by Professor Karol Koranyi, *Powszechna historia państwa i prawa* ("Universal History of the State and Law") (second edition; Warsaw: Państwowe Wydawnictwo Naukowe, 1952), contains in Vol. III, part 1, an article entitled, "England from the XVII to the Second Half of the XVIII Century," and in Vol. III, part 2, "The United States up to the End of the XVIII Century," with bibliographic information and scholarly materials for which the students are responsible.

[8] This idea was expressed clearly by a leading Marxist historian of Polish law, Juliusz Bardach, in "Nauka prawa w pierwszym dziesięcioleciu Polski ludowej, 1944-1954," ("Teaching of Law in the First Ten Years of People's Poland, 1944-1954"), *Nauka Polska,* II, No. 3, 42-87. "In bourgeois landlords' Poland," he wrote, "the entire legal science had been holding an idealistic position. ...A considerable majority of

This Marxist outlook on law requires "the acceptance that law as a part of the superstructure depends entirely on the economic basis and system of production. . . . .The real character of state and law was made clear by the Marxist doctrine that showed the state as an instrument of compulsion serving the ruling class, and law as an expression of the stately will of this class. In this way the real role of the exploitative state and law as an instrument of oppression of the laboring masses has been unmasked."[9]

Apparently, Polish scholars achieved quite a degree of skill in defense of this Marxist method.[10] The factual aspect of their studies is unbiased and scholarly,[11] so that the ideological concepts of Marxist interpretation seem to be a questionable addition to what is basically responsible

research staff up to 1948 did not understand the need for studying the Marxist-Leninist theory. In the sphere of theoretical problems, they did not go beyond submission to the reactionary legal 'theories' such as: psychologism, normativism, neothomism, solidarism, and legal positivism."

On the schools of legal thought in Poland, see: Kazimierz Opałek and Władysław Wolter, *Nauka filozofii prawa karnego w Polsce* ("Teaching Philosophy of Penal Law in Poland") (Cracow: Polska Akademia Umiejętności, 1948); and Ludwik Ehrlich and Jerzy Stefan Langrod, *Zarys historii prawa narodów, politycznego i administracyjnego w Polsce* ("An Outline History of the International, Political and Administrative Law in Poland") (Cracow: Polska Akademia Umiejętności, 1949), issued respectively as Vols. XVII-b and XVII-d of *Historia Nauki Polskiej w Monografiach* ("Monographic History of Polish Learning by Polish Academy of Arts and Sciences").

[9]Bardach, *ibid.,* p. 43. In the curricula of the law schools in 1954-55 were included such required subjects as: Foundations of Marxism and Leninism, and Dialectical and Historical Materialism. Interpretation and extent in application of this method underwent strong criticism in 1956 and 1957.

[10]Bardach, in the above-mentioned article, points to some names of the historians of law whom he considered full-fledged Marxists, others whom he thought beginners, and some branded as non-Marxists. Also see his article, "Perspektywy rozwoju nauki historii państwa i prawa," ("Perspectives in the Development of Teaching History of State and Law"), *Czasopismo Prawno-Historyczne,* III (1951), 1-11, in which he refers to Stalin's teaching on linguistics as the source of orientation for historians of law.

[11]Complaints have been raised by some younger scholars that the standards of scholarship in the legal professions was lowered in Poland in the 1950's. On this topic see the discussion at the Committee of Juridical Sciences of the Polish Academy of Sciences (Polska Akademia Nauk), *Państwo i Prawo,* XI, No. 8-9, 382. Also see Gustaw Auscaler, "Aktualne zagadnienia ideologiczne nauki prawa," ("The Present Ideological Problems in Teaching Law") *Państwo i Prawo,* XI, No. 7, 3-21. He says, "The basic question is, however, that the Soviet theory by the mere fact that it is Soviet, not necessarily has to be automatically correct and convincing."

13

scholarship.[12] There is much added interest in new fields of study and such new problems as the historical situation of peasants, burghers, and workers. An ensuing strong concern for social justice resulting from such studies might enrich the democratic culture and humanistic prospects of the nation.

Another institutional factor that contributed to the development of historical studies in Polish law was the creation of a number of Polish learned societies during the nineteenth century, partly for the study of Poland's past. The most prestigious was the Academy of Arts and Sciences, born of the Cracow Learned Society in 1872; it was called the Polish Academy of Arts and Sciences *(Polska Akademia Umiejętności,* or *PAU).* It was dissolved in 1951 and superseded by the Polish Academy of Sciences *(Polska Akademia Nauk, or PAN).* The *PAN* maintains its offices abroad, as did the *PAU* prior to its dissolution.[14]

Since the end of the nineteenth century, Polish learned societies have been founded in larger cities over the entire territory of the former Polish Commonwealth. The interwar period of Poland's independence contributed further to their development.[15]

[12]Probably the most convincing general criticism of the dogmatic application of the Marxist method in research and studies in Poland was formulated by Kazimierz Ajdukiewicz in his "O wolności nauki" ("Freedom of Learning"), *Nauka Polska* ("Polish Learning"), III (July-Sept. 1957), 1-20. A very interesting discussion of historical studies in contemporary Poland was supplied by Professor Marian Kukiel in his "Historiografia w Kraju," ("Historiography in Poland") *Teki Historyczne,* VIII (1956-57), 192-202.

[13]Stanislaw Kutrzeba, *Polska Akademia Umiejętności, 1872-1938* (Kraków, 1939).

[14]Bronisław Biliński, "Rzymska Stacja Naukowa PAN i polskie tradycje naukowe w Rzymie," ("The Roman Study Center of *PAN* and Polish Learning Traditions in Rome"), *Nauka Polska* ("Polish Learning"), XI, No. 1 (Jan.-Feb. 1963), 91-112; and Janusz Lech Jakubowski, "Polska Stacja Naukowa w Paryżu," ("The Polish Study Center in Paris"), *Nauka Polska* XI, No. 2 (Mar.-Apr. 1963), 99-102.

[15]The first Polish learned society was active in Cracow from 1488 to 1490 as the *Sodalitas Literaria Vistulana,* with Conrad Celtes and Philippo Buonacorsi (Kalimach) as members. On the activities of the Warsaw Learned Society since 1770, and on other associations of this type, see Bogdan Suchodolski, *Rola Towarzystwa Warszawskiego Przyjaciół Nauk w rozwoju kultury umysłowej w Polsce* ("The Role of the Warsaw Society of Friends of Learning in the Development of Intellectual Culture in Poland") (Warsaw: Nakł. Towarzystwa Naukowego Warszawskiego, 1951), and its review by Antonina Kłosowska, *Nauka Polska* ("Polish Learning") I, No. 1 (Jan.-Mar. 1953), 207-13.

Activities of Polish learned societies, including the study of Polish law, are discussed in numerous articles published by *Nauka Polska, Przegląd Nauk Historycznych i Społecznych* ("Survey of Historical and Social Sciences"), and other periodicals.

14

Besides local organizations of this type, others were created for special purposes.[16] The Polish Historical Association *(Polskie Towarzystwo Historyczne)* came into existence in 1886[17] and extended its organizational activities to some thirty-one centers. Since 1939, for various reasons, Polish historical learned societies have pursued research and developed studies in foreign countries–especially in Great Britain, the United States, France, and Italy.[18] Such studies have dealt with the history of Polish law within an historical, philosophical, and social framework. Often special departments, institutes, committees, and sections have been organized exclusively for study of the subject. For this purpose the *PAU* established its Legal Commission *(Komisja Prawnicza).* In 1952 the *PAN* created a Committee of Legal Studies *(Komitet Nauk Prawnych),* and, in 1956, an Institute of Legal Studies with departments studying the History of Polish State and Law and the Universal History of State and Law. The last two subjects were finally placed under control of the Historical Institute of the *PAN.*[19] The work accomplished resulted in a special series of studies in legal history and in the publication of historical sources.[20] Their main themes included the history of Polish law

[16]*Instytut Śląski* (The Silesian Institute) (Opole), *Śląski Instytut Naukowy* (The Silesian Scientific Institute) (Katowice), *Instytut Bałtycki* (The Baltic Institute) (Gdańsk), *Instytut Zachodni* (The Western Institute) (Poznań), *Żydowski Instytut Historyczny* (The Jewish Historical Institute) (Cracow), etc. A list of the learned societies existing in 1956 and connected with the *PAN* can be found in "Spis placówek Polskiej Akademii Nauk," ("Index of Agencies of the Polish Academy of Sciences), *Nauka Polska* ("Polish Learning"), VI, No. 4 (Oct.-Dec. 1958), 161-250. The *PAN* directory lists them currently for each year.

[17]See *Polskie Towarzystwo Historyczne, 1886-1956* ("Polish Historical Association, 1886-1956"), ed. Stanisław Herbst and Irena Pietrzak-Pawłowska (Warsaw: Państwowe Wydawnictwo Naukowe, 1958), with French and Russian summaries.

[18]Marian Kukiel, "Historia Polski na Zachodzie," ("History of Poland in the West"), *Teki Historyczne,* VIII (1956-57), 192-202.

[19]The organization and scope of the legal studies at the *PAN* is presented by Cezary Berezowski, "O pracach i zadaniach Instytutu Nauk Prawnych," ("About Work and Tasks of the Institute of Legal Studies"), *Nauka Polska* (Polish Learning) IX, No. 2 (Apr.-June, 1961), 109-16.

[20]A selection of the most important bibliographies of Polish legal materials, including the history of all the branches of law, is provided by a publication in English: Peter Siekanowicz, ed., *Legal Sources and Bibliography of Poland* (New York: Praeger, for Free Europe Committee, 1964). It was prepared in the framework of the Mid-European Law Project under the general editorship of V. Gsovski. Among the best bibliographies in the Western languages are: Józef Feldman, "Historical Studies in Poland; a Bibliographic Survey," *Slavonic Review,* II (1923-24), 660-66; Oskar Halecki, ed., *Poland* (New York: Praeger, for

in the broadest sense, together with studies of those non-Polish systems of law which had been in force in the territory of the Polish Commonwealth. Also included were Western European, Slavic, and other systems of law, as

Mid-European Studies Center of Free Europe Committee, 1957), 572-86; J. K. Kochanowski, "Le développement de l'historiographie polonaise dans la séconde moitie du XIX-e siècle," *Atti del Congresso internazionale di scienze storiche* (Rome: 1906), III, 599-605; International Committee of Comparative Law, *Catalogue des sources de documentation juridique dans le monde* (Paris: UNESCO, 1953), 233-5 (very poor); and Michał Sczaniecki, "Chronique des travaux d'histoire du droit polonais parus en Pologne de 1939 a 1946," *Czasopismo Prawno-Historyczne,* I (1948), 206-36. Among the bibliographies in Polish, Wiktor Hahn's *Bibliografia bibliografii polskich* ("Bibliography of Polish Bibliographies") (second edition; Wrocław: Zakład im. Ossolińskich, 1956) lists legal bibliographies of monographies, serials, and periodicals. The list of legal bibliographies includes: Jan Wincenty Bandtkie-Stężyński, *Bibliografia prawa polskiego od najdawniejszych czasów do r. 1823* ("A Bibliography of the Polish Law from the Oldest Times to 1823") (Manuscripts of Biblioteka Jagiellońska No. 4917). *Bibliografia prawnicza polska XIX i XX wieku* ("The Legal Polish Bibliography of the XIX and XX Centuries") compiled by Adolf Suligowski (Warsaw: M. Arct, 1911) contains the books and articles published in Latin and in Polish from 1800 to 1910. It was supplemented by Roman Longchamps de Berrier, *Polska Bibliografia prawnicza 1911-1912* ("Polish Legal Bibliography") (Lwów: Drukarnia K. Jakubowskiego, 1916) for the years 1911-1912. The years 1930-37 are covered by a quarterly publication of Artur Miller, *Bibliografia prawnicza za okres pięcioletni 1930-1934* ("A Legal Bibliography for Five Year Period, 1930-1934") (Warsaw: Hoesick, 1935). Dąbkowski compiled *Powszechna kronika historyczno-prawna, 1920-1925* (Vol. 5 No. 1 of *Pamiętnik Historyczno-Prawny;* Lwów, 1927). Karol Koranyi published *Bibliografia historyczno-prawna za lata 1926-1936* ("Historical Legal Bibliography") (Lwów: Towarzystwo Naukowe, 1938-9) and "Bibliografia historii prawa państw słowiańskich i baltyckich, 1930-1931," ("Bibliography of History of Law of Slavic and Baltic Countries, 1930-1931"), *Rivista di storia del Diritto Italiano,* IV (1931), 726 ff., and V (1931), 776 ff. The Institute of Legal Studies of the Polish Academy of Sciences published under the editorship of K. Koranyi *Polska bibliografia prawnicza, 1944-1959* ("Polish Legal Bibliography, 1944-1959") (Warsaw: Państwowe Wydawnictwo Naukowe, 1962). The Institute was planning to publish complete listings of Polish legal publications since 1912, the years 1944-59 being the first step in the retrospective project. Concerning this period, Jakub Sawicki publishes periodically a selective bibliography, "Materiały do polskiej bibliografii historyczno-prawnej" ("Materials of a Polish Historical and Legal Bibliography") in current issues of *Czasopismo Prawno-Historyczne.* Materials important for the history of Polish law are also found in *Polska bibliografia prawa kanonicznego od wynalezienia druku do 1940* ("Polish Bibliography of Canon Law from Invention of Print to 1940"). Its Vol. II (1800-1940) was compiled by Joachim R. Bar and Wojciech Zmarz and published by *Towarzystwo Naukowe Katolickiego Uniwersytetu Lubelskiego* w Lublinie (Learned Society of the Catholic University of Lublin) in 1947. Vol. I has not appeared as yet. Basic to the history of Polish law are the general bibliographies:

well as the universal history of state and law, Church law, universal canon law, Roman law, and other selected topics.

Two tendencies in comparative law studies appear in the recent approach to Slavic legal systems. One of these tendencies aims at the consideration of Slavic law as separate from other law.[21] In this spirit, the

Karol Estreicher, *Bibliografia polska* ("Polish Bibliography") (Cracow: Wydawnictwo Towarzystwa Naukowego Krakowskiego, 1872-1951) and supplements. For full bibliographic description of this multivolume national bibliography see Wiktor Hahn, *Bibliografia bibliografij polskich* ("Bibliography of Polish Bibliographies") (second edition; Wrocław: Zakład im. Ossolińskich, 1956), items 59-79; *Przewodnik Bibliograficzny, 1878-1928,* issued in Cracow, and its continuation for 1929-38, as well as the current bibliography of the same title published in Warsaw, from 1946 on. Of fundamental value is *Bibliografia historii polskiej,* ("Bibliography of Polish History"), compiled by Ludwik Finkel in the years 1891-1914, with Henryk Sawczyński (Lwów: Komisja Historyczna Akademii Umiejętności w Krakowie, 1891) and its Part II, published in Cracow, 1895-1901; Part III, Fascicule 1, published in Cracow, 1904; Part III, Fascicule 2, published as Supplement I in Cracow, 1904; Part III, Fascicule 3 published in Cracow, by the Academy of Arts and Sciences as all other volumes, in 1906. Supplement II (1901-10) to this work was compiled by Finkel with H. Sawczyński and E. T. Modelski (Cracow: Akademia Umiejętności, 1914). A new edition of this work was issued in three volumes (Warsaw, 1956). Bibliographic essays in this field include: Stanisław Estreicher, "Przegląd najnowszej literatury z zakresu historii prawa" ("A Survey of the Most Recent Literature from the Field of Law"), *Czasopismo Prawnicze i Ekonomiczne,* I (1900), 215-32, and III (1902), 295-317; Stanisław Kutrzeba, "Rozwój nauki historii prawa polskiego," ("The Development of Studies in History of Polish Law"), *Kwartalnik Historyczny,* ("Historical Quarterly"), LI (1937), 338-61; Kazimierz Tymieniecki, *Zarys dziejów historiografii polskiej* ("An Outline History of Polish Historiography") Vol. XIX-a of *Historia Nauki Polskiej w Monografiach* ("Monographic History of Polish Learning") (Cracow: Polska Akademia Umiejętności, 1948); Władysław Smoleński, *Szkoły historyczne w Polsce* ("The Historical Schools of Thought in Poland") (new edition; Wrocław: Zakład Narodowy im. Ossolińskich, 1952); M. H. Serejski; "Rzut oka na historiografię polską w dobie kapitalizmu od początku XX wieku; stan badań, główne tendencje ideologiczne," ("A Glance at Polish Historiography in the Period of Capitalism From the Beginnings of the XX Century; the Situation in Research, and Main Ideological Tendencies"), *Przegląd Nauk Historycznych i Społecznych* ("Survey of Historical and Social Sciences"), I (1950), 98-121; Bogusław Leśnodorski, "Nauka historii w pierwszym dziesięcioleciu Polski Ludowej" ("Teaching History in the First Ten Years of People's Poland"), *Kwartalnik Historyczny* ("Historical Quarterly"), LXII (1955), 1ff.

[21]Wojciech Hejnosz took such a stand in his report to the Seventh and Eighth Congress of Polish Historians, as revealed in his "W sprawie badań porównawczych nad historią praw słowiańskich," ("Concerning Comparative Studies of the History of Slavic Law"), *VIII Powszechny Zjazd Historyków Polskich: Historia Państwa i Prawa* (VIII All-National Convention of Polish Historians of State and Law)

courses of comparative study of the history of Slavic law were introduced in the late 1800's at the Lwów University and then offered at various universities in the period between the world wars. The first chair of the History of Slavic Law, conceived as a separate discipline, was founded not in Poland but in Bohemia, at the Charles University of Prague in 1903. Dr. Karel Kadlec was the first to occupy it.[22]

Others consider that Slavic legal systems can be examined concomitantly with other systems of law in comparative study of legal institutions in their historical evolution.[23]

Polish interest in Slavic law was heightened and given scholarly dimension by Wacław A. Maciejowski. Oswald M. Balzer devoted himself to studying "the main features and essential purposes of comparative

(Warsaw: Polskie Towarzystwo Historyczne, 1959), pp. 77-82. The first historians of Polish law who began comparative studies of Slavic law were Wacław A. Maciejowski and Romuald and Józef Hube.

[22]Professor Kadlec was assisted in his endeavor to create this chair by an outstanding Polish historian of law, Oswald M. Balzer. See: Jerzy Pogonowski, "Oswald Balzer a katedra praw słowiańskich w Pradze," ("Oswald Balzer and the Chair of Slavic Law in Prague") *Česko-polský sborník vědeckých prací,* ed. Milan Kudělka (Prague: Statní Pedagogické Naklad, 1955), I, 550-55. Kadlec's disciples, Rudolf Rauscher and Richard Horna, continued comparative studies of Slavic law. Russian scholars traditionally have paid much attention to the history and comparative study of Slavic law. Such subjects as Lithuanian and Ruthenian (Ukrainian) law as well as the problem of Marxist interpretation of common or analogous institutions (for example, feudalism in Eastern Europe) have found particular coverage in Russian and Soviet legal studies. For a bibliography on older Russian literature see: Stanisław Kutrzeba, *Historia ustroju Polski w zarysie; tom drugi: Litwa* ("An Outline History of Poland's State and Social Organization; the Second Volume: Lithuania") (second edition; Lwów and Warsaw: Nakładem Księgarni Polskiej Bernarda Połonieckiego, 1921), pp. 161-70; V. Gsovski, "Medieval Russian Laws," *American Slavic and East European Review,* VI (Dec., 1947), 152-8, which is a review of George Vernadsky, ed., *Medieval Russian Laws* (No. 41 of the *Records of Civilization: Sources and Studies;* New York: Columbia University Press, 1947). Bardach's *Historia Państwa i Prawa Polski* ("History of the State and Law of Poland"), quoted above, includes Soviet Russian literature. The question of Slavic law, treated comparatively, is not foreign to the French and German historians of law.

[23]Bardach, in the discussion about Hejnosz's report to the Eighth Convention of Polish Historians, as quoted above, took a stand against the study of Slavic law as a separate discipline. According to him, comparative study of Slavic law should not develop on the assumption that it is a separate discipline but that it is a method only, which might yield some results if submitted to a Marxist interpretation of history.

18

However, before Balzer, B. Ulanowski and Michał Bobrzyński, the research in this field was not based on source materials. Monographic study of Polish private law was rather rare and did not allow for generalizations and synthesis. The need for research based on adequate sources was critically presented by Balzer in his *O obecnym stanie nauki prawa prywatnego polskiego i jego potrzebach,* ("About Current Conditions in the Study of Polish Private Law and Related Needs").[36]

A particular place in this field belongs to Przemysław Dąbkowski, author of several basic monographs and of a system of Polish private law in his two-volume work, *Prawo prywatne polskie* ("The Polish Private Law").[37] Its outline was published as a textbook for the use of students.[38] Another book on old Polish law, *Dawne polskie prawo sądowe* ("The Old Polish Judicial Law"), containing criminal law and judicial procedures, was published by Kutrzeba.[39] Józef Rafacz wrote *Dawne polskie prawo karne* ("The Old Polish Penal Law").[40]

Although the subject was peripheral to their main interest, Władysław Abraham, Rafał Taubenschlag, Marceli Handelsman, and Juliusz Makarewicz have enriched our knowledge of particular problems of Polish judicial law. The disciples of Dąbkowski (K. Koranyi, J. Adamus, P. Skwarczyński), of Kutrzeba (A. Vetulani),[41] and of Rafacz (S. Borowski), as well as W. Hejnosz, J. Bardach, J. Matuszewski, W. Sobociński, K. Kolańczyk, S. Roman, and others are maintaining the highest tradition of research in this field.

The term "Polish law," a part of which constitutes Polish private law, has several meanings. First, it includes all the law systems, general and particular, and universal and local, that have been in force in the territory

[36]Poznań, 1889. See Vetulani, *Dzieje,* pp. 34-5. The author also quotes Michał Bobrzyński's "O dawnym prawie polskim, jego nauce i umiejętnym badaniu" ("About the Old Polish Law and Its Knowledgeable Study") in *Szkice i studia historyczne* ("Sketches and Historical Studies") (second edition; Cracow, 1922). II, 298 ff.

[37](Lwów: Nakładem Towarzystwa dla Popierania Nauki Polskiej, 1910-11).

[38]*Zarys prawa polskiego prywatnego* ("An Outline of the Polish Private Law") (second edition; Lwów: K. S. Jakubowski, 1921).

[39]Lwów: Wydawn. Zakładu Narodowego im. Ossilińskich, 1921.

[40](Warsaw: Gebethner i Wolff, 1936). In Polish literature, private law, criminal law, and civil and criminal procedure are called *prawo sądowe,* translated often as *"court law",* or better, "judicial law."

[41]Vetulani holds honorary doctorates of the Universities in Nancy and Strasbourg, is Professor at the Jagiellonian University in Cracow, and a world renowned scholar in history of law. His contributions to the history of Polish law and to the editing of historical sources constitute an outstanding example of scholarship.

of the Polish Commonwealth during any period in its history. As such, the term embraces canon, German, Jewish, Lithuanian, Ruthenian, Armenian, Wallachian, and Gypsy law as developed and used among specific ethnic groups of Poland.

We can also approach the legal order in Poland from the point of view of social strata regulated by special sets of laws. As such, the term includes the law of the clergy, the gentry, the burghers, and the peasants. Some professional groups developed their own legal order, sanctioned by ancient usage and applied in court decisions; examples are the customary law of beekeepers, shepherds, and millers. University members, professors and students had separate laws relating to their autonomus position and institutional status. The armed forces had their own military laws and courts.[42] There was also maritime law, applicable primarily in the city of Gdańsk (Dantzig), "issued either by the kings of Poland who were sovereign rulers of the city or by its municipal authorities. . .to 1793, i.e., . . .when Gdańsk was an integral part of Poland."[43]

The term "Polish law" is also used in a restricted sense as a set of norms, customary and statutory, that evolved in the territory of Poland for the regulation of the legal relations of those not under jurisdiction of other laws, and for defining state and social institutions and their organization. In this sense, Polish law includes public and judicial law (private as well as criminal and procedural). Public law expressed and shaped the state organization, the power of the kings, and the privileges and obigations of estates: clergy, gentry, burghers, and peasants. To it belonged the creation and organization of the Polish parliament, the political character of the Polish Commonwealth, and the civil rights and privileges of the citizens.

Originally, Polish law was in force among the inhabitants of the Kingdom of Poland, called the Crown, as opposed to Lithuania, another part of the Polish Commonwealth. It was applied to those who were not under other systems of law. The provinces that constituted the Kingdom of Poland were *Wielkopolska* (Great Poland) and *Małopolska* (Little Poland).[44] Polish law gradually expanded to include the territories

[42]Dąbkowski, *Prawo prywatne*, I, 17-31.

[43]Stanisław Matysik, *Prawo morskie Gdańska: studium historyczno-prawne* ("The Maritime Law of Gdansk; a Study in Legal History") (Warsaw: Wydawnictwo Prawnicze, 1958). English summary, p. 339.

[44]There is a continuous inconsistency noticeable in the English terminology used for Polish names of legal institutions and geographical units. In the case of *Wielkopolska* and *Małopolska*, for example, Kutrzeba calls them, in his article cited above and published in the *Encyclopaedia of Social Sciences*, "Greater Poland" and "Lesser Poland." However, most authors use "Great Poland" and "Little Poland."

incorporated into the Crown as well as to those which entered into feudal relations with the Crown and Lithuania jointly or with the Crown alone.[45] Sometimes Polish public law was granted first to the inhabitants of the new provinces, while the local judicial law was preserved without change. In other instances, judicial law was accepted in new provinces before public law could be granted to them.

Polish law often influenced other systems of law, as in the case of Mazovia. This province was incorporated into the Crown gradually during the fifteenth and sixteenth centuries. The final act of incorporation came in 1529, when Mazovia accepted the public law of the Crown as its own but continued to preserve her own judicial law. This law was codified in 1532 and 1540. In spite of her determination to preserve it intact, the Mazovian judicial law became more and more influenced by the Polish law, until the Mazovian gentry acceded fully to the Polish law in 1576.[46] Only forty-six provisions were left from the old system and confirmed by the Polish king. This situation lasted until the end of the Polish Commonwealth. The Lithuanian judicial law was also influenced by the Polish law, a fact which is noticeable in the Third Lithuanian Statute of 1588.[47] The territory under Polish law increased steadily with the extension of the boundaries of the Polish commonwealth, although the adoption of Polish law was not always tantamount to the accession to the Polish commonwealth. Within the boundaries of the Crown, other systems of law were strongly influenced by Polish law. The German town law was changed to such an extent that it became fully polonized. It was called Polish town law, *ius municipale polonicum,* as early as the sixteenth century.[48] Reciprocally, Polish law underwent the influences of canon, Lithuanian, Ruthenian, German, and other legal systems in force in the commonwealth.

[45]In the course of history, Great Poland, with Mazovia and Royal Prussia, and Little Poland, including Ruthenian (or Ukrainian) lands, Volhynia, Podolia, and Podlachia came to belong to the Crown. The Crown, together with the Grand Duchy of Lithuania and their fiefs, formed the Polish or Polish-Lithuanian Commonwealth.

[46]Soon after, the principal city of Mazovia, Warszawa (Warsaw), became the capital of Poland.

[47]See fn. 59 and 60.

[48]The problem was treated in a broader context by M. Z. Jedlicki, "German Settlement in Poland and the Rise of the Teutonic Order," *Cambridge History of Poland,* (Cambridge: University Press, 1950) I, 125-47. The term *ius municipale polonicum* was used by Bartłomiej Groicki, author of *Porządek sądów i spraw miejskich prawa majdeburskiego w Koronie Polskiej* (1559). A compilation of Prussian town law of 1580, the *Nowe Miasto Revision,* had to be translated into

Division of the history of Polish law into historical periods has aroused much controversy since a very early date. Two leading legal historians, Balzer and Kutrzeba, discussed the matter at the beginning of this century. The political development of the four estates, as well as social and economic changes, suggested considering the period between the Koszyce Privilege of 1374 and the Polish-Lithuanian Union of 1569, together with the first interregnum, in 1572, as one period. Professor Kutrzeba calls it "the period of the estates."[49] The following period, of supremacy of the gentry, lasted until the last interregnum and the beginning of reforms in 1768. The final period, although unfinished because of the partition of Poland, produced the work of the Great Diet and the Constitution of May 3, 1791. This division is based on the development of public law.

Contrary to public law, Polish private law is sometimes presented, by Dąbkowski for instance, without a "periodization" which would correspond to the development of political institutions. Dąbkowski's work on Polish private law is rather a cross-section of the system in the last stage of its development before Poland's partition, with references to the historical growth and changes of particular institutions of private law.

Marxist historians proposed a new division of history.[50] It corresponds to the noted Marxist scheme in the development of each society from primitive socialism and slavery to feudalism, and from feudalism to capitalism, socialism, and communism. This scheme is also binding on historians of law. Therefore, Marxist periodization includes the entire history of Polish law up to the partition of Poland in the period of feudalism. This feudal period is subdivided into the "gentry's democracy,"

Polish for its use in the cities by 1623. See Bardach, *op. cit.*, II, 239-40. Also *Ius Culmense (prawo chełmińskie)* had to be translated from German into Latin in 1553 in order to make it accessible for the population. See Józef Matuszewski, *Najstarszy zwód prawa polskiego* ("The Oldest Codification of Polish Law") (Warsaw: Państwowe Wydawnictwo Naukowe, 1959), p. 60.

[49]This term was also used by J. Siemieński in his article, "Constitutional Conditions in the Fifteenth and Sixteenth Centuries," *Cambridge History of Poland,* I, 416-40. P. Skwarczyński uses the term "Commonwealth of the Gentry" in relation to the entire period before the partitions as in "The Constitution of Poland Before the Partitions," *Cambridge History of Poland,* II, 67.

[50]Bardach, *op. cit.* (fn. 4), I, 21-77. The problem was discussed at the First Methodological Conference of Polish Historians in 1953. Stanisław Arnold opened the discussion with his report, "Niektóre problemy periodyzacji dziejów Polski" ("Some Problems Relative to the Periodization of Poland's History"), in *Pierwsza Konferencja Metodologiczna Historyków Polskich; przemówienia, referaty, dyskusja* ("The First Methodological Conference of Polish Historians; Addresses, Reports, Discussion") (Warsaw: Państwowe Wydawnictwo Naukowe, 1953), I, 155-93. Participating in the discussion were Z. Kaczmarczyk, B. Leśnodorski, K. Tymieniecki, and others.

"the magnates' oligarchy," and "the reforms and fall of the republic of the nobility." All the branches of Polish law, including judicial law, are similarly divided. The current study of various institutions, however, is based on sources which often do not fit the rigid schemes of Marxist historical interpretation.

Polish law was chiefly customary. Custom and usage, the main source of law in the first period, retained an important place along with other sources of law. However, by the end of the eighteenth century public law had been formalized by constitutions establishing fundamental law of the country. This tendency had been reflected in particular institutions since the sixteenth century *(pacta conventa)*. These were primarily the Cardinal Laws of 1768 and the Constitution of May 3, 1791, which started the epoch of modern constitutionalism in Poland—interrupted of course by the partitions. Polish private law remained basically customary until the termination of Poland's independence at the end of the eighteenth century.[51] Some of its branches, nevertheless, underwent statutory changes. The new branches of private law, such as the law of negotiable instruments and the law of business associations, were primarily established by the constitutions and statutes. Activities of the central legislative bodies as well as local ones such as dietines (provincial conventions of the gentry) increased.

The legislative activity of the kings during this period included work on diet constitutions issued in the king's name and with his assent. Kings also issued edicts, decrees, and manifestoes. Individual and provincial privileges, so important in the first period, lost their place, together with the rights granted to the whole clergy and gentry. However, similar functions were carried out regarding newly acquired lands and lands united with the Polish Commonwealth.

The dietines performed an important function in enacting some rules of Polish judicial law. Their enactments, called *lauda*, constituted a source of law until the end of the Commonwealth. The ordinances or articles of the marshals *(marszałków)*, hetmans *(hetmanów)*, and other central and local officials also created law. These same functions were performed by insurrectionist authorities in the 1794 uprising against Russia under the leadership of Tadeusz Kościuszko.

The role of the courts in the creation of law was significant, although different from that in the English common law. It consisted of the interpretation of customs and existing laws. However, the courts did not develop the doctrine of *stare decisis*. One written provision about

[51]For a general presentation of this subject, see Konstanty Grzybowski, "Loi et la coutume en Pologne, depuis le X-eme siècle jusqu'à 1795," *Rapport polonais présenté au sixième Congrès international de droit comparé* (Warsaw: Comité des sciences juridiques, 1962).

rule-making in the course of judicial process is worth mentioning. According to the Constitution of 1578, cases were to be sent to the diet, acting as a court, if the Court of Referendars could not find any applicable legal rule. Such judgments of the diet would have the force of law. Also, judgments of the Crown tribunals had the character of precedents[52] and might be considered comparable to the systems of common law. Decisions of higher town courts *(ortyle)* in the town law had also rule-making features.

In analyzing the sources of Polish law, special mention is due to contemporary systematic compilations and commentaries of the existing law. Some of them acquired much authority. Their exposition and emphasis of the institutions and rules of customary origin influenced the interpretation and enactment of law to a considerable extent. However, their main value to us is that they provide us with the sources of existing laws and deepen knowledge of them.

The sources of Polish town law and peasant law require some discussion. For the town law, the most important sources are the noted German compilations which comprise *Der Sachsenspiegel* ("The Saxon Mirror"), compiled by Eike von Repgow between 1215 and 1235, as well as town charters and privileges, decisions of town authorities, orders and decisions of feudal lords, and decisions of the municipal supreme courts. Customs also retained their significance. Regarding the peasant law,[53] the same sources as for the town law were valid with respect to villages chartered under the German law. In the course of time, the feudal power of the lords increased until they became the predominant source of law in all villages. Such law was expressed in ordinances, village constitutions, and decisions. Up to the end of this period, the constitutions enacted by the diets, the *lauda* of the dietines, the acts of kings, and the decisions of stewards in the royal domains, as well as the customs, played their roles as sources of law for peasants.[54] The documentary sources of Polish law

[52]Bardach, *op. cit.* (fn. 4), II, 239. See also Kutrzeba, "La réforme judiciaire en Pologne à l'époque d'Etienne Batory," *Etienne Batory, roi de Pologne, prince de Transylvanie* (Cracow: Académie polonaise des sciences et de lettres, et Académie des sciences hongroise, 1935), p. 292-3 ff.

[53]See Vetulani, "W sprawie prawa chłopskiego w Polsce feudalnej," *Państwo i Prawo*, XI, No. 10 (Oct. 1956), 618-32. Also, in his introduction to *Księgi sądowe wiejskie klucza Łąckiego* ("Village Judicial Books of Łąck Estates") (Wrocław: Zakład Narodowy im. Ossolińskich, 1961-3), he affirms the existence of a separate system of "peasant law." So do other scholars, such as Wojciech Hejnosz and Stanisław Szczotka. Bardach questions the existence of the "peasant law."

[54]Some records of the peasant courts were discovered by Bolesław Ulanowski. Vetulani currently directs the publication of the sources of Polish law: *Pomniki Prawa Polskiego* ("Monuments of Polish Law"). Division II of this project contains

preserved from this period have been re-edited and republished in modern times.

The major part of the customary Polish law was not reduced to written form. Only a few segments, indeed, were codified or written down. The codification of Casimir the Great, in the middle of the fourteenth century, remained in force in the following centuries. Also the Elbląg Book of Polish Customary law,[55] called by B. D. Grekov and other Russian historians *Polskaîâ Pravda* ("Polish Truth"), was used. At the end of the fifteenth century, a collection of the customary law of the Cracow province appeared in Polish rather than in Latin. It is known as *Artykuły sądowe* ("Judicial Articles"). In the sixteenth century were compiled *Consuetudines terrae Cracoviensis (Zwyczaje ziemi krakowskiej* or "Customs of the Cracow Province"), *Processus iuris,* and *Cautelae quaedam in iure terrestri tentae et observatae.*

Since 1576 the constitutions of the diets have been issued systematically and continuously in printed form; since 1543 they have been issued in the Polish language. They were included, together with various legislative and other acts, in a collection of laws compiled by Jan Łaski and published in 1506 under the title *Commune incliti Poloniae regni privilegium constitutionum et indultuum publicitus decretorum approbatorumque.* The journals of the diets *(diariusze)* constitute still another source of knowledge of the Polish legal order. Acts of the officials, legal transactions of private individuals, and the minutes of the sessions of courts were registered in the records of the district and castle courts.[56]

the records of the peasant courts, as well as other sources of peasant law. Vetulani discussed this topic at the Eighth General Convention of Polish Historians in Cracow, Sept. 14-17, 1958, in his report: "Wartość badawcza ksiąg sądowych wiejskich" ("Research Value of the Village Judicial Records"), *Pamiętnik VIII Powszechnego Zjazdu Historyków Polskich w Krakowie* ("Memoir of the VIII General Convention of Polish Historians in Cracow") (Warsaw, Państwowe Wydawnictwo Naukowe, 1958), p. 1 ff., Kutrzeba also contributed to the development of this field in the history of Polish law. He published, together with Alfons Mańkowski, *Polskie ustawy wiejskie XV - XVIII wieku* ("Polish Village Enactments"), Vol. XI of *Archiwum* of the Legal Commission of the PAU (Cracow: Polska Akademia Umiejętności, 1938). Stanisław Szczotka added to this research his article, "Uzupełnienia do zbioru polskich ustaw wiejskich" ("Supplements to the Collection of the Polish Village Enactments"), *Czasopismo Prawno-Historyczne,* II (1949), 459-66.

[55]See fn. 48 and Vetulani, "Niemiecki spis prawa zwyczajowego; uwagi źródłoznawcze" ("A German Collection of Customary Law; Remarks Related to the Knowledge of Sources"), *Czasopismo Prawno-Historyczne* ("The Legal Historical Review"), V, 180-97.

[56]*Akta grodzkie i ziemskie, 1244-1768* ("Castle and Land Records, 1244-1768"), published in 25 volumes by Ksawery Liske, Antoni Prochaska, and Wojciech

There were many attempts at codification of some of the branches of Polish law. The first and the only successful one, in the sense that it was formally approved and accepted, was a codification of the laws of procedure: the *Formula processus* of 1523, containing 123 articles. The next, a project of 1532, known as *Correctura iurium* or *Mikolaj Taszycki's Correctura,* contained 929 articles and is considered a remarkable work for its time. However, the *Sejm* (diet) of 1534 rejected this project.

The last and, perhaps the most interesting, codification projects were prepared at the end of the eighteenth century. Codification was ordered by the *Sejm* of 1764. A codification commission, acting under the chairmanship of Andrzej Zamoyski, published its draft in 1778. This project reflected the theories of natural law of the Enlightenment period. It proposed some modern principles, such as granting the protection of law to peasants, emancipating some of them, and extending all rights to burghers. However, it was rejected by the *sejm.*

Another codification began during the Great Diet (1788-91). A commission under the chairmanship of Hugo Kołłątaj produced a project known as the Code of the King Stanislaus Augustus *(Kodeks Stanisława Augusta).*[57] The same reform tendencies characteristic of the Zamoyski code and the enormous work accomplished by the Great Diet were reflected in the project. From the technical point of view, this code was interesting in that it drew a sharp distinction between civil law and penal law and greatly curtailed and quickened judicial procedures. The events which brought forth the partition of Poland, however, prevented the acceptance and implementation of this codification.

Some provinces of the Polish Commonwealth were more successful than others in codifying their laws. To survey these achievements in detail is beyond the scope of the present chapter, but it is necessary to mention the most important of them: the three codifications of the Mazovia province.[58] The Royal Prussia which was incorporated in to the Crown preserved its laws, partially codified in *Korektura prawa pruskiego,* which was confirmed by the Sejm of 1598. Since it had been based on the law of

Hejnosz (Lwów: Zakład Narodowy im. Ossolińskich, 1869-1935), include materials from Little Poland and the Ukraine. J. von Lekszycki, *Die ältesten Grosspolnischen Grodbücher* (Leipzig: S. Hirzel, 1887-89) was the first collection of castle and land records from Great Poland. At present, similar publication projects are being carried out.

[57]Stanisław Borowski, ed., *Kodeks Stanisława Augusta; zbiór dokumentów,* ("Code of Stanislaw August; a Collection of Documents") (Warsaw: Nakł Towarzystwa Prawniczego, 1938).

[58]Bardach, *op. cit.* (fn. 4), II, 28-9. Balzer devoted to this question his *W sprawie sankcji Statutu Mazowieckiego Pierwszego, z roku 1532* ("Concerning the Sanction of the First Mazovian Statute of 1532") (Cracow: *PAU,* 1900).

the Crown, this codification was used as a subsidiary source of law in all the territories of the Crown. The most advanced codifications were successfully carried out in Lithuania. The First Statute, containing 244 articles, was compiled in 1522 and came into use in 1529. A supplementary edition, the Second Lithuanian Statute, containing 368 articles, went into use in 1566. The Third Lithuanian Statute, containing 488 articles, was confirmed by the king with the agreement of the diet of the Polish Commonwealth and came into effect in 1588. All three of the statutes codified the existing Lithuanian customary and statutory law, both public and private. Although the influence of Polish law, especially noticeable in the Third Statute, as well as of Russian, Ukranian, and German law, is undeniable, the Lithuanian character of the law and its codification is beyond question. This has been one of the most controversial subjects among Polish and Russian historiographers. The latter emphasize the influences of *Russkaia pravda* as the most essential,[59] while Balzer saw the Polish influence as prevailing.[60] Soviet historiography maintains the point of view of the tsarist scholars; and apparently its allegations must be accepted without criticism by Polish scholars, as is evidenced in Bardach's treatise. The importance of the codification was proven by the fact that it remained in force after the partition of the Polish Commonwealth until 1840. In this case the law survived the state and then was partially absorbed by Russian legislation of the nineteenth century.[61]

Special laws of the Church and clergy, of the Jews and Armenians, and of miners, beekeepers, shepherds, and millers were compiled and codified,

[59] A survey of the Russian point of view up to 1934 was given by I. I. Lappo, *Litovskiĭ Statut 1588 goda* (Kaunas: "Spendulio" B-vés spaustuve, 1934-38), especially in "Nauchnoe izuchenie Litovskago Statuta 1588 goda," I, pt. 2, 484-563; in this work (see p. 541) Lappo takes issue with some statements by Oswald Balzer in his *Przygodne słowa* (Lwów, 1912).

[60] A summary of Polish studies on the subject can be found in Stefan Ehrenkreutz, ed., *Księga pamiątkowa ku uczczeniu czterechsetnej rocznicy wydania pierwszego Statutu Litewskiego* ("Festschrift to Commemorate the Four Hundredth Anniversary of the First Lithuanian Statute") (Wilno, 1935); and *Studium historii prawa litewskiego* ("Study of History of the Lithuanian Law") (Wilno, 1938).

[61] Also, Lappo emphasizes this fact: "Statutovoe pravo. . .perezhilo razdiely soedinenoi Pol'sko-Litovskoĭ Rechi Pospolitoĭ i ostavalos' dĕistvuiushchim na territorii gosudarstva Litvy poslĕ eiá prisoedineniiá k Rossiiskoi Imperii, vplat' do 1840 goda. Ono bylo v znachytel'noĭ mierĕ retsepirovano i Rossiiskim zakonodatel'stovom." ("The Law of the Statute *[3rd of 1588]* survived the partitions of the Polish-Lithuanian Commonwealth and remained in force in the territory of the state of Lithuania after its incorporation into the Russian Empire, through the year 1840. It was in a significant measure absorbed by Russian legislation.") Lappo, *op. cit,* 1, pt. 1, vi.

29

with various results. Two types require further discussion: the town law and the peasants' law. Throughout the sixteenth century, attempts were made at the codification of town law. The most successful was the so-called *Revision of Nowe Miasto,* used in Latin from 1580 on. Although it was never enacted, it was used in the courts as a subsidiary collection of laws. Another partial codification of the cities' "self-governing rules" *(Willküren, wilkierze)*[62] was compiled in 1597 and printed in 1732. The sixth edition of this codification was published in 1761. The enactments of landlords, being a kind of codification, were granted to various private cities. The Customary Law of Kulm *(Chełmno),* in force in Ducal Prussia, was revised and confirmed in 1620 as an official codification under the name *Ius provinciale ducatus Prussiae.*

Codification of peasant law was not known. Comprehensive enactments issued by some landlords for their estates contain systematic sets of dominial rules established for the peasants. Among the best-known are *Ustawy powszechne dla dóbr moich rządców* ("Common Rules for the Administrators of My Estates") issued in 1783-5 and in 1786 in eight volumes by Princess Anna Jabłonowska. The law itself derives from legal acts such as peasant wills, contracts, court cases, and records. Such material has been preserved and is being edited.[63]

All such codes (even if not enacted), as well as private compilations of laws, systematizations, commentaries, inventories or indexes, and text-books, constitute significant sources of Polish law.

The most important published works of this group include *Leges seu statutaʹ privilegia regni Poloniae* ("Laws or Statutes and Privileges of the Kingdom of Poland"), by Jakub Przyluski (1533), and *Statuta regni Poloniae in ordinem alphabeti digesta* ("Statutes of the Kingdom of Poland Alphabetically Compiled"), by Jan Herburt, author of still another later compilation: *Statuta i przywileje koronne z łacińskiego języka na polskie przełożone, nowym porządkiem zebrane i spisane* ("Statutes and Crown Privileges Translated From Latin into Polish and in the New System Gathered and Rewritten") (1570). From the sixteenth century are *Statuta i metryka przywilejów koronnych* ("Statutes and Records of Crown Privileges"), by Stanisław Sarnicki (1594) and *Statuta, prawa i konstytucje koronne* ("Statutes, Laws, and Crown Constitutions"), by Jan Januszowski (1600).

---

[62]Concerning the town law terminology as used in English, the present study is based on *A General Survey of Events, Sources, Persons and Movements in Continental Legal History,* Vol. I of *Continental Legal History Series* (Boston: Little, Brown and Co., 1912), pp. 327-31.

[63]See fn. 53 and 54.

The seventeenth century brought some other publications: *Prompt-uarium statutorum*, of Paweł Szczerbicz (1604), and *Compendium*, by Teodor Zawacki. These two works finally attracted more attention and exerted more influence than the previous ones. Antoni Trzebicki's *Prawo Polityczne i cywilne Korony Polskiej i W. X. Litewskiego* ("Public and Civil Law of the Polish Crown and Lithuanian Grand Duchy"), issued in 1789-91 in two volumes, and Teodor Ostrowski's *Prawo cywilne narodu polskiego* ("Civil Law of the Polish Nation") (1784) appeared just before the downfall of Poland.

The synopses, sytematic presentations, and compendia of town law were also important. The oldest in this group is *Farrago actionum civilium iuris Magdeburgensis,* by Jan Cervus Tucholczky (1531). Four editions were issued before 1540; the last one was supplemented and enlarged. In this form, four other editions were issued before 1607. The most popular and authoritative synopses, however, were Bartłomiej Groicki's *Artykuły prawa majdeburskiego* ("Articles of the Magdeburg Law") (1588) and *Porządek sądów i spraw miejskich prawa majdeburskiego w Koronie Polskiej* ("Order of Courts and Municipal Matters of the Magdeburg Law in the Polish Crown") (1561).[64] These and other works of Groicki preserved their usefulness until the end of the Polish Commonwealth. In the second half of the eighteenth century, criminal law and the procedure in town law became the subject of a popular textbook by J. Czechowicz, under the title, *Praktyka kryminalna, to jest wzór rozumnego i porządnego spraw kryminalnych sądzenia* (1769).

An influential role in the formation and interpretation of law was played by theoretical treatises and studies. As yet, this part of the Polish legal past has not been explored sufficiently. In recent times, numerous monographic works on individual Polish lawyers, philosophers, and historians before the partition have been published by scholars such as Ludwik Ehrlich,[65] Karol Koranyi,[66] Eugeniusz Jarra,[67] and Kazimierz

[64]The most recent critical edition of Groicki's works was provided by K. Koranyi: *Porządek sądów i spraw miejskich, Artykuły* prawa majdeburskiego, *Postępek sądów około karania na gardle, Ustawa płacej u sądów, Tytuły prawa majdeburskiego* ("Order of Courts and Municipal Matters; Articles of the Magdeburg Law; Court Procedure in Cases Involving Capital Punishment; Rules on Judicial Fees; Titles of the Magdeburg Law") (Warsaw: Wydawnictwo Prawnicze, 1954.)

[65]*Paweł Włodkowic i Stanisław ze Skarbimierza* (Warsaw: Wydawnictwo Prawnicze, 1954) and *Polski wykład prawa wojny* ("Polish Explication of the Law of War in the XV Century") (Warsaw: Wydawnictwo Prawnicze, 1954).

[66]"O postępowych tradycjach w polskim piśmiennictwie karnym XVI i XVII wieku" ("About Progressive Traditions in Polish Penal Writings of the XVI and XVII Centuries"), *Państwo i Prawo*, VIII, No. 4, 550 ff. Also see the Introduction in

Grzybowski,[68] who are internationally famous, and also by the younger generation of legal historians, such as Krystyna Bukowska,[69] Teresa Janusz,[70] Zygmunt Kolankowski,[71] Irena Malinowska,[72] Lesław Pauli,[73] and Zbigniew Zdrójkowski.[74]

Bartłomiej Groicki, *Artykuły, op. cit.*, p. viii; Koranyi, *J. Cervus Tucholiensis i jego dzieła* ("J. Cervus Tucholiensis and His Works"), a reprint edition of *Przewodnik Historyczno-Prawny* (Lwów, 1930); and "Z dziejów polskiej literatury prawniczej XVI wieku" ("From History of Polish Juridical Literature of the XVI Century"), *Sprawozdania Towarzystwa Naukowego we Lwowie,* IX (1929), 225 ff.

[67]"Andrew Wolan; Sixteenth Century Polish Calvinist Writer and Philosopher of Law," *Studies, op. cit.* (fn. 1), pp. 124-55. Under the supervision of Prof. Jarra, many monographs on Polish legal writers were prepared by his students as doctor's theses at the University of Warsaw between the two world wars.

[68]"Polish Doctrine of the Law of War in the Fifteenth Century: A Note on the Geneology of International Law." *Jurist,* XVIII (Oct. 1958), 386-411.

[69]*Tomasz Drezner, polski romanista XVII wieku i jego znaczenie dla nauki prawa w Polsce* ("Tomasz Drezner, a Polish Romanist of the XVII Century and His Significance to the Study of Polish Law") (Warsaw: Wydawnictwo Prawnicze, 1960), issued as Vol. III of the series, *Dawni Pisarze Prawnicy* ("Old Writers-Jurists"), ed. Vetulani, Koranyi, and Zdrójkowski.

[70]"Konstantego Swięcickiego De jure naturae et gentium in generale et de jure belli et pacis in specie z 1763 roku" ("About Konstanty Swięcicki's Law of Nature and of Nations in General and About Law of War in Particular, Issued in 1763"), No. 22 of Series A, *Prawo* of *Zeszyty Naukowe Uniwersytetu Wrocławskiego* ("Research Papers of Wrocław University") (Wrocław: Uniwerystet Wrocławski, 1959), VI. 77-109.

[71]*Zapomniny prawnik XVI wieku Jan Łączyński i jego "Kompendium sądów Króla Jegomości;" studium z dziejów polskiej literatury prawniczej* ("Jan Łączyński, a Forgotten Jurist of the XVI Century and His Compendium of the Courts of His Majesty the King; a Study From the History of Polish Legal Literature"), Vol. 63, No. 2 of *Roczniki Towarzystwa Naukowego w Toruniu* (Toruń, 1960).

[72]*Mikołaj Zalaszowski, polski prawnik XVII stulecia na tle ówczesnej nauki prawa* ("Mikołaj Zalaszowski, a Polish Jurist of the XVII Century, Against the Background of Contemporary Legal Science"), Vol. 2 of *Zeszyty Naukowe Uniwersytetu Jagiellońskiego; Rozprawy i Studia* ("Research Papers of the Jagiellonian University, Dissertations and Studies") (Cracow, 1960).

[73]*Jan Nixdorff, 1625-1697, pisarz prawa procesowego* (Jan Nixdorff, 1625-1697, a Writer in Procedural Law"), Vol. 2 of *Dawni Pisarze Prawnicy* ("Old Writers-Jurists") (Warsaw: Wydawnictwo Prawnicze, 1957).

[74]"Tomasz Kuźmirski, nieznany osiemnastowieczny, polski prawnik humanista i jego pisma na tle współczesnej literatury humanistycznej" ("Tomasz Kuźmirski, an Unkown Polish Jurist and Humanist of the Eighteenth Century and His Writings Against the Contemporary Humanistic Literature"), *Czasopismo Prawno-Historyczne,* VII (1955), No. 2, 35-162.

Some of their findings shed light on the Polish law of the past that cannot be ignored in the present study, although its scope is limited to introductory observations and is far from offering a complete treatment of the subject. Polish legal treatises, especially those from the period through the first half of the seventeenth century, as well as those of the second half of the eighteenth century, reveal alertness to general legal problems equal to that in Western Europe. Polish authors sometimes preceded those West European writers who in the future were to become classics of the legal thought in the world. In some instances, Polish writers manifested a keener understanding of particular issues. Such was the case with Stanisław ze Skarbimierza and Paweł Włodkowic z Brudzenia in the early fifteenth century. In their doctrine was the principle of the inadmissibility of the forceful conversion of pagans; they emphasized that violation of the rules of charity was worse than failure to enforce a dogma. These problems were later taken up by Francesco de Vitoria. Jakub Przyluski continued studies of war, peace, and international arbitration, adding to legal discussions the same issues that were later treated by Gentilis and Hugo Grotius, considered founders of international law. The doctrine of equal rights for all inhabitants of the country, defended by Frycz Modrzewski[75] and held as their own by Gentilis and Grotius, proved to have been well presented in Poland in the sixteenth century. Doubts concerning the inquisitorial use of torture were very early expressed in that country.[76] Opposition to witch trials, which never proliferated in Poland to the extent known in Germany, was very strong. "Poland was one of the first countries in Europe to abolish torture by a special act of 1776."[77] Groicki was opposing torture before the birth of its most famous adversaries, Adam Tanner and Paul Laymann.[78]

[75]Waldemar Voisé, *Frycza Modrzewskiego nauka o państwie i prawie* ("Frycz-Modrzewski's Teaching about State and Law") (Warsaw, 1956), and "O ideologii społeczno-ustrojowej Andrzeja Frycza Modrzewskiego" ("About the Socio-Political Ideology of Andrzej Frycz-Modrzewski"), *Czasopismo Prawno-Historyczne*, IV (1952), 1-36. See also Stanisław Kot, *Andrzej Fryez Modrzewski; Studium zdziejów kultury polskiej w. w. XVI* ("Andrzej Fryez Modrzewski; A Study from the History of Polish Culture in the Sixteenth Century") (Second revised edition; Cracow: Nakł. Krakowskiej Spółki Wydawniczej, 1923).

[76]Koranyi, "O postępowych tradycjach w polskim piśmiennictwie karnym XVI i XVII wieku" ("About the Progressive Traditions in Polish Penal Writings of the XVI and XVII Century"), *Państwo i Prawo,* VIII, No. 4, 550 ff. See also his introduction to Groicki's *Artykuły,* p. viii.

[77]Koranyi, "O postępowych tradycjach," *op. cit.,* English summary, p. 2.

[78]*Ibid.,* p. 551.

This stand exemplifies the courage and intellectual ability of some Polish authors. (The position is still more noteworthy if we recall that Jean Bodin, whose works are considered classics of legal thought, accepted the torture and inquisitorial trial of witches.) To the same category of advanced thought belong treatises on toleration and equal rights for the Jews.[79] The Polish voice in these matters emphasizes the need for further study to obtain a truthful idea of the variety of European civilization.

The sources of law discussed above are available in printed form in both early and modern publications.[80] The first and most important is *Volumina legum*, a compilation of constitutions and other enactments. The collection, called the *Statut* of Jan Laski (1505), mentioned above, constitutes the first part of this compilation. *Volumina legum* was started by Andrzej Zaluski and Stanisław Konarski; six volumes appeared between 1732 and 1739. Volumes VII and VIII, issued by the Piarist Friars, contained the legislative acts up to 1780. All eight volumes, together with an index prepared by the Piarist Friars, were republished by Józef Ohryzko in 1859-80 in St. Petersburg. In 1889 the Legal Commission of the *PAU* issued Volume IX of *Volumina legum*, containing the Grodno Diet resolutions of 1793. This was edited by Z. Kaczmarczyk and published by *Poznańskie Towarzystwo Przyjaciół Nauk*.

A collection of international treatises compiled by another Piarist priest, Maciej Dogiel, under the title, *Codex diplomaticus Regni Poloniae et Magni Ducatus Lithuaniae*, won recognition. The first and fifth volumes were published in Wilno in 1758-59. The fourth appeared in 1764 after the death of the compiler. The second and third volumes were not published. G. F. Martens noticed that Poland had richer collections of treatises than any of the partitioning countries.[81]

[79]Bardach, *op. cit.* (fn. 4), II, 432-34.

[80]A special Commission for the Publication of Legal Historical Sources was created at the Institute of Legal Sciences of the *PAN*. See Stanisław Roman, "Działalność Komisji Redakcyjnej Wydawnictw Źródłowych Komitetu Nauk Prawnych Polskiej Akademii Nauk" ("Activities of the Editorial Commission for Source Publications of the Legal Sciences Committee of the Polish Academy of Sciences"), *Czasopismo Prawno-Historyczne*, VII, 1, 395-408. Concerning the related field of Church laws in Poland, a plan, partially carried out by now, was described by Jakób Sawicki, "Programme et état actuel des travaux préparatoires relatif à la publication du 'Corpus Conciliorum Poloniae'," *Czasopismo Prawno-Historyczne*, II, (1949), 209-26.

[81]Quoted by L. Ehrlich and J. S. Langrod, *Zarys Historii prawa narodów, politycznego i administracyjnego w Polsce* ("An Outline History of International Political and Administrative Law in Poland"), Vol. 17-d of *Historia Nauki Polskiej w monografiach* (Cracow: Polska Akademia Umiejętności, 1949), p. 11.

Akta grodzkie i ziemskie, records of territorial and castle courts as well as township offices[82] in Lwów, have a basic significance in the study of the history of Polish law. Publication of this type of record has been started again in the new series of the *Starodawne Prawa Polskiego Pomniki.*

Judicial books on peasant courts (minutes, judgments, and other records) are now being published by the *PAN* in the subseries *Pomniki Prawa Polskiego* ("Monuments of Polish Law") dział II, *Prawo wiejskie* ("Village Law"), under the editorship of Adam Vetulani.

Meanwhile, the publication and annotation of source documents[83] contributes to the growing body of research materials. The number of monographic studies and subjects covered in them increases. Polish private law, together with the old Polish penal law and procedures, is still the least elaborated branch of the subject. Bibliographies of bibliographies on the subject facilitate access to publications in all fields of legal history in Poland.[84]

The history of Polish law is a challenging subject for students of European civilization as well as for specialists in Russia's place among the Slavic nations. Some institutions which developed early in Poland bear a mark of originality. They were not known in Russia at all, or had barely appeared until the late eighteenth century.[85] At least two of these institutions should be mentioned. First is the alodial ownership of land. This constituted the material basis of the individual rights of the gentry, a class which constituted approximately one-tenth of the country's inhabitants. Feudal *divided* ownership, which allowed the establishment of absolute monarchies in Western Europe, did not develop in Poland. The lack of similar alodial ownership of land in Muscovite Russia heavily influenced the formation of her autocracy. Alodial ownership, with its attendant privileges, was responsible for the evolution of elective, limited

[82]See fn. 56.

[83]See fn. 54.

[84]See fn. 20.

[85]*Bolshaia sovetskaia entsiklopediia,* 2nd ed., s. v. "Feudal'noi stroi." Russian feudalism had flourished in the 17th century, as a result of the tsar's grants of land to his new vassals. The existence and character of feudalism in Russia is presented by Iwo Jaworski in *Zarys powszechnej historii państwa i prawa* ("An Outline of the Universal History of State and Law") (Warsaw: Państwowe Wydawnictwo Naukowe, 1961) pp. 218-20.

monarchy in Poland and affected the Polish concepts of society and personal freedom so different from those in Russia.[86]

Another institution peculiar to Polish law is related to the privileges of *Nec bona recipiantur* ("No goods shall be seized") and *Neminen captivabimus* ("No one shall be apprehended"). Those privileges were granted by the king to the Polish gentry in 1422, 1425, 1430, and 1433.[87] They established the rule that the lands of the gentry could be confiscated without due process and that no one could be arrested or imprisoned without an order of the court, except in well-defined urgent cases.[88] It is true that these privileges were granted originally to the gentry only; even so, they represent very advanced legal concepts, and their implementation gave the right of *habeas corpus* to large groups of people in the country. They protected the personal freedom of the people against the arbitrariness of state authorities down to the time of the partition. The right of *habeas corpus* granted by those privileges was extended to the burghers in 1764 and to the Jews in 1792.[89] Legal protection was given to the peasants in 1791, and amelioration of the peasants' position was prepared for implementation during the Kościuszko uprising in 1794. The process was interrupted by the partition. By that time, the French nation was building revolutionary barricades in the struggle for political rights which were to be given to much less than 1 per cent of the population. In England, before 1832, no more than one out of thirty-two citizens had the right to vote. By 1820, less than five hundred men, most of them members of the House of Lords, selected a majority of the House of

[86]Z. Wojciechowski, "Z zagadnień rodziny kulturalnej polskiego ustroju średniowiecznego," ("Some Problems Relative to the Cultural Family of the Polish Medieval State and Social Organization"), *Studia z historii społecznej i gospodarczej, poświęcone Prof. Dr. Franciszkowi Bujakowi* ("Studies in Social and Economic History; A Festschrift for Professor Franciszek Bujak") (Lwów, 1931), p. 67-81, and French summary, p. 600-2. In relation to Lithuanian law, a question of feudalism was raised by Oswald P. Backus III in "The Problem of Feudalism in Lithuania, 1506-1548," *Slavic Review*, XXI, No. 4, 639-59.

[87]Jan Wincenty Bandtkie, ed., *Ius Polonicum* (Warsaw, 1831), p. 221-23; A. Prochaska, "Przywilej czerwiński z 1422" ("Czerwinsk Privilege of 1422"), *Przegląd Historyczny*, IV (1907), 283-96; S. Kutrzeba, "Przywilej jedlneński z r. 1430 i nadanie prawa polskiego Rusi" ("Jedlno Privilege and Granting Polish Law to Ruthenia") in *Ku czci Ulanowskiego* ("A Festschrift for Ulanowski") (Cracow, 1911); Bardach, *op. cit.* (fn. 4), I, 422-28, 540-43; and, in English, J. Siemieński, "Constitutional Conditions," *Cambridge History of Poland*, I, 420.

[88]Kutrzeba, *Historia ustroju Polski w zarysie: Korona, op. cit.*, p. 62; Bardach, *op. cit.* I. 428.

[89]*Ibid.*, II, 433-34.

Commons.[90] By 1850 in Prussia "one large property owner had as much voting power as hundreds of working people."[91] The situation was much worse before that time. The basis for political rights was land ownership and the amount of taxes paid. Possession of lands and other property and payment of taxes defined rights and freedoms of people up to the beginnings of the twentieth century. This basis might be considered as more modern than the feudal hereditary basis, since now, from the legal point of view, everybody could acquire property, pay corresponding taxes, and acquire for himself a broader range of rights and freedoms. In the most recent times, rights and freedoms of individuals have been made independent from the property possessed or taxes paid. They are considered due to all people equally, as rights of man and citizen. In some countries, the commoners gained full rights in a long democratic process that was stimulated by struggle and by enormous intellectual and moral effort throughout the nineteenth and twentieth centuries; and in many countries this process has not been fully accomplished yet. These political rights were extended to the burghers and Jews in Poland before the partition at the end of the eighteenth century, and to the peasants in the first year of regained independence in 1918.

No absolute monarchy was established in Poland, contrary to the pattern of development in most other European countries. True, Polish society was dominated by an omnipotent gentry, which resulted in the paralysis of cities and the submission of the peasants to landlords. As a result, some basic economic functions in the society, such as commerce, degenerated. Also, the defense of the country and the execution of court decisions became stagnant. Society—i.e., the needs and claims of people and the "golden freedoms" of various social groups—took precedence over the rights of state and the strength of state organization. The state organization was well developed, interesting, and even artful in contrast to the uncurtailed and relatively unconfined power exercised by society; but it was crushed by the imperialistic pressure of Prussia and Russia, joined by Austria, at the end of the eighteenth century. The society could not be crushed, however. Therefore, after the partition, "the Poles discovered a national identity and engaged in one of the most potent independence movements of the last two centuries."[92]

The history of Polish law, together with the history of Russian and other Slavic legal systems, constitutes a challenge to the theory that there

[90]R. R. Palmer, *A History of the Modern World* (second edition; New York: A. A. Knopf, 1963), p. 459.

[91]*Ibid.*, p. 402.

[92]S. C. Easton, *The Western Heritage* (New York: Holt, Rhinehart and Winston, 1961), p. 524.

37

are two systems of law in Europe: common law and civil law. Neither Polish nor other Slavic law can be explained by such a theory. Unwritten Polish law was basically customary. It was influenced by judicial precedents.[93] In general, judgments of the Polish courts did not create the law, except in a few instances such as those mentioned above.[94] Nor did Polish law undergo at any time the influence of Roman law to the extent noticeable in France, Italy, and Germany. The influence of Roman law on Polish law was, however, strong. Such influence is seen in the canon and Church laws, and resulted from a long tradition of the study of Roman law at the universities.[95] People in each generation studied it at the Western universities and brought it back to their country, where it was taught in Polish universities. However, Roman law was never considered in Poland as the common law of that country or as the civil law of its citizens. Nor was it a subsidiary source of law, except in Royal Prussia,[96] in town law, and in Lithuanian law. Polish law was both customary and statutory; it was independent from Roman law, although markedly influenced by it. It was, in short, highly developed, and had a tradition of its own.

[93]Precedents or prejudicates (in Polish, *prejudykaty*) in early Polish law attracted the attention of some legal historians. See, e.g., O. Balzer, in his introduction to *Statuty Kazimierza Wielkiego,* ("Statutes of Casimir the Great"), edited from Balzer's materials by Zdzisław Kaczmarczyk, Michał Sczaniecki, and Stefan Weymann, published as Vol. 19 of *Studia nad Historią Prawa Polskiego* ("Studies on History of Polish Law") (Poznań: Nakładem Poznańskiego Towarzystwa Przyjaciół Nauk, 1947), p. xii.

[94]See fn. 52.

[95]This problem is discussed in a recent book on Tomasz Drezner by Krystyna Bukowska (fn. 69). It was studied by most outstanding specialists in the field, including Rafał Taubenschlag, in "La Storia della recezione del diritto romano in Polonia fino alla fine del secolo XVI," *L'Europa e il diritto romano; studi in memoria di Paolo Koschaker* (Milan: Giufré, 1953), I. 227-42; and in his earlier article, "Zur Geschichte des römischen Rechts in Polen," *Zeitschrift der Savigny-Stiftung für Rechtsgeschichte,* Abteilung III (1932), 325 ff. See also Stanisław Kutrzeba, "Il diritto romano in Polonia fino alla fine del secolo decimottavo," *Le relazioni fra l'Italia e la Polonia dell eta romana ai tempi nostri* (Rome, 1936). Wacław Osuchowski devoted his article "Les études du droit romain en Pologne," *Czasopismo Prawno-Historyczne,* II (1949), 508-13, to this problem. Juliusz Wisłocki wrote *Prawo rzymskie w Polsce* ("The Roman Law in Poland") (Warsaw, 1945).

[96]Zygmunt Lisowski, "O prawie rzymskim w korekturzye pruskiej i uwagi krytyczne," ("About the Roman law in the Prussian Correction, and Critical Remarks"), *Czasopismo Prawno-Historyczne,* VI (1954), No. 2, 194-220. In Royal Prussia, the reception of Roman law took place concomitantly with the reception of Roman law in Germany.

WOJCIECH WASIUTYŃSKI

Origins of the Polish Law,
Tenth to Fifteenth Centuries

Introduction
POLAND IN THE MIDDLE AGES

The oldest document concerning Poland dates from 963 A.D. Of the country's history before then, we have only vague reports, legends, and the testimony of buildings. In other words, the Middle Ages began in Poland in the tenth century. They ended, by the consensus of historians, at the close of the fifteenth century. By 1500 Poland manifested all the fundamental characteristics of a newer political structure: an elective monarchy; a parliamentary system; the political monopoly of the nobility; the *glebae adscriptio* (villeinage) of the peasants; a vast extension of her frontiers toward the East; and the multinational character of her state, resulting from the union of the Kingdom of Poland and the Grand Duchy of Lithuania (with the Catholic church powerful in the West and the Greek Orthodox church in the East). None of those features had been found in tenth-century Poland.

At the time of Poland's emergence, her territory corresponded rather closely to that of the Polish state today. It was comprised of the basins of the two major rivers (the Vistula and the Oder) and formed a near-rectangle bounded by the Carpathian and the Sudeten mountain chains and reaching the Baltic shore. No permanent territorial changes occurred until the second half of the fourteenth century, when Poland lost Silesia for almost seven centuries and gained Red Ruthenia. In 1386 Poland and Lithuania were united as the result of a royal marriage. The huge Lithuanian state, comprised of the Lithuania, Byelorussia, and the Ukraine of today, was originally to have been incorporated into the Polish kingdom. However, after preliminary conflict, the two parts of the future commonwealth remained linked only by a personal union (the hereditary grand dukes of Lithuania were elected kings of Poland) until the end of the Middle Ages.

Because the Grand Duchy of Lithuania had a separate legal system, differing basically from the Polish system in both public and private sectors, and because the Polish legal system influenced the territories east of the Vistula basin only later, we shall deal in this brief survey only with the Polish law proper.

By the tenth century, the Polish state, newly emerged from historical obscurity, had already existed for some time. The authority of the ruler was well established, and the old tribal forces were on the wane. The population was ethnically homogeneous and composed of tribes belonging to the northern branch of the Western Slavs as opposed to the southern branch (the later Czechs and Slovaks) and to the Eastern Slavs (the later Russians, Ukranians, and Byelorussians). The dialectal differences between the Polish tribes were slight; to this day the Poles are unique among the major European ethnic groups in their dialectal unity.

The Polish state took its name from the dominant tribe of *Polans* or Poles, living on the banks of the Warta River around the cities of Poznań, Gniezno, and Kalisz, which still exist. In the tenth century the center of the state shifted to Cracow, in the southwestern part of the country, and remained there until the end of the Middle Ages. These two areas — Old (or Great) Poland and New (or Little) Poland — developed somewhat different customary laws, and in the fourteenth century, when the first codification of Polish law was attempted, two separate statute books were compiled. However, these books did *not* include laws of certain other areas such as Masovia (near the Warsaw of today) and Silesia.

SOURCES AND LITERATURE

The study of Polish medieval law became popular in Poland in the nineteenth century. Publication of its sources and fundamental works on its history date from the second half of that century. In independent Poland (1919-39) at every Polish university there were two chairs: one of the History of Polish Political Institutions and one of the Old Polish Private Law.

Unfortunately most of the works on Polish medieval law are published only in Polish, although many of them include resumés in French, German or (less often) English. A selected list of document collections and of those books which are either fundamental or have been published in one of the Western European languages is given below. There is, happily, no such linguistic difficulty with the sources as with the books of commentary, as all Polish medieval documents are in Latin, even if the collections bear Polish titles.

The main collections of Polish medieval documents are: *Akta Grodzkie i Ziemskie z Czasów Rzeczypospolitej Polskiej* (Documents of Borough and County Archives), vol I-XXV (Lwów: 1868-1935). *Codex Diplomaticus Cathedralis ad S. Venceslaum Ecclesiae Cracoviensis.* Cracow: 1874. *Codex Diplomaticus Maioris Poloniae,* I-V. Poznań: 1877-1908. *Codex Diplomaticus Poloniae Minoris,* I-IV. (Cracow: 1876-1905). *Codex Diplomaticus Poloniae,* I-III. Warsaw: 1847-58. *Kodeks Dyplomatyczny Księstwa Mazowieckiego, (Documents of the Duchy of Masovia).* Warsaw: 1863. *Monumenta Medii Aevi Historica,* I-XIX. Cracow: 1874-1927. *Monumenta Poloniae Vaticana,* I-VIII. Cracow: 1918-1946. *Starodawne Prawa Polskiego Pomniki, (Monuments of the Old Polish Law)*I-XII. Cracow: 1856-1921. *Volumina Legum.* 2nd ed., I-VIII. Petersburg, 1859-60.

There are also many collections of abbey, town and county documents. Among these are the very valuable *Codex of the Abbey of Tyniec* and the *Book of the Abbey of Henryków.* For more detailed study there are the Court Books (*Księgi Sądowe*), some edited on a large territorial basis (such as the *Księgi Sądowe Mazowieckie*), and others comprising documents of one village only. The most interesting among these is the Court Book of Kasina Wielka.

Major reference books on public law are: Balzer, Oswald. *Genealogia Piastów* ("The Genealogy of the Piasts"). Cracow: 1895 (Resumé in French). Balzer, Oswald. *Historia ustroju Polski ("History of Polish Public Law Institutions").* Skrypt wykładów uniwersyteckich. Lwów: 1933. Kutrzeba, Stanisław. *Historia ustroju Polski w zarysie ("History of Polish Public Institutions").* I-IV. Lwów: 1917. Tymieniecki, Kazimierz. *Procesy twórcze formowania się spoleczenstwa polskiego w wiekach srednich. ("The Formative Processes of Polish Medieval Society").* Warsaw: 1921. (Resume in French). Tymienecki, Kazimierz. *Historia Chlopów Polskich ("History of Polish Peasantry").* I-III. Warsaw: 1965-67. Major reference books on private law are: Dąbkowski, Przemysław. *Prawo prywatne polskie. ("Old Polish Private Law").* 2 vols. Lwów: 1911. Rafacz, Józef. *Dawne polskie prawo prywatne* ("Old Polish Private Law"). Warsaw: 1938. Taubenschlag, Rafal. *Prawo karne polskiego sredniowiecza ("Polish Mediaeval Criminal Law").* Lwow: 1934. Balzer, Oswald. *Przewód sądowy polski w zarysie* ("Old Polish Judicial Procedure"). Lwów: 1935.

Important works in Latin are: Abraham, W. *Ius canonicum particulare in Polonia tempore decretalium Gregorii IX* (Acta Congressus Iuridici Internationalis, III). Rome: 1936. Bandtkie, J. V. *Ius Polonicum.* Varsoviae: 1831.

Important works in French are: Grodecki, R. *Les marchés en Pologne à l'époque antérieure à la colonisation organisée d'après le droit de*

Magdebourg. Bulletin International de l'Académie Polonaise des Sciences et des Lettres: 1922. Jedlicki, M. Z. *Les rapports entre la Pologne et l'Empire Germanique au point de vue de l'histoire des institutions politiques.* La Pologne au VII-e Congrès International des Sciences Historiques, III. Warsaw: 1933. Tymieniecki, K. *Les paysans libres en Pologne à la fin du Moyen Age. Ibid.* I. Wojciechowski, Z. *L'état polonais au Moyen-Age, Histoire des Institutions.* Paris: 1949.

Important books in German are: Arnold, S. *Die Städte Westeuropas und Mitteleuropas.* La Pologne au VII-e Congrès International des Sciences Historiques, III. Kutrzeba, S. *Grundriss der polnischen Verfassungsgeschichte.* Berlin: 1912. Wojciechowski, Z. *Das Ritterrecht in Polen vor den Statuten Kasimirs des Grossen.* Wrocław: 1930.

Institutions of Public Law: The Two Periods

In prehistoric Poland the primary social institution was the patrilineal clan (*ród*). In early historical times it claimed great popular loyalty, but it had two strong rivals. One of these included the ruler (duke or king) and his knights (*comites*); the other, following the adoption of Christianity by the country in 966, was the Church. However, unlike the majority of Western European states, the Polish state had not been formed as the result of external invasion, and so lacked the strongest traditional basis for stable class division among the freemen. Therefore the feudal system was not fully developed in Poland. In that respect Polish medieval history was closer to the Scottish than the English example.

Polish historians distinguish two periods in the history of medieval Polish law. 'n the first, the ruler (king or duke) was the main source of law, and his power was almost unlimited by public institutions. In the second, several estates were formed, each with autonomous laws which greatly limited the ruler's powers. The transition from the first to the second period occurred during the thirteenth century.

THE FIRST PERIOD

In the first of the two periods, the state, in accordance with old Slavic and popular custom, was regarded as the property of the royal clan (the Piasts). Every male member of the Piast clan had the right to inheritance. This might be a share in common ownership of the territory, or, more usually, a separate portion of that territory. The right to inheritance did not mean the right to a voice in collective rule. Only one man of the clan, the Senior Prince, was the actual ruler, and the right to designate the future

Senior Prince belonged exclusively to him. Sons had precedence over collaterals, and there was a tendency to designate the eldest son as Senior, but this was not a binding rule. The same principles governed inheritance among free clansmen. A strong individual on the throne was often able to get rid of his brothers and assume *direct* control over the whole territory of the state, as did the first fully historical ruler of Poland, Mieszko (died 992).

A great change was introduced when the second historical ruler, Boleslas the Brave (*Chrobry*) (992-1025), obtained the crown and assumed the royal title. The crown lifted its wearer above all other members of the royal clan. Still more important, the king had the right to appoint bishops, and in this way controlled the new power in the state, the clergy. By the end of the eleventh century, Poland had been considerably weakened by a pagan uprising, foreign invasions, and an internal struggle among the Piasts, and was unable to withstand claims to suzerainty by the German emperor. Poland's rulers had to abandon their royal titles, and thereafter the old inheritance system returned.

A later king, Boleslas the Wry-Mouth (*Krzywousty*), attempted to give this system a more regular and stable form. In his testament of 1138 he divided the state among his four sons, leaving the central and most important part (including the capital, Cracow) to the Senior Prince, in addition to his hereditary domain. He provided that in the future the eldest of the princes should always be the Senior. It is interesting to note that similar arrangements had been made somewhat earlier in the two neighboring Slavic states of Russia (1054) and Bohemia (1055). The Russian system was more complex, for with every change of the Senior Prince all the princes changed their lands, advancing according to age.

The system devised by Wry-Mouth lasted less than a generation. The Junior Princes ousted the first Senior Prince, and a long struggle for the Cracow throne ensued. Meanwhile the prolific Piasts partitioned their lands through succession into ever-smaller units. The constant struggle among the princes and the partitioning of the territory had two important consequences for the future of Poland. First, the position of the prince in relation to his more important subjects – especially the clergy – was considerably weakened. As early as the Synod of Łęczyca (1180), the Church obtained from the princes general privileges, judicial as well as fiscal. At the same time, the princes lost the power to appoint Church dignitaries. Other privileges for abbeys, knights, and towns followed, changing the whole pattern of legal relations. The second consequence of the burgeoning of small Piast principalities was that the full feudal "ladder" was never developed in Poland. In these principalities, all of which belonged to members of the same clan, there was no place for hereditary dignitaries or for a graded vassalage. Every free man remained

43

directly subordinate to the local prince, and the princes regarded themselves as equals, acknowledging the Duke of Cracow only as *primus inter pares.* Here lay the roots of the future principle of equality among all Polish nobles.

During that first period the prince was not only the ruler and lawgiver, but also the greatest proprietor by far. He retained the rights to all uncultivated land and all forests, waterways, game, minerals, highways, beehives, and market places. These rights were called *regalia* and could be yielded to commoners. There was no permanent council to advise the prince. Although according to tradition, Boleslas the Brave had twelve councillors, there was no such institution after his reign. The *wiec,* or council of higher court and territorial officers, appeared later, but with no fixed composition or times of meeting.

When the whole of the state territory was directly under the control of the king, he sometimes entrusted the government of a province — for example Masovia or Silesia — to a governor. In East Pomerania this office became hereditary and the area became a separate principality: the only example in Poland of what was a familiar process in Western Europe.

The early royal court was organized on the Franconian pattern. The two most important offices were those of *wojewoda,* or palatinus, and of chancellor, usually held by a cleric. There was no fixed capital city, and the court usually resided in one or another of the cities. When the court was on the move, the population had the duty of supporting and lodging them. This duty was called the *stan.*

In the country, public authority was exercised by the *kasztelani* (burgraves). This office probably derived from the old tribal chieftainships. The *kasztelan* was assisted in his duties by a deputy called *wlodarz,* by a military leader (*wojski*) and by a judge. The *kasztellania* (district under the jurisdiction of the *kasztelan*) was divided into several *opole,* or rural regional units responsible for settling all crimes committed within their boundaries and for levying taxes; they were, in short, judicial, fiscal, and military precincts.

There was but one permanent, clear legal distinction made with respect to the early inhabitants of the Polish state; the populace was divided into the free and the slaves. The free belonged to clans in which there were further social (but not legal) distinctions. The others were slaves of the clan or the prince. Slaves of the prince usually lived in slave villages and served the court or the neighboring borough or church. There were slave villages of groups such as swineherds and shepherds, wine growers, shield makers, and blacksmiths.

After the Christian conversion of the country, there appeared also a milder form of slavery known as *ascriptio.* The *ascripticii* usually served the church. They had no liberty to leave the area and could not be sold without the land. Legal jurisdiction over slaves as well as free men belonged to the *kasztellan.*

THE SECOND PERIOD

During the period when Poland was partitioned among the members of the Piast family (twelfth to fourteenth centuries), similar court and rural offices were established in every principality. In the fourteenth century the last of the Piasts, Ladislas the Short and Casimir the Great, effected the reunion of most of the national territory under their direct rule and introduced a strong royal government. Although they did not abolish the existing local offices, they reduced all but the Cracow offices to merely ceremonial importance. As the mainstay of their territorial authority the kings of the fourteenth century introduced a new office, that of *starosta* or, in Latin, *Capitaneus.* This office had originated in Lombardy,[1] was adopted in Bohemia, and from there came to Poland. In the later Middle Ages there were two kinds of starosta in Poland. The first, the starosta general, administered a large province comprising the territories of several former principalities. Such were the starostas of Great Poland, Cracow, and later, of Red Ruthenia and Podolia. The second, the borough starostas, were much more numerous and were charged with the administration of boroughs and surrounding regions. The borough starostas also possessed some judicial authority, primarily in penal cases (involving murder, rape, arson, and robbery) described in the four so-called Borough Articles.

During the same period great social and legal changes occurred. The upper stratum of the free population became a distinct class of knights by obtaining charters called Immunities, which granted them freedom from fiscal duties and from the jurisdiction of the royal officers, and in most cases also granted them permission to colonize or resettle their lands and to assume jurisdiction over the inhabitants. By means of other charters the establishment of self-governing towns was permitted, and a new class, the townsmen, appeared. A wave of colonization, which had begun a century earlier in Western Europe, swept over Poland. It was given its initial impetus by foreigners, mostly Germans and Flemings, but it soon developed into a general movement of internal recolonization by the indigenous population.[2] The slave villages gradually vanished, the slave and free rural populations were integrated, and the majority of the villages were resettled under the rule of the municipal law of Magdeburg. A

[1]Wojciechowski, *L'état polonais . . ., op. cit.* p.   .

[2]Tymieniecki, *Procesy twórcze . . ., op. cit.* p.   .

minority of the villages continued under the rule of the old Polish customary law for several centuries, but they too were strongly influenced by the rural self-rule system.

The estates thus formed were patterned upon those of Western Europe, but were not preceded by full development of the feudal system. However, the Magdeburg law introduced some feudal elements. The "locator" or settlement manager, who was usually also the mayor of the town or village, was regarded as a vassal of the landlord. The landlord in turn had only one liege: the duke or the king. There were no intermediate lords. The only exception to this pattern developed during the later Middle Ages in a few of the remaining Piast principalities, where the knights were vassals of the king's vassal. Generally however, the knights, later called nobles, were of equal rank. Until the fifteenth century there were, along with the knights of full rank, the lesser knights *(wlodykas),* who used no coats of arms. The wergild, or capitation fee *(głowesczyzna)* for a *wlodyka* was half that for a knight. The knight of full rank was distinguished from the rest of the population by three legal privileges: higher *Wergild,* free tithe (see below), and exemption from taxes on land worked with his own oxen.

In the second half of the fourteenth century, the Polish attitude toward the state underwent a basic change. Until then the Polish state had been considered the hereditary domain of the royal clan of Piasts. However, not only was King Casimir the Great without sons or brothers, but he was also a man of new ideas: in some ways a forerunner of the Renaissance. He left the crown not to any of his more distant clansmen, but to his sister's son Louis, King of Hungary. This development met with some misgivings among the upper classes, and in order to keep the Cracow throne, Louis had to grant general privileges to the nobility and the clergy. Moreover, he had to grant further privileges later, because he in his turn had no male descendants and so wished to secure the Polish crown for one of his daughters. Thus the real power of the state passed from the king to the so-called Cracow Lords, who later arranged the marriage of Louis' daughter Hedwige to the Grand Duke of Lithuania, thereby fostering the union of the two countries, which together formed the largest territorial unit in the Europe of that day.

The concept of the Piast patrimony was thus replaced by the concept of the Crown. The importance of the change is perhaps best illustrated by a declaration of the Piast princes of Masovia. When requested to pay homage to Jagiello, who was the first ruler to be called both King of Poland and Grand Duke of Lithuania, they replied that they were ready to pay homage "only to your person and not to the Crown of the Realm": i.e., to the King Jagiello but not to the Kingdom of Poland, since such allegiance would mean that any citizen of the realm could then consider the princes as his own vassals.[3] The state, in short, was no longer the property of the dynasty. It had become the heritage of all citizens: i.e., all nobles.

This new belief had serious legal consequences. On a number of occasions even prior to this when there had been no heir apparent, an election by the knights had taken place. When Louis of Hungary acceded to the Polish throne, he had to seek recognition by eight delegates sent from Cracow to Buda. Later, in order to secure the succession of his daughter, he had to obtain the approval not only of deputies of the nobles, but also of the more important towns and of the clergy. After his daughter's death, his widowed son-in-law, Jagiello, had to ask for the sanction of both the Royal Council, which had been in existence since the reign of Casimir the Great (1333-70), and the assembly of the nobility. Jagiello's sons were elected by the Royal Council and confirmed by the county assemblies and the major royal towns. Beginning in 1493, the county assemblies of the nobility, or dietines, sent one delegate each to the general meeting. By the end of the fifteenth century, therefore, there were three powers in the state: the king, the Royal Council (since that time called the Senate) and the House of Deputies. Finally, in the famous Constitution, *"Nihil novi,"* of 1505, the king was forced to declare that he would refrain from any future legislation with respect to matters "pertaining to common law or public liberty" without the consent of the Senate and the House.

One of the most characteristic features of the old Polish judicial system was that, in contrast to West European and especially the Teutonic courts, the assessors in Polish tribunals acted only as advisers to the judge but never participated in handing down the decision.

The supreme court was the Royal Court Tribunal, presided over by the king himself or by the court judge in the name of the king. The jurisdiction of this tribunal comprised cases of *status* (freedom, legitimacy and nobility), *haereditas* (cases of succession to landed property), and *crimen* (cases threatened by the penalty of death, mutilation, infamy, or confiscation of estate), and also cases against royal officers.

After the period of Immunities and the Resettlement, the courts of the royal officers, except for those of the borough starostas previously mentioned, declined in importance. From then on the proper forum for the hearing of a case was dependent upon the status of the parties in litigation. Cases against the clergy were heard by the ecclesiastical courts beginning in 1210. The only exceptions to this rule were cases concerning succession of a cleric to landed property *(causae haereditariae)*. Cases involving knights were generally heard in a county court, which could sit

[3]Wojciechowski, *L'état polonais . . ., op. cit.* p.

47

as a great or a little assize. In the latter cases the court was composed of the judge, a vice-judge *(podsędek)* and a clerk *(pisarz)*; in the former case, an unspecified number of assessors was added. Candidates for court offices were nominated by county nobles. The nominations were then presented by them to the king, who appointed the judges. Boundary disputes were tried before a special court, presided over by an official called the vice-chamberlain *(podkomorzy)*. Appeals from the county courts went to the Royal Court Tribunal.

A townsman was judged by the Court of Aldermen of his town. The High Court of German Law at Cracow Castle acted as an appellate court for the town courts. The Tribunal of Six Towns, presided over by the Cracow starosta, served as the supreme court. Cases against Jews were tried by the court of the vice-palatine *(podwojewodzi)*.

In the rural areas, *causae majores* (important cases) were usually brought before the Court of the Landlord, while *causae minores* (of minor importance) were tried by the mayor *(soltys, scultetus)*, aided by some aldermen, usually seven in number. In villages where the landlord did not receive the Immunity and which were governed by the old Polish customary law, *causae majores* were originally judged by the starosta and later by the county court. Until the end of the Middle Ages, the borough starosta courts also acted as appellate courts for the courts of the Landlords. Toward the end of that epoch, the landlords began to buy out or evict the hereditary mayors of the villages and assimilated both the *judicia majora* and the *judicia minora,* so that they had jurisdiction over all cases. At about the same time, in 1496, a law was passed providing that even for crimes committed or debts incurred by the peasants, a city trial was to be held in the landlord's patrimonial court and not in the municipal court.

Institutions of Private Law

CIVIL LAW

The rights and obligations of a person depended upon his social status, sex, and age. In earlier times, by far the most important social differences stemmed from the dichotomy between the free and the slaves. Although slavery was never predominant in Poland, in the tenth and eleventh centuries it was fairly widespread. In subsequent centuries its importance diminished, but it did not vanish completely until the fourteenth century. In Red Ruthenia, slavery existed until the sixteenth century.[4]

[4]Dąbkowski, *Prawo prywatne . . ., op. cit.* p.

A person could be relegated to slave status in several ways: by being born of slave parents; by being taken as a prisoner of war; by being sold into slavery for punishment (e.g., instead of receiving the death sentence); by incurring debts; or by committing prostitution. A man could also be pawned into slavery. However, slaves were not completely deprived of the protection of the law, and in some cases were subject to the jurisdiction of the royal courts. A slave could be freed by manumission, by working his way to freedom or, sometimes, as a punishment to his master. Also, if he were turned out by his master during a famine, he gained his freedom automatically.

In later times, the free were classed into four estates: the clergy, the nobility, the townspeople, and the peasantry. Originally the Church had been organized on the Franconian pattern, but following the close of the twelfth century the bishops were no longer appointed by the king but were elected by the chapters. In the second half of the fourteenth century, after the reunification, the kings again appointed the bishops, until the fifteenth century, when the following procedure was established: the king proposed his candidate for a bishopric in a formal writ — *litterae instantiales,* the chapter then elected the candidate and the Pope ratified the election. This system was tantamount to the appointment of the bishops by the king. At the Council of Constance (1416), the title of Primate of Poland was bestowed upon the Archbishop of Gniezno. Clerics enjoyed the *privilegium fori,* which meant that they could be tried only by ecclesiastical courts, except in cases of succession to landed property. On the other hand, the ecclesiastical courts judged laymen in cases of a moral nature, taking jurisdiction over such matters as those of matrimony. Generally the church estates enjoyed the privileges of the nobility and were the first group to be granted judicial and fiscal immunities. The monasteries, especially the Benedictine and Cistercian orders, were pioneers in the resettlement process and in the propagation of new agricultural techniques and new municipal law.

The knight or noble held a favored position in the legal order. For him, the wergild, or capitation fee, was higher. He paid no taxes on the land he ploughed with his own oxen and was not obliged to deliver his church tithes, which the vicar had to collect from the knight's field. In later times the knight was exempted from appearing before the royal magistrates; instead he was tried by the king or by his peers. After 1374 only a nobleman could be elected to a county office, and beginning in 1422 his estate could be confiscated only by judicial decree. After 1496 he was not required to pay customs duties, and in the same year it was established that only three to five plebeians were allowed to sit in a chapter, of which the other members were to be of noble descent. Beginning in 1433, a noble could not be arrested except when caught *in flagranti* (the law

"Neminem captivabimus"). The most important prerogative of the nobility, however, was their right to inherit or acquire the land *iure militari*. After the fifteenth century, the *ius* usually included the nobleman's right to judge his tenants in *causae majores* and to receive from them, in addition to rent, customary gifts *(honores)* and a definite number of days of unpaid labor each year, exacted from every *łan* (about sixty acres). After 1374 he was required to pay no more than two pence per *łan* in ordinary taxes. In return for these privileges, the knight or noble was under a duty to present himself armed and on horseback with armed servants whenever called upon by the king, under penalty of confiscation of his estate. However, he was entitled to receive pay for his military service outside the frontiers of the realm. He had other obligations toward his clansmen, and could not freely dispose of his landed property because the clansmen had the right of "nearness": i.e., in case of sale, the land had to be offered to them first.

Until the end of the Middle Ages there was no rigid distinction between knights and townsmen. Rich townsmen (patricians) bought up landed estates and moved into the noble class, while poorer nobles moved into the towns and became townsmen. A townsman enjoyed the freedom of his town and the use of its self-governing institutions, much the same as his Western European counterpart. The charters and customs of the towns were modeled upon the German municipal law *(Sachsenspiegel, Magdeburger Schoffenrecht)*, except that the role played by the town council was larger in the Polish than in the German towns. At the beginning of the development of the towns, a hereditary mayor *(wójt)* headed each town. Later, the towns bought out this office and replaced the hereditary mayors with elected ones. The Jews formed a separate segment of the town population and did not participate in the town government. They were granted a general privilege in Great Poland by Prince Boleslas the Pious, and this privilege was extended throughout Poland in the fourteenth century by Casimir the Great. The Jews were under the king's protection and could be tried only by special officers (vice-palatines). In 1423 the proscription for debts claimed by Jews was shortened to three years, although it was longer in general practice.

The Polish towns might be said to have missed a significant political opportunity in the fourteenth century, for when the nobility and the clergy received their general privileges from Louis of Hungary, the towns failed to act jointly, but received their privileges separately. Consequently, they later had no valid claim to joint representation as a third estate in the Diet, and the political power was monopolized by the nobility, first through the county dietines and subsequently through the Diet.

The law recognized several classes among the rural population of the early ages. These included the free landholders *(haeredes);* the free landless *(hospites);* the half-free *(ascripticii),* who served a church or borough and were not permitted freedom of movement; and the slaves. Free landholders were obliged to render their services as footsoldiers until the end of the thirteenth century. They could be deprived of their fields only by the king. Beginning in the twelfth century with the development of grain agriculture (wheat and rye instead of barley and oats) most of the hitherto free landowners moved in search of a higher living standard to the lands of the Church and the nobles. They merged there with the half-free and slave workers to form gradually a single peasant class. As the market and money economy developed, their obligations of work and duties gradually devolved into the payment of rents. At about the same time most villages were resettled and obtained municipal rights.[5] The peasants thus became hereditary tenants who paid rent, presented customary gifts, and supplied free labor to the landlord for a fixed number of days in a year. The law governing inheritance and tutelage among the peasants differed from that among the nobles. Peasants were tried, in minor cases, by their mayor *(sołtys)* and aldermen, who were usually appointed by the mayor. In major cases they were tried by their landlord and could appeal his sentences at the court of royal magistrates. They were also permitted to sue their lords before a royal court. After 1496 only one peasant a year could leave a village, and this marked the beginning of a new *glebae adscriptio,* or *villainage,* which had its origins in early modern times.

The *sołtyses* formed a separate subclass among the villagers. The *sołtys* was considered a vassal of his landlord. With the approval of his lord, he had the right to sell his office. During wartime, he was obliged to serve on horseback. He owned some fields free of rent, collected rents for the lord, and received some income from the village court payments. In 1423 the nobles acquired from the king a privilege to oust some of the *sołtys* (the law known as *"de sculteto inutili aut rebello"*).

Sex was an important factor in the determination of rights. While women received special privileges, they were also subject to special limitations. The wergild for a woman was twice that for a man. Women also held a privileged position in judicial procedure. For example, while the prescription against a man ran for three years, it ran six years for a widow and ten years for a married woman. Among the primary limitations for a woman were the prohibition from marriage without the consent of parents or relatives, the limitation of her right to acquire landed property, and the prohibition from retaining guardianship over children of her former marriage when she remarried.

The age classifications of the population were several. A person yet unborn could be subject to the law, and there were cases concerning

[5]Tymieniecki, *Historia . . ., op. cit.* p.

obligations drawn in favor of a *nasciturus*. In order to acquire the rights of a legitimate offspring, a child had to be symbolically lifted up by his father. At the age of seven, a boy was adopted into the clan by a ceremony which included the shearing of his hair. These customs prevailed for a long time. In earlier times a person was regarded as a minor until the time of his physical maturity. Later the age of twelve was held to mark the end of minority. By the statutes of Casimir the Great in the fourteenth Century, the end of minority was established at twelve for girls and fourteen for boys. However, even after attaining this age, a person was not yet considered completely adult and could not, for example, sell, pawn, or mortgage property. Full majority was achieved only at the age of twenty-four.

In historic Poland, there was no marriage by kidnap or by purchase, although traces of these may possibly be found in older nuptial customs. The old Polish marriage consisted of two separate acts: the betrothal *(zrękowiny)* and the wedding *(pokładziny)*. The Church wedding does not appear until some time after the Christianization of the country. In 1197 the papal legate Peter had to urge that marriage be concluded *in facie ecclesiae*. Jurisdiction over all marital matters belonged to ecclesiastical and not to royal courts. Women were subjected to very strict rules of mourning.

Generally, spouses were required to live under the system of separate estates, or dowry. In earlier times dowry consisted of movables only. In principle, a husband was entitled to a dowry *(posag)* but forfeited this right if the marriage was concluded without the assent of the bride's parents or relatives or through elopement, or if he married into the nobility, above his own station. In consideration of dowry, the husband gave the jointure *(wiano)*, usually in the form of security on his possessions, the enjoyment of which was reserved for his wife in case of widowhood. Property acquired during the married life of the spouses was regarded as the husband's property.

The power of the father in the family was very wide. He had jurisdiction not only over his wife and children but generally over all *chlebojedźcy*, "those who ate his bread." On his demand the courts had to help him in executing his verdicts. However, there was one significant exception to this rule: if he remarried, he could not ask for assistance from the courts in carrying out his judgments against his stepchildren. On the other hand, he was responsible for all offenses committed by any member of his household, as if he himself were the culprit, unless he delivered the culprit to the authorities. He could be deprived of his jurisdiction by public courts.

The primary duties of children toward their parents included maintaining them in their old age or when they were deprived of their property and providing surety for them at any time. In later times it was common practice for parents to leave their property to their children during the parents' lifetime, in return for a promise of adequate maintenance. In earlier times the entire large family dwelled in a community of landed property, and even toward the end of the Middle Ages the institution of "undivided brothers" *(bracia niedzielni,* or *fratres indivisi)* was widespread. This meant that after the parents' death, male descendants and their families continued to dwell in the community of immovable property. An occasional practice was that of the *pobratymstwo,* or adoption into brotherhood, by which an adopted brother was given all the legal rights and duties of a blood brother.

The position of illegitimate children became progressively more difficult. The clan had no right to any wergild for the slaying of such children. Furthermore, bastards could not succeed to nobility and were not permitted to receive gifts, either *inter vivos* or testamentary, from their natural parents.

There were three kinds of tutelage. The most common was natural tutelage *(opieka przyrodzona),* in which the guardian or guardians of a child were appointed by the clan and responsible to it. The second kind was official or state tutelage (rare in the Middle Ages), practiced in cases in which for some reason the clan could not appoint a guardian. The third type was self-tutelage *(opieka samowładna),* which left the minor to handle his own affairs and perform any acts which a guardian would have performed.

At first, inheritance applied only to movables, since the land belonged to the clan in common. Only when a clan died out (i.e., when there were no male descendants) did its property become "void" and subject to royal claim. The situation was different when the property was not under clan ownership, but consisted of land given by the king or prince *iure militari* as to a knight, for then only the sons of the owner could succeed to the land; otherwise it returned to the king. Under the statutes of Casimir the Great in effect in Great Poland, daughters could inherit landed property if it had been acquired by their parents in some way other than from the king or the clan. This was subject, however, to the right of their brothers to buy them out. Under the statutes of Little Poland, daughters could inherit any type of property if there were no sons, but were subject to the right of the paternal uncles and their sons to buy out the inheritance.

Because of these conditions, testaments were a rarity until the end of the Middle Ages, and a child commonly received his portion of inheritance through an *inter vivos* gift from his parents, who were under no obligation to divide the property into equal portions. Division of the inheritance might be made by choice or by lot, but custom required that the family home be left to the youngest son, just as in the old English law of the pre-Norman period. The approval of the king was sometimes sought in order to make the property division all the more secure.

The order of succession under Polish medieval law was generally as follows: first to descendants, then to siblings, then to ascendants, and last to collaterals. In this last category were, originally, all members of the clan. Later, under the influence of canon law, the right to succession was limited to relatives up to the eighth degree of consanguinity.

Property included movables and immovables, but the line of distinction between the two classifications was quite arbitrary. In earlier times, for example, slaves were considered movables, while herds of cattle were immovables. A wooden house might be regarded as a movable, while corn still growing in the fields was an immovable.

Originally there were three kinds of property: personal property (mostly movables); common or clan property, including arable land, slaves and cattle; and royal property. Hogs were important to primitive husbandry; the oldest known Polish tax was that assessed on the basis of the number of hogs owned by the taxpayer *(narzaz).*[6] Horses were a luxury and oxen were used for field work. Uncultivated land, forests, rivers, and underground resources belonged neither to individuals nor to clans but the king or prince. Eventually the kings abandoned these rights, yielding them up to landlords or to towns through special charters or general immunities. Until the end of the Middle Ages the royal rights, or *regalia,* and compulsory obligations based upon them, prevailed. *Regalia* covered mining, hunting, fishing, beehives, mills, inns, and ferries. To commence mining operations, it was necessary to obtain the king's license, for which a special payment, called *olbora,* was charged. Some of the more important mines, such as the big salt mine in Wieliczka, or the silver mines in the Olkusz area, remained in the Crown's possession, while smaller enterprises were undertaken by brotherhoods of *gwarki* (free miners).

When granting land or the right to settle anew a village under the German law, the king usually conceded the right to small game hunting, but reserved the right of big game hunting. As part of the preparations for a war, kings often organized large-scale hunts to provide the army with meat. Similarly, the Crown retained the right to big-catch fishing, allowing the landlords the right to angling and to fishing with smaller nets.

Beekeepers in the royal forests were independent of the lords and, not unlike the *gwarki,* formed a community of free royal licensees.

The term "mill," for purposes of the regale, included not only flour mills and sawmills, but also breweries, tanneries, paper mills, powder mills, fulling facilities and similar buildings. Every plant with water-propelled machinery was known as *mollendinum seu industria* — (mill or industry).

[6]Oswald Balzer, *Narzaz* (Lwów: 1928).

By the middle of the epoch most of the landlords had acquired privileges to build their own mills. However, some of the more important city *industriae*, as well as some of the larger flour mills, remained the property of the king.[7]

The inhabitants of a village or town were required to mill their grain or tan their hides in the mill of the person to whom a territorial milling monopoly had been granted. The same monopolistic regulations governed inns. This type of privilege came to be known as "banal rights" throughout medieval Europe.

Real property was subject to ground servitude laws. The local population had the rights of passage to their homes, of driving their cattle through a strip of land, digging for stone, chalk or clay, and drawing water. They also had the rights of pasture and of hewing, in the woodlands, as well as water rights, which included the rights of fishing, watering horses and cattle, and bathing.

This short survey permits but a brief mention of some of the outstanding features of the old Polish law of obligations, one of which was the extensive concept of surety. The responsibility of the guarantor was a personal one, which also extended to his entire estate. In the very early stages of the development of a related institution, called *załoga*, a person surrendered himself into slavery to his creditor. In historical times, a person in *załoga* was required to promise not to leave a place (e.g., a borough, inn, or precinct) until the debt on which he had provided surety was paid.

Because of the great importance of personal honor among people of medieval times, one of the most effective means of coercing payment from a negligent debtor was the creditor's right to scold him in solemn fashion in a public place. This right was known as *prawo łajania,* or "the right to scold."

Written documents were used only in major transactions, so the presence of witnesses to all other agreements was of primary importance. The act of purchase was usually accompanied by *litkup,* a ceremonial drinking by the witnesses.

A remnant of the old common clan property was the right of "nearness," previously mentioned, under which the seller was required to inform all his clansmen, or in later times relatives, of his intention to sell hereditary property and to offer them priority of purchase.

[7]W. Wasiutynski, *Regal młynny w średniowiecznym prawie polskim* ("Regale of the Mills in Polish Medieval Law") (Warsaw: 1936).

Polish medieval penal law stems, like all other old Eurpoean criminal systems, from the right to vengeance. This right belonged to the clan of the wronged individual, which was permitted to inflict a similar wrong on the culprit or his clan or could agree to a composition for judicial compromise. In earlier times, the ruler intervened only when the offense was committed against the King's Peace: i.e., on a public road, in the place where the ruler dwelled, or against one of the ruler's agents on a mission. The field of public intervention gradually increased, but until the end of the Middle Ages some traces of the old right of vengeance remained, and even in cases of serious crime, the possibility of composition remained open. The concept of collective responsibility never vanished completely. In Masovia the idea was supported until the end of the thirteenth century. The collective responsibility of all of the members of a household for a crime committed there was abrogated theoretically in the fourteenth century, but the practice was actually retained for a much longer time. The master of the house was responsible for bringing complaints in behalf of members of his household; by the end of the Middle Ages, however, this role was circumscribed and he then merely assisted them in court proceedings.

The *opole,* or rural region, bore a collective responsibility for the murder of any corpse found within its boundaries and could avoid liability only by indicating the guilty village within its territory. This practice was abrogated by the Statutes of Casimir the Great. Until the fifteenth century, a village bore collective responsibility for refusing its help to judicial authorities. The doctrine of collective responsibility also applied to the cities.

Upon its full development at the end of the Middle Ages the Polish criminal law had the following general features. Each individual consequence of an unlawful act (e.g., each wound inflicted) was regarded as a separate offense. There was no distinction among intentional, negligent, and accidental acts. However, the criminal intent and state of mind of the accused were taken into account. Preparation to commit a crime might be punished as an attempt to kill. The wrongdoers were jointly responsible. In earlier times, abetting a crime was of only minor importance in the penal law, but in later times an abettor could be punished in place of the absent actual wrongdoer. An accessory was always punished less severely than the wrongdoer.

If the offense were instigated by strong provocation, there was no punishment. Until the middle of the fourteenth century, neither the slaying of a prostitute nor the killing of a thief caught *in flagranti* was punished. In Masovia a rapist could also be killed with impunity.

The old Polish law did not recognize degrees of murder, and even abortion was punishable by death. However, as a relic of the old right of vengeance, the right to ransom was recognized. Even after the death sentence had been passed, if the wronged party agreed to take a ransom, the convict was freed. The ransom for slaying (wergild) was called *główszczyzna*, and its amount was determined by the status of the person slain.

The inflicting of bodily injury was one of the commonest crimes, and the law recognized four degrees of this offense. The most serious was maiming which necessitated amputation of a limb. Second to that came crippling or laming, third was the "bloody wound," and fourth was the "blue wound" or bruise. In case of bodily injury, a *concordia* or composition was always permitted. Under the Statutes of Casimir the Great, if a person were injured in a brawl after dark in a building, the person who extinguished the light was held responsible for the injury. Wounding was prosecuted only on the demand of the person wronged, and not on the initiative of the public authority. The culprit, besides incurring a penalty, had to pay damages to the plaintiff. Sometimes the *pokora*, or act of public penance, could be substituted for punishment; it consisted of symbolic acts by which the plaintiff supposedly took revenge upon the defendant.

Defamation, in extreme cases, was punished by cutting of the tongue, but usually the cases ended in composition, which included the retraction of the injurious statements and payment of damages. A special form of penalty for defamation was the *odszczekanie* or "rebarking," in which the culprit appeared in a public place, under a table, and retracted his words.

The crime of trespassing against a person included such acts as kidnapping a girl, a wife, or a serf; imprisoning a free man; exerting duress in marrying another; and rape. The crime of trespassing on property included invasion of a house or land; expulsion from an estate; resistance to the action of a judicial authority; sowing of another's ground; pasturing on another's land; and hewing another's wood. Robbery on the highways was regarded as a highly serious case of trespassing. The crime of trespassing was prosecuted upon the initiative of public authorities only when it was practiced as a profession by the culprit. Composition between the parties in cases of trespassing was permissible. Extortion was treated as a kind of trespass, and in some cases was punished by the assessment of treble damages.

Larceny was prosecuted by the state only when committed by professional thieves, and then it was punished by death, infamy, or cutting of an ear. Theft from a closed place was punished more severely than other types of theft. A thief was frequently permitted to remunerate his victim instead of receiving punishment.

Embezzlement was subjected to the penalty of three hundred *grosze*, a rather high fine. Forgery of documents was punished by the penality of fifteen *grosze*, a much lower fine.

Adultery committed by a wife was, in principle, punished by the husband himself.

The crime of lese majesty was rather extensive in scope, and even an assault upon a public official could fall under this category of offense. An offense against the Court's Peace was punished usually by fine and only exceptionally by death.

For military desertion the penalty was confiscation of all property owned by the deserter.

Probably the most ancient of penalties was the outlawing of a person. In a tightly knit clan society it amounted to civil, and later, often physical death. From this original punishment three main types of penalty developed. The first was banishment, accompanied by the confiscation of property. The second was infamy and other lesser penalties assessed against the honor of the offender. The third was the death penalty, which was later mitigated by the development of slavery and corporal punishment. Imprisonment later devolved from the penalty of slavery, while fines stemmed from the old ransom from state's vengenace.[8]

PROCEDURE

Polish medieval judicial procedure was, like most contemporary European procedures, slow and formal, but manifest with a high regard for the rule of law. There was a double division of cases: one according to the subject matter of the case, the other according to the amount in controversy. In the former division, cases fell into two classes; *causae haereditariae* and *causae personales.* The former concerned landed property or business establishments. The latter included disputes arising from obligations, controversies over chattels, and questions over real estate if the relief asked for were other than vindication. It also included cases on questions of status, particularly those involving nobility, which had to be proven by the testimony of witnesses – usually clansmen.

On the basis of the amount in controversy, cases were divided into *causae majores,* which included all cases of succession to real property and cases in which the value of the matter in controversy exceeded a specified sum (forty, sixty or one hundred *grzywna,* or pounds, depending upon the period and region); and *causae minores.*

Judicial proceedings were initiated by certain preliminary steps, some of which were obligatory and others mandatory. A judge could be notified

[8]Taubenschlag, *Prawo karne . . ., op. cit.* p.

of a complaint, but this had no binding initiatory force. More important, but still not absolutely necessary, was the protest, or *manifestum*, introduced into the record. As the courts had no permanent seat in one place, the protest was usually filed in the borough starosta's office. The actual proceedings opened with the citation (*pozew*). The citation, until the fourteenth century, was usually oral. Later, the citation of a nobleman was required to be in writing. The citation had to indicate the court, time of hearing, the object of litigation, and the names of plaintiff and defendant. The delivery of a citation to a defendant sometimes posed difficulties, so that the procedure for delivery was regulated in detail. The citation of a propertied person had to be delivered to his home, and in his absence was to be nailed to the door or gate. When this latter course was impracticable, the citation could be put in a split rod and "planted" on the property. Similarly, when an unpropertied person could not be found, the citation could be put in a split rod in his birthplace or the place of his last residence, and eventually such a person could be arrested. The court bailiff was responsible for delivery of the citation, and after delivery he was required to write an account of the service of process and join it to the court's records. A second citation (*przypozew*) was necessary in certain cases: e.g., upon death of the reigning king and ascension of a new king to the throne, or upon a change of presiding judge, plaintiff, or defendant.

Every court kept files where all of the main proceedings were noted and the sequence of cases settled. The time of trial, in earlier times, was stated rather vaguely (*"ut tertia die post nostrum felicem ingressum compares"*: "that thou compareth in the third day after our lucky arrival"). Later, one had to appear before the Royal Court Tribunal immediately, before other courts in major cases within three weeks, and in minor cases within a day. The *rok zawity* (*terminus peremptorius* or peremptory term) was of particular importance, and the absence of a party could be prejudicial to his case. Every term of the Royal Court Tribunal was a *rok zawity*. In the other courts, however, postponement of a trial was not difficult.

The trial was open to the public, the only limitation being on the number of persons accompanying the parties. The proceedings were oral, but a summary record was kept.

The trial itself was divided into the *Instantia Procedendi* and the *Instantia Respondendi* and each instance was subdivided into *accessoria*. The first instance was preparatory, concerned with the registration, term, and jurisdiction of the forum. The second instance consisted of the plaintiff's presentation of his case, followed by the defendant's reply. Originally the burden of proof was on the defendant, who could either acknowledge the plaintiff's claim or swear to his own innocence or claim. According to the legal reasoning of the time, the plaintiff had the right to prove and the defendant the duty to prove. The legal adage ran, "Negans

59

proprior est ad probandum" ("It is more proper that he proves who denies").

The oath was at once the most common and the most important type of evidence. It was taken not only by the defendant but also by the witnesses produced by him. These were not witnesses to the facts of the case, but witnesses to the good character and honor of the defendant. The testimony of eyewitnesses, documents, and the court's visit to the scene were utilized only as secondary means of evidence. Excluded from testifying as sworn witnesses were those of a lower status than any of the parties, the infamous, the excommunicated, near relatives, women, minors, and lunatics. Excluded as eyewitnesses were the infamous, the excommunicated, minors, and lunatics. However, proof of nonliability by the use of oath-helpers was limited, and a person availing himself of this device three times previously for the same kind of accusation was, on the fourth occasion, held responsible without evidence.

A defendant who failed to appear before the court at the first time (except for the Royal Court Tribunal) was fined. If again absent, he paid another fine. However, if absent at the third term, he lost his case by default. A plaintiff lost by default if he failed to appear at the first term.

A decision could be final (*stanowczy*) or interlocutory (*przedstanowczy*), and in the latter case the court could order *impositio vadii primarii* (escrow) and could also pass a conditional judgment, e.g., a judgment on condition that a party would swear afterwards.

The proper means of appealing from a sentence was determined by whether the judgment was rendered after a trial in the presence of both parties, or by default. In the latter case the appellant took action for *male obtendum*, asserting that the judgment was invalid. In the former case the appellant could only claim that the judgment was unjust and had to take action against the judge, in an action called *Nagana* (censure). In such an action the appellee and the judge were considered as a single party, while the appellant was the opposing party. The judge could refuse a party the right to censure him, in which case the party was required to undertake another kind of action against the judge, called *pro gravamine*. In Masovia, there was still another kind of appeal: if the judge refused the right to censure, the appellant could ask the prince to order a new trial. Such an order, if issued, started a *processus per litteras informatorias.*

The judgment was, in principle, executed immediately after the delivering of the decision, by payment, by giving a surety, or by depositing a sum of money in escrow. If the losing party did not comply he was fined, and if he were not present at the delivery of the judgment, the winner had to send him a *przypowiest* or *concitatio*, requiring him to appear at the new term (*astitio*) under penalty of fine.

The oldest form of execution was not levying on property but levying on the person, which meant giving the losing party into slavery. In later times, when clan property was replaced by individual property, this form of execution was retained for unpropertied persons only, and slavery was replaced by imprisonment.

The execution on property was directed primarily to chattels. Only if the object of the litigation was landed property or a building was the execution directed to it at once. In other cases the levying on real property was only subsidiary, usually resorted to only when the value of chattels was not sufficient to satisfy the judgment. Execution on chattels could be conducted either by the court or by the winning party himself. Execution on real property was a lengthy procedure conducted not by the court but by the state executive power in the person of the starosta.[9]

Conclusion

The Polish medieval system of law, public as well as private, is clearly distinguishable from the systems prevailing to the east and west of Poland's frontiers. It differed from the Western system primarily because of the absence in Poland of a strictly feudal structure. Poland did not pass through the Roman rule and did not have the prerequisites of feudalism in the form of "protection" and vassalage. The medieval partitioning of the territory occurred at about the same time as it did in continental Western Europe, after the crumbling of the Carolingian Empire, but in Poland all the princes belonged to the same family or clan of Piasts, and there was no room for hereditary dignitaries or for a many-runged feudal ladder. Moreover, the patriarchal character of the Polish state feudalism made possible the early reunification of the national territory under one king, which occurred in the fourteenth century, earlier than in Western Europe. However, in contrast to the later Western European monarchies, the restored Polish kingdom never became absolutist. The dying out of the national dynasty and the installation of foreign rulers such as the absentee Louis of Hungary, his daughter Hedwidge and her "barbarian" husband Jagiełło had an effect similar to that of the introduction of a foreign dynasty in England much later. It gave the real political power first to the aristocratic oligarchy of the Cracow Lords, and later to the nobiliary democracy.

On the other hand, Poland came under the strong influence of three Western European institutions that in many ways shaped her social and

[9]Balzer, *Przewód sądowy . . ., op. cit.* p. .

cultural character. They were: first, the Roman Catholic church, with its hierarchy independent from the state, and its universities, orders of monks, and canon law; second, the self-governing municipality, urban and rural; third, the concept of Christian chivalry, with its code of honor and its coats of arms. These institutions never reached the Eastern Slavs. In contrast, Russia was subjugated by the Mongols in the thirteenth century and consequently influenced by their system of law.

In Polish private law, three coexistent currents, differing in origin, influenced each other and in some ways merged. The first, the old Slavonic law, was customary and particularist. The second, Roman law, was represented in the canon law. The third was the German municipal law.

The ecclesiastical courts rendered their judgments according to canon law, the municipal courts and the High Court of German Law at Cracow according to the Magdeburg law, and the county courts and the Royal Court Tribunal according to the old Polish law which had been codified in part by Casimir the Great in the fourteenth century.

Two processes mark the close of the Middle Ages in Polish law and the beginning of a new period. One of these is the establishment of a political monopoly of the nobles, and the other is the gradual reception of the Roman civil law by way of university teaching and court decision. The two trends had a disastrous effect on the situation of the peasant population, for the ideas of Roman law substituted for the medieval concept of divided property in land (useful and direct) the Roman notion of indivisible and absolute property vested in the landlord.

WACŁAW SZYSZKOWSKI

The Law of Nations in Poland from the Middle Ages to Modern Times

In accordance with a view which is gaining an ever-growing acceptance among students of the law of nations and which is supported by authoritative statements of some well-known scholars, it is no longer possible to maintain that Hugo Grotius was "the father of international law." Indeed, it is now possible to trace the development of the law of nations, and especially the concept of a "just war," to the works of the Canonists of the thirteenth century.

It was quite natural that the law of the Empire and the ecclesiastical law of the Church during the Middle Ages cannot be treated as identical with the law of nations in the modern sense. How could this law flourish under the medieval tradition of interdependence between lord and vassals? The transformation of *ius gentium* into international law coincided with the decline of the Empire (specifically, the fall of the House of Hohenstaufen, circa 1254) and the weakening of the Papacy, as a result of the Avignon captivity, which occurred half a century later. It was then that the law of nations began to supplant the unitarian philosophy characteristic of the medieval world.

As Professor Halecki says in his history of East Central Europe:[1]

It is now more and more generally admitted that in the course of European history the real Middle Ages ended toward the end of the fourteenth century and are separated from the modern period, in the proper sense, by two centuries of transition which correspond to the flowering of the Renaissance and of its political conceptions.

We have chosen as the topic of our inquiry the law of nations in Poland in the fifteenth and sixteenth centuries — the period of transition from the

[1]Oscar Halecki, *Borderlands of Western Civilization — A History of East Central Europe* (New York: Ronald Press, 1952), p. 117.

Middle Ages to modern times — because, apart from its being intellectually fertile (in the special sense in which transitional periods usually are), the period demonstrates revolutionary ideas of international law in force long before the works of Vitoria and Grotius saw the light of day.

Feudal law in its Western European sense (formalizing the interdependence of lord and vassal) was unknown in Poland; instead, a modern approach to international relations developed at the close of the Middle Ages from the authority exercised from 1320 by Władislaw Lokietek over the whole unified kingdom.

As early as the fourteenth century, Poland had begun to suffer from the onslaught of the Teutonic Order, whose members were popularly called Knights of the Cross. With strong military organization and considerable political influence in the Western world, in the Holy Roman Emperor's court, in the Church, and among the ranks of Western knighthood, the Order was a powerful enemy of Poland. It accused the peoples of Lithuania, Samogitia, and Russia of paganism and claimed that their supposed conversion to Christianity had not been accomplished. The Order acted on the theory that an aggressive war against pagans was not only permissible but laudable. Transferring their activities from the Mediterranean region to that around the Baltic Sea, the Knights of the Cross began to make regular raids and to pursue a policy of extermination which would now be branded as genocide. Their appeal to the rest of Christendom for help found the greatest response among other Western knights — heirs of the crusaders, adventurers, and soldiers of fortune. At the same time the Teutonic Order attacked Poland under the pretext that she was an ally of the "pagan" peoples. As the Order considered any war against the pagans a "just war" *(bellum justum)*, and as it had some support in the West, the moral justification of the war was a vital problem for Poland.

Success in the war of ideas required not only military, but also spiritual and intellectual strength. To use modern terms, any political action implies a solid philosophic preparation, which was, in fact, furnished in this case by the oldest Polish university, the University of Cracow, founded in 1364. The problem of the "just war" has attracted the attention of the best philosophic minds. The ancient Romans had developed the idea of a *bellum justum et pium.* The confrontation of war and ethics runs through the speculations of Cicero, Archbishop Isidore of Seville, and Thomas Aquinas, among many others. Thus the intellectuals in Cracow were concerned with a subject of traditional interest.

It is a general rule that the evolvement and diffusion of state theories is a matter of political necessity. Machiavelli, for instance, did not offer an abstract philosophy, and Bodin would probably have been silent had he not wished to consolidate the power of his monarchs. Grotius's early work, *De iure praedae commentarius,* was written, his contemporaries believed, as a result of legal doubts which had arisen after the Dutch East India Company had taken spoils from conquered Portuguese cargo ships. Gentili and Bynkershoek developed their expertise in the law of nations as the result of specific and practical legal cases. The same was true of Stanislas and Paulus Vladimiri, whose doctrines we are now going to outline.

Stanislas of Scarbimiria, (a small town near Cracow) was a professor of canon law and rector of the University of Cracow from 1400 to 1413. His most remarkable work was the sermon *"De bellis iustis,"* delivered probably in 1409, dealing with the problems of a "just war" as well as with the dilemma of cooperation with pagans, which in practice meant cooperation with the Moslem Tartar contingents belonging to the Lithuanian forces. The sermon is the earliest known systematic treatise on the law of public war and covers this subject exclusively.

Stanislas expressed his views on the philosophical and legal problems of war in a sermon; however, given the medieval admixture of secular and holy instruction, one can include Stanislas's sermon in the category of scientific lectures destined for an academic audience. Another example is Francisco Vitoria's set of two well-known lectures on the American Indians given in 1532.

Stanislas's conception of war, and especially of a "just war," is not original. He based it on the numerous sources: on St. Augustine, on *Decretum Gratiani,* and on other canon collections; on Raymond of Penyafort, William of Rennes, St. Thomas Aquinas, Margarita Decreti, Martinus Polonus; and of course on the Scriptures, Roman law, and Cicero. However, many of these older ideas were developed by Stanislas in an original way. In discussing "just war," for instance, he forbids clergymen to start or take part in it. This idea is obviously taken from the *Summa Theologica* of St. Thomas Aquinas, and is meant as an argument against the wars of the Teutonic Order. War *is* admissible, however, for the recovery of property and in defense of one's country. There must exist a just cause *(causa)* – the restoration of peace, for instance. No war can be waged because of hatred, vengeance, or greed, though it is permissible to wage war for God's love or for justice. Authorization by the Church or a monarch also provides the necessary license for battle.

In contrast to preceding writers, Stanislaus refuses to justify the concept of private war; a "just war" for him can be only that in which a public armed force is used. This concept shows how advanced Stanislas is, especially when one remembers that Grotius, two hundred years later, includes a section on private war in the second book of his great work, *On the Law of War and Peace.*

In another respect Stanislas is also in advance of his contemporaries: he is more humane than they, and deprecates wars of punishment which older writers would have considered as the administration of justice.

Further, Stanislas advocates a doctrine of religious toleration and belief in the equality of the pagan and the Christian states. To be sure, this was nothing new in the theological teaching; Pope Innocent IV (Sinibaldo de' Fieschi), who had died in 1254, recognized the right of pagans to possess a state, though in practice this principle was forgotten among Christians in the next century. Instead of the collaboration of Christians with pagans in a community of states, an idea which Stanislas set forth, the fourteenth century was dominated by a spirit of proselytism which found its expression in forcible conversions and even the destruction of infidels. Stanislas emphasized the subjection of all men to the natural law established by God, and accorded a sense of dignity to all of mankind. Before him, medieval theologians had seen the pagan as nothing except an object for conquest.

Because he believed in the equality of Christians and pagans, Stanislas wished to reject the papal privileges granted those who waged an aggressive war against the pagans; and he questioned the right of the West to rule over the entire world. He precedes by one century Vitoria, who also criticized this kind of aggression.

In that era, any political association or coalition with non-Christians was held by the Church as illicit, although the Byzantine emperors did not have any scruples about entering into political alliance with the "pagans." Thus, Stanislas had to justify the partnership with infidels which became a political necessity in the war against the common enemy, the Teutonic Knights. Stanislas made a simple analogy: as it is prohibited to fight against a human being who has done no harm to us, so it is also dishonorable to attack any such kingdom. Similarly, as men are entitled to self-defense, so are states. On this basis, he made an important statement in his sermon about the permissibility of alliance with infidels. This part of Stanislas' reasoning appears as his most original idea. He conceived of self-defense as a natural human right. Stanislas dealt with the problem of self-defense in a way never encountered before in medieval doctrine; that is to say, he envisaged the political or military help of the infidels, should it be necessary in achieving peace, as not in conflict with Christian doctrine. It was an incontestable right of Christians to use war machines: the siege machine, for instance. If we agree on this point, so Stanislas argues, can we not use for the same purpose of self-defense the *human* force, as man is the most worthy creature on earth? The Christian prince, so the argument goes, is not responsible for the wrongdoing of his non-Christian partners. Such an interpretation of self-defense can be found in Article 51 of the Charter of the United Nations.

In the era when the decrees of the Popes and Church councils prohibited trade with the Saracens, the theory of alliance with the infidels preached by Stanislas was a serious challenge to the old order and to the customs of the Christian world. Supported by scriptural quotation and stressing the equality of *all* states, the sermon advocated the legality of pagan states and their property rights, and denied to the Pope the right of arbitrary organization of Crusades. Thus, a hundred years before modern times, an ecclesiastic from Central Europe gave a new spirit to the traditional doctrine of "just war" and created the foundation on which the idea of the sovereignty of nations was later developed. This was a great step in the direction of the modern international law.

Stanislas required of a "just war" not only a just cause but also honorable conduct in war. While the war is being waged, he said, any malicious action or unnecessary cruelty, destruction or deportation should be avoided. With regard to the methods of warfare, Stanislas uses several times the expression "inevitable necessity" *(necessitate inevitabili)* when some really strong action is required. We can find such a concept articulated in a document signed five centuries later – the Hague Regulations (1899, 1907) attached to the Convention Respecting the Laws and Customs of War on Land. Article 23g forbids the destruction and seizure of the enemy's property unless it be "imperatively demanded by the necessities of war."

Stanislas also considered the problem of reparation for war damages. His theory anticipated the contemporary practice of decision by arbitrary tribunal. (Paragraph 17 states "Oportet siquidem omnem obliquitatem ad equalitatem reduci et omne damnum iniuste illatum resarciri.") ("At least all the obliquities must be resolved and the harm illegally done must be repaired.") The term "resarciri" will later be used by Vitoria and Grotius.

Stanislas also pioneered in his approach to the problem of executing the orders of superiors, which played such a considerable role in the trials of war criminals after World War II. How could one define the responsibility of a soldier acting on the order of his superior? Stanislas makes a significant distinction between a commander (a person in charge) and the people who are bound to obey. The superiors (monarch and knights) should not wage a war without proper justification. The people bound to obedience must obey, unless it is obvious that the war is unjust. A similar attitude was taken in the Charter of the International Military Tribunal (annexed to the London agreement of August 8, 1945), in which Article 8 states that the defendant is responsible for his crime even if he was acting in pursuance of a higher order, although that fact may be taken into account in mitigation of the punishment. The Nuremberg Tribunal was based on the London agreement.

A review of the legal treatises written in Europe during the fifteenth century reveals no work so far-sighted, so reflective of legal thought in our own times, as Stanislas's sermon.

In summary, Stanislas's significance in the history of international law is based mainly on his formulation of the principle of the equality of pagans and Christians, on the admissibility of alliances with the pagans, and on his view concerning reparation of war damages.

Now let us consider the work of another learned person: the treatise presented to the Council of Constance by Paulus Vladimiri in the years 1415-17. After the Battle of Grunwald (known also as Battle of Tannenberg), in which the united Polish and Lithuanian forces had achieved a major victory (July 15, 1410), the power of the Teutonic Order was broken forever. However, despite the peace treaty signed in Toruń on February 1, 1411, the antagonism between the Order and Poland and Lithuania did not lessen. The situation required from Poland a public explanation that she had defended herself against Teutonic aggression. The proper occasion came soon, at the time of the Council of Constance.

Such councils compared in importance with meetings of the United Nations today, although one must remember that the authority of the councils was much greater. The presence of the Pope and the Emperor gave to the debates an especial splendor; and at the same time the presence of many eminent scholars, together with the contributions which they brought to the meetings, increased the worldly influence of such universities as the Sorbonne, Oxford and Bologna. These universities gradually tried to replace in philosophic influence the declining though still powerful Papacy and the Empire. The University of Cracow celebrated its entry into the family of the first universities of the world. At the Council of Constance (1414-18) the Polish delegates, headed by Nicholas Trąba (Archbishop of Gniezno and Primate of Poland, and one of the candidates for the Papacy), joined the group which advocated the supremacy of the Council over the Pope. Among the many important items on the agenda, the Council was called upon to decide in the matter of the dispute between the Kingdom of Poland and the Teutonic Order. A member of the Polish delegation, the rector of the young University of Cracow, Paulus Vladimiri of Brudzeń, presented to the Council on July 5, 1415, a treatise, *De potestate papae et imperatoris respectu infidelium*, conceived in a modern spirit of international law.

First of all, Paul declared himself a scholar, and not a diplomat. He was, in short, not merely an advocate of the Polish cause; he was able to rise above partisan interests and to represent the noblest ideals of mankind. Considering the circumstances, his outlook was bold and courageous. According to his view, the forcible conversion of pagans to Christianity and the destruction by fire and sword was not to be allowed. Proselytism was to be conducted by way of the cross and love for the pagans, who were neighbors of the Christians and who also had the right to existence. Christian faith was to be spread by word and example, and not by acts of violence. One was not to invade the pagans and take over their lands under cover of devotion to Christianity. Neither the Pope nor the Emperor was to authorize this course of action, nor could privileges be granted, as neither the Pope nor the Emperor had the right to dispose of pagan lands. Paul's treatise won the support of the majority of the Council. Besides gaining an extraordinary political success, he developed some ideas new and even revolutionary in contemporary thought, especially regarding national self-determination and religious toleration. It will be noted that many of Paul's theses are in full harmony with the principles of Stanislas's sermon; these form the basis of what we can call the Polish school of international law. When Paul declared that it was not permissible to war against the infidels under the pretext of conversion to Christianity, and that one should not convert by coercion (*"cum praetexto pietatis non est impietas facienda"*), and when he emphasized the necessity of peaceful relations with Eastern neighbors regardless of their faith, he was formulating a set of principles new in the field of international law which had to await the Renaissance to find general acceptance; not until the sixteenth century (Vitoria and Las Casas) and later (Suarez, 1613) do we find similar objections to the use of the sword in conversion. The tradition of thought which followed Paul's treatise could not have been unknown to Vitoria. Indeed, Paulus was a precursor of the twentieth-century idea of colonial self-determination, an idea of paramount importance for many nations at this moment.

One cannot neglect another writer who belongs to the Polish school of state and international legal theory — Jan Ostroróg, who as early as 1475 developed to a considerable extent the idea of the sovereignty of the state in his work, *Monumentum pro reipublicae ordinatione.*

One must bear in mind that a Frenchman, Jean Bodin (1530-1596) published his famous work, *Six livres de la République* in 1576. Ostroróg, like Bodin, was inspired by the idea of strengthening the government of his country. Sovereignty to them was vested in the person of the monarch. Both of them rejected imperial and papal supremacy. The king of Poland, according to Ostroróg, was not subject to a higher temporal power and did not recognize any superior except God. Similarly, according to Bodin, sovereignty was vested in the person of the monarch, who maintained only the supremacy of God and of the law of nature.

It is significant that Ostroróg proclaimed the theory of freedom of the roads and rivers long before similar proclamations of the French revolutionists and the Congress of Vienna, when the principles of free navigation on the so-called international rivers were proclaimed.

The political literature in Poland of the fifteenth and sixteenth centuries was imbued with a pacific spirit directly resulting from the peaceful policy of Poland and the aggressive action of the Teutonic Order. This spirit can be found in Andrzej Frycz Modrzewski *(De republica emendanda,* 1551-54), who did not rely for his authority exclusively on the medieval and scholastic masters, but also on the more rational thought of Cicero.

It would be difficult to omit the name of Laurentius G. Goślicki (1530-1607), a Polish scholar, although he was not, in the strict sense, a writer in the field of the law of nations. His book, *De optimo senatore* (Venice, 1568; second edition printed in Basel, 1593), is an excellent treatise on constitutional law, and was used in England in the struggle of Parliament against the Crown. There were at least three translations of the work into English – in 1598, 1607, and 1733. It is also very likely that *De optimo senatore* influenced the founding fathers of the United States.

Jakób Przyłuski, who belonged to the same Protestant group in Poland as Modrzewski, published a giant work, *Encyclopedia of Polish Laws and Political Problems* (*Leges seu Statuta ac Privilegia Regni Poloniae,* 1548) in which he deals, in chapter XV, part 5, with problems of legations. Przyłuski includes in the law of nations all rules pertaining to the security of foreign envoys and merchants, and discusses the degree of hospitality to be accorded to foreigners. He emphasizes the obligation of keeping one's promises even to enemies. The above principles, Przyłuski says, can be considered as part of the natural law of nations, for they have always been accepted internationally by common agreement, have been maintained, and cannot be violated without punishment. Przyłuski concludes that the rules governing the use of force are included in the positive law, since the positive law provides a formula in keeping with the customs of a particular country.

Przyłuski, as we can see, is confronted with one of the topics most essential to the establishment of international law: the transformation of international clauses into the municipal law. He resolves the problem of transformation in a way which still has many eminent followers. To appreciate fully the novelty and originality of Przyłuski's contribution, one has to remember that he lived three and one-half centuries before Triepel, Anzilotti, and Kelsen, and at a time when the famous dichotomy between monism and dualism did not exist.

Jan Tarnowski, Commander-in-Chief of the Polish Army, published in 1558 a book dealing with military topics, but covering also some subjects of legal and philosophical nature. He analyzed the elements of war from the humanitarian point of view, and levelled strong objections against aggressive wars: an interesting view, considering his military rank.

Towards the end of the sixteenth century (1595), there appeared a booklet of Krzysztof Warszewicki entitled *De legato et legatione liber*. The booklet is of only moderate value, but it deserves attention for the fact that its author adduces examples from modern rather than ancient history. It thus demonstrates a new spirit and technique of inquiry, as pointed out by the Belgian scholar Ernest Nys in his *Les Origines du droit international*.[2]

We have seen above how the idea of the law of nations was developed in the works of Polish writers of the fifteenth and sixteenth centuries. Some concepts described by them can be traced far back through centuries to the time before our era. To such concepts Polish writers often gave a new meaning, but in other instances their ideas were new. The ideas were developed in a spirit of peace, loyalty, and international understanding at the time when new trends were about to make themselves known – in the Renaissance.[3]

[2](Brussels: A. Castaigne, 1894), pp. 356-7.

[3]Compare also Stanislaus F. Belch, *Paulus Vladimiri and His Doctrine Concerning International Law and Politics* (2 vols.; London: Mouton, 1965), *passim*; and Ludwik Ehrlich, *Works of Paul Wladimir (A Selection)* (3 vols.; Warsaw: PAX, 1968-69), *passim*.

WACŁAW W. SOROKA

Main Institutions of
the Polish Private Law, 1400-1795

Law Regarding Persons

The Polish private law of the period 1400-1795 distinguished natural persons from juridical persons.

Everybody born alive was the subject of law and legal action. A fetus was also under the protection of law, as evidenced by the facts that abortion was a crime, that legal protection was given to pregnant women, and that pregnant women were not subject to capital punishment, except for witchcraft, in which case, in Poland just as in Germany, England, and France, even they were burned alive if convicted.

The law distinguished between two kinds of death: natural death and civil death. Natural death was manifest or presumptive. Even manifest death had to be stated officially by public authorities or by priests, physicians, or witnesses. In the case of a soldier, for example, a positive statement by his commanding officer was conclusive in establishing death.

Presumptive death had to be declared in judicial proceedings. Most often such a case arose from the disappearance of a person during combat or some other calamity. For example, if a soldier was declared missing or fugitive by his commanding officer, judicial action was undertaken. The missing person was summoned to the court in a manner prescribed by law. Failure to appear in court within a prescribed time constituted the basis for legal presumption of his or her death. The declaration of the presumptive death carried all the consequences of natural death.

In the case of disappearance, a time lapse alone could constitute the basis for declaring legal death. The length of time that justified the presumption of death was prescribed by law; it was increased, under the influence of canon law, during the period under study. The declaration of presumptive death was made by the court in answering a request of the interested parties – most often the family of the missing person.

The institution of civil death, as well as the rules concerning it, developed at the end of this period from the institutions of infamy *(infamia)* and banishment *(banitio)*.[1] "Infamy" meant that the convicted person was deprived of the protection of law. Such people lost all rights; not only could they be assassinated with impunity, but their assassins were granted a reward (including noble status if the assassins were commoners) and a share in the real and personal estates of the victim.[2] Together with *banitio*, this institution constituted the basis for the legal concept of civil death. This concept had earlier been known in French law.[3] As early as the sixteenth century, Polish law considered both outlaws and banished persons as dead.

The concept of the juridical person developed early in the first period of the Polish law, and underwent further evolution and refinement into its two characteristic types: corporations and foundations. The juridical personality of the Crown of the Polish Kingdom *(corona regni Poloniae)*, elaborated in the fourteenth century,[4] was separate from the person of the king. Particularly, the dukes of Mazovia as well as the Mazovian gentry at large distinguished the Kingdom of Poland as a political body separate from its king. This was evident especially in their deliberations over the relation of Mazovia to the Polish Crown at the beginning of the fifteenth century, before Mazovia became fully incorporated into Poland. This principle of separation of the state from the person of the ruler developed in Poland without resistance. The Polish kings could not say, "I am the state," as the French kings did.

The Church and religious orders, as well as the ecclesiastical foundations – another group of juridical persons – were limited in their legal

[1]The ambiguity of the terms *infamia* and *banitio* is emphasized by Juliusz Makarewicz, *Polskie prawo karne, część ogólna* ("Polish Penal Law, Part General") (Lwów: Księźnica Polska, 1919), p. 5.

[2]Juliusz Bardach, *Historia państwa i prawa Polski do roku 1795* ("History of the State and Law of Poland Until the Year 1795") (Warsaw: Państwowe Wydawnictwo Naukowe, 1957), II, 326.

[3]*Ibid.*, p. 485.

[4]The problem has been discussed in numerous publications by, among others, Jan Dąbkowski, *Korona Królestwa Polskiego w XVI wieku; studium z dziejów rozwoju polskiej monarchii stanowej* ("The Crown of the Polish Kingdom in the XVI Century; A Study From the History of the Development of the Polish Feudal Monarchy") (Wrocław: Zakład im. Ossolińskich, 1956) and Konstanty Grzybowski, "'Corona Regni' a 'Corona Regni Poloniae'," *Czasopismo Prawno – Historyczne*, IX, No. 2 (1953), 299-331.

74

capacity to perform some acts in that period. For example, beginning in the seventeenth century, they could no longer acquire property, either by purchase, by gift, or by testamentary disposition. Secularization of the property of the Church and its institutions was not known in Poland,[5] but the increase of land owned by the Church and the clergy has been checked throughout the ages. Special laws (the so-called amortization constitutions) were enacted by the Polish *sejm* (parliament) in the seventeenth century and later.[6] They prohibited or limited the acquisition of landed property by the Church or by the clergy: i.e., the acquisition *manu mortua.*[7]

At the end of the eighteenth century, companies and corporations for production, trade, and construction work appeared in Poland. The development was reflected in the creation of corporation law. Two features characteristic of corporations could be seen at that time: the departure from monopoly toward economic liberalism, and the limitation of responsibilities of shareholders to their shares. Both were advanced legal concepts.

The Polish law distinguished legal capacity (legal power to be subject to law, or *status*) from capacity for legal action (power to create, change, or extinguish legal relations.)[8] Legal capacity as well as capacity to legal action could be limited by such factors as age, health, religion, nationality, alien status, captivity, wealth, the kind of property possessed, social status, morality, criminal record, sex, marital status, education, profession, and domicile.

[5]Two particular cases of secularization, however, should be mentioned here: secularization of the Teutonic Knights, in 1525, and the secular takeover of Jesuit real estates after the dissolution of the order by Pope Clement XIV in his *breve Dominus ac Redemptor noster* of July 21, 1773. The real estate of the Jesuits in Poland passed to the Commission of National Education and was to be used for educational purposes. These decisions were made by foreign authorities and were alien to Polish law; therefore they do not disprove the contention of this paragraph.

[6]The enactments of the Polish parliament were called "constitutions." The full parliament, composed of the King, the Senate, and the Chamber of Deputies, met periodically after 1493. After the 1505 *Nihil novi* constitution, nothing new could be enacted without the agreement of the full *sejm.*

[7]The "dead hand" (*manus mortua*) or mortmain property was acquired by religious houses or other organizations of the Church. Such property was considered as being held in one "dead hand." The alienation of mortmain property was restricted by various limitations including permission of the Pope.

[8]German law also distinguishes clearly between the capacity to possess rights and duties (*Rechtsfähigkeit*) and the capacity to act in a legal sense (*Geschäftsfähigkeit*).

75

Three major age periods were distinguished by Polish law: minority, which ended with physical maturity; the age of puberty; and the age of majority *(competentia annorum)*. In addition, children up to the age of seven and people older than seventy (or sixty, at the end of the period under consideration) were subject to special rules relative to their legal capacity and capacity for legal action.[9]

Minority, which first ended at twelve years, was later fixed at fourteen and then fifteen, and was established at the end of this period at eighteen for boys and thirteen for girls. The Constitution of 1768 set twenty as the limit of minority, and twenty-four for ending puberty and start of complete maturity. Before twenty-four a person could not encumber his real estate, make bequests without the assistance of his father or guardian, acquire commodities on credit, make loans, or issue bills of exchange. The Constitution of 1768 also limited minors and adolescents in other ways: for example, one could not join a religious order (except the Piarist Friars) before the age of twenty-four.

Although the clergy enjoyed more rights in some respects than other estates, clergymen were limited in their capacity for legal action in such matters as guardianship, the charging and collection of interest, and the purchase of real estate.

Among other peculiarities of Polish law, legal limitations due to ill-health are of interest. A serious illness justified the establishment of guardianship. A person prevented from court attendance by illness was not allowed to act as a guardian. The seriously ill were limited in making wills; however, their sickness required certification by, for example, a priest administering the sacraments of Communion and Extreme Unction. The mentally sick also had to be certified as such. Such certification could be made only by a royal commission, and only after a thorough investigation conducted at the domicile of the person alleged to be mentally ill. Such a procedure was required by the Constitution of 1638. The mentally ill were not liable, but they could accept inheritance.

Legal Aspects of Religious Affiliation

In private law, a person's religious affiliation decided the extent of his rights and limitations as a citizen. Jews were subject to various limitations but on the other hand were granted special privileges. They were considered servants of the state treasury *(servi camerae)* entitled for their services and contributions to special royal protection of their persons, temples, and cemeteries. Their status in public and private life in Poland

[9]Dąbkowski, *op. cit.,* 111-2.

was regulated by the Privilege of 1264, issued by Prince Bolesław Pobożny and subsequently confirmed and often extended by other Polish kings. The need for such confirmation and extension of old laws and privileges resulted from the influx of new groups of Jews into Poland following their persecution in Western and Central Europe. They had been expelled from Spain in 1492, following similar expulsions from England in 1290, France in 1306, and Germany throughout the fourteenth century. In England the legal status of Jews did not improve until the middle of the seventeenth century, in Brandenburg not until the second half of the seventeenth century, and in France not until the revolution of 1789.[10] Some of these exiles settled in Poland. They were provided with full legal protection under the Privilege of 1264, which was never revoked nor suspended. This privilege was confirmed, broadened, and extended to cover the whole territory of Poland by Casimir the Great in 1334, 1364, and 1367 and by other Polish kings. Of particular importance was the Privilege of King Stefan Batory, issued in 1580 initially for the Jews in Great Poland and then extended to all Jews throughout the country. This privilege and others issued by the kings of the Polish-Lithuanian Commonwealth were by 1669 compiled — a collection which constituted the law in force for Jews in that country and which was broadened in 1765. It guaranteed individual freedom for Jews; protection of their lives, and property, temples, and cemeteries; freedom of residence and movement; religious liberty; and the due course of justice.

The Jews were considered to be under the direct protection of the king as exercized by the palatines *(voyevods)*. They enjoyed extensive self-government. Jurisdiction over them, in matters of high treason and blood accusation, was reserved to the king after 1633. Until the eighteenth century they were under restriction in the acquisition of landed estates, which, however, they could lease.[11] They could not extend loans

[10]For a brief survey see R. R. Palmer and Joel Colton, *A History of the Modern World* (3rd ed., New York: Alfred A. Knopf, 1965), p. 63. An English translation of excerpts of the Privilege of 1264 can be found in Waclaw W. Soroka, ed., "Basic Sources Related to the History of Eastern and Central Europe; A Selection," (mimeographed) (Stevens Point, Wisconsin, 1966), pp. 17-9. See also *The Universal Jewish Encyclopedia, s.v.* "Poland." For more extensive treatment see Michał Maksymilian Borwicz, *1000 i.e. Mille ans de vie juive en Pologne. 1000 Years of Jewish Life in Poland. 1000 lat życia Żydów w Polsce* (Paris: Centre d'Études Historique, 1966); Majer Balaban, *Die Juden in Polen* (Wien: Hobrith Verlags-Gesellschaft, 1927); Semen Markovich Dubnov, *History of the Jews in Russia and Poland From the Earliest Times Until the Present Day* (Philadelphia: The Jewish Publication Society of America, 1916-20); and Aleksander Hertz, *Żydzi w kulturze polskiej* ("Biblioteka 'Kultury'," Vol. LXVI) (Paryż: Instytut Literacki, 1961).

[11]Bardach, *op. cit.*, II, 264, 394-5.

guaranteed by real estate or accept as security liturgical vestments *(vestes sacrae)*, bloodstained dresses *(vestes sanguinolentae et malefactae)*, or objects obtained by theft. They could not marry Christians or hire Christians as servants or domestics. They were also bound to some additional formalities, such as, for example, exact bookkeeping concerning securities.

The privileges granted to the Jews gave them some freedom in commercial dealings not enjoyed by the Christian population, such as the power to lend money at interest. Jews and Christians were subject to the same tariffs, as provided in a royal privilege in 1527. After 1532, Jews were granted the right of free trade throughout the country. A further privilege was their exemption from military service. The legal inability of non-Christians to hire Christian domestics and servants was removed in 1775, together with the prohibition against owning landed estates as perpetual lease (emphyteusis).

Civil rights and privileges of Jews were further extended in the final period of the Polish-Lithuanian Commonwealth. The Jews then received some rights previously reserved to the nobility alone, such as the right of freedom from arbitrary arrest without due course of justice. This right was included in the privilege *Neminem captivabimus nisi jure victum* enjoyed by the nobility since 1430 and extended to cover Jews in 1792.

Members of the Orthodox and Protestant churches did not favor marriages with Catholics. Catholics themselves were not allowed to marry non - Catholics. This situation was reflected in the legal prohibition of marriage between Catholics and non - Catholic Christians, a prohibition which was abolished, however, in 1768.

The legal position of "heretics" (Arians or Anti-Trinitarians, Unitarians, Quakers, Mennonites, and Anabaptists) as well as atheists was the result of the spirit of tolerance expressed in the Warsaw Confederation of 1573 and permeating Polish public law for almost one hundred years thereafter. In that act of the Warsaw Confederation, sworn to by the newly elected king in his own name and those of his successors, the nobility, burghers, and all free men were granted complete freedom of religious affiliation. No limitation in public position or private law could result from religious conviction or church affiliation. This act was passed just eighteen years after the Peace of Augsburg, which, in contrast, provided such freedom only to Catholics and Lutherans, and established the submission of religious matters to secular princes according to the principle of *cuius regio eius religio*. The Warsaw Confederation was accepted a few months after the St. Bartholomew Massacre, which took place in France in 1572 and which led toward the Edict of Nantes of 1598 through a period of passionate religious wars and persecutions. The Warsaw Confederation, expressing modern concepts of tolerance, was respected in Poland in law

78

and in practice until the Anti-Trinitarians were banished from the country in 1658, a time of national calamity resulting from the Swedish invasion and the Polish-Cossack wars. At that time, the "heretics" were deprived of their legal rights, and their properties could be confiscated if they did not comply with the requirements of the law. These limitations did not apply to other Protestant churches, although all of them were affected by the victory of the Counter Reformation and the offensive of the Catholics in Poland. This offensive, however, did not produce major enactments (except briefly in 1717) against Protestants, as did the repeal of the Edict of Nantes by Louis XIV in 1685. The French Huguenots could, and did, come to Poland to escape persecution in their own country.

Social Status and Law

The broadest differences in the extent of legal rights were related to social status. The most extensive rights belonged to the nobility, who constituted more than 10 percent of the total population. Within this group even the king and the aristocracy were limited by the rights of the community of nobles. Such freedom contrasted with that of the clergy and lower estates. However, even the nobility was limited by the rights reserved to other states. For example, the nobles could not own city real estate until the second half of the eighteenth century. They could not engage in trade until 1775, when this limitation was removed by a constitution.[12] The nobility were also subject to certain limitations related to possession or nonpossession of landed property.

The king himself was limited *vis-à-vis* the nobility by private law and by the *Pacta Conventa* and Henrycian Articles.[13] After 1504, he was limited in the distribution of the Crown's estates. This provision indirectly affected the magnates and other prospective beneficiaries of new grants. Mere possession by the king of lands of the nobility did not establish rights to such lands for the king and did not extinguish the property rights of the owners and their successors. This provision limited the king's prerogatives in disposition of lands acquired against any property rights of nobles. He also was limited in contracting his own marriage, which required the consent of the Diet. He could not acquire hereditary landed estates for his

---

[12]Jan Ptaśnik, *Miasta i mieszczaństwo w dawnej Polsce* ("Towns and Town Populations in Old Poland") (Cracow: Polska Akademia Umiejętności, 1934), 431.

[13]The political significance of *Pacta Conventa* and Henrycian Articles constituted the subject of a thorough monograph: Władysław Sobociński, *Pakta Konventa* (*"Wydawnictwa Wydziału Prawa Uniwersytetu Jagiellońskiego,"* No. 6) (Cracow, 1939).

family, nor could he travel abroad.[14] The king, however, enjoyed special privileges which were proper to his office, such as the appointment of candidates to office.

As early as the sixteenth century, the concept of the superiority of law to the king was firmly established in Poland and was never discarded.

Some limitations were imposed also on the upper class of nobility and clergy, the magnates, and the aristocracy. An authorization of the Diet was required to create entails. A general rule which applied to the entire nobility, this law actually affected only the magnates, who alone had real power to establish entails. The political movement of the nobility directed toward the "execution of laws" and "execution of royal estates" which developed in the sixteenth century, resulted in further limitation of magnates. The Diets of 1504 and 1565 ordered prohibition of new grants of royal lands without their permission. Tenants of such lands, mostly magnates spiritual and temporal, were urged to return their tenancy to the treasury of the Commonwealth. Finally after 1792 all royal lands could be auctioned only to the broader strata of nobility. This land could then pass to the other social groups (burghers, aliens) allowed to own land at that period.

Those estates politically and socially inferior to the nobility were limited by private law. The serfs, for instance, were subject mainly to dominial law and the power of their lords.

The burghers were at first prohibited from acquiring and owning landed estates. This rule was embodied in a constitution adopted in 1611. This situation was undermined in many ways; for example, exceptions were established in favor of some cities (treated as juridical persons) and their inhabitants. Enjoying such exceptions were Lwów, Wilno, Lublin, Poznań, Kalisz, Toruń, and Gdańsk. However, after 1775 in Lithuania and 1791 in the rest of Poland, the burghers were permitted to acquire and possess landed estates without limitation.[15]

Peasants were further limited by law. They could not marry without the lord's permission, and had limited capacity to make wills. They could not lend money nor make guarantees without dominial permission.

[14]In the public law, the most essential limitations on kings were the rights of the nobility to resist illegal royal actions and to refuse the king obedience (*ius resistendi* and *de non praestanda oboedientia*). After 1573, these rights became law. The prescribed formalities for implementation were: (a) an admonition by the Primate of Poland or by any senator; (b) a formal remonstration against some acts of the king by any dietine; and (c) a vote of the Diet. For a brief survey of this matter see Bardach, *op. cit.* II, 130, 293-4.

[15]*Ibid.*, II, 432-4.

Generally they could not acquire or possess landed property independently. In this matter there were, however, substantial differences between the various groups of peasants, depending on the period of time under examination. The situation differed in the villages under the German and Wallachian law, the colonies originated by the Dutch immigrants *(Olędry)*, and the king's estates. The peasants in those areas could trade their land and mortgage or lease it. They also retained rights of inheritance, which could be transferred to their heirs through testaments.

Aliens were to some extent limited in their legal capacity and capacity to legal action.[16] In the sixteenth century, they could transfer their property only to those heirs who were living in the Polish-Lithuanian Commonwealth. In the case of their absence, the inheritence passed to the king. They could not acquire landed estates. The wealth possessed by them in Poland could not be exported to other countries. An exception to this rule was established in 1590: the aliens living in larger cities (Cracow, Poznań, Lwów, and Wilno) could remove their possessions after having paid to their city of residence 10 percent of their value. After 1792 foreign citizens were encouraged to settle and invest in Poland. The aliens in that period were given the right to acquire landed estates and were promised Polish citizenship.

Family Law

The secular mode of contracting marriage prevailed until the second half of the sixteenth century,[17] when the Constitution of 1577 prescribed a ceremony before a pastor as obligatory for Catholics. Other groups maintained their own forms, and secular legislation supplemented ecclesiastical rules on marriage. Marriages between Catholics and non-Christians were void, and the Constitution of 1616 prohibited marriages with the Tartars under the penalty of death. Marriages between Catholics and other Christians were prohibited but were not void. This situation, however, underwent change. The Constitution of 1768 granted dissidents (the Greek Orthodox, Calvinists, and Lutherans) the right of marriage with the

[16]The problem of the position of the foreigners in Polish law has been exhaustively presented by Paweł Skwarczyński, *Stanowisko cudzoziemców w dawnem prawie polskiem koronnem* ("The Position of Foreigners in the Old Polish Crown Law"), ("Pamiętnik Historyczno-Pawny," I, No. 1 [1931]), 14-27, 239-51. On landed property, see Bardach, *op. cit.*, II, 201-21, 317, 433.

[17]Władysław Abraham, *Zawarcie małżeństwa w pierwotnem prawie polskiem* ("The Act of Marriage in Early Polish Law") ("Studya nad Historyą Prawa Polskiego," Vol. IX) (Lwów: Towarzystwo Naukowe, 1925), p. 475.

Catholics. Marriages between Christians and Jews were considered by the town law as adulterous and were punishable as such.

The validity of marriage depended upon fulfillment of a prescribed set of requirements. Except in the case of a Catholic marriage, failure to meet such requirements could result in nullification. Prohibitive requirements could be removed and a marriage could be validated by dispensation or by a new ceremony when the impediment ceased to exist. Some rules were immutable. For example, a girl under the settled age who got married without the permission of her parents or guardian lost the right to a dowry from her parents or family.

Separation was known. It could be established by an agreement between the married persons or through a decision of the court. The ecclesiastical courts (Catholic, Greek Orthodox, and Protestant), as well as the proper authorities of the Jews and Moslem Tartars, had jurisdiction in the matter of marriage. Civil courts respected the decisions of these ecclesiastical courts.

There were several marital property regimes in Poland in that period. As a rule, the so-called dotal system or dotal regime (*rząd posagowy*), related to dowry, prevailed. It consisted in the legal separation of the husband's and wife's real estate under the husband's management. The dowry, which was brought in cash by the wife, was secured on a part of the husband's real estate. The dotal estates could not be used for the satisfaction of debts or other obligations of the husband. They were always at the disposition of the wife. After her death, they were inherited by her children. If there were no children, the estates returned to her family if not disposed of otherwise. The wife's other property (acquired through gift, bequest, purchase, etc.) was treated in the same way as the dotal estates. In particular, the estates (called *oprawa*) given by the husband as a reciprocation of the dowry or guarantee of contractual provisions were subject to the same provisions.

There were other systems of property arrangement between husband and wife. The principal ones were the community property system, the division of property, and the common management of the divided properties. In the cities placed under Magdeburg law, the system of separation of properties prevailed, while under the law of Chełmno the community of property was the usual regime.

An important part of family law was devoted to the position of children. Two kinds of children were known to Polish law: legitimate and illegitimate or natural. Legitimate children had the right to parental assistance and were under parental authority. They inherited the name and status of their parents as well as the right to an established part of the parental estate, according to circumstances.

The natural children did not inherit the status of nobility or the right to inherit property. They could be legitimized, at the beginning of the period under consideration and also after 1768, through subsequent marriage. They could also acquire the status of legitimate children by living in particular orphanages (in Gdańsk and Warsaw) that obtained the legitimizing privileges from the king after 1736.[18]

Special family relationships were created through adoption. Various kinds of adoption were known to the Polish law: adoption of an unrelated child by a family or a single person, adoption of a son-in-law, and brotherly adoption of an adult person. Receiving anyone to the coat of arms of the grantor constituted a special kind of adoption. However, a noble could not adopt a commoner, under the threat of losing his own nobility. This rule, established by the Constitution of 1616, was not changed until the end of the period under consideration.

Adoption did not require special formalities, but it could not be freely revoked. When established, it constituted a situation in which the adoptee accepted the rights and also the obligations of a legitimate child, such as the obligations of respect, reverence, and obedience.

Guardianship Law

In the period under consideration, Polish law recognized guardianship over minors, over the seriously ill and insane, and over widows and unmarried women who had no relatives. There were provisions for special guardianship over prodigal persons incapable of managing their affairs and for guardianship of children mistreated by parents or next of kin.

The institution of guardianship in its fullest development was known in territorial law as well as in town law. Guardianship could be established by a private act or through court decision. Guardianship over prodigal gentry members was established by a decision of the king based on the initiative of the family. After 1638, the guardianship over the mentally ill was decided by the king. Such a decision could be made only on the basis of findings of a special investigating committee assigned to examine the case.

Inheritance Law

Three kinds of inheritance were known in Polish law: necessary *(ab intestato,* or against the provisions of the will, contrary to the law), testamentary, and contractual. The subject matter of an estate consisted of

[18]Bardach, *op. cit.,* II, 320.

real or personal property, or both. The property of the nobility was different in its content and legal character from the property of the burghers and peasants.[19] The rules of succession varied with each situation.

During this period, the right to succession belonged to all legitimate children of the deceased. All sons enjoyed equal rights, except in the case of entail estates, in which the oldest son inherited the indivisible landed property: primogeniture was the essential element to succession in the entail estates. In some regions, among the peasants, only the sons had the right to succession.

The right of daughters to landed property developed slowly from the thirteenth century on, but remained limited except under town law, which provided for the equal treatment of sons and daughters. Elsewhere, daughters inherited one-fourth of the paternal landed property, three-fourths being inherited by the sons. The dowry of the daughters was included in the total estate to be inherited by the successors. The daughters participated equally in the inheritance of maternal goods and estates. The inheritance of serfs depended on the limits of the lord's rights and on local customs defining the rights of peasants to the lands and chattels in question.

Descendants inherited to the exclusion of the brothers and sisters, ascendants, and collaterals, who in the order given (including collaterals up to the eighth degree of affinity) entered the succession in the absence of descendants.

Widows and widowers had legal rights to the usufruct of the estate of the deceased and to life annuities.[20] Such rights of widows did not develop in some regions among peasants and serfs. In some places, sons inheriting a peasant possession had the obligation to endow their sisters and to support their widowed mothers.

Testamentary inheritance developed early in the first period of Polish law and then underwent essential modifications. The will could include disposition of personal property and real estate. However, disposition of real estate through wills steadily became more limited until it was almost

[19]The question is a subject of renewed attention in historical studies. Two basic publications related to it are Jósef Rafacz, *Włościańskie prawo spadkowe w Polsce nowożytnej* (Warsaw, 1929) and Kazimierz Dobrowolski, *Włościańskie rozporządzenie ostatniej woli na Podhalu w XVII i XVIII w.; studia i materiały* ("Prace Komisji Etnograficznej," No. 15) (Cracow: Polska Akademia Umiejętności, 1933).

[20]Stanisław Roman, in his article "Stanowisko majątkowe wdowy w średniowiecznym prawie polskim," *Czasopismo Prawno-Historyczne,* V (1953), 80-108, expressed the opinion that the situation of widows was stronger in the early Polish law than has been indicated in the literature on the subject.

completely denied. Early constitutions (of 1505 and 1510) prohibited the disposition of real estate beyond the descendants. Wills were either private or public. The latter were made in the presence of the king or his representative, as well as in courts or before the notary public. There were also military wills (*in procinctu*). Throughout Polish history, substantive and formal requirements for securing the validity of wills, as well as procedures for their revocation and execution, were developed. Polish law knew various types of limitations or exclusions from inheritance. Illegitimate children, for example, were ineligible to inherit. Unworthy of inheritance were persons who had attempted to murder the testators, women agreeing to their abduction, a kinsman's assassin and his progeniture, and the children of persons married despite nullifying kinship. The Polish territorial law did not allow disinheritance, but this legal institution was recognized in the town law as well as in Lithuanian law.

Property Law

Man's dominion over things constituted the content of property law. It could be eternal or limited to a certain period, and complete or partial. Very early, Polish law distinguished between possession, usufruct, and management of property, and the right to dispose of it in favor of successors or other persons. The most inclusive right in property was ownership. Although such a relation of man to property had been known since earlier times, the term 'ownership' *(własność)* itself was developed in the sixteenth century. The use of property, or a limited hold over it, was called "possession" *(posiadanie, dzierżenie)*.

In the period under consideration, the distinction between ownership of movables or personal property and of real estate was clear, and produced different sets of laws.

Real estate was classified by type. The most consequential distinction was that between hereditary property (*bona hereditaria*) and granted or purchased estates (*bona acquisita*).

Individual ownership prevailed under Polish law. Traces of collective ownership or of tenancy in common (*coniuncta manu*) disappeared under the pressure of laws which protected individual ownership.[21] Legislation

[21]This question was studied by Juliusz Bardach in "Własność niepodzielna w Statutach Litewskich," ("Indivisible Ownership in the Lithuanian Statutes"), in *Studia Historica; w 35 – lecie pracy naukowej Henryka Łowmiańskiego,* Tom przygotowany przez Aleksandra Gieysztora et al. (Warsaw: Państwowe Wydawnictwo Naukowe, 1958). This problem was also included in the *Encyclopaedia of Social Sciences,* in the article by Stanisław Kutrzeba, s.v. "Law, Slavic." On

favored liquidation of family or brotherly tenancy in common. If such property was divided factually without legal action, the right to institute legal proceedings underwent prescription in three years and three months. After that time, factual division was considered final. The property was granted reduction of taxes and dues if it was divided in a legal way. The rights of a community to woods, pastures, and waters which originally constituted communal property changed in the course of history into easements.

Ownership could be either allodial (*dominium directum*) or subordinate (owing allegiance). The same property might belong to a landlord entitled to hereditary unlimited ownership and to a tenant granted hereditary or temporary possession and usufruct of the lord's land dependent upon the fulfillment of some services. The presence of both elements constituted divided ownership (*dominium divisum*). This type of ownership, therefore, incorporated both the allodial rights of ownership and the inferior rights of vassals, burghers, and peasants or guests (*hospites*). Those inferior rights relating to property or subordinate ownership were also called usufruct ownership (*dominium utile*).

The typical ownership under Polish law of the period was the land ownership of the gentry, allodial and undivided. Feudal, or subordinate, ownership was exceptional, and it tended to disappear. Professor Wojciechowski gives the following accurate comment on the situation:

> The lack of the concept of divided ownership should be recognized as the characteristic feature of the Polish structure which made the state and social organization of Poland saliently different from that of Western Europe. Due to this fact, a homogenous stratum of gentry was created which did not fit into the feudal ladder of West-European gentry.[22]

Nor was Polish ownership similar to the Russian type of gentry ownership. The gentry in Poland was sovereign in relation to its land possessions and stood in direct contact with the king. In many respects, its ownership matched that of the territorial overlordship known in Western Europe. It necessarily decreased the power of the king, and because of the shortage of

collective ownership of peasants in the early period, see Jan Gerlach, "Nawsie, wspólna własność gromadzka wsi staropolskiej," in *Czasopismo Historyczno-Prawne*, IV (1952) 260-73.

[22] Zygmunt Wojciechowski, "Z zagadnień rodziny kulturalnej polskiego ustroju średniowiecznego" ("From the Problems of the Cultural Family of the Polish Medieval State and Social Organization"), in *Studia z historii społecznej i gospodarczej poświęcone Prof. Franciszkowi Bujakowi* ("Studies from the Economic and Social History Devoted to Professor Franciszek Bujak") (Lwów, 1939), pp. 67-81, and its French summary, pp. 600-2.

authorities sufficiently strong to master the gentry, it contributed to the partition of the country at the end of the eighteenth century.[23] Many institutions and legal rules were developed to protect and defend the gentry's ownership in Poland. These laws were directed against the dissolution of hereditary estates through inheritance by women, as well as against the endeavors of the clergy to increase their land holdings and the attempts of burghers and peasants to gain possession of landed estates.

In this respect, as previously mentioned, the kings were limited in their disposition of royal demesnes by the Constitutions of 1504 and 1565. In 1745, a reform in the tenancy of royal demesnes (*starostwa*) under the regime of perpetual lease (emphyteusis) was carried out.[24] It extended the scope of allodial ownership of the gentry farming on those demesnes. The Constitution of 1786 changed the feudal tenancy of the Tartar nobility in Lithuania into allodial ownership. The Great Diet of 1788-92 retrospectively converted all feudal ownership in Lithuania into allodial ownership.

Municipal studies reveal both allodial and subaltern ownership. Divided ownership prevailed in the beginning of the period. In all types of cities under Polish,[25] German, or Wallachian law,[26] allodial ownership of royal, ecclesiastical and nobles' estates belonged to the overlords. Their real estate holdings increased as they bought off the privileges and positions of bailiffs and headmen (*sołtys* and *wójt*). This practice developed in the fifteenth and sixteenth centuries.

However, burghers in the cities and towns were struggling for rights of full ownership. In fact, ownership of arable lands, city lots with buildings, and orchards or gardens became allodial at the end of this period. After 1791, full allodial ownership over real estate in royal towns and cities became legally established.

Divided ownership existed in peasant holdings. Sovereign rights belonged to the king, ecclesiastical lords, gentry, and cities as juridical persons. The scope of peasant ownership was reduced in some cases to

[23]Concerning Russia, see Bardach, *op. cit.*, in fn. 2, II, 172.

[24]According to *Black's Law Dictionary, s.v.* "Emphyteusis," we read this is "a contract by which a landed estate was leased to a tenant, either in perpetuity or for a long term of years" under certain conditions. The same contents are found in the emphyteusis known to Polish law.

[25]See an article by Gerard Labuda devoted to the problem of cities placed under Polish law: "Miasta na prawie polskim" ("Cities Under Polish Law"), *Studia Historica*, pp. 181-97.

[26]Stanisław Szczotka, "Studia z dziejów prawa wołoskiego w Polsce" ("Studies from the History of Wallachian Law in Poland"), *Czasopismo Prawno-Historyczne*, II (1949), 355-418.

nothing. In many places, however, the peasants maintained some property rights.[27] Bailiff property was hereditary and legally protected. The most privileged groups of peasants in this respect were the colonists of Dutch origin called *olędry* ("from Holland").[28] Peasants in the villages located under the German law as well as peasants in the royal demesnes, especially in southern Poland, preserved their rights of ownership. The peasant land allotments were called hereditary estates (*hereditas*). The peasants maintained the right to make transfers of real estates through transactions *inter vivos* as well as by wills. Conveyances of land were made in some cases without the necessity of the lord's approval. Landlords desiring to buy off the peasants' allotments had to pay off the tenants. At the end of the eighteenth century, new reforms amplified hereditary rights of peasants to their land holdings under perpetual lease or emphyteusis. This process grew in the royal desmesnes under the supervision of the courts of the referenderies.[29]

During the period under study, Polish law recognized both original and derivative ways of acquiring property. In the first group was the appropriation of things belonging to no one *(res nullius)* and loot, shore rights *(ius naufragii),*[30] hunting and fishing acquisitions, and *usucapio,* or prescription based on *justa causa* (or a title) and *bona fides* (or ignorance of defects in possession). To the second group belonged the transfer of ownership through inheritance, through grants of the ruler (unconditional, conditional, or feudal) or through property contracts (*umowa rzeczowa*). In this type of contract, the law distinguished the transfer of property (*wzdanie*) from the transfer of possession (*wwiązanie*). After the fifteenth

[27]Stanisław Śreniowski, "Problematyka historii chłopów w Polsce Przedrozbiorowej ("Problems Connected with the History of Peasants in Poland"), in *Przegląd Nauk Historyczno-Społecznych* I (1950), 122-36.

[28]Władysław Rusiński devoted his special attention to this question. His findings were published in his *Osady tzw. "Olędrów" w dawnym woj. poznańskim* ("Settlements of So-Called 'Olędry' in the Old Poznań Palatinate") (Vol. V of "Prace Komisji Atlasu Historycznego Polski" [Poznań and Cracow: Polska Akademia Umiejęstności, 1939-47]). See also the review of this book by Zdzisław Kaczmarczyk in *Czasopismo Prawno-Historyczne,* II (1949), 493-6.

[29]On this institution, see Jósef Rafacz, *Sąd Referendarski Koronny; z dziejów obrony prawnej chłopów w dawnej Polsce* ("The Referendar Crown Courts; From the History of Legal Defense of Peasants in Old Poland"), (Vol. XX, No. 1, of *Studia nad Historią Prawa Polskiego* [Poznań: Poznańskie Towarzystwo Przyjaciół Nauk, 1948]).

[30]The right to appropriate objects that were washed up by the sea or by the rivers, lakes or other inland waters. Such objects included amber, fish, etc. When cast on the shore, vessels with crew, passengers, and cargo were also included.

century, transfers of real estate were made by means of entry into the judicial register.

Property could be lost through abandonment, cession of rights to other persons, or confiscation, the last procedure subject to limitation in many respects by Polish law.[31] Grants of royal land by the king, if made unconditionally, included transfer of the royal property rights to the grantees.

Two main groups of institutions limited the rights of ownership in Polish law. One was derived from old social institutions and the rights of the ruler. The second answered to the new needs of the developing society. The first group was still known in the period under consideration, and included the *regalia,* the rights of proximity (*propinquitas, proximitas*), and the rights of neighborhood. The second developed throughout this period and involved expropriation laws and the prohibition or regulation of certain activities of owners.

The *regalia* constituted the economic prerogatives of the ruler, as exercised either by himself or by his delegates, granted usually in return for payment of royalties, rents, tolls, or excises. It was a kind of a primitive monopoly derived from the rights of the ruler as they had existed before the ownership became individualized, and before such prerogatives were ceded to the nobility. The *regalia* included establishment of markets, fairs, inns, mills, and mines, the hunting of larger game, fishing, beekeeping, building and possession of castles, coinage of currency, and sale of salt. In all these spheres private freedom of action was limited. The ruler's prerogatives in these spheres underwent a transformation; either they were granted to the nobility by special privileges, were gradually abolished by legislation, or disappeared with changing conditions. Thus, for example, the mining *regalia* came to an end about 1573, when the ownership of land was redefined to include ownership of natural resources under the surface. The beekeeping *regale* was abolished by 1538. The inn and tavern rights of the ruler were earlier granted to the gentry (1496). In France, the problem of the king's hunting privileges, as well as those of the gentry, took on considerable importance in the complaints of the French people before and during the great Revolution. This problem was settled in Poland in 1775 by means of the general prohibition of hunting on the property of others without their permission — a prohibition which extended to the king and his court. Water *regalia* and shore rights in relation to navigable rivers were abolished

[31]The privilege that nobody could be arrested without due process was issued finally in 1430 and 1433, and is known as *Neminem captivabimus nisi jure victum.* In Czerwień as early as 1422, the nobility were also granted a privilege which ensured that their lands could not be confiscated without due process. This privilege is known as the *Nec bona recipiantur* privilege.

as waterways were declared public in 1447, 1496, and 1511. On the Baltic Sea around Gdańsk, the shore rights were abolished in 1454; until that time they constituted a prerogative of the Teutonic Knights under a grant from Polish kings. Exercise of this prerogative by the Knights conceivably was hurting the interests of the Pomeranian and Prussian burghers and gentry. Seashore rights were definitely abolished by 1775. In the same year, inland shore rights relating to wrecked vessels and rafts were abolished. The landowners obtained exclusive rights to extract natural resources by 1573.[32] By 1776, the rights of all landowners to the interior resources of their land were confirmed.

The remaining ancient limitations on ownership included the rights of proximity and neighborhood. The first related to the remnants of the old Slavic family communities and their collective possessions. Throughout the ages, family members preserved some rights to the hereditary properties of their relatives. They could exclude from acquisition or succession to hereditary possessions not only nonrelatives but also persons of more distant kinship. The right of proximity developed into the right of pre-emption and the buying up of property. Relatives had the right to purchase hereditary possessions offered to the next in order of kinship or to people not related to the seller. If they were not offered this possibility to pre-empt before a transfer of the possession was executed, they could buy up the property in question from the purchaser for the amount of money he paid. This obviously placed a limitation on the individual disposition and favored those who had an interest in preserving the hereditary lands and privileges.

The rights of neighborhood limited reciprocally land ownership by neighbors and formalized the right to graze cattle on neighborhood fields after harvest and the obligation to clip trees that spread over neighborhood lands. The neighbors could appropriate fruit that fell naturally on their ground. In some cases, neighbors could be required to support common agricultural projects.[33]

Gradually limitations on individual ownership were removed. First, the rights of proximity were limited to the sales of hereditary possessions; they lost their significance in relation to exchanges and donations or grants. At last, a law of 1768 abolished the rights of proximity entirely.[34]

On the other hand, some new limitations on property rights appeared. They included expropriation laws and the prohibition or regulation of some activities of landowners. The Diet, for instance, could expropriate lands (with compensation) for public projects such as highways and canals.

[32]Bardach, *op. cit.* in fn. 2, II, 173.
[33]Cf. Bardach, *op. cit.* in fn. 2, II, 300.
[34]*Ibid.*, p. 472.

After 1591, such cases belonged to the jurisdiction of the National Treasury Commission. When a river was declared public, the riparian owners could not maintain any obstructions impairing navigation. The owners of land at the Ogiński Canal, for example, could not dig ditches on their land nor connect them to the canal without special permission from the state authority. No one could burn his own forests in order to change them into arable land, since it was prohibited by the King's Manifesto of 1778. By that time hunting privileges were also limited. The protection of game was established and regulated and hunting seasons were introduced.

Legal protection of possessions independent of ownership was developed very early in Polish law. This protection, known in the fifteenth century, was expressed by 1543 in a possessory action. The mere fact of possession of land was sufficient ground for initial legal action to restore possession without examination of the legal title if the holder of the property was evicted from the possession or challenged in his rights. By 1699, a constitution required that possession be recovered, or restored to those who possessed it, without examination of the title. A petition for the determination of ownership could be filed when possession of the land had been restored.

By virtue of the statutes which Casimir the Great enacted in the middle of the fourteenth century, real estate possession could change into ownership (for example, through prescription) in the short time of three years and three months. The requirements for prescription, depending on the object possessed, origin of the claim of possession and on its character (i.e., whether it was just or unjust) (*iusta vel iniusta, indebita possessio*), were precisely regulated by particular laws.

Limited property rights (*prawa rzeczowe*) included the exercise of easements, usufruct independent and collateral with other rights, and lien or deposit. In the period under study, Polish law recognized the lien on movables and the lien on real estate. The latter could be arranged without possession or with possession. A lien with possession was recognized earlier and was more common at the beginning of the period. A lien could be usufructal (in which case the fruits of possession could be consumed without effect on the debt), or the fruits could be used toward the satisfaction of the debt. Under another arrangement, the real estate could become the property of the lienor after a certain period of time.

In all three of its forms, the lien with possession resulted in the creation of hidden interests. As early as 1264, the Jews were granted permission to take advantage of primitive liens (except for liens which could result in ownership of the land) under a special privilege. The lien with possession, in which the income from the property reduced the principal of the debt, was endorsed and recommended by various synodal statutes of the Catholic church in Poland. The property could in turn be the object of another lien or could be underpledged.

A lien without possession could be established by an entry into judicial records. This was the institution of mortgage in its original form. The Constitution of 1588 prescribed that the entries had to be public, accessible to everybody, and detailed. Priority was granted to entries according to their date. Poland utilized one of the most highly developed mortgage systems in Europe. It was supplemented in Gdańsk by a special file with one card for each holding.[35] Entries were kept, however, only if the courts were so interested. The Constitution of 1768 ordered the transfer of all entries into the court records of the place where the real estate was located. The record of loans secured by real estate after 1776 was to be entered into separate files.[36]

Polish law also recognized the ownership of intangible goods. With the growing use of the printing press from the sixteenth century onward, the interests of publishers became protected in Poland. This protection was granted through a privilege of either the king, a bishop, or the city authorities. As early as the first half of the sixteenth century, publishers were protected against unauthorized republication of entire works, excerpts, and illustrations. This protection could be arranged for a stated period of time (ten to fifteen years), for the time of the sale of the edition, or for life of the publisher. Toward the end of the eighteenth century, the protection of publishers was extended to cover periodical publications for twenty years. There developed a general tendency toward longer periods of protection.[37]

Obligations

In Polish law, obligations originated in contracts or in torts.[38] One or more persons could be a party on either side of the obligation. A number of persons could be bound jointly (*manu coniuncta*) or separately (*pro parte rata*).

The creation of obligations through contracts required that contracts be made without constraint. The subject matter of the obligation could not be contrary to the law or to the teachings of the Church. By virtue of the Constitution of 1507, it could not obligate anyone "to betray others or to impair justice." Personal pledges, such as alienation of one's liberty, were abolished at the beginning of the period under consideration.

[35]Bardach, *op. cit.* in fn. 2, II, 176-7.

[36]*Ibid.*, pp. 473-4.

[37]*Ibid.*, pp. 175, 473.

[38]"Obligations arise from manifestations of the will or from acts and other facts which the law considers as the source of obligations," as Dąbkowski, *op. cit.*, I, 3, states. A similar formula was used in subsequent Polish codes.

Contracts could be oral or in written form; written contracts were made primarily for purposes of evidence. If a written document did not exist, it was necessary to provide witnesses to prove the information and define the scope of a contract. There was no prescribed form for contracts, although some symbolic gestures had been maintained from ancient times and their meaning preserved. On the other hand, some forms were elaborated in use as a convenient pattern as early as 1523 (*formula processus*). Their use was recommended, but the Constitution of 1543 prescribed that the established forms were not compulsory and that the contracting parties could use any form they liked, paying a higher fee for recording their own version of the contract.

Later, requirements for the registration of contracts dealing with real estates developed and became compulsory. Other legal transactions could be registered upon request of the interested parties. The requirements for registration varied in different Polish provinces. In principle, contracts had to be made personally. Seriously ill persons and monks could act through their representatives. The clerks keeping the records had to check on the legal capacity of the parties and on possible restrictions on their ability to enter into transactions.

Legal capacity to make contracts depended on the age, status, and character of the party. Peasants, as noted earlier, were limited in their contract-making capacity. In many regions they could not borrow money without the permission of their landlords. Burghers were also under some restrictions. However, they enjoyed more freedom than the gentry in some fields: for example, in the use of negotiable instruments that were developed at the end of this period.

Secured transactions, as noted above, and guarantees were known. The sanctions of the loss of liberty (*sub illibertate* or *sub servitute*) or of ecclesiastical *caesurae* (such as excommunication) for breaking a contract or not fulfilling an obligation were abolished during the sixteenth century, while some other sanctions, to be applied to particular contracts, were developed.

Torts originated in damages resulting from crimes and other wrongful acts. Original consequences included fines and indemnities. Torts, therefore, developed at first in conjunction with penal law. A peasant committing a tort was under liability both to the injured person and to his own landlord, to whom he owed a fine.

The types of contracts known in the period under consideration originated in earlier centuries. They were: exchange (*zamiana*), donation (*darowizna*), purchase and sale (*kupno-sprzedaż*), contracts for service (*umowa usługi*), labor contracts (*umowa o pracę*), contracts for work (*umowa o dzieło*), commission (*umowa-zlecenie*), lease of goods and chattels (*najem rzeczy*), lease of real estate (*dzierżawa*), loan (*pożyczka*), partnership (*spółka*), and deposit and pledge (*wierna ręka, pokład, depozyt*). Also, the practice of representing abstract and transferable obligations in promissory notes originated in the fifteenth century.

Particular rules developed relating to each of these types. For example, a pledge by third persons in contracts of sale, exchange, load, etc., became an auxiliary contract. The guarantor was held responsible only if the debtor did not fulfill his obligation. Until 1577, pledges by landlords could be made for peasants who wanted to move to another place and could not carry out all of their legal obligations or pay off all their legal debts before moving. Usually future lords of the peasants about to move offered pledges for their debts to their previous lords.

Concerning loans, the concept of a moratorium (of the court, or through the king's script) was developed in this period. Execution on the goods of the debtor in the town law was sped up; all deadlines of procedure in the town law were shortened. The Jews, being allowed at all times to lend money on interest, were prohibited from making loans against promissory notes. The securing of a loan by a pledge was necessary; this was to remind some lightminded nobles of the seriousness of the transaction.

Real estates could not be donated if the donor wanted to retain a lifelong usufruct of subject property. Such a donation constituted a hidden form of will prohibited by law. The apparent reason for this limitation was to make impossible a will by which the landed property would be transferred in violation of the rights of legitimate successors.

Contracts of lease were elaborated and defined more precisely than before. An inventory had to be made at the beginning of the lease, and was to be used at the end as the basis for the account. Legal consequences of acts of God, accidents, plagues, hurricanes, cattle epidemics, lightning fire, enemy plundering, floods, pests, droughts, and hail were regulated. Such events could decrease the rent agreed upon, or postpone the fulfillment of obligations. These happenings, however, were to be reported to the courts within a prescribed time. The law of that period also maintained the principle of self-help in the execution of obligations; the lawless tenant could be removed forcefully from his possession by means of a legally regulated foray.

Contracts for service and labor underwent further regulation and change. After 1593, employers were punished if they hired anyone without a certificate from his previous employer. Contracts were generally drawn up for a year. Notices of resignation or termination had to be given at least six weeks in advance (1505). In time of war, the nobles working as employees could not quit their jobs, under the sanction of infamy. From 1565 until the second half of the eighteenth century, Christians could not be employed as servants of Jews or Tartars. In 1493 provisions were enacted that cities and towns could not admit to residence persons who were not to be employed there for at least a year. There was also forced employment; peasants about to migrate abroad to work could be forcibly retained and employed by their landlords.

In the seventeenth century, the use of bills of exchange appeared first in trade in the bigger cities. Law regarding negotiable instruments was at first customary, but later supplemented and unified by statutes. The first laws regulating bills of exchange were enacted in Gdańsk and Elbląg.[39] Polish law defined the bill of exchange as an abstract loan contract in the form of a handwritten draft by which the drawer (or debtor) was obligated to pay a stated sum of money at some fixed or determinable time, or at sight, to some designated person (a creditor).[40] The creditor could be mentioned by name, or the bill of exchange could be payable on order of the bearer. The law made such contracts quick and rigorous, and available in the same form to all estates; the regulations were truly all-persuasive in the state, and contributed much to the development of commerce. In the eighteenth century, commercial companies were developing in Poland. There were companies created for production, for import and export of goods, and for conducting various works (such as the construction of canals). Originally, partners of commercial companies were liable for the entire obligations of their companies. Already in the eighteenth century, a tendency to limit the risk of shareholders to their shares only was visible in Polish corporation law.[41] Like the law of bills of exchange, the law concerning business associations was uniform for all the inhabitants of the country. As such, the law predated the growth of equality among the estates in more recent times.

[39]Bardach, *op. cit.* in fn. 2, II, 323.

[40]*Ibid.*, pp. 475-6.

[41]The newest literature on the subject is represented by Grażyna Bałtruszajtis, "Kompanie akcyjne w Polsce w drugiej połowie XVIII w.; z zagadnień prawa akcyjnego," *Czasopismo Prawno-Historyczne,* XI, No. 2 (1939), 77-128.

WENCESLAS J. WAGNER

ARTHUR P. COLEMAN

CHARLES S. HAIGHT

Laurentius Grimaldus Goslicius and His Age—Modern Constitutional Law Ideas in the Sixteenth Century*

I

Of all the struggles that have engaged man in the course of his uphill climb from barbarism, none has absorbed him more persistently than the struggle to master the art of government.

The crucial problem in that struggle, wherever man has taken it up and at whatever time, has been that of striking a balance among conflicting interests within the state so that harmony and good will might prevail and, as the Benthamites put it, "the greatest possible good accrue to the greatest possible number."

Though all nations and races are, by the very nature of things, at all times to some degree occupied with this problem, all do not attack it with the same intensity at the same time. In the seventeenth century it was England which witnessed the most positive efforts to harmonize a political organism with man's essential needs and aspirations, while in the eighteenth century it was France and in the nineteenth England again and the United States of America.

In the sixteenth century it was Poland which for the moment became the principal scene of the struggle for balance and harmony in political relationships.

*The responsibility for this study is divided among the co-authors as follows: Dr. Wagner, Part I; Dr. Coleman, Part II; Mr. Haight, Part III. It was originally published in the *Polish Review,* III, 37 (New York, 1958), and is reprinted, with minor editorial changes, by permission of the *Review.*

In other parts of Europe the return to lay authority which followed Papal withdrawal from direct influence on lay matters gave rise to the theory of a sovereign state and subsequently to its natural corollary, an all powerful prince. In Poland, however, the development went in another direction.

The emergence of Poland as a constitutional monarchy in a period when in other countries absolutism was being reinforced was not sudden nor unexpected. The process of limiting the king's power began as early as the fourteenth century. One of the first important landmarks was the Privilege of Koszyce, in 1374, in which King Louis agreed not to impose any taxes on the nobility without their consent, except a small levy on real property.[1] In 1430, by the famous Privilege of Jedlnia, *Neminem captivabimus*, King Ladislas Jagiełło "promised and swore that no member of the gentry will be imprisoned or ordered to be imprisoned, or afflicted with any penalty whatsoever, unless he will be duly convicted by a law court."[2] Thus, at the beginning of the fifteenth century, Poland had its "due process" clause, the right of the king to arrest any full-fledged citizens without judicial warrant having been abolished. In most other continental countries, this was achieved three or four centuries later; in France, e.g., until the end of the *ancien régime*, the king could not only incarcerate anyone who displeased him, but also distributed the ill-famed *lettres de cachet* as a token of a special favor to his subjects; the *lettres* were royal orders of arrest in blank, and by filling in a name, the possessor could have any of his personal enemies put into jail.

From a Polish royal council, which can be traced back to the end of the twelfth century, a parliamentary body began to develop. By the fifteenth century this body had features of a senate. The development of a House of Representatives was prompted by the Law of Nieszawa of 1454, in which provincial assemblies were given legislative powers.[3] At the end of the fifteenth century, the parliamentary system of government was well established in Poland. While in France, Germany, Italy, Russia, and Spain, the power of the rulers remained absolute for centuries, in Poland the authority of the king became ever more limited. This development reached a climax in the adoption of the famous *Nihil novi* constitution in 1505, in a parliamentary session held at Radom in which King Alexander announced, in the first words of that document: "Whereas common laws and public constitutions concern not one individual, but the whole nation, therefore it is ordered that hereinafter and forever nothing new will be

[1]Halecki, *A History of Poland* (1943), p. 66.

[2]Kridl, Malinowski, and Wittlin, *Polska myśl demokratyczna w ciągu wieków ("The Polish Democratic Thought Through the Ages") (1945), p. 5.*

[3]Sigel, *Lectures on Slavonic Law* (1902), p. 110.

decided by us or our successors without the concurrence of the counsellors and the deputies...," or members of the Senate and House of Representatives (Sejm).[4]

The dignity of the kingship of Poland became elective at the time of Ladislas Jagiełło, but in order to safeguard the Polish-Lithuanian Union, the nation never elected anybody outside the new dynasty.[5] Only after the last king of the Jagiełło dynasty, Sigismund Augustus, died without heir, were Polish monarchs freely elected. This constitutional principle, extremely rare, was applied for two centuries, until the downfall of Poland at the end of the eighteenth century. It was believed that this was the best safeguard of the famous Polish "golden freedom," and that the highest office in the great state should go to a person who had proven his qualities and capacities. Thus, the position of the king in the constitutional monarchy of Poland was comparable to that of a president elected for life. This fact found its expression in the traditional name of the Polish-Lithuanian state, which was called a republic or commonwealth more often than a kingdom.

In 1573, with the first actual "free election" of the king, a practice was established by virtue of which the new ruler entered into a kind of agreement with his electors, called *pacta conventa*,[6] in which he affirmed all the laws of the country and privileges granted by his predecessors and promised to fulfill some special conditions. In a clause called *de non praestanda oboedientia*, it was declared that the nation was entitled to defy the orders of the king should they be contrary to the established constitutional system and laws of the country.[7]

There remained, however, the problem of establishing a sound balance between the governmental bodies in the first democratic power on the European continent. The attempt to solve this problem produced an abundant crop of political theories and a rich vintage of political and legal treatises in sixteenth-century Poland. Some of the treatises were mere

[4]Kridl, Malinowski and Wittlin, *op. cit.*, p. 6.

[5]Halecki, *op. cit.*, p. 131.

[6]*Ibid.*, p. 133.

[7]Poland never knew absolute monarchy, which for so many years was the system in other continental countries. All full-fledged citizens, or the nobility, participated in the government of the country, as noted by W. Komarnicki, "The Spirit of Polish Constitutional Law and Its Recent Development," in *Studies in Polish and Comparative Law* (1945) pp. 1-2. Contrary to the situation in other countries, the noble class comprised a large number of the population. At the end of the eighteenth century, the percentage of nobles in France was about 0.1. In Poland, the percentage was about 10. (Lednicki, *Life and Culture of Poland as Reflected in Polish Literature* [1944], p. 44.)

run-of-the-mill discourses "on the ideal government based on the Greek and Roman classics,"[8] but many were both original and of enduring significance.

Among the topics most frequently discussed in this rich literature were the problems of civil liberties, organization of executive power, diplomacy, equality of all before the laws, religious freedom, and the fate of the peasants.[9]

One of the foremost political and legal thinkers of sixteenth-century Poland was Andrzej Frycz-Modrzewski (1503-72); his *Commentarii de republica emendanda* was a book translated into many languages and known all over Europe.

Many ideas expressed by Frycz-Modrzewski were a few centuries ahead of their time. He advanced the concept of universal freedom and equality between citizens and between nations. He was the strongest proponent of the "government of law." In a time in which wars were so frequent that peace sometimes seemed to be abnormal, he suggested the substitution of armed conflicts between nations by peaceful settlement of international disputes. On the equality of everyone before the law, he wrote:

Laws are like medicines. No expert physician has regard for the status of the individual. It is sufficient for him to know the disease. He does not inquire whether his patient is a peasant or a lord, a noble or a serf. He knows only him who has to be cured. In the same manner ought laws to apply to citizens.[10]

Frycz-Modrzewski, a firm Protestant, found a vigorous opponent in an able Catholic writer, Stanisław Orzechowski (1515-67), who in *Oratio Reipublicae Poloniae* (1563), *Quincunx* (1564), and many other publications opposed his political and religious ideas, criticized his liberalism, and expressed greater respect for the concept of authority, which, he claimed, derived from God himself.[11] Another outstanding Catholic philosopher

[8]Filipowicz, "The Accomplished Senator," *Proceedings of the American Society of International Law* (1932), p. 234. The address was translated into Polish and published under the title "Goślickiego *De optimo Senatore*" in *Przeglad Współczesny* ("Contemporary Review"), XLVIII (1934), p. 68. See also "Wawrzyniec Goślicki, biskup poznański" ("Wawrzyniec Goślicki, Bishop of Poznan") in *Obrona Kultury* ("Defense of Culture"), January 1, 1939, p. 3. The last-mentioned article is an excellent survey of Polish and British references to Goślicki. There is a copy in Columbia University Library.

[9]Lednicki, *op. cit.*, p. 39.

[10]*Ibid.*, p. 53. See Halecki, "Andrzej Frycz-Modrzewski," in Mizwa, ed., *Great Men and Women of Poland* (1941), pp. 51-66.

[11]Jarra, *Twórczość prawna duchowieństwa polskiego* ("Legal Writings of the Polish Clergy" (1954), pp. 45-7; Lichtensztul, "Poglądy filozoficzno-prawne St.

and jurist was Stanisław Cardinal Hozjusz (1504-79); among his many contributions to the development of legal thought in Poland the following are particularly noteworthy: discussion of the idea of justice and its close connection with love, and a well-reasoned disapproval of frequent changes in the legal system of a country, (particularly of abrogation of laws based on ancient customs) as dangerous to the nation and undermining the authority of the law in the minds of the people.[12]

Besides Frycz-Modrzewski, another outstanding thinker and statesman, Andrew Wolan (1530-1610), also emphasized equality of rights. In spite of the fact that he was a prominent leader of the Protestants in Poland and bitterly fought Catholic thought, he served as secretary to three consecutive kings of the Polish-Lithuanian Union, and in 1581 became a justice of one of the two highest courts of the Union in this predominantly Catholic country. His career is a testimony to the principle of religious tolerance observed in Poland, even in times when bloody religious wars raged all over Europe.

From his principal work, *De libertate politica seu civili – libellus lectu non indignus* (1572)[13] and his other numerous writings (Professor Jarra enumerates thirty-four items),[14] Wolan appears as a deeply educated and original philosopher and jurist. A believer in natural law, he rejected the idea of laws as simple commands of those who govern. He correlated law to morality and denied the obligatory force of laws which tend to deprive the people of freedom.[15] Law is "deaf and merciless"[16] and must be applied in the same way to all. Its unequal application violates justice and creates a danger to the state. However, if the spirit of the law is contrary to its letter, equity must intervene to avoid an undesirable result: *summum ius – summa iniuria*.[17]

Orzechowskiego" ("Philosophical-Legal Ideas of St. Orzechowski"), Vol. III of Jarra, *Prace Seminarium Filozofii Prawa Uniwersytetu Warszawskiego*, ("Studies of the Seminar of Legal Philosophy of the University of Warsaw") (1930).

[12]Jarra, *op. cit.*, pp. 35-6.

[13]Jarra, "L'idea della libertà nella litteratura politica Polacca del Secolo di Decimosesto" ("The Concept of Liberty in the Polish Political Literature of the Sixteenth Century") *Rivista Internazionale de Filosofia del Diritto VIII* (1928), p. 617.

[14]Jarra, "Andrew Wolan–Sixteenth Century Polish Calvinist Writer and Philosopher of Law," in *Studies in Polish and Comparative Law* (a symposium, 1945), pp. 124, 131-4.

[15]*Ibid.*, p. 145.

[16]*Ibid.*, p. 144.

[17]*Ibid.*, p. 147.

A strict correlation between liberty and equality was found by Stanisław Sokołowski (1536-93) who in his numerous writings also discussed the problems of the obligatory force of the laws, of natural law and justice, and stability and certainty of the law.[18]

Krzysztof Warszewicki (1524-1603) was one of the few politico-legal philosophers who defended the power of the king and was willing to curtail the excesses of the Polish "golden freedom."[19] His best-known treatise, however, *Ambassador–De legato et legatione* (1595), was devoted to international relations and described the duties of ministers to foreign countries.[20] The legal status of foreign representatives was also discussed in an earlier treatise, *Leges seu statuta ac privilegia Regni Poloniae* (1553), by Jakub Przyłuski (? -1554), who likewise gave a good discussion of some other problems of international law and of the laws of war.[21]

The ideas of Łukasz Górnicki (1527-1603) were similar to those of Warszewicki. In his *Conversation Between a Pole and an Italian*, published in 1588 and written in Polish (most books in his times were written in Latin,[22] he expressed the fear that the growth of the sense of freedom was dangerous, criticized the election of the kings, and exhorted the nation to be just and united.[23]

Among the writers who displayed less originality but gave valuable contributions to the development of political and legal sciences, a special place is due to Marcin Kromer (1512-89). In his *Polonia sive de situ, populis, moribus, magistratibus et republica Regni Polonici libri duo* (1578), he gave a keen analysis of the Polish constitutional and legal system of his times.[24]

[18]Jarra, *op. cit.*, fn. 13, pp. 37-8.

[19]*Ibid.*, p. 56-7.

[20]For translation of some excerpts from Warszewicki, see Lednicki, *op. cit.* fn. 8, pp. 59-63.

[21]Ehrlich and Langrod, *Zarys historii nauki prawa narodów, politycznego i administracyjnego w Polsce* ("Outline of the History of the Science of the Law of Nations, Political and Administrative Law in Poland") (1949), pp. 8-10.

[22]Lednicki, *op. cit.*, fn. 7, pp. 67-8. Another well-known book by Górnicki, *The Polish Courtier,* published in 1566, was inspired by Castiglione's *Cortegiano.*

[23]For analysis of Górnicki's philosophical and legal ideas, see Chróściechowski, "Poglady filozoficzno-prawne L. Górnickiego" ("Philosophical-Legal Ideas of L. Górnicki"), in Jarra, *Prace Seminarium Filozofii Prawa Uniwersytetu Warszawskiego,* Vol. VII (1937).

[24]Ehrlich and Langrod, *op. cit.*, fn. 21, p. 26, and Jarra, *op. cit.*, fn. 13, pp. 61-3.

It is unnecessary to discuss the work of many other politico-legal thinkers of the sixteenth century, such as Jan Dantyszek (1485-1548),[25] Jan Demetriusz Solikowski (1539-1603),[26] Jakub Górski (1525-85),[27] Stanisław Karnkowski (1525-1603),[28] Fabian Birkowski (1566-1636) [29] and others, to prove that the abundance of writing and the liveliness of discussion on matters most important to the nation was in that century amazing. In view of the fact that this phenomenon corroborated the splendid development of science, arts and letters, it may well be understood why the period under consideration is called the golden age of Polish culture.

This was the atmosphere in which Laurentius Grimaldus Goslicius (in Polish, Wawrzyniec Grzymała Goślicki) lived and created his works,[30] the most important of which was *De optimo Senatore*.

II

I discovered *De optimo Senatore* entirely by accident, having it called to my attention in 1937 by an article on "Poland Before the First Dismemberment," which appeared in John Mitchell Kemble's propaganda journal for the Great Emigration, *The British and Foreign Review*, in the issue of October, 1843.

As I hastened to investigate the possibilities of studying the treatise in the United States, I was gratified to learn that we had in the library at Columbia University and in the Newberry Library in Chicago copies of the original edition of the celebrated work, published in Venice by Giordano Ziletti in 1568. I found further that of the three translations which had been made of *De optimo Senatore* into English, we had all but the first one of 1598, called *The Counsellor*,[31] where we could get at them in the

[25]Jarra, *op. cit.*, fn. 13, pp. 47-8.

[26]*Ibid.*, pp. 40-1.

[27]*Ibid.*, pp. 41-3.

[28]*Ibid.*, pp. 43-5.

[29]*Ibid.*, pp. 52-3; see also Petzówna, "Prawo i Państwo w Kazaniach ks. Fabiana Birkowskiego," ("The Law and State in the Sermons of Rev. Fabian Birkowski"), in Jarra, *Prace Seminarium Filozofii Prawa Uniwersytetu Warszawskiego*, Vol. VIII (1938).

[30]A student on Goślicki includes six items in the list of his works (Stankiewicz, *The Accomplished Senator of Laurentius Goslicius* [1946] p. 40).

[31]*The Counsellor. Exactly pourtraited in two Books. Where in the Offices of Magistrates, the happie life of Subjectes, and the felicitie of Commonweales is*

United States. The translation of 1607, entitled *A Commonwealth of Good Counsaile*,[32] is in the Folger Shakespeare Library in Washington, and the third English version, published under the title *The Accomplished Senator* in 1733, is at both Harvard and Illinois and at the Newberry Library as well as in the Library of Congress.

My next discovery apropos of *De optimo Senatore* was made in Poland in the summer of 1939, when I learned from Mr. Tytus Filipowicz, Poland's first ambassador to the United States, that he had done some pioneer work, while he was in Washington, in the direction of exhuming Goślicki's treatise and of securing for the Polish Aristotle the place he deserves to hold in the hierarchy of political and legal thinkers.

I learned from Mr. Filipowicz that he had propounded to the 1932 meeting of the American Society of International Law the idea that Goślicki should properly be regarded as an ancestor, in a demonstrably direct line, of the fathers of the American Declaration of Independence and the American Constitution.[33]

Back of Thomas Jefferson and Tom Paine, the "fathers" familiar to everyone, were such figures as Blackstone and Helvetius, Montesquieu and Jean-Jacques Rousseau, John Locke, and Algernon Sidney. Sidney, runs Mr. Filipowicz's argument, is perhaps the most important of all in this "family tree," for he was not only the arch-smiter of Stuartian Divine Right-ology[34] but the one who supplied a clue to "fathers" more remote than himself.

For Sidney, when he struck as with the very sword of St. George at the lion of the Stuarts' preposterous doctrine, directed his blows not in general but toward a specific individual, namely, that mouthpiece of Stuart ideology, Sir Robert Filmer, whose writings clearly proclaimed the king to be free from all save divine control.

Sidney might never have been stirred to the point of giving form and substance to the idea of government as a "mutual compact" if the idea of "divine right" had not been so flaunted, and if a doctrine contrary to that of "divine right" had not already possessed currency in his day.

Here Mr. Filipowicz's reasoning leads us close to Goślicki, for the fact that such a contrary doctrine was in circulation in seventeenth century England, despite the efforts of Filmer's Stuart patrons to root out all

pleasantly and pithily discoussed. 155 pp. Published by Richard Bradocke, a London printer from 1581 to 1615, who learned his trade from the great London printer Henry Middleton. A copy of this translation is in the British Museum.

[32]Subtitle: *Policies chiefe Counselor, portraited into two Books.* Evidently translated by one "P.B.," and printed by N. Lyng.

[33]See fn. 8.

[34]Especially in his *Discourses Concerning Government.*

expression of it by the most severe censorship, is due, as we know from Filmer's own reference to the work he himself used as a springboard,[35] to the political writings of a man writing during the latter part of Goślicki's own century.

The man whose work was Filmer's starting point in his apology for the theory of "divine right" was Cardinal Robert Bellarmine.[36] Filmer hated the man and his theories, as well he might, for Bellarmine was the author of a famous definition of the principle undergirding all democratic government:

> The multitude itself is always and always remains the supreme head, and the prince is the vicar of the multitude.[37]

and his ideals were as forward-looking as Filmer's were reactionary.

But who, asks Mr. Filipowicz, was the "father" of Bellarmine, as Bellarmine was Algernon Sidney's "father"? He was "an author of influence" in the period immediately preceding the great cardinal, "who expounded similar theories,"[38] Wawrzyniec Goślicki, author of *De optimo Senatore*.

The Polish political theorist who, through his *De optimo Senatore*, thus fathered from a distance our own founding fathers, Jefferson, Mason and Paine, is more generally known by the Latin version of his name, Laurentius Grimaldus Goslicius, than by the Polish, Wawrzyniec Grzymała Goślicki.

Goślicki was born about 1533 of a very good and very old family in the vicinity of the Mazovian village of Goślice, long owned by his family, which lies not far from the fine cathedral town of Płock, a little to the north and west of Warsaw.

The first thing we know for certain about Goślicki is that on a winter day in 1557 he registered as a student in the Faculty of Philosophy at the Jagiellonian University in Cracow. Goślicki was older than most of the students who entered with him. He was tall and handsome, with the long head and nose of the typical Polish nobleman, and he stood out among his colleagues not only because of his looks but also because of an unmistakable air of high breeding which most of them lacked, since most were the sons of burghers or country folk.

The Jagiellonian University had been in Copernicus' day (1491-4) a center of intellectual life and its teachers had been world figures as well as outstanding Humanists. Even up to the death of the great Humanist,

[35]*De Laicis,* by Bellarmine, which Filmer translated.

[36]James Scott Brown's address on "Robert Bellarmine and our Political Heritage," *Georgetown College Journal*, LX (1931), p. 17.

[37]Bellarmine, *Apologia*, cited by Brown, *op. cit.*, p. 26.

[38]Filipowicz, *op. cit.*, fn. 8, p. 234.

Bishop Tomicki, guardian of the University's destiny until 1535, it had continued to generate intellectual heat and light. But in Goślicki's time Cracow was not an international meeting place any longer and the university had become a purely national Polish school. "The school was not designed for Poles alone, yet where now are the Hungarians and the Germans and the others too from more distant regions? " lamented one of the school's few remaining Humanists. Alas, they were not in Cracow, for the Polish University was not, as it had once been, a place where free minds loved to clash and set each other on fire. Liberal and creative thinking had migrated to the royal court and to the courts of the wealthy noblemen, a class rapidly increasing in power in Goślicki's day, yet shunning, the more it rose in prestige, all contact with the university it once had passionately supported.

Despite the reactionary air and bourgeois atmosphere of the Jagiellonian school, Goślicki remained in Cracow for five years, pursuing first the course in philosophy and then going on to complete the work leading to a Master's degree in the Arts. Long before he left, all his other Cracow colleagues who later became famous had deserted the city, some leaving in order to escape the terrible plague that visited it in 1559, others in order to study at more animated universities like Frankfurt-on-Oder, which was enjoying a period of intense activity since its reopening in 1539, or Wittenberg, where Melanchton lectured until his death in 1560. Goślicki was persuaded to remain in Cracow by two things: patronage on the part of high ecclesiastics who saw in him a great churchman, and the magnetic force of a single great and eloquent teacher, the Humanist Jakub Górski.

Beyond the stifling chambers of the university, if not within them, Goślicki heard, all through his student days in Cracow, rumbling that foreshadowed the onrush of modern times and modern ways of thinking. The old ideal of "learning for learning's sake" was breaking down and a new ideal of what constituted a desirable education was crystallizing. A "Republic of the Nobles" was in the process of formation in Poland, and, as this became more and more of a reality, thoughtful members of the noble class came to believe increasingly that the purpose of education was to train young men to serve the state nobly and wisely. They wished to see the universities offer studies calculated to help men solve the practical problems of political and social life.

> I have no use for teachers who feed our young men on useless speculative learning, so that instead of deriving true enlightenment they are plunged into any abyss inscrutable to the ordinary intelligence and thus, far from extending, they actually obscure learning and truth. . . .

declared Chancellor Zamoyski at the opening of his own ideal Academy at Zamość in 1595, while Nicholas Rey, one of the first "modern men" in

Poland, laid down the principle that

...for the living of an upright life no branches of learning are necessary save only such as are conducive to a canny intellect and sound virtues.

Goślicki was powerfully influenced by this exceedingly practical, and, if one may say so, political type of thinking. In *De optimo Senatore* he divided learning into two distinct categories, calling one category the theoretical or contemplative, the other the utilitarian – with ethics, politics, law, history and the like included in the latter – and he made his Excellent Senator above all else a capable and upright public servant.

Goślicki left Poland to complete his studies abroad soon after he received his Master's degree in 1562. He went first to Padua, one of the great centers of legal learning, where Torquato Tasso was a student and Goślicki's own compatriot Jan Zamoyski was presently to be made Rector (President) of the University at the age of twenty-two.

Like Tasso, Goślicki soon left Padua for Bologna, to study toward a doctoral degree in both civil and canon law at the fine university at the foot of the Appenines. Goślicki belonged to the first generation of Bologna students to attend classes in a building belonging to the university. Hitherto classes had been conducted haphazardly about the city in any corner where the professors could find a free hall. Sometimes the professors had met the students in their own homes. In 1562, however, the great archigimnasio was built at the order of Pope Pius IV, a Medici, and the tumultuous students began to listen to lectures in quarters of their own. Thus Wawrzyniec Goślicki undertook the study of law in an edifice whose charming arcaded courts remind one of nothing in the world so much as the courts of his own alma mater in Cracow.

As soon as he received his Doctorate, Goślicki left Bologna to follow the trail, already well marked by his compatriots, to Rome. Reaching the city early in January 1567, he was greeted on his arrival by his old teacher from Cracow, Jakub Górski, and by Joseph Zamoyski, at whose promotion to the Doctorate he soon stood as a witness. Not long after, Goślicki made an excursion with a number of other Poles to Naples. Along the way, near the village of Terracina, the party was set upon by bandits and robbed of both clothes and money!

It was in Rome that Goślicki completed the work he had long had in mind, "dreaming" the Excellent Senator into existence, as he reported to Cardinal Hozjusz, "on Italian nights."

Goślicki published *De optimo Senatore* in Venice rather than Rome; printing costs were only about a third as great there and, in addition, the Venetians were more expert than other Italians in circumventing rigid censorship. Goślicki was undoubtedly assisted in the work of finding a publisher for his *Senator* by the most distinguished publisher of his day,

Paolo Manutius, son of the Venetian who founded the Aldine Press and a close associate of Goślicki's teacher, Górski.

Almost immediately after the publication of *De optimo Senatore* (1568), Goślicki returned to Poland. Still a young man of only thirty-five or thereabouts, he went back to a long and splendid career in the service of his country and the Church. First under Sigismund Augustus, that "Most Serene and Powerful Prince" to whom he dedicated his *Senator*, and later under Stefan Batory and Sigismund III, Goślicki headed important embassies and missions both at home and abroad and filled with distinction one high post in the ecclesiastical hierarchy after another, until he became at the climax of his career Chancellor of Poland and later Bishop of Poznań. Three kings of Poland in succession found Goślicki "a man faithful and honorable." Although he was a dignitary of the Catholic church, he showed a remarkable spirit of tolerance for any religious beliefs. Together with Chancellor Zamoyski, he greatly contributed to the official recognition by the state of equality of all in religious matters (1573), and in his unfinished manuscript, *Discursus de hereticis* (in possession of the Załuski Library), he strongly advocated the rights of dissenters.[39]

Goślicki died on the 31st of October, 1607, at the place of his final residence, the Bishop's Palace at Ciążeń in Great Poland. He was buried in Poznań in the cathedral of Poland's first kings, in a separate chapel where, to this very day, his tall, imposing figure, clad in liturgical robes and crowned with the Bishop's mitre, still may be seen represented in marble, above a massive sarcophagus.

III

When the Huns were overrunning Europe in the fifth century of the Christian era, they came upon a church in which a cross had been worked in the masonry above the altar. In an effort to wipe out the cross, the Huns covered over the masonry with gold leaf. After a time the outline of the cross was seen to come through. A second, a third, and a fourth covering of gold leaf were placed over the masonry, but on each occasion the outline of the cross continued to come through. In succeeding years, after the shadow of the Huns had been lifted from the church, men and women came from great distances to witness the miracle of the ineffaceable cross.

In the same way, Goślicki's *De optimo Senatore* has "come through" all attempts that have been made to obliterate it. Censorship did its best to kill the work first in Venice, where at the very moment of its publication

[39]Stankiewicz, *op. cit.*, fn. 30, pp. 9, 12, and 40.

it was scanned with suspicion. In 1593 another Latin edition was published in Basle. In 1598 the first English translation was confiscated as soon as it came from the press by the reactionaries who tried to stifle the printed word at the end of the reign of Elizabeth. Nine years later the treatise met the same fate again at the hands of the watchful agents of the Stuarts, when "P.B.'s" new translation was published in the year of Goślicki's own death, 1607.

But there was immortality in the *Senator*, and in 1733, when but three copies of the original Latin text were known to exist, the work was again translated into English, this time by William Oldisworth, a professional hack writer for the London booksellers and publishers, of whom Pope said that he could turn an ode of Horace into English, "the quickest of any man in England." Oldisworth's translation, like the others before it, was quickly confiscated lest it inflame the already restive spirits of the Jacobites.

Again Goślicki's *Senator* did not die. Passed furtively from hand to hand, it lived on, to become for English political theorists and revolutionaries what the pamphlets of Rousseau were for liberal thinkers in pre-revolutionary France.

The political belief of Goślicki was that "in the private happiness of the subjects consists the general and publick happiness of the common-wealth,"[40] and the ideal system of government was to him the one which rendered all the citizens happy. The similarity of this idea to the credo of the Declaration of Independence is striking.

The title which Goślicki gave to his immortal dissertation is somewhat misleading.[41] The treatise is not, as its title might lead one to expect, a picture of some ideal Senator

... nowhere really extant but in the mind; and whose shining original is only to be found in heaven, without casting the least shadow or resemblance of it on earth[42]

but rather an intensely practical handbook of good constitutional law and statecraft in which Goślicki first endeavors to find the figure he sees every state as requiring and then tries to invest that figure with form and substance.

What Goślicki was searching after in *De optimo Senatore* was a harmonizer, a buffer to stand in the midst of yet always above and

[40]Goślicki, *De optimo Senatore*, p. 27 (Oldisworth's edition).

[41]Besides works referred to in other notes, comments on *De optimo Senatore* and Goślicki in general were written by Jarra in "Wawrzyniec Goślicki jako filozof prawa" ("Wawrzyniec Goślicki as Legal Philosopher"), *Themis Polska* (1931), p. 92.

[42]Goślicki, *op cit.*, p. 3.

removed from party strife, resolving and harmonizing hostile interests. Goślicki's fellow-countryman and fellow-Paduan, Jan Zamoyski, came to the conclusion, on the basis of his study, *De Senatu Romano* (1563), that the Roman office of *tribuni plebis* answered most satisfactorily the universal need of states for such a figure, and when he returned to Poland, Zamoyski took with him a fixed determination to see created in his homeland an office corresponding to the Roman tribunate. Goślicki, on the other hand, saw the senator as the ideal harmonizer and the guarantor of a free yet orderly state.

In Poland, the necessity for finding a harmonizer was acute in the middle sixteenth century because, as we have seen, the upward thrust of the people was both positive and aggressive at that moment and at the same time successful. Moreover, freedom was sometimes being abused and endangering the intrinsically good evolutionary movement.

It became clear indeed to Goślicki that the "golden freedom," of which Poland had so much, was not enough, and that freedom, to profit a people, must be implemented by wise and cunning statecraft.

Reviewing the state of his homeland from distant Padua and later from Bologna and Rome, Goślicki reached the conclusion that the principles undergirding the noblemen's revolt against senatorial domination were without exception good. He embodied them in *De optimo Senatore*, thereby tacitly approving them all, even the new and dangerous principle of the right to revolution:

> Sometimes a people, justly provoked and irritated by the tyranny and usurpations of their kings, take upon themselves the undoubted right of vindicating their own liberties; and by a well-formed conspiracy or by open arms, shake off the yoke, drive out their lords and masters, and take the government entirely into their own hands.[43]

But how, Goślicki was obliged to ask as he pondered over the problems of government, how were harmony and balance to be achieved in a state where freedom was the possession of the people? What man or body of men could most satisfactorily serve as a barrier to reaction and tyranny on the one hand and unbridled license on the other? How, in a word, could freedom be implemented so that the state, in cherishing freedom and the equality of its citizenry, both of which principles Goślicki fervently believed in, would not wreck itself and imperil its very existence?

Goślicki saw the Senator as the answer to this question. The Senator, calm, poised, elevated above party strife, standing midway between the king and the noblemen's mass, was the axis Goślicki sought.

> As the balance turns, he (the Senator) may provide accordingly, and timely prevent a daring and licentious people from running into

[43]*Ibid.*, pp. 32-3 (spelling modernized).

anarchy and confusion, or an ambitious monarch from aspiring to tyranny and usurpation.[44]

The ideal senator appears as a background upon which Goślicki develops his ideas of a good system of law and government. Although *De optimo Senatore* is a fairly extensive treatise, consisting of two books and many chapters, only four principles are set forth in it. These four principles are, however, fundamental ones:

1. There must be laws which are greater than any individual— including those who rule the state.
2. Such laws must be founded upon the basis of the Christian faith.
3. There must be mediation between conflicting points of view.
4. Both the nation and the individual derive their true purpose and dignity from Christian principles – and without them must perish.

Let us consider, one by one, the principles stressed by Goślicki, illustrating what he meant us to understand by them with passages quoted from his own work.

1. There must be laws greater than any individual – including those who rule the state.

"The king," notes Goślicki, "can do no public act of government without the advice and authority of the state."[45] And later,

The King of Poland, in the administration of his government, is obliged to make the law the sole guide and rule of his conduct. He cannot govern according to his own will and pleasure, nor make war or peace, without the advice and consent of the senate. He cannot go beyond, or break in upon their decrees, nor exceed the bounds which they and the laws have set him.[46]

No Pole of Goślicki's time could possibly have held a contrary attitude toward the transcendent authority of the laws and their place above both king and senate, for the laws were the people's guarantee of justice, the sure foundation of their dearly prized liberty. How clear, at the same time, is Goślicki's reverence for the senate! That sentiment too was characteristic of the highborn Mazovian lords to whose ranks he belonged, for ever since 1529, when King Sigismund Augustus had tried to persuade the nation to establish a precedent for abandoning the electoral idea of the kingship and for making the Jagiellonian dynasty hereditary, these lords had regarded the senate increasingly as the guardian of liberty against royal usurpation.

The contention set forth in the first part of this study that Goślicki was a forerunner of our own founding fathers is plainly supported by the

[44]*Ibid.*, p. 61.

[45]*Ibid.*, p. 51.

[46]*Ibid.*, p. 52.

above quotations. The very words of the English translation, "with the advice and authority of the senate," are echoed in our own Constitution, especially Article II, Section 2, which grants the President the power to make treaties "by and with the advice of the Senate."

While we are noting similarities in Polish custom to our own, it is worthwhile to call attention, as Goslicki does, to the Polish manner of oath-taking. Goslicki shows that in Poland all officers of the government were solemnly sworn to keep, observe, and maintain the laws. Such an oath was the forerunner of the oath administered to officials of the United States government, charging them to "preserve, protect and defend the Constitution of the United States." The purpose of the Polish oath is fully explained by Goslicki:

> This oath, which is mutually administered to every order, and by which they are bound to the observance of the laws, and the maintenance of the liberties of their country, is in the Polish language called KAPTUR, that is, a covering for the head; for as such a covering defends the head from all the assaults of frost and snow, snow and tempest; so is this oath a sure covering and defense for the public, against all attempts upon its laws, liberties and happiness.[47]

Goslicki was careful to show that the judges, or the magistrates, were themselves to be bound by the laws. On this point, Goslicki referred to a quotation from Cicero, "that the law is as much above the magistrate, as the magistrate is above the people." After referring to the quotation, Goslicki carried it further and added: "... whence it may be truly said that the magistrate is a speaking law, and the law a silent magistrate."[48]

Goslicki's "reign of law," under which "both the rulers and the ruled have to obey the law" is identical with the ideas of Frycz-Modrzewski and the American concept of "government of law."

2. *The Laws must be founded upon the basis of the Christian faith.*

Goslicki based his system of laws not upon the will of the ruling powers, but upon the broad principles of natural justice, which he defined in the following language:

> Natural justice has its rise from the first principles and dictates of Nature, which had kindled up a certain light in us, whereby we are enabled to discern between the good we ought to choose and the evil we ought to shun and avoid. This is the great law of equity, that we abstain from all injuries; and never contrive or attempt anything which may be hurtful or displeasing to others. Mutual benevolence or good will to mankind, is that great and fundamental virtue, by which men are drawn together, and united in one common body, or public society.[49]

[47]*Ibid.*, p. 51.
[48]*Ibid.*, p. 54.
[49]*Ibid.*, p. 215.

112

Goslicki did not base his system of laws upon "natural justice" alone, but also upon "divine justice," about which he wrote:

Divine justice, or the justice due to our Maker, is an obligation laid upon us by Nature, to acknowledge, to worship, to fear, to love, and to reverence Him. This is a privilege, as well as a duty, peculiar only to man. For Nature, in the formation of all living creatures whatsoever, took care that the notion of a Deity should be fixed and implanted only in the mind of man. To our creator, we look up, whilst the animals beneath us prone and intent upon the earth, and stoop down to their several pastures, for food and nourishment. Man, therefore, of all other animals, in their several kinds and orders, is the only being in the world with whom Nature has entrusted the high and honorable office of worshipping and adoring his Maker, and of giving Him the reverence and honor due unto His Name.[50]

The fact that Goslicki based his system of laws upon the Christian faith is made abundantly clear by this passage:

Since, therefore, we are in effect associated with our Maker, and are so nearly allied and related to Him we ought to look upon this world as our great city, or society, the right ordering and government of which is committed to us by and in common with our Great Creator. And since He is the Author of all things, and the architect of the Universe, from whom, as the One Great Parent, all other beings derive their original, for this reason, we ought to resort to him, for whatever counsels, laws, and edicts, are necessary to the good government of the world, his creature; that the world may know it is not managed and directed by the will of man, but under command and by the wisdom of its eternal maker, and according to His good will and pleasure.[51]

It has been said that faith "is a grasping of Almighty power, the hand of man laid on the arm of God." The hand of Góslicki truly was laid upon the arm of the Divine Being.

In quite a few passages, Goslicki makes it clear that the principal objective of the law is to build up an orderly society, not to punish criminals.

This modern idea is a sequence of Goslicki's general concepts of social philosophy. It is reflected in many passages, and finds its best expression in the statement:

It is better in framing laws to aim them rather at the preventing than the suppressing of evil.[52]

And again:

[50]*Ibid.*, p. 217.

[51]*Ibid.*, p. 5.

[52]*Ibid.*, p. 175.

In my opinion all our counsel and wisdom ought first to be employed in bringing men to justice rather than to execution.[53]

Legal order is, according to Goślicki, a necessary element of every state, the other two being a definite territory and a population. In this approach, Goślicki was first, and preceded by nine years the ideas of Jean Bodin.

3. There must be mediation between conflicting points of view.

It is here that Goślicki sets forth the true rôle of the good senator. Goślicki recognized that

... differences and contentions will often arise between King and people; whilst one party is pressing forward, and aiming at too much power, and the other falling back into an excess of liberty.[54]

To bring about a middle course between these extremes was the purpose assigned by Goślicki to a good senator. He pointed out that it was

... a necessary part of his knowledge, to be able to set out the true legal limits and boundaries of the royal prerogative, grandeur and jurisdiction; and of the rights and liberties of the subjects.[55]

And in a later passage Goślicki stated:

To prevent these evils, the Senator must interpose with all his diligence, and use his best endeavors to preserve the just, undoubted liberties of his fellow subjects, in that regular and legal state, in which they are held in common by all the members of the body politic. From the midway station, where he is properly posted, he must look out constantly, and keep a watchful eye upon the public welfare, and exert his utmost diligence in preserving the commonwealth, from whatever dangers of detriment it may possibly be exposed to, either by the ambition of a few, who are aiming at more power; or the seditions of the multitude contending for more liberty. For the Senator, in his proper post, and by the very nature of his office, is really a judge and arbiter between the quiet and peaceable, and the violent and unruly; between liberty and servitude, between King and people.[56]

The essential requisites for the good senator are clearly set forth by Goślicki, and are four in number. First, he must be "well endowed with those particular virtues, which tend to the promotion of public good and welfare."[57] Second, he must be well settled and confirmed in his religious judgment and sentiments, "for constancy in religion is the foundation of true wisdom, virtue and honor."[58] Third, he must be a true lover of the

[53]*Ibid.,* p. 176.

[54]*Ibid.,* p. 149.

[55]*Ibid.,* p. 149.

[56]*Ibid.,* p. 150.

[57]*Ibid.,* p. 55.

[58]*Ibid.,* p. 224.

114

constitution of the government in which he is to be employed, and "desirous to live quietly under it, without attempting any changes or alterations, in prejudice to an old and well grounded establishment."[59] Fourth, he must look upon the power and trust, which is reposed in him by the public, "to be intended for no other use or purpose, but to be employed in their service and for the common good."[60]

Goślicki points out that just as in the constitution of human bodies "the separation of the head and heart is sure and immediate death," so, in the body politic, "a separation between King and Senate is proportionately dangerous; is always followed with civil discord, dissention and confusion, and easily brings on the ruin and overthrow of a government."[61] On the other hand, he shows the benefits which result from close co-operation and complete understanding and union between king and the senate:

> A King therefore, who will be under the direction of the Senate, and collect together within himself the united wisdom of a great and wise body, and govern by the rules and dictates of it, must be truly perfect in reason, in counsel, and in discipline, and by far superior to the mixed multitude and mass of people over whom he presides. Such a monarch cannot but govern wisely, and with the most consummate prudence; because he never relies upon his own private opinion, which may often vary, and lead him into errors, but on the common reason and united counsel of his Senate, by which his own private reason is made perfect.[62]

That the senate, during the time of Goślicki, came up to the high standards set by him, is shown by the dedication of his work to Sigismund Augustus, in which he said:

> You are doubly happy in this, that you have a Senate to assist you, in a wise and prudent administration, chosen according to your own wishes, and by your own direction, and as remarkable for their prudence and justice, as for their illustrious birth and nobility; by whose moderation and wisdom, our country enjoys peace and quiet, and the fullness of reputation and renown.[63]

And in another portion of the dedication, Goślicki stated that "no government can be happy or miserable, without involving its people in the same state and condition,"[64] and then attributed the good fortune of

[59]*Ibid.*, p. 56.
[60]*Ibid.*, p. 56.
[61]*Ibid.*, p. 36.
[62]*Ibid.*, p. 37.
[63]*Ibid.*, p. xxix.
[64]*Ibid.*, p. xxvii.

Poland and her people to "the consideration of your Majesty's personal character, and the right use you make of power and authority."[65]

4. *Both the nation and the individual derive their true purpose and dignity from Christian principles – and without them must perish.*

After showing that man only, of all animals, was appointed not only an inhabitant and citizen of the world, but the lord and master of it, Goślicki shows the depth of man's religious faith when he says:

This high and extensive dignity he attained immediately from the Divine Being, the one Supreme Governor both of heaven and earth; who took him to be, as it were, his partner in the government of this world, made for the common residence of human beings, and capable of communication with those of a celestial nature. Accordingly, He breathed into him a divine mind and understanding, the better to enable him, by his reason and counsel, to govern the world in a godlike manner, with truth, sanctity and justice.[66]

There was no doubt in Goślicki's mind that man had a choice, and was free to decide for himself whether or not he would abide by Christian principles; and that if he did not, then he would reap the consequences thereof. In words which, if we did not know their source, might well be taken to come from the Bible, Goślicki says:

There is a heavenly seed sown in our nature which, if well received and improved by the good husbandman, will bring forth fruit agreeable to its nature and original; but if neglected, or depraved, it perishes in a barren soil; or, instead of fruit, produces nothing but thorns and briers.[67]

Goślicki made no distinction between the individual man and the state with respect to the evil consequences which follow upon a failure to abide by the fundamental laws of the Christian faith. Thus he states:

Where there are neither laws nor magistrates, there cannot be so much as a shadow or appearance of any human society; and such a country may be looked upon as forsaken both by God and man.[68]

Goślicki was most direct and forceful in his condemnation of tyrants. We may be sure that the following passage must have been one of the principal reasons why his work was suppressed:

Many are the artifices of tyrants, by which they set themselves to invade and make spoil of their people's liberties. As it is natural for them to entertain a jealousy and suspicion of all about them, who are justly noted for their virtue, goodness and wisdom; so their first and greatest care is to remove all such out of the way; and when

[65]*Ibid.*, p. xxviii.
[66]*Ibid.*, p. 5.
[67]*Ibid.*, p. 5.
[68]*Ibid.*, p. 55.

116

they are removed, all other opponents, either by force and violence, or by their own cowardice and weakness, are easily brought under and enslaved; and the will and lust of the usurper are the only measure and rule of government.[69]

The most important duty of the kings is to serve their nations, as they "were made not for their own, but for the people's sake."[70]

The finest insight into the philosophy and teaching of Goślicki is given to us, at the close of his great work, in these words:

All the appetites and desires of our souls, and all our endeavors to attain the sum and perfection of all virtue whatsoever, ought to return back to the fountain whence they issued and were at first derived. The great end and aim of all our lives, and of all our labors and industries, is this; that (if possible) we may bring ourselves to resemble our Maker in virtue and goodness, and rise by degrees to an imitation of the divine excellencies and perfections.[71]

As Oldisworth said of Goślicki in his dedication of the English translation to the Dukes of Beaufort and Argyll, to the Lord Bishop of Oxford, and to a number of other illustrious English dignitaries:

His reasoning proceeds altogether upon such principles (namely), those of Divinity, Law, Policy and Philosophy, and terminates in such conclusions as are of Eternal Veracity, and of perpetual use to all states and societies of men.[72]

Goślicki himself would have been delighted with this dedication, for he desired above all else to have his work serve forever the practical needs of the race of man.

The principles expounded by Goślicki not only survived all attempts made to destroy the work in which they were set forth, but they were largely carried over into and embodied in the Polish Constitution of May 3, 1791, and influenced constitutional and legislative enactments in other countries.

We may be certain that, as in the miracle of the ineffaceable cross, these principles will continue to emerge from every present and future attempt to obliterate them.

[69]*Ibid.*, p. 150.
[70]*Ibid.*, p. 32.
[71]*Ibid.*, p. 330.
[72]*Ibid.*, p. al.

WACŁAW W. SOROKA

The Law in the Polish Lands
During the Partition Period

The partitions of Poland in 1772, 1793, and 1795 brought about changes in the legal order of that country. The sovereignty of the partitioning powers (Austria, Prussia, and Russia) replaced the independence of the Polish-Lithuanian Commonwealth, and the source of authority for law changed. The governments of Vienna, Berlin, and St. Petersburg determined the validity of the laws, their interpretation, the procedures to be applied in administration of justice, and the sanctions provided by the state. The legal orders of the partitioning countries were extended to those parts of Poland now incorporated into them.

Laws of the Polish-Lithuanian Commonwealth remained, however, in force under specified circumstances for a given period of time. Polish law was applicable to matters not covered by new legal rules in the Duchy of Warsaw, 1807-14, in the Kingdom of Poland created at the Congress of Vienna, and in the Cracow Free Republic, 1815-46. Polish legislative action produced a special group of autonomous statutes specifically for use in Poland.

The national uprisings of the Poles against the occupying powers in 1794 (with Tadeusz Kościuszko as the head of the state), in 1830-1, in 1846-9, and in 1863-4 created a special legal order. The revolutionary authorities and the national governments that headed those uprisings developed their own legislative activities and enacted new laws.

The systems of law in the parts of Poland incorporated within Austria, Prussia, and Russia also underwent evolution as legislatures of the partitioning powers developed in the nineteenth and twentieth centuries. The establishment in 1871 of the German Empire also affected the Prussian section of Poland.

119

The prevailing religion in Prussia was Protestant and in Russia, Orthodox. In Poland, these occupying powers, however, enacted special laws for resident Catholics and Jews. The laws governing these religious groups were determined by political objectives, and not by the desire for justice or internal peace. During some periods, in fact, persecution of these groups became especially intense. Martial law and authoritarian action on the part of the occupants resulted in oppression, an element characteristic of the whole period of Poland's partition.

Other oppressive laws hampered and restricted the national objectives of the Polish nation. Together with the laws discriminating against the Poles in favor of the ruling nations of Austria, Russia, and Prussia (and later Germany), other oppressive laws evoked Polish opposition to the legal order. The law of the occupants was often considered an unjust and arbitrary expression of force. Opposition to the legal system established by the occupants[1] became a major characteristic of the period. This resentment largely contributed to the struggle for independence which was regained in 1918.

The Laws of the Partitioning Powers

The legal orders of the partitioning powers left some Polish laws and institutions in force until the whole of life in the incorporated territories could fully be absorbed by the three ruling nations and regulated by them.

The first book of the Josephin Civil Code of 1786 was introduced as law in the Austrian part of Poland as early as May, 1787. The Austrian procedural law of 1781 was made applicable to the incorporated territories, together with the rest of the Code of 1786, after the third partition of Poland. By January 1, 1798, Austrian law, with amendments and specific exceptions, came into effect in the Polish provinces incorporated by Austria.[2]

In the Prussian part of Poland, the *Allgemeines Landrecht* of 1794, supplemented in 1806, was enacted as law. The organization of the

[1]Leon Duguit, *Traité de droit constitutionnel* (2d ed., Paris: E. de Boccard, 1922-5), III, 659-81. See also Jean Dabin, *La philosophie de l'ordre juridique positif spécialement dans les rapports de droit privé* (Paris: Librairie du Recueil Sirey, 1929), pp. 668-71, 696-700, 712-15.

[2]Przemysław Dcąbkowski, *Prawo prywatne polskie* ("Polish Private Law") (Lwów: Nakł. Towarzystwa dla Popierania Nauki polskiej, 1910-1) I, 12. See also: Władysław Sobociński, *Historia ustroju i prawa Księstwa Warszawskiego* ("History of State Organization and Law of The Duchy of Warsaw") (Vol. 70, No. 1, of *Roczniki Towarzystwa Naukowego w Toruniu*) (Toruń: 1964), pp. 42-3. Stanisław Kutrzeba surveys the legal order in the partitioned Poland in Vols. III and IV of his *Historia ustroju Polski w zarysie* ("History of State Organization of Poland: An Outline") (Lwów: Nakł. Księgarni Polskiej Bernarda Połonieckiego, 1917).

judiciary and the procedure of the courts were regulated by the *Allgemeine Gerichtsordnung* from the years 1793-5. Particular statutes, dealing with deposits and mortgages, were separately extended to the annexed Polish lands. Territorial diversification of the Prussian legal order was also reflected in that part of Poland which was subdivided into Süd Preussen (South Prussia) and Neu-Ost-Preussen (New East Prussia) each of which was submitted to a different system of law. A part of the Bydgoszcz province was incorporated into the East Prussian Territorial Law, or *Preussisches Landrecht*, of 1721.[3]

Polish-Lithuanian Law after the Partitions

As mentioned above, the law of the Polish-Lithuanian Commonwealth was not abrogated in its entirety by the partitioning powers immediately after the downfall of the Kingdom. Even when the legal systems of the occupants were extended to the territories of the Commonwealth, the old law was accepted as a subsidiary source of the law, as well as a source of information on the interpretation of laws, customs, and jurisprudence. In that respect, the law of the Polish-Lithuanian Commonwealth survived, in some cases, until the middle of the nineteenth century.

In the Austrian part of Poland, Count Pergen, the Governor of Galicia, ordered in 1772 that the judges exercise their jurisdiction according to the "ancient custom and legal order."[4] Empress Maria Theresa stated in her Patent (decree) of 1775 that Polish law was to continue to be applied in matters of inheritance. Sources subsidiary to Polish law were the Lithuanian Statute and the Prussian Book of Law, a Polish codification called *Korektura pruska*.[5] By 1798, however, Polish law had lost its validity as a primary source of law in the territories which were annexed by Austria.

For some time, Polish law was maintained in force in the Prussian parts of Poland, either as the primary source of legal order or as a subsidiary system of law. Therefore, a treatise used commonly for acquainting one with the existing Polish law, *Prawo cywilne* (the "Civil Law") by Teodor Ostrowski,[6] was translated into German.

[3]Sobociński, *op. cit.,* p. 43. See also Kutrzeba, *op. cit.,* IV, 123; and Dąbkowski, *op. cit.,* I, 145.

[4]Dąbkowski, *op. cit.,* p. 6.

[5]This is a codification of the laws in force in Royal Prussia that was incorporated into Polish law in 1454. The codification was approved by the Polish Diet of 1598 as *Ius terrestre nobilitatis Prussiae,* or *Korektura pruska.*

[6]Teodor Ostrowski, *Prawo cywilne albo szczególne narodu polskiego z statutów i konstytucji koronnych i litewskich zebrane* ("Civil or Particular Law of the Polish

121

The law of the Polish-Lithuanian Commonwealth remained in force longest in territories incorporated into Russia. The Third Lithuanian Statute was retained after the partitions. It was translated into Russian in 1811, and its effectiveness was maintained in the Vitebsk and Mohilev provinces until February 18, 1831. The Statute was also maintained in the Kiev, Volhynia, Podolia, Wilno, and Grodno *guberniias* (provinces) and in the district of Białystok until June 25, 1840, when the Russian *Svod Zakonov Rossiiskii Imperii*) "The Code of Laws of the Russian Empire") of Nicholas I became applicable. In the *guberniias* of Chernikhov and Poltava, the Lithuanian Statute was effective, at least in part, until 1842. The rules of the Statute regarding inheritance were incorporated into the Russian *Svod* in 1842 and 1857. Some of them, indeed, were adopted for use in Russia by the Governing Senate (*Pravitel' stvuiushchyi Senat*).[7]

Special professional or occupational Polish laws remained in force after the partition. An example was the law of the beekeepers preserved in some regions (such as Jedlna) until 1835.[8]

The Law and the Legislative Activities in the Duchy of Warsaw

In the years 1807-31, Polish law was re-established in the Duchy of Warsaw, and then in the Congress Kingdom of Poland, and in the Free City of Cracow, a part of the pre-partition Polish-Lithuanian Commonwealth. This law included the common territorial law (*ius terrestre*), all the "constitutions" or enactments of the *seym* (parliament), the Lithuanian Statute, the Magdeburg and Chełmno Laws, and other civil and criminal laws which had been in force before the partition. The laws of the occupants which had been enacted between the partitions and the creation of the Duchy of Warsaw were retained as subsidiary law. In matters of criminal procedure these laws proved to be more efficient than the old Polish laws, which had not been codified.

The diet of the Warsaw Duchy upheld the effectiveness of the Polish law and established criteria for applying the existing laws in 1809. Substantive Polish criminal law was held to be applicable when it was more favorable to the accused and when it defined more precisely various offenses than the law of the occupants.

Nation Compiled from the Polish and Lithuanian Statutes and Constitutions") (2d ed., Warsaw, 1786-7). Its German edition is titled, *Civilrecht der polnischen Nation* (Berlin: Herausgegeben von Beni, 1797).

[7]Dąbkowski, *op. cit.,* p. 16. Also see Kutrzeba, *op. cit.,* IV, 123, and III, 160.

[8]Dąbkowski, *op. cit.,* I, 34.

A special situation was created in Cracow, which was proclaimed, together with the adjoining territory, as a free state in the form of a republic at the Congress of Vienna. The Republic of Cracow returned to the legal order in force before the partition, during the time Cracow had belonged to the Duchy of Warsaw. (It was annexed to the Duchy by Napoleon in 1809).[9] After the insurrection of 1846, Cracow and its vicinity were incorporated into Austria with the agreement of the Prussian and Russian governments. Until the First World War, Cracow shared the law of the rest of Austrian Poland.

The applicability of the old Polish law was sharply limited by the enactment of new fundamental laws of the Duchy and of the Kingdom of Poland, as well as of the Code of Napoleon (May 1, 1808), the French Commercial Code (1809), and French procedural law and judicial organization in the Duchy of Warsaw. In addition, some statutes were enacted to regulate special problems such as military organization.[10]

The reception of the Code of Napoleon was to be prepared, and the French texts translated, by a special committee. This committee, like others of its type, extended its prerogatives over preparation for the reception of all the Napoleonic codes, including the commercial code, the procedural codes, and penal code, as well as over the organization of judiciary and military laws. The short period of the existence of the Duchy prevented the full reception of the entire French legal order in the Duchy of Warsaw.

The legislation of the Duchy of Warsaw, based on the Napoleonic Code, survived the Duchy itself. Some political and military institutions established in the Duchy of Warsaw lasted until 1831, some administrative institutions lasted until 1863 or 1867, some judicial institutions until 1876, and the civil law system until our own time. The last was recently abrogated by Polish legislation.[11]

A large portion of the legal system in the Duchy of Warsaw, as well as in the Congress Kingdom, resulted from legislative action of the kings and *seyms,* as well as of other branches of the government.

[9]In 1809 the territory between the Pilica River and the Bug River with the district of Zamość was also incorporated into the Duchy of Warsaw. Concomitantly, the validity of the Polish law was re-established there. The Code of Napoleon was extended over those territories in 1810.

[10]Szymon Askenazy, *Sto lat zarządu w Królestwie Polskiem, 1800-1900* ("A Hundred Years of Government in the Polish Kingdom") (Lwów: Nakł. Księgarni H. Altenberga, 1903), p. 96. A thorough study of the legal situation in the Warsaw Duchy was published by the Learned Society in Toruń. It was written by Sobociński (*op. cit.*)

[11]Sobociński, *op. cit.,* pp. 300-1.

Nikolai Reinke, Russian author and high official, characterized this period, especially with respect to the Congress Kingdom, as follows:

> The first fifteen years of its existence represents the development of the stately and national idea of the Kingdom. Under the protection of the Throne,[12] the general upheaval of spirit, particularly in the first half of this period, found its expression in fine legislative acts, from among which many survived all later catastrophies.[13]

Three of the legislative acts enacted in the Congress Kingdom proved to be particularly significant: the law on mortgages of 1817, the penal code of 1818, the civil code of 1825, which replaced the part on persons and the family law in Book I of the Napoleonic Code. There was a project to replace entirely the Napoleonic legislation with the Kingdom's own legislation.

Development and Change in the Law until 1918

The partitioned Poland was subject to four legal systems: Austrian, Prussian, (after 1871, German), Russian, and Franco-Polish. The last was established in the territories influenced by the *Code Napoléon* and by other sources of law of the Duchy of Warsaw and of the Congress Kingdom.

The laws of the occupants underwent, of course, continuous development. In the Austrian part of Poland, the Austrian Civil Code of 1811, *Allgemeines Zivil-Gesetzbuch,* and the Austrian Commercial Code, *Oesterreichisches Handelsgesetzbuch,* were introduced as law.[14] They were amended and supplemented by subsequent enactments.

The criminal law in Austrian Poland was finally codified in the Austrian Code of 1852.[15] Particular laws, including emergency and martial laws, were enacted by special acts. All above codes and statutes were in force in southern Poland until 1918.

[12]Of Alexander I.

[13]Nikolai Reinke, *Ocherk zakonodatel'stva Tsarstva Pol'skogo (1807-1881 g.)* (*"An Outline of the Legislation of the Polish Kingdom"*) (St. Peterburg: Senatskaia Tipografiia, 1902), p. 4. The author was a judge in Warsaw and St. Petersburg and the Associate Attorney-General of the Senate. The book is an outline of the legal order in force from a historical perspective.

[14]Zygmunt Nagórski, "Codification of Civil Law in Poland (1918-1939)," in *Studies in Polish and Comparative Law: A Symposium,* issued by the Polish Lawyers' Association in the United Kingdom (London: Stevens and Sons, 1945), pp. 44-69.

[15]Stefan Glaser, "Some Remarks on the Polish Criminal Code," in *Studies,* p. 10.

In the Prussian (and later German) parts of Poland, private law was finally codified in the German Civil Code, *Deutsches Bürgerliches Gesetzbuch,* effective as of January 1, 1900, and enacted together with the Introductory Law to the German Civil Code. In addition, the German Commercial Code, *Deutsches Handelsgesetzbuch,* was extended to those territories.[16]

All acts supplementing the basic German codifications were applied in German Poland. Special legislation discriminating between the Poles and the Germans was enacted for special reasons.[17] The German Criminal Code of 1871 was in force, together with the German criminal procedure, in penal matters.[18]

In the Russian part of Poland, a distinction should be made between Central Poland, restricted to the lands belonging to the Duchy of Warsaw and the Congress Kingdom, and the eastern part of the Polish-Lithuanian Commonwealth. The evolution of the legal systems was somewhat different in each of those territories.

After the November uprising of 1830-31, the Constitution of the Congress Kingdom was suspended and its autonomy was significantly curtailed. The Organic Statute promulgated by Tsar Nicholas I became the fundamental law for that part of the country. It abolished parliamentary institutions, imposed restrictions on individual freedom, and attempted to curtail national aspirations.

Russia sought a nearly complete merging of the Polish central territories with the Empire. Polish armed forces were abolished as separate units and were incorporated within the Russian army. In 1841 departments for handling matters of the Polish Kingdom were created as Departments IX and X of the Governing Senate in St. Petersburg and were made the supreme administrative organs for the Polish provinces. Soon the country was divided into five *guberniias*: Warsaw, Lublin, Radom, Płock, and Augustów, according to the territorial division of Russia.[19] The separate coronation of the tsar as king of Poland was abolished.

In the civil law, the first changes affected marriage and family law. The new law of 1836 replaced the Polish law of 1825.[20]

[16]Nagórski, *op. cit.,* p. 44.

[17]For details, see pp. 000-00.

[18]Glaser, *op. cit.,* p. 10.

[19]Askenazy, *op. cit.,* pp. 48-50; Reinke, *op. cit.,* pp. 70-72.

[20]Nagórski, *op. cit.,* p. 45. Also see Kazimierz Alexandrowicz, "Marriage Law in Poland: A Problem of Comparative Law," in *Studies,* pp. 156-67. It is a brief but thorough analysis of the changes in this field from 1825 to 1918.

The eastern provinces of the Polish-Lithuanian Commonwealth were subject to all Russian laws, institutions, and customs regarding the autocracy of the tsar and the administration of the country immediately after the partitions. In the matter of private law, the Third Lithuanian Statute was left in force until the codification of Nicholas I was accomplished. Then, Part I, Volume X of the *Svod Zakonov Rossiiskii Imperii* ("The Code of the Russian Empire") became law in this province unified with other provinces of the Russian Empire.

In penal matters, the Polish Code of 1818 was replaced by the Code of the Capital and Correctional Punishments, promulgated by Nicholas I in 1847. This was almost a literal translation of the Russian Criminal Code of 1845.

The criminal laws in Russia were in a state of constant flux. A new codification was promulgated in 1903.[21] The Russian Criminal Code was in force in all the provinces of Poland under the Russian rule at the dawn of Poland's independence.

The Legal Systems of Poland and the Occupying Powers

The imposed legal orders of Austria, Prussia, and Russia substantially differed from the laws of the former Polish-Lithuanian Commonwealth. These differences appeared, of course, most clearly in the sphere of public law and were reflected in the criminal law. They were deeply rooted in the institutions, scope, and interpretation of the private law as well.

Before the downfall of the state, Poland had the written Constitution of May 3, 1791. It was the second written constitution, conceived as fundamental law, in the modern world, after that of the United States in 1787. It provided for a constitutional monarchy in which the law was unquestionably superior to the king. This concept had been growing since 1573, as reflected in the Articles of Henry (*Articuli Henriciani*) and *Pacta Conventa*,[22] and the ever-stronger position of the *sejm* and *sejmiki* (general and local legislative organs). Historically, the king's position in Poland was weak. The executive competencies of the king were fully

[21]Glaser, *op. cit.*, p. 10.

[22]An explanation of the limitations on the power of the king can be found in Oskar Halecki, *Borderlands of Western Civilization: A History of East Central Europe* (New York: The Ronald Press Company, 1952), pp. 225-9 and *passim;* and in Francis Dvornik, *The Slavs in Eastern History and Civilization* (New Brunswick, N. J.: Rutgers University Press, 1962), p. 338 and *passim*. On superiority of the law, see also Kazimierz Grzybowski, "From Contract to Status: Some Aspects of the Reception of Soviet Law in Eastern Europe," *The Jurist*, XI (1953), pp. 64-5.

reorganized and re-established in the Constitution of May 3, 1791. The legislative competencies of the king were expressed in his two votes in the Senate. The principle that the authority of the government is founded on the will of the people was fully incorporated into the Constitution of May 3, 1791.[23]

The acts of the king as the chief of the executive branch of the government were to be countersigned by a minister who was responsible to Parliament.

Such institutions and the political freedom which they reflected were incompatible with the autocratic and militaristic governments of the absolute monarchies in Austria, Prussia (or the German Empire), and Russia. No constitution was known in Austria until 1848, and after the revolutionary upheaval of that year, not until 1861-7. Prussia did not accept constitutional guarantees and institutions until 1850, and did not have a representative government until the Weimar Republic. In the Russian autocracy any idea of a constitution was contrary to the foundations of Russian tsardom. Even the October Manifesto of Tsar Nicholas II (1905) and the Fundamental Law of April, 1906, did not provide Russia with representative constitutional institutions comparable in terms of political freedom to those established by the Polish Constitution of 1791. Parliamentary control over the executive was not developed in the Prussian (or German) constitutions, nor in the Russian Fundamental Law until the revolution of 1917.

Therefore, the imposed laws of Austria, Prussia (or Germany), and Russia extended absolute and autocratic regimes over the Polish provinces, a situation which had not been known previously in Poland. On the contrary, the slightest threat of absolutism had evoked such an opposition in Poland that even reforms had not been adopted, or were short-lived because of fear that they might infringe on the "golden freedom" of the citizens.

Guarantees against arbitrary imprisonment and full recognition of private ownership existed in Poland as the foundations of freedom from the beginning of the fifteenth century[24] down to the end of the

---

[23]Wacław Komarnicki, "The Spirit of Polish Constitutional Law and Its Recent Development," in *Studies*, pp. 1-6. About the representation of the cities in the Polish parliament, see Jerzy Reder, "Posłowie miasta Lublina na sejmy dawnej Rzeczypospolitej," *Czasopismo Prawno-Historyczne*, VI, No. 2 (1954), 253-86.

[24]The privileges were the *Neminem captivabimus* and *Nec bona recipiantur* of 1422-35. On the historical meaning of those privileges see Stanisław Kutrzeba, "Przywilej jedlneński z r. 1430," in *Ku czci Bolesława Ulanowskiego* (Cracow, 1911), pp. 271-301; and Antoni Prochaska, "Przywilej czerwiński z 1422," in *Przegląd Historyczny*, IV (1907), 283-96.

Commonwealth. The privilege against arbitrary imprisonment was incorporated into the Constitution of May 3, 1791, and extended to burghers. It also was granted to Jews in the entire territory of Poland in 1792. Such guarantees were not known in Russia until the end of the tsardom. They did appear with significantly reduced scope, in Austria and Prussia, but not earlier than the middle of the century.[25]

The people of Poland opposed legal restrictions on the freedom of speech and press and also opposed the prohibition of travel abroad. All such restrictions were traditional in Russia, however, until the revolution of 1917. (The extent and intensity of such limitations changed slightly during some periods of her history.) Censorship and restrictions on freedom of speech were also practiced in Austria and Prussia. In those countries, however, guarantees of these freedoms were assured in the nineteenth and twentieth centuries. After 1867 some civil liberties were granted to the population of the Austro-Hungarian Empire by enactments providing for the use of national languages in administration, courts, and schools, and for cultural autonomy. The early achievements of the Polish nation in those matters were remarkable.

Torture has never been legally acceptable in Poland.[26] It was, however, used in exceptional cases from the fifteenth to the eighteenth century.[27] In contrast, the *Constitutio Criminalis* of Maria Theresa, the Austrian empress, as well as the Prussian criminal laws, condoned its use in the criminal process until the middle of the nineteenth century. The criminal laws of Russia included punishment by torture which varied according to the gravity of the offense. Chaining of the condemned to the wheelbarrow

[25]This is an issue related to the broader human problem that what is just is often weak, and what is strong is often unjust and in many respects inferior. Very often individual freedom and privilege jeopardize the social strength and cohesiveness of the society. On this point, the objectivity of researchers, including historians, faces the most challenging test, and not always with success. The interpretation of Polish historical events in connection with this problem is often biased.

[26]Karol Koranyi, "O postępowych tradycjach w polskim piśmiennictwie karnym XVI i XVII wieku," ("About the Progressive Tradition in the Polish Penal Writings of the 16th and 17th Centuries"), *Państwo i Prawo* (State and Law), VII, No. 4 (1952), 550-1.

[27]Koranyi noticed that Groicki opposed using torture before its known adversaries, Adam Tanner (1572-1632) and Paul Leymann (1575-1635), formulated their stand. Later Daniel Wisner published in Poland a treatise against the tortures: *Tractatus Brevis De Extra Magis Lamii, Veneficis Aliisque Malefactoribus a Consociis suis in quaestionibus seu torturis nominatis inculpatisque* (Posnaniae: In Officina Alberti Reguli. Excudebat Paulus Böttcher, 1639). Also a Polish version of this book appeared in Poznań in 1639.

for life in the mines of Siberia was a punishment typical of the penitentiary system in tsarist Russia.[28]

Oppressive and Discriminatory Laws

Oppressive and discriminatory laws reflected the power which militaristic and autocratic states imposed on the divided country. Examples cited below typify that movement toward oppression and discrimination which is so very important in European history, yet which so often goes unnoticed.

The oppressive and discriminatory laws of the occupants were intended to limit the rights of the Polish population with respect to land, property, possessions, religion, and national language and aspirations.

Landed property was totally confiscated from those who had participated in the national uprisings. The occupants distributed it to the generals and officials. Russia made extensive use of such procedures after the uprisings of 1830-1 and 1863.

The legal basis for such confiscations was provided by the *ukaz* (edict) of 1835 on confiscation. Administrative and judicial methods were used to establish the system of confiscations. After the promulgation of this law, 2,339 estates were confiscated.[29] In 1861, governmental instructions were directed toward the intensification of this process.[30] The purpose of such action was to weaken Polish independent element, to provide punishment as a deterrent against revolt, to accumulate land as a reward for faithful government agents, and to create a loyal element in the population by distributing to them larger confiscated estates on the basis of indivisible entails. By the end of the 1860's, 350 entails had been created from the confiscated lands of Polish gentry and placed in the hands of the Russians. Thus, the most enlightened Polish element was eliminated from the area,

---

[28]On the broader aspects of the administration of justice in Russia, see Samuel Kucherov, "Administration of Justice Under Nicholas I of Russia," *American Slavic and East European Review,* VII, No. 2, 125-38, and "The Jury as Part of Russian Judicial Reform of 1864," *Ibid.,* IX, No. 2, 77-90. Concerning the punishments developed and applied in Polish Kingdom, see Monika Senkowska, *Kara więzienia w Królestwie Polskim w pierwszej połowie XIX wieku* ("Prison Penalization in the Kingdom of Poland in the First Half of the 19th Century") (Vol. XI, series II of *Studia nad Historią Państwa i Prawa,* Wrocław: Zakład Narodowy im. Ossolińskich, 1961), pp. 9-17. See also George Kennan, *Siberia and the Exile System* (New York: Century, 1891).

[29]Reinke, *op. cit.,* p. 79.

[30]*Ibid.,* pp. 79-80.

and its place was taken by the Russian newcomers. As a result, the Polish element was weakened.[31] This process became more intense after 1863. At that period, some confiscated lands were distributed among the local peasants: mostly White Russians and Ukrainians who, therefore, were allotted larger plots of land in the reform of 1861-83 than the peasants in the rest of Russia.[32]

The struggle for land became particularly acute in the Prussian part of Poland. There, Chancellor Bismarck held the belief that national minorities should be fully absorbed or eliminated by the ruling nation. There was no peace between the ruling nation and minorities which had owned lands for 900 or more years. Bismarck was convinced that Poles of the territories incorporated into Prussia had remained attached to the thought of their national independence. On February 7, 1872, he wrote to Count Friedrich zu Eulenburg, Minister of the Interior, "I have the feeling that in our Polish provinces the ground under us, even if it still does not visibly quake today, has been so undermined that it can break up soon as Polish-Catholic-Austrian politics can develop."[33] Bismarck urged zu Eulenburg, in words which did not leave much doubt as to his intention, to carry out an interior war against Poles who had not submitted entirely to Prussian rule. This program, put forth by a Chancellor who spoke of "iron and blood," was implemented by several laws favoring the German purchase of Polish lands.

Through such legislation the Polish nobility were deprived of credit to improve their estates or to save them from bankruptcy. The Polish Land Credit Society was limited in its action in 1849 and dissolved in 1877. In 1872 Bismarck wrote to zu Eulenburg: "My proposal goes toward a principal removal of all Poles who have no rights of citizenship, with exceptions which the government will permit in its grace."[34] On March 26, 1885, a law was issued under which the inhabitants of Prussia who

[31]*Ibid.*, p. 80.

[32]Michael T. Florinsky, *Russia; A History and Interpretation* (New York: The Macmillan Company, 1967), II, 916-7.

[33]"Ich habe das Gefühl, dass auf dem Gebiete unserer polnischen Provinzen der Boden unter uns, wenn er heute noch nicht auffällig wankt, doch so unterhöhlt wird, dass er einbrechen kann, sobald sich auswärts eine polnisch-katholisch-österreichische Politik entwickeln kann." Heinrich von Polschinger, *Fürst Bismarck und der Bundesrat* (Stuttgart and Leipzig: Deutsche Verlags-Anstalt, 1898), III, 199.

[34]*Ibid.*, III, 199. Bismarck's attitude toward the Poles resulted from his convictions of the importance of the Polish question. "The Prince considered the Polish question as the most important after the social-democratic problems," writes Hermann Hofmann, *Fürst Bismarck, 1890-1898* (Stuttgart and Berlin: J. G.

remained stubbornly Polish would be exiled. About 30,000 people were ejected by force from their lands.

In 1886, the German emperor announced a further struggle against the *Polentum* (Polish element). A Colonization Commission was created as a governmental agency for this program. The social support of German nationalists was mobilized through the Society of Eastern Marches, *Der Ostmarkverein.* Three founders of this society won particular fame: Hansemann, Kennemann, and Tiedemann, who provided the name *Hakata* for the organization.

The organization was supported with appropriations voted by the Reichstag from the taxes which, of course, were collected from the Poles as well. As early as 1887, 100 million Reichsmarks were appropriated for this purpose. By 1908, half a billion marks had been spent on that program. Then, in 1913 alone, 995 million Reichsmarks were appropriated. To make impossible the transfer of lands to Polish peasants, the peasants were prohibited from building homesteads.

The efficiency of this oppressive legislation in the Prussian (and later German) part of Poland was limited by economic counteraction of the Poles, as well as by economic, social, and cultural factors which drove the Germans from the East toward the West. A German scholar, Dr. Wilhelm Volz, professor of Leipzig University, noticed that 1,100,792 Germans fled from the East to the West in 1840-1937, despite the support given

Cotta'sche Buchhandlung Nachfolger, 1922), I, 145. Still in 1894 Bismarck spoke: "For centuries we have existed without Alsace-Lorraine, but no one yet has dared to think of what our existence would be if today a new kingdom of Poland were founded." (Louis L. Snyder, *The Blood and Iron Chancellor; a Documentary Biography of Otto von Bismarck* [Princeton, N. J.: D. Van Nostrand Company, Inc., 1967], p. 374.) See also *Bismarck the Man and the Statesman, Being the Reflections and Reminiscences of Otto Prince von Bismarck* (Leipzig: Bernhard Tauchnitz, 1899), III, 57-60. In his *Reflections and Reminiscences,* T. S. Hamerow (New York and Evanston: Harper and Row, 1968), pp. 214-5, we read: "...statistical data proved beyond doubt the rapid progress of the Polish nationality at the expense of the Germans in Posen and West Prussia, and in Upper Silesia the so far sturdy Prussian element of the "Wasserpolacken" became Polonized; Schaffranek was elected there to the Diet, and it was he who, speaking in parliament, confronted us in the Polish language with the proverb of the impossibility of the fraternization of Germans and Poles.... Upon complaints being made to the Prince-Bishop, Schaffranek was forbidden on his re-election to "sit" on the Left; as a consequence of this order, the powerfully built priest stood as upright as a sentinel before the benches of the Left for five or six hours...and was thus spared the trouble of rising when he wished to make one of his anti-German speeches."

them by the government.[35] It does not change the fact that the legislation of that period is a dramatic example of German oppression.

The struggle against the national language was used by the occupants in the process of Germanization and Russification of the people of the former Polish territory. The legislators provided the formal basis for such a program involving the army, the schools, and the Church.

In the Eastern Polish provinces incorporated into Russia, the official language was Russian. In the Congress Kingdom, Polish remained the official language. French could be used in the Administrative Council. Then, after 1832, Russian translations were supplied with the Polish texts. In 1851, Russian became the official language in the postal service. Following 1875, Russian became the official language; Polish was eliminated from offices and schools. Its use was prohibited even in private life. Polish books and publications were accessible to the youth often only in secrecy.[36]

Oppressive laws regarding the language were also intensively developed in Prussia. The elimination of Polish from the schools constituted the last step in the struggle against the Polish language. Kindergarten could be open only to children who spoke German and did not use Polish. In the public schools German was the language of instruction. In private schools, Polish could be used until the end of the nineteenth century. In the public

[35]Wilhelm Volz, *Die ostdeutsche Wirtschaft; eine wirtschaftsgeographische Untersuchung über die natürlichen Grundlagen des deutschen Ostens und seine Stellung in der gesamtdeutschen Wirtschaft* (Fascicule 1 of *Veröffentlichungen des Geographischen Seminars der Universität Leipzig*) (Berlin: Verlag von Julius Beltz, 1930), pp. 34-43. The findings in this book were based on an earlier study of the shortcomings of the German colonization of her eastern territories. This is: *Der ostdeutsche Volksboden; Aufsätze zu den Fragen des Ostens,* Wilhelm Volz (2d ed., Breslau: Verlag Ferdinand Hirt, 1926). Particularily the chapters, "Die historische Entwicklung der Ostdeutschen Agrarverfassung und ihre Beziehungen zum Nationalitätenprobleme der Gegenwart," by Gustav Aubin, pp. 340-74, and "Innere Kolonisation; Grundsätzliches und Praktisches," by Graf Baudissin, pp. 375-88, reflect the dimensions of the failure of German colonization. The significance of their desire to colonize is expressed in the last sentence of the last article: "Möge solche deutsche Siedlungsarbeit in diesen Schicksaljahren deutschen Aufstieg vorbereiten! " ("May such a German colonization work prepare in these fateful years the German assent! "), p. 387.

[36]A shocking example of the Russian approach to national languages was provided by an order issued in 1887 that the Lithuanian language should be written in the Cyrillic alphabet. For comments on laws dealing with the use of national languages in the Russian Empire of the 19th century see Georg Morris Brandes, *Polen* (Paris and Leipzig, 1898), pp. 64-6 and *passim.*

132

grade schools and in the lower classes of high schools, Polish could be used at that time only for teaching religion. Then the private schools using the Polish language were closed, and German was imposed as the language of instruction in all classes on religion. The children opposed this order. A teacher's flogging of fourteen children in Września in 1901 for refusing to answer in German became a symbol of that oppressive order. In 1906, a strike involving 50,000 children broke out against such measures in the schools of the German part of Poland.

Oppressive and discriminatory laws were also enacted in the field of religion. The German *Kulturkampf* affected first of all the Catholic church in the Polish provinces. The arrest of Archbishop (then Cardinal) Mieczysław Ledóchowski was an episode in the war against the Church in Germany, brought to an end in 1881. The persecution of the Church in the Polish territories did not end until 1918.

The Russian position toward the Church was shaped by three major considerations: the Church in Russia served the tsars; in Poland the Catholic religion was the religion of the majority, so that it was difficult to distinguish religious objectives from national ones; and the Greek Catholics had constituted a threat to the orthodoxy of the Russian Church and the unity of the Russian nation since the Union of Brest of 1595-6. Since then the Ukrainian Uniates had revealed a new and distinct endeavor toward their own independence.

In the first period after the November uprising of 1830-1, St. Petersburg signed a concordat with the Holy See in 1847 and thereafter maintained the relationship between the State and Church more or less within the framework of its provisions. Before and after the January uprising of 1863, however, the government increased its control over the Catholic monasteries and then over the secular clergy as well. In 1866 Tsar Alexander II declared the Concordat of 1847 as no longer in force. The *ukaz* (edict) of 1867 made illegal any direct contact between the Catholic clergy and the Holy See. Such contacts were made possible only through the Roman Catholic Collegium in St. Petersburg. All the bulls, breves, and letters of the popes were to be presented by the representative of the Collegium to the Ministry of the Interior for approval before their circulation. Before assenting, the Ministry was to take into consideration any infractions of Russian laws. In addition the government established strict control over the economic basis of the Church.[37] A period of constant harassment and persecution continued until 1905 when it was eased.

Major attacks were directed against the Greek Catholics. Various oppressive laws were enacted in order to obtain forced conversions to

[37]Reinke, *op. cit.,* pp. 140-3.

Orthodoxy. In 1875 a union of the Greek Catholic eparchy of Chełm with the Orthodox Church was imposed over the clergy and faithful. This act was considered the end of the process which had been started by the Union of Brest.[38] The implementation of this legal provision was left to the clergy of the Orthodox Church, which was completely at one with the objectives of the Russian autocracy.

The situation of the Protestant churches in the Polish provinces was the same as their situation in the Russian Empire in 1849. Protestantism was regarded as "a relatively minor evil" by the Slavophiles of the middle of the nineteenth century.[39] Administrative matters over those churches belonged after 1832 to an Evangelical-Lutheran General Consistory in St. Petersburg. Protestant religions were considered foreign and at best were only tolerated. Often, however, Protestants were restricted and persecuted. Persecutions grew particularly during the reigns of Alexander III and Nicholas II before 1905, when religious toleration was established.[40]

The Jews lost some of the privileges they had acquired in Poland during the period of the Constitution of May 3, 1791. Prussian legislation of 1806 introduced a ghetto in Warsaw for the masses of Jews. Those with education and money were exempted from the prohibition against living in certain sections of the city. In the Duchy of Warsaw, the political rights of Jews were at first suspended and then limited. Their civil rights were also restricted to some extent.[41]

At the time of partition, there were approximately one million Jews in the provinces united with the Russian Empire. Following Catherine's *ukaz* of December 4, 1762, the Jews were not permitted to settle in Russia. The Jews of the Polish-Lithuanian provinces were kept in those provinces outside the historical Russian territories. They were subjected to legal rules limiting their rights and discriminating against them. The autonomy of the Jews, which had been traditional in Poland since 1264, was suspended in 1844. Forcible assimilation was carried out on the basis of special laws of 1804, 1823, 1827, 1835, 1844. Russification of Jews was the foundation of Russian policies toward the Jews until the end of tsardom. "In the years of general reaction that characterized the latter portion of the reign of the

[38]A brief but detailed presentation of this problem can be found in Reinke, *op. cit.,* pp. 145-57.

[39]Florinsky, *op. cit.,* II, 998, 1117, and 1257.

[40]Erik Amburger, *Geschichte des Protestantismus in Russland* (Stuttgart: Evangelisches Verlagwerk, 1961), pp. 98-105.

[41]Sobociński, *op. cit.,* pp. 88-91. Concise information on the subject is provided by Jesse D. Clarkson, *A History of Russia* (New York: Random House, 1963), pp. 251-3, 256-8, 270, 330-5, and *passim.*

'Liberator,' anti-Semitism began to grow in official circles and among the Russian masses."[42] And in 1881, "violent pogroms took place in Yelizavetgrad in New Russia, at Kiev, and in a number of other towns and villages; Odessa suffered again. The pogrom of Warsaw was the most conspicuous, for Catholic Poland had been free from such excesses of barbarism."[43] The tsarist police and administration, and the clergy of the Orthodox Church who supported the nationalistic "Union of the Russian People" and its "Black Hundreds" instigated and often directed the pogroms.

Resistance to the Law of the Occupants and Struggle for Self-Determination

The first upheaval against the invaders[44] and the imposed law developed in 1794. Aspirations toward national independence were expressed in the established national government headed by Tadeusz Kościuszko, a hero of the American War of Independence.

Two other major uprisings took place, in 1830-1 and in 1863. The upheaval of 1846-8 was supported by the populations of the Austrian and Prussian parts of Poland. During these periods, national governments were established and new legal systems were originated by the national authorities of those uprisings.

Three aspects of these periods should be emphasized: the protests against the imposed rule of the occupants, the connection of the Polish question with the progressive movements of Europe, and the attempts at social reform.

None of the occupying powers was able or willing to devise a program to assure peace, progress, or respect for the basic rights and freedoms of its captive Polish population. Not a single plan for loyal cooperation with the partitioning states, formulated on the assumption that the Polish nation could develop its individual life within broader state organization, found sufficient support from those states and their rulers. Thus failed the

[42]Clarkson, *op. cit.,* p. 331.

[43]*Ibid.,* p. 332.

[44]A characteristic expression of the opposition toward the occupant was visible in Gdańsk (Danzig). After the second partition, the city councilors voted a period of mourning and wore black dresses. See Władysław Pniewski, "Przywiązanie do Polski i polskości w gdańskiej literaturze niemieckiej XIX wieku," in *Studia z dziejów kultury polskiej; książka zbiorowa.* Redaktorzy: Henryk Barycz i Jan Hulewicz ("Studies From History of Polish Culture; a Collective Work") (Warsaw: Gebethner i Wolff, 1949), pp. 479-87.

program of Aleksander Wielopolski, Włodzimierz Spasowicz, and Erazm Piltz in the Russian part of Poland. Thus failed similar attempts by Gołuchowski, Dunajewski, and Badeni in Austrian Poland, and projects advanced by Prince Radziwiłł and Mielżyński in the German part of Poland. The conclusion drawn by the Polish nation from the experience it had under the rule of the occupants was that a fight for independence should be waged in every way. The leaders of the national struggle related the Polish question to the progressive movements of Europe: the Carbonari and Constitutionalists, democratic programs, and the fight against the autocrats and absolute monarchs.[45] The programs of the Polish national governments organized during the uprisings included the full emancipation of the peasants, allotment of land, and restoration of full political rights and social justice. Such was the program proposed by the Manifesto of Kościuszko issued on May 7, 1794, at Połaniec. The decrees of the temporary national government of January 22, 1863 granted land to the peasants and to the landless.[46]

The opposition to the occupants and the struggle for independence were purposely misinterpreted by the rulers of the partitioning powers. Nicholas I said: "These Poles are the people without faith, law and religion; they sacrifice all to one phantom of nationality.[47] And Metternich added:

> Polanism is nothing but a formula, a word behind which hides Revolution in its most brutal form; it is a *Revolution* itself, and not a portion of it; it is this that is proved by the noted manifestations of the Polish emigration. Polonism does not declare war on the three powers which are presently in possession of Polish territory; it declares war on all existant institutions, it preaches the reversal of all of the foundations on which society is based; to combat polonism it is not the task of the three powers only; it is an obligation which imposes itself on all powers.[48]

[45]The Polish Democratic Society, founded in France, as well as some socialist organizations, serve as examples.

[46]"Materiały do historii powstania 1863-1864;" some excerpts are available in English in "Basic Sources Related to the History of Eastern and Central Europe; a Selection," ed. Waclaw Soroka, mimeographed (Stevens Point, 1966), pp. 64-6.

[47]Translated from Wilhelm Feldman, *Dzieje polskiej myśli politycznej, 1864-1914* ("History of Polish Political Thought, 1864-1914") (Warsaw: Instytut Badania Najnowszej Historii Polski: 1950), p. 56. "Ces Polonais sont des gens sans foi, sans loi, sans religion; ils sacrifient tout à un fantôme de nationalité."

[48]"Le *polonism* n'est qu'une formule, un mot derrière lequel se cache la Révolution sous sa forme la plus brutale; il est la *Révolution* elle-même, et non pas une fraction de celle-ci; c'est ce que prouvent les manifestations connues de

In defiance of the European reactionaries, twentieth-century society embraced self-determination and international cooperation as the surest and shortest way to freedom, justice, peace, and progress. Aiming at such goals, the Polish nation remained in conflict with the imposed legal orders of Austria, Prussia-Germany, and Russia until it regained its independence, supported by the thirteenth of the Fourteen Points of President Woodrow Wilson and the stand of the progressive world favoring the self-determination of nations.

l'émigration polonaise. Le polonism ne déclare pas la guerre aux trois puissances qui sont en possession du ci-devant territoire polonais; il la déclare à toutes les institutions existantes, il prêche le renversement de toutes les bases sur lesquelles repose la société; le combattre n'est donc pas la tâche de trois puissances seulement, c'est un devoir qui s'impose à toutes." *Memoires, documents et ècrits divers laissés par le prince de Metternich,* publiés par son fils le prince Richard de Metternich (Paris: E. Plon et c-ie, 1883), VII, 211. Concerning broader aspects of repressive action of Vienna government and its attacks against the Polish emigration see *Ibid.,* pp. 169, 172-3, 194, and *passim.*

BRONISŁAW HEŁCZYŃSKI

The Law in the Reborn State

Diversity of Legal Systems Inherited from the

Period of Partition and the Necessity of Unifications

When Poland was reborn as a state in 1918, four different and distinct legal systems were in existence in her constituent territories.

Central Poland still used some codes and laws introduced during the Napoleonic wars when the so-called Duchy of Warsaw was established, and also some laws which had been put into force when − according to the stipulations of the Congress of Vienna in 1815 − the so-called Congress Kingdom was formed. After crushing the 1863 insurrection, the Russians gradually introduced their own legislation, but some of the former laws and regulations still remained in force.

In the Northeastern territories, Russian legislation was adopted and only a few traces of the former Lithuanian-Polish law of the pre-partition period were left. In Western Poland, Prussian or German law replaced completely the former Polish law. In Southern Poland, which was under Austrian rule, Austrian legislation formed the basis of the law, although some laws and regulations derived from the autonomous authorities of the province of Galicia, especially after 1867, had the force of law.

To be exact, one should mention that there was even a fifth legal system still in force in a small part of the southern territory. Parts of the districts of Spisz and Orawa, which belonged, before the First World War, to Hungary, were, on the basis of the treaties of Trianon and St. Germain, incorporated into the Polish Republic because their populations were ethnographically and linguistically Polish. In these small areas Hungarian law was in force at that time.

It is obvious that such a situation could not continue and that the new − or rather reborn − state could not tolerate the prolonged existence of such a diversity of legal systems in its territory. It hampered the economic unification of the Republic and also presented some moral problems: in some parts of Poland certain acts were prohibited by law as criminal offenses, whereas in other parts the same acts were legal. This situation may not seem shocking to Americans, who are accustomed to differences in the law in separate states, but the United States is a federation, whereas Poland was politically a unitary state in which there was no reason to maintain laws and regulations inherited from the partitioning powers, especially in view of the fact that many of them were contrary to traditional Polish legal concepts and did not serve the needs of the Polish population.

First of all, there was the problem of determining the basis of the uniform legal system to be established under the constitution of the Republic.[1] Only one question pertaining to the constitution should be mentioned here, and that is the question of what organ was vested by the constitution with legislative power. In principle, the law-making power rested, as in all democratic states, with the parliament. Quite soon, however, it became clear that the parliamentary procedure was far too slow to permit a speedy replacement of the laws inherited by the new state from the partitioning powers by a unified Polish law. This was one of the main reasons why the constitution was revised in 1926, allowing parliament to delegate its legislative power to the administration in the form of decrees of the President of the Republic.[2] Furthermore, the revised constitution itself vested the administration with legislative power from the time when the parliament was dissolved until new elections were held. These principles were maintained by the new constitution of 1935.[3]

Looking today from a historical point of view at the whole body of Polish law in the interwar period, we can easily see that the most numerous and important laws were promulgated in the form of such decrees by the President of the Republic. This is particularly true of those laws which replaced the laws issued by the partitioning powers.

In the vast body of these laws one can clearly distinguish two kinds of enactments. There were, on the one hand, the large codifications for application mainly by the courts, such as the Civil, Commercial and Criminal Codes and the Codes of Civil and Criminal Procedure. They

[1] 1921/267. Nearly all quotations refer to the Polish Journal of Laws (*Dziennik Ustaw R.P.*), the first number indicating the year in which the enactment in question was promulgated, and the second or subsequent figures to the numbers of entries under which it was published. In most cases, citations refer to the original text only, even if some subsequent changes were adopted and promulgated.

[2] 1926/442.

[3] 1935/227.

comprised a vast and compact set of rules which were intended to stay in force for a long period and were not to undergo frequent changes. These codes were based on long experience and the legal problems that they were to solve had been dealt with in numerous papers and judicial decisions.

On the other hand, there were many rules and regulations intended to satisfy some of the more or less transitory needs or regulate some rather specific problems arising not in the whole community but among specific classes or groups of citizens. These laws and regulations related mostly to administrative law and were to be applied in the first instance not by the courts but by the various administrative authorities and organs. It is true that while in the area of administrative law there were also some rather comprehensive enactments (for instance, in the field of fiscal law), their character differed from that of the so-called judicial law. In general, they were not as intricate and did not arouse as great an interest on the part of theoreticians and scholars as other fields of law.

In view of this difference between the judicial and administrative law, it was decided to confer the task of unifying and codifying the former not to any ministerial departments but to a special Codification Commission. This commission, established by a law of 1919,[4] was composed of very distinguished scholars and practitioners. It was subdivided into various committees and subcommittees, each of them entrusted with the task of preparing drafts of different codes and laws.

Judicial Law

Even before the Codification Commission seriously started its work, one part of the civil law, in a branch of the business associations law, had been unified. As early as 1920, when Poland was still at war with her Eastern neighbor, Soviet Russia, a unified law on cooperative societies had been promulgated.[5] Its draft was prepared by a special commission under the chairmanship of one of the most eminent Polish jurists, Professor Wróblewski. (The author of this chapter was the commission's secretary.) The commission advanced voluminous legislative reasons for the draft. This achievement should be mentioned not only because it was the first Polish codification in the area of civil law but also because the method adopted by the special commission served as a model for drafts of many subsequent laws, especially those prepared by the Codification Commission. This method consisted in comparing the laws then in force in various areas of the Polish territory and then attempting to maintain the principles

[4] 1919/315.

[5] 1920/733.

which were common to all or most of them. The laws of other countries were also taken into consideration. Some of the provisions of the new law were an original product of the commission itself, based on experience with and views of the Polish cooperative movement. Nearly all other laws in the area of the judicial law were prepared by the Codification Commission.

CIVIL LAW

The essential rules of civil law of the states to which parts of Polish territory belonged during the partition period were embodied in the civil codes of these states. The Codification Commission came to the conclusion that it would be rather difficult to replace these civil codes at once by a complete new Polish civil code. It adopted, therefore, a piecemeal method of preparing drafts for separate fields of civil law in order to replace parts of the civil codes, one after another.

The Commission began with the part of the Civil Code most important to the economic life of the country – the law of obligations: contracts and torts. This Code of Obligations was promulgated as a decree of the President of the Republic in 1933[6] and came into force on the first of July, 1934. It cannot be called in any way a revolutionary enactment. The differences between the German, Austrian, and French Civil Codes in this field are not particularly important – all three of these great codes derived their essence from a common heritage of Roman law. The main difference between them consisted in the method of approach. The French and Austrian legislators were trying to lay down some general principles while leaving the field open to the courts to develop more precise rules in the course of judicial practice, and they did not worry about leaving gaps in the vast fabric of the law. The method of the German legislature consisted in trying to foresee all possible situations and gave to the judges explicit guidance as to how to solve them. The Codification Commission clearly followed the French-Austrian method and was also guided to some extent by the rules formulated in the Swiss Code of Obligations.

The other parts of the Civil Code containing the general principles, the real estate law and the law on movables (chattels), the family law and the inheritance law were prepared by the Codification Commission and were ready to be promulgated as laws when the Second World War broke out. The Communist regime established in 1945 promulgated most of these drafts, with very small changes, as unified codes, but came very soon to the conclusion that they did not fit into the pattern of a Communist state

[6]1933/598.

142

and replaced them, one by one, with other codes modeled more or less on the corresponding enactments in force in the U.S.S.R.

Coming back to the 1918-39 legislation on civil law, we must mention two important pieces of work prepared by the Codification Commission and promulgated as laws in 1926: one covering the law on copyrights,[7] and the other covering international private law.

The law on copyrights is, of course, modeled on similar laws passed in other civilized countries and by the International Convention on Copyrights, but it has one pioneering feature in this area. Whereas the municipal laws of other countries enumerate as the subjects of copyright specific kinds of creative activities (works of literature, science, plastic arts, music, etc.), the Polish law tries to give a general definition covering all these kinds of activities and works. It defines as a subject of copyright any phenomenon of spiritual activity having the character of personal creative work if it is put into a form of any kind. This definition, which was elaborated by one of the outstanding Polish legal scholars, Professor Zoll, should be recorded as an example of original Polish juridical thought.

The Polish international private law of 1926[8] (better known in Anglo-Saxon terminology as "conflicts of law") is to be noted as another creative achievement of Polish jurists. In most countries the principles of conflicts of law are either not codified at all or are codified very briefly in the introductory parts of their civil codes. The Codification Commission tried to embody the principles established by judicial decisions of civilized nations in a quite comprehensive code in order to provide guidance to the judges in making specific decisions. The only other codification comparable to this (and, by the way, even more detailed) is the so-called *Codigo Bustamante* adopted by the Latin American states as an annex to the Convention of Havana of 1928.

Two features of the Polish law are worth noting. One is that in matters of personal rights and of the law on inheritance the principle of nationality is to be applied and not that of domicile. The second is that Poland modeled its rules concerning contracts on the resolutions of the International Law Association's conference held in Florence in 1908 — the first application in practice of these resolutions.

A so-called interprovincial private law was promulgated in 1926[9] together with the international private law. It contains rules on the question of which law should be applied in cases of conflict between the various laws in force in different parts of Poland as a result of partitions.

[7]1926/286.

[8]1926/581.

[9]1926/580.

In this area, of course, the principle of domicile, and not that of nationality, had to be applied in matters of personal rights and inheritance. The interprovincial private law was to be, by its very nature, of short existence, because with every new unified Polish law it lost justification for its application.

COMMERCIAL LAW

Commercial Code

The Polish Commercial Code came into force together with the Code of Obligations on the first of July, 1934.[10] It was prepared by the Codification Commission and promulgated by a decree of the President of the Republic.

Although it follows in most of its rules the ideas laid down by the French and German law (the commercial code which was in force in Austria was in fact the General German Commercial Code of 1861), and in part by the Swiss law, it contains some important innovations introduced by the Polish Codification Commission.

It is based not on the objective but on the subjective system. This means that certain contracts, called "acts of commerce" (in French, *actes de commerce;* in German, *Handelsgeschaefte*) are not ruled by the commercial law irrespective of who enters them, but that this law applies to all activities of merchants performed in pursuit of business. This subjective system is not only in accordance with the tradition of the merchant class in the Middle Ages, but meets also the practical requirements of the modern times, and, therefore, has been adopted in recent German and Swiss enactments.

The particular achievement of the Polish legislature was its new definition of the term "merchant." All previous statutes and codes gave a rather incomplete and illogical answer by specifying a certain list of activities which they called, quite arbitrarily, acts of commerce, and by conferring upon those performing them professionally the status of "merchants." The Polish code had the merit of having drawn its final conclusions from a long historical evolution which has continually enlarged the conceptions of merchants and of acts of commerce. It defines as a merchant any person who conducts any profit-making business. It deliberately refrains from considering the question of what should be understood as a profit-making business, leaving the answer to the investigation of economists. It is, therefore, an extremely elastic definition, leaving the door open to further development.

[10]1934/502.

144

Apart from this new definition of a merchant there are also some other features of the Polish Commercial Code which were new and which it is quite impossible to enumerate in a short article. However, at least two points should be made. One of them is the increased importance of entries in the Commercial Register, which allows the public to rely on them nearly as fully on the entries in the Land Register. The second is an interesting way of protecting the interests of the minorities in the business associations law. Leaving the conduct of the affairs of a corporation and especially the election of its board in the hands of the majority of the shareholders, the Code gave the minority the right to elect its representatives to the so-called corporation control commission, which had access to all its books and could, therefore, verify whether its affairs had been conducted fairly and reasonably. In the event that any irregularity was detected, the minority had the right to sue those responsible in the courts, even if they enjoyed the support of the majority in the general meeting of the shareholders.

It is to be noted that the Commercial Code of 1934 did not embrace all the rules and regulations which should form part of it. Two other parts of the Code—one dealing with maritime law and another with private insurance law—were still being worked on by the Codification Commission when the war broke out in 1939.

Laws on Bills of Exchange and Checks

The first laws prepared by the Codification Commission were the laws of 1924 on bills of exchange and checks.[11] This was rather easy work because Poland has adhered to the rules of the Geneva international conventions on both these matters and the task of the Polish legislator consisted only in filling in some gaps left by the conventions in reserving some of their rules for decision of the signatories. Both these laws were repealed by new laws in 1936[12] which resulted from transactions of the Geneva conventions of 1930 on bills of exchange and 1931 on checks.

Law on Patents, Industrial Patterns, and Trademarks

The law on patents, industrial patterns and trademarks promulgated in 1928[13] as a decree of the President of the Republic belongs partially to

[11] 1924/926 and 927.

[12] 1936/282 and 283.

[13] 1928/384.

the commercial and partially to the administrative law. This unified law, modeled mostly on the British law on these subjects, proved an inadequate protection to the Polish economy which was, of course, interested in the exploitation of various inventions covered by foreign patents. For this reason it was inteded to be replaced by another law which covered these needs. Its draft, prepared by the Codification Commission, was nearly ready at the time of the outbreak of the Second World War but was not promulgated as law before that date.

Law Against Unfair Competition[14]

If it is true that free competition is one of the essential principles of a capitalistic society, it is also true that there must be some safeguards against unfair competition. One of the most frequent instances of such competition is to advertize the products of one manufacturer in such a way that they seem to be products of another one which enjoys a high reputation in the eyes of the public. It is the most common and important example of unfair competition. Another frequent device is known in English legal practice as slander of title or disparagement of goods. In addition to these cases, the Polish Law against unfair competition of 1926 dealt also with such other cases as the starting, by a salesman or former employee of a firm, of a competitive business based on knowledge of the trade secrets of the former firm or the so-called avalanche contract (a promise not to claim the full purchase price of an article if the buyer induces a certain number of persons to buy such articles under the same conditions). The Polish law gave to those who suffered losses through unfair competition a means to obtain injunctions against the practices of unfair competitors and substantial damages.

Law on Cartels (Anti-Trust)

In 1933 a law on cartels[15] was enacted in order to protect the public against the high prices they imposed by such devices as contracts in restraint of trade, regulation of the supply of goods, and price-fixing. All cartels were required to be registered in a special Register of Cartels kept at the Ministry of Industry and Trade. Secondly, a special Cartel Court, composed of justices of the Supreme Court and lay judges who were experts in production and commerce, was instituted. The Cartel Court

[14]1926/559.

[15]1933/270.

could dissolve existing cartels or alter cartel agreements if it felt that the effects of their activity were detrimental to the public interest.

In 1939 this law was replaced by another law.[16] One of the main differences between them was that the new law allowed any party who signed the cartel agreement to denounce it and to withdraw its signature if the cartel restrained it in its business activities in specified cases. In case of a dispute between the parties, solution rested with the Minister for Industry and Commerce, subject to an appeal to the Cartel Court. The second main difference between the new and the previous law was that the right to dissolve a cartel if its effects were detrimental to the public interest belonged not to the Cartel Court but to the Minister, against whose decisions the parties could appeal to the Cartel Court.

Law on Debentures

Just before the outbreak of the Second World War in July, 1939, a law on debentures was passed by the Polish Parliament.[17] According to this law, the right to issue debentures was restricted to corporations, either private or public, and to big unions of cooperative societies. In order to safeguard the interests of the owners of the debentures, the law prescribed that the issuing corporation had to convoke, in certain cases, general meetings of the owners for the election of representatives. The corporation had to give to these representatives access to its books and furnish them with the data necessary to determine how the corporation business was conducted. Any decision of the corporation could be impeached by these representatives if it affected the rights or interests of the owners of the debentures in a way contrary to *bonos mores*.

CRIMINAL LAW

Criminal Code

The Criminal Code of 1932[18] was another work of the Codification Commission. The replacement of the penal codes of the partitioning powers with a unified Polish Criminal Code was looked upon as an especially urgent task of the Commission, because it was very disturbing that an act might be classed as a criminal offense in one part of Poland

[16]1939/418.

[17]1939/379.

[18]1932/571.

while being permitted in another part of it. Prolonged coexistence of differing systems of criminal repression and prevention in one state seemed also intolerable. However, as the very principles of a new criminal code suitable to the times had to be thoroughly discussed, about eleven years of preparatory work and discussion were needed to produce the final draft of this code. It was promulgated in 1932 as a decree of the President of the Republic.

The Code adopted the principle of subjectivization (or individualization) of guilt as well as of punishment. The courts were given a wide discretion to decide what would be just and fair after full consideration of a given case, and were advised to take into account the individual characteristics of the accused as well as the circumstances which led him to commit the criminal act.

As to the general principles of criminal responsibility, the Code stressed the following requirements: the accused must have understood what he was doing, and he must have been able to control his actions by his will. Where one of these conditions was lacking (either that of intellect or that of will) there was no criminal responsibility. These principles were developed in detail with regard to the responsibility of minors, attempts at crime, and the abuse of the right of self-defense.

With regard to penalties, the Code did not eliminate capital punishment, although such suggestions were made. It limited, however, the kinds of cases in which capital punishment might be imposed by the court. The principal punishment was imprisonment. For minor offenses the punishment was "arrest," which meant imprisonment from one week to five years. Apart from imprisonment and arrest, or instead of arrest, the court might impose fines and was required to do so when unlawful financial gain was the motive of the criminal act. Incorrigible or professional criminals could be institutionalized even after they had served their sentences. This was meant not as repression but to prevent further crimes. The Code included, of course, procedures for reprieve of a sentence, placing of the accused on probation, release from prison or arrest in the event of good conduct, and erasure of a sentence from criminal records in certain cases.

Law on Misdemeanors

The law on misdemeanors, dealing with minor and unintentional offenses, was promulgated in 1932 together with the Criminal Code.[19] The penalties for these misdemeanors were limited to either arrest or fine. Those proven guilty of misdemeanors were to be punished in the first

[19]1932/572.

instance not by courts but by administrative authorities. If, however, the accused was not satisfied with the administrative decision, he could ask for the transfer of the case to a court. In such a case, the administrative decision was simply put aside as non-existent and the case was tried by a competent court in the first instance (not by way of appeal). In most cases, however, the accused did not object to the administrative decision (which was not reported by the press) and accepted it as final, in order to avoid publicity, costs, and loss of time.

Law on Emergency (Martial) Courts

In 1928 a law on emergency (martial) courts was promulgated;[20] it remained in force after the enactment of the Criminal Code. This law had as its object the repression of mass waves of certain crimes, especially of a political character. It gave the government the right to introduce, under certain circumstances, emergency, or martial courts. Such circumstances included, in particular, the proclamation of a state of emergency or of war. In such a case, specified crimes were to be tried not by the ordinary courts but by the emergency courts, the decisions of which were final and incapable of appeal. The law can be classified as belonging to the field of criminal procedure. However, it vitally affected the substantive criminal law as well, particularly by directing the emergency court, if it should find the accused to be guilty, to inflict on him a much more severe punishment than an ordinary court could mete out for the same crime: in many cases, capital punishment.

It should be added that this law was applied rarely, and only in some parts of the country and for short periods of time, mostly against espionage.

The Military Criminal Code

The general Criminal Code applied only to civilians. Members of the armed forces were tried in accordance with rules laid down by the Military Criminal Code of 1932.[21] Actually, the difference was not very great, as the Military Code prescribed that for all common crimes committed by the military personnel the general Criminal Code should be applied with only small changes and that special provisions of the Military Criminal Code would apply only to the so-called military crimes and offenses: desertion,

[20] 1928/315.

[21] 1932/765.

insubordination, etc. But even in such cases the general principles of the Criminal Code (e.g., rules concerning self-defense, criminal attempts, abetting, accomplices, etc.) applied to members of the armed forces.

Other Provisions Belonging to Criminal Law

The above-mentioned codes contained the most important rules of law dealing with crimes of a general character. Far more regulations, however, than could be collected in these enactments were required. In particular, the vast area of administrative law, which will be discussed later, requires thousands of specific rules, which must be enforced by the threat of punishment. These threats generally had features of criminal laws, although they were included in various administrative laws and regulations. Even in some civil and commercial law enactments (particularly in the field of corporation law), there were provisions threatening violation by fines, arrest, or even prison. It would be useless to try to summarize these provisions. It should be said, however, that in constructing them, only the general rules of the Criminal Code and of the law on misdemeanors could be applied either by the courts or by the administrative authorities.

PROCEDURAL LAW

Organization of the Courts

At first, the organization of the courts was based on statutes inherited from the partitioning powers, with one exception: the Supreme Court was organized on the basis of a decree of the Chief of State as early as the beginning of the year 1919.[22] All other courts functioned on the basis of the old laws until 1927, when a decree of the President of the Republic, unifying the structure of the common courts (i.e., courts judging all civil and criminal cases) was promulgated.[23] These courts were of four kinds: city courts, district courts, appeal courts, and the Supreme Court.

To the jurisdiction of the city courts belonged criminal cases in which the maximum penalty could be two years of imprisonment or a fine up to 2000 zł. (about $400, according to the 1939 rate of exchange), and civil cases in which the value of the matter in controversy did not exceed approximately 2000 zł. An appeal from a city court would go to a district court (a special appellate division), and from its decisions the parties could

[22] 1919/195.

[23] 1928/93.

appeal to the Supreme Court when the appellant claimed that the lower court had violated some rule of either substantive or procedural law. The Supreme Court could affirm or reverse the judgment of the lower court, but normally, instead of delivering a final decision, it would remand the case to the same or another district court with instructions binding on the lower court. Only exceptionally would it give a final judgment by way of a so-called revision.

Cases exceeding the jurisdiction of city courts were tried by district courts in the first instance, and an appeal from their judgments would go to the appeal courts (there were seven such courts in the whole country). Apart from that, the appeal courts had important organizational and administrative functions. Following the decision of appeal courts, the parties could appeal to the Supreme Court on the ground that the court of appeal had violated some substantive or procedural rule of law. The decision of the Supreme Court would usually consist in either dismissing the appeal or reversing the judgment and remanding the case to the same or another appeal court with binding instructions.

Whenever the Supreme Court laid down a legal principle, it had to be published together with the whole judgment, in a special periodical publication,[24] to serve as guidance in handling similar matters in the future. At the request of the Minister of Justice, the Supreme Court also had to give advisory opinions on legal problems.

One of the most important features of the organization of the courts in a country governed by the rule of law is the principle of the independence of the judicial power. The Polish law proclaimed this principle as one of its most important features, stating that the judges were independent from any other authority and that they should obey only the law. This meant that they could not be required to account for their judgments, nor could they be prosecuted for them. In cases of misbehavior in office, such as abuse of their authority or negligence in performance of their duties, they could be tried only by special disciplinary courts consisting of judges of higher courts, also fully independent and immune from outside pressure. Also, the judges could not be dismissed or transferred to judicial posts in other districts against their will. Finally, the principle of judicial independence had its guarantee in the manner in which judges were appointed.

In Poland, as in most states on the continent of Europe, the judges formed a special branch of the legal profession and were not recruited, as it is usual in common law countries, from the ranks of practicing lawyers. To become a judge one had to obtain a diploma at the school of law of one of the universities, to spend at least three years as a kind of apprentice

[24]*Zbiór Orzeczeń Sadu Najwyzszego* ("Collection of Decisions of the Supreme Court").

(or "applicant," as they were called), and after such a training to undergo a special examination. He could then be appointed as a judge of a city court. Further promotion depended mostly on the reputation the young judge acquired in professional circles. Appointments to the post of judge of a higher court were made on the basis of proposals or suggestions of special administrative colleges, elected by members of each court. For every vacancy the administrative college had to nominate three candidates, one of whom was appointed by the President of the Republic on the proposal of the Minister of Justice. One fifth of the judges of each court could, however, be selected by the Minister from candidates not nominated by the administrative college. The bulk of the judges were selected from the body of professional judges: some, however, were appointed from among other branches of the legal profession (attorneys-at-law, public prosecutors, professors of faculties of law at universities, or civil servants having legal education).

There were special cases in which some members of the court were selected not from the legal but from other professions. Of these cases three were most important.

First of all, there were commercial judges who took part in judging cases arising out of commercial contracts in which the defendant was a merchant. The commercial judges were selected from among businessmen proposed for this function by chambers of commerce. They sat in special commercial sections of the district courts, which were always presided over by a professional judge.

Then there were labor courts functioning either as separate courts or as sections of the city courts. The labor courts had jurisdiction over disputes between employers and their employees and were composed of one professional judge as president and two lay judges, one selected from among the employers and the other from among the employees by the court from rosters presented by competent professional organizations.

Lastly, there were jurors sitting in on the more important criminal cases. There was one curious peculiarity about trials by jury. In all three of the partitioning states, (Russia, Austria, and Prussia) the institution of the jury was introduced before the First World War as a contemporary liberal reform, but use of the jury was not extended to the Polish territories of either Russia or Prussia. The governments of these states feared that juries composed of Poles would be too lenient when trying political crimes committed by their fellow countrymen, so that only in the Austrian part of Poland were juries functioning at that time. This institution was inherited by the reborn Polish state.

It must be admitted that for similar political reasons the jury was not introduced in these territories even then. The new Polish Code of Criminal Procedure of 1928 (which will be discussed later) provided for the establishment of jury trials in the whole country, but the implementation of this provision was postponed indefinitely, and a special law of 1938[25] repealed it altogether, so that jury trials ceased to exist even in the former Austrian territory.

Codes of Procedure

The unification of the laws of court procedure was easier than the unification of substantive law and could be accomplished quite independently of it.

The Code of Civil Procedure was promulgated by decree in 1930.[26] The preparation of its draft was comparatively simple, since the codes of civil procedure then in force in Russia, Austria, and Prussia did not differ basically from each other. According to this code, the proceedings were started by way of a writ, which could be answered by the defendant with a counterwrit. The parties could exchange further written documents stating or explaining their positions, but were not compelled to do so. These documents served as preparatory materials for the main hearing, which was public and obligatory. The proceedings at the main hearing were oral and were recorded by the court clerk.

The most important difference between the codes of civil procedure in force in the partitioning states consisted in the handling of cases by the Supreme Court. In the former Russian territories, the French principle of recognizing this court as a "breaking court" (*cour de cassation*) was adopted; this meant that the court could either affirm the decision of the lower court or reverse it, but it could not decide the case on its merits by delivering a judgment differing from that of the lower court. In contrast, the Supreme Court in the former Austrian and Prussian territories could revise the decision of the lower court. According to the Polish Code of Civil Procedure the Supreme Court could either reject the appeal or reverse the decision of the lower court and remand the case to be tried again, as mentioned before. By way of exception, however, the Supreme Court could revise the judgment, but only on the motion of one of the parties and only when no rule of procedure had been violated by the lower court but its decision could not be affirmed because of the violation of some rule of substantive law as construed by the Supreme Court.

A peculiarity of Supreme Court proceedings in civil matters was the participation of the procurator. This participation was modeled on the French notion of procurators as guardians of the rule of law not only in criminal matters (as public prosecutors) but also in civil matters.

[25]1938/213.

[26]1930/651.

In 1932 the Code of Civil Procedure was supplemented by the addition of a second part dealing with the execution of court judgments in civil cases, (particularly in regard to the attachment or seizure of a debtor's property).[27]

The Code of Civil Procedure dealt only with adversary proceedings. The Codification Commission also prepared the draft of a Code of Non-Adversary Procedure, but this code was promulgated only after the Second World War.

Finally, the bankruptcy law of 1934 prepared by the Codification Commission and promulgated as a decree should be mentioned.[28] It did not differ basically from similar laws in force before the unification.

Criminal procedure was unified by the Code of Criminal Procedure prepared by the Codification Commission and promulgated by a decree of 1928.[29] Again, this law did not differ basically from the codes of criminal procedure inherited from the partitioning process. The role of the Supreme Court as a court of last instance was the same in criminal and civil cases. The Code of Military Criminal Procedure was promulgated in 1937.[30]

Administrative Law

However great the number of enactments dealing with the judicial law, and however comprehensive the problems which they cover, they cannot match the number and volume of enactments belonging to the field of administrative law. If we look through the volumes of the Polish Journal of Laws (generally two thick volumes per year) the texts of "judicial" laws appear like *"rari nantes in gurgite vasto"* (few swimmers in a vast abyss).

What are the common characteristics of these enactments? First of all, many of them were intended to meet the current needs and were thought of *ab initio* as temporary measures to be replaced again and again by new enactments adapted to changing social and economic conditions.

Secondly, there is in most cases no difficulty in tracing the models which they imitate more or less closely. The drafts of these laws and regulations were not prepared by the Codification Commission, whose members had learned their law in many countries — mostly in Austrian, German, and Russian, but also in French and Swiss universities. They were

[27]1932/934.

[28]1934/834 and 836.

[29]1928/313.

[30]1936/537.

prepared by lawyers who had served in various government departments as civil servants. Now, how did the reborn state recruit its civil servants in 1918 and the following years? In Russia, as well as in Prussia, Poles had not been reputed sufficiently loyal to the occupying powers to be allowed to pursue administrative careers. The whole body of civil servants employed in the administration of these territories had been composed of Russians or Germans brought from other parts of the Russian or Prussian state. Only in the provinces belonging to Austria was the attitude of the central government different, dating from the second half of the nineteenth century, so that the civil servants there were almost without exception Poles. It was only natural that these civil servants, having adequate experience and training, became the cadres of the new Polish administration, especially in the various ministerial departments. It was equally natural that when they were entrusted with the task of preparing drafts of new unified laws and regulations, they usually looked for models in Austrian laws and regulations, which were well known to them. On the other hand, much of Austrian legal thought had developed under the strong influence of German legal doctrines, and many of the Austrian enactments were to some extent modeled after German legislation. It would be rather difficult to find in Polish administrative law any corresponding French influence, and still more difficult to find evidence of Russian law, which was completely inadequate to the needs of the new republic. It would be, however, a great exaggeration to say that these Polish laws and regulations were merely translations of Austrian or German texts. In time there appeared quite a number of enactments which were products of original Polish juridical thought.

The third characteristic feature of Polish administrative law statutes and regulations was that most of them contained rules belonging to the sphere of substantive as well as procedural law. There were, however, some enactments dealing exclusively with procedural matters.

STRUCTURE OF ADMINISTRATIVE AUTHORITY

In order to understand Polish administrative law, it is necessary to know about the structure of its administrative hierarchy.

At the top of the public administration there were, of course, the ministries, whose number and jurisdiction varied with the time. In 1939 there were eleven ministries, to which all administrative authorities were subordinated. Of local administrative authorities there were two sets: the so-called general administrative authorities and the separate administrative authorities.

The country was divided into provinces bearing the old Polish name, *województwa*, with a provincial governor called a *wojewoda* at its head. There were, altogether, sixteen provinces, and the capital city of Warsaw formed a type of a municipal province having at its head on one hand an elected president and on the other a governmental commissioner or *wojewoda grodzki* (municipal governor), as he was called sometimes. The relationship between these two officials will be explained later. The provinces were subdivided into 264 districts, the bigger towns forming special municipal districts, of which there were 23. At the head of each district was an official bearing the old Polish name of *starosta*. In municipal districts, besides the *starostas*, there were elected town mayors or presidents. The administrative authority in the provinces and districts was vested in the *wojewoda* or *starosta*. There were in existence various councils and committees, but their functions were merely consultative. The chiefs of the general administration were responsible in the first instance to the Minister of the Interior but, as far as special matters were concerned, to all other ministers according to their competence. The structure and functioning of the general administration was settled by a law of 1919,[31] replaced later by a presidential decree of 1928.[32]

By virtue of the Constitution, the province of Silesia had a special position. It enjoyed a certain autonomy,[33] with its own provincial *sejm*, or parliament.

Besides the authorities of the general administration, there also existed separate administrative authorities as special organs of various ministries. There were, for instance, local authorities of the military, fiscal, educational, forestry, mining, railway, and postal administrations not subordinate to the general administration authorities. The chiefs of the general administration had the task of coordinating the activities of these separate authorities in their respective territories. The courts did not form a part of the public administration, and their own hierarchy was subordinate in matters of personnel and budgetary administration to the Ministry of Justice.

These administrative authorities, appointed by the government, should be distinguished from those which were elected either by the whole population or some classes of it. There were in Poland three kinds of self-government: territorial, economic, and professional.

The basic unit of territorial self-government was the commune, either rural or urban. Its supreme organ was a communal council elected by the whole adult population of the commune. The council elected in its turn a

[31] 1919/395.

[32] 1928/86.

[33] 1920/497.

board of management and a president or mayor as the chief executive. The communal authorities had, apart from their own competence, a so-called entrusted competence; i.e., they had to perform certain functions on behalf of the central government, and received for the performance of these duties a special remuneration from the state.

The communal self-government was truly autonomous. On a higher level there were also district and provincial councils and boards of management, but their budgets were rather meager. Moreover, these boards were not presided over by elected chairmen, but by the *starosta* or *wojewoda* as chairmen *ex officio*. In towns having the status of municipal districts or provinces, there were no district or provincial councils or boards of management. Their competence was included in the broader competence of town councils and boards of management, and the municipal government was headed by the town president or mayor. The powers of the municipal *starosta* or *wojewoda* were limited to matters relating to the state administration.

Toward the end of this period, the territorial self-government was based on the decree of 1932 concerning the structure of territorial self-government[34] and on the electoral law of 1938 regulating the procedure of election to communal councils and other bodies of the self-government.[35]

The so-called economic self-government comprised three sets of self-governing bodies: the chambers of agriculture, the chambers of industry and commerce, and the chambers of artisans. These chambers grouped all persons professionally active in their respective fields of economic activity. They were entitled to elect the councils and, through them, the boards of management of these chambers. The districts of the respective chambers roughly corresponded to the territories of the provinces, although they were not identical to them. The provincial chambers were organized into unions. The structure and duties of these chambers were regulated by statutes: the decree of 1928 concerned the chambers of agriculture,[36] and the decrees of 1927 the chambers of industry and commerce[37] and the chambers of artisans. Some modifications were brought about by later enactments.[38] The role of these chambers was quite important: the administration had to consult them on many matters, and tax money was allocated by law to them so that they

[34] 1932/294.

[35] 1938/479,480 and 481.

[36] 1928/385.

[37] 1927/591.

[38] 1927/1003 and 1933/638.

could develop useful activities. The Union of the Chambers of Industry and Commerce was quite an important pressure group within the Polish community.

In regard to the professional self-government, five professions were organized by law into specific self-governing bodies: attorneys-at-law,[39] public notaries[40] (who are, in Poland and other civil law countries, lawyers specializing in particular fields of law), the medical profession,[41] the medico-dental profession,[42] and pharmaceutical chemists.[43] All members of these professions were required to belong to their respective chambers, which were autonomous in their activities, although they acted under the supervision of the Ministry of Justice or the Ministry of Social Welfare. In addition to the local chambers, there existed national chambers. The councils of the national chambers were elected by the local chambers. The main objective of these chambers was to act on behalf of their members and to supervise their professional activities. They kept registers of their members and had important disciplinary powers over them. In view of the very great number of attorneys, which exceeded the actual needs of the population, a law of 1938[44] gave the Minister of Justice the power to introduce a *numerus clausus* in those districts which were especially overcrowded. The boundaries of the districts of chambers of attorneys and notaries public did not correspond with the administrative provinces, but with the districts of the appeal courts.

Both of the Polish constitutions (1921 and 1935) provided for the establishment of a Supreme Economic Chamber, but the implementation of this provision was postponed until all branches were called into being. The organization of chambers of technicians was regarded as especially important. Preparatory works were under way but were not finished before the outbreak of the Second World War.

It should be stressed that, in addition to the compulsory economic and professional chambers, there existed voluntary professional and productive associations, which were quite active and in some cases even more influential than the official bodies.

[39] 1932/733.

[40] 1933/609.

[41] 1921/763 and 1934/275.

[42] 1938/33.

[43] 1939/346.

[44] 1938/289.

158

ADMINISTRATIVE PROCEDURE

In most countries, rules of administrative procedure have not been codified and are contained either in special laws regulating specific branches of administrative law or have been established in practice by administrative authorities themselves or by administrative courts. In Poland, however, administrative procedure was codified and promulgated by a decree of 1928.[45] This decree is modeled quite closely on an Austrian law on administrative procedure of 1925. This law, although enacted only after the fall of the old Hapsburg empire, was based on preparatory drafts completed before the First World War, and was well known to Polish lawyers serving in the Austrian ministries in Vienna.

What were the essential features of this administrative procedure? It prescribed the method by which administrative proceedings were to be started and conducted, in order to safeguard the interests of the parties concerned as well as the public interest, and prescribed the rights the parties had during those proceedings. It also contained rules about the production and evaluation of evidence and about the conduct of the main hearing and the issuance of administrative decisions, and outlined the methods of appealing against them. The decision issued in the second instance (i.e., by the administrative authority immediately superior to that which had issued the first decision) was final. However, such a "final" decision did not end the matter. The party who was not satisfied with this decision could sue the respective administrative authority before the Supreme Administrative Tribunal.

This tribunal was created by a law of 1922[46] which was modified by a decree of 1932.[47] The Tribunal had a status equal to that of the Supreme Court, and was composed of judges who enjoyed full independence from any other authority and had to obey only the law. The members of the Tribunal were appointed by the President of the Republic from candidates presented by the so-called administrative college of the Tribunal itself, and could not be removed from office against their will before reaching the retirement age, unless as a result of disciplinary proceedings conducted before the Tribunal itself. (However, no such proceedings were ever instituted during the interwar period). The judgments of the Tribunal were binding on the administrative authorities. Important judgments of the Tribunal were published in a special publication.[48]

[45]1928/341.
[46]1922/600.
[47]1932/806.
[48]*Zbiór Orzeczeń Najwyższego Trybunału Administracyjnego* ("Collection of Decisions of the Supreme Administrative Tribunal").

The Polish law concerning the Supreme Administrative Tribunal was modeled on the Austrian law, which in turn was modeled on the prototype of all administrative courts, the French Council of State (*Conseil d'Etat*).

The law on the administrative procedure of 1928 had its corollaries in two other enactments of the same date: the law on the penal administrative procedure[49] and the law on the implementation of the administrative decisions.[50]

The penal administrative procedure regulated proceedings before the administrative authorities in cases of minor criminal offenses. It was mentioned above that, by virtue of the law on misdemeanors, the administrative decisions in minor criminal matters had only a provisional character, which meant that the accused who was not satisfied with such a decision could appeal either to a higher administrative authority or to a court. In the latter case the administrative decision was simply put aside and the court had to pass over the case as if it had never been tried before, the original administrative decision being treated as a kind of indictment.

The law on the implementation of administrative decisions had as its model the rules laid down in codes of civil procedure dealing with the execution of the courts' judgments.

In this connection, another problem should be mentioned. What happened when doubts arose as to whether a certain case should be decided by the courts of general jurisdiction or by administrative authorities with the Supreme Administrative Tribunal as the final authority? There could be either "positive conflicts" of competence, when both a court of general jurisdiction and an administrative authority asserted their competence over the matter, or "negative conflicts" of competence, when both the court and the administrative authority declined to take jurisdiction. Both the positive and negative conflicts of competence were finally decided, if not previously settled within the judicial or administrative hierarchy, by a special Competence Tribunal established by a law of 1925.[51] This Tribunal was composed of an equal number of judges of the Supreme Court and the Supreme Administrative Tribunal, appointed by the President of the Republic in conformity with recommendations put forward by the administrative colleges of these courts, and of further judges appointed by the President of the Republic from among professors of law at state universities. The presidency of the Competence Tribunal rotated among judges of the Supreme Court and the Supreme Administrative Tribunal, according to appointments made by the President of the Republic.

[49]1928/365.

[50]1928/342.

[51]1925/897.

During the discussions on the draft of the Polish constitution of 1921, a motion was put forward to create a Constitutional Tribunal to decide cases in which conformity of a law to the Constitution was in dispute. This motion, however, was not adopted, with the result that the legislative branch itself was empowered by the Constitution to ensure that no provision of the Constitution was violated by a statutory enactment.

The rule that no one had the right to question the validity of laws or decrees duly promulgated in the Journal of Laws did not apply to rules and regulations deriving from administrative authorities (i.e., various ministers or the Council of Ministers). The validity of such rules and regulations could be challenged before the courts or before the Supreme Administrative Tribunal. The number of cases, however, in which such rules or regulations were declared invalid by the courts was very limited.

PERSONNEL ADMINISTRATION

An important branch of administrative law was concerned with personnel administration. The personnel of various branches of the state administration had their own peculiar "service pragmatics" as these laws were often called. A general law on the rights and duties of civil servants was enacted in 1922[52] and modified by later statutes and decrees. There were similar laws concerning teachers of primary and secondary schools,[53] professors and other teaching staff members of the academic schools,[54] officers and career soldiers,[55] functionaries of state railways[56] and post offices,[57] members of the police force,[58] prison personnel,[59] and – quite apart from them – judges and procurators,[60] the former enjoying a degree of independence unknown to any other branch of the public administration. These basic laws and decrees were supplemented by more detailed rules and regulations issued either by the prime minister or by ministers in charge of the respective governmental departments.

[52]1922/164.

[53]1926/530.

[54]1928/204.

[55]1922/257 and 1924/698.

[56]1929/447.

[57]1934/25.

[58]1928/257.

[59]1932/667.

[60]1928/93.

To this branch of administrative law belonged a number of fundamental rules developed from certain provisions of the Constitution itself. Such were the laws on Polish citizenship of 1920[61] and on the status of aliens of 1926;[62] the decrees on the state of emergency[63] and on the state of war of 1928[64] (revised in 1937);[65] the law on possession and trade of arms, munitions, and explosives of 1932;[66] the legislation on press and printing enterprises; the law on associations[67] of 1932 and on public meetings and gatherings of the same year;[68] and many others which cannot be enumerated in a short article.

Because of their fundamental importance in establishing relations between citizens and the administration, some of these laws should be examined.

The legislation concerning the press and printing enterprises forms a separate chapter in Polish legal history. At first, of course, the old Austrian and Prussian laws on this subject remained in force. Only in the former Russian territories was any provisional Polish legislation enacted. This legislation was passed as early as the beginning of 1919,[69] because the Russian law based on the principle of strict censorship did not fit into the pattern of the Polish democracy. In 1927 there was an attempt to unify this branch of law by a decree of the President of the Republic.[70] This decree gave the administration broad powers over the press and was criticised as placing upon it unreasonable restrictions. According to the amendment to the Constitution of 1926, the decrees of the President of the Republic had to be immediately brought to the attention of the parliament (*sejm*), which could abolish them by a simple resolution without observing normal and, to a certain extent, cumbersome legislative procedure. The criticism of the decree on the press could not, for

[61] 1920/44.

[62] 1926/465.

[63] 1928/307.

[64] 1928/54.

[65] 1937/1080.

[66] 1932/807.

[67] 1932/808.

[68] 1932/450.

[69] 1919/186.

[70] 1927/398.

complicated political reasons, be expressed in this way until the beginning of 1930, when such a resolution was finally passed and promulgated in the Journal of Laws,[71] thus abolishing the 1927 decree. This case demonstrates that the provisional character of legislation by decree was not a mock provision of the Constitution.

The abolition of the 1927 decree meant the reinstatement of the previous Austrian, Prussian, and the provisional Polish laws of 1919. They remained in force until 1938, when at last a unified law on the press and printing establishments was enacted in a decree which met with much less opposition than the previous one.[72] Like its predecessor, this decree did not introduce any preliminary press censorship. However, it gave the administration the power to seize and stop the circulation of newspapers, books, or any printed matter the contents of which had, in the opinion of the administration, the features of a criminal offense. This measure was effective because the first copies of any printed matter had to be submitted to the competent administrative authority. In the case of such a seizure the newspaper (or any printed matter) could be put in circulation only after the incriminating parts were deleted. The administrative decision was, however, not the end of the matter. It was possible to submit it to a competent court. The judgment of this court could either uphold the administrative decision and order the confiscation of the seized copies, or reverse the decision, in which case the publisher had the right to be indemnified for the illegal seizure. In case of more serious offenses, the court could suspend the publication of a newspaper or periodical for a period from six months to five years.

The decree on associations of 1932 provided for three kinds of associations: ordinary associations, registered associations, and associations of higher public importance. Ordinary associations could be organized by way of a simple notification of the intention to establish such an association to the district administrative authority, together with the submission of its charter and bylaws. During the four weeks after such a notification, the authority could forbid the establishment of the association if its aims were deemed contrary to the law or could endanger the public safety, peace, or order. A registered association had the rights and privileges of a legal person. The registers of these associations were kept by competent district administrative authorities who could refuse registration for the above-mentioned reasons or if the formation of the association in question was deemed not in the public interest. Associations of greater public importance (such as the Polish Red Cross, the League for Defense Against Air Attacks, etc.) could be established only with the consent of

[71]1930/92.

[72]1938/608.

the Council of Ministers. Such associations could enjoy special and important privileges: for instance, the exclusive right to conduct certain activities.

The district administrative authorities had the right to control the activities of ordinary and registered associations and could suspend or even dissolve them if their activities proved to be contrary to the law or public order. Purely religious associations and trade unions were not regulated, however, by this law. Religious associations were governed by the rules of the respective established churches and denominations, and the trade unions were regulated by a special statute.

The decree on meetings and gatherings of 1932 distinguishes between public and private meetings. Private meetings (for instance, meetings of members of any association or meetings purely social in character) could be held without any interference of administrative authorities. A public meeting in a building could be convened by any adult person, who was, however, obligated to notify the appropriate administrative authority, which had the right to send its representative to such a meeting. Public meetings in open spaces could be convoked only with the consent of the competent authority, which normally sent to it its representative. A public meeting could be terminated by the representative of the authority if it threatened, in his opinion, to endanger the public safety or order. Traditional fairs, gatherings of a religious character, and meetings of students of academic institutions were permitted without any interference from the administrative authorities.

A state of emergency could be proclaimed by the government with the consent of the President of the Republic during war, under the threat of war, or in case of serious internal riots or other demonstrations which could endanger the security of the country. A state of emergency had to be proclaimed at once to Parliament, which, if necessary, was convoked at once. Parliament could repeal such a proclamation if, in parliamentary opinion, it was not justified by the circumstances. The state of emergency could be proclaimed either for the whole country or for specific areas.

Such a proclamation had as its effect the suspension of the basic freedoms guaranteed in normal circumstances by the Constitution to the citizens. The suspension of personal freedom meant that persons endangering the security of the country could be, by administrative decisions, confined or interned, or deported to parts of the country where the state of emergency had not been declared. Administrative authorities also had the right to arrest suspected persons for not longer than six months without referring the matter to the courts. The suspension of the inviolability of the home gave administrative authorities the right to search premises without the consent of a court. Likewise, the suspension of the liberty of the press gave the administration the right to introduce censorship and confiscate newspapers and printed matters without the court consent. The suspension of the right of secrecy in correspondence allowed the introduction of the censorship of letters. The suspension of the liberty of associations and public meetings and gatherings meant that new associations could not be established and public meetings convoked without express consent of the competent administrative authority.

The proclamation of a state of war had similar effects. The main difference was that it was proclaimed not by the government but by the commander-in-chief of the armed forces and that quite important powers passed immediately from the civil to the military authorities.

Military Administration

Legislation dealing with the military administration was rather scarce when compared with other branches of administration. Besides the Military Criminal Code, the Code of Military Criminal Procedure, and the laws on the rights and duties of officers and career soldiers (under personnel administration), only the statutes concerning compulsory military service,[73] requisition of vehicles for transportation, and the supply of other goods and labor for military purposes,[74] the law on fortresses and military bases,[75] and the decree on the organization of the supreme military command will be mentioned here. The organization of the supreme military command, and especially the position of the General Inspector of the Armed Forces, was highly controversial and was one of the reasons for the *coup d' état* of 1926, after which the Inspector was placed under the direct responsibility of the President of the Republic as the supreme chief of the armed forces.[76] Thus, the relationship between the President and the armed forces resembled to a certain extent the American pattern.

FISCAL LAW AND ADMINISTRATION

In contrast to the legislation on the military administration, that concerning the fiscal administration was so abundant that only the most important fiscal laws and regulations can be mentioned here.

[73] 1924/609.

[74] 1934/859.

[75] 1927/483.

[76] 1926/444 and 445.

First of all, there were statutes on various kinds of taxation. The most important of them were the laws on the income tax,[77] the industrial tax on the gross receipts of business enterprises,[78] the real estate tax,[79] and the very complicated and sophisticated law on stamp duties.[80] On the other hand, numerous statutes dealt with different kinds of indirect taxation: customs and excises,[81] state monopolies (tobacco,[82] alcohol,[83] and match monopolies,[84] the state lottery,[85] and others of lesser importance), and various others.

Most interesting from the legal point of view are, however, not so much rules defining these various objects of taxation but the procedure which the fiscal authorities had to observe in order to safeguard the rights and interests of the citizens. The rules of this procedure were laid down in the special tax ordinance of 1934.[86] This law applied only to direct taxes paid by individual taxpayers after being assessed by the fiscal authorities. The procedure of this assessment was to a certain extent patterned after the general administrative procedure. It differed, however, in many respects. Normally, the assessment procedure started when the taxpayer filed a return. The law laid down special rules on commercial bookkeeping and accounting as the basis for assessment of taxes payable by businessmen and business associations, and provided that appeals from decisions of the fiscal offices (i.e., fiscal authorities of the first instance) were not to be examined by the fiscal chambers (i.e., authorities of the second instance), but by special appeals commissions functioning at the fiscal chambers and composed of taxpayers. Members of these commissions were appointed by fiscal authorities nominated by the organs of economic and professional self-government. The ordinance on taxes also included rules on punishment for fiscal misdemeanors. Such procedures were modeled on the general administrative penal procedure, the fines being imposed, of course, by fiscal authorities and not by the general administrative authorities.

[77]1923/521 and 1924/110.

[78]1925/881.

[79]1936/144.

[80]1926/570.

[81]1930/276 and 1932/732.

[82]1922/409.

[83]1927/289.

[84]1931/45.

[85]1920/180.

[86]1934/346.

The procedure relating to criminal offenses against the laws on indirect taxation was governed by the fiscal penal law of 1926[87] (replaced by another law of the same name in 1932).[88] The penalty imposed by this law could be either a fine, or confiscation of untaxed or illegally produced goods, or even imprisonment. Offenses which could be punished by imprisonment were within the jurisdiction of special fiscal penal departments of district courts, composed of judges well versed in this branch of law. Misdemeanors were punished by the competent fiscal authorities, but the defendant had the right to transfer the matter to a court if he was not satisfied with the punishment inflicted upon him.

ECONOMIC ADMINISTRATION

The vast area of legislation on economic matters belonged primarily to the judicial law, but some matters had to be taken care of not by the courts but by the administrative authorities. Among these were measures aimed at protecting the public interest, which could easily be violated by unrestricted economic activities. Sometimes it is rather difficult to draw the dividing line between judicial and administrative law, as in the case of cartel legislation (discussed above), which really belongs to both.

The best example of administrative economic law is the industrial law of 1927.[89] It proclaimed the principle that the conduct of industrial and other business enterprises was free from regulation — with some important exceptions: in order to establish some kinds of enterprises, especially those which could affect the defense policy (for instance, production of arms and explosives) one first had to apply for a license from the administration. Other regulations related to projects of industrial installations (factories, etc.) and to enterprises using power-moved machinery or machinery which might endanger the public safety or health. Such projects had to be approved by administrative authorities, which had the right to inspect the new installations before production could be started. The industrial law prescribed in detail the procedure to be observed in these cases. Some kinds of non-licensed industrial production could be conducted only by persons having necessary training and experience, who were required to produce a so-called proof of ability to conduct these actitivies. The law also regulated the training of industrial apprentices competing for a proof of ability. This was especially the case with artisanship, which was a special kind of industry within the meaning of the

[87] 1926/609.

[88] 1932/355.

[89] 1927/468.

law. The various branches of industry were organized compulsorily into industrial corporations bearing, in the case of the artisans, traditional guild names and organization. Furthermore, the law contained some provisions on peddlers, who had to apply for special licenses to carry on their business.

The industrial law did not apply to many branches of business activity which were governed by special laws. Such was the case with banking enterprises (decree of 1928),[90] stock exchanges and grain and other goods markets (law of 1924),[91] private insurance companies (decree of 1927)[92] and electricity plants (law of 1922).[93] All of these types of economic activity were subjected to a stricter administrative supervision because of their importance to the nation's economy, and could be engaged in only after a license had been obtained from competent administrative authorities.

The mining industry was governed by the mining law of 1930.[94] Mining rights did not accrue automatically to the land owners, except in the case of some minerals, such as oil and natural gas, which belonged to them by law. Some minerals, such as potassium, were declared by law to be handled by state monopolies. The mining law prescribed how mining enterprises should be conducted. They were to be controlled by special mining authorities subject to the Ministry of Industry and Commerce. Litigation between the owners of neighboring mining fields (i.e., special units of mining property) and between the land owners and those who held mining rights was not under jurisdiction of mining authorities but under that of the ordinary courts. It is impossible to give here a more detailed account of the provisions of the Polish mining law, which was in many respects an original product of the Polish juridical thought and experience.

A special branch of economic law dealt with the use of land and water.[95] Here were the politically very important and very controversial laws on land reform,[96] which aimed at the compulsory distribution of bigger estates among the peasant population. This problem was so difficult and complicated that a special branch of administration, the land offices,

[90]1928/321.

[91]1924/687.

[92]1928/64.

[93]1922/277.

[94]1930/654.

[95]1922/936.

[96]1920/462 and 1926/1.

168

had to be created to accomplish the task, which was still far from complete when the Second World War erupted.

Legislation on various branches of agricultural activity (breeding of animals,[97] production of seeds, etc.) was rather uncontroversial. There were special laws on forestry,[98] hunting[99] and protection of wild animals, and fishing.[100]

Legislation on public transportation (railways,[101] public roads,[102] motor vehicles,[103]) communications (mail, telegraph, and telephones),[104] the merchant navy,[105] and air transportation (e.g., the air law of 1928,[106] modeled to a great extent on a draft of an international convention on this subject) was quite extensive. There were also many other laws dealing with some other aspects of economic activity (for instance, the 1928 decree on building and town planning)[107] but it is not possible to mention all of them here.

LAW ON CULTURAL ADMINISTRATION AND RELIGIOUS PROBLEMS

First, legislation on the school system should be noted here. The basic laws concerning this problem date from the very first years of the reborn state: the 1919 decree on compulsory primary education,[108] the 1920 law on the structure of educational authorities,[109] and the 1921 law on academic schools.[110] These laws were later replaced by new laws: the

[97] 1928/332 and 361, and 1933/639.

[98] 1927/504 and 1936/533.

[99] 1927/934.

[100] 1932/357.

[101] 1928/102.

[102] 1921/32 and 1933/55.

[103] 1932/336.

[104] 1931/392.

[105] 1920/285.

[106] 1928/294.

[107] 1928/202.

[108] 1919/147.

[109] 1920/304.

[110] 1921/447.

1932 law on the school system[111] and the 1933 law on institutions of higher learning.[112]

According to the laws on primary education and the school system, every child of seven years of age had to begin primary education either in a state school at the cost of the state, in a private school, or at home. The curriculum of primary schools lasted in principle seven years; after five years, however, the child could be transferred to a secondary school. Its curriculum lasted for six years. Apart from secondary schools giving a general education, the 1932 law created professional secondary schools. Most of the primary and secondary schools were run by the state, but there also existed private schools. Their functions were regulated by a special law of 1932[113] which provided that they could be granted, on certain conditions, the rights of public schools. It provided also that some of them might be recognized as experimental schools, in which case they enjoyed special privileges granted by the educational authorities. The supervision and control of all schools was in the hands of the Ministry of Education, which exercised control through local educational authorities: the curators of educational districts and the school inspectors.

Most institutions of higher learning were also run by the state. There also existed, however, private academic schools which had to fulfill requirements imposed on them by a law of 1037.[114] Both state and private academic schools enjoyed a vast autonomy, i.e., the rectors (presidents), deans, and senates were elected by the members of faculty, and new professors and lecturers were appointed only on motions of fully autonomous academic bodies. The fundamental provision of the law on academic schools was the one which proclaimed that they should enjoy full freedom of scientific and educational work.

Apart from the legislation on schools, there were enactments dealing with other aspects of cultural administration, such as libraries[115] and archives,[116] the preservation of historical monuments,[117] and cultural foundations.[118]

[111]1932/389.

[112]1933/247.

[113]1932/343.

[114]1937/89.

[115]1932/347.

[116]1919/182.

[117]1918/30 and 1928/265.

[118]1928/372.

170

To this branch of law also belonged legislation on religious matters. All recognized religious denominations enjoyed a vast autonomy guaranteed by the Constitution. The relationship between the state and the Catholic church was regulated in detail by an international agreement (concordate) between the Holy See and the Polish state.[119] Other denominations were dealt with by special laws regulating their relations with the state. One important principle was laid down in all these laws: the supreme religious authority of each recognized denomination was to have its seat in Poland and not abroad. There was an important political reason for the strict application of this principle: the Orthodox Church on the Polish territory formed during the partition period a part of the Russian Orthodox church, and the Protestant churches on the territory which belonged to Prussia during that period had been under jurisdiction of the respective Prussian protestant hierarchies. The new state could not tolerate interference of these Russian or Prussian religious authorities on the Polish soil. These churches functioning in Poland had to become *autokefalous* to use the proper technical term.

LABOR AND SOCIAL LEGISLATION

An important branch of Polish law was that law through which the new state tried to put into effect its social policy. It is worthwhile to discuss in more detail for two reasons: (1) little about it was and is known in the Western world apart from those circles which had to do with these matters professionally (e.g., those who were acquainted with the activity of the International Labor Office in Geneva), and (2) the Communist regime now in power in Poland tries to represent the social policy of the interwar Polish state as one dictated by reactionary tendencies, and to give the impression that only the Communist regime has introduced a progressive social legislation for the well-being of the working classes.

As will be shown below, the contrary is true. The Polish social legislation of the interwar period was more advanced than that of most other countries and, what is even more striking, it provided greater and better care of the interests of the working classes than the legislation introduced by the new regime after 1945.

Protection of Labor

The fundamental rules for the protection of workers were contained in the decrees of 1928 concerning the labor contracts of manual workers [120]

[119] 1925/501 and 502.

[120] 1928/324.

and white collar employees.[121] Until the promulgation of these decrees, the contents of such contracts were left to the discretion of the employer and the employee – a consequence of the *laissez-faire* doctrine. In practice, the employers, as the economically stronger party, could dictate the conditions of such contracts to their economically weaker partners. The decrees of 1928 discarded the *laissez-faire* principle, prescribing that certain terms of these contracts, if less favorable to the working people than those set out by the law itself, should be voided and replaced by those which the law prescribed. (Such terms might be those relating to working hours, the termination of a contract, etc.)

In practice, most labor contracts were not negotiated individually between one employer and one employee, but were subject to collective bargaining between associations of employers and organizations of employees (trade unions). Collective bargaining procedures were regulated by a law of 1937[122] providing for compulsory arbitration when agreement between bargaining parties could not be reached.

Some conditions of labor were regulated by the law itself. As early as 1918, a decree promulgated the principle that a worker should work no longer than eight hours a day and forty-six hours a week.[123] A law of 1922[124] went into more detail, prescribing among other things that under certain circumstances the time could be extended on the condition that there was higher pay for overtime and for work on Sundays and public holidays. (See also the law of 1924 on work on holidays[125] and the 1928 decree on working hours in the shops.)[126] A very important law was that of 1922 concerning vacations.[127] It provided that manual workers could get holidays with pay up to two weeks, and white collar workers up to one month per year.

A special law of 1924 provided for the protection of women and minors,[128] and allowed for compulsory maternity leave and for the compulsory establishment of orphanages in bigger factories. Some kinds of hard work, as well as work during night hours, were prohibited to women by this law. As to minors, they were not permitted to work until fifteen

[121] 1928/323.

[122] 1937/242.

[123] 1918/42.

[124] 1920/7 and 1922/127.

[125] 1924/928.

[126] 1923/551.

[127] 1922/334.

[128] 1924/636.

years of age, and had to be given free time and an opportunity to learn in order to achieve greater general or professional education.

In 1928 a decree on safety and hygiene of working conditions was enacted.[129] It prescribed technical requirements under which the work had to be carried out in the interests of the safety and hygiene of the workers. There were two safeguards which prevented these laws from merely remaining on paper and not being enforced. One was the "inspectorate of labor" introduced by a decree of 1919 as a special administrative branch subordinate to the Ministry of Labor and Social Welfare.[130] Labor inspectors were required to inspect periodically all factories and places in which work was being conducted. They had the right to impose fines on employers violating labor legislation and to bring more serious offenses before the labor courts (mentioned above), which could impose penalties, including imprisonment, on those responsible for these offenses. The second safeguard was legislation on trade unions (a decree of 1919),[131] which enjoyed more liberal treatment than ordinary associations and could efficiently defend the rights and interests of their members. Their right to strike was protected by the Constitution of 1921.

It may be noted that both of these safeguards were practically destroyed after 1945 by the new legislation and practice. The inspection of labor was abolished as a special branch of administration and its task allocated to trade unions, which do not possess qualified and trained bodies of labor inspectors and which are deprived of the most effective means of enforcing the protection of labor — namely, the right to impose fines on management. As to the second safeguard, the trade unions ceased to fulfill their role as the defenders of the rights and interests of the workers, a role which is allegedly obsolete in a non-capitalist system. They have been transformed into organs of the state and of the ruling party with the assignment of controlling and disciplining the workers.

Social Insurance

Prussian Poland inherited a very comprehensive system of social insurance. (Actually, Germany played a pioneering role in this field.) Austria had copied most of the German laws on this subject, but her social insurance system was somewhat less developed than the German one. However, both the Prussian and Austrian provinces of Poland had fairly

[129] 1928/325.

[130] 1919/90 and 1927/590.

[131] 1919/209.

well-established systems of social insurance. In contrast, such legislation in the Russian provinces of Poland was almost non-existent.

The Polish legislation had as its object a gradual unification of the social insurance law without, however, diminishing the rights acquired by the workers under the German or Austrian legislation. Towards the end of the interwar period this objective was achieved, and there existed the following branches of social insurance:

1. Health insurance, providing for illness benefits and free health service.[132] The insurance contributions were paid half by the employer and half by the employee.

2. Insurance against accidents, paid for exclusively by the employers.[133] This insurance covered the cost of medical treatment and pensions for invalid workers, as well as annuities for their dependents in the event of death.

3. Old-age insurance, which was introduced (except in the former Prussian province, where it already existed) in 1927 for white collar workers[134] and in 1934 for all other workers.[135] Forty percent of the contribution was paid by the employee and sixty percent by the employer.

4. Insurance against unemployment, providing benefits for a period not exceeding seventeen weeks.[136] Twenty-five percent of the contribution was paid by the employee and seventy-five percent by the employer.

Social insurance was administered by the Social Insurance Board through local social insurance offices (there were sixty-four such offices in the country), under the supervision of the Ministry of Labor and Social Welfare.

The final development in social insurance law was a 1939 law on social insurance courts. Until the promulgation of this law, decisions on the amounts of insurance contributions and benefits were issued by various bodies of a semi-judicial and semi-administrative character, originally instituted by the German, Prussian, or Austrian law; in the formerly Russian provinces these bodies were of a markedly administrative character. The new law replaced these bodies by real courts enjoying full judicial independence: the district social insurance courts and the Social Insurance Tribunal, which was a court of appeal from the decisions of these courts. This law, promulgated in August 1939,[137] was to have

[132] 1919/122 and 1933/396.

[133] 1921/413.

[134] 1927/911.

[135] 1934/855.

[136] 1924/650.

[137] 1939/476.

become effective as of the first of April 1940. Because of the war, it came into force only after the end of the hostilities.

Unemployment Legislation

Insurance against unemployment, mentioned above, provided unemployment benefits only for a limited period and only to those who lost their employment after working at least twenty-six weeks. It did not provide any remedy against initial unemployment and, what was far more important, against unemployment lasting longer than seventeen weeks. Unfortunately, the economic crises suffered by Poland as by many other countries in this period usually lasted much longer, so that this insurance could not provide a satisfactory solution to the problem. A special law of 1924 supplemented the scheme.[138] It provided for the creation of an unemployment fund, which was transformed into a labor fund in 1933.[139] This fund was used to organize public works, and paid complementary unemployment benefits to those who did not get such benefits from insurance and to whom the fund could not provide adequate work.

Social Welfare Legislation

In 1923 a fundamental law on social welfare was passed by Parliament.[140] It stated that the care of those in need of assistance was one of the duties of the state and of the communal self-government. A network of social wardens under the supervision of the communal administration was created. The formation of benevolent associations was encouraged, and their work as well as the charitable work of religious orders and associations was subsidized from public funds. Special care was taken of minors. A network of orphanages and kindergardens was created, and summer camps were organized for young people, with financial support from public funds.

[138] 1924/650.

[139] 1933/163.

[140] 1923/726.

Considerable legislation was passed on hospitals and sanatoria,[141] on health resorts,[142] on the State Institute of Hygiene,[143] on the medical profession,[144] and on the fight against epidemics[145] and socially dangerous diseases (tuberculosis, trachoma, and others).[146]

Conclusion

As a result of the activity of the Codification Commission and the legislative bodies and ministries, the primary task of giving to the reborn state a unified Polish law was nearly completed during the twenty years of independence. An important counterpart of legislative work was the activity of the courts — especially the work of the Supreme Court and of the Supreme Administrative Tribunal on the one hand, and the contributions of scholars to legal literature, which was abundant, on the other. Owing to this activity, the new law was translated from the abstract into the language of practice and everyday life. It was made more accessible and comprehensible not only to the members of the legal profession but also to the general public. On the whole, the new law was well received by the population, which felt that those who had created and applied it in practice had tried to fit it to the requirements of modern times and the needs of the whole nation.

One must admit that many rules of the new Polish legal system were not original products but adaptations of foreign legal institutions to specifically Polish conditions. The Polish law frequently followed paths cut through by others. It could hardly be otherwise. The industrial revolution, the emergence of the labor class, the developments in transportation and communication and science in general in the nineteenth and the first part of the twentieth centuries called for legal regulation at the time when Poland was under the rule of other nations. Upon being reborn, she had to select from among various solutions already adopted by foreign legal systems. Nevertheless, there was an element of originality; and new ideas were reflected in the interwar Polish law.

[141] 1928/382.

[142] 1922/254.

[143] 1927/477.

[144] 1921/762.

[145] 1919/402.

[146] 1927/676.

VINCENT C. CHRYPIŃSKI

Postwar Developments in Polish Law:
A Survey of Criminal and Civil Legal Rules

The rebirth, in 1918, of an independent Polish state established an obvious need for the creation of a unified and truly national legal system. Unification was no mean task, however. While in most societies the process of legal adaptation to changing conditions forms a continuum of law from past to present, Poland was faced with an entirely different situation. After almost 150 years of partition and foreign rule, there was no genuinely Polish law that could serve as a basis for modernization. Instead there were four or five legal systems, each dating back to a different period — some as far back as the 18th century — and each reflecting a distinctive stage in the socio-economic development of the dominant society.

To commence the massive undertaking, the Polish parliament (*Seym*), already within the first few months of its existence, opened a debate on the issue.[1] Consequently, on June 3, 1919, a bill was passed creating the Codification Commission and giving it the task of preparing a uniform system of civil and criminal law for the entire country. The commission, independent from the council of ministers, consisted of forty-four members, including some of the most prominent theoreticians and practitioners of law in the land. Professor Xawery Fierich, the rector of Jagiellonian University in Cracow, became its first president.

At first the commission consisted of two departments, civil and criminal, which were divided into sections: the civil department into three (civil law, procedure, and commercial law) and the criminal department into two (criminal law and procedure). In addition, a special subcommission was formed for the purpose of establishing rules for the

[1]Z. Nagórski, "Codification of Civil Law in Poland 1918-39," The Polish Lawyers' Association in the United Kingdom, *Studies in Polish and Comparative Law* (London: Stevens and Sons, Ltd., 1945), p. 44.

organization of courts. In later years the departments were abolished and the commission operated through the five sections and the subcommission. The section on civil law was divided into three subsections which devoted their efforts to the areas of family law, property law, and general rules of law, which included the law of contracts.

The Codification Commission operated under dual and frequently conflicting interests. On the one hand, political considerations prompted the commission to speed up the work and offer the reborn state uniform laws that would accelerate national unification. On the other hand, the Codification Commission wanted to prepare not merely a mechanical amalgamation of existing rules, but a system that would incorporate the most modern ideas and provide a firm legal foundation for future development.

In spite of the difficulties, the commission worked at a rapid pace and in the course of years prepared a number of important legal drafts which, later enacted in the form of statutes or decrees, gave Poland her most-needed criminal and civil laws. They included three procedural codes (criminal, civil, and administrative); a penal code; and laws on the judiciary, the bar, and public notaries; as well as uniform rules regulating important branches of civil relations: obligations (in particular, torts and general and commercial contracts), rights concerning intangible goods (copyright and patent laws), and law on the structure and operation of commercial enterprises. The work accomplished included important sections of a civil code and two statutes on conflicts of law in international and inter-provincial relations.

At the outbreak of World War II, however, the task of codifying Polish law was only partly finished. Especially in the area of civil law, there still existed a heterogeneous and complicated conglomerate, devoid of uniform rules in such important branches of civil law as property and family law.

The First Period

After World War II, political, social, and economic changes resulting from the war and from the establishment of a Communist-dominated government again caused a basic transformation of the entire Polish legal system. The process, still continuing, went through certain stages which can be broadly identified with the cycles of political development in the country. Of course, there are no definite dates or formal pronouncements to mark the end of one cycle and the beginning of another. Quite naturally, certain manifestations of one phase have appeared in advance or continued through the following cycle.

The first period, between 1944 and 1948, was marked by an intense struggle between the Communist Party (PPR) and its allies, and the opposing forces, united around Mikołajczyk. For the opposition the prize of this contest was not so much the recapture of Poland from Communist domination, for the presence of Soviet troops made that impossible, but rather a symbolic victory in the forthcoming elections of 1947.

In discussing the laws of this period one should remember certain important factors which had some significant and interesting effects upon the lawmaking.

First, the pre-1939 governmental apparatus was totally destroyed by the Germans and the Soviets in their zones of occupation. The new machinery set up progressively in 1944 and 1945 in the parts of the country taken over by the Red Army was from the very beginning controlled by the members or nominees of the Communist Party. The admission, in June of 1945, of Mikołajczyk and his followers to the government did not substantially alter the power relationship established before that date.[2] Thus the composition of governmental bodies by itself predetermined the political content of future lawmaking.

An additional matter should be mentioned at this point: the peculiar legislative technique frequently resorted to during this period. While normally important matters should be regulated by statutes or decrees, during the years 1944-5 many vital issues were decided by internal instructions, often unpublished and sometimes issued by unauthorized officials.[3]

Second, most enactments of the first period were intended to accelerate the consolidation of political power placed by the Soviets in the hands of Polish Communists. Surely the tutelage of the Red Army had a decisive influence in maintaining Communist control over the country with or without the popular acceptance of the regime imposed on it. Yet it was important, for international and domestic reasons, to gain the support of, or at least to neutralize, the masses. Hence the laws of this period clearly displayed two aspects: the carrot and the whip.

This explanation may help one to perceive the motives behind these laws, but one must resist the temptation to ascribe all evils and nothing but evils to the Communist Party. It is not inaccurate to say that even the opposition honestly believed in the necessity of many of the laws passed in these years and genuinely desired their socio-economic effects.

[2]Stanisław Mikołajczyk, *The Pattern of Soviet Domination* (London: Sampson Low, Marston and Co., 1948).

[3]For examples see Kazimierz Grzybowski, "The Draft of the Civil Code for Poland," K. Grzybowski *et al, . Studies in Polish Law* (Leyden: A. W. Sythoff, 1962), p. 13.

Third, if a general survey is made of the laws of the 1944-8 period, it is apparent that, with a few striking and important exceptions, the legal system of those years was based on statutes in force in prewar Poland. Whether this circumstance represented a necessity that hampered the tasks of the Communist Party[4] or a tactical device used by this party to its advantage is a matter for a separate discussion. Regardless of the answer, the fact is well established.

Finally, the skeleton of the new legal system established during this period apparently was temporary in character, as was clearly demonstrated in the official designations of some of the statutes [5] and newly created institutions.[6] To quarrel over the justification or purpose of the attitude behind this is again a very difficult matter. Even in Poland opinions differ on this subject. While earlier writers condemned it as a "rightist deviation" expressing a tendency to return to the capitalist system,[7] recent authors attribute it to the noble desire of waiting for the "authoritative decision of the people."[8] Neither of these views is entirely convincing; this paper seeks only to register the existence of this transitory phase. Certainly, the provisional character of the new legal system had some effect upon the laws that were then made.

It is in the light of these general considerations that a review of the enactments in the period between 1944 and 1948 is undertaken.

CRIMINAL LAW OF THE FIRST PERIOD

It is important to emphasize that in Poland — as well as in other socialist countries of Eastern Europe, with the possible exception of

[4] Władysław Wolter et al., "Węzłowe zagadnienia prawa karnego w świetle konstytucji Polskiej Rzeczypospolitej Ludowej" ("Main Problems of Criminal Law in the Light of the Constitution of the Polish People's Republic"), Zagadnienia Prawne Konstytucji Polskiej Rzeczypospolitej Ludowej ("Legal Problems of the Constitution of the Polish People's Republic"), ed. Gustaw Auscaler (Warsaw: Państwowe Wydawnictwo Naukowe, 1954), I,259.

[5] For example, "Statut tymczasowy Rad Narodowych" ("Provisional Status of the National Councils").

[6] For example, the law of July 21, 1944, in Dziennik Ustaw ("Journal of Laws"), No. 1, Item 1, described the Polish Committee of National Liberation (PKWN) as a "provisional executive authority."

[7] Gustaw Auscaler and Władysław Wolter, "Prawo karne" ("Criminal law"), Dzięsieciolecie Prawa Polski Ludowej, 1944-1954 ("Decade of Law of the Polish People's Republic, 1944-1954"), ed. Leon Kurowski (Warsaw: Państwowe Wydawnictwo Naukowe, 1955), p. 283.

[8] Andrzej Burda and Romauld Klimowiecki, Prawo Państwowe ("State Law"), (Warsaw: Państwowe Wydawnictwo Naukowe, 1958), p. 91.

Yugoslavia — the Communist regime did not follow the Soviet example set by the famous Decree No. 3 of 1918 and did not forbid the courts to use prewar criminal law. On the contrary, the Criminal Code of 1932 was retained in force. Of course, its "old forms" were filled with new "socialist content" and supplemented by new regulations whenever the need arose.

The first of the new criminal laws issued in People's Poland was the Military Penal Code of September 23, 1944,[9] which replaced the code of 1932. The provisions of the new code included several measures the sole purpose of which was to protect the new political system (articles 85 through 88). They were directed against soldiers and civilians alike, and significantly contributed to the destruction of the underground movement which was oriented towards the exiled Polish government in London.[10]

The Code of 1944 is still in force. It is interesting to note that Poland is one of only two European socialist states — the other is Rumania — that have distinct military and civilian criminal codes. The existence of special military courts further defines this difference.

The protective measures of the 1944 code were extended by the decree on the protection of the state of October 30, 1944,[11] which, among other sanctions, introduced punishment for publishing anti-Soviet propaganda. The repressive nature of this law was excused by the necessities of war. Later on, however, its duration was extended — with editorial modifications — by the decrees of November 16, 1945[12] and June 13, 1946.[13] Both decrees had a significant title: "On Crimes Particularly Dangerous in the Period of Rebuilding the State." Although their title and the contents of certain articles imply that these two measures are temporary, the 1946 decree is still in force.

The comparison of these three decrees shows two significant differences. First is the appearance in the two later decrees of a difference in certain criminal sanctions. The acts qualified as socially dangerous were to be punished more severely than the ones free of this stigma. It was up to the court, helped by a procurator, to determine the existence of that vaguely defined characteristic. Second, minimum penalties were higher for crimes against the security of the state.

[9]"Kodeks Karny Wojska Polskiego," *Dziennik Ustaw* ("Journal of Laws"), No. 6 (1944), Item 27.

[10]Exemplified by the trials of Niepokólczycki, Rzepecki, and others.

[11]*Dziennik Ustaw* ("Journal of Laws"), No. 10, Item 50.

[12]*Ibid.*, No. 53, Item 300.

[13]*Ibid.*, No. 13, Item 192.

A different type of punitive measure was provided for in the decree of August 31, 1944,[14] directed against members of Nazi organizations (the S.S., the Gestapo, etc.) and their collaborators who during the German occupation of Poland had participated in the extermination of the population or committed other criminal acts of a similar nature. The decree served as a legal basis for the prosecution of many war criminals, including the infamous Hoess, Goeth, and Greiser. For this reason the decree undoubtedly received the approval of the entire nation. Later on, however, the decree was used — and utterly abused — for strictly partisan political purposes. Indiscriminately and unjustly classifying as Nazi collaborators all those who during the war professed an anti-Soviet position, the Communists used the decree as an intimidating measure against all potential enemies of their regime.

The months immediately preceding and following the end of hostilities witnessed a large rise in offenses against property, accompanied by bribery, corruption, and a black market. Extreme economic disorder, brought about first by the war and then by the sudden collapse of the German system of controls, was further complicated by the socialization of the main branches of the national economy and of formerly German property in the so-called Recovered Territories. The novelty of this type of ownership, the misunderstanding of its nature, and the lack of proper supervision and protection, greatly contributed to the growth of activities detrimental to the well-being of the nation.

The decree of June 13, 1946, mentioned above, included certain rules referring to economic offenses (articles 39 through 42). Most of them created new crimes unknown in prewar law, such as lowering the quantity or quality of production in socialized enterprises, selling on the open market of supplies intended for planned distribution, and arrogation of property left unprotected because of war.

One matter which must be briefly commented upon is the peculiar manner in which the law was used in the fight against corruption of public officials. The peculiarity consisted of a double-pronged operation in which the provisions of the prewar Criminal Code (article 292) were first extended by the decree of June 13, 1946 (article 46) to include a wider circle of culprits and then further extended by doubtful legal interpretation to the utmost limits.

In conclusion, the existence of another decree — that of November 16, 1945[15] should be mentioned. It subjected the accused to a special procedure which allowed additional punishment, ranging from a three-year

[14]*Ibid.*, No. 7, Item 29.

[15]*Ibid.*, No. 53, Item 301.

imprisonment to the death sentence. Whatever justification there may be for such measures, it is doubtful whether such harshness was required.

Socio-economic reforms introduced by the new regime — especially the land reform[16] and the nationalization of industry and commerce[17] — were accompanied by punitive provisions or by concurrently enacted criminal laws, the purpose of which was to prevent frustration or delay in the application of reform acts. Thus such provisions and laws were contained in the decrees of October 30, 1944 (article 2), November 16, 1945 (article 15), and June 13, 1946 (article 20), as well as in the nationalization law of January 3, 1946 (article 9).

Merely to nationalize ownership of the means of production was not sufficient. It was equally important to ensure that the new system produced. Thus it was necessary that the peasants who received their plots immediately start to cultivate them, seed and then harvest their crops, and above all deliver assigned quotas of foodstuffs to hungry cities. To achieve the production goal, the decree of March 30, 1945,[18] made the cultivation of all arable land compulsory, and failure to comply fully with this obligation was made punishable. This decree was strengthened by another, of September 12, 1947,[19] on "neighborly aid," which introduced the obligation of agricultural assistance and punished refusals to comply and demands for payment exceeding the limit determined by law (article 8). Some provisions of the well-known decrees of October 30, 1944 (article 10), November 16, 1945 (article 17), and June 13, 1946 (article 21), penalized farmers who were delinquent in making obligatory deliveries.

The effects of these punitive measures were highly intimidating. The decrees — especially that of March 30, 1945 — forced some peasants to abandon individual tilling and to join collective farms.[20]

Nationalization of commercial activities presented the regime with a special problem that could not be solved simply by a single order transferring ownership from private individuals to the state or to co-operatives. In this area the authorities decided to achieve their goal by gradual strangulation of private enterprise. Strict licensing and controlling

[16] Decree of September 6, 1944 as amended January 17, 1945. Full text in *ibid.*, No. 3 (1945), Item 13.

[17] Statute of January 3, 1946, *ibid.*, No. 3, Item 17.

[18] *Ibid.*, No. 11, Item 69.

[19] *Ibid.*, No. 59, Item 320.

[20] Z. Nagórski, Sr., "The Legislation of the Polish People's Republic, 1945-1957," *Law in Eastern Europe*, ed. Z. Szirmai (Leyden: A. W. Sijthoff, 1958), p. 29.

of inventories, prices, and profits,[21] accompanied by constant harassment by specially created commissions,[22] led to the slow but effective elimination of the private distributive sector.

Accompanying such measures was a multiplicity of criminal regulations, often inconsistent and difficult of application. It is understandable, therefore, that codification appeared to be of primary importance to the government.

The first move in this direction began in 1947.[23] Characteristically, the objective was to improve the Criminal Code of 1932 rather than to institute a radical departure from it. Consequently, the changes suggested usually related to particular rules and not the principles of the 1932 code. Even the most radical proposals tended to correct and supplement the old code only in the parts which were directly in opposition to actual practice. Renewal and reform, rather than a complete break with the past, were clearly dominant in the pattern of thought and action on the subject.

The period of moderation did not last very long. Its end came in 1948 without causing a great stir either among the practitioners or theoreticians of criminal law.

CIVIL LAW OF THE FIRST PERIOD

There were at least three reasons for the sense of urgency felt by the new regime in the area of civil law. First, the unfinished task of the prewar Codification Commission had left untouched many rules introduced by the conquering powers after the partition of Poland. Some of them could be traced as far back as the eighteenth century. Clearly enough, they reflected socio-economic relations of an era long gone and thus were totally unacceptable to the Communist regime.

The fact that the civil law traditionally formed a part of "private" law was no protection against interference. The Communists, following Lenin, rejected the traditional division of continental law into "public" and "private" law and treated the whole system as serving a single set of socio-political goals. To them, it was unthinkable that a single branch of law could lead an autonomous life independent of their reformative zeal.

[21] Statute of June 2, 1947, *Dziennik Ustaw* ("Journal of Laws"), No. 43, Item 21.

[22] Decree of the Council of State of June 13, 1947, *ibid.*, No. 44, Item 228.

[23] Igor Andrejew, *Nowy Kodeks Karny* ("New Criminal Code") (Warsaw: Wydawnictwo Prawnicze, 1963), pp. 17-9.

Second, Poland acquired territories in the West which for many years belonged to Germany, and it was important for international as well as domestic purposes to integrate these lands with the rest of the country. Introduction of Polish law into these provinces was intended to pave the way for social and economic unity.

Finally, radical changes of the socio-economic order — especially the land reform and nationalization of the basic branches of the economy — significantly affected the civil law. For instance, the land reform led to the creation of novel types of ownership and to new contractual relations. Nationalization caused many legal-civil problems as well: for example, the question of mortgages and other obligations due on the enterprises taken over by the state.

These and similar reasons prompted the government to start work on a project known as "the unification of the civil law." Its purpose was to replace the remaining enactments inherited from the partitioning powers. Reform of the branches of the civil law which had already been regulated between the wars appeared to be less urgent at that time.

The decision initiating the operation was made by the Council of Ministers as early as June 12, 1945. It left the preparation of specific projects to the Ministry of Justice, whose experts began their work with the elaboration of socio-economic guidelines for individual enactments. The directives were then submitted for evaluation to a special commission composed of representatives of political parties and mass organizations, in addition to governmental officials.

The unification work was greatly influenced by the traditions established by the prewar Codification Commission. The draftsmen, apparently not fully aware of the impact that current socio-political events were about to exert on the concept of law, proceeded to produce progressive provisions the sole intention of which was to embody, systematize, and modernize the applicable legal rules.[24]

These efforts produced amazing results. Within seventeen months not less than nine decrees (two of them passed in 1945) unified all branches of the civil law that had been left intact in the interwar period. There were rules on legal and physical persons, marriage, family, guardianship and curatorship, inheritance, property, mortgages, and general principles of civil law.[25] In addition, new regulations on the maintenance of civil registers,[26] a subject closely related to the family law, were issued.

[24] Jan Topiński, *Prawo Bliżej Życia* ("Law Closer to Life") (Warsaw: Książka i Wiedza, 1964), pp. 46-7.

[25] In chronological order they were:
a. Law on persons, of August 29, 1945, *Dziennik Ustaw* ("Journal of Laws"),

It is self-evident that putting these laws into effect required many subordinate regulations. When one realizes that this formidable undertaking was accomplished after the terrible destruction of the war, during which many of the best Polish lawyers had been killed in concentration camps and the archives and libraries had been ruined or pillaged, the accomplishment must be praised as truly remarkable.

At first it would appear that the most significant merit of the project was the introduction of uniform laws throughout the state. Undoubtedly this is true. Yet we would misunderstand profoundly the significance of this action if we thought of it as intended for a single purpose only. Actually it attempted, and achieved, a number of goals. Unification and reform of the civil law went hand in hand. For instance the marriage law reflected complete secularization, with state courts acquiring exclusive jurisdiction in all pertinent matters. Less thorough were the changes made in family, inheritance, and property law. Characteristically, enactments in the field of property law did not lay down special provisions for the socialized sector, but covered all property rights in one piece of legislation, irrespective of the type of ownership.

As laws were enacted in the course of unification, the idea that their essential role was to protect the public interest was underlined very strongly. It went without saying that the "public interest" was to be interpreted in accordance with the expressed or implied intentions of those who made the laws: i.e., those in whose hands rested the control of the state. The political character of the civil law was made obvious to the courts.

The hint was meant to be heeded, and the judges — not without opposition — began to apply civil law rules, including the prewar ones, in a new class spirit diametrically opposed to the original concept of "private" law. Once begun, the practice played an increasingly influential role in the process of transition from private ownership and free enterprise to a socialist system.

No. 40, Item 223.
b. Law on Marriage, of September 25, 1945, *ibid.*, No. 48, Item 270.
c. Law on Family, of January 22, 1946, *ibid.*, No. 6, Item 52.
d. Law on Guardianship, of May 14, 1946, *ibid.*, No. 20, Item 135.
e. Law on Marital Property, of May 29, 1946, *ibid.*, No. 31, Item 196.
f. Law on Inheritance, of October 8, 1946, *ibid.* No. 60, Item 328.
g. Law on Property, of October 11, 1946, *ibid.*, No. 57, Item 319.
h. Law on Mortgages, of October 11, 1946, *ibid.*, No. 57, Item 320.
i. Law on General Principles of Civil Legislation, of November 12, 1946, *ibid.*, No. 67, Item 67.

[26]Decree of September 25, 1945, *ibid.*, No. 48 Item 272.

In the light of these circumstances, it may seem strange that, in 1947, the Minister of Justice set up a commission the purpose of which was not to create a new civil law, but to produce only a collection of enactments in existence, systematized and improved technically. However, it became clear almost at the beginning that such an effort could not be effective in the rapidly changing environment. A first project, a code of obligations, prepared in 1947, was never enacted. Poland began to enter the second period of its postwar history.

The Second Period

The elimination of Mikolajczyk in 1947 marked the beginning of the second phase in the political and socio-economic conversion of Poland, characterized by the crushing of the "rightist opposition" and the adoption of long-range economic planning. It also signaled the next stage in the transformation of Polish law. Both processes took place in the shadow of growing international conflicts arising out of the "cold war" that ultimately erupted in the Korean War of 1950. No doubt these events exercised a great influence on domestic developments in Poland.

A survey of the changes made in the civil and criminal enactments of that period illustrates once again a strictly pragmatic concept of law. The law was treated merely as a machine effecting orders and interdictions, devoid of the moral and philosophical nature that traditionally justified its existence. The role of law as a humanistic discipline oriented toward the definition of the ethical personality of man was completely disregarded. "Legality" as a concept was utilized strictly to attain for the rulers the most advantageous position in pursuing their socio-political ends. The application of rules so conceived was determined not by their actual formulation, but by their underlying purpose. Criminal law was applied in a specific manner contrary to well-established principles of the rule of law. "Legality" now resulted from "understanding and realizing of Party and government policy."[27] In the civil law, greater emphasis was placed on procedural rules than on legal definition.

CRIMINAL LAW OF THE SECOND PERIOD

The second period witnessed a dual quest. On one hand, the regime wanted to strengthen its position and to enhance its prestige. The yearning

---

[27]Tadeusz Rek, "O roli i zadaniach sądów powszechnych w walce o utrwalenie socjalistycznej praworządności" ("On the Role and Tasks of the Ordinary Courts in the Fight for the Consolidation of Socialist Legality"), *Nowe Prawo* ("New Law"), No. 9 (1951), 4.

for safeguards was paramount. It represented a reaction to the rebellious attitudes of a subdued country and to the growing discords of a divided world. In this sphere, criminal rules were used, as in the first period, to meet current needs and to tune old norms to actual exigencies. As earlier, the repressive and intimidating character of these measures was strongly accentuated.

The attempt to impose a protective straight jacket upon the Polish people through the medium of criminal law manifested itself especially strongly in the decree of August 5, 1949, entitled "On the Protection of the Freedom of Soul and Confession."[28] This law, presumably directed against religious coercion, was in fact another step in the political warfare aimed at a potential enemy not yet subordinated to Party control, the Catholic church. The decree in a significant way helped the regime to interfere with the internal affairs of the Church and to infiltrate her organization with men weakened by the threat or actual application of repression.

While this decree had the intention of disunifying an alleged enemy, the decree issued on October 26, 1949,[29] on the protection of state and service secrets, was enacted to prevent the disclosure of compromising information. Neither of these enactments was concerned with espionage, which was punishable under article 7 of the decree of June 13, 1946.[30] Their purpose was, actually, to stop the spread of adverse news stories.

There was more, however, than a narrow partisan purpose in the statute of December 29, 1950, "on the defense of peace."[31] This law, enacted during the Korean War in line with world-wide Communist propaganda, was surely not free from utilitarian motivation. Yet it was distinguished by an admixture of sound political realism that saw in the war a grave threat not only to the rulers but to the entire nation.

A distinct group of criminal rules was enacted in an attempt to curb so-called "anti-social" crimes. The Marxist expected, somewhat naively, that the abolition of capitalism would *ipso facto* generate among the masses an idealistic attitude toward the socialist state, toward the obligations imposed by "people's authorities," toward labor, and toward socialized property. The reality was disappointing. Not only did the old vices fail to disappear, but they flourished as never before. Encouraged by meager wages, heavy demands, the inability of the legitimate market to satisfy needs, and by organizational deficiencies in the system of

[28]*Dziennik Ustaw* ("Journal of Laws"), No. 45, Item 334.

[29]*Ibid.*, No. 55, Item 437.

[30]See *supra*, fn. 13.

[31]*Dziennik Ustaw* ("Journal of Laws"), No. 58, Item 521.

production and distribution, the "anti-social" crimes reached dangerous proportions. The Communists were unwilling to admit this occurrence. They tried to explain it as a "peripheral" phenomenon resulting from bourgeois mentality. They also undertook to combat it by drastic criminal repressions.

Evidence is easily provided by the statute of April 19, 1950,[32] on the discipline of labor. The preamble to this law sought to justify it as an exceptional act directed against anti-social individuals who harmed the efforts of the great majority of workers displaying "a socialist attitude toward labor." The statute listed penalties for various offenses: among others, absenteeism was punished by "corrective labor," a measure new to Polish codes but long used in the Soviet Union.

Another persistent problem, the poor quality of industrial production, was dealt with in a similar manner. The decree of March 4, 1953[33] was expected unrealistically, to provide a cure by imposing repressive sanctions.

Crimes against socialized property were attacked by the so-called March decrees of the same date. The first of these rules,[34] strictly in accordance with the Soviet model, defined the fraudent conversion of socialized property and provided severe penalties for all forms of such a crime. The second[35] dealt with petty thefts, punishable by imprisonment from six months to one year. It is characteristic that in both cases the restraint of freedom was recognized as the principal and almost exclusive way of protecting socialist property.

While these laws were focused on "anti-social" industrial workers, similar measures were applied against peasants who were not too friendly toward the new rulers and their orders. Here again criminal penalties were provided for propaganda against the regime and for attempts of kulaks and other enemies of the new social system to influence uninformed peasantry.

Criminal repressions in this sphere were basically oriented toward the same old problems. One of the main questions was the food supply of the

[32]*Ibid.*, No. 20, Item 168.

[33]*Ibid.*, No. 16, Item 63.

[34]*Ibid.*, No. 17, Item 68.

[35]*Ibid.*, No. 17, Item 69. For a discussion of this problem, see Leszek Lerner, "Ochrona własności społecznej w polskim prawie karnym dwudziestolecia" ("Twenty Years of Protection of Socialized Property in Polish Criminal Law"), *Państwo i Prawo* ("State and Law"), No. 7 (1964), 64-5.

cities. The laws on the delivery of grain,[36] potatoes[37] meat,[38] and milk[39] all included criminal penalties for those who were derelict in performing their duties. When the shortages still persisted, the government eased restrictions on free market sales by farmers in January 1953; but shortly afterward, several punitive and intimidating criminal sanctions were imposed by the decree of March 4, 1953.[40] Unsatisfactory use of arable land was a constant problem. To deal with it more effectively, the decree of March 30, 1945 was amended by another one of February 9, 1953.[41] It provided a variety of penalties, including fines, corrective labor, and imprisonment, as well as confiscation of property and expulsion from the place of residence.

As the process of lawmaking continued, the need for codification became an urgent matter. Another reason for undertaking this task, perhaps even more important at this time, was the growing desire to create an entirely new criminal law in the spirit of basic ideological, philosophical, and socio-economic concepts of the socialist state. On September 27, 1950, the government passed a resolution[42] to prepare a new criminal code.

Poland was one of the last socialist states of Eastern Europe to take this step. While other socialist countries, except East Germany and Rumania, had already enacted new or partly new criminal codes or were about to do it, the old Polish Criminal Code of 1932 had been retained almost without changes. The reasons for this were plain.[43]

Perhaps the most important was the circumstance that the old code, properly interpreted and supplemented by additional regulations, was found adequate to carry out the criminal policy of the new regime. Another reason was the necessity of utilizing persons trained in old law.

[36]Law of July 23, 1951, *Dziennik Ustaw* ("Journal of Laws"), No. 39, Item 297, replaced by statute of July 10, 1952, *ibid.,* No. 32, Item 214.

[37]Law of October 8, 1951, *ibid.*, No. 52, Item 368, replaced by decree of August 28, 1952, *ibid.,* No. 37, Item 255.

[38]Law of February 15, 1952, *ibid.,* No. 8, Item 46, replaced by decree of December 1, 1953, *ibid.*, No. 50, Item 244.

[39]Law of April 24, 1952, *ibid.,* No. 22, Item 142, replaced by decree of December 1, 1953, *ibid.,* No. 50, Item 245.

[40]*Ibid.,* No. 16, Item 64.

[41]*Ibid.,* No. 11, Item 40.

[42]*Monitor Polski* ("Polish Monitor"), No. A-106, Item 1339.

[43]Igor Andrejew, "W drodze do nowego kodeksu karnego" ("On the Road to a New Criminal Code"), *Państwo i Prawo* ("State and Law"), No. 2 (1966), 196-7.

Certainly not without importance was the emotional attachment of the whole generation of Polish lawyers to the code that had been produced by them and had survived the German occupation. Equally significant was the widely recognized fact that the Criminal Code of 1932 was a truly modern work, highly praised for its excellent content and for the "classic architectural lines"[44] of its structure.

The task of preparing a new criminal code was assigned to the Minister of Justice, who acted through a special consulting scholarly commission of legal experts. The project was expected to be ready by the fall of 1951. The commission was quite expeditious and finished the assignment on time. The project was submitted to an extensive review which continued until 1954 and resulted in the publication of a revised version in 1956. By then, however, a new climate already prevailed and the project was severely criticized. Consequently, it was decided to start the work all over again.

Future legal historians probably will be able to inquire into and discover all the causes of this failure. However, a view may be already advanced that the project was defeated not only because of the unreasonable harshness of its provisions, but also because of the radical departure from its Polish predecessor in favor of the Soviet model, the Federal Penal Code of 1926.[45] The anonymous consultants and specialists decided, for ideological reasons, to apply elements quite novel in Polish law. Their zeal carried them so far that they radically changed not only the content of legal provisions, but also their terminology and style. This approach was resented by many Polish lawyers. They understood and accepted the need for new institutions, and realized the benefits of a new and harmonious code. But they questioned the wisdom of change for its own sake. When in 1956 their voices could be heard more clearly, the project met its ignominious end.

CIVIL LAW OF THE SECOND PERIOD

The development of the civil law in general during the second period was influenced by the contents of various statutes issued in response to the needs of the socialized economy. These rules and subordinate regulations

---

[44]Mieczysław Szerer, "Uwagi na temat projektu kodeksu karnego"" ("Remarks on the Subject of the Project of the Criminal Code"), *ibid.*, No. 3 (1963), 414.

[45]Z. Szirmai, ed. *The Federal Criminal Law of the Soviet Union* (Leyden: A. W. Sythoff, 1959).

brought into existence novel forms of ownership, placed everyone in planned economic orbits, and determined the substance of legal relationships.

To understand this process, let us recall the effects of the decree of October 26, 1950,[46] on state enterprises. This law, establishing for those enterprises a new and less centralized organizational structure, included several provisions of importance to the civil law. In particular, it amplified the rule that a state enterprise was invested with a special legal capacity circumscribed by the plans specifically assigned to it. Dealings beyond those limits had no legal consequences. In addition, the decree laid down several other rules that could become the source of rights or obligations under the civil law.[47]

The effects of the three laws of May 21, 1948,[48] and of the statute of December 20, 1949,[49] which drastically reformed the system of co-operatives, were similar. Among others, they led to the creation of the first co-operatives of agricultural production, a goal long sought by the regime in its drive for the collectivization of farming.[50] The formation of this type of socialist agriculture resulted in specific, often highly complicated, legal relations. As an example, the question of ownership may be mentioned. Production co-operatives consisted of members who had brought into the association their land and farm stock without legally transferring the ownership. Their enjoyment of property rights was restricted, however. A member could not, except by a testament, dispose of his share, and the use of it was reserved to the co-operative. The creation of such co-operatives introduced a novel form of property right previously unknown to the Polish civil law.[51] In case of a withdrawal, the members could claim only an equivalent amount of land situated on the fringes of the co-operative's total holdings.

Many of these laws had a far-reaching impact on consensual obligations arising out of economic relations between socialized enterprises. Thus far

[46]*Dziennik Ustaw* ("Journal of Laws"), No. 49, Item 493.

[47]Stefan Buczkowski *et al.*, "Prawo cywilne" ("Civil law"), *op. cit.* in fn., 7, pp. 175-6.

[48]*Dziennik Ustaw* ("Journal of Laws"), No. 30, Items 199, 200, and 201.

[49]*Ibid.*, No. 65, Item 524.

[50]Z. Nagórski, Sr., *op. cit*, fn. 20, p. 27.

[51]Józef Fiema and Henryk Świątkowski, "Problematyka prawna rolnictwa" ("Legal Problems of Agriculture"), *op. cit,* in fn. 7, p. 261.

their dealings had been governed either by the prewar codes[52] or by administrative acts which established legal obligations and rights between the parties. The latter procedure, applied to the distribution of the so-called "deficit articles," was clearly predominant. In both cases the situation was not satisfactory.

New laws, reflecting stricter discipline, amplified the use of contracts. In the majority of cases, contractual relations were subject to new rules.

The first enactments in this field were the statute of November 18, 1948,[53] and the order of the Council of Ministers of February 19, 1949,[54] which was based on this enactment. Jointly, they established legal foundations for contracts entered into by state enterprises among themselves, with the co-operatives and in some cases with private parties. These acts were later supplemented by the statute of April 19, 1950, [55] the decree of October 29, 1952,[56] and by other regulations.

It is interesting to note, in this connection, the role played by judicial and arbitration tribunals.[57] The latter, created especially for the settlement of disputes between socialized enterprises,[58] became not only official interpreters of the laws enacted after World War II, but also reformers of the prewar rules established by the Code of Obligations and the Commercial Code. Modifications resulted either from the appearance of new institutions, or, more often, from the necessity of adjusting old rules to rapidly changing economic relations. Frequently the arbitration tribunals went even further and completely disregarded prewar laws. Sometimes, however, their decisions were in accordance with traditional principles.

The government also found it necessary to take care of other particularly urgent matters. Thus were passed the two acts of 1950

---

[52]The Code of Obligations of October 27, 1933, and the Commercial Code of June 27, 1934.

[53]*Dziennik Ustaw* ("Journal of Laws"), No. 63, Item 494.

[54]*Ibid.*, No. 12, Item 73.

[55]*Ibid.*, No. 21, Item 180.

[56]*Ibid.*, No. 44, Item 301.

[57]Witold Czachórski, *Zarys Prawa Zobowiązań* ("Outline of the Law of Obligations") (Warsaw: Państwowe Wydawnictwo Naukowe, 1962, pp. 23-5.

[58]Decree of August 5, 1949, *Dziennik Ustaw* ("Journal of Laws"), No. 46, Item 340, amended by statute of May 25, 1951, *ibid.*, No. 31, Item 239.

reforming the patent law;[59] the statute of March 28, 1952, on state insurance;[60] and the statute of July 10, 1952, on copyrights.[61]

As time passed and the enactments multiplied, the need of a new codification became increasingly urgent. The necessity was accentuated by the fact that a number of regulations enacted in previous years became, for various reasons, obsolete. For example, the rules on testaments and on contractual matrimonial property relations were not applied almost from the date of their inception.

The first reformist step was taken with the passage, on July 18, 1950, of two statutes[62] which comprised the General Principles of Civil Law. The enactment of those general provisions was justified by the desire to provide a common ground for a uniform application and interpretation of rules promulgated outside of the existing codes. However, the impact of the General Principles, with but a few significant exceptions was rather trifling.[63]

Of greater importance was the reform of the marriage law accomplished in the statute passed on June 27, 1950.[64] This new code introduced, to a much greater degree than those of 1945 and 1946, socialist concepts of family organization and relations. It is interesting to note that the reform was prepared by a commission composed of both Polish and Czechoslovakian lawyers.

The drive for reform was reinforced by the resolution of the government of September 27, 1950 which instructed the Minister of Justice to prepare a new civil code. The task was declared "an urgent and indispensable matter." The Minister, in turn, appointed a commission composed of a few experts from among theoreticians, justices of the Supreme Court, and representatives of the arbitration commission. The work was begun.

Codes grow slowly, however. Four years elapsed between the government's resolution of 1950 and the publication of the first draft in 1954. An extensive debate ensued afterwards and caused a revision of the

---

[59]Statute of July 18, 1950, *ibid.*, No. 36, Item 331, and decree of October 12, 1950, *ibid.*, No. 47, Item 428, amended by statute of December 29, 1951, *ibid.*, No. 3, (1952), Item 17.

[60]*Ibid.*, No. 20, Item 130.

[61]*Ibid.*, No. 34, Item 234.

[62]*Ibid.*, No. 34, Items 311 and 312.

[63]"Prawo cywilne w XX-leciu PRL" ("Twenty Years of Civil Law of the PPR"), *Prawo i Życie* ("Law and Life"), No. 25 (1964), 5.

[64]*Dziennik Ustaw* ("Journal of Laws"), No. 34, Items 308 and 309.

project. The modified text again appeared in print toward the end of 1955. By that time, however, the "thaw" or more liberal trend, was being felt and the draft had no chance of becoming law. Actually, it was never submitted by the government to parliamentary scrutiny.

What was the main cause of the failure? Several factors contributed to it, but two reasons were particularly significant. The first was political. The years 1948-56, later euphemistically called "the time of errors and distortions," brought forth numerous laws and bureaucratic regulations which attempted to change radically the socio-economic order of the country and to adjust it to the Soviet scheme. The nature and speed of the superimposed reforms left no chance for legal principles to ripen and become worthy of inclusion in a civil code. The second cause, closely related to the first, was organizational. The task was assigned to small groups of men who, though experts in law, were unable to assess correctly the needs of their society. At first, acting in the spirit of the time, they worked in isolation and disregarded public opinion. Later, the public condemned their work. Thus the fate of the draft civil code was similar to that of the criminal code.

The Third Period

The events of 1956 opened a third period of postwar Polish history. It appeared, at this time, self-evident that in order to eradicate the "errors of the past" and to erect an effective bulwark against a new "personality cult in government", it was imperative to raise the laws to their proper place in national-life. A fundamental reform of both criminal and civil laws became a *conditio sine qua non* of the intended revival of legality.

The voice of public opinion, spurred by the Polish Lawyers' Association and the press, found official approbation. On August 23, 1956, the Council of Ministers[65] established a new Codification Commission for the purpose of preparing criminal and civil codes. The commission was expeditious in its efforts and as early as March 1957 the first reports on its progress appeared in the press. Significantly, contrary to the 1951 development, the advance in the criminal field lagged behind.

CRIMINAL LAW OF THE THIRD PERIOD

A draft of the penal code was prepared by a team of a dozen theoreticians and practitioners of law; characteristically, there was not a

---

[65]Order No. 227, *Monitor Polski* ("Polish Monitor"), No. 70, Item 856.

single attorney among them. The group was chaired by a Justice of the Supreme Court, Dr. Mieczysław Szerer. After four years of work, at the end of January 1961, a three-man commission (Jerzy Sawicki, Włodzimierz Winawer, and Władyslaw Wolter) prepared a final text, incorporating proposals of the team's members, introducing uniform terminology and style, and adding a short legal dictionary. In February 1961 the draft was reviewed by the entire team, and on March 5, 1961, the weekly, *Prawo i Życie ("Law and Life")*, reported on its first page that the draft was accepted and would be submitted to a public discussion prior to official governmental action.

For reasons not generally known, the draft was not published until January 1963.[66] The printed text, preceded by a preamble, traditional in socialist codes, consisted of 433 articles, of which 124 formed a general part and the remainder a part dealing with particular offenses. The 1963 draft code contained approximately 140 articles more than the Criminal Code of 1932. It was also more extensive than criminal codes enacted at about the same time in other socialist states such as Hungary (340 articles) or Czechoslovakia (301 articles).

Two basic causes accounted for the difference from the 1932 predecessor. First, the new project included provisions on new offenses not covered by the old code, especially on transgressions against the security of the state and the so-called economic crimes. Second, while the 1932 code was highly synthetic, the new project was very casuistic, full of hair-splitting distinctions, and abundant in lengthy explanations. Obviously it was prepared not only for the use of qualified lawyers but also less qualified enforcement personnel. The project became an object of a wide public discussion in which not only lawyers participated but representatives of other social groups, including workers. The media of mass communication (press, radio and television) gave the debate very extensive publicity. Unquestionably, the issue aroused public opinion.

On the whole, the project was widely and aggressively censured. Criticism was shared by lawyers and laymen alike. Apologetic voices were rare and timid.

When one examines the objections raised by the critics, one finds, without much surprise, that the technical side of the project became the principal target of the attackers. The critics pointed out that the new draft only refashioned the old code, destroying in the process the qualities of the prototype, especially its compactness, clarity, and elasticity. They gave

---

[66]Komisja Kodyfikacyjna przy Ministrze Sprawiedliwości (Codification Commission by the Minister of Justice), *Projekt Kodeksu Karnego* ("The Criminal Code Project") (Warsaw: Wydawnictwo Prawnicze, 1963).

concrete examples to demonstrate how certain paragraphs, articles, and even whole chapters could be shortened or entirely eliminated.

In addition, however, the critics discovered and emphasized the incompleteness of the draft; its authors, contrary to the purpose of codification, had not included all of the most important criminal laws. Thus, they omitted rules on juvenile delinquency, on the protection of socialized property, on smuggling, and on many other topics. The justification advanced by the authors — that they had omitted only matters of a more or less transitory character — was found entirely unconvincing. It is worthwhile to add at this point that among the most significant omissions were the rules of the penal military code.

In addition to these formal objections, much criticism of a deeper nature was expressed. To describe all points raised is beyond the scope of the present inquiry. A few must be mentioned, however.

A problem was repeatedly discussed which was crucial to the future of the entire project. Its nature was ideological. The Marxist theory regards the law as a superstructure originating from economic relations and firmly linked with the state, with which it will gradually "wither away" as socialism develops. Consequently, the evolution of criminal law should constantly reflect the tendency toward step-by-step elimination of intimidating and coercive measures as they are replaced by a socio-educational and corrective approach.

The project, however, appeared to represent a step backward. Instead of relenting, the new code showed a tendency toward excessive penalizing. Indeed, it appears at the first sight that this was the main purpose of the code. If this conclusion appears premature, one can hardly escape it after further considering at least two aspects of the matter.

The first one is the system of penalties. It is evident that the proposed criminal rules would interfere with the personal and family life of the citizens. It is significant that such statements were enunciated not only by private persons but also by the Minister of Justice and the chairman of the Codification Commission.[67] Surveying the project, a critic, Maria Ossowska, voiced what seemed to be a general anxiety that the code could, if so applied, keep all in terror, for certain of its provisions would make everyone feel like a criminal.[68] Furthermore, the authors of the project demonstrated their indifference to doctrinal demands also in other respects. The Marxists assert that the socialist states are already moving toward communism and that this transition is reflected in a gradual

[67]*Trybuna Ludu* ("People's Tribune"), April 19, 1964.

[68]Maria Ossowska, "Ogólne refleksje związane z projektem nowego kodeksu karnego" ("General Reflections in Connection with the Project of a New Criminal Code"), *Państwo i Prawo* ("State and Law"), No. 5-6 (1963), 898.

transfer of state functions to social organizations. The "people's courts" and the "people's militia" are quoted as two examples of this process. The project, however, did almost nothing to emphasize and facilitate the fulfilment of this idea. It did not provide for a possibility of transferring certain cases from the jurisdiction of regular courts to social courts and did not make any effort to delimit their future jurisdiction.

The system of penalties has been branded as orthodox, indiscriminate, out of step with contemporary findings of sociology and psychology, and above all, eminently repressive and intimidating. The death penalty was not only retained, but the number of cases in which it could be imposed was significantly increased. Altogether eighteen articles of the draft allowed the application of capital punishment. Characteristically, eight of these articles referred to political crimes directed against the regime. What a striking, though surely inadvertent, admission of the authors' feelings about the popularity of the government! Did their attitude reflect the rulers' sense of insecurity?

It may be suggested that this supposition is a little farfetched. The harshness of penalties for political crimes, and the priority given to them above crimes against humanity, might be a good indication of the actual situation, but one could hardly say that it seriously indicated that the government was sitting on a powder keg. Rather, it demonstrated the authors' over-zealousness and their inadequate understanding of the intricacies of Marxist dialectic. Whatever the causes, the comminatory character of the proposed code was not imaginary.

The intimidating character of the project was further amplified by the inclusion of provisions punishing offenses which, for all practical purposes, could not be proven, such as the production of substandard goods or the refusal to render services. This approach, based on the concept of a legal rule known as *lex imperfecta*, was applied solely for the purpose of deterring potential offenders.[69]

Other comments on the substance of the project centered around a different shortcoming of the draft: its lack of coherence. Several features could be cited to illustrate this criticism. Two, however, seem to be most representative.

One feature contrasted strongly with the project's overall casuistry and tendency toward detail. This was the appearance of the so-called normative provisions which, contrary to the old code, left to the judge the determination of whether an act was criminal or not and how "socially dangerous" it was. This matter, apparently of a technical nature, had, in fact, great social and political significance. One critic has very properly

[69]Jerzy Milewski, "Projekt kodeksu, czyli: co nowego? " ("Project of a Code, or: What's New? "), *Życie i Myśl* ("Life and Thought"), No. 3-4 (1963), 8.

noted that the retention of many of the "normative provisions" would create a potential danger to the concept of legality.[70]

Of course it could be said that in criminal proceedings the total elimination of judicial discretion in the evaluation of facts is practically impossible. It could be also theorized that the inclusion of normative provisions manifested trust in the judges who would have to interpret the norms and evaluate factual situations. Both arguments are unquestionably reasonable. But why then, asked another commentator, after endowing a judge with such power, put on him a straitjacket of extremely detailed rules?[71]

A second objection against inconsistency was related to the avowed harshness of the penalties. Here the critics pointed out that while the proposed code was in general highly, even excessively, repressive, the penalties for certain offenses were surprisingly mild. For instance, the punishment of persons convicted of major economic crimes was rather light.

The list of unfavorable comments could be easily continued, yet it would be wrong to conclude that there was nothing good in the draft. Positive elements existed as well, and they were praised by the critics. Two examples, at least, deserve mention. One is the abolition of imprisonment for life. The limits of time of confinement were set from one month to twenty-five years. Another is the concept of a "combined guilt," new to Polish law. While the 1932 code, following the Roman tradition, recognized as offenses only acts in which either wrongful default (*culpa*) or wilful injury (*dolus*) could be proven, the new project introduced a third kind of guilt. Its essence consisted in the conscientious creation of a situation fraught with danger. The consequence is of decisive importance. The value of this theoretical development will surely be appreciated by all dealing with traffic offenses.

But the merits of the project could not conceal its many and grievous shortcomings. The fact that even the authors did not think of their work as destined for long existence[72] did not help. The intensity of public interest in the draft code was great; and open, almost unanimous, disapproval was expressed. In the post-October political climate the *vox populi* could not be ignored.

On April 16, 1964, the Presidium of the Codification Commission met in the presence of the Minister of Justice and decided to appoint a new

[70]*Ibid.*

[71]Eugeniusz Bartkowicz, "Blaski i cienie kodyfikacji" ("Lights and Shadows of Codification"), *ibid.*, p. 22.

[72]Filip Graboś, "Chcemy dociec prawdy" ("We Want To Find the Truth"), *Prawo i Życie* ("Law and Life"), No. 4 (1963), 5.

team for the purpose of redrafting the penal code. The size of the group was increased to twenty-two. Among the members were five university professors, one member of the bar, and three men not identified as to profession. The remainder was more or less equally divided among judges and other public officials, including the Vice-Minister of Justice, Kazimierz Zawadzki. Significantly, the list of new appointees did not include the names of Messrs. Szerer, Winawer, and Sawicki. To head the team, the Presidium appointed the President of the Criminal Chamber of the Supreme Court, Franciszek Wróblewski. As section chairmen were appointed Dr. Igor Andrejew, Professor of Criminal Law, University of Warsaw; Dr. Jerzy Bafia, Director of the Legislative Division in the Ministry of Justice; and Mr. Kryspin Mioduski, Justice of the Supreme Court. The draft was to be ready by the end of 1965.

However, this deadline was not met, and by the middle of 1966 nothing had come out publicly about the team's work. In May of 1966 an editorial in *Prawo i Życie*, signed by Kazimierz Kąkol, himself a member of the drafting group, mentioned *in passim* that the preparations were in progress, but he did not hint when the work might be completed. As to the direction of the team's efforts, Mr. Kąkol only stated that some "anachronistic" rules of the early periods of "building socialism" in Poland would be discarded. He added that certain demagogic demands of a "liberal character" would be rejected as well.[73]

While the time when a new penal code will be adopted is still uncertain,* the country faces two problems of unusual proportions. One is the question of juvenile delinquency, and the other the question of economic crimes.

The problem of juvenile delinquency, though not limited to socialist countries alone, is played down by their governments in an obvious effort to show the superiority of the socialist system. Officials quote statistics emphasizing either a decline, or at least a stabilization, in the number of offenses committed by teen-agers in postwar years. When the figures show a relative increase in the crime rate, it is always explained by "infiltration from without" by ideologically alien publications, films, etc. But in spite of these efforts, the issue remains, and has caused serious concern for all responsible elements.

In Poland, as in other socialist states,[74] the problem is twofold. Not only is the percentage of offenses committed by juveniles increasing, but

*Finally adopted in 1969.

[73]Kazimierz Kąkol, "Praworzadność ("Legality"), *ibid.*, No. 10 (1966), 1.

[74]Maria Regent-Lachowicz, "Przestępczość nieltnieh" ("Criminality of Teenagers"), *ibid.* No. 22 (1964), 1 and 5.

their character becomes progressively more dangerous.[75] It is interesting to note the growing number of crimes "for kicks."

Obviously, the problem requires a new approach and new regulations. As yet, however, the question is still handled in Poland on the basis of the 1932 Criminal Code. Luckily, its elasticity permits the application of old rules to novel situations. Although the need for new rules is generally recognized, there is a lack of agreement on how they should be enacted. While some favor the separation of law on juvenile delinquency from the penal code, others insist on its inclusion.

In postwar Polish criminal law, the rules directed against economic offenses, together with those aimed at "counter-revolutionaries," have occupied a prominent place. While, however, the latter have remained basically unchanged since 1946, the former have been constantly revised and sharpened.

The so-called "March decrees" of 1953[76] were replaced by new laws which tried to meet new forms of economic crime. As before, they were highly repressive and their primary purpose was to prevent such crimes by intimidation.[77]

A typical example is the statute of January 21, 1958,[78] which established as the minimum punishment for stealing socialized property valued over 50,000 zł. or 100,000 zł. imprisonment of five or eight years, respectively. To the same category belonged the statutes of May 29, 1957,[79] on the conditional release of prisoners, and of June 18, 1959,[80] on criminal liability for economic offenses, as well as many others.

There appeared, however, a new feature distinguishing the laws of the third period from their predecessors. It was the introduction of penalties of an economic character. They took one of three forms: obligatory fines, compensation for loss, and "smart money" (additional damages assessed

---

[75]Kazimierz Wągiel, "Margines" ("Margin"), *ibid.*, No. 13 (1966), 5 and 7.

[76]See *supra*, fn. 34, 35.

[77]Leszek Lerner, *Przestępczość Gospodarcza ("Economic Crimes")* (Warsaw: Wydawnictwo Prawnicze, 1965), p. 195.

[78]"Ustawa o wzmożeniu ochrony własności społecznej" ("The Statute on the Increase of Protection of Socialized Property"), *Dziennik Ustaw* ("Journal of Laws"), No. 4 (1958), Item 11.

[79]"Ustawa o warunkowym zwolnieniu osób odbywających karę pozbawienia wolności" ("The Statute on Conditional Release of Persons Serving Prison Terms"), *ibid.*, No. 31, Item 134.

[80]"Ustawa o odpowiedzialności karnej za przestępstwa przeciwko własności społecznej" ("The Statute on Criminal Responsibility for Crimes against Socialized Property"), *ibid.*, No. 36, Item 228.

against a defendant for gross misconduct). The tendency to move from imprisonment as the principal sanction, toward economic punishment was first expressed in the statute of January 21, 1958, and found its full expression in the statute of June 18, 1959.

However, this development did not appeal to all. In 1960 the official organ of the Association of Polish Lawyers, *Prawo i Życie*, opened a debate on the criminal policy regarding economic crimes.[81] The discussion, in which many practicing attorneys participated, emphasized many important aspects of the problem. It was unanimously stressed, for example, that the repressive economic policy could serve only as a subsidiary force in the fight against economic offenses.

The discussion was concerned very largely with the question of distinguishing between big and small offenses against socialized property. It was suggested that the penalties for serious crimes should be made still more severe, perhaps by an automatic invocation of martial procedure. On the other hand, it was proposed that the repressive policy against lesser offenders be modified by substituting short-term jail sentences, by limiting certain socio-economic rights of the lawbreakers, by simplifying judicial procedures, and by transferring certain transgressions from regular to social courts.

While some of these proposals were resented (e.g., the limitation of socio-economic rights), others were generally approved. Consequently, the Polish parliament (*Seym*) passed a bill transferring petty offenses against socialized property from regular courts to social courts in the spring of 1966. The main purpose of the statute was the substitution of harmful short-term jail sentences applied by the regular courts by economic repression to be applied and executed in a speedy and simplified manner. The most severe penalties allowed under the new law are a fine of 4,500 zł. or a three-month arrest. In special cases, the social judges may abstain from imposing a penalty and may pronounce an admonishment or other correctional measure instead. In other cases, the chairman of the social court may transfer the case to the offender's place of work without initiating formal criminal proceedings.

On the whole the law was well received. An enthusiastic admirer did not miss the opportunity of praising the statute as a manifestation of the "withering away" of the state.[82]

[81]Walery Namiotkiewicz, "Uwagi w sprawie polityki represyjnej" ("Remarks on the Policy of Repressions"), *Prawo i Życie* ("Law and Life"), No. 22 (1960), 1 and 7.

[82]Michał Grendys, "Odpowiedzialność za drobne przestępstwa" ("Responsibility for Petty Offenses"), *ibid.*, No. 14 (1966), p. 2.

The third period finally set the stage for a successful codification of civil law in Poland. It was not accidental that this important feat was accomplished during the years marked by a general change in the political climate. Obviously the earlier era was not conducive to the fruition of legal thought. One may point out the sudden surge in codifying activities in almost all states of Eastern Europe after the Stalinist era. Hungary and Czechoslovakia adopted new civil codes, and other countries started preparatory work. In the Soviet Union, the well known "Principles of Civil Law" of December 8, 1961, led to the enactment of civil codes in many union republics.

Codification is not an easy task under any circumstance, but it is particularly complicated in a socialist state determined upon a rapid, revolutionary transformation of existing relations. A constantly changing situation made the pursuit doubly difficult. On the one hand, it was difficult to determine which rules had already achieved stability and deserved to be incorporated into the code. On the other, the rules could not be petrified to a degree destroying their adaptability to changes in the socio-economic system. Last but not least, codifiers could not violate Marxist dogma and create a legal superstructure which preceded developments in the economic base.

The task of preparing a project of the Polish civil code was assigned to a team of nearly a dozen people, presided over at first by Marowski and later by Szer.[83] The main section chairman of the draft was Professor Wasilkowski, Chief Justice of the Supreme Court, assisted by Professor Wolter. Other members of the team prepared papers on particular aspects of the project. The team started to work in December 1956 and completed the assignment in about five years, during which the members held 223 meetings.

The proceedings were marked by three stages, or readings. After the first stage was completed, the draft was printed in 1960 and submitted to public discussion.[84] The debate lasted for several months and included many participants from within and without the legal profession. In the meantime, the team completed a short second reading devoted mainly to technical legal questions. The third reading started in October 1960 and consisted mainly of an analysis of opinions and views expressed during the

[83]Aleksander Wolter, "Nowy projekt kodeksu cywilnego" ("New Project of the Civil Code"), *Państwo i Prawo* ("State and Law"), No. 2 (1962), pp. 210-8.

[84]K. Grzybowski, *op. cit. supra*, fn. 3, pp. 11-37. Also see Jan Wasilkowski, "Zagadnienia kodyfikacji prawa cywilnego" ("Problems of Codification of Civil Law"), *Nowe Drogi* ("New Ways"), No. 11 (1960), pp. 27-38.

public discussion of the project.[85] In the last round, the draft was discussed by the Presidium of the Codification Commission which, after introducing a few amendments, decided to submit the project to the Minister of Justice for further action. The final version of the draft was published in December 1961.[86]

Following publication, the project underwent inter-ministerial consultations during which several proposals were suggested by interested officials. The suggestions were referred back to the Presidium of the Codification Commission and served as the basis for appropriate modifications. This new version was approved by a collegium of the Ministry of Justice and then submitted for the approval of the Council of Ministers. On February 7, 1963, after introducing about fifty changes, the Council of Ministers resolved to submit the proposal for enactment by the *Seym*. One of the main changes consisted in the exclusion from the draft of rules on the inheritance of farms, as another bill specifically devoted to that subject was simultaneously being prepared.

In the Seym, the draft was referred to the Judiciary Committee[87] for detailed examination. This committee, acting through specially created subcommittees and in co-operation with other permanent committees of the Seym, scrutinized the project for about two years with the help of experts from all pertinent fields. The work of the committee was prolonged by the decision of the government to re-introduce into the project the rules on the inheritance of farms which in the meantime had been passed by the Seym.[88] With more than 100 of the amendments introduced by the committee, (none of a basic nature),[89] the project was adopted by the Seym on April 26, 1964. On May 18 of that year the Civil Code was published in the official journal,[90] and on the same day a part of it, referring to limitations on the subdivision of agricultural land,

[85] Jan Wasilkowski and Aleksander Wolter, "Wyniki dyskusji publicznej nad projectem Kodeksu Cywilnego" ("The Results of Public Discussion on the Project of the Civil Code"), *Prawo i Życie* ("Law and Life"), No. 22 (1961), 1.

[86] *Projekt Kodeksu Cywilnego* ("The Project of the Civil Code") (Warsaw: Wydawnictwo Prawnicze, 1961).

[87] For more information, see Vincent C. Chrypiński, "Legislative Committees in Polish Lawmaking," *Slavic Review*, XXV, No. 2 (June 1966), 250.

[88] "Ustawa z 29 kwietnia 1963 r.o ograniczeniu podziału gospodarstw rolnych" ("The Statute of April 29, 1963 re: Limitations on Subdividing of Agricultural Households"), *Dziennik Ustaw* ("Journal of Laws"), No. 28, Item 168.

[89] Jan Winiarz, "KC," *Prawo i Życie* ("Law and Life"), No. 1 (1965), 5.

[90] "Kodeks Cywilny PRL" ("The Civil Code of the PPR"), *Dziennik Ustaw* ("Journal of Laws"), No. 16 (1964), Item 93.

became operative. The remaining parts of the Code became effective on January 1, 1965. It is interesting to note that on the very same date the Family Code[91] and the Code of Civil Procedure[92] went into effect as well.

A few important features of the new code should be pointed out, mainly to show its differences from the old law and to indicate some of the more interesting solutions.

Perhaps it should be mentioned first that with the enactment of the Civil Code, the Code of Obligations of 1933 and the Commercial Code of 1934 were abrogated. Many rules particular to these codes are included in the Civil Code and may be found there either grouped in special sections (e.g., Part III: Obligations) or in provisions spread over other parts. The elimination of the two old enactments was explained as an adjustment of the legal superstructure to changes in the economic base. The old rules regulated relations existing among private persons, physical or legal, and served their private economic interests. Socialization of the means of production eliminated transactions motivated by private goals and regulated by private law norms. Instead, the new relations were motivated by "integrated social goals" and subordinated to some other overriding principles, especially those concerning economic planning. However, the rules on planning itself are not of a civil nature and cannot be found in the Civil Code.[93]

Another aspect deserves brief mention as well: the omission of rules on family relations, which are normally found in civil codes. The issue was hotly debated by the Codification Commission, which at first decided to return to the traditional approach and re-incorporate the Family Code of 1950, with appropriate changes, into the Civil Code. Accordingly, the draft submitted to public discussion in 1960 included a section on family relations. Finally, however, the Commission decided to prepare a separate family code.[94]

This decision resulted from a combination of factors. Probably crucial was the tendency of socialist legal theoreticians to treat family law not as a

[91]"Kodeks Rodzinny i Opiekuńczy z 25 lutego 1964 r." ("The Family and Guardianship Code of February 25, 1964"), *ibid.*, No. 9, Item 59.

[92]"Kodeks Postępowania Cywilnego z 17 listopada 1964 r." ("The Code of Civil Procedure of November 17, 1964"), *ibid.*, No. 43, Item 296.

[93]Jan Topiński, "Nowy kc w gospodarce uspołecznionej" ("The New Civil Code in Socialized Economy"), *Prawo i Życie* ("Law and Life"), No. 1 (1965), 5.

[94]Adam Zieliński, *O Nowym Kodeksie Rodzinnym i Opiekuńczym* ("On the New Family and Guardianship Code") (Warsaw: Wydawnictwo Prawnicze, 1965), pp. 25-8.

portion of civil law, but as a distinct branch of its own.[95] Undoubtedly of great influence was the existence of separate family codes in other socialist states, including Bulgaria (1949), Czechoslovakia (1963), Hungary (1952), Rumania (1953), and Yugoslavia (1946). Finally, public discussion reinforced the position of those who from the beginning were in favor of separate solutions.

Finally, it is worthwhile to note that the codification did not cover matters relating to mortgages, but left in force the rules already in existence. This topic, though not of primary importance in a socialist system, must be resolved in the near future because of its applicability to some private property as well (e.g., single-family homes).

Labor law, which is generally recognized as a separate branch of law, also remains outside of the Civil Code. The same is true of some other fields, such as the law on bills of exchange, on checks, on copyrights, and on patents. The authors of the project do not claim to provide complete rules on civil relations. It seems, in fact, that this was not their purpose. Instead, they wanted to cover the most important aspects of these relations and to establish broad principles which might be helpful in the application of more detailed rules. In the light of this idea, it is significant that the Civil Code has a special "general part" laying down such principles. It should be added that this approach did not receive the unanimous praise of socialist scholars.

However, another controversial branch, the so-called economic law, was included by the commission in the project and became an integral part of the Civil Code. Some objections to this action were expressed.[96] In their zeal to be theoretically pure, some opponents considered it necessary to isolate the area of economic relations among socialized enterprises and leave it to a separate law. Others argued that a civil code may have only subsidiary character in this sphere, which was basically regulated by enactments of the superior administrative organs. Still another group wanted to see the auxiliary operation of the civil law applied only to the nationalized sector. Finally, certain writers questioned the timing of the civil codification. They maintained that the whole operation was prema-

[95]Seweryn Szer, *Prawo Rodzinne* ("Family Law")(Warsaw: Państwowe Wydawnictwo Naukowe, 1966), pp. 12-4. It should be noticed, however, that the issue is controversial. For a different view see Witold Czachórski, *Droit de Famille des Pays Socialistes Européens* ("Family Law of the European Socialist Countries") (Warsaw: Państwe Wydawnictwo Naukowe, 1965), p. 3.

[96]Stefan Buczkowski, "Problematyka obrotu uspołecznionego w kodeksie cywilnym" ("Problems of Socialized Transactions in the Civil Code"), *Państwo i Prawo* ("State and Law"), No. 10 (1964), pp. 479-89.

ture because relations in the economic sector, as well as the rules to regulate them, were still in a state of flux.

What effect did all these arguments have upon the commission? In what ways was this body impelled to adjust to the objections? One answer — which already has been indicated — was to disregard the demands of the "purists." Instead, the commission constantly enlarged the area of relations in the socialized sector regulated by the code. The trend resulted from the pressure of views expressed by the economists, who were all in favor of codified rules.

A further word of clarification is needed. The proponents of a separate economic law were unable to produce convincing arguments in support of their views. To make their position worse, similar attempts in the Soviet Union had also ended unsuccessfully. Earlier concepts promoted by Stuchka and Pashukanis were abandoned and the new ones advanced by Pavlov and Tadevosyan heavily assailed. The practice in other socialist states turned against the "purists" as well. The Soviet "Principles of Civil Law" and the Hungarian Civil Code of 1959 both cover economic relations among socialized enterprises.[97]

While the commission favored the principle of the unity of the civil law from the very beginning, its position on the role of the code underwent a certain expansion. At first the commission saw in the code only a subsidiary instrument to be applied when no other governmental regulations existed.[98] Later on, this view was changed so that the code was recognized as a binding source of law for relations in the socialized sector.

The commission stopped short of making the code a supreme and immutable foundation of rules, however. Instead, it gave the government the right to regulate economic relations in the socialized sector in a manner different from those established in the code. Thus, the Council of Ministers or the bodies empowered by it may, whenever they deem it fit, issue regulations without seeking the special authority of enabling acts.[99] In absence of these special enactments, however, the Civil Code is the basis for legal relations in the socialized sector.

The above short summary of how the Civil Code evolved permits one now to take a bird's-eye view of the technique exemplified by that body of law. Following a traditional approach, the first part is devoted to general principles, the common purpose of which is to help the practitioners of law to meet the problems of daily practice. Here, for example, are included rules on the application and interpretation of the

[97]*Ibid.*, p. 480.

[98]K. Grzybowski, *op. cit. supra*, fn. 3, p. 15.

[99]Jan Topiński, *op. cit. supra*, fn. 93, p. 5.

law, on the minimum age for legal transactions, on evidence, on prescription, etc.

The second part contains rules on ownership and other property rights. In Polish legal terminology,[100] property law means rules regulating the content, acquisition, transfer, and loss of positive rights that have reference to things. The concept of "things" covers, in Polish as well as in Soviet law, material parts of nature, in their original or converted form, set apart in a sufficiently definite way to be treated in socio-economic relations as goods existing by themselves. Thus the notion excludes, with a few insignificant exceptions, all which is intangible (e.g., literary and artistic works) as well as material goods forming an integral part of a certain whole (e.g., trees and houses attached to the land).

The third part regulates matters related to basic institutions and principles of the law of obligations. Here belong rules applicable to contractual relations and torts. In addition, this part lays down specific rules on certain obligations (e.g., those based on unjust enrichment).[101]

The fourth part comprises rules on inheritance. It is significant that here are found also regulations on the devolution of peasant farms, earlier incorporated into a special statute. Without question, this is a very sensible addition. Under the existing conditions, the law of inheritance finds application primarily among individual farmers.

It is an established practice in Polish lawmaking that a new statute either includes so-called "introductory provisions" or, if it is a more extensive piece of legislation, is accompanied by a separate introductory law. The purpose of such a practice is to introduce the new law into the complex of legal enactments already in existence. Thus, introductory provisions state which rules are repealed or left in force, what should be done with transactions started under old provisions, what the exact meanings of the terms used are, and what subordinate regulations should be issued (and by whom) in order to make the new statute fully operative.

The Civil Code itself, a highly intricate and comprehensive enactment, is introduced by a special set of provisions. They were, like the code itself, prepared by the Codification Commission and by the *Seym* as a separate statute. Among the provisions of this introductory statute, perhaps the most interesting are those which deal with economic relations among socialized enterprises. While the statute repealed a number of rules of

[100]Jan Wasilkowski, *Zarys Prawa Rzeczowego* ("Outline of the Law of Real Property") (Warsaw: Państwowe Wydawnictwo Naukowe, 1963), pp. 8-9.

[101]For a more detailed examination see W. J. Wagner, "The Interplay of Planned Economy and Traditional Contract Rules in Poland," *American Journal of Comparative Law*, XI (1962), 348-75 and the chapter on General Features of Polish Contract Law in the present volume.

statutory rank, it left intact regulations issued by the Council of Ministers and other central bodies directing the national economy (article 9). The *Seym*, however, adopted a resolution calling on the Council of Ministers to repeal all rules that differed from the provisions of the Civil Code, unless specific needs of the socialist economy required their retention.

The Civil Code includes twenty-five provisions by virtue of which the government is empowered to enact subordinate regulations.[102] The great majority of them are directed to the Council of Ministers and to the Minister of Justice. This rather large number was justified by the desire to leave definite questions, especially those that might require specific changes, to the determination of the government. About two-thirds of these delegations of power are obligatory (i.e., they impose the duty to make appropriate regulations), while others are left to the discretion of the officials to whom they are directed. The extent of the grants of power varies in extent and complexity.

Every law to a certain degree captures and reproduces the spirit of its time. The best way to discover this spirit is to look at the so-called general clauses. They lay down principles serving multiple purposes. They express the principal moral and political character of the legal system. Phrased in broad terms, they form a bridge to extra-legal systems of human behavior. They establish the limits for individual rights. When life outdistances specific rules, general clauses indicate the direction of supplements and corrections. In short, they form the backbone of a system of law and determine its "personality."

Usually the general clauses amplify certain principles. They are often used to declare tenets that are difficult to express in legal terms, and in such cases they serve primarily as directives for the future application of statutes. Without question, general clauses — especially those of the last category — may endanger the stability of the law and increase its ambiguity. Consequently, they may be easily abused for political ends. Their use in postwar Poland offers very convincing proof of such practices.

The Civil Code of 1964 contains general clauses, although their number is not great. A few of them deserve special attention.[103]

The first one is self-explanatory. It is embodied in article 4, which states that the provisions of the Civil Code must be applied and interpreted in conformity with the political system and the goals of the Polish People's Republic.

[102]Adam Zieliński, "Przepisy wykonawcze do k. c. " ("Transitional Laws for the Civil Code"), *Prawo i Życie* ("Law and Life") No. 12 (1965), 3.

[103]Andrzej Stelmachowski, "Klauzule generalne w kodeksie cywilnym" ("General Clauses of the Civil Code"), *Państwo i Prawo* ("State and Law"), No. 1 (1965), 5-20.

Another formula is more complex. It refers to "principles of community life" and may be found in numerous articles of the Civil Code, including article 5, which not only prohibits the exercise of rights contrary to the "principles of community life" but also declares that actions based on such rights are not recognized at all and shall not be protected by the law.

The "principles," modeled after the Soviet prototype, were first introduced into the Polish civil law system in 1950.[104] As a general directive, these principles became criterion by which judgments were rendered in courts and which permitted the curtailment of formally justified individual rights in the name of "socialist morality." The tenet was raised to constitutional rank in the Constitution of 1952 (article 76) to equal such others as conscious fulfillment of one's duties toward the state and the socialist discipline of labor.

The formula has been hailed as a superior substitute for such "meaningless bourgeois principles" as "good faith," "good morals," and "honest dealings."[105] In contrast to such "abstract formulas," the "principles of community life" have been characterized as a concrete social norm that "introduced an objective evaluation of care required in socialist intercourse."[106] Allegedly, they express "the convictions of the majority of society, or of the working people of the towns and villages in their striving to build socialism and liquidate the remnants of the capitalist structure."[107] In the establishment of such principles, "the leading role is played by the consciousness of the workers' class, having hegemony in the society, and being led by its *avant-garde* – the party."[108] Once established, the principles acquire a mandatory force "irrespective of the passive attitude or even resistance of the elements which continue to represent retrogressive or clearly inimical ideas (remnants of the capitalist class)."[109] The principles serve as a "general safety valve" against abuses of rights which, as a general rule, are left by the civil law to be taken advantage of by the interested parties who are entitled to do so.

[104]"Przepisy ogólne prawa cywilnego" ("General Rules of the Civil Law"), article 3.

[105]Jadwiga Goławska, "Zasady współżycia społecznego a nowy kodeks cywilny" ("Principles of Social Co-existence and the New Civil Code"), *Prawo i Życie* ("Law and Life"), No. 12 (1965), 3 and 7.

[106]S. Szer, *Prawo Cywilne, Część Ogólna* ("Civil Law, General Part") (Warsaw: Wydawnictwo Prawnicze, 1955), p. 30.

[107]A. Wolter, *Prawo Cywilne, Część Ogólna* ("Civil Law, General Part") (Warsaw: Państwowe Wydawnictwo Naukowe, 1955), p. 63.

[108]*Ibid.*, p. 64.

[109]*Ibid.*

This argumentation is not very convincing. The lofty phraseology used in an attempt to strengthen the illusion that "socialist principles" are superior to all others, as well as the tendency to equate the "principle of community life" with moral norms[110] cannot conceal the fact that the concept is far from being "concrete." It should not be forgotten that, thus far, the encomiasts failed to give examples of factual situations illustrative of their reasoning. The courts and arbitration commissions are, of course, applying the principle in concrete cases, but they have not succeeded in expounding the doctrine in clear and plain terms. Their decisions, including that of the Supreme Court, are disparate, inconsistent, and inseparably related to highly specific circumstances.[111]

Apologists,[112] however, still look to judicial or arbitration bodies to provide a solid background for satisfactory formulations. Unfortunately, in the absence of theoretical analyses, the courts and arbitration commissions cannot but follow an erratic and often erroneous course from case to case.

While the search for solution continues, critics express fears that imprecision in the formulation of the principle may jeopardize the security of contractual dealings and endanger the entire legal system. They recall the situation that existed under the rule of a similar general formula in the previous period. The careless and mistaken application of the clause, caused either by political motives or simply by ignorance, resulted in dangerous "legal nihilism,"[113] "undermining the obligatory force of legal rules on the ground of their pretended repugnancy to the principles of community life."[114] The apprehension is phrased much more clearly and strongly by Polish legal scholars living in the West who flatly state that the clause "opened the door for ... arbitrariness"[115] and to a "free legal interpretation."[116]

[110] Jadwiga Goławska, *op. cit. supra* fn. 105, p. 3.

[111] Andrzej Stelmachowski, *op. cit. supra* fn. 103, p. 10.

[112] E. g., Jadwiga Goławska, *op. cit. supra*, fn. 105, p. 7.

[113] J. Różański, "O błędach w orzecznictwie niektórych sądów powiatowych w stosowaniu art. 3 p.o.p.c." ("On Errors in Judicial Decisions of Some County Courts in the Application of Article 3 of the P.O.P.C."), *Nowe Prawo* ("New Law"), No. 11-12 (1956), 138.

[114] A. Wolter, *Prawo Cywilne, Zarys Części Ogólnej* ("Civil Law, Outline of the General Part") (Warsaw: Państwowe Wydawnictwo Naukowe, 1963), p. 61.

[115] P. Siekanowicz, "Contracts in Postwar Poland," *Highlights*, No. 5 (1957) (Washington, DC: Library of Congress, mimeographed) p. 493.

[116] Z. Nagórski, "Draft of a New Civil Code for Poland", *Studies of the Association of Polish Lawyers in Exile in the United States,* I (1956), 51, 57.

Whatever variation there may be in emphasis, the common feature in this criticism is the apprehension that the application of the "principles of community life" leads in practice to the disregard of binding laws. The past has been abundant in examples of such practices. There is no guarantee against the reappearance of such abuses in the future.

Similar difficulties are encountered in an effort to define another general clause found in the Civil Code of 1964 – that which speaks about the "socio-economic purpose of the law". The clause is combined with the one on "community life," but its extent is narrower since it applies only to property relations. The exact content of the principle is again a matter for future theoretical analyses and judicial pronouncements.

The new principle is meant to be as a barrier against the "individualistic tradition" of the civil law.[117] Traditionally, legal systems have envisaged the civil law as a body of rules proclaiming, in general, subjective rights, the exercise of which was left to private individuals. These rights served the interests of private persons who, within the legal and moral order of society, could freely determine the goals of their economic activities. Whatever the interested parties agreed upon in their contracts, it received the legal sanction of the state. In the case of violation of a consensual obligation, the injured party could always ask the courts for help.

In a state where the means of production and distribution are socialized, all economic activities, including those of private persons, are subordinate to a single goal determined by national economic plan. Consequently, the civil law has lost its character as the backbone of private economic relations and has become merely an instrument for the realization of the superior purpose of the socialized economy. In addition, the civil law has lost its exclusive position. Instead of being nearly the only element of law in the organization of the national economy, it has become one of a series of lawmaking tools, in addition to administrative, financial, criminal and procedural rules, by which the state arranges its economic life.[118]

The tendency to protect the superior interests of the socialized economy is especially noticeable in the functional concept of property rights.[119] The Civil Code not only introduced a distinction between private and socialized property, but also assigned to the latter, and especially to the nationalized property, a dominant role in the economy of

[117] Andrzej Stelmachowski, *op. cit. supra,* fn. 103, p. 17.

[118] Jan Topiński, *Rozwój, Postęp, Prawo* ("Development, Progress, Law") (Warsaw: Wydawnictwo Prawnicze, 1964), p. 63.

[119] Andrzej Stelmachowski, *op. cit. supra*, fn. 103, p. 17.

the country.[120] This principle, formulated in general terms in article 129, is also expressed in other provisions of the Civil Code. For example, article 127 declares that the protection of socialized property is a duty of every citizen, and article 355 requires special care in the fulfillment of obligations regarding socialized property. The inclusion of the principle of "socio-economic purpose" in the very notion of property (article 140) permits a highly flexible application of the clause in relation to all other appropriate provisions of the Civil Code.

A short account of the three general clauses described above does not exhaust the whole problem. The Civil Code includes many other principles, and almost all of them could serve as topics for a special monographs. Unfortunately, lack of space does not permit even their enumeration. Generally, like the clauses mentioned, they represent an attempt to arm future practitioners of law, and particularly judges, with flexible tools for the continuous development of civil law — along lines conceived by the authors of the Civil Code.

How can the Civil Code be assessed? The answer is not easy. Surely no work is absolutely perfect, and no codification is free from loopholes and uncertainties which open it to future controversies and different interpretations. The Code of 1964 is definitely not free from shortcomings. The critics already complain that the authors sacrificed the clarity of its structure for socio-economic dictates. Instead of completely eliminating the legal confusion brought about by the accumulation of enactments issued at various periods, the Code only partially accomplished this task. Many related rules and institutions were still left outside of the Code.[121]

Yet it would be premature to express a negative opinion about the Code. It is expected that, despite its structural imperfection, the Code by its very existence will form a barrier against a flood of "mimeographed laws"[122] made by administrative bodies. It may also be hoped that the Code will better satisfy the needs of society and its members than a series of administrative rules.

---

[120] Jan Wasilkowski, "Metoda opracowania i założenia kodeksu cywilnego" ("The Method of Drafting and the Principles of the Civil Code"), *Państwo i Prawo* ("State and Law"), No. 5-6 (1964), 740.

[121] Aleksander Wolter and Zofia Policzkiewicz-Zawadzka, "Przedawnienie roszczeń według kodeksu cywilnego" ("Prescriptions of Claims According to the Civil Code"), *ibid.*, No. 3 (1965), 373-4.

[122] Stefan Buczkowski, *op. cit. supra*, fn. 96, p. 482.

CONCLUSION

In a socialist state, the law appears to be only a companion to the administrative direction of the national economy. Actually, however, the role of the law is much broader and much more complicated. To understand and evaluate it correctly, legal analysis alone is not enough. This is simply inadequate and misleading. A comprehensible picture can be formed only on the basis of socio-political and economic inquiries. The understanding of factors which led to the enactment of legal norms and which continuously affect their operation is not only indispensable, but absolutely primary.

It may be assumed that the role of law will increase in the new system that is slowly emerging in Eastern Europe. The new economic model, presently in its experimental stage, will definitely require clear legal concepts and well-defined judicial rulings. One of the essential features of the new approach lies in the demand that the law should be used to a greater degree and in a different manner than before. It is certain that in the coming period not only the economists, but lawyers as well, will play an important role.

To meet this important challenge, Polish legal scholars must become bolder and more perceptive in their proposals and criticisms. They must free themselves from slavish repetitions of phrases taken bodily either from Marxist classics or from Soviet sources, and avoid abstract analyses of legal concepts. They must utilize to the fullest the degree of freedom allowed by Moscow since 1956[123] and by all the means at their disposal continue their struggle against the abridgment of individual liberties.[124] The job cannot be done by critics residing abroad, if only for the reason that they are not engaged deeply enough to comprehend fully the role of the law and legal institutions in today's Poland.

[123]John Hazard, "The Soviet Legal Pattern Spreads Abroad," *University of Illinois Law Forum,* Spring 1964, p. 278.

[124]Kazimierz Grzybowski and Jonathan L. Alder, "Eastern European Legislative Trends," *Problems of Communism,* XIV, No. 2 (March-April, 1965), 130.

LUDWIK KOS-RABCEWICZ-ZUBKOWSKI

Polish Constitutional Law*

The Polish state has a history extending over a thousand years into the past. In order to study the development of Polish constitutional law, it is helpful to divide the long history of the Polish state into periods. Scholars differ as to the criteria for the establishment of these constitutional periods.

The author of this study used the growth of participation of citizens in the affairs of the state as the criterion and divided the study into the following periods:

1. *Ius ducale*, starting in the eighth century and ending with the granting of the first privileges in the twelfth century
2. The divided state and the development of the rights of the society until the privilege of Kościce (1374)
3. The development of the estates and the formation of the diet (*sejm*) until the union of Poland with Lithuania (1569)
4. The nobiliar state until the reforms started in 1764
5. The period of reforms, interrupted by the partitions of Poland in 1795
6. The rule of three foreign powers until the reconstitution of the Polish state in 1918
7. The Republic of Poland, 1918-45
8. The Polish People's Republic

The Polish State Until the Twelfth Century

The first reliable information on the Polish state concerns the second half of the tenth century. This source indicates that Poland as a state was

---

*This study is dedicated to the memory of Jàn Laski (1456-1531), Grand Chancellor of the Kingdom of Poland, author of the "Laski Statute" of 1506, and member of my maternal family — LudWik KoS-RabCewicz-ZubKowski.

already well organized at that time. Therefore, it seems quite safe to accept the theory that the Polish state was born as early as the ninth and perhaps even the eighth century. This theory is confirmed by an early written tradition about three predecessors of the first historical prince, Mieszko, of the Piast dynasty, and about the legendary pre-Piast monarch, Popiel. Archeological findings seem to corroborate this contention, and there is no evidence to disprove it.

According to the available sources there were no legal limitations on the prince's power in the early Polish state. Nevertheless, the clans played an important role and exercised some influence on the ruler of the country. The country's organization and legal system, however, were based on *ius ducale* — rules enacted by the prince.

The Divided State, Twelfth Century Until 1374

PRIVILEGES

In the twelfth century, during the period when Poland was divided into several provinces, the warring princes often had to rely on ecclesiastical and secular magnates. In order to obtain support, the princes granted various persons immunity from fiscal duties or exempted them from the jurisdiction of certain officials. Such privileges had at first the character of a personal obligation assumed by the prince and, while irrevocable during prince's life, terminated at his death. Later these privileges were considered as granted in perpetuity.

Furthermore, princes began to grant privileges to certain groups to ensure their loyalty: for example, the clergy and knights of a given area. Such was the privilege granted by Władyslaw Laskonogi in 1228 at Ciernia to the clergy and knights of the lands of Cracow and Sandomir, and such was another privilege granted in 1291 at Lutomyśl. These privileges expired with the prince's death.

As early as 1180 the Roman Catholic church benefited from a privilege granted at tęczyca which abolished the prince's *ius spolii* (taking over of moveables left by a deceased bishop) and revised certain tax abuses of *ius ducale*. This privilege was granted after the church recognized the principle of succession of the junior line of descendants of Casimir the Just, thus according succession to the prince's eldest son. Until that time the principle of the senior had prevailed; it called for succession by the oldest male (thus often by a brother instead of a son of the deceased prince).

The first privilege given to all of Poland, including the cities, was granted in 1355 at Buda by Louis d'Anjou, king of Hungary, to become effective at the time of his ascension to the throne of Poland in 1370.

216

MONARCHS

The first historical ruler of Poland, Mieszko (Mieczysław I), who baptised Poland in 966, did not have the title of king. His son, Bolesław Chrobry (the Brave), was crowned king of Poland, with papal consent, in 1025.

The second crowned ruler was Mieszko II, crowned in 1025; he had to renounce his title after being defeated by the German emperor about 1034. Next was Bolesław Śmiały (the Bold) (1058-79), crowned in 1076. During the following two centuries there were no crowned rulers of Poland.

The succession to the throne was governed by the rules of private law, the state being considered as the prince's property – a patrimonial concept – with the possibility of division at his death. Each of the male descendants could claim the inheritance of a province, but the prince reserved the right to decide in his will which province would be left to a given descendant. Were there no male descendants, the prince could will his land to one or several collaterals, not necessarily the closest relatives. However, the Polish state remained undivided until 1139, one of the heirs in each case banishing his co-heirs.

The last will of Bolesław Krzywousty (the Wry-Mouth) of 1138 divided the state among four of his sons. In order to maintain the unity of the Polish state he created by this last will the institution of a *princeps*, senior to all the princes of Poland and ruling directly over its central and biggest part. After the death of the *princeps*, the next eldest prince was supposed to succeed him.

This principle was changed, probably in 1180, to the principle of succession by the eldest son after his father. In time, the entire concept of *princeps* lost its importance.

As a result the process of inheritance, which caused partition of the country, more than twenty Polish principalities existed towards the end of the thirteenth century. The practice of allowing men related through women to the prince's family to be appointed as successors (begun in the thirteenth century) contributed further to partition. Struggles among the prospective successors increased the influence of knights, who sometimes elected one of the prospective heirs to the throne. In spite of partitions, the unity of Poland was maintained by the inter-provincial clan links and by the Roman Catholic church, subordinated to one primate of Poland with his seat at Gniezno.

Wacław (Wenceslas) II of Bohemia unified Poland and was crowned king in 1300. Around 1306 Władysław Łokietek took over the southern part of the country (Little Poland) and in 1314 the western part (Great Poland). He was the first Polish king crowned at Cracow (in 1320) and not at Gniezno.

The Kingdom of Poland was known in the second half of the fourteenth century under the name *Corona Regni Poloniae*. However, the provinces kept their particular laws.

STRUCTURE OF SOCIETY

The primitive division of society into freemen and serfs changed gradually; in the twelfth and thirteenth centuries there were already owners of landed property, referred to in Latin sources as *nobiles* and *milites*. They were bound to serve in the army when called by the prince.

The freemen still laboring on the land gradually became serfs. The *milites*, in return for land from the prince, were bound to render services and give supplies in kind according to the *ius ducale*. The lands granted *iure militari*, at first for life, gradually became subject to inheritance by all male descendants and therefore were often divided in the case of two or more male heirs.

While the primitive clan organization underwent great economic changes and group ownership of land evolved into individual ownership, new clans were formed by *milites*, using so-called *proclamationes* (names) to distinguish one clan from another. Crests of arms were introduced under the influence of Western Europe.

Milites, who were economically weak, were called in the thirteenth and fourteenth century *media militia,* or *media nobilitas* or individually *squirio* or *scartabellus*. Gradually they became either full-fledged nobility or, more frequently, peasants. As a separate class they disappeared in the fifteenth century.

ROMAN CATHOLIC CHURCH

After the baptism of Poland in 966, the Catholic church was protected by the prince and granted several privileges. Beginning in the thirteenth century, the bishops were elected by the cathedral chapters (*electio canonica*), and approved by the Pope. The ecclesiastical courts had jurisdiction over *causae spirituales* concerning religion and later over *causae spiritualibus annexae* (for instance, the validity of marriage, of oaths, etc.). As the ecclesiastical courts were well organized, the litigants often also submitted to these courts cases otherwise not under their jurisdiction, under the Polish principle of choice of tribunal (*prorogatio fori*). The Church owned extensive landed properties given by the prince or donated by the *milites*.

218

PEASANTS AND COLONIZATION ACCORDING TO GERMAN LAW

In order to encourage colonization of virgin lands, the prince could grant to the landlords a privilege allowing the replacement of the Polish *ius ducale* by the German law, under which the landlords could grant a certain autonomy to the colonists. In return, colonists paid rent to the landlord. The "locator," or organizer, chosen by the landlord, became a hereditary chief of the village (in German, *Schultheiss*; in Polish, *sołtys*). The villages had their own tribunals. The German law was used either for German colonists or for purely Polish peasants, provided that the latter lived in villages governed by German law. (Villages under Polish law, however, did not have a village chief or their own tribunals; they were completely under the jurisdiction of the landlord.)

CITIES

Most Polish cities did not follow the gradual evolution toward autonomy characteristic of Western Europe but accepted, starting in the thirteenth century, the already extant German municipal institutions, of which the law of Magdeburg serves as an example. The "locator" became the hereditary chief of the city (in German, *Vogt*; in Polish, *wójt*). He performed his functions with the help of assessors. Subsequently a municipal council with a mayor was formed. The *wójt* and his assessors usually continued to act as a tribunal, while the council administered the city.

The Jews fleeing persecutions in Western Europe settled in Polish towns in great numbers. They were granted special privileges, were protected by the prince, were considered *servi camerae* (serfs of the treasury) and as such were under the personal protection of the king. They enjoyed a certain judicial and administrative autonomy in their religious commons, or autonomous communities.

OFFICIALS

The duties and titles of officials were patterned after the organization of the state of Charlemagne. At the prince's court were *comites*, the highest of which was the *comes platinus (wojewoda)*, or chief court official. Next was the *subcamerarius* (there was no *camerarius*), supervising the prince's property. The *cancellarius* (chancellor) prepared documents. A *iudex* helped the prince as a supreme judge. The *subthesaurarius* was the highest treasury official. The *dapifer* cared for the prince's food, the *pincerna* took care of the prince's store of alcoholic beverages, the *gladifer* kept the prince's sword, the *vexilifer* held the prince's standard, the *agazo* cared for horses, and the *venator* was in charge of hunting. The *nutritor*, or *paedagogus* taught the prince's sons. All were appointed and recalled at the prince's pleasure.

After the division of the Polish state, the personal relations between the prince and his officials faded away gradually. This was one of the consequences of the weakening of the power of the prince. Officials acquired gradually the character of provincial administrators, linked with the given province regardless of a change in princes. As the court officials could not handle the administration of the whole country, local officials were appointed with their seats at the fortresses (*castella* or *grody*); they were called *comites castellani*. Later such an official was called for short *castellanus* (*kasztelan*). A *castellanus* was aided in military matters by a *tribunus* (*wojski*) appointed by the prince, in the economic field by a *villicus* or *vlodarius* (*włodarz*), and in the administration of justice by a *iudex castellani* (*sędzia*).

The villages surrounding a fortress (*gród*) rendered services to it. (For example, one village produced shields, another cared for horses, etc.).

Sometimes the peasants bound to render such services were organized in groups of one hundred and subdivided into groups of ten. A group of several villages was called an *opole*. The *opole* made payments in kind or money which exceeded the capacities of one peasant (for instance cows, sheep, etc.). The *opole* had a certain common responsibility to other parties and certain policing powers.

Gradually the power of the *castellani* diminished; in the fourteenth century their sole task was to lead the *milites* in time of war. Toward the end of the thirteenth century new officials appeared — primarily the *capitanei* (*starostowie* or in singular, *starosta*). They were lieutenants of the prince and acted in his name. However, they could not grant privileges. Gradually the *capitanei* took over almost all the functions executed formerly by other officers. The *capitanei* were the officials who executed the prince's orders.

When several princes met they brought with them their officials. In the twelfth and thirteenth centuries the princes called meetings (*colloquia*, or *wiece*) with officials of various provinces. Furthermore the princes lost *de facto* a part of their power and had to look for support from their officials and prelates. Such meetings always had a provincial character; they did not concern the whole country.

COURTS OF LAW

A wronged person could look for redress and enforce it using his own power. The prince and his officials sat in judgment. The prince had jurisdiction over *milites*, decided in litigation about landed property, crimes against the state and his person, complaints against officials, etc. With certain exceptions, peasants were under the jurisdiction of the *castellanus* on the estates of the prince, or of a knight or church official on their estates.

Beginning in the fourteenth century, the *starostowie* administered justice on the prince's behalf. In the fifteenth century a special judge acted under the supervision of the *starosta*. In Little Poland, where the office of *starosta* did not exist, judges appeared in the fourteenth century. However, the prince could judge any case he called before him. The clergy submitted to secular tribunals only in matters concerning land; in all other matters ecclesiastical tribunals had exclusive jurisdiction over them.

The law applied was in general customary. However, written statutes occur as early as the reign of Casimir the Great (1333-70).

In the villages and cities organized under German law, there were courts composed of the *sołtys* and seven benchers and also courts having jurisdiction over the *sołtys* in which the landlord and seven *sołtyses* sat.

In case of doubt, inquiries were made in the courts of bigger cities — sometimes even in Magdeburg. In 1356 Casimir the Great organized a higher court for the crown estates and big church estates, called the Court of Six Cities at the Cracow Castle.

THE TREASURY

The prince's treasury received funds from his landed estates, administered by the *castellani* and later by the *starostowie* (except in Little Poland where a special manager was appointed). The administration was either in trust (*ad fideles manus*) or in leasehold, with a fixed rent to be paid by the *starosta* or in pledge as a guaranty for a loan to the treasury.

Furthermore, the peasants had to render to the prince either certain services or payments, at first mostly in kind but later also in money, according to *ius ducale*. Other sources of revenue were customs and toll duties. A mineral monopoly (mostly salt mines) also belonged to the prince.

The largest expenses were the upkeep of the prince's court and the construction of fortresses, castles, and churches. Officials were paid directly either in land or with the services and taxes of the local inhabitants. *Milites* and headmen of the villages under German law were obliged to serve without pay in the army in time of war.

GENERAL FEATURES

The primary feature of the structure of the Polish state between the ninth and fourteenth centuries was the predominance of the ruler. The prince emancipated himself from the influence of the clans and ruled the entire country. However, the size of the state limited the prince's influence. Therefore, the victims of local injustice often had to avenge themselves without the help of the state. The patrimonial concept of the state as the property of the prince permeated the state structure. For that reason, the rules of private law were applied to the public law, especially in the matter of dynastic succession. The central offices were the offices at the court of the ruler.

As the development of the state in Poland came later than that of Western Europe, several legal concepts and institutions already developed there were remoulded and adopted in Poland.

The Western feudal system, however was not introduced into Poland. The lands granted to *milites* by virtue of military law (*iure militari*) did not create a special class of property owners and were rapidly assimilated to other landed properties. Moreover, there were no intermediate links between the sovereign and the "vassals." All *milites* were directly subordinated to the monarch and were legally equal among themselves. The offices never became hereditary in Poland, although some of them (the so-called landed offices) were held for life. Only certain principalities were considered fiefs (among the territories inhabited by Poles there was just one: the principality of Mazowsze).

The Development of the Estates and the Formation of the Diet: Sejm

FORMATION OF THE *SEJM*

The right of dynastic succession resulted in the division of the Polish state into loosely linked principalities; even after the state became re-united, the provinces maintained their identity. Under the foreign king Louis d'Anjou and later under the Lithuanian king Jagiełło, the provinces banded together in dealing with the king. Therefore, instead of provincial meetings there appeared the *sejm*, or a supra-provincial meeting of deputies. This development was a gradual one. At the beginning the Kingdom of Poland did not include all of its later Polish provinces. Furthermore, in addition to the provinces considered to be within the "Corona Regni Polonaie," other territories, often non-Polish in origin, were incorporated with the Kingdom. These incorporated lands did not participate in the election of kings or the members of the *sejm*. They were administered directly by the king, who was *dominus et haeres,* according to their separate laws. However, these lands were gradually assimilated to other parts of Poland, with the exception of East Prussia (incorporated in 1454), which maintained special legal institutions.

222

Sometimes a land was immediately granted all public rights as they existed in all parts of Corona Regni Poloniae.

SUCCESSION TO THE THRONE

In his testament, Casimir the Great designated as his successor Louis d'Anjou of Hungary, whose mother was of the Polish Piast dynasty. A certain part of Poland (Kujawy, Sieradz, Łęczyca and Dobrzyń) was bequeathed to Casimir's grandson, Kaśko of Szczecin, but the Polish leaders opposed a new division of Poland. As Louis d'Anjou had no male descendants entitled to succeed him as king of Poland, he called the Polish nobles to Košice in Slovakia and obtained their approval for the ascension to the Polish throne of one of his daughters, to be chosen by himself or by his wife.

Two years after Louis's death, his daughter Hedvige (Jadwiga) became the queen of Poland. The Grand Duke of Lithuania, Jagiełło, was chosen as her husband and baptized, and after their marriage he was crowned king of Poland. After the death of Jadwiga (her only daughter had died previously), Jagiełło remained the only ruler of Poland, and remarried. Contrary to the principle of hereditary monarchy under the Piast dynasty, the country became an elective kingdom under the Jagiellonian dynasty. This was possible only when the concept of the state as property of the ruler had been completely discarded. The election of kings, paralleling the increase of the influence of the nobles and the development of the parliamentary system, was unique in a world in which hereditary monarchs, exercising absolute power in most countries, were not accountable to anyone for their deeds.

In 1434, the son of Jagiełło, Wladislaus III, was elected to the throne. Subsequent kings were either brothers or sons of their predecessors: Casimir Jagiellończyk was elected in 1445, Jan Olbracht in 1492, Alexander in 1501, Sigismund I in 1506, and Sigismund Augustus in 1530.

All the nobles had the right to vote at the election. Representatives of the cathedral chapters and of the most important cities also took part in the elections. The vassals, or heads of fiefs not forming part of the Polish kingdom, however, were excluded from the vote in sixteenth century. The prevailing influence on the results of elections was exercised by the king's council.

The election of the king was followed by his coronation in Cracow by the archbishop of Gniezno. The king took a liturgical oath and a state oath. After coronation, the king was free to govern the country.

From the reign of Wladislaus III onward, each king issued a general confirmation of the previously established rights (*confirmatio iurum generalis*) of the citizens.

A candidate for kingship limited his power by promising privileges in return for election support. Kings also granted privileges when requesting the nobility to serve in the army in foreign lands or to pay taxes. Such privileges were granted by Louis d'Anjou to all estates in 1355 at Buda (a promise only until he became king in 1372) and to the nobility in 1374 at Kośice. Later, Jagiełło granted similar privileges to the nobility and clergy in 1388 at Piotrków, in 1422 at Czerwień, in 1425 at Brześć, in 1430 at Jedlno, and in 1433 at Cracow. This practice was followed by their successors. An important privilege was granted in 1454 at Nieszawa.

From the end of the fifteenth century on, the king's power was limited by the resolutions of the *sejm*, called "constitutions." In principle, the king had all power, aside from those prerogatives he or his predecessors had relinquished. In particular, legislative power belonged to him. At first, he exercised it as an absolute sovereign, and later, with advice of the king's council; finally, ratification of the *sejm* was required. However, the king could not infringe on rights that he or his predecessors had granted as privileges, so that the scope of his power became ever more limited. Concerning matters not affected by privileges (for instance, the cities, the Jews, etc.), the *sejm* did not claim jurisdiction and the king himself could freely legislate.

The king possessed the entire executive power and appointed all officials, with the exception of four provincial judges, whom he had to choose from among candidates submitted to him. The king's council had only advisory power. However, the lifetime appointment of officials often weakened the king's position.

The king was the supreme commander of the armed forces and he represented the state in international relations. He was the supreme judge and could adjudicate any litigation. He was not responsible to anyone in the execution of his duties.

THE NOBILITY

Noble status became hereditary. There were nobles owning landed properties (*possessionati*) and landless nobles (*impossessionati*).

The landless nobility (the so-called *gołota*) were not bound to serve with the army and did not enjoy certain rights: for instance, they could not hold office.

From the fourteenth century onward, one could enter the ranks of the nobility in only two ways—as the result of adoption by a noble family or ennoblement by the king. A crest of arms was the exterior sign of nobility.

Privileges were granted at first to one person or to the nobility of a certain province; beginning in 1374 at Košice, they were granted to all the nobility.

The Košice privilege limited the taxes to be paid by the nobility to two *grossi* from a unit of land called *łan* or *laneus*, worked by peasants, (known as *łanowe* or *poradlne*). It was an important concession, as under Casimir the Great this tax had amounted to twelve *grossi* per *łan*. Still more important was the fact that this privilege exempted the nobles from the imposition of other taxes (except by their consent) once and for all. Furthermore, the nobility was now under the obligation of military service, although this privilege provided that in case of war beyond the frontiers of the country the king should pay ransom for captured noblemen as well as compensate them for damages which they might sustain. The privilege also provided that only natives of a province should be appointed to landed offices in the province. Later the privilege was extended. In 1388 it was decided that nobility should be paid for serving in the armed forces beyond the boundaries of the state.

The privileges of 1422, 1425, 1430, and 1433 granted to the noblemen *possessionati,* the right to be exempted from arrest save through a judgment. In its final form, the privilege was granted in Jedlna and is known as the Jedlneński privilege. The principle it proclaims is frequently referred to as "Neminem captivabimus nisi iure victum," the first words of the privilege. Thus, as early as in the first half of the fifteenth century, Poland had its *"Habeas Corpus* Act," for which England had to wait another two and a half centuries, and most other countries much longer.

However, a noble could be arrested if caught *flagrante delicto* in murder, arson, rape or abduction of a woman, or robbery. After 1454 the nobility in Little Poland and Ruthenia – and after 1496 *all* the nobility – were exempted from customs duties on all products from their landed properties transported to a market in Poland (internal duties) or abroad and, furthermore, on merchandise brought for their own use.

THE ROMAN CATHOLIC CHURCH AND OTHER RELIGIONS

Following the conversion to Christianity of Mieszko I in 966, the Roman Catholic religion remained the religion of the majority of the Polish people.

The fact that the Roman Catholic bishops were at the same time high state officials prompted the kings to promote their own candidates for bishoprics. After the Church was organized in Poland during the reign of Mieszko I, his successor, Bolesław the Brave, obtained from the German emperor, Otto, the right to appoint bishops. Subsequent monarchs did not retain this power. In 1211 Bolesław Laskonogi allowed the chapter of Poznań to elect its own bishop. Hughes de Saint-Cher (1215-54), the papal legate, promulgated a decree to the same effect, reserving to the Pope the right to confirm the result of the elections. Usually confirmation was a matter of course. From the end of the sixteenth century on, the king's candidates were appointed bishops by the Pope, even without formal election by the chapters. After 1430 only a nobleman could be appointed bishop.

High church offices were gradually reserved for the nobility, except for some offices to which the holder of a doctor's degree could be appointed even if he were not a nobleman. The church did not pay taxes, except for two *grossi* per *laneus* of land; however, when the nobility voted extraordinary taxes, the clergy offered of their free will a certain amount called *subsidium charitativum*. The clergy were exempt from military service.

During the early period, the judgments of ecclesiastical courts could be enforced by the state. However, the constitutions of 1563 and 1565 deprived the ecclesiastical judgments of state enforcement.

Only the Roman Catholic church had special privileges. However, other religions such as the Jewish faith and the Orthodox denomination enjoyed complete freedom. After the Reformation, Protestantism was not prohibited. In the sixteenth century, many prominent Polish families accepted the Protestant creed. Later many returned to Catholicism, but the spirit of tolerance was so deeply imbedded in the nation's tradition that the bloody and devastating religious wars which ravaged all Europe were never waged in Poland – another unique feature of her history.

THE PEASANTS

In addition to the above-mentioned colonization of certain villages and cities under German law, peasants emigrated from the Balkans into southeast Poland and settled under the régime of Valakh law.

Generally the legal situation of the peasants was the same in all parts of the country. A peasant could leave his village, usually during the Christmas period, and settle elsewhere if he complied with certain conditions, which varied from one part of the country to another.

The local government of villages under the German and Valakh law was the same. After 1423 a landlord could remove from office the hereditary head of the village only if he was *inutilis* or *rebellis* (useless or rebellious).

The peasants could appear before the state courts or village courts (the latter presided over by the *soltys* in the villages located under the German law, or by the landlord elsewhere).

Toward the end of the fifteenth century, the importance of the *pospolite ruszenie* (mobilized noblemen) decreased as paid regiments were used as the main force in the army. No longer a warrior, the nobleman became an agricultural producer. The devaluation of money decreased the relative value of rents, and the noblemen started to intensify production from manor lands not leased to peasants. Flanders, Holland, and England increased their import of Polish grain and so encouraged this development, which in turn required new labor. At the beginning of the sixteenth century, new laws drastically restricted the right of the peasants to leave the land on which they worked.

At the same time the peasants were excluded from city courts and the king's courts. The landlords purchased the privileges of *sołtys* and appointed their own officers as *sołtys* (*Schultheiss*, or bailiff). Appeal from the landlord's decisions was barred. The landlords then increased the obligation of work by the peasants. Generally speaking, this period reduced peasants to serfdom — a condition which existed to a still greater degree in most Western European countries.

CITIES

In certain royal cities, a new council was elected by the outgoing council. In others the councils were elected in various ways — sometimes by the entire population. The *starosta* often had a decisive influence upon the election. However, in the majority of private cities the landlord exerted decisive control. The councillors were elected for one year, except in a few of the larger royal cities where they were elected for life.

At the end of the fourteenth century, Cracow (and later other cities) started to legislate without any interference from the king. Gdańsk (Danzig) even obtained formally such a privilege in 1457. Cities imposed taxes for their own needs.

The mayor was sometimes appointed by the council and sometimes by the *starosta* or landlord. The municipal court, composed of seven members (*ławnicy*), was usually elected for one year by the council.

In the sixteenth century there appeared in the cities a body representing all the burghers and usually composed of 20 or 40 members (hence the names *viginti viri* and *quadraginta viri*). Half of them represented the trades and the other half — the craftsmen. Their main purpose was to control pecuniary matters and to supervise the activities of the council.

Cities were administered in various ways. Originally the *wójt* was the "locator" (organizer of the city, or *zasadźca*), who organized the city in virtue of a charter granted either by the king in royal cities or by the landlord-nobleman in other cities. The *wójt* was a hereditary post. The *wójt* was aided by a bench, usually composed of seven benchers. It is not clear who appointed the benchers, the practice probably varied. Toward the end of the thirteenth century appeared an additional organ called the city council (*rada miejska*). This council was elected every year either by the outgoing city council or sometimes by the landlord. Gradually the bench kept municipal judiciary power while the council took over the general administration of the city. With the passage of time all the burghers (*pospóstwo*) started to participate in the election of councillors, although this happened only in some of the cities. Sometimes the elections had to be confirmed by the *starosta*. In private (non-royal) cities the landlord usually appointed the councillors. Councils were usually composed of six to eight councillors. The council was presided by a burgomaster (*burmistrz* or *Bürgermeister*). The benchers became gradually to be elected by the city council.

The king ruled over the problems of public markets (*targ, jarmark*) and granted certain fiscal privileges such as tolls, monopolies of transport of beer, etc. Certain cities, such as Cracow, Wilno (1568), and Lwów (1658), obtained the privilege of participating in the *sejm*. The king could intervene in important city disputes and could enact new laws.

Important rights consisted in the so-called *ius emporii, ius stapulae,* whereby foreign merchants were bound to sell imported merchandise only wholesale to the traders of the city. Sometimes the foreign merchants were not allowed to continue to transport some of their merchandise at all, and sometimes they could do so if within a certain period of time, such as two weeks, the local traders did not purchase such merchandise.

The craftsmen were organized in unions which followed the German pattern, so that membership was obligatory. The unions usually elected four aldermen annually. These unions tried to eliminate unfair competition and regulated the training and examinations for master craftsmen. Special charters were adopted and confirmed by the municipal council or landlord.

The state designated obligatory routes for the transportation of goods in such a way as to force the traders not to by-pass cities and custom points. In 1509 new customs regulations, providing payment points at the boundaries of the state, eliminated the charge of duty on internal roads.

One could become a burgher by birth or by the grant of city rights (*ius civile*) by the municipal council. Peasants could work permanently in the cities only if they submitted a written permit issued by their landlords. In 1496 and in 1538 it was decreed that the burghers should not purchase landed property, a rule which had been generally followed in practice anyway. On the other hand the nobility was prohibited from engaging in any city trade (1505, 1550).

Jews enjoyed a special position granted by royal privileges, the most important being that of 1367 obtained from Casimir the Great. The Jewish commons, mostly in cities, enjoyed almost complete autonomy and were only loosely supervised by the *wojewoda*. The Jewish communities entered into speical agreements with the cities concerning professional practice. Their main occupations were trade, the granting of loans, and, to a limited extent, craftsmanship.

PROVINCIAL OFFICES

The old provinces (*ziemie*), where the provincial offices were maintained, were called from the fifteenth century onward *wojewódz twa* (voivodships) and each was headed by a *wojewoda*. Smaller provinces in which there was no *wojewoda* were called *ziemie* (lands).

In each voivodship, or province, there were several territorial subdivisions called *kasztelanie*, each headed by a *kasztelan*. However, in the second half of the fourteenth century, new district divisions *powiaty* gained more importance.

Certain offices could not be held simultaneously by one person: for instance, *starosta* and *wojewoda* or *kasztelan* after 1454 or *sędzia ziemski* (provincial judge) after 1422. This prohibition was called *incompatibilitas*. Appointment to a provincial, like that to a crown, or court office, was usually for life.

Each of the provincial officers had specific duties. The *wojewoda* brought to the king the *pospolite ruszenie* (mobilized noblemen) of his voivodship, supervised the Jews and, from the fifteenth century on, took charge of problems concerning weights and measures. He also chaired provincial meetings of nobility (*sejmiki*). In Little Poland he had, in addition, certain judicial supervisory powers.

The *kasztelan* (*castellanus*) brought to the *wojewoda* the *pospolite ruszenie* from his district. Both the *wojewoda* and the *kasztelan* were members of the senate. The *podkomorzy* (*subcamerarius*) decided litigation involving boundary lines between landed properties. The *sędzia* (judge), *podsędek* (assistant judge), and *pisarz* (scribe) staffed the provincial courts. All other provincial offices were purely honorary. *Sejmiki elekcyjne* (electoral assemblies of nobility) elected four candidates for each of the four provincial judiciary offices: *podkomorzy* (*subcamerarius* or chamberlain), *sędzia* (judge), *podsędek* (vice-judge), and *pisarz ziemski* (scribe), and submitted these candidates to the monarch, who could appoint only one from among such candidates but not other persons.

229

In Greater Poland and in newly incorporated territories, the *starosta* administered a district. He was considered a representative of the king, and had certain judicial powers (*sądy grodzkie*). He also administered the king's landed properties. In Little Poland, the *starosta* appeared only after the death of Casimir the Great. Their jurisdiction gradually increased but remained less extensive than that of the *starostas* in other parts of Poland.

Provincial officers were appointed for life by the king. After the fifteenth century, judicial officers were appointed from among four candidates elected by the nobility (*sejmiki elekcyjne*).

CROWN AND COURT OFFICES

The office of marshal gradually became the most important of court offices. At first he was called the King's court marshal (*regis curiae*), but later, – crown marshal (*regni*). After 1409 there were two marshals: crown marshal (*koronny*, or *marsalcus regni Poloniae*), and court marshal (*nadworny*, or *marsalcus curiae*). Their functions were alike; the court marshal assisted the crown marshal in the general court administration. The provincial offices of chancellor and vice-chancellor (*kanclerz* and *podkanclerzy*) gradually disappeared, but the Cracow chancellor, known as the crown chancellor, became a *de facto* minister of foreign and internal affairs. The chancellor was helped by scribes (*notarii*); the more eminent of them were in the sixteenth century called *protonotarii*; the highest had the title of *supremus secretarius*.

The treasurer of Cracow assumed the title of crown treasurer (*podskarbi koronny* or *thesaurarius regni*). He was helped by subordinate officers, the highest of which, *custos thesauri*, was called, from the second half of the fifteenth century on, court treasurer (*podskarbi nadworny*, or *vice thesaurarius curiae*).

The king was the supreme commander of the armed forces, but he often appointed a special commander (*campiductor* or *capitaneus exercitus*) for certain campaigns. When commanding all forces such a commander was called *generalis*. Under Casimir Jagiellończyk, a permanent commander, called a *hetman*, appeared. In 1539 his second-in-command (*hetman polny*, or *capitaneus campester*) was appointed for the first time.

Besides these important offices there were minor court offices such as chief cook (*kuchmistrz* or *magister coquinae regiae*), butler (*podczaszy*, or *pincerna curiae*), tailor (*krojczy* or *incisor regni*), and manager (*ochmistrz*, or *magister curiae*). In 1507 two *referendarii* were appointed to assist the king in judicial activities.

Sometimes other offices appeared temporarily. The most important among them was the maritime commission appointed in 1568 by

Sigismund Augustus. It ceased to exist, however, with his death. This commission supervised the navigation in the Baltic Sea. It had judiciary powers over freebooters (*nad kaprami*).

THE KING'S COUNCIL

The king's council was known by the Latin names of *consilium domini regis, consilium maius,* or *consilium supremum*.

At the time of the death of Casimir the Great no all-Polish assemblies having the features of a parliament were being held; each province deliberated separately. Such meetings were known as *wiece*.

The general meetings of all provinces of Poland were called conventions (*sejmy*); in fact, they were the assemblies of the king's council and not of the *sejm* (diet), which was formed later. These meetings were attended by ordinary bishops (heads of dioceses) and provincial officials, and were called together by the king. Those ministers who attended such meetings were the chancellor, vice-chancellor, crown marshal, court marshal, and treasurer. During the sixteenth century some members of the nobility having special rank also attended. When the lower house was formed, the original king's council, previously called the *sejm*, became the senate, an assembly which included Catholic bishops (heads of dioceses), *wojewodas, castellani,* and the five ministers. Those crown officials whose offices were created later were not members of the senate. In the middle of the sixteenth century the senate had a membership of seventy-three. As new territories were incorporated, this membership gradually increased: in 1569 there were 140 members.

The king's council had in principle only advisory functions. The king convened the council for deliberations lasting only a few days. Usually, the king's council met in the centrally located city of Piotrków. The lords of the council (*consiliarii*) often expressed opinions differing from that of the king. The council considered only matters submitted by the king and within his discretion. The councilors expressed their opinion in turn and then the king announced his decision (*conclusio*). Privileges created formal prerogatives; thus, after the privilege *czerwiński,* the king could not mint coins without the approval of his council.

By the end of fifteenth century, a new *sejm* was formed and the king's council became one of its component elements. The Constitution of 1505 formally provided that the king's council (later called the senate) would co-operate in legislating.

In the fifteenth century kings sometimes invited noblemen, members of the clergy, and burghers who were not members of the council to express their opinions or even to concur with the king in important acts, such as international treaties and acts of union with Lithuania.

CONFEDERATIONS AND PROVINCIAL ASSEMBLIES

In times of special need, so-called confederations (groups of persons promoting a particular object) were formed. They were dissolved upon realization of their purpose. The confederates were bound under oath to support the purpose for which the confederation was organized. These confederations functioned independently of all state organs and sometimes fought against state officials. Usually confederations were established by the nobility or the cities; sometimes, the clergy confederated, as in 1407.

Provincial assemblies of nobility were called *sejmiki*. The king was represented at the *sejmik* by his legate (*legat*). The names of the various *sejmiki* corresponded to the reasons for which they were convened: the *przedsejmowe*, to elect and instruct deputies to the *sejm*; the *elekcyjne*, to elect provincial tribunal officials; the *kapturowe*, to maintain order after the death of a king and before the crowning of a new king (after 1572); the *deputackie*, to elect deputies to the crown tribunal (created in 1578); and the *relacyjne*, to report on the activities of the *sejm*.

The deputies met together with senators at the *conventiones generales* (*sejmiki generalne* or *generały*): one for Little Poland, one for Great Poland, one for Mazovia, and one for Lithuania.

The constitution (*bydgoska*) of 1520 allowed the *sejmiki* to send any number of deputies to the *sejm*, but not more than six per province (*ziemia*) were paid by the king.

In Great Poland provincial groups (*wiece*) acted as tribunals and as local legislative bodies. Their resolutions were known under the name of *lauda*.

In the first half of the sixteenth century, a provincial *wiec* was subdivided into two parts: a tribunal composed of a few provincial officials under the chairmanship of a *starosta*; and a local legislative body (*sejmik*, or *conventio particularis*) composed of all the noblemen of the province and presided over by a *wojewoda*. At first, *sejmiki* were unknown in Little Poland, but were introduced there in the fifteenth century. In the sixteenth century there were in the Polish Commonwealth about seventy *sejmiki*, of which ten were in Masovia.

THE HOUSE OF DEPUTIES

Because of the privilege of freedom from taxes given in 1374, the consent of all the nobles was necessary to impose new taxes. Such consent was to be given by the *sejmiki*. The provincial assemblies, in order to discover the views of other provinces, would send deputies to the king's council and to other meetings. In Great Poland these deputies met in Koło, and in Little Poland and the Ruthenian provinces they met in Korczyn.

232

After 1493 all the deputies met in one place for a general diet called the *sejm walny* or *wielki* (*conventio magna, conventio solémna*, or *parlamentum generalis*). Each province usually sent two deputies. Therefore, at the beginning of the sixteenth century the *sejm walny* was composed of about forty deputies, while there were eighty-seven senators. These numbers increased upon the incorporation of new provinces and as more deputies were sent (up to six from older provinces). In 1569 there were in the *sejm walny* 120 deputies, of which 95 were from the crown lands. There were also 140 senators from the crown lands. At that time nineteen deputies from newly incorporated territories, forty-eight deputies from Lithuania (two per province), and a few from Prussia were added to this number. The deputies were bound to follow instructions given them by the *sejmiki*. The clergy did not send deputies but a few cities, such as Cracow, did. However, city deputies played an insignificant role in legislation.

The diets were convened at the king's pleasure and in various cities, but usually in Piotrków. The *sejm* was supposed to sit in session every year. Gradually the *sejm* was convened every two years for a session lasting six weeks. This was rather often in comparison to the West European practice. For example, during 24 years of the reign of Henry VII there were in England only seven sessions of parliament, and during the thirty-year reign of Henry VIII there were nine parliaments, of which one, elected in 1529, held eight sessions. The Estates General did not convene in France between 1484 and 1561, after which time it met only in 1576-7, 1588-9 and 1593.

During an interregnum (after the death of a king, and before the election of his successor), the Catholic primate had the right to convene the *sejm*. The convening procedure was established by custom. The king convened the senators and, through the *starosta*, asked the provincial assemblies to elect their deputies. The king sent delegates to those assemblies to explain the reasons for which the diet was convened and the proposed program of deliberations. After the sixteenth century, the *sejmiki* sat under the chairmanship of an elected marshal. The central diet also elected a marshal.

At the opening of the session, the king appeared before the two houses and explained the agenda. Then the senators delivered speeches, after which the houses separated for deliberation.

General resolutions were called constitutions (*konstytucje sejmowe*); resolutions on taxes were called *uniwersały podatkowe*. The constitutions could be permanent (*constitutiones perpetuales*) or temporary (*temporales*).

The king could not infringe on the privileges without the consent of the *sejm*; this rule was particularly applicable to taxes. Moreover, the king

233

could not call a general mobilization without the consent of the *sejm*, although he did not need such consent in order to wage war using only professional troops (Constitution of 1496).

On occasion the deputies also discussed matters which were within the sole jurisdiction of the king. From time to time, in order to obtain the consent of the *sejm* in matters protected by privileges, the king had to yield on matters ordinarily left within his authority. The jurisdiction of the *sejm* gradually increased. The constitution *Nihil novi* of 1505 provided that any bill onerous to the Commonwealth, burdensome to any individual, changing the common law, or limiting public freedom could be enacted into law only with the consent of the diet. This date marks the firm establishment of a predominantly parliamentary system, which had had its origin in the previous century. Among other rights of the *sejm* was the appointment of tax collectors.

In 1538 the king undertook, in his name and in that of his successors, to enforce the laws. At that time it was further established that he could issue constitutions only with the consent of the *sejm*. The diet did not, however, limit the traditional power of the king to legislate alone for cities and the Jews, or in the matters relating to the vassal states. King's legislative acts were called edicts, decrees, or *uniwersaƚy*.

The consent of all the deputies and senators was required to change a privilege (principle of unanimity). Deputies from one province, and subsequently even a single deputy, could prevent the passage of a law by the exercise of his *liberum veto*. Only the dexterity of the marshal of the *sejm* and the pressure of the majority against minority groups could assure the functioning of the *sejm* under this principle. If unanimity could not be obtained, the king could ask the *sejmiki* to change their attitude after the dissolution of the *sejm*, and then submit the matter to a subsequent *sejm*. In practice the adoption of laws was not prevented by the opposition of a small minority until the mid-seventeenth century.

Certain acts of the diet required only a majority vote: for instance, the election of the marshal. Also, a majority vote determined the validity of a deputy's mandate. The practice in the Polish *sejmy* during the sixteenth century was to consider resolutions of the *sejm* as valid even if opposed by a minority. The king considered the reasons (*rationes*) submitted by the opposing deputies and decided whether to accept or to reject the opposing view. This was not yet the practice of *"liberum veto,"* allowing one deputy to interrupt the session of the *sejm*. Many examples show the adoption of resolutions opposed by a minority. This was possible, as according to the contemporary concept the king created laws (*condit leges*). The chamber of deputies submitted to the king the resolution of the majority and the opposition submitted reasons for their opposition. The king then decided whether to confirm the resolution of the majority and transform their resolution into law or to agree with the minority and refuse his sanction.

While in England the development of parliamentary practice culminated in the victory of the principle of majority, the changes in Poland resulted in the *liberum veto* (principle of unanimity). Among the reasons for such an evolution in Poland are the insignificant role of the cities in the Polish *sejm*, the introduction to the *sejm* (after the union with the Grand Duchy of Lithuania in 1569) of deputies from northern and eastern provinces where the nobility was under greater influence of the magnates than in ethnic Poland, and the elections, after the death of Sigismundus Augustus in 1572, of foreign kings who had not been educated in Poland and so were not able to dominate the *sejm* as fully as the kings of the Jagellonian dynasty.

The principle of unanimity was especially dangerous because all resolutions of a session of the *sejm* were considered together, and the lack of unanimity on one of them could wreck the work of that session. A *sejm* which decided to "confederate" in the manner mentioned above was not bound by the rule of unanimity.

COURTS OF POLISH LAW

There were separate courts for each of the estates.

Through gradual evolution, the tribunals for nobility took specific form at the turn of the fifteenth century.

The courts of first instance were called *ziemskie, grodzkie,* and *podkomorskie.*

A *ziemski* court was composed of a judge (*sędzia*) and associate judge (*podsędek*), (both of whom could be replaced by officials appointed by them and called *komornicy*), and a clerk (*pisarz*).

In many provinces the courts were assisted by five or six local noblemen sitting as assessors (assistant lay judges). Each voivodship or province (*ziemia*) had one *ziemski* court, which held sessions in each district of the province, usually three or four times per year. These courts had jurisdiction over all cases having a nobleman as defendant except cases explicitly reserved for other courts.

Courts *grodzkie* or *starościńskie* were under the jurisdiction of the *starosta*. Usually the *starosta* was replaced in these courts by officials appointed by him (*burgrabia* or *podstarości*), and sometimes by an official called *sędzia komisarski*. These courts had jurisdiction over the landless nobility (*gołota*) and over landed nobility in matters involving crimes such as arson, assault on a public road, invasion of home, and rape. In all these cases the *grodzki* court acted as a tribunal (*iudicium*). Besides, this court also acted as *officium*: it executed the judgments of all other courts and took care of registering such documents as land contracts, written declarations, and testimonies.

The *podkomorski* court determined the boundaries of landed property owned by the nobles. The *podkomorzy*, or an official appointed by him, called *komornik*, presided in the field, where investigation was being conducted.

Among superior courts was the *wiec* – usually one per voivodship. Its origin was in the court of a regional prince. The composition of the *wiec* varied among provinces. In Great Poland a *starosta* presided over the *wiec*, and in Little Poland a *wojewoda* presided, with *castellani* and other officials sitting as assessors. These courts originally sat three times a year, and after 1454 once a year. They disappeared when their responsibilities were assumed by the crown tribunal created in 1588. The *wiec* functioned in the fourteenth and fifteenth centuries as a court for more important litigations, for magnates, for *causae haereditariae* of the nobility, and for some other cases. In the sixteenth century it became a court of appeals from the judgments of the *ziemski* and *grodzki* courts.

The king's tribunal was superior to all other courts. The king could decide any case he chose or any case submitted to him. The king's tribunal was called *in curia*. It could sit without the monarch; it was then called the assessor's tribunal (*sąd asesorski*). The king's tribunal had original jurisdiction in cases of public law (*causae iuris communis*), in certain criminal cases against the state (especially treason cases which could be punished by loss of civic rights, freedom, or life, or by confiscation of all property), in complaints against officials, and in all matters concerning the king himself, especially when his properties or revenues (*causae fisci*) were involved. When in the sixteenth century the right to appeal was finally established, the king's tribunal acted as a court of appeal in the second or third instance.

In the sixteenth century the sessions of king's tribunal held during the *sejm* gained more importance because the senators and later also the deputies of the nobility acted as assessors. Moreover, an appeal from the king's tribunal *in curia* to the court at *sejm* gradually became possible.

The courts of Polish law were governed by the customary law and certain statutes – mostly those of the fifteenth century. The most important of these statutes codified the procedure (the *formula processus* of 1523). The attempted codification of the law as expressed in judicial decisions (the *correctura iurium* of 1532) was not adopted by the *sejm* of 1534. Following the initiative of the *sejm* of 1505, the crown chancellor Jan Łaski published the collection of the laws of Poland in 1506. The first part, dealing with Polish law, was confirmed by the king, acquiring thereby an official character. The second part contained foreign law elements — particularly German law.

COURTS OF GERMAN LAW AND OTHER COURTS

The municipal bench (*ława miejska*) and sometimes the municipal council (*rada miejska*) acted as courts in the cities. The most important cases, however, were decided by the landlord. In case of doubt on a legal point, these courts could request advice from the higher courts of municipal law: from the fourteenth century on, either those organized under German or Polish law, or the higher court of German law in Cracow, or the royal court of six cities at Cracow castle.

The same procedure applied to appeals when they were introduced in the fifteenth century. However, in the sixteenth century the landlords started to direct appeals to their manorial courts. In smaller royal cities appeals could be brought to the tribunal of the *starosta*, and in bigger royal cities to the king's court *asesorski*.

In the villages under Polish law the landlord's court was the only tribunal. In the villages under German law there were *ławy wiejskie* and *ławy wielkie* — rural benches and benches dealing with more important matters. In the villages under the *Valakh* law the *kniaź* administered justice.

After the purchase of the *sołtys* office, the landlords gradually increased their influence over the administration of justice and often acted as appeal judges.

The *wójt* in the city and the *sołtys* in the village were under the jurisdiction of the *leńskie* courts, usually composed of seven members. These courts sometimes acted as courts of appeal from the judgments of village courts.

Armenians of the Eastern rite had their own courts and applied customary Armenian law. The Armenian statute was finally confirmed by Sigismund I in 1519.

Jews also had separate Jewish courts. Appeals from those courts, important cases in first instance, and litigations between Jews and Christians were submitted to the *wojewoda*'s court for Jews, usually composed of one Christian judge and one Christian clerk. Beginning in 1539, Jews in private cities were subject to the jurisdiction of the landlords' courts and in smaller royal cities to the courts of the *starostas*.

Ecclestiastical courts retained their traditional jurisdiction.

THE TREASURY

The treasury was not divided into a "state treasury" and a "king's treasury"; nevertheless, the *sejm* requested an audit of that part of the revenue and expenditures that corresponded to the sums voted for taxes. In 1563 a special treasury called *rawski* (because it was located at Rawa) was created especially for military expenses.

The king used his revenue without restriction. This revenue included the income from landed property, salt mines, customs and tolls, ports, land tax (in the amount of two *grossi* from the *laneus* paid by the nobility and slightly more by the clergy), one-tenth of the lead and silver extracted from the Olkusz mines, the *podwodne* (a sum paid in lieu of the cost of transportation which the royal cities were bound to furnish for royal messengers), and the *stacyjne* (a sum paid by certain convents, cities, and Jews in lieu of supplying accommodations and upkeep for the royal court when traveling). Furthermore, special taxes were paid at the time of coronation. The king had also income from the mint. Finally, the popes sometimes transferred to the royal treasury the sums obtained from the Polish faithful.

Extraordinary taxes were voted from time to time and income therefrom was subject to control by the diet. The *sejm* of 1562 introduced a permanent state tax known as *kwarta* representing one-fifth of the income paid by all persons holding the king's properties.

THE ARMED FORCES

All noble landowners were subject to general mobilization (*pospolite ruszenie*). Women, children, priests, and invalids owning land had to send someone to replace them. The number of men and horses and the amount of equipment to be supplied depended on the importance of the landed property.

The nobility was not obliged to serve outside the boundaries of Poland unless paid. The cities were bound to furnish such supplies as carts and food. Peasants were free from military service. The king alone could call for general mobilization; after 1496 he had to obtain the consent of the *sejm*. The noblemen who failed to respond to the call for general mobilization had their property confiscated. From the fifteenth century on, the king usually transferred confiscated property to the informer (*delator*).

The *sołtys* of the villages under German law and the *kniaź* of the villages under Valakh law were under the same obligation of military service. However, this system of nobility cavalry was unwieldy and, following the general development of weapons, mercenary troops started to appear in the fifteenth century. At first these troops were hired only in time of war. From 1562-3 on, a part of income from the crown land served to maintain a permanent contingent of paid troops.

LANDS ATTACHED TO THE POLISH CROWN

Masovia (Mazowsze)

Masovia was a fief at first bound only to supply troops in case of war (acts of 1351, 1355, and 1359). In the fifteenth and the early sixteenth centuries the dukedoms forming Masovia were gradually incorporated into the Crown of Poland (1462-1505.)

Prussia

After the defeat of the Teutonic Order in the fifteenth century, a part of the lands controlled by the Order (so-called Royal Prussia) reverted back to Poland. Another part became a fief of Poland. In 1525 the last Grand Master of the Order, Albrecht, assumed the rule over the territory known as "Ducal Prussia" as its first duke, with the title of "Duke in Prussia," while the king of Poland was the "Duke of Prussia." The Duke in Prussia had the right to sit in the senate of the Polish Commonwealth and to intervene in Prussian matters. The judgments of Prussian ducal courts were subject to appeal to the king's court.

In 1526 the Pomeranian dukes confirmed the lands of Bytów and Lęborek, formerly belonging to the Teutonic Order, as fiefs of Poland.

Inflanty

The Order of the Knights of the Sword submitted to the Polish king Sigismund Augustus, in 1561. From part of their land a vassal dukedom of Curland and Semigalia was formed. The remainder, under the name of Inflanty, was placed under the joint jurisdiction of Poland and Lithuania. It was ruled by a governor appointed by the king of Poland. Local laws, privileges, and institutions, including a diet and offices, were maintained. The estates of the clergy, the nobility, and the cities had a certain individual autonomy and the right of participation in the offices of state. The Jews and peasants had some autonomy but practically no voice in government.

Lithuania

After the election of Jagiełło to the throne of Poland and his marriage with Queen Jadwiga in 1386, Poland was in personal union with Lithuania: the kings of Poland were at the same time grand dukes of Lithuania. Through various acts this union was reinforced, with the co-operation of the Polish nobles and Lithuanian boyars. By the union of Horod/o (1413), forty-seven Catholic families of Lithuanian boyars were granted the crests of arms of Polish nobility.

Gradually the Lithuanian institutions were reorganized along Polish lines. The landowners (boyars or *milites*) were transformed into nobility by several privileges in the fifteenth and the sixteenth centuries. In Lithuania there were no villages governed by German law, and, despite a few cities, the character of the country was primarily rural.

The voivodships and *castellani* were introduced to Lithuania in the fifteenth and sixteenth centuries. Central offices were organized according to the Polish pattern, and a grand duke's council was established. Finally, in 1566, the boyars' participation in general legislative meetings was established through the organization of *sejmiki* who elected two deputies to the *sejm* from each district.

Court law was codified in 1529 and 1566. The Second Lithuanian Statute introduced, in addition to the courts of *starosta* the land courts: *ziemskie, grodzkie,* and *podkomorskie.*

The Polish-Lithuanian Union was climaxed in 1569, when the *sejmy* of the two countries met in Lublin and established a federal union, with one *sejm* and one monarch. Lithuania kept her offices and a separate administration. The voivodships of Podlasie, Volhynia, Brac/aw, and Kiev were directly incorporated into Poland. The Union of Lublin created the first modern close federation in the world. It was referred to as *Rzeczpospolita Polska* (the Polish Commonwealth, or, literally, the Polish Republic), while the designation of *Korona* (Crown) attached to Poland proper.

The Nobiliar State, 1569-1764

GOVERNMENT

After the death of Sigismund Augustus, the last of the Jagiellonian dynasty, the electors of kings of Poland saw their choice no longer limited to the members of one dynasty. The king was elected by the nobility. The period between the death of the king and the coronation of his successor was called the interregnum. The chief officer, or *interrex*, of the state during the interregnum was the Catholic primate, the archbishop of Gniezno. The *interrex* did not exercise all powers of the king; however, he represented the state on the international scene and directed the internal administration if it was not directed by a confederation of the nobles. The primate proclaimed the interregnum and called the *sejmiki*. The latter, called *kapturowe*, sent deputies to a *sejm* called *convocatio*. The *convocatio* protected the interests of the state during the interregnum and prepared an election. This *sejm* also voted a general act of confederation. An act of confederation had the character of a personal undertaking by all the signatories and, therefore, could be signed even if there was no unanimity. The new king was elected at the electoral *sejm*, which deliberated in tents on a field at Wola, near Warsaw. All noblemen could vote in the elections (*viritim*). In principle, the election had to be unanimous. The primate proclaimed the new king-elect (*nominatio*). This was followed by the drafting of an agreement (*pacta conventa*) with the representatives of the elect. The electoral *sejm* determined the date of coronation, which took place during the coronation *sejm*. Coronations took place in Cracow, with the exception of those of kings Leszczyński and Poniatowski, who were crowned in Warsaw. After the coronation the king confirmed the laws (*confirmatio generalis iurum*), certified that he was sworn in (*literae iuramenti preastiti*), and proclaimed the coronation (*denunciatio regis coronati*).

After the death of the last king of the Jagiellonian dynasty in 1572 and the beginning of the reign of Henri Valois, the king's power was based on the agreement called *pacta conventa*, mentioned above. Furthermore, the fundamental constitution of the state (including such items as election of the king, freedom of religion, *sejms*, taxes, and procedures for general mobilization) was usually confirmed by the king-elect in so-called *articulae henricianae*. Henri Valois did not confirm the *articulae*, Stefan Batory did. Beginning with Władysław IV, these provisions were simply included in the *pacta conventa*. If the *pacta conventa* were breached by the monarch, the nation was freed from obedience to the king (*articulus de non preastanda obedientia*, introduced in 1573). The Constitutions of 1607 and 1609 specified admonitions to be given to the king three times: by the primate, by the senators, and finally by the *sejm*. The king was required to cease violating the law; otherwise he could be dethroned.

Constitutions could not be enacted without unanimous approval of the *sejm* and the king. Between the sessions of the *sejm* the king had a free hand in his policy; the so-called senators resident, chosen by the king (sixteen beginning in 1573, twenty-eight after 1641) played only an advisory role. The resolutions (*senatus consulta*) of such senators were recorded and reported to the *sejm*. After 1717 these resolutions were binding on the king, but in practice the senators resident were never of great importance. They were replaced by a permanent council, appointed by the *sejm* in 1775, which became the supreme executive power and reduced the king's role to representation of the state.

After 1569 the Polish Crown was composed of twenty-two voivodships and a few separate lands, and subdivided into 119 districts (*powiaty*). The Grand Duchy of Lithuania was composed of eight voivodships subdivided

241

into twenty-two districts and of the Duchy of Samogitia (Żmudź). The Polish Commonwealth represented both nations on the international scene.

In the internal administration, Lithuania followed the Polish example. Even the private law, incorporated in the Third Lithuanian Statute of 1588, showed the strong influence of Polish law. The main Lithuanian tribunal, established in 1587, was modeled on the Polish one.

Within the Crown (Poland), Royal Prussia maintained a slightly different organization of offices and had a special compilation of laws, the *Korektura pruska* of 1598. The Prussian dukes ceased to be vassals of Poland in 1657. In the same year, Bytów and Lęborek were given to the electors of Brandenburg, who formally recognized the Polish sovereignty over these lands for the last time in 1698.

The seventeenth and especially the eighteenth century showed a decline in the strength of the Polish state. In 1617-21 Poland lost the major part of Inflanty to Sweden; in 1667 the lands of Smoleńsk, Siewierz, Czernihów, and Kiev were lost to Moscow. In 1772 the first partition of Poland was accomplished by Russia, Prussia, and Austria. A territory of 81,900 square kilometers with a population of two and a half million was annexed by the neighbors of Poland. In 1793, through a second partition, Poland lost 521,000 square kilometers with eight million inhabitants to Russia and Prussia. Finally the last partition in 1795 divided the remainder of Poland between Russia, Prussia, and Austria.

During the second half of the eighteenth century, the official concept of "fundamental laws" (*prawa kardynalne*) was embodied in the treaty of 1767 with Russia, and was incorporated in the Constitution of 1768. These laws were declared as "eternally valid and unchangeable." They dealt with the election of the king, the jurisdiction of the *sejm*, the principle of unanimity, the privileges of nobility, the jurisdiction of landlords over peasants, the Catholic religion, and similar matters.

Several enlightened writers and statesmen saw the necessity of political reform, and especially of strengthening the executive power of the king, abolishing the principle of unanimity, increasing treasury revenues, and improving the situation of cities and peasants. These reforms were embodied in the famous Consititution of May 3, 1791, and the day of its adoption became the national holiday.

From the seventeenth century on, the nobility strove to close its ranks to new candidates. In fact, the Constitution of 1601 provided that only the *sejm* could confirm ennoblement. This rule applied, after 1641, to the admission of foreign nobility, (*indygenat*). Additional conditions and restrictions followed. Within the nobility there was a trend for legal, if not economic, equality.

242

Hence, in 1638, the acceptance and use of specific titles and orders was prohibited, except for those titles included in the acts of the Polish-Lithuanian union of 1569. In 1705, notwithstanding this prohibition, Augustus II instituted the Order of the White Eagle, and Stanislaus Augustus later granted several titles of "prince." The nobility had a monopoly on ownership of landed property except for the burghers of three cities (Cracow, Wilno, and Lublin) who shared it. Landless nobles were in an inferior position. The economic structure of the society had changed to some extent after the union with Lithuania and the incorporation of vast Ruthenian (Ukrainian) domains (*latifundia*). Wealthy families usually gathered the poor nobility around themselves.

CHURCHES

The Roman Catholic religion enjoyed a special position. The king of Poland was required to be a Catholic. In 1589, Pope Sixtus V granted to Polish kings the right to appoint bishops. The nobility tried to curtail the expansion of the landed holdings of the Church, and in the sixteenth and seventeenth centuries several constitutions restricted transfer of hereditary landed properties to the Church. After the abolition of the Jesuit Order in 1773, its properties were taken over by the state for the purpose of education.

The Eastern Rite clergy, united with the Catholic church through the Union of Brześć of 1595, did not obtain the political privileges granted to the Roman Catholic clergy; the Eastern Rite bishops were not admitted to the senate.

While Protestants and Orthodox church members did not suffer discrimination (the freedom of religion was confirmed by the Warsaw confederation of 1573 and by the subsequent *pacta conventa*), their clergy did not enjoy the same status as that of the Roman Catholic priests. In 1632 a period of discrimination began, especially against Arians (called also Trinitarians) who refused to fulfill the duty of military service. This partial discrimination was ended in 1768 when the status of non-Catholics was practically equalized with that of the Catholics. However, certain limitations on non-Catholics were reintroduced in 1775.

PEASANTS

From the end of the sixteenth century to the end of the eighteenth century, the landlords had full power over the peasants in the economic, administrative, and judicial fields. The peasants could not leave the land on which they labored except by permission of their landlords. However, some peasants managed to flee; and such fugitives could not be easily found. There were also free peasants; and in the mid-eighteenth century a number of foreign peasants came to Poland, settled under Dutch law, and kept their freedom.

A peasant, subject to his landlord, could appear as defendant before the state courts only with authorization of his landlord (*cum assistentia domini*). Landlords issued regulations concerning the rights and duties of peasants in their landed properties.

In some villages there were organs of self-government: especially in old villages organized under German or Valakh law and also in all villages under Dutch law. However, the landlord could always intervene and supersede the decisions of the village government. A *gromada* (common) included all subjects of the village along with those who were landless. As a legal entity, a gromada had common property (pastures, woods, gardens); it imposed taxes, entered into contracts, and performed other similar functions. The members met in general assembly and often had the right to elect the *sołtys* and *przysiężnych ławników* (sworn benchers).

The *sołtys* and the assessors decided minor penal matters. Their decisions could be appealed to the landlord. A *gromada* was responsible as a whole for taxes and other duties of its members. The peasants were bound to pay rent to the landlord and to work on his land: usually a total of eight man days per week was required from one *laneus*. The landless peasants also had certain obligations towards the landlord. The landlord often had a monopoly on the production and sale of liquor, on milling, and on other services. Because of the high birthrate, homesteads were subdivided among the heirs, and in consequence most peasants in the sixteenth century were settled on one fourth of a *laneus*. (A *chełmiński laneus* was equal to 30 mórg, or 16.8 hectares; a *frankoński laneus* was 43 mórg, or 24.2 hectares; one hectare is equal to 2.47 acres).

In the seventeenth century there was a definite trend in political literature toward advocating an improvement in the condition of peasants. As a result, the kings issued new regulations improving the lot of peasants in the Crown properties.

Several big landlords followed this lead. Often the duty to work for the landlord was replaced by a rent. Sometimes the peasants opposed it, as it placed the risk of production on their shoulders. In the general legislation there were no great changes. It was established in 1768 that the landlord could not punish the peasant by death; he was required to submit capital cases to the nearest *grodzki* tribunal. This confirmed previous practice.

CITIES

The entire population of a city (*communitas*) was called to meetings to debate public matters — particularly taxes and regulations. However, the king could intervene in the legislation of royal cities, and private landowners did the same in private cities. Moreover, landlords and royal *capitanei* (*starosta*) intervened even in the local administration. Certain persons in cities were exempt from municipal law (*jurydyki*) and sometimes were the privileged competitors of normal burghers, as they did not pay municipal taxes and did not have other duties.

Cities were economically weakened by wars, and gradually the burghers came to be considered socially and politically inferior to the nobility. A constitution of 1633 decided that a nobleman resident in a city and trading or holding municipal offices lost the privileges of nobility.

Only in the second half of the eighteenth century did the state begin to introduce measures improving the situation in the cities. In 1764 some of the exemptions from municipal law (*jurydyki*) were abolished. In 1765 the assessor's court (*sąd asesorski*) established a commission of good order (*boni ordinis*) for Warsaw and later for Lwów. Similar commissions were created for other important royal cities and their work proved beneficial.

In Lithuania municipal self-government was abolished, except in the eleven biggest cities. However, the burghers in Lithuania could, after 1775, purchase landed property outside cities. This was prohibited in the Crown lands, where only burghers of a few important towns were allowed to acquire rural land.

JEWS

The Jews were ruled by privileges confirmed by all monarchs, by ordinances issued by *wojewodowie*, and by agreements with cities. They had self-government.

The Jewish common (*gmina*, or *kahał*) was ruled by a college whose members were called *parnassim* or *rashim* (*seniores*, or *starsi żydowscy*). They were elected by a commission appointed by taxpayers. The commons sent deputies to general meetings, one for Poland and one for Lithuania (*Waad*). These meetings were abolished in 1764.

The Period of Reforms

OFFICES

The landed offices kept their medieval character. The king could dismiss an official only for causes determined by law.

The constitution of 1775 revised the appointment procedures for *starostowie*; the *sejmiki* elected four candidates, from which the king chose one. Furthermore civil-military commissions, created toward the end of the period of the kingdom, assumed executive powers much broader than those of the *starostowie*.

In 1764 reform of the central executive offices was begun. The economic council of the treasury (*rada ekonomiczna skarbu*) was established; it was composed of two treasury commissions: one for the Crown and another for Lithuania. A military commission for the Crown was succeeded by a similar commission for Lithuania. In 1773 a commission of education was created: the first ministry of education in the world. The treasury commission was headed by the grand treasurer (*podskarbi wielki*) assisted by the court treasurer (*podskarbi nadworny*); it was composed of senators and noblemen. It took over the fiscal administration and the administration of justice in this field; the treasury tribunals ceased to exist. The commission also sat as a tribunal in controversies oncerning letters of exchange and other commercial matters.

In 1776 the military commissions were abolished and their functions were in part restored to the commanders-in-chief (*hetmani*), and in part transferred to military department of the permanent council created in 1775; this council was composed of the king, eighteen senators, and eighteen noblemen; one of the latter was called Marshal of the Knights. It was subdivided into five departments: foreign interests, police or good order, military, justice, and treasury. The departments were headed by ministers. This council was abolished in 1789.

THE SEJM

The senate increased to a maximun of 163 senators in 1768, while the number of the deputies to the *sejm* reached 236, of which 135 were from Poland (Crown), 49 from Lithuania, 6 from Inflanty, and 46 from Prussia. The deputies from cities disappeared.

After 1573 the *sejm* was required by law to meet every two years. The term of office of the *sejm* of 1788 was extended by special resolution. In 1792 new deputies were added, raising the total to 354. This *sejm*, which adopted many reforms and deliberated for four years, is known in Polish history as the "four-year *sejm*." After 1569 the *sejm* usually met in Warsaw; after 1673 every third session was held in Grodno.

The principle of unanimity began to be strictly applied in the seventeenth century. In 1652, for the first time, one deputy caused the dissolution of a *sejm*. Under the reigns of Augustus II and of Augustus III in the eighteenth century, only a few *sejmy* managed to adopt valid resolutions.

From the beginning of the seventeenth century, the *sejm* had the last word on treaties of peace and alliance, war, taxes, and supervision of state revenue. In 1717 the first budget was voted. Even some administrative matters such as ennoblement, commission appointments, tax collection, and the granting of rewards were reserved to the *sejm*. The senate, being a part of the *sejm*, also acted as an advisory body or king's council.

Some order was brought into the sessions of the *sejm* through regulations enacted during the reign of the last king, Stanisław August, after 1764. In economic matters the principle of majority instead of unanimity was applied. Finally, the *sejmy* of 1773-5 and 1788-92 acted totally under the principle of majority, the deputies having formed a *sejm* confederation.

THE *SEJMIKI*

In the seventeenth century the *sejmiki* gradually acquired ever more power. The deputies to the *sejm* were bound by their instructions. Often it was necessary to call certain *sejmiki* after the end of the *sejm* session in order to appeal for confirmation of new taxes voted by the *sejm* against the instructions given to deputies by some *sejmiki*. The principle of unanimity also prevailed at the *sejmiki*. Landless nobility could participate. The *sejmiki* even voted local taxes and organized local troops. The Constitution of 1717 abolished these usurpations by the *sejmiki*. Other reforms followed, (especially in 1768), introducing the principle of decision by majority at the *sejmiki* and in principle eliminating the power of the landless nobility, who could be easily influenced by the magnates on whose lands they lived.

CONFEDERATIONS

Confederations, which had disappeared in the fifteenth century, reappeared after the death of King Sigismund Augustus to fill in the vacuum caused by the monarch's death. In theory, the nobility took over the power. The confederations were usually headed by a marshal. Later, confederations were sometimes formed during a king's life even to oppose his policies.

COURTS

In 1678 a supreme crown tribunal was established. It was composed of deputies of the nobility (one or two per province or voivodship) elected annually at special *sejmiki*. If a priest were a party to litigation, half of the seats in the tribunal were reserved for the deputies of the clergy, elected by certain chapters. This tribunal was headed by a marshal elected by the deputies. The deputies of the clergy had their president. The tribunal heard appeals directly from the *sąd ziemski* (land court) and from the *grodzki* court. Therefore, the intermediate court of appeals (*wiec*) disappeared. The tribunal's judgments were not subject to appeal, except when no majority decision could be reached in cases involving the clergy, in which instance the litigation was referred to the court of the *sejm*. Furthermore, the tribunal acted in first instance in cases against *capitanei*, or *starostonie*, and associated officials if the latter had violated their duties in administering justice. The court of *sejm* retained some jurisdiction over criminal and civil cases of general jurisdiction, as well as over misfeasance in office.

The assessors' court (*sąd asesorski*) was presided over by a chancellor; it heard cases against cities, appeals from city courts, and cases involving certain fiscal matters of the nobility.

The *sąd relacyjny*, with the king presiding, heard appeals against judgments of princes and vassals, interpreted privileges, decided litigation about church property between the Orthodox and the Uniates, and judged charges of the bribery of tribunal deputies. The *sąd referendarski* was formed at the beginning of the sixteenth century. It heard complaints of peasants living on the royal properties against the *starosta* and the lessees. The *sąd marszałkowski* (marshal's court), with the marshal of the royal court presiding, heard criminal cases in the place of sojourn of the king.

During an interregnum all courts lost their jurisdiction, which had actually been a delegation of power by the king. Therefore, the *sejmiki* elected *sądy kapturowe* to maintain public order and security. The members of the general *kapturowy* court were elected by the electoral *sejm*. In 1768, however, it was decided that normal courts would continue to function during the interregnum.

In the second half of the eighteenth century, some confederations appointed temporary courts. In the cities, a bench (*ława*) and the city council (*rada miejska*) functioned as courts. The higher vassal courts (*leńskie*) disappeared except for the supreme court of German law at the Cracow castle.

THE TREASURY

In 1590 the treasury was divided into two parts: the king's treasury and the state treasury.

248

THE ARMED FORCES

A general mobilization was seldom called; changes in the technique of fighting and the nobles' lack of discipline made it undesirable. The basic unit of the armed forces was a standing army (*wojsko kwarciane*) reinforced in case of need by new regiments recruited by captains (*rotmistrz*) under the authority of the king.

The *sejm* of 1578 created an infantry from the peasants on the king's landed properties (*piechota łanowa*). However in 1649 this obligation was replaced by the payment of a small tax.

In 1572 the Cossacks were organized under an elected *ataman*. When their autonomy was curtailed, they revolted. In 1699 the last Cossacks ceased to be an organized part of the Polish armed forces.

THE CONSTITUTION OF MAY 3, 1791

The Constitution of 1791 is a major achievement of modern Polish political thought. It declared that all power emanates from the will of the people (article V). It eliminated the election of kings by providing for the election of a dynasty and ascension to the throne through succession. All acts of the king were to be countersigned by one of the five ministers. The king appointed all officials.

This constitution and additional statutes maintained the division of the society into estates but improved the situation of the cities and facilitated the ennoblement of burghers. The inhabitants of the cities were granted the privilege of *neminem captivabimus* (freedom from arbitrary arrest). The peasants were placed under the protection of the law and of the national government. This implied state control over the landlord's jurisdiction. In theory, agreements between landlords and peasants were binding on both parties, but the peasants still were left under the jurisdiction of landlords.

The Roman Catholic religion was maintained as the national faith, but the freedom of other religions was assured.

The supreme executive power was vested in the Guard of Laws (*"Straż praw"*), composed of the king, the primate, and five ministers responsible to the *sejm*. The prince's heir and the marshal of the *sejm* were also given membership in the Guard. In case of disagreement between the king and the other members of the Guard, the *sejm* decided the issue. The *sejm* could request dismissal of a minister by a two thirds majority vote.

The *sejm* held the legislative power. The deputies were not elected for a session but for two years. The *sejm* was composed of the senate (king, *wojewodowie, castellani,* bishops, ministers: altogether, 132 members) and of the chamber of deputies (204 deputies sent by the nobility and 24 deputies sent by the cities). The senate had the right of veto. The chamber of deputies could override a senate's veto at the subsequent session.

The principle of majority or qualified majority replaced the old requirement of unanimity. The king had only one vote, as had other members of the senate.

The *sejmiki* were reformed; the landless nobility was excluded from them. The *sejmiki* could no longer vote local taxes, and their instructions were no longer binding on the deputies to the *sejm*.

The administration of the cities was reorganized. The city assemblies were open only to property owners (*possessionati*). The country was divided into departments. Each department had an assembly, to which deputies were sent by city assemblies. The departmental assemblies elected deputies to the *sejm*, elected officials, and could vote local taxes with consent of the state commission of police. The city officials were elected for two years. The supervision of the *starostowie* over the cities was abolished.

The courts *ziemski, grodzki,* and *podkomorski* were replaced by the landowners' courts (*ziemiańskie*), staffed by judges elected for four years by the *sejmiki*. The Crown tribunal remained as a court of appeals and the courts *relacyjny, referendarski,* and *sejmowy* were maintained.

The previous courts in the cities were replaced by a uniform set of new courts, to which the judges were elected for two years. The former assessors' court was confirmed as a supreme court of appeals with its seat in Warsaw.

THE LAST YEARS OF INDEPENDENCE

Under Russian pressure, the *sejm* at Grodno, held in 1793, replaced the Constitution of 1791 by a new counter-reform constitution reintroducing the election of the king and the *pacta conventa* but maintaining such provisions of the 1791 constitution as the increased rights of the cities. A permanent council composed of the king, ten senators, and fourteen deputies held the supreme power.

The Russian intervention was followed by the national insurrection in 1794 in which Tadeusz Kościuszko became Head of State (Act of March 24, 1794), assisted by the Supreme National Council (Act of May 10, 1794). On May 7, 1794, several provisions improving the lot of the peasants were proclaimed (*Uniwersał połaniecki*).

The third partition of 1795 overthrew the insurrectionist authorities and abolished the peasant reform.

The Rule of Three Foreign Powers, 1795-1918

Through the three partitions of 1772, 1793, and 1795, Russia, Prussia, and Austria (which did not participate in the 1793 partition) liquidated the Polish-Lithuanian Commonwealth and took over its territories and population.

The reforms of the second half of the eighteenth century came too late, at the moment when the neighboring powers, strong, united, and governed in an absolutist manner, decided to stop the liberal movements in Poland, which, they believed, could "contaminate" their states with democratic ideas.

Of course, the Poles did not submit voluntarily to foreign rule. Patriots organized various independence movements in the country and abroad. The most important military group was organized into auxiliary legions of the French Republic and later of Napoleon.

GRAND DUCHY OF WARSAW

In consequence of his victorious campaigns, Napoleon was able to reorganize Europe. From the Polish territories recovered from Prussia, he created the Grand Duchy of Warsaw. On July 22, 1807, he signed its constitution, which proclaimed equality of all citizens (article 4). However, the peasants did not receive the land in which they toiled. They were legally equal to other citizens but were landless. The hereditary ruler (the king of Saxony) held the executive power. A diet composed of two chambers was established. The deputies to the lower house were elected for ten years by both the *sejmiki* of the nobility (sixty deputies) and the municipal assemblies (forty deputies). Owners of immovables, craftsmen, merchants, artists, clergy, meritorious citizens, and army officers had the right to vote at municipal assemblies. The senate was composed of six bishops, six *wojewodowie*, and six senators appointed for life by the ruler. The diet met for fifteen days once every two years. Only members of three commissions and of the state council (ministers and councillors) had the right to speak at the plenary meetings. If disagreement between two houses occurred, the ruler's decision prevailed.

The country was divided into departments, the latter subdivided into districts and administered by prefects and subprefects. The constitution proclaimed the independence of tribunals. The Napoleonic Code was made the civil law of the Duchy. The constant necessity for approval by the king, who resided in Dresden, made the task of the council of ministers in Warsaw particularly difficult.

The territory of the Grand Duchy of Warsaw was extended by the treaty of Schönbrunn of October 14, 1809, which incorporated into the

Duchy a part of southern Poland with Cracow, Lublin, Zamość, and Wieliczka.

Napoleon's defeat marked the end of the Duchy of Warsaw. The Russian-Prussian and Russian-Austrian treaties of May 3, 1815, together with the treaty of the Congress of Vienna of June 9, 1815, partitioned the Grand Duchy of Warsaw. Its western part, under the name of Grand Duchy of Poznań (Posen), was annexed by Prussia; Cracow was given the status of a "free city"; and the bulk of the territory was put under Russian control and given the name of the Kingdom of Poland.

THE KINGDOM OF POLAND OF 1815

The Treaty of Vienna created the kingdom of Poland, with about 3,200,000 inhabitants and a territory of 127,000 square kilometers. This consisted of about one-sixth of the Polish-Lithuanian Commonwealth.

On November 27th, 1815, Tsar Alexander signed the constitution of the kingdom, which provided that it was to be forever united with the Russian Empire. The Russian tsar was to be the king of Poland and was to be represented there by a deputy.

The constitution proclaimed freedom of religion and freedom of the press. However, the formula *neminem captivabimus* was replaced by *neminem captivare permittemus nisi iure victum* ("We will not permit arrest unless when condemned according to law"), which appeared to indicate that the tsar could decide otherwise.

The lower house of the diet was composed of seventy-seven deputies elected by the nobility at the *sejmiki* and fifty-one deputies elected by municipal assemblies. The senators were appointed by the king for life. The king could refuse to sanction the resolutions of the diet.

The viceroy, with the council of state, governed the kingdom. This council, presided over by the viceroy, was composed of ministers, councillors, and other persons appointed by the king. The real executive power was in the hands of the viceroy and the administrative council of five ministers; however, the ministers had only advisory powers, while the viceroy had the decisive voice. The tribunals were declared independent.

On the whole it was a liberal constitution for its time. However, in actual practice, the commander of the Polish armed forces (the Russian Grand Duke Constantine) and the tsar's commissar (Novosiltsev) imposed an arbitrary rule over the country.

After the Polish-Russian war, known as the November Uprising (begun on November 30, 1830), the victorious Tsar Nicholas I abolished the constitution of the Kingdom of Poland and introduced on February 26, 1833 the so-called Organic Statute, which organized the kingdom as a province of the Russian Empire, with separate administration and some autonomy. Supreme power was vested in the viceroy, who was assisted by an administrative council. The council of state took over certain functions of the diet. This statute remained ineffective, however, and the Russian Fieldmarshal, Paskiewicz, appointed Duke of Warsaw, held absolute power.

In the eastern provinces (east of the boundaries of the Kingdom of Poland as established in 1815), the peasants received the right to hold land by the tsar's decree (*ukaz*) of March 3, 1861. A similar reform in the Kingdom of Poland went into force on October 1, 1861. While it abolished serfdom, it did not grant land to the peasants.

During the January Uprising of 1863, the Polish insurrectionist National Government finally granted land to the peasants. After the defeat of the insurrection, the tsar's *ukaz* of March 2, 1864 repeated almost word for word the Polish National Government's decree granting land to the peasants.

THE FREE CITY OF CRACOW

The Vienna treaty created the Free City of Cracow with the Constitution of May 3, 1815. This free city had a territory of 1000 square kilometers and had 60,000 inhabitants.

The senate of the Free City was composed of twelve members (six of whom were elected) and the president. The assembly of representatives was elected. The peasants had the right to elect the deputies in an indirect vote.

In fact, the entire administration was under the supervision of a committee with residents representatives appointed by Russia, Prussia, and Austria.

The Free City survived until the uprising of 1846, when it was incorporated into Austria.

GALICIA

This territory under the Austrian regime covered about 77,000 square kilometers with a population of 3,500,000 (in 1815). It was approximately co-extensive with lands called Little Poland.

The government of Vienna governed Galicia through a "land president."

The Austrian Patent (statute) of 1817 established a territorial diet of estates with the participation of clergy, magnates, nobility, and the city of Lwów. At first, the diet had only advisory powers.

Under pressure of Polish democratic elements, the peasants in Galicia obtained the right to own land on April 19, 1848, a few months earlier than in other countries of the Austrian monarchy. Later, an autonomous land diet was called into being; it met for the first time in March 1861, in Lwów.

THE GRAND DUCHY OF POZNAŃ

The territory annexed by Prussia had 29,000 square kilometers with 850,000 inhabitants. In 1826 a provincial diet was created. It was composed of four hereditary lords and of the representatives of three estates: the nobility, (twenty-two deputies) the cities, (sixteen deputies) and the rural commons (eight deputies). The king of Prussia was represented by Prince Antoni Radziwiłł (*namiestnik*). A German land-owner, Zerboni di Sposetti, was *Oberpräsident*.

In 1823 the peasants obtained land for a modest indemnity paid to landowners.

Silesia and West Prussia were considered German lands, and no special institutions for the Polish population existed there. Gradually the Grand Duchy of Poznań came to be called, without any legal act, the Province of Posen. After 1866, Bismarck suppressed the use of the Polish language in government offices and tribunals.

The Republic of Poland, 1918 - 45

ORGANIZATION OF THE POLISH STATE BETWEEN WORLD WAR I AND 1921

World War I resulted in the resurrection of the Polish state. The general governors of the Central Powers occupying Polish territories established (by their decree of December 13, 1916) the first authority for a vaguely discribed Kingdom of Poland. It was designated as the Provisional Council of State and was composed of twenty-five members who elected a Crown Marshal from among their members. This council had only advisory powers and was supposed to give opinions on organization of the Kingdom of Poland.

On September 12, 1917, the Central Powers called into being a Regency Council, composed of three members appointed by them. On February 1, 1918, the Regency Council created a Council of State, composed of fifty-five members elected by the *sejmiki* of districts and municipal councils of bigger cities, twelve members "ex officio" and forty-three members appointed by the Regency Council.

On November 14, 1918, the Regency Council transferred its powers to the Polish military leader Józef Piłsudski and declared the dissolution of the Council. The decree of November 22, 1918, established the provisional structure of the state. Piłsudski was the provisional Head of State. He appointed a government responsible to him. The electoral law granted the right to vote to all citizens over 21 years of age. The *sejm*, elected on January 26, 1919, met on February 9th, 1919. It adopted the so-called Little Constitution of February 20, 1919, which proclaimed the supremacy of the *sejm*, to which the Head of State and ministers were responsible. During the Polish-Soviet war, a Council of Defense of the State was created (July 1, 1920). This council was composed of the Head of State, marshal of the *sejm*, ten deputies designated by the *sejm*, the president of the council of ministers, three ministers designated by the council of ministers, and three representatives of the armed forces appointed by the supreme commander.

THE CONSTITUTION OF MARCH 21, 1921

The first *sejm* of the reconstituted Polish state had as its principle task the preparation of a constitution.

The Polish-Soviet war menaced the very existence of the reborn Polish state. Although it terminated victoriously for Poland, it delayed the work of the diet. The constitution was enacted on March 17th, 1921.[1] Its preamble began with the words: "In the name of Almighty God" and thanked Providence for the "delivery from one and a half centuries of slavery." The merits of the past generations were gratefully acknowledged, and the new constitution was linked with "the glorious tradition of that of May 3rd, 1791," which represented the summit of the Polish constitutional thought before the partitions of Poland. The preamble dedicated the constitution to the "good of the new renascence of humanity" and proclaimed equality of all citizens and special protection of work. The constitution was composed of seven chapters subdivided into 126 articles. It declared that the supreme power in the Republic of Poland resided in the people.[2] The *sejm* and the senate held the legislative power; the

---

[1]*Dz. U.* ("Journal of Laws of the Republic of Poland"), 1921, No. 44, Item 267. The author decided to limit footnotes in large part to the references to the Journal of Laws of Poland in the twentieth century. Otherwise references to sources would exceed in length the text of this summary of the history of Polish constitutional law.

[2]Article 2.

President of the Republic, together with responsible ministers, acted as the executive organ, and independent tribunals administered justice.

The president had the power to appoint and to recall the prime minister and, on the latter's request, the ministers.[3] All the president's acts had to be countersigned by the prime minister and by the proper minister.[4]

While the president was not responsible for official acts, the cabinet of ministers and each of the ministers had to resign on a request of the *sejm*. The president was to play a coordinating role in political matters. However, he could not act without the cooperation of his ministers. The prime minister had the title of President of the Council of Ministers. He was only *primus inter pares*.

Articles 65 to 67 provided for territorial self-government on the levels of urban and rural commons, districts (*powiaty*), and provinces (*województwa*). Article 68 dealt with economic self-government: agriculture, trade, industry, crafts, and labor chambers linked with the Supreme Economic Chamber of the Republic were provided for.

The legality of central administrative governmental acts and those of local governments was subject to the control of the administrative tribunals, the highest of which was the Supreme Administrative Tribunal.[5] Deputies to the *sejm* and senators were elected by a universal, secret, direct, equal, and proportional (d'Hondt) voting system. Deputies to the *sejm* were required to have reached the age of twenty-five years, and were elected by voters at least twenty-one years old, while senators had to have reached forty and were elected by voters at least thirty years old. The number of deputies was fixed at 444, and that of senators at 111. All were elected for five years. Twentieth-century terminology applied the name *sejm* to the lower chamber only, while in the pre-partition Kingdom of Poland the word *sejm* had usually been applied to the whole diet, composed of the king, the chamber of deputies, and the senate. The proportional d'Hondt electoral system allowed parliamentary representation of minor groups, resulting in a great number of parliamentary parties — a situation similar to that in the Third French Republic. Article 6 of the constitution stated that the extension of state loans, the sale of immovable state property, the imposition of taxes and customs duties, the creation of monopolies, the establishment of a monetary system, and the extension of financial guarantees by the state required laws enacted by the *sejm*.[6] Both the executive branch of the government and the *sejm* had the

[3]Article 45.

[4]Article 44.

[5]Article 73.

[6]Article 6.

right to introduce new legislation. Deputies and senators were not bound by instructions from their electors.[7] This provision, modeled after a similar one in the Constitution of 1791, abolished the system by which deputies were bound by instructions given by their electors at the *sejmiki*. The *sejm* and the senate were presided over by their marshals, elected by each of the two chambers from among its members.

The *sejm* and the senate, united as the National Assembly, elected the President of the Republic for a term of seven years.[8] There was no vice-president; if necessary, the marshal of the *sejm* replaced the president until the election of the new president.[9] The President of the Republic convened, opened, adjourned, and closed the sessions of the *sejm* and senate.[10]

The *sejm* could be dissolved by its own decision, providing at least half of its members were present and an affirmative vote of two-thirds were achieved. The President of the Republic could also dissolve the *sejm* with consent of three-fifths of the total number of senators. Upon dissolution of the *sejm*, the senate was also automatically dissolved.[11] It is to be emphasized that the executive branch alone could not dissolve the diet.

The independence of the tribunals was assured by a provision that their judgments could not be changed by either the executive or the legislative branch of the government.[12] The judges could not be recalled[13] and could not be prosecuted or arrested without the decision of a competent tribunal.[14] On the other hand, the tribunals were not entitled to examine the validity of laws properly published.[15]

Chapter V, articles 87-124, enumerated the general duties and rights of citizens. Article 95 assured protection of the life, freedom, and property of all, regardless of national origin, ethnic group, language, race, or religion. Other rights included legal equality for all citizens,[16] personal

[7] Article 20.

[8] Article 39.

[9] Article 40.

[10] Article 25.

[11] Article 26.

[12] Article 77.

[13] Article 78.

[14] Article 79.

[15] Article 81.

[16] Article 96.

freedom (i.e., no arrest for more than forty-eight hours without a court order),[17] trial by a proper tribunal,[18] protection of private property,[19] protection of home,[20] freedom of choice of residence and type of work,[21] protection of work and social insurance,[22] freedom of opinion,[23] freedom of the press,[24] protection of secrecy of correspondence,[25] petition,[26] free association,[27] observance of rights of ethnic, religious or linguistic minorities,[28] freedom of conscience and religion,[29] the right to teach and study and the right to attend the state schools free of charge,[30] and the right to obtain compensation from the state for damages caused by illegal acts of officers acting in their official capacity.[31]

Article 113 granted spiritual and economic autonomy to churches (called "religious unions" – *związki religijne*). Article 114 stated that the Roman Catholic religion, which was that of the majority of the population, was to have the first place in the state among religions which were, however, equal in their rights. "The Roman Catholic Church is governed by its own rules," stated the constitution. It foresaw an agreement with the Apostolic See. A concordat with the Vatican was signed on February 11th, 1925.[32]

Silesia, separated for centuries from Poland, was granted autonomy. This voivodship was the only one to obtain its own legislative organ: the

[17] Article 97.

[18] Article 98.

[19] Article 99.

[20] Article 100.

[21] Article 101.

[22] Articles 102, 103.

[23] Article 104.

[24] Article 105.

[25] Article 106.

[26] Article 107.

[27] Article 108.

[28] Articles 109, 110.

[29] Article 111.

[30] Articles 117-119.

[31] Article 121.

[32] *Dz. U.*, 1925, No. 72, Item 501.

sejm of Silesia, composed of forty-eight deputies. Silesia also had a separate treasury.[33]

AMENDMENTS OF AUGUST 2, 1926

After the *coup d'état* of May 1926 by Marshal Józef Pilsudski, the powers of the President of the Republic and of the executive branch of the government were broadened.[34] The president was authorized to issue decrees having force of law when the *sejm* was not in session. These decrees were to be submitted to the *sejm* at its session, to be either approved or disapproved. However, the president acting alone could not change the constitution or the budget, decree the number of men to be drafted into the armed forces, ratify international treaties, nor declare or terminate war.

The *sejm* ceased to have the right to dissolve itself. The president could dissolve the *sejm* even without the senate's consent.

A no-confidence motion against the cabinet could not be voted at the meeting at which it was made. If the *sejm* did not approve a budget within three and one-half months (and the senate within thirty days), the president could decide to promulgate a budget identical either to the previous one or to the one submitted by the government.

THE CONSTITUTION OF APRIL 23, 1935

The governmental party, *B.B.W.R.* (*Bezpartyjny Blok Współpracy z Rządem*), considered the 1921 constitution, even as amended in 1926, inadequate. It wanted a strong executive. As the governmental party could not secure the two-thirds majority required for the change of constitution, it managed to have a change approved by the *sejm* on January 26, 1934 by taking advantage of the temporary absence of the deputies of the opposition parties. Several legal requirements were not observed: for instance, the fifteen days' notice of the motion to amend the constitution was not given.

One year later, on January 16th, 1935, the senate approved the new constitution with several changes. The *sejm* agreed to those changes on March 23, 1935, and the president signed the new constitution on April 23, 1935.[35] It became known as the April Constitution. It contained

[33]Constitutional law of July 15, 1920.

[34]*Dz. U.*, 1926, No. 78, Item 442.

[35]*Dz. U.*, 1935, No. 30, Item 227.

fourteen chapters subdivided into eighty-one articles. Furthermore, twelve articles of the previous so-called March Constitution (of 1921) were maintained in force (from Chapter V, dealing with duties and rights of citizens).

The 1935 constitution declared that the one and undivided power of the state was concentrated in the person of the President of the Republic[36] and that the government, the *sejm*, the senate, the armed forces, and the tribunals, and the state audit were subordinate to him.[37] The president had the right to veto laws voted by the *sejm*,[38] and changes to the constitution.[39] He could institute legislation in order to change the constitution.[40] His prerogatives, by which he could act without having the countersignature of a minister, included: nominating of a candidate for the office of the President of the Republic and calling a universal vote; appointing his successor in time of war; approving and recalling the President of the Council of Ministers, the Chief Justice, the President of the Supreme Audit Chamber, and the Supreme Commander and the Inspector General of the Armed Forces; appointing a certain number of senators; dissolving the *sejm* and senate before the expiration of their term; and a few other powers.

The president was declared to be responsible only to "God and history."[41] He was elected by fifty electors designated by the *sejm*, twenty-five electors designated by the senate, and five electors *ex officio*, (marshal of the *sejm*, marshal of the senate, President of the Council of Ministers, Chief Justice, and Inspector General of the Armed Forces). However, the outgoing president had the right to designate his own candidate and to call for a universal vote in order to choose between two candidates.

The marshal of the senate chaired the Assembly of Electors. If necessary he replaced the President of the Republic.

The power of the diet was curtailed by the fact that, in case of a no-confidence vote, the President of the Republic could either recall the cabinet or the minister in question, dissolve the *sejm* or senate, or simply wait for the vote of the senate. Only if the senate confirmed the no-confidence vote was the president under the obligation either to recall the minister involved or to dissolve the diet.

[36]Article 2.

[37]Article 3.

[38]Article 35.

[39]Article 80.

[40]Article 80.

[41]Article 2.

The electoral law of July 8, 1935,[42] reduced the number of deputies to the *sejm* from 444 to 208. The proportional system was abolished. A severe blow to the opposition parties was the new system of nomination of candidates to the lower house. They were to be nominated exclusively by electoral assemblies (*zgromadzenia okręgowe*) placed under the chairmanship of an electoral commissioner appointed by the Minister of Interior Affairs. These assemblies were composed predominantly of representatives of territorial, economic, and professional governing bodies. The minimum age was raised to twenty-four years for electors and thirty years for deputies.

The electoral law governing the senate, enacted on the same date,[43] provided for ninety-six senators, of which thirty-two were to be elected by the President of the Republic and sixty-four by provincial electoral colleges. The right to vote in senatorial elections was reserved to those who had been decorated with certain orders, had university diplomas, were officers in the armed forces, or had been elected to certain offices in economic and professional self-government, associations of public utility, etc.

The above mentioned voters elected provincial electors, who then convened and voted for senators.

WORLD WAR II, 1939-45

After the invasion of Poland by the German Reich and the Soviet Union in September 1939, the Polish government was transferred to France and, after the defeat of France, to London. In 1945, the Great Powers, following agreements with the USSR, withdrew the recognition of the Polish government in London and recognized the communist-dominated Polish government established by the Soviet Union. At this time Soviet policy was supported by numerous Soviet armies stationed in Poland. The Polish government in London continued to exist and maintained embassies and consulates in the countries that did not recognize the communist government in Poland. Due to circumstances characteristic of a government in exile, special powers and means were resorted to, but there was no significant change in the official Polish constitutional system.

The Polish People's Republic

The Soviet Union, which had recognized the Polish government in London after the German invasion of the USSR in 1941, broke off

[42]*Dz. U.,* 1935, No. 47, Item 319.

[43]*Dz. U.,* 1935, No. 47, Item 320.

diplomatic relations with this government when the latter favored an impartial investigation by the International Red Cross of the massacre of thousands of Polish officers in the Katyń forest.

A Polish communist group was formed, under Soviet protection, and was named the Polish Committee of National Liberation.[43a] The committee published its manifesto on July 22, 1944.[44] This document, while referring to a new social and economic structure in Poland, declared the 1935 Polish constitution illegal and proclaimed that the fundamental principles of the 1921 constitution would be applied until the election of a constitutional assembly. Commentators in Poland maintained that, while the "fundamental democratic principles" of the 1921 constitution were in force, that did not mean that the whole 1921 constitution had the force of law.[45] Thus the legality of the constitution was nebulous. The communist leaders organized a body not provided for in any previous law: the National Home Council (*Krajowa Rada Narodowa*) which acted as a legislator, decided in important political and international matters, supervised the executive organs, including the Polish National Liberation Committee (*Polski Komitet Wyzwolenia Narodowego*), and exercized the supreme authority over the newly created territorial national councils (*terenowe rady narodowe*).[45a] The National Home Council (*KRN*) was headed by a presidium composed of seven members. This new body exercized, when the *KRN* was not in session, all functions of the latter except the legislative ones.[46] The presidium acted as Head of the State until September 11, 1944, when the chairman of the National Home Council was invested with the majority of powers of the President of the Republic (as in the 1921 constitution).[47]

[43a]*Dz. U.,* 1944, No. 1, law of July 21, 1944, on creation of the Polish Committee of National Liberation (Item 1) and law of August 15, 1944, on the temporary powers to issue decrees with the force of law (Item 3).

[44]The text of the manifesto was annexed to issue No. 1 of the *Journal of Laws of the Republic of Poland* of August 15, 1944. Under the communist rule numbers of the *Journal of Laws* started again with No.1.

[45]See Andrzej Burda *Prawo Państwowe* ("State Law") (Warsaw, 1959), p. 88.

[45a]This body was organized extra-legally. Detailed provisions concerning it appeared subsequently in the law on organization and sphere of activities of national councils of September 11, 1944 (*Dz.U.,* 1944, No. 5, Item 22).

[46]Article 26 (2), *Dz. U.,* 1944, No. 5, Item 22, published on September 20, 1944.

[47]Law of September 11, 1944 on the powers of the Chairman of the National Home Council (*Dz. U.,* 1944, No. 5, Item 23, published on September 20, 1944).

The Polish Committee of National Liberation (*Polski Komitet Wyzwolenia Narodowego*, the corresponding Polish abbreviation being *PKWN* acted as the government.[48] The law of December 31, 1944 replaced it by the provisional government.[49] National councils (territorial, existing at all levels of the administrative division of the state) mentioned in the July 22, 1944 manifesto, existed parallel to, and until the final abolition (1950) of, the previous organs of territorial self-government and administration.[50] This dualism is explained sometimes by the fact that the national councils created during foreign occupation of Poland, in a conspiratorial way, were not sufficiently known to the masses of the population, so that an early transfer of powers to these councils was not advisable.[51] The law of August 15, 1944 provided that the Polish Committee of National Liberation (and later its successor, the provisional government) had the right to issue decrees having force of laws.[52] These powers were widely used. The *KRN* and *PKWN*, non-elected provisional bodies, completely changed the legal structure of Poland, and nationalized landed properties[53] and industrial and commercial enterprises.[54] The whole economy was subordinated to central economic planning.[55]

[48]Law of July 21, 1944 on creation of the Polish Committee of National Liberation (*Dz.U.*, 1944, No. 1, Item 1, published on August 15, 1944).

[49]*Dz.U.* 1944, No. 19, Item 99, published on December 31, 1944.

[50]Law on territorial organs of the uniform state power, of March 20, 1950 (*Dz.U.* No.14, Item 130, published on April 13, 1950). This law was subsequently replaced by the law on national councils of January 25, 1958 (*Dz.U.*, No. 5, Item 16).

[51]Andrzej Burda, *op.cit.supra,* p. 92.

[52]*Dz.U.* 1944, No. 1, Item 3, published on August 15, 1944.

[53]As to labored land, see decree on land reform of September 6, 1944 (*Dz.U.*, No. 4, Item 17, published on September 13, 1944). As to forests, see decree on taking over by the state of certain forests, of December 12, 1944 (*Dz.U.*, No. 15, Item 82, published on December 27, 1944).

[54]These confiscations were described in the law of January 3, 1946 on taking over by the state of the main branches of national economy (*Dz.U.*, No. 3, Item 17, published on Feburary 5, 1946).

[55]Decree of November 10, 1945 on creation of the Central Planning Office at the Economic Committee of the Council of Ministers (*Dz.U.*, No. 52, Item 298, published on December 7, 1945).

Formation of new industrial and trade enterprises was subject to new rules.[56]

Thus, under the rules of non-elected bodies, all landed properties exceeding the area of 50 hectares of labored land or 100 hectares of any land were confiscated entirely, together with equipment, buildings, and installations and all domestic animals, no land whatsoever being left to the owners. The enterprises were nationalized if either their production was in one of numerous categories listed in seventeen groups or if the number of employees working in one shift in an enterprise exceeded fifty, regardless of type of enterprise.[57] The referendum of June 30, 1946, brought about the abolition of the senate.

The National Home Council and the Presidium were supposed to cease functioning when a legislative assembly convened.[58] After rigged elections marked by intimidation and violence, the new diet held its first session on February 4, 1947. The next day, the members of the legislative assembly elected the President of the Republic and the latter appointed the government. On February 19, 1947, the legislative assembly adopted a "Little Constitution"[59] that declared in force the "fundamental principles" of the 1921 constitution, the principles of the manifesto of the Polish Committee of National Liberation, the principles of legislation of regional national councils, and social and governmental reforms. It was not entirely clear which articles of the 1921 constitution were confirmed by the "Little Constitution." It permitted the legislative assembly to delegate legislative powers to the government during the time when the legislative assembly was not in session. Governmental decrees were to be ratified by the Council of State and submitted for approval or rejection at the next session of the legislative assembly.

The President of the Polish People's Republic was elected for seven years by the majority of the legislative assembly, the required quorum being two-thirds of the deputies. He appointed and recalled the premier and, upon the latter's motion, appointed other ministers.

The Council of State was a new type of institution in which certain legislative and executive powers were vested. It was to a certain extent the continuation of the Presidium of the National Home Council. The Council of State was composed of the President

[56]Law of January 3, 1946 on foundation of new enterprises and promotion of private initiative in industry and trade (*Dz.U.*, No. 3, Item 18, published on February 5, 1946).

[57]Article 3, *Dz.U.*, 1946, No. 3, Item 17.

[58]They acted until the election to the *sejm* on January 19, 1947 (*sejm ustawodawczy*).

[59]*Dz.U.*, 1947, No. 18, Item 71.

264

of the Republic acting as president of the council, the president of the diet, three vice-presidents of the diet and the president of the Supreme Audit Chamber; in time of war the Supreme Commander of the Armed Forces was also to be a member. The Council of State ratified the decrees of the government, and could initiate legislation, control the activities of national councils, determine a state of emergency (but not of war) and examine the report of the Supreme Audit Chamber. Besides legislative and executive powers, the Council of State had also some judicial powers. The law concerning the procurator general [60] stated in its article 4:

> The Procurator General of the Republic can submit to the Council of State motions on interpretation of laws in effect and for establishment of principles of application of such laws. The interpretation and principles of application of provisions of law, as established by the Council of State, are binding universally and shall be published in an official periodical determined by the Council of State.

The Council of State was not accountable to anyone. It stood above the national councils. These councils were established by a decision of the National Home Council of January 1st, 1944, followed by a law of September 11, 1944, and another law of March 20, 1950, concerning the "local organs of unified state power." The concentration of all powers — legislative, executive and judicial — in the Council of State was, and still is, the characteristic feature of the Polish People's Republic. The "Little Constitution" was amended by the constitutional law of March 20, 1950,[61] which was necessary to adjust the constitution to the abolition of territorial self-government and the creation of "local organs of unified state power," called "national councils".[62]

The resolutions of the national councils could be declared void by a council of higher level or the Council of State if such resolutions were deemed illegal or against the basic policy of the state. The national councils were given wide powers in local affairs. The "Little Constitution" was replaced by the Constitution of July 22, 1952.[63] The name of the state was changed into the Polish People's Republic, described in the preamble as "a state of people's democracy." The chief organs of the state are: a unicameral diet, the Council of State and the Council of Ministers. The office of the President of the Republic was abolished, and

[60]*Dz.U.*, 1950, No. 38, Item 346.

[61]*Dz.U.*, 1950, No. 14, Item 129.

[62]*Dz.U.*, 1950, No. 14, Item 130.

[63]*Dz.U.*, 1952, No. 33, Item 232.

most of his functions were assigned to the Council of State, the latter consisting of a president, four deputy presidents, a secretary, and nine other members. It has broad jurisdiction, including the power to interpret laws and to issue decrees. The electoral law of August 1, 1952,[64] designated political, professional, and co-operative organizations, the Peasant's Mutual Aid Union, the Polish Youth Union, and other mass organizations of the working people as qualified to nominate candidates. This law has been replaced by a similar one of October 24, 1956.[65] In theory, the one-party system, characteristic of many communist countries, has not been officially introduced into Poland. There is, of course, the communist party, known as the United Workers' Party (a name established after the forced merger of the Socialist Party with the Communist Party), but in addition there are the United Peasants' Party (to correspond to the second social class, after the workers) and the Democratic Party, which is supposed to reflect the opinions of the intellectuals, although this group is not considered a separate class. Furthermore, there is a small group of Roman Catholic deputies — a concession toward the feelings of the vast majority of the population. All the deputies are chosen by a pre-electoral nomination of candidates completely controlled by the United Workers' Party, so that the nomination of enemies of the regime is unthinkable. Both the Peasants' Party and the Democratic Party are controlled by persons loyal to the communist system, so that under the facade of a multi-party system, the government rules the country without any organized political opposition. Another law concerning election to national councils was adopted on October 31, 1957.[66] The candidates can be nominated by political, professional, co-operative, and other mass organizations. The list may contain 50 percent more names than there are seats to be filled. A national council member may be deprived of his seat by resolution of the council or by his constituents. The new law governing national councils (January 25, 1958)[67] decentralized the administration. The Supreme Audit Chamber, abolished by the law of November 22, 1952,[68] was restored by the law of December 13, 1957,[69] amending the constitution, and by the law on the Supreme Audit Chamber of the same date.[70] However, this chamber was not granted independence. It is

[64]*Dz.U.*, 1952, No. 35, Item 246.

[65]*Dz.U.*, 1956, No. 47, Item 210.

[66]*Dz. U.*, 1957, No. 55, Item 270.

[67]*Dz.U.*, 1958, No. 5, Item 6.

[68]*Dz.U.*, 1952, No. 47, Item 316.

[69]*Dz.U.*, 1957, No. 61, Item 320.

[70]*Dz.U.*, 1957, No. 61, Item 321.

supervised by the Council of State. Under the decree of February 9, 1953,[71] the creation, change or abolition of ecclesiastical offices, the assumption of such offices or the removal or transfer of the incumbents required prior consent of the state. The subsequent decree of December 31, 1956,[72] abolished these and some other restrictions on religious freedom, but it provided for prior agreement of the state on the creation, change, and abolition of dioceses and parishes, as well as for changes in their boundaries and the residence of their leaders. The government has the right to veto the appointment of such heads.

Land reform was proclaimed by the manifesto of the Polish Committee of National Liberation. According to the decree of September 6, 1944, amended on January 17, 1945,[73] any land owned by individuals or legal persons, if larger than 100 hectares or including more than 50 hectares of arable land and more than 25 hectares of forest was nationalized without compensation. A law favoring establishment of collective farms was enacted.[74] After 1956, the mass withdrawal of peasants from agricultural co-operatives restored individual peasant farms. Numerous decrees enforced the compulsory delivery of produce at prices established by the state. The sale of small peasant holdings was permitted, subject to certification of the farming abilities of the purchaser by the local national council.[75] The former landowners were given pensions equal to that of a state employee of middle rank. The newly formed farms could not exceed a maximum size of five hectares, and vegetable gardens or orchard properties were limited to two hectares. The main branches of the national economy were nationalized by the law of January 3, 1946.[76] The state took over, without compensation, industrial, mining, transportation, and insurance enterprises previously owned by the Germans or persons who had fled to the enemy. As to other enterprises, the owners were supposed to obtain compensation and to pay their liabilities, except those toward the state. In fact, assessments of the amount of compensation were never established. Except for mining, oil, natural gas, electricity, gas, water distribution, iron, steel, armaments, aircraft, sugar, yeast, printing, and large and medium-size textile mills, large breweries, and grain mills, no enterprises employing fewer than fifty employees were nationalized. In

[71]Dz.U., 1953, No. 10, Item 32.

[72]Dz.U., 1957, No. 1, Item 6.

[73]Dz.U., 1944, No. 4, Item 17; 1945, No. 3, Item 9; and 1945, No. 3, Item 13 (amended complete text).

[74]Dz.U., 1950, No. 37, Item 344.

[75]Dz.U., 1957, No. 39, Item 172.

[76]Dz.U., 1946, No. 3, Item 17.

addition, the building and installation industry was not nationalized. Transport and communication enterprises were nationalized. In certain cases the Council of Ministers raised the maximum number of employees to 100 or even 150 or 200 employees. Banks were either liquidated or nationalized. Pharmacies were nationalized by the law of January 3, 1951.[77] Printing firms that had not obtained licenses before July 28, 1949 had to cease business.[78]

All land within the limits of the city of Warsaw became state property.[79] All river navigation crafts above 30 tons, if not fitted with engines, and all motor boats with engines of over 25 horsepower, with the exception of sport boats, were nationalized by the decree of February 2, 1955.[80] The former owners received pension allowances. In larger cities, all dwellings and office accommodations were subjected to public administration.[81] This meant that no premises could be used without assignment by the proper housing authority. The law of May 28, 1957 exempted from public administration one-family houses and apartments in co-operative buildings.[82] However, exemption from public administration may be claimed only in cases in which the house or apartment is occupied by its owner, his children or parents, or by members of the co-operative which owns the house. The rents were fixed at a very low rate and based on the area of the premises.

The law of January 30, 1959 [83] provided that provincial national councils and national councils of cities forming separate administrative units could create a public housing administration within their territorial jurisdiction. Where such an administration is established, an allotment of space for it is provided; tenants may be transferred and other measures taken. Even in the localities not subject to public housing administration, the local national councils are entitled to allot free space to state agencies and institutions, socialized economic units, and political organizations. If an owner fails to maintain his building properly it can be taken over by the state. Any professional activity in industry, trade, or services not socialized

[77]*Dz.U.*, 1951, No. 1, Item 1.

[78]Executive Order of the Council of Ministers of May 12, 1949 (*Dz.U.*, 1949, No. 34, Item 245).

[79]Decree of October 26, 1945 (*Dz.U.*, 1945, No. 50, Items 279 and 280; *Dz.U.*, 1950, No. 14, Item 130).

[80]*Dz.U.*, 1955, No. 6, Item 36.

[81]Decree of December 21, 1945, published on February 13, 1946 (*Dz. U.*, 1946, No. 4, Item 27).

[82]*Dz.U.*, 1957, No. 31, Item 131.

[83]*Dz.U.*, 1959, No. 10, Item 59.

requires a license.[84] The law on workers' councils, enacted on November 19, 1956,[85] in the wake of the "October thaw,"[86] was replaced on December 20, 1958 by the law on workers' self-government.[87] The workers' councils lost the autonomy they gained in 1956 and openly became subordinate to the communist party.

A new element in the administration of justice was provided by the law of July 20, 1950 concerning the organization of courts.[88] This law introduced two peoples' assessors — laymen sitting together with a professional judge of the first instance. Provisions concerning judges as to their decisons at trials are applicable to assessors as well, except that an assessor cannot preside at the court. The role of the assessors was somewhat reduced by the amendments to the code of civil procedure of March 28, 1958 and to the codes of criminal procedure of March 28, 1958 and June 18th, 1959.[89] Among the state monopolies is the important monopoly on foreign trade.[90] The whole economy, in fact, is subject to the national plan.[91] Article 8 of the constitution lists as national property: mineral resources, waters, state forests, mines, roads, railways, water and air transportation, means of communication, banks, state industrial establishments, state agricultural enterprises, state machine centers, state commercial enterprises, and communal enterprises and establishments. Article 11 of the constitution supports the development of co-operative property. Finally, Article 12 protects, according to the laws in force, individual property and the right of inheritance of land, buildings, and other means of production belonging to peasants, craftsmen, and individual workers.

Arbitration commissions were established for the purpose of securing discipline in implementing the national economic plans, safeguarding the

[84]Law of July 1, 1958 (*Dz.U.*, 1959, No. 40, Item 224).

[85]*Dz.U.*, 1956, No. 53, Item 238.

[86]Events of 1956 which led to a more liberal trend in Poland. However, many hopes aroused at that time were frustrated by subsequent revocation of concessions granted to the citizens.

[87]*Dz.U.*, 1958, No. 77, Item 397.

[88]*Dz.U.*, 1950, No. 39, Item 360.

[89]*Dz.U.*, 1958, No. 18, Items 75 and 76; and 1959, No. 36, Item 229.

[90]Article 7 (2) of the Constitution of July 22, 1952 (*Dz.U.*, July 23, 1952, No. 33, Item 232).

[91]Article 7 (1) of the Constitution of July 22, 1952.

principles of economic clearing, and securing the execution of contracts.[92] The arbitration commissions have jurisdiction over disputes between state enterprises, co-operatives, and enterprises in which the state has an interest greater than 50 percent. All members of arbitration commissions are state employees. The awards rendered by district commissions may be appealed to a main commission.

Summary

The official introduction of the Christian faith in Poland in 966 by Mieszko brought Poland into closer contact with Western Europe. The Polish state was already well organized, but very little is now known about its foundation and early structure. However, it seems that the power of the prince was somewhat curtailed by the clans. The organization of the clans and the rights of their members are indicated by certain legal institutions that survived to the known period of Polish history. Thus, a clan member was not allowed to donate his own landed property to the church unless a waiver was signed by all other members of his clan. This resulted from the right of all members of the clan to acquire land belonging to one of the members before such land could be offered for sale outside the clan. Furthermore, the institution by which brothers could hold jointly undivided landed property (*bracia niedzielni*) survived as late as the fourteenth century. This was another example of the tightly knit clan structure.

While there was no direct reception of Roman law in Poland, it influenced the Polish legal system indirectly through canon law ("Ecclesia vivit lege Romana"). The ecclesiastical courts were almost totally independent and their judgments, until the mid-sixteenth century, were enforced by the state. As these courts were well organized, parties often submitted to them even those cases which normally were not within the jurisdiction of such courts.

The publicity of debates and hearings held before the prince, assisted by officials and prelates in *wiec* (colloquium), was obviously beneficial to the administration of justice and to debates on the matters of state. While the customary law already excluded arbitrary decisions, major enactments that strengthened the rule of law appeared as early as the fourteenth century (the so-called Statutes of Casimir the Great). Meanwhile, the foundation of cities and villages under German law assured self-government for their inhabitants.

[92]Decree of August 5, 1949, amended on May 29, 1957 (*Dz.U.*, 1949, No. 46, Item 340; 1957, No.31, Item 135; 1951, No. 31, Item 239; 1954, No.23, Item 86; 1956, No. 14, Item 75; 1953, No. 2, Item 2.

The princes limited their power over certain persons and, from the thirteenth century on, over certain groups of persons by granting privileges exempting them from fiscal duties or from the jurisdiction of certain officials. This trend toward granting privileges became a factor of major importance in the development of constitutional law. The general feeling of security engendered by respect for law in Poland compared favorably with the situation in other European countries. Thus, as early as the fourteenth century, the Jews fleeing persecution in Western Europe settled in Poland in great numbers.

During the division of Poland, after the death of Bolesław the Wry-Mouth (1138), the knights sent deputies to general meetings in each of the principalities. After the reunification of the state, deputies were sent to such meetings in each of the provinces. The ascension of foreign kings to the throne of the unified state toward the end of the fourteenth century prompted the provinces to unite in order to deal effectively with the monarch. A supra-provincial convention of deputies (*sejm*) served this purpose. After the privilege of Kościce of 1374, by which Louis d'Anjou (king of Poland and Hungary) exempted the nobility from taxes (except for two *grossi* from one *laneus* of land), a vote of the *sejm* was required in order to impose additional taxes on the nobles. As to the clergy, the *sejm* did not vote taxes to be paid by them; however, the clergy, of its own will, paid a so-called *subsidium charitativum*. The statutes of Łęczyca of 1180 are generally considered as the first important grant of rights to the clergy. They abolished *ius spolii*, in virtue of which the prince could take over the moveables left by a bishop after his death, and revised certain charges of *ius ducale*.

The statutes of Nieszawa (1454) and of Piotrków (1496) provided for important limitations on the monarch's power. Thus, for instance the consent of the deputies of the nobility was necessary to call them to arms, and certain offices could not be held simultaneously by one person. In 1505 the constitution *Nihil novi* provided that the king alone could not enact new measures that could damage or weaken the state, cause prejudice against anybody, change the common law, or reduce public freedom. The consent of the king's council (senate) and of the deputies in the *sejm* became indispensable for the promulgation of new laws. The parliamentary system was well established.

The beginning of the fifteenth century brought the important privilege *Neminem captivabimunisi iure victum* which protected the noblemen not only against confiscation of their property but also against imprisonment, unless ordered by a competent court. There was also a marked trend toward administering justice according to customs and laws chosen by certain ethnic or economic groups; thus, there were special laws for cities and villages founded under German law, and a certain autonomy for such

271

groups as Jews, Armenians, and Valakhs. While the Roman Catholic religion was considered first in the state, and Catholic bishops were members of the senate, a complete religious tolerance (with minor exceptions) brought to Poland French Huguenots, English Catholics, Jews, and other persecuted groups. This atmosphere was propitious for a *rapprochement* of churches, as evidenced by the Union of Brest, which reconciled some of the Orthodox Eastern Christians with the Pope.

After the extinction of the Jagellonian dynasty in the seventeenth century, the individual freedoms, enjoyed especially by the nobility, which was in Poland a large group, became excessive. However, at the end of the eighteenth century, a national cultural and legal renascence culminated in the great Constitution of May 3, 1791, very advanced for its time. Further reorganization of the state was interrupted by the partitions of Poland by three absolutist military powers: Russia, Prussia and Austria. After a brief Napoleonic interlude in the Grand Duchy of Warsaw, the Congress of Vienna maintained the partitions. However, the constitution of the rump Kingdom of Poland, united with the Russian Empire, provided for a governmental structure much more liberal than that of Russia.

The twenty years of the Republic of Poland, 1918-1939, were characterized by a democratic regime, although after 1926 it was dominated by the authoritarian rule of Marshal Piłsudski. Here again, the return to a normal democratic regime was interrupted by German aggression in the wake of the Molotov-Ribbentrop pact.

At the end of World War II, Poland was left within the Soviet sphere of influence. The communist rulers, supported by Soviet might, introduced a system called a "people's democracy" that was completely foreign to all Polish traditions. This system puts all decisions as to general policy in the hands of the Communist Party, a tiny minority in Poland. Even in this system may be felt a trend toward greater individual freedom and co-operation with non-communist states than in some other "people's democracies." The spirit of freedom, respect for justice, and tolerance — characteristic features of Polish constitutional law throughout its one thousand years history — remains alive, even if unable to manifest itself freely during this short period of the history of the Polish nation.

RICHARD SZAWŁOWSKI

"State Control" in Poland in the Nineteenth and Twentieth Centuries*

Introduction: "State Control" in the East and the West

The organs which in the terminology adopted by the successive Congresses of Havana (1953), Brussels (1956), Rio de Janeiro (1959), Vienna (1962), Jerusalem (1965), and Tokyo (1968) are called "supreme public finance audit institutions" (in French, *institutions supérieurs de contrôle des finances publiques;* in German, *die obersten Rechnungskontrollbehörden*) are in Eastern European countries (although their activities now go far beyond purely financial audit) called "state control." This term derives from nineteenth-century Russia (*gosudarstvennyj kontrol*) and was rendered into Polish (*kontrola państwowa*), and after World War II into Czech (*státna kontrola*), German (*Staatskontrolle*–term used in the GDR), and several other East European languages.[1]

---

*The task of this chapter is to give a short historical review and a summary of recent Polish "state control." It must be stressed that for lack of space we have concentrated only on matters of first importance and reduced the legal and bibliographical documentation quoted in this chapter to the minimum. Research has been done in the following archives: the Archiwum Główne Akt Dawnych in Warsaw, Manuscript Division of the Czartoryski's Museum and the District State Archives in Cracow, and the Polish Library in Paris (for the nineteenth century); the Archiwum Akt Nowych in Warsaw (for the period between the two world wars); and the Archives of the Supreme Board of Control in Warsaw (for the period after World War II). The results of this research are made use of in this chapter, but the author has dispensed with quoting the particular files.

[1] Due to the fact that for the Anglo-Saxon reader the term "state control" as a synonym of concrete names given to the individual supreme public finance audit institutions in different countries may, in spite of the explanations given in the

273

It is a *terminus technicus*, and its specific designations in various countries are the General Accounting Office (and its counterparts in the individual states, e.g. the Auditor General in California) in the United States, the Exchequer and Audit Department (Comptroller and Auditor General) in the United Kingdom, the *Cour des comptes* in France, the *Bundesrechnungshof* (and the *Rechnungshöfe* of the *Länder*) in the Federal Republic of Germany, the Committee of People's Control of the Council of Ministers of the USSR (and its replicas in the Union's republics and autonomous republics) in the Soviet Union, as of December 1965.[2]

To determine the apparatus of "state control" in a given country, whether in the East or in the West, one must consider a number of points: who is examined, which areas of activity are examined, what criteria for examination are adopted, what kinds of examination are applied, what post-audit powers the "state control" possesses, what position "state control" occupies within the framework of the division of governmental powers into the three main branches, and finally, how "state control" is organized.

To begin with, we will discuss briefly these aspects of "state control" as it operates in both East and West.[3]

[1] Introduction to this chapter, be confusing, we will use in this text the term *state control organs* (*apparatus, institutions*) or "state control" in quotation marks. Apart from that, one should bear in mind that in the Slavonic languages the word "control" is a synonym of "examination" or "inspection," and does not have the meaning of the same word in English.

[2] "State control" in the USSR has, during the past fifty odd years, undergone frequent and radical changes. Between 1918 and 1965 there have been approximately ten reforms, connected with changes in the names of the respective organs. To mention only the reforms which took place starting with World War II: in 1940 the People's Commissariat for State Control of the USSR was created (and rebaptized as "Ministry" in 1946). In 1957 the Ministry of State Control was abolished and replaced by the Commission for Soviet Control of the Council of Ministers of the USSR. The latter was abolished in 1961 and replaced by the Commission for State Control of the Council of Ministers of the USSR. This commission, in turn, was abolished in November 1962 and replaced by the Committee for Party and State Control of the Central Committee of the CPSU and the Council of Ministers of the USSR. Finally, by an act of December 9, 1965, the latter organ was abolished and the current Committee of People's Control of the Council of Ministers of the USSR was created. Indeed, this is a kaleidoscope of frequent changes, quite the reverse of the highly stabilized supreme public finance audit institutions in the West.

[3] Valuable relevant material can be found in the papers presented by the state control institutions of many countries to the successive congresses of the supreme public finance audit institutions (1953, 1956, 1959, 1962, 1965, and 1968), mentioned at the beginning of this chapter. These papers, however, cover only those topics which were discussed at the congresses, and thus do not give a full picture of

As far as the problem of who is examined is concerned, state control organs in all countries first of all concentrate their activities on the state administration. In the West, however, "state control" does not generally deal with local government, which is audited by other organs (an exception to this rule is, e.g., the French *Cour des comptes*). Contrary to this, in the Eastern countries, where the whole public administration is organized according to a uniform pattern, "state control" examines the functioning of the entire administrative apparatus, central and local.

Apart from public administration, the state (nationalized) industries may be an additional area for examination. In those Western countries possessing such industries, examination is provided in various ways. In the United Kingdom, for instance, the Exchequer and Audit Department does not audit the nationalized industries. In France, although there is a special body charged with the task here under discussion — the *Commission de vérification des comptes des entreprises publiques* — this body is located in the *Cour des comptes* and has one of its presidents as chairman. High-ranking officers of the *Cour des comptes* preside over its sections, and the majority of the Commission's members having deliberative vote are magistrates of the *Cour des comptes*. On the other hand, the Austrian *Rechnungshof* examines directly the nationalized industries of that country. In Eastern countries the entire economic apparatus is examined by their organs of state control.

the problems involved. In addition, some countries abstained from participating in these congresses (for example, some Anglo-Saxon countries, headed by the United States).

A German work by Kurt Heinig, *Die Budgetkontrolle,* (Vol. I of *Das Budget*, Tübigen, 1949) gives useful information about state control institutions in many countries. Some countries have monographs dealing with their own state control organs: e.g., H. C. Mansfield, "The Comptroller General" (New Haven, 1939), for the United States; B. Chubb, "The Control of Public Expenditure" (Oxford, 1952), for the United Kingdom; the anniversary publication *Cent-cinquantenaire de la Cour des comptes 1807-1957* (Paris, 1957) for France; the anniversary publication *200 Jahre Rechnungshof* (Vienna, 1961) for Austria; the anniversary publication *250 Jahre Rechnungsprüfung. Zur zweihundertfünfzigjährigen Wiederkehr der Errichtung der Preussischen Generalrechenkammer* (Frankfurt-am-Main, 1964). About the *Bundesrechnungshof* see, in English, Hillhous-Lang, "The German Federal Audit Court," *Accounting Review,* XXVII (1952), p.530. As to the "state control" in tsarist Russia and in the USSR (including the reform of November 1962), see R. Szawlowski, "Die Staatskontrolle im alten Russland und in der USSR" in *Osteuropa-Recht,* No. 2, 1963 (with English, French, and Russian summaries). For a shorter history of "state control" in the USSR (including only the reform of July 1961) compared with the *Prokuratura* (public prosecutor's office exercising general supervision over legality in the public administration), see R. Szawlowski, "Le contrôle étatique dans l'Union Sovietique" in *Revue Internationele des Sciences Administratives,* No. 3, 1962.

Finally, the state control organs in Western countries sometimes audit the social insurance programs (e.g., the West German *Bundesrechnungshof* or the French *Cour des comptes*) and also some categories of social or even private organizations if subsidized by the state (e.g., the U.S. General Accounting Office audits local administrations, universities, and other institutions receiving federal funds — including contractors and sub-contractors). In Eastern countries, in general, almost all non-state organizations, including the cooperatives, are systematically examined by "state control."[4] (The Polish Supreme Board of Control offers some exceptions to be discussed below.)

Thus "state control" in the East generally has a far broader scope of activity in this field than in the West.

As regards the problem of which areas of activity are examined, in some Western countries state control organs are interested exclusively in financial problems (e.g., the Italian *Corte dei Conti* or the Belgian *Cour des comptes*). Other Western state control organs (e.g., the U.S. General Accounting Office, the West German *Bundesrechnungshof,* and the Austrian *Rechnungshof*) are, in addition, concerned with problems of management, organization, and even production.[5] In the East nearly all aspects of the activity of the controlled units are examined by "state control." Thus, again, Eastern state control organs have a broader field of activity than their counterparts in the West.

[4]Excluded are, for instance, the Communist Parties' apparatuses. These parties have their own auditing bodies, called, at the national level, the Central Auditing Commission, and a hierarchy of lower-level auditing commissions. The Central Auditing Commission of the Polish Communist Party (PZPR), apart from auditing the Party's income and expenditure, also reports on the examination of the handling of complaints, petitions, and letters received by the Central Committee and local party organizations, and investigates the state of care over "meritorious activitists, veterans of the working class movement, and the families they left behind," about which see the report of the Central Auditing Commission presented at the Fifth Party Congress in 1968, and published in *Życie Warszawy* of November 12, 1968. The Party auditing commissions should not be confused with the Party control committees (or commissions), whose task it is to verify the members' observance of the party program and statutes, "party and state discipline," and "party ethics."

[5]How far, for instance, the scope of the activities of the U.S. General Accounting Office goes beyond the mere auditing of accounts may be well illustrated by a few examples taken from its most recent practice. Thus the office reviewed the army management of its tractor-trailer fleet in Europe and U.S. aid to the Republic of Korea; reported on the need to strengthen controls by the agricultural research services over public sales of pesticides; and presented a survey of the adequacy and effectiveness of U.S. Air Force practices in disposing of repairable spare parts, for example. See *GAO Newsletter* of February 12, 1968; August 15, 1968; October 15, 1968; and November 15, 1968, respectively.

276

Concerning the examination criteria, the state control organs in some Western countries traditionally limit themselves to the criterion of legality (e.g., the Belgian *Cour des comptes,* the Luxembourg *Chambre des comptes,* and the Italian *Corte dei Conti*). But today the majority of Western state control organs are also extensively concerned with far broader examination criteria: especially, for example, that of economy and financial efficiency (e.g., the General Accounting Office in the U.S., the French *Cour des comptes,* and the *Bundesrechnungshof*). In Eastern countries "state control" adopts very broad examination criteria which include not only legality, economy, and financial efficiency, but also a criterion which could be called "political expediency."

Two kinds of examination are generally exercised within the framework of financial audit: pre-audit and post-audit. The first (sometimes also called "a priori" − or "preventive" audit) is exercised *before* a payment decision is taken or a payment order is fulfilled, the latter (which is also called "a posteriori" audit) is performed *after* payment.

The state control organs of some Western countries (e.g., the Italian *Corte dei Conti,* the Belgian *Cour des comptes,* the Swiss *Contrôle fédéral des finances*) perform different kinds of pre-audit, but the majority of them concentrate on post-audit. State control organs in Eastern countries, in general, do not perform pre-audits. Especially characteristic of state control procedures in the East is the so-called "actual control" (*faktitsheskij kontrol* in Russian, *kontrola faktyczna* in Polish), which is an examination performed on the spot during the course of activity (such as production, storage, or a cash transaction).

As far as the post-examination powers of state control organs are concerned, differences may be noted. In the West, "state control" in the Romance countries (e.g., the French and Belgian *Cours des comptes,* the Spanish *Tribunal de Cuentas* and the Brazilian *Tribunal de Contas*) is given judicial power similar to that of civil tribunals to deal with state employees in charge of making payments (*comptables*) and sometimes even with those empowered to decide on payment orders (*ordonnateurs*). Normally, however, Western state control organs have no imperative post-audit powers; their role is confined to notifying the units concerned and the parliament of detected irregularities and to monitoring correctional procedures. In contrast, Eastern state control organs normally possess some imperative post-examination powers. Soviet "state control," for instance, can inflict disciplinary punishments or hand down decisions on repayment of damages caused to the State (limited in amount to three month's salary of the employee involved). However, it must be stressed that this is not the main "weapon" of state control organs in the East, which, like their Western counterparts, are required above all to notify and to watch.

277

Finally, the question of the placement and organization of "state control" remains to be outlined. In the West "state control" is normally either an organ of the legislative branch of government (e.g., in the Anglo-Saxon countries, Belgium, and Austria) or, at any rate, maintains independence from the executive branch and has contacts with the legislature (e.g., in West Germany or Japan). It is normally organized into chambers, boards, or offices of high status. In a number of new African states which were formerly French, "state control" functions as one of the departments of the supreme court.[6] Only in some small Western countries, such as Switzerland and Denmark, does "state control" still remain administratively within the framework of the Department or Ministry of Finance and yet maintain direct contact with the legislature.

The position of state control organs in the East differs in many respects from that in the West. First of all, with the exception of the Polish Supreme Board of Control, "state control" is an organ of the executive. In 1963 things even went so far that in some East European countries the state control organs were merged with the control apparatus of the Communist parties and with the so-called "social control of the masses." Thus in the USSR and Bulgaria, committees of party and state control, and in East Germany the Worker's and Peasants' Inspection (*Arbeiter-und Bauerninspektion*) were created. The first was liquidated in 1965, but the two others still exist. In Czechoslovakia, on the other hand, following the liquidation of the Ministry of State Control in 1961, the Central Office of State Control and Statistics (*Ústřední Úřad Státní Kontroly a Statistiky*) was created. This office, in turn, was replaced in 1963 by a new system headed by the Central Commission of People's Control and Statistics (*Ústřední Komise Lidově Kontroly a Statistiky*). Finally the latter was divorced from the statistical branch and replaced in 1967 by a system headed by the Central Commission of People's Control.

Summing up, one can say that Eastern and Western countries exhibit great differences in "state control" organization and procedure, the powers given to such agencies, and the scope of their activities. However, although the tasks of "state control" in socialist countries are broader, if the notion "public finance examination" is understood *lato sensu* (thus comprising the examination of the whole economic activity of the state, which always has its financial counterpart), it can be said that the *main* task of socialist "state control" is a financial examination, too. Thus, apart from all profound differences, a certain "common denominator" between the state control organs in the East and in the West does exist.

[6]See, for example, the state constitutions of the Republic of Gabon of February 21, 1961 (art. 59); of the Republic of the Congo (Brazzaville) of December 8, 1963 (art. 71); and of Dahomey of January 11, 1964 (art. 85). Texts are found in J. A. Peaslee, *Constitutions of Nations* (3rd ed.; The Hague: Martinus Nijhoff, 1965), I.

Following these introductory remarks, let us consider the Polish "state control." These institutions have a tradition which, though not uninterrupted, goes back to the beginning of the nineteenth century.

The Audit of Public Finance in Pre-Partition Poland until the End of the Eighteenth Century

In the old Polish state, which existed until the partitions of the country at the end of the eighteenth century, there was no "state control," though in some of its neighbor states such organs already existed: the Prussian *General-Rechen Kammer* was created in 1713 or 1714, and the Austrian "state control" was founded in 1761 but gradually lost much of its importance and was totally abolished in the period between 1801 and 1805. Russia, however, created its "state control" only in 1811.

It should be mentioned that the so-called Fiscal Tribunals (*Trybunały Skarbowe*), which existed in pre-partition Poland from the sixteenth until the beginning of the eighteenth century, were not state control organs, although some authors have thought so.[7] These tribunals had jurisdiction over civil servants who had committed offences in connection with the administration of public funds and also had jurisdiction in tax-evasion cases. A Fiscal Tribunal acted as a kind of special criminal court which started proceedings only on the petition of the so-called instigator and generally pronounced penalties of banishment and confiscation of property.

Thus the Fiscal Tribunals were not organs of state control established to audit systematically the state accounts. In pre-partition Poland the only body which was concerned with control over the state accounts (although not systematically) was the Diet (Parliament) itself.[8]

"State Control" in the Duchy of Warsaw, 1808-15

In Poland state control organs were created for the first time in the so-called Duchy of Warsaw (*Księstwo Warszawskie*), brought into being by Napoleon in a small part of the former Poland in 1807 and lasting until

[7] See, e.g., Antoni Puljanowski, "Najwyższa Izba Obrachunkowa Królestwa Polskiego 1808-1866" ("The Supreme Audit Board of the Kingdom of Poland 1808-1866"), published in *Biblioteka Umiejętności Prawnych* (Warsaw) Nos. 42-44, series III, year VII (1880), p. 1, asserting that the General Audit Board of the Duchy of Warsaw "replaced" the Fiscal Tribunals.

[8] See, e.g., for the seventeenth century, *Volumina Legum*, IV, 314-315, 597 ff., 774 ff. and 714 ff; and for the eighteenth century, *Volumina Legum*, VIII, 190 ff. and 888 ff.

1815.[9] The decree of December 14, 1808,[10] established the General Audit Board (*Główna Izba Obrachunkowa*) of the Duchy of Warsaw. The main task of this board was the post-audit of state accounts from the point of view of legality; it did not have any imperative post-audit competences. Some broader audit criteria (particularly that of economy) stipulated by the decree were to have been adopted (as far as one can understand today on the basis of the archival documents still in existence) in what amounted to general remarks of the board on the audited state accounts as a whole, and not vis-à-vis individual audited accounts.

The General Audit Board of the Duchy of Warsaw was not, as some authors have thought,[11] a replica of the French *Cour des comptes*. During the drafting of the decree of December 1808 (end of May and beginning of June 1808) a suggestion was made to model the "state control" in the Duchy of Warsaw on the French "state control," with modifications; but this was never done, and a comparison of the French act (*loi*) of September 9, 1807 concerning the *Cour des comptes* with the Polish decree of December 14, 1808 substantiates this. This is interesting, as it is generally known that in the period of the Duchy of Warsaw a number of French legal institutions relating to civil law and organization of public administration *were* adopted in central Poland.

The practical activity of the General Audit Board was, as a result of war conditions, very limited and played a smaller role than might have been expected. An immense number of unaudited accounts accumulated, the standard of the account-keeping was generally low, and the whole budgetary system was imperfect. The stormy political scene of those years (including the temporary occupation of Warsaw by the Austrians in 1809 before Austerlitz and by the Russians in 1813 after Napoleon's defeat in the Moscow campaign) even caused a lengthy cessation of General Audit Board activity.

Some initiatives undertaken by the board itself (1810) and by a prominent deputy (Joseph Godlewski) during the session of the Diet in 1811, aiming at enlargement of the scope of state control activity and at making it more efficient, were not realized.

[9]For a more detailed analysis of the "state control" in the Duchy of Warsaw and in the Kingdom of Poland, see R. Szawłowski, "Kontrola państwowa w Polsce w XIX.wieku" ("State Control in Poland in the XIX Century") in *Kontrola Państwowa* (organ of the Polish Supreme Board of Control), No. 6, 1958, pp. 1-16.

[10]*Dziennik Praw Księstwa Warszawskiego* ("Law Gazette of the Duchy of Warsaw"), I, 120.

[11]See Henryk Rosman, "Rys historyczny budżetu w Polsce" ("Historical Outline of the Budget in Poland"), in *Ekonomista,* No. IV, 1865; Nos. I and II, 1866 and No. II, 1868. The allegation which interests us here is in No. II, 1868, p. 222.

Generally one can consider the six to seven years' activity of the "state control" in the Duchy of Warsaw as a kind of elementary school for the first apparatus of its kind in Poland's history. This experience was not without importance in the creation and operation of later state control organs in the Kingdom of Poland.

"State Control" in the Kingdom of Poland, 1816-66

The Congress of Vienna (1815) created the so-called Kingdom of Poland, now a small "buffer state" under the rule of the Russian tsars, who were at the same time to be kings of Poland.

In the Kingdom of Poland a Board of Audit (*Izba Obrachunkowa*) was created in 1816[12] on the basis of the "state control" which had existed in the former Duchy of Warsaw. This board was reorganized in 1821[13] and existed for almost fifty years under the name of the Supreme Audit Board (*Najwyższa Izba Obrachunkowa*).

We shall concentrate here on the state control organs which existed from 1821 on.

If one compares the two decrees – that of December 1808 establishing the former General Audit Board and that of August 1821 establishing the Supreme Audit Board – one can see great differences. Certainly, the main task of "state control" under both regimes was the post-audit of state accounts. But, as was mentioned above, "state control" in the Duchy did not have any imperative post-audit competences. If something irregular was detected (for example, any improper use of public moneys or embezzlement), the General Audit Board was required only to report it to the king. On the other hand, the Supreme Audit Board was empowered to pronounce judgments concerning compulsory restitution of pecuniary damages caused by civil servants to the State.

This solution was undoubtedly inspired by the legislation respecting the French *Cour des comptes,* which could – and can – pronounce such judgments. But there was a difference in this respect between the state control organs of the two countries: the judgments of the *Cour des comptes* were absolutely restricted to the *comptables,*[14] whereas the Supreme Audit Board of the Kingdom of Poland – at any rate beginning

[12]*Dziennik Praw Królestwa Polskiego* ("Law Gazette of the Kingdom of Poland"), II,160

[13]*Dziennik Praw Królestwa Polskiego,* VII, 230.

[14]In 1948, the so-called *Cour de la discipline budgétaire,* composed of representatives of the *Cour des comptes* and the *Conseil d'Etat,* was created in France; it has a restricted jurisdiction over the *ordonnateurs.*

281

with 1842 — extended its judgments also to the *ordonnateurs* and even to third persons.[15]

There were also two other features which clearly demonstrated the widening of the tasks of the "state control" in the Kingdom of Poland compared with that of the Duchy of Warsaw.

First, the Supreme Audit Board was represented by its president or its senior officers in the preparation of the state budget of the kingdom. Second, it extended its examinations to the execution of the state budget as a whole by presenting a final closing statement on the yearly state accounts and general remarks on the execution of the state budget. These tasks were almost never performed by the General Audit Board of the Duchy of Warsaw.

These distinctions make clear the great differences between the state control organs in the kingdom of Poland and the Duchy of Warsaw: something which has not always been noticed in literature.[16]

In discussing the practical activities of the Supreme Audit Board, we will confine ourselves to two major problems.

First, there was the problem of mutual relations between the "state control" and the parliament of the Kingdom of Poland. All the Diets convoked between 1818 and 1830 (their power very much limited by the Constitution of the Kingdom) demanded closer relations with the "state control". They wished to use the Supreme Board's reports and to appoint leading board members from among the ranks of the parliament and to ensure that its president was a senator. However, this was never agreed to by the Russian tsars, who also functioned as Polish kings and were obsessed by their belief in the famous *samoderzhavie* (absolute power of the tsar).

Only during the uprising of 1830-1 could the Diet in liberated Warsaw — after having amended the Constitution of the Kingdom in this respect — elect (in March 1831) the president of the Supreme Audit Board (Andrzej Horodyski).[17] This was, for that period, a revolutionary act, stressing the close relationship and, at the same time, the auxiliary role of "state control" to the parliament: before and after the uprising the chief of the

[15]See the bilingual (Russian and Polish) *Zbiór przepisów administracyjnych Królestwa Polskiego. Wydział Skarbu. Tom XVI o rachunkowości i kontrolli* ("Collection of Administrative Rules of the Kingdom of Poland. Division of the Treasury, Vol. XVI, Concerning Accountancy and Audit"), pp. 366-73.

[16]See Stanisław Kutrzeba in *Historia ustroju Polski w zarysie. Tom III: po rozbiorach* ("An Outline of the History of the Polish Governmental System." Vol. III: "After the Paritions") (3rd ed.: Lwów, 1917), III, 127. He asserts that in the Kingdom of Poland "the Audit Board was preserved without changes."

[17]Michał Rostworowski, ed., *Dyaryusz Sejmu z r.1830-1831* ("The Minutes of the Diet 1830-1831"), II, 303-8.

"state control" was appointed by the king (and tsar) at the proposal of his lieutenant in the Kingdom of Poland. The only precedent then known was in the newly independent Belgium, where, in an act passed in December 1830 (replaced by an act of 1846 which is still in force), the parliament decided that the leading members of the Belgian *Cour des comptes* should be elected by the parliament itself.[18]

The defeat of the uprising several months later brought the suppression by the Russians of any kind of parliamentarianism in the Kingdom of Poland and thus made any cooperation between "state control" and legislature pointless.

The second point to be discussed is that of the audit criteria adopted by the Supreme Audit Board and the scope of its audit results.

It is evident that the fundamental audit criterion was legality. But at the same time other criteria, especially those of economy and expediency, were also used to a certain extent.

With regard to the audit results of the Supreme Audit Board, one is struck, when reading its annual reports, by their wide scope. Although the majority of these reports were destroyed in Polish archives during World War II, some of the reports which were saved, dating back to the early 1860's, present interesting data. They deal, for instance, with the methods of evaluation of budgetary incomes and the budgetary scheme; they propose modifications of tax law; they suggest the development of savings banks; and they demand the extension of the government's supervision over private woodlands because of their national importance. Some of the state control's proposals have an outspokenly progressive social character, as, for instance, the demand to lower the price of salt, which is described as "being too burdensome for the poorer working class of the country," and the demand to enlarge the network of elementary schools in the country because the peasants required more education.

All of this useful and interesting activity of the Supreme Audit Board of the Kingdom of Poland came to an end in 1866 when, after the failure of the new uprising of 1863 - 4, the remaining autonomy of the so-called Kingdom of Poland was crushed by the Russians. Beginning in 1867 they replaced the Supreme Audit Board by their own "state control."[19]

[18]How revolutionary this solution seemed in the nineteenth century one can see from the fact that even at the end of that century the well-known German scholar Max von Heckel wrote about it in *Das Budget* (Leipzig, 1898) pp. 299-300: "The whole organization of the Belgian Supreme Audit Board is a dogmatic exaggeration of the constitutional principle. . . . Such caricatures of constitutional ideals are often more damaging to the vital functions of the state than they theoretically serve the realization of constitutionalism."

[19]*Dziennik Praw Królestwa Polskiego*, LXVI, 365.

The Period between 1867 and 1917-8

In the fifty years between 1867 and 1917 there was no Polish "state control." There existed only the state control institutions of the occupation powers: the Russian *Vedomstvo Gosudarstvennovo Kontrolja* (with headquarters in St. Petersburg and the branch offices in the *goubernias*), the Prussian *Rechnungshof* in Potsdam (at the same time — under the label of the *Reichsrechnungshof* — the state control organ for the German Empire) and finally, in Vienna, the *Gemeinsamer Oberster Rechnungshof* for the Austrio-Hungarian Empire (finance, war and external affairs) and the *Oberster Rechnungshof* for Austria itself. Many Poles worked in the Russian and Austrian state control offices, sometimes even in very high positions, but this was not their own "state control."

An embryonic Polish "state control" was created after a period of fifty years, in 1917. It followed the establishment by the Germans and Austrians in 1916, during World War I, of the so-called Kingdom of Poland in a part of the Polish territories they had taken over from the Russians. In August 1917, within the framework of the newly-organized central administration, an Audit Office (*Urząd Obrachunkowy*) was created.[20]

"State control" in Poland between the Two World Wars: 1918-39

A new chapter in the history of the Polish "state control" began when the country regained its independence in November of 1918.

At the beginning, the Supreme Board of State Control (*Najwyższa Izba Kontroli Państwa*, 1919-21)[21] was established. Shortly thereafter it was replaced by the Supreme Board of Control (*Najwyższa Izba Kontroli*, 1921-39).[22] The main reason for the reform of 1921 was the pre-audit performed by the first state control organ, which led to serious friction with the executive branch. We will concentrate here on the "state control" which existed between 1921 and 1939.

"State control" was a separate governmental agency of ministerial rank, independent from the cabinet and directly subordinate to the President of

[20]This was done by an act voted by the plenum of the Provisional State Council (*Tymczasowa Rada Stanu*) which has never been published. Its text is in the *Archiwum Akt Nowych* in Warsaw.

[21]*Dziennik Praw Państwa Polskiego* ("Law Gazette of the Polish State"), No. 14 1919, Item 183.

[22]*Dziennik Ustaw Rzeczypospolitej Polskiej* ("Law Gazette of the Polish Republic"), No. 51, 1921, Item 314.

the Republic. The president of the Supreme Board of Control was appointed by the President of the Republic, following a proposal of one candidate by the cabinet. According to article 9 of the Constitution of March 1921, senior staff members of the "state control" were independent and had the status of judges; they could be removed only by a resolution of the Diet adopted by a three-fifths majority. However, the new Constitution of April 1935 gave the President of the Republic a free hand regarding the appointment and revocation of the president of the Supreme Board of Control.

Apart from its headquarters in Warsaw, a number of "state control" branch offices were created; they were the District Boards of Control (*Okręgowe Izby Kontroli*) and a Control Office (*Urząd Kontroli*) for Upper Silesia. The total staff amounted to about 600 in 1939.

The main task of the Supreme Board, according to the 1921 act, was the audit of the "income and expenditures of the state and of the condition of its properties." In addition, the "state control" could also — if asked to do so by the cabinet — audit the local administration and corporations, foundations, and associations managed with the financial participation of the state or under its guarantees.

The pre-audit performed by the "state control" starting in 1919 was abolished in 1921. Thereafter it exercised local examination (*kontrola faktyczna*) and post-audit. A big role was played by local examination, which is that exercised on location during the course of an activity such as construction or production, or on the current condition of such property as stores or cash.

As for the criteria adopted by the state control organs, the act of 1921 provided for those of legality, economy, and expediency from the economic point of view.

Regarding the post-audit powers of the Supreme Board of Control, there was a discrepancy between the provisions of the act of 1921 and actual practice. The act provided that, upon the discovery of an irregularity, the "state control" should deliver to the responsible units so-called control decisions (*orzeczenia kontrolne*). Such units were obligated to comply without delay with the orders given in these decisions. The intent, it seems, was to provide "state control" with the power to enforce prompt and complete fulfillment of its demands. However, these provisions of the 1921 act were not quite clear and were a typical *lex imperfectum*. Especially in regard to recovery of damages caused to the State by civil servants, the system of these control decisions did not function well. Such cases were generally brought to court, where they often remained many years before final judgment. State control organs could also demand the suspension of the employees responsible for detected irregularities, but this rarely happened in practice.

285

Under these circumstances the main weapon of the state control organs against irregularities was simply written notification of the unit concerned, which was required to answer within one month. If an answer was either not forthcoming or unsatisfactory, the "state control" referred the matter to the unit immediately superior to that which was responsible. Eventually the matter could be presented to the President of the Republic and to the parliament.

The climax of the yearly activities of the Supreme Board of Control was the presentation of two documents to the President of the Republic and to the parliament (copies were also sent to the Prime Minister and the Minister of Finance): (1) remarks concerning the execution of the state budget, with a motion concerning the provision or refusal by Parliament of approval (*décharge*) to the cabinet; and (2) a yearly report on the activities of the "state control" during the previous budgetary year. Apart from these documents, the "state control" was given the right to present at any time to the President of the Republic and to parliament additional reports and conclusions concerning important and urgent matters.

Concluding these observations on the Polish "state control" between the two World Wars, mention must be made of the role it played within the framework of the whole state apparatus in this period of the country's history.

During its twenty years of activity, highly skilled state control officers, including lawyers, economists, accountants, engineers, and other professional specialists, made an important contribution to the establishment and efficiency of the state administration, the improvement of which during this period was striking.

On the other hand, the relations between "state control" and parliament and cabinet became less and less close in the thirties as compared with the twenties. This was the result of the development of the general political situation which – starting with Piłsudski's *coup d'état* of 1926 – gradually shifted from full political democracy towards an authoritarian system of government.

In the twenties the "state control" was considered by many political leaders and also by its own president between 1921 and 1926 (Jan Żarnowski) as an organ of the parliament. There existed some working contacts, insufficient though these were, between the Supreme Board of Control and the parliament: representatives of the "state control" took an active part in the sittings of the budgetary committees of both houses of parliament, and the Supreme Board exercised audits, upon parliamentary demand, and reported special cases, on its own initiative, to the legislative bodies.

In the thirties these contacts were either sharply reduced or ceased to exist. Even the yearly reports of the "state control" ceased to be printed after 1928-9, allegedly for reasons of economy, and were only mimeographed and distributed in such small numbers that they were not easily available to the general public.

"State Control" under the Polish Government in Exile during World War II

Nazi aggression and the occupation of Poland in September 1939 brought an end to Polish "state control" within the country itself.

The Polish government in exile (which until the capitulation of France in 1940 resided in Angers and afterwards in London) adapted the "state control" to meet the new circumstances.

The decree of the President of the Republic dated February 14, 1940,[23] which was "enacted for the period of special circumstances caused by the war" (and at the same time repealed the act of 1921), preserved the major fundamentals of the former "state control". The new Supreme Board of Control, like the old one, was a separate governmental agency of ministerial rank, independent from the cabinet and directly subordinate to the President of the Republic. The "state control" administration was reduced in size to the Supreme Board of Control alone, however, and no branch offices were provided for by the decree of 1940.

The main task of "state control" was, as before, audit of the "income and expenditures of the state and of the condition of its properties." The optional audit of local administration as well as corporations, foundations, and associations managed with the financial participation of the state or under its guarantees was also maintained.

The decree of 1940 provided for the same kinds of activities (local examination and post-audit) and the same audit criteria (legality, economy, and expediency from the economic point of view) as the act of 1921. However, regarding the post-audit powers, the decree of 1940 did not provide for the "control decisions." The "state control", as in prewar times, merely notified the "proper authority" of irregularities and ensured that appropriate consequences were carried out. As in the prewar period, the "state control" could demand the suspension of the employee concerned.

As the end result of the whole year's activity, the Supreme Board of Control was, as before the war, to present to the President of the Republic and the National Council of the Polish Republic (*Rada Narodowa Rzeczypospolitej Polskiej*, a quasi-parliament in exile) remarks concerning the execution of the state budget and a yearly report about its own activity in the past budgetary year (with copies of both these documents

[23]*Dziennik Ustaw Rzeczypospolitej Polskiej*, No. 5, 1940, Item 5.

to be sent to the Prime Minister and the Minister of Finance). However, the Supreme Board no longer motioned for parliamentary acceptance or refusal of the executed budget, as the parliament was now not empowered to make such decisions.

Concerning the practical activity of the Polish "state control" in exile, the Supreme Board functioned until June 1940 in Paris, and afterwards in London. It was a relatively small body, with a staff reaching a total of twenty-seven in 1944.[24]

The audit of state income was pointless in these years: there were no taxes, and the receipts of the state budget consisted of lump sums loaned to the Polish Ministry of Finance by the British Treasury. (The budget amounted, for instance, to more than 77 million pounds in 1944.) The Supreme Board of Control concentrated on the audit of expenditures of the government, primarily for the administration and the armed forces. For the efficiency of on-the-spot audits, three very small branch offices of the Supreme Board were created in the United States, Iran, and Palestine.

"State Control" in Poland after World War II, 1944-56

After the liberation of Poland from German occupation in 1944-5 (which, contrary to the expectations of the overwhelming majority of the population, did not come from the West) the state control organs in Poland underwent profound reforms several times, as a result of radically changed political, social, and economic conditions.[25]

The prewar Supreme Board of Control was not restored, and only a very few of its former officers were permitted to work in the new "state control."

In the years between 1944 and 1949, a special Control Bureau (*Biuro Kontroli*) existed in Lublin and afterwards in Warsaw, with its branch offices. This bureau was affiliated first with the Presidium of the so-called Country's National Council (*Krajowa Rada Narodowa*) and, after 1947, the State Council (*Rada Państwa*).

[24] I should like to express my gratitude to Mr. Okoniewski, vice-president of the Polish Supreme Board of Control before 1939 and afterwards it vice-president and president-in-exile, for the information concerning the activity of the "state control" in the years 1940-5, which he kindly gave me during our talk in London in September 1962.

[25] See R. Szawłowski, *W obliczu nowej reformy kontroli państwowej w Polsce"* ("On the Eve of a New Reform of the State Control in Poland") in *Państwo i Prawo* ("State and Law," organ of the Institute of Legal Sciences of the Polish Academy of Sciences), No. 4-5, 1957, pp. 752-69.

The legal basis for the functioning of the Control Bureau was article 16 of the act of September 11, 1944, respecting the so-called national councils;[26] this act, among other things, enlarged the scope of the "state control" to deal with organizational and administrative problems.[27] As a result of this, the examination criteria were also expanded to include *general* efficiency and expediency. As far as other problems were concerned, "state control" from 1944 to 1949 was based, in principle, on prewar legislation—especially on the act of 1921 and the general audit instruction of 1922, which were repealed as late as 1949 and 1950, respectively.

In the two years following World War II, the Control Bureau was primarily concerned with administrative and organizational problems. According to unpublished and, at that time, confidential reports of the bureau, it controlled, for instance, the implementation of the land reform, the organization of public administration, and settlement on recovered territories east of the Oder-Neisse border, and performed on-the-spot investigations on the basis of complaints of the population, especially against the police (illegal requisitions). Financial audits, especially the post-audit, did not regain their former importance until 1947.

The second post-war period in the history of the Polish "state control" began in 1949, when the Supreme Board of Control was recreated by the act of March 9 of that year.[28]

According to this act, the Supreme Board of Control was "independent of the cabinet." Its president was to be elected and dismissed by the Diet. The "state control" was directly subordinate to the State Council and had branch offices (*delegatury miejscowe*). The scope of units examined by the Supreme Board was practically the same as that of the former Control Bureau. The subjects examined and the criteria adopted were as broad as those applied by the former bureau; in addition to others, administrative and organizational problems, such as the training of employees in state administration, were subject to bureau control.

The act of 1949 provided for three kinds of examination: preventive, local, and ex-post-facto. The scope of preventive examination was to have been defined by special State Council instructions, which, however, never

[26]*Dziennik Ustaw Rzeczypospolitej Polskiej*, No. 5, 1944, Item 22. This decree was afterwards amended and its uniform text was published in the *Dziennik Ustaw*, No. 3, 1946, Item 26.

[27]This was not noticed by Maurycy Jaroszyński in *Polskie Prawo Administracyjne* ("Polish Administrative Law") (Warsaw, 1956), p. 451. He asserts that "in the scope of the state control itself, during this starting period, no formal changes were introduced."

[28]*Dziennik Ustaw Rzeczypospolitej Polskiej*, No. 13, 1949, Item 74.

appeared, so that this kind of examination was exercised only in special cases.

Regarding the post-examination powers of the Supreme Board of Control, the main weapon (as in prewar times and during the existence of the Control Bureau) was the notification of irregularities to the unit responsible or to that unit immediately superior to it. A special type of notification was the information sent to the public prosecutor's office to initiate penal proceedings. Another kind of post-examination power of the Supreme Board, this time of an imperative nature, was the issuing of decisions (*postanowienia*); beginning in 1951, the Supreme Board could, among other things, order reparation of damage caused to the state by an employee, but in an amount not exceeding three months of his salary, and the so-called immediate orders (see below).

The Supreme Board was to submit to the State Council, together with the report about the closing of the state accounts for the expired budgetary year, a motion concerning the Diet's giving approval to the cabinet.

As a result of the wave of Stalinization of Polish public life, the Supreme Board of Control was abolished in November 1952 and replaced by the Ministry of State Control,[29] modelled on the Soviet Ministry of State Control. Similar reforms had been carried out earlier in other East European countries (witness, for example, the creation of the Ministry of State Control in Czechoslovakia and the Commission of State Control in East Germany).

Thus the new state control apparatus was this time, even formally, organized as part of the executive branch. As the Ministry of State Control submitted its reports only to the cabinet and maintained no contact with the Diet, the legislative branch was deprived, even formally, of any specialized and independent body which could help to exercise control over the executive branch. But on the other hand one must remember that the role of the Diet during the whole Stalinist period was practically nil. The jurisdiction of the Ministry of State Control was extended to the co-operative sector of the national economy.

In conclusion, at least some words must be said about the *activity* of the Polish "state control" in the years from 1949 to 1955.

In either of its guises between 1949 and 1955, the state control apparatus operated without its best men, who had been dismissed mainly for political reasons but also because they were sometimes too highly qualified in comparison with the representatives of the "new class." It was headed by a former workman who was followed everywhere by his personal bodyguard and who tolerated no criticism. The officers were

[29]*Dziennik Ustaw Polskiej Rzeczypospolitej Ludowej* (Law Gazette of the Polish Peoples Republic"), No. 47, 1952, Item 316.

intimidated, everything was "top secret," and procedures were bureaucratic in the extreme. The "state control" did deal with smaller irregularities, but was often indifferent, powerless, or tolerant when it came to major problems involving higher party and state officials: a state of affairs which was openly admitted in the wave of criticism which broke out before and after the so-called Polish October of 1956.

In general one can say that the "state control" of these years did not serve the country well. However, its ineffectiveness was not inherent in the concept of the "state control" itself: it resulted mainly from the political situation in which the country found itself — a situation imposed from without.

"State Control" in Poland after the "Polish October" of 1956

In the wake of the anti-Stalinist political events in Poland in October 1956, a long and broad discussion on a far-reaching reform of the "state control" took place. A new Supreme Board of Control was provided for by an amendment to the Constitution of 1952 and was created in December 1957.[30] The initial decision to scrap the Ministry of State Control and to replace it by a new Supreme Board of Control was made by Gomulka and announced in his program-making speech of October 1956. Gomulka was, after his dismissal from the highest party and state posts in 1948, and before his arrest in 1951, one of the vice-presidents of the 1949-52 Supreme Board of Control.

One of the most important features of the new Supreme Board of Control is the fact that, contrary to its forerunner, it is an organ of the Diet and not of the executive.

The main task of the current Supreme Board of Control is to supervise the activities of the state administration and the nationalized economy. It can also audit co-operative and even private enterprises, but only in connection with deliveries of goods and services rendered by them to the state economic sector and in connection with the payment of taxes to the state. It may also audit organizations operating with state aid or performing tasks delegated to them by the state or spending money derived from contributions of the public (e.g., for the construction of a school or a monument).

[30]See the Polish Constitution of 1952 (as amended in 1957), chapter IIIa, articles 28a, b, c, and d, in *Dziennik Ustaw,* No. 61, 1957, Item 329; the act of December 13, 1957, concerning the Supreme Board of Control, in *Dziennik Ustaw,* No. 61, 1957, Item 330; and the resolution of the Diet of the same date, concerning the procedure for the submission to the Diet of reports of the Supreme Board and the Diet's ordering of examination tasks to the Supreme Board of Control, in *Monitor Polski*, No. 99, 1957, Item 578.

The scope of this examination and audit is very wide: it includes the economic, financial, organizational, and administrative activities of the controlled units. Some of the problems considered by the Supreme Board of Control in the early 1960's have been: illegal construction of houses (without permission, approved plans, etc.); social assistance to old and disabled people; economy in the activities of the state-owned theatres; functioning of housing offices and apartment renovation activities; problems of state construction standards; problem of reserves in the national economy; state administration improvements; co-operation among the state-owned factories; investment program revisions; the realization of anti-alcoholic measures; urban communication; co-operation between state foreign trade organizations and state industry; and the conservation and construction of public roads and bridges.[31]

Nevertheless, article 2, point 3, of the 1957 act expressly stipulates that "the *main* task of the Supreme Board of Control is control of the execution of the state budget and of the National Economic Plan, of the preservation of social property and of financial discipline" (italics added). This clear legal formulation certainly reflects the situation in other communist countries — namely, that the *main* task of "state control" is a broadly conceived financial audit.

As previously, the criteria applied in the work of the Supreme Board are very broad and embrace first of all legality, economy, and expediency from the economic point of view.

Two main kinds of examination are carried out: (1) the local examination, already mentioned, and (2) ex-post-facto examination. No preventive examination has been practiced up to the present time, though such a possibility is provided for in the 1957 act, after a joint decision of the State Council and the Council of Ministers is taken.

The main weapon of the Supreme Board of Control against irregularities is written notification of the institution concerned or of its superior organ (*wystąpienia pokontrolne*). These notifications contain appropriate remarks and conclusions concerning the elimination of the detected irregularities, and must be answered within a period prescribed by the state control organs. They generally have no imperative character.

If the answer received is found unsatisfactory, the Supreme Board of Control can present the matter to a higher administrative level and also to the Diet. The authority and effectiveness of these notifications relies primarily on the high qualifications of the Supreme Board officers, among whom engineers, economists, accountants, lawyers, and other professional

[31] See, e.g., the Warsaw daily *Życie Warszawy* of August 10, November 10, November 14, November 18, December 3-4, and December 21, 1960; January 19, March 9, and September 12, 1962; November 17-18, 1963; and May 7, 1968.

men are represented.[32] The total number of the staff of the Supreme Board is almost 1,400.[33] The fact that the Supreme Board is an organ of the Diet adds to its authority. The total number of its written notifications reaches several thousand yearly; for instance, over 6,200 were issued in 1967.[34]

As exceptions to the general rule, in two cases the notifications of the state control organs have a binding effect on the addressee: first, when disciplinary measures (including dismissal from service) are demanded against guilty employees, and second, when the "state control" requests the addressee to sue in tort a person who has caused damage to the state by his action or negligence.

In practice, only the first of these cases plays an important role. In 1959, for example, well over 1,000 persons were disciplinarily punished as a result of the state control organ's motions. In contrast, requests to sue in tort have been adopted only rarely, notwithstanding the fact that many cases have arisen in which recovery of damages might be expected. In this connection it has been suggested on occasion that the Supreme Board of Control be empowered to decide the amount of liability — perhaps limited to three months' salary of the employee responsible — for damages to the State.[35]

Thus a problem spoken of in 1957, when the new Supreme Board of Control act was being drafted,[36] still exists. It will have to be solved sooner or later. It would seem that if decisions concerning liability — even unlimited in amount — were handed down by the Supreme Board and administered by a team of men with legal training and the status of judges, the problem could be dealt with more efficiently and quickly, and at the same time due process of law would be guaranteed.

A provisional device to which the "state control" *can* resort is "immediate orders" (*zarządzenia doraźne*). Their aim is to prevent further damage or danger, to safeguard property and evidence, and, when

[32]As the president of the Supreme Board of Control informed the Diet in 1964, 70 percent of the Board's officers had a university level education, and they represented over thirty different specialties. See *Życie Warszawy* of November 13, 1964.

[33]This figure, which includes the employees of both the Supreme Board of Control in Warsaw and its field offices in districts all over the country, is taken from annex 2 to the budget act for 1968, in *Dziennik Ustaw,* No. 47, 1967.

[34]See *Życie Warszawy* of July 6, 1968.

[35]See Z.J. Leski, "Po dwuletniej działalności Najwyższej Izby Kontroli" ("After Two Years of Functioning of the Supreme Board of Control") in *Państwo i Prawo,* No. 1, 1960, p. 28.

[36]See e.g., R. Szawlowski, *op. cit.,* pp. 766-7.

embezzlement has been discovered, to suspend the guilty employee. A typical situation in which such immediate orders are issued is when "state control" discovers, for example, that the storerooms of a state factory are not sufficiently secure against burglary or fire.

When a situation is covered by the provisions of the criminal code, the public prosecutor's office is notified by the state control organs. The annual number of such notices, about 500 some years earlier, had decreased to fewer than 150 (involving about 350 persons) by 1962.[37]

Another procedure of the Supreme Board of Control, unknown in the practice of Western supreme public finance audit institutions, provides for so-called post-examination conferences (*narady pokontrolne*). This procedure, typical of "state control" in other Eastern European countries also, is specially valuable in units involved in production. The conference is convened to inform the employees and workers of the examined enterprise (or at least the "activists" in it) about the results of the examination and to discuss them thoroughly in order to find the best solution to the existing difficulties. The number of such conferences, far smaller than that of the written notifications, nevertheless amounted to almost 1,000 in 1959.

Besides administering its own examinations, the Supreme Board of Control co-ordinates its own activities and those of other state organs of audit, revision, and inspection. To this end these organs are obliged to agree with the Supreme Board on their periodical examination plans, to carry out immediate inspection at the demand of the Supreme Board, and to submit to it periodical reports of activities and the results of the more important inspections. It should be noted that while the 1957 act empowered the Supreme Board to co-ordinate the activities of "other state organs of control, revision and inspection," the executive rules of 1958[38] restricted its scope to those organs which exercise these functions in the field of economy and public finance only. Thus, such organs as for instance the Sanitary Inspection or the Water Protection Inspection are not included. This may be considered additional evidence that the emphasis in the activity of the Supreme Board is on broadly understood financial problems.

Summing up its yearly activities, the "state control" presents two documents to the Diet: (1) remarks on the report of the Council of Ministers about the execution of the state budget and the National Economic Plan, with a motion concerning approval to be given by the Diet to the cabinet; and (2) a report concerning results of examination of more important problems of the national economy and the activities of the state

[37] See *Życie Warszawy,* November 28, 1963.

[38] *Monitor Polski,* No. 95, 1958, Item 517.

administration. These documents, unfortunately, are treated as "internal" and are not published.[39]

The problem of the relationship between the Diet and the Supreme Board of Control must be viewed in the light of the role of the Polish parliament after 1956. Of course, the Polish parliament is not equivalent in power to Western legislatures. For instance, it contains no opposition party and the number of plenary sessions is very small. On the other hand, there are a few Catholic representatives, who are sometimes very critical of the executive, and the number of committee sessions is rather large. The bulk of parliamentary work is now done in committee and the questioning of ministers and under-secretaries which takes place (the committee members are supported by expert officers of the Supreme Board) is not a mere formality. This is a unique situation in Eastern Europe, where, except in Poland, the role played by the legislatures (with the obvious exception of Czechoslovakia during the 1967-8 period) is rather decorative.

The Polish Supreme Board of Control is, as mentioned before, an organ of the Diet. This is clearly stipulated both in the Constitution (article 28b) and in the Supreme Board of Control act of 1957 (article 1). It is an arrangement which resembles that in some Western countries: for example, the United States, where the Comptroller General of the U.S. and the General Accounting Office are "a part of the legislative branch of the Government".[40] In the East, however, this situation is exceptional; the state control organs of the Soviet Union and the "people's democracies" form part of the executive branch and are in most cases completely divorced from the legislature. It was not until the summer of 1967 that the situation changed in this respect in Czechoslovakia.[41]

[39]The nonpublication of reports of the state control organs is typical of the situation in all Communist countries. This is in sharp contrast to procedures in all Western democracies, where such reports are published routinely and sometimes even extensively discussed in the press (e.g., the reports of the French *Cour des comptes* are discussed in several consecutive issues of *Le Monde* each year). An even broader reportage prevails in Japan, where during a recent visit to the Board of Audit in Tokyo, the writer was shown two versions of that institution's annual report – a fully detailed version intended for politicians, civil servants, scholars, etc., and a smaller, condensed version intended for the general public.

[40]United States Code, (1964 edition; Washington, D. C.: 1965), I, title 5, ch. 1, 133 z-5.

[41]Already under the People's Supervision and Economic Recording Act of March 6, 1963, some attempt in the direction of a *rapprochement* between the "state control" and the National Assembly was made in Czechoslovakia. The National Assembly was to elect the ordinary members of the Central Commission (not its chairman, deputy chairman, or assistants to the chairman) and mention was made in the act that the Central Commission should submit a report on its activities to

The subordination of the Supreme Board of Control to the parliament is worthy of further examination.[42] First, the Diet appoints and dismisses the president of the Supreme Board. Second, as already mentioned, the Supreme Board must submit every year to the Diet its remarks regarding the report of the Council of Ministers on the execution of the state budget and the National Economic Plan with a motion concerning approval to be given by the Diet to the cabinet. This must be done not later than three months after receipt of the reports from the Council of Ministers. The presidium of the Diet transmits these remarks and motions to the competent parliamentary committees, which analyze the appropriate parts of the report of the Council of Ministers together with the related parts of the Supreme Board's report. Authorized representatives of the president of the Supreme Board of Control provide additional explanations and information to the members of the committees. At plenary sessions of the Diet, the remarks and motions of the Supreme Board are reported by its president.

Within three months after the year's end, the president of the Supreme Board of Control presents to the presidium of the Diet (after examination

the cabinet *and* to the National Assembly. But the Central Commission of People's Control and Statistics was directly subordinated to the cabinet "as its objective control body," and its chairman was a member of the cabinet with the rank of a minister. The basic subordination of the "state control" was formulated in section 2, paragraph 3 of the 1963 act, reading "The activity of the people's control bodies shall be developed in the closest possible co-operation with the organs and organizations of the Communist party of Czechoslovakia and under its leadership."

The 1963 act was replaced by that of June 29th, 1967 on the Commissions of People's Control. According to this act the Central Commission of People's Control is an examining organ of the National Assembly *and* of the cabinet. (This solution, incidentally, corresponds to that adopted, also in 1967, by the new Swiss legislation on the *Contrôle fédéral des finances* and the new French act on the *Cour des comptes.*) Its members are elected by the National Assembly; the chairman is appointed by the President of the Republic from among the elected members and recalled by him; and the chairman's two deputies are elected by the Central Commission out of its own ranks and recalled by it. The Presidium of the National Assembly votes on the working plan of the Central Commission after its discussion in the cabinet. The Central Commission of People's Control is to present reports on its activities to the National Assembly and, as far as the realization of the tasks given to it by the cabinet is concerned, to the latter. This new model of the Czechoslovak "state control," corresponding to the rapid democratization processes in that country of 1967-8 lost, of course, much of its importance after the Soviet-led invasion of August 1968.

[42]On this subject, see R. Szawłowski, *"Legislatywa a kontrola państwowa w Polsce Ludowej"* ("The Legislature and the State Control in People's Poland"), *Państwo i Prawo*, No. 8-9, 1959, pp. 283-96.

by the State Council) the annual report on the Supreme Board's activities. The report is then transmitted to the competent parliamentary committees for analysis, but is not discussed at a plenary session.

However, the Diet and the Supreme Board of Control collaborate even more closely during the consideration by the parliament of the drafts of the state budget and the National Economic Plan, and, afterwards, during the execution of these two acts. On its own initiative the Supreme Board reports during the year to the Diet the results of the examination of more important problems of the national economy and state administration; administers examinations at the request of the Diet; and, finally, presents to the Diet its remarks concerning the drafts of parliamentary and other legal acts.

It must be emphasized that the Diet and the Supreme Board of Control meet and work together mainly during the meetings of the parliamentary committees, and less so during plenary sessions of parliament. During 1958, the first year of its existence, the new Board's representatives took part in 204 committee meetings out of a total of 265.

As a final comment it should be added that the Diet highly appreciates the contacts with the Supreme Board and the materials furnished by it.

Conclusions

In concluding this brief survey of the history of the Polish state control institutions during the past 160 years, I should like to make some remarks on these organs in the early years (in the Kingdom of Poland) and today, as compared with state control institutions in other countries.

It can be said that the "state control" in the Kingdom of Poland between 1821 and 1866 was one of the most progressive state control organs in the world. Many countries (for example, the United States, which created its General Accounting Office as late as 1921; the Scandinavian countries; and Switzerland) had no state control organs at that time. Until the reform of the 1860's, the Russian "state control" was largely fictional, as is admitted in Russian pre-revolutionary literature (e.g., Ozerov and Sakovich).[43] But what matters more is that the Polish "state control" and its activities contained a number of features absent from the state control organs in other countries at that time.

Among these novel features were its participation in the preparation of the state budget; the handing down of judgments of liability for damage caused to the State by *comptables, ordonnateurs,* and even third persons;

[43]See Oserov, *Osnowy finansowoj nauki* ("Principles of the Science of Public Finance") (last edition: Riga, 1923), II, 59; and Sakovich, *Gosudarstvennyj kontrol w Rossii* ("State Control in Russia") (St. Petersburg, 1898).

its presentation of final closings of yearly state accounts; and — perhaps most striking — the extremely broad scope and degree of generalization, criticism, and proposals adopted in the remarks of the "state control" to the tsar and king.

All this demonstrates the importance of its position in comparison with the state control institutions of other countries during the nineteenth century.

The "state control" in present-day Poland (since 1957) is an organ of the parliament and has daily contact with it.[44] This is an almost unique situation in the Eastern camp. However, even in most of those Western countries where a similar system exists, such intensive daily cooperation between the legislature and the supreme public finance audit institutions is not to be found. Apart from the United States, the Polish system, under which the "state control" furnishes to the parliament, on a large scale, reliable and up-to-date information concerning the functioning of the state apparatus at any time, is indeed hardly to be found anywhere in the world.

Generally speaking, the Polish "state control" has rendered (apart from the gloomy period of 1948-1955) and still renders a valuable service to its country.[45]

[44]While stressing the originality of the Polish Supreme Board of Control, a book published under the auspices of the Inter-Parliamentary Union (*Parliaments. A Comparative Study of the Structure and Functioning of Representative Institutions in Fifty-five Countries* [2nd ed.: London, 1966,] p. 303) classifies that institution wrongly and lists it in one breath with the "ombudsmen" in Scandinavia and New Zealand, and also with the West German "defense commissioner." In fact, the Supreme Board should be classified as a supreme public finance audit body, and the fact that it is an organ of the Diet does not change anything in this respect. Similarly, the fact that the U.S. General Accounting Office is an organ of Congress does not classify it as an "ombudsman" institution.

[45]One thing, though, should be borne in mind. Under the post-World War II political system in Poland, where the decisive role is played by the Communist Party, there are certain limitations to the activities of the "state control," dictated by "political wisdom" as interpreted by the party or some influential cliques within it. Thus certain embarrassing affairs involving highly placed personalities may not be disclosed, and the culprits escape the consequences. In the spring of 1968, in the wake of the well-known purges of the Jews which took place after the March 1968 riots, the Polish press reported that there was, allegedly, such a clique in the Supreme Board itself; it was headed by one of the Board's vice-presidents (a former member of the Politbureau) and some other people who were later dismissed (see, e.g., *Życie Warszawy,* 5 April and 13-14-15 April, 1968). Some quite recent examples of manipulations and of hushing up are known to the present writer. Although this is probably only a relatively small margin in the activities of the Supreme Board which, *grosso modo,* should be considered as useful to its country, it is nevertheless intolerable.

GEORGES S. LANGROD

MICHALINA VAUGHAN

The Polish Psychological
Theory of Law

Introduction

According to available sources, Polish legal scientists have been interested
since the Middle Ages in searching for the human values integral in legal
phenomena. From that remote period onward, each generation of authors
and teachers has made repeated, and often valid, attempts to investigate
the general problems of law. Using foreign sources of contemporary
philosophical thought, and remaining in close touch with Western
specialists, those authors sought to base legal technique upon a theoretical
discipline. Their works show an intuitive grasp of the notion that a mere
exegesis of positive texts, without consideration of pre-established
principles, is sterile and misleading. Thus, several Polish authors, at various
stages of the evolution of Polish thought, have endeavored to investigate
the system and the spirit of the legal rules in force, to determine their
intrinsic nature, and to define the very function of law (its links with
public order, the scale of values to which it corresponds, and its position in
relation to ethics).

No systematic history of the successive trends of Polish thought in the
philosophy and theory of law has been written as yet. Therefore, the
individual contributions of various authors throughout the centuries have
not been properly assessed. As such contributions are comparatively
numerous, it is all the more difficult to undertake an assessment now.
Even when Polish writers used Latin (as was the case until the sixteenth
century), so that the problem of linguistic barriers did not arise, their
writings remained little known abroad. Only in isolated cases did the
works of some particularly eminent specialists cross national frontiers to
assume an important place in the context of European culture. A few

Polish legal scientists became known in foreign countries where they had studied and retained a considerable reputation; however, their treatises have not been preserved.[1] There would certainly be great interest in studying the evolution of Polish legal scientists' philosophical thought and in assessing the steady Western influence on Central and Eastern European legal thought, as well as the often underrated contribution of Polish researchers (working either in Poland or abroad) to the philosophy of law.

Whatever one might believe at first, and despite the important and at times overwhelming influence of Western theories at certain periods, Polish authors did not lack originality. Several of them provided creative and wholly original contributions: even when assessing contemporary world thought or doctrines, their works retained a truly personal character and contained new ideas geared to reform or inspired by constructive criticism.

Thus, in the sixteenth century, Andrzej Frycz Modrzewski (1503-72), secretary to the king and political philosopher and reformer, wrote the famous treatise *De Republica emendanda* ("Of the Need to Reform the Republic"), the first edition of which is dated 1551. He was continuing thereby the work of his fifteenth century predecessors: particularly Jan Ostrorog (1436-1501), author of *Monumentum. . .pro Reipublicae ordinatione* ("Moment. . .for the Organization of the Republic), dated 1456 and 1477, by studying social laws and relating abstract thought to practical life. However, Frycz Modrzewski distinguished between law and ethics, stressed the superiority of written law over custom, and considered justice as the natural basis of any law with social content. His social and legal system was derived from a concept of natural law, which he considered the rational element of legal science. His influence on world thought, on Grotius[2], on Hotman[3], and on many others[4] is fully acknowledged. Jean Bodin engaged in a controversy with him and, beginning with political considerations, disagreed with his democratic and egalitarian approach to

[1]Thus at the end of the sixteenth century, Hieronim Gorecki, doctor of the Roman *Sapienze* and professor at the Law Faculty of Cracow University, was considered in Rome as "oraculum Lachiae. . . .quem docta stupuit iurisperitum Italia." See H. Barycz, *Historia Uniwersytetu Jagiellonskiego w epoce humanizmu* ("History of the Jagellonian University in the Age of Humanism") (Cracow, 1935), pp. 587-8.

[2]See Hugo Grotius, *Via ad pacem ecclesiasticam* ("The Way to Ecclesiastical Peace") (1642).

[3]See Jean Hotman de Villiers, *Syllabus* (1628).

[4]See, e.g., Waldemar Voisé, *Frycza Modrzewskiego nauka o panstwie i prawie* ("The Study of the State and Law by Frycz Modrzewski") (Warsaw, 1956) and *Poczatki nowozytnych nauk spolecznych* ("The Beginnings of Modern Social Sciences") (Warsaw, 1962), p. 277. See also P. Bayle, *Dictionnaire historique et critique* ("Historical and Critical Dictionary") (1669), and Gaspard de Réal, *La science du gouvernement* ("The Science of Government") (1751).

public order.[5] The interest inspired by Frycz Modrzewski is shown by the number of translations of his works[6] and of new editions in Latin,[7] as well as by its impact abroad and the praise widely given to it.[8]

Other Polish legal thought during the Renaissance was represented by lesser writers, such as Andrzej Wolan (1530-1610), author of *De Libertate politica seu civili* ("In Political and Civil Liberty") (1572); and Pawel Szczerbic, author of *Politica* ("Politics") (1595), a study in the Thomist tradition, and translator of the famous *Sachsenspiegel* by Eicke von Repkow (1581). Both were influenced by Aristotelian thought and endeavored to transcend contemporary national politics in order to make theoretical generalizations in accordance with the trend of the time. The political writers of the sixteenth century, such as Stanislaw Orzechowski (1513-66), author of *Fidelis Subditus* ("Faithful Subject") and *Policy of the Kingdom of Poland* (in Polish, 1566); Sebastian Petrycy, translator of Aristotle; Lukasz Gornicki; Krzysztof Warszewicki; and Wawrzyniec Goslicki played an important part in shaping new concepts of political philosophy and dealt with the reform of public law.[9]

In the seventeenth century, the tradition of Frycz Modrzewski and Orzechowski was continued by writers who, like Aron Alexander

[5]See Jean Bodin, *De Republica* ("The Republic") (Lyons: 1593, 1636). See also in this connection J. Moreau-Reibel, *Jean Bodin et le droit public comparé* ("Jean Bodin and Comparative Public Law") (Paris, 1933), pp. 209 ff.

[6]E.g., into German by Wolfgang Weissenburg (Basle, 1557); into Spanish (extracts only) by Giovanni Giustiniano (Padua, 1555); and into Polish, French and Russian several times.

[7]E.g., Basle (Oporyn), 1554 and 1559.

[8]The work of Frycz Modrzewski was praised by Milton and Locke. Giustiniano wrote in 1555 that "a study of this kind, so useful to society and both so beneficial and so pleasant to read, has not been published for a thousand years. I appreciate it so much that I would like to see it translated in all languages. . ." (*Works* [1555], I, 637).

[9]P.Rybicki, "Z dziejow polskiego arystotelizmu" ("From the History of Polish Aristotelian Thought") in *Studia i materialy z dziejow nauki polskiej, Seria A, Historia nauk spolecznych* (Polish Academy of Science: Warsaw, 1959), pp. 87-8, says: "In the middle of the 16th century, Polish political theory had a European character. It was characterized by participation in Western intellectual trends — a participation which was sometimes creative. The best representative of this participation is Frycz Modrzewski, who in *De Republica emendanda* based political considerations on an analysis of the elements which create and unite the human community, and on detailed descriptions of contemporary social life. A theoretical effort in the same direction is reflected in the works of Orzechowski, particularly his *Policy of the Kingdom of Poland*, in which he tried to provide a theoretical concept of the state in the sixteenth century, based on Aristotle, but unfortunately in a

Olizarowski (1618-59), author of *De politica hominum societate* ("On the Policy of Human Society") (1651), and Szymon Starowolski (? -1656), author of *Accessus ad iuris utriusque cognitionem*. . . . (1654), represented a humanistic theory influenced by Aristotelian thought.[10]

During the Age of Enlightenment, the theory of natural law, with an increasingly rationalistic bias, found eminent representatives. Among them were Hugo Kollataj (1750-1815),[11] Hieronim Stroynowski (1752-1815),[12] Antoni Poplawski (1739-86),[13] and several others.[14] Their contributions remain important for the assessment of trends in the Polish philosophy of law and of attempts at constitutional reform, but they were strongly influenced by foreign ideologies. They blended the natural law theory with physiocratic thought and economic utilitarianism. All these authors were eclectic and endeavored to draw from the Western philosophical trends of the time some practical conclusions geared to reform of the state during a crucial period in Polish history.

The classic conception of natural law theory reigned over Polish literature at the beginning of the nineteenth century, when fashionable foreign writing set a pattern. Thus, Felix Slotwinski faithfully imitated the Viennese school when he translated Zeiller's works and used them and those of Martini as a basis for his own studies.[15] Ignacy Oldakowski[16] and

theological context which limits the problem. Another pamphlet (by Goslicki), *De optimo senatore* proved a wide intellectual culture and a knowledge of the notions of political theory to which the author owed his considerable audience and reputation."

[10]*Ibid.*, pp. 89 ff. See also S. Kot, *Aron Alexander Olizarowski* (Wilno, 1929) and E. Jarra, *Aron Alexander Olizarowski jako filozof prawa* ("Aron Alexander Olizarowski as Philosopher of Law") (Wilno, 1929).

[11]See H. Kollataj, *Porzadek fizyczno-moralny* ("The Physico-Moral Order") (Cracow, 1810). This is a defense of empiricism applied to factual knowledge.

[12]See H. Strojnowski, *Nauka prawa przyrodzonego politycznego, ekonomiki politycznej i prawa narodow* ("The Study of Natural Law, Political Law, Political Economy, and the Law of Nations") (Wilno, 1785). This treatise was generally admitted in Poland as a basis for the teaching of natural law.

[13]See A. Poplawski, *Podania z nauki prawa natury i politycznego* ("Data from the Study of Natural and Political Law") (Cracow, 1781).

[14]E.g., Mlocki, Markiewicz, Garycki, Michalowski, Szaniawski, Karczewski, and Ladowski.

[15]See F. Slotwinski, *Prawo natury prywatne* ("Private Natural Law") (Cracow, 1825) and *Rozprawa o poczatkach i postepach w nauce prawa natury* ("Treatise on the Beginnings and Progress of the Study of Natural Law") (Cracow, 1825).

[16]*O prawie przyrodzonym i filozofii prawa* ("On Natural Law and the Philosophy of Law") (Warsaw, 1882).

Michal Czacki[17] remained faithful to natural-law rationalism stemming from Kant. The metaphysical concept of natural law was retained by Gustaw Roszkowski.[18] Modern theories — historicism and positivism (as opposed to natural law and to the quest for *a priori* principles), as well as the "encyclopedic" eclecticism represented by countless writers throughout the nineteenth century[19] — were to prevail later. The Polish theory and philosophy of law then followed the methodological trends of the time by stressing the merits of an experimental approach and by investigating the true causes of empirically studied phenomena. Such positivists as Franciszek Kasparek[20] and Jozef Kasznica[21] based their work on dogmatic studies and identified the essence of law with the legal texts in force. In his writings and his teaching, Kasparek adopted the ideas of Adolphe Merkl, while advocating the study of history and legal policy together with the exegesis of laws. The works of twentieth-century authors reflect the concepts of Ihering's realism, the return to idealism according to Stammler, and later, following Kelsen, the concept of psychosociological realism.[22] A particularly wide range of trends was represented, and they became increasingly original and less and less dependent on foreign theories in the second quarter of the century.

[17]*O prawie przyrodzonym czyli o powinnosciach i stosunkach czlowieka moralnego* ("On Natural Law or on the Duties and Relationships of a Moral Being") (Warsaw, 1803).

[18]*O istocie i znaczeniu filozofii prawa* ("On the Essence and the Meaning of the Philosophy of Law") (Cracow, 1871).

[19]See, e.g., Jan Klodzinski, *Encyklopedia i methodologia obejmujaca ogolny zarys nauk i wiadomosci prawnych* ("Encyclopedia and Methodology Covering a General Outline of Legal Sciences and Data") (Warsaw, 1842); Leopold Jakubowski, *Filozofia historii prawa* ("The Philosophy of the History of Law") (St. Petersburg, 1874); and Wladyslaw Daisenberg, *Dzieje filozofii prawa i panstwa przedstawione na tle dziejow cywilizacji* ("History of the Philosophy of Law and of the State in the Context of the History of Civilization") (Cracow, 1874).

[20]*Zadania filozofii prawa i jej stanowisko w dziedzinie nauk prawnych* ("The Tasks of the Philosophy of Law and Its Position in the Field of Legal Studies") (Cracow, 1887).

[21]*Kilka uwag z powodu niektorych pism filozoficznoprawnych* ("Some Remarks About Certain Writings on the Philosophy of Law") (Warsaw, 1874) and *Pojecie i system nauk spolecznych* ("Notion and System of Social Sciences") (Warsaw, 1870).

[22]See K. Opalek, "Zarys dziejow filozofii prawa w Polsce" ("Outline of the History of the Philosophy of Law in Poland"), in K. Opalek and W. Wolter, *Nauka filozofii prawa i prawa karnego w Polsce* (Cracow, 1948), pp. 11 ff.

In this context, at the end of the nineteenth and the beginning of the twentieth century Leon Petrazycki composed his works. It has been said of Petrazycki that he was an "original genius,"[23] "a first-rate thinker whose innovating ideas are so advanced for their period that their true meaning appeared only after some time had elapsed,"[24] and that "with a truly genial perspicacity he foresaw the direction in which the philosophy and the science of law were to develop today."[25] As "the greatest contemporary legal philosopher in Russia and in Poland,"[26] he "reached the highest scientific knowledge of law. . .his death having deprived science of a rare genius. . . ."[27] He "was the first legal philosopher who went beyond theoretical statements about the necessity of treating law as part of reality and beyond merely speculating that this reality was sociological or psychological."[28] He has been called:

> the Copernicus of the legal sciences. . .whose doctrine caused a scientific revolution in legal science by the discovery of the intrinsic nature of the phenomenon "law" and by the revelation of its sphere of existence and of action, by the explanation of the influence of law on human behavior and on the politico-social life of mankind in all its magnitude. . . .[29]

He was a real innovator.[30]

The psychological theory of law, devised and elaborated by a Polish specialist (who spent most of his life abroad, however, and wrote either in

[23]Hugh W. Babb, "Petrazhitskii: Science of Legal Policy and Theory of Law," *Boston University Law Review*, XVIII (1938), 797.

[24]Georges Gurvitch, "Une philosophie intuitioniste du droit: Léon Petrazycki" ("An Intuitionistic Philosophy of Law: Leon Petrazycki"), *Archives de Philosophie du Droit et de Sociologie Juridique*, 1931, p. 403.

[25]*Ibid.*, p. 419.

[26]*Ibid.*, p. 403.

[27]Elemer Balogh (in German), *Leo v. Petrazycki, 1864-1931* (Volume 22 of Mémoires de l'Academie Internationale de Droit Comparé), 1st part (1934), p. 64.

[28]Nicholas S. Timascheff, "Introduction," *Law and Morality: Leon Petrazycki* (trans. H. W. Babb) (Cambridge, Mass.: Harvard University Press, 1955), p. xxxvi.

[29]Peter Michailowski, *Copérnico das ciências juridicas* (The Copernicus of Legal Sciences") (Rio de Janeiro: 1 Revista de Direito Publico e Ciência Politica, 1960), pp. 140 ff.

[30]For other evaluations of Petrazycki's works, see G. Langrod, "L'oeuvre juridique et philosophique de Léon Petrazycki (Essai d'introduction analytique)" ("The Legal and Philosophical Work of Leon Petrazycki [An Attempt at an Analytical Introduction]"), *Revue de l'Institut de Sociologie Solvay* (Brussels, 1956).

Russian or in German) represents the most important modern contribution by a Pole to the field of legal science and a landmark in its history. It is precisely in Poland — where Petrazycki spent the last years of his life — that a philosophical school continued, interpreting and at times revising the Master's work. Monographs and biographies were written, Petrazycki's works were translated into Polish, and his manuscripts and the memory of his words were preserved despite the vicissitudes of war and foreign occupation. It was said:

> The heritage of Petrazycki should be studied not only by every theoretician of law who wishes to become truly competent, but also by every researcher, every thinker who deals with the living problems of methodology in the human sciences, of the theory of civilization, of socio-technique, whether he is or not in sympathy with the psychological theory of law, whether he adheres to the theses and arguments of its authors or not....Petrazycki's creative spirit introduced his contemporaries to several questions which became very significant from then onwards. By his perceptive and continuous work he ensured a privilege for his writings: they acquired a right to be read...[31]

Thus the psychological theory in legal science, according to which "law is the psychological element of social life and acts on the psychic level,"[32] provided an original contribution to contemporary law. Thanks to its creator's genius and to his disciples' fidelity, it remained alive and still applies to various legal spheres. Until the middle of this century its impact seemed to be limited and it was almost forgotten or even unknown abroad. But its influence has grown since and has been felt by many thinkers in both hemispheres, including lawyers, philosophers, psychologists, and sociologists, some of whom seemed to be far removed from Petrazycki's own specialty and uninclined to imitate him. It has been observed:

> An extremely unusual phenomenon in the history of science at any time, Petrazycki, a lawyer by training, holder of a chair of law, whose studies had law as their main object and whose life was dominated by a legal ideal, extended the horizons of his thought in widely differing fields — logic, psychology, ethics in the broad sense of the word, sociology, general theory of evolution — and in all these

[31]Tadeusz Kotarbinski, "Introduction" to Leon Petrazycki, *Wstep do nauki prawa i moralnosci (Podstawy psychologii emocjonalnej)* ("Introduction to the Science of Law and Ethics [The Bases of Emotional Psychology]"), ed. Jerzy Lande (Warsaw, 1959), p. 5.

[32]*Ibid.*, p. 14.

spheres he was able to express highly individual concepts of particular importance, without ever being an amateur. . . .[33]

We are dealing therefore with a *system,* the various parts of which (explored in the course of interconnected research programs and throwing light upon each other) are logically linked. At a time of increasing specialization, there is hardly any contemporary counterpart; in fact, it has been said that one had to go back to Herbert Spencer's "synthetic philosophy" in order to find a suitable parallel.[34]

The Founder

HIS LIFE

Leon Petrazycki was born on April 13, 1867, on the manor of Kollontaievo, near Vitebsk.[35] His family belonged to the Polish nobility, his mother tongue was Polish, and although, several authors mistakenly consider him Russian[36], there is no doubt that he was in fact Polish. His

[33] Jerzy Lande, "Leon Petrzycki," *Przeglad Filozoficzny,* I-II (1932). Cf. J. Lande, *Studia z filozofii prawa* (Warsaw, 1959), pp. 559.

[34] *Ibid.,* p. 2.

[35] His father, Jozef Petrazycki, took part in the Polish insurrection of 1863. His estates were confiscated by the czarist government as a reprisal for his anti-Russian activity during the uprising. He died early. See Giorgio del Vecchio, *Lehrbuch der Rechtsphilosophie* ("Handbook of Philosophy of Law") (2nd ed.; Basle, 1951), p. 322. See also Babb, *op. cit.,* p. 793, n.l.

[36] Several authors insist on considering Petrazycki Russian. See, e.g., Claude du Pasquier, *Introduction à la théorie générale et à la philosophie du droit* ("Introduction to the General Theory and Philosophy of Law") (2nd ed.; Neuchâtel, 1948), p. 299; P. Michailowski, *op. cit.,* p. 140; and S. N. Timascheff, *Introduction à la sociologie juridique* ("Introduction to the Sociology of Law") (Paris, 1939), p. 53. However, in his 1955 edition, Timascheff (p.xxi) admits that Petrazycki's family was Polish and that he belonged to the Polish cultural sphere.

The fact that until 1917 he lectured in Russian in St. Petersburg and that he wrote mostly in Russian is misleading. Petrazycki actually considered himself a Pole. When he lectured in Russian, he constantly borrowed expressions from the Polish (see e.g., N. S. Timascheff, *Introduction. . . , op. cit.* (1955), xxi. This caused difficulties (as is proved by the historical archives of Leningrad) and even attacks in the press (*Nowoje Wremya,* No. 12975, January 27, 1912, signed "Zemshtch"). See also in this connection, Adam Podgorecki, *Socjologia Prawa* ("Sociology of Law") (Warsaw, 1962), p. 137. While teaching at St. Petersburg University, Petrazycki was chairman of the Society of Polish Economists and Jurists of this city, and, from 1912, a full member of the Polish Academy of

secondary schooling was in Vitebsk, and he studied medicine for two years at the University of Kiev, where he was later to read law. As a student of law, he published in 1883 a translation into Russian of the *Roman Pandects* by Baron, then commonly used as a textbook in Russian universities.[37] Being a particularly brilliant student, he obtained, as a professorial aspirant, a study grant which enabled him to work in Germany under the great German Romanist, Dernburg. A special seminar for Russian research workers in Berlin under the auspices of the Russian Ministry of Education existed at that time.

Sciences and Letters (*P.A.U.*) in Cracow. See *Mémoire de l'Académie Internationale de Droit Comparé* ("Memoir of the International Academy of Comparitive Law") I, (The Hague, 1928), 1149. He went back to his country as soon as it recovered political independence, (in 1918). As a deputy to the first Russian Duma (parliament) in 1905-6, he did not join the circle of Polish deputies; but this was due to the fact that he represented the Russian capital city and not the Polish territories of the Empire. For the same reason, Alexander Lednicki, deputy for Minsk and a member (as was Petrazycki himself) of the Russian political party "KD," did not join the circle, in spite of being a Polish national leader in Russia.

See also the text of the Latin diploma of doctorate *honoris causa* granted to Petrazycki in 1929 by the Polish University Stefan Batory in Wilno (quoted by Babb, "Petrazhitskii...," p. 793). There is much evidence of Petrazycki's national sentiment, and all misunderstandings are due to insufficient information. The names "Petrazhitskii" or "Petrazhicky" (Petrajicki) are Russian transcriptions of the original Polish name.

If Carl-August Emke, among others, refers to Petrazycki as the Russian-Polish philosopher of law, in *Errinerungen eines Rechtsphilosophen* ("Souvenirs of a Philosopher of Law"), in *Studium Berlinense* (Berlin, 1960), he appears to refer to the places where he taught rather than to his nationality.

At the time Petrazycki was criticized in Poland because his activity abroad and his use of foreign languages deprived Poland of the prestige to be derived from his reputation; see Stanislaw Posner's article in *Gazeta Sadowa Warszawska,* XXIV (1909). However, one should take into account that difficult historical conditions in Poland compelled many Poles to work abroad and to acquire a mixed cultural allegiance without losing their national character. A series of similar examples (Maria Curie-Sklodowska, Ignacy Paderewski, Ludwik Gumplowicz, Joseph Conrad Korzeniowski, Bronislaw Malinowski, Gabriel Narutowicz, Dr. Babinski, Florian Znaniecki, and others) shows that the vicissitudes of an eventful life and of working in two cultures did not prevent strong devotion to one's country of origin. It was so in the case of Petrazycki. His work belongs to mankind's intellectual heritage. To acknowledge his Polish nationality is only to pay tribute to the truth and to reject a misinterpretation occurring in several biographies. See, e.g., Waclaw Lednicki, *Life and Culture of Poland* (New York, 1944), p. 112.

[37]Second edition, 1899-1908; third edition, 1908-10.

During the two years he spent in Berlin, Petrazycki acquired a thorough knowledge of German legal science, thus improving his background and widening his horizons, particularly in regard to methodology. As German specialists were at this time engaged in contributing to the draft of the new civil code, which was to come into effect in 1900,

> ...young Petrazhitsky was directly immersed in the problem of scientifically treating law-in-the-making. The German jurists sought to accomplish this task on the basis of the doctrines of the historical and legal positivistic schools. This precluded the use of philosophical, sociological, or psychological points of view and caused the draftsmen to concentrate on the technical perfection of their product.[38]

Far from being overwhelmed by the sheer weight of German science —

the merits of which he fully appreciated, but without underestimating its weaknesses — the young scientist determined, at the age of twenty-five or twenty-six, to rethink the essence of law. He conducted an attack against the manner in which the reform of the civil code was conceived in Germany. From this criticism he derived theoretical consequences by an intellectual process which has been compared to that of Auguste Comte, with whose works Petrazycki was fully acquainted. Wishing to base social reform upon scientific foundations and aware that no empirical science of society existed, Petrazycki decided to create such a science. In addition, Petrazycki, seeking means of improving the laws in force, realized the need for a new applied science, that of legal policy.[39]

> This was the turning point in his scientific development. In addition to becoming an excellent "dogmatic" jurist, able to interpret the most complicated legal texts, he developed an empirical theory of law reflecting many elements then present in both Russian and German jurisprudence, but in its main aspect quite original, testifying to his superlative creative ability.[40]

The nature of law being empirical, Petrazycki had to seek a theoretical basis for legal science: he considered the reality of law to be psychological. His approach was related to Bierling's and Jellinek's, and to that of Korkunoff in Russian jurisprudence, but he drew all the logical conclusions deriving from it. He refused to consider legal phenomena as pertaining to the sphere of the outer world, but related them to individual psychology. Being a psychological phenomenon, law (like ethics) could

[38]Timascheff, *op. cit.* (1955), p. xxxii.

[39]*Ibid.*, p. xxii.

[40]*Ibid.*

not be explained by resorting to biological concepts alone. By linking the psychological aspect of *all* legal problems not only to the action of law, to the reactions it stimulates and the results it yields, but also to its *cause*, or motivation, Petrazycki sought the basis of law in *emotions*: in emotional attraction or repulsion. As will be stated in section II, he endowed legal science with inexhaustible possibilities of investigating legal problems through psychological study. Neither transcendental elements nor purely biological concepts were, in his opinion, to play a determining part in this quest. This is what a commentator noted:

> Petrazhitsky turned for assistance to psychology, but the psychology of his day was inadequate for the construction of the theory he needed. Boldly, he decided to create a new psychology, and in large measure he repeated the achievement of Spencer who, without previous training in psychology, wrote a remarkable treatise on the subject. While working on both his legal theory and his new psychology, [Petrazycki] saw that the teachings of contemporary logicians as to the formation and definition of concepts were insufficient, and he thereupon decided to construct a new logic, at least with regard to concepts. This he succeeded in doing.[41]

He acquired a growing belief in the truth of his early ideas, which were to shape the whole of his later work. The psychological theory of law was derived from them.

While studying in Germany, Petrazycki published two well-known works, both in German: *Fruchtverteilung beim Wechsel des Nutzungsberechtigten; Drei zivile Abhandlungen* (1892) and two volumes entitled *Die Lehre vom Einkommen vom Standpunkt des gemeinen Civilrechts* (1893, 1895). To the second work was appended a study of civil policy and political economy[42] which went beyond the dogmatic interpretation typical of the German pattern and anticipated his future doctrine on legal policy, particularly regarding "active love" as a decisive element guiding the legislator toward better law. As soon as they appeared, those works were considered in Germany[43] as a..."first rate performance which ensured to the author a place in the ranks of the masters in the scientific milieu of German jurists."[44] Jerzy Lande, the Polish philosopher of law who was Petrazycki's disciple and who continued his work, wrote:

[41]*Ibid.*, p. xxiii.

[42]*Die Lehre vom Einkommen. . . ,* II, 437-628.

[43]E.g., P. I. Novgorodtseff stated that Petrazycki represented a truly Russian version of the doctrine of progress and an original outlook on the renaissance of natural law. This he considered as too specifically Russian to be understandable to Westerners. Cf. Timascheff, *op. cit.* (1955), p. xxxiii.

[44]Leonhard, *Die Vollendung des Deutschen bürgerlichen Gesetzbuches* ("The Completion of the German Civil Code") (Marburg: N. G. Elwert, 1897), p. 7. He

These volumes, which were in principle monographs devoted to certain problems of Roman law and exceptionally complete monographs at that, achieved another aim also: ... without advocating radical changes, they brought in their dispassionate and objective developments and in the conclusions of specialized analyses – a complete revolution in contemporary legal science.[45]

When he returned to Russia, Petrazycki published in Russian an extract from his "Fruchtverteilung," an article devoted to problems of the dowry in Roman law.[46] In 1896-7 he published in Russian the final appendix to his *Lehre von Einkommen* under the title "Introduction to the Science of Legal Policy."[47] On the strength of this publication he was granted a master's degree (*Magister iuris romani*). A study on the "Bona Fides in Roman Law" followed; it was a comparative extension of works previously published in German.[48] In 1898, there appeared two volumes in Russian under the title *The Joint-Stock Company*. This work, which was concerned with commercial law, political economy, and legal psychology, stemmed from the author's activity in connection with the committee which drafted the Russian legislation on joint-stock companies.[49] He obtained the doctor's degree for this study and was admitted

added: "The achievements of Petrazycki's work are valuable enough to retain a lasting influence even if they are not fully appreciated immediately...." See also Oertmann, in *Grünhuts Zeitschrift für Privat – und öffentl. Recht der Gegenwart*, No. 20 (1894), p. 575; No. 22 (1895), p. 301; and No. 23 (1896), p. 136. He states that "this memorable work, indubitably quite first-rate...will cause any reader with a social outlook (or, as Petrazycki himself says, interested in 'civil policy') to think and will thereby teach him much...."

[45] *Op. cit.*, p. 3 (quoted from the offprint).

[46] *Kijewskiya Univiersitietskiye Izwiestia*, VI (1896).

[47] *Ibid.*, VIII and X (1896), and No. 9 (1897), pp. I-CCL. See also *Boston University Law Review*, XVII (1895), 793 ff.

[48] First edition (with "The Rights of a Bona-Fide Possessor" appended), 1898. Second edition, St. Petersburg, 1903. The first edition was subtitled "Shares and Speculation"; the second, "Shares, Stock Exchange and Theory of Economic Crises."

[49] The First volume was translated into German in 1906 under the title *Aktienwesen und Spekulation. Eine ökonomische und rechtspsychologische Untersuchung*. Its economic and phychological content was highly appreciated, as Balogh, *op. cit.*, p. 66, notes: "This book is the last longer work by Petrazycki in civil law. His later writings dealt with the boundless field of the philosophy of law. A brilliant civilist appeared there, whose starting point was not general philosophy, but the laboratory in which the German Civil code was drafted. Petrazycki showed also there the precise and meticulous way of thinking of the civil law specialist."

to the professorship (*privat-dozent*) in 1897. Petrazycki was given the chair of philosophy of law at the law faculty of the University of St. Petersburg in 1898.[50] He remained a member of this great faculty for twenty years and became its first elected dean when the university was granted autonomous status.

Petrazycki thus chose the chair of philosophy of law rather than that of civil or Roman law, for which his early works would seem to have qualified him. From then on he elaborated his original theories and gave them increasingly precise formulation. At a time in which dogmatic science reigned supreme over doctrine and university teaching alike, and in which the theory of law was taught at best in a descriptive manner, he stimulated a growing interest in the philosophy of law. He did not neglect ethics, logic, psychology, sociology, economics, the philosophy of history, epistemology, biology, educational and social problems, or politics. His interests were truly encyclopedic and his numerous writings were never purely critical and negative, but always embodied a constructive approach to the subject. As a teacher, he gave intellectual stimulus to an entire generation and his great personal impact had lasting echoes. Although he was faced with linguistic difficulties[51] and expressed his thoughts in a somewhat involved style, in German fashion[52], he always had thousands of assiduous and enthusiastic students, including some who were not enrolled at the law faculty.[53] "His lectures were a tremendous success and were an event for all the faculties of human sciences at St. Petersburg University".[54] Those lectures were "alive" and the audience felt with pride that they were participating in the creation of deep thought, in the

[50]See Babb, *Petrazhitskii. . .*, p. 795: "From the early 1900's he was easily the most conspicuous figure in the law faculty. His classes were enormous, overflowing the largest lecture hall (which seated over a thousand students). His annual income, measured in part by student attendance, reached the unprecedented figure of forty thousand roubles."

[51]See fn. 36 and Balogh, *op. cit.*, p. 67. See also Podgorecki, *op. cit.*, pp. 137-8.

[52]The saying went in St. Petersburg at the time that Petrazycki thought in Polish, mentally translated his thought into German, and then spoke in Russian. It seems that the way in which he expressed his thought was not a very important problem to him.

[53]Babb, *Petrazhitskii. . .*, p. 796; Balogh, *op. cit.*, p. 67; and Podoreck, *op. cit.*, p. 138.

[54]Podgorecki, *op. cit.*, pp. 138 ff. See also N. N. Shulgowskyi (in Russian), *The Circle of Philosophy of Law of L. J. Petrazycki* (St. Petersburg, 1910). It should be noted that Petrazycki lectured also at the Bestujeff Higher Courses in St. Petersburg.

elaboration of a philosophical system. The testimonials of all former students prove that

> the majority were simply fascinated; some expressed admiration and agreement because Petrazhitskii was fast becoming the fashion among students of the University.... But...only a few could understand the more subtle aspects of the new doctrine.... Demolition was not an end in itself. From the ruins of these destroyed theories, a scientific edifice, beautiful in consistency and dramatic expression, emerged.[55]

Apart from his great teaching and research activity, Petrazycki did not shirk civic responsibilities. His true nature, deeply humanistic, expressed itself in his participation in Russian political life during the constitutional era. This commitment involved serious personal risks which he assumed without hesitation in order to express freely his political ideas. He was far from being a conformist at all costs and did not seek to avoid disagreements with those in power.[56] In 1906, he was persuaded to take

[55]Timascheff, *op. cit.* (1955), p. xxiv.

[56]A personal friend of Petrazycki's seems to have held a different opinion, for which see A. Meyendorff, "The Tragedy of Modern Jurisprudence", in *Interpretations of Modern Legal Philosophy* (1947), pp. 521-41. See also Podgorecki, *op. cit.*, pp. 141 ff. Facts disprove his assessment. As Petrazycki was a Pole and a Roman Catholic in an orthodox country in which Poles had no access to power, he was placed in an invidious position, particularly because of his personal influence at the university. This alone would invalidate Meyendorff's thesis. Neither in public life, professional life, nor in his private life could Petrazycki be considered a conformist. As will be shown, he did not hesitate to affront public opinion. He risked his career and even faced prison and disgrace, although he could have retained the favor of the government at the price of minor concessions.

When he was in favor with the government (the Prime Minister, Siergiey Witte, invited him before 1905 to participate in the consultative committee summoned after the peace negotiations with Japan, at Portsmouth, N.H.), he sat on the central committee of the great Russian party of liberal opposition, "KD" (Constitutional Democrats), and was elected deputy from the capital city. He adopted a highly moral attitude at the time of the Duma's dissolution by Stolypin and the Viborg manifesto of 1906 (see below, fn. 58). He showed equal courage in 1908 when his university position was threatened by the Ministry of Education because of his political ideas. Finally, in 1913, he published in the well-known Russian legal review *Pravo* (of which he was ·a co-director) a study on "Ritual murders" (1913, pp. 2403 ff. and 2423 ff.) in connection with the trial of Mendel Beilis, accused of having killed a boy, A. Joshtshinski, on ritual grounds. Thus he took sides publicly against the anti-semitic policy of the Russian government and threw the whole weight of his scientific authority on the side of the committee headed by M. Gorki. This attitude, adopted by a time when emotion ran high, proves beyond doubt that Petrazycki was prepared to share in the fight when

an active part in Russian political life and was elected to the new Duma as a deputy from the capital city. The consequence was that he lost his position as dean of the law faculty and even his chair. For the next ten years, he was reduced to the rank of associate professor. He therefore sacrificed his position for many years in order to serve the public good in parliament. When the Duma was dissolved in 1906, Petrazycki, together with other former deputies and members of the KD party, signed the Viborg Manifesto, dated July 9-10, 1906, in protest against this dissolution. The manifesto advocated refusal (1) to pay taxes other than those voted by the Duma, (2) to accept draft into the army, and (3) to comply with other public obligations until the election of a new parliamentary assembly. Petrazycki's stand was all the more remarkable because, although he opposed this manifesto, he signed it in a spirit of solidarity, even though he was aware of the personal consequences involved.[57] In fact, he was sentenced under article 129 of the Russian Penal Code to three months' imprisonment and was barred from future election to the Duma. In spite of his moral and professional prestige, he served this sentence and was the object of discrimination in his career for several more years. It was only in 1913-5 that he recovered his position as full professor and dean of the faculty.[58]

human and ethical values and intellectual responsibility were, in his opinion, at stake.

[57] See Babb, *Petrazhitskii. . .*, p. 796; Balogh, *op.cit.*, pp. 68-9; and Lande, *op.cit.*, p. 8.

[58] As soon as the Duma was dissolved in 1906, the university proposed the re-establishment of Petrazycki as full professor. This request was rejected in view of the penal proceedings against him in connection with the Viborg Manifesto of 1906. In 1908, the president of St. Petersburg University was ordered by the Ministry of Education to obtain from Petrazycki a confidential written statement that he was not participating and would not participate in any activities directed against the state or the government, and that he would not do anything prohibited by penal law, civil service regulations, or oath to the crown. A refusal was to be punished by dismissal.

In his answer, dated October 25, 1908, Petrazycki refused to sign any statement, even with reference to future activities. He explained that his position with regard to the need for a State and for the State power was outlined in his writings and was evidenced by his public activities. His books dealt also with the objectivity and impartiality to be expected from scientists and university teachers; this meant that their lectures were to be free from politics, *a priori*, but also from governmental interference. It would be against political ethics and personal dignity to sign a promise not to participate in organizations opposed to the changing programs of governments.

After several weeks, the ministry answered Petrazycki through the president, pointing out that, as a civil servant, a professor was not entitled to criticize his

When the revolution of March 1917 started in Russia, Petrazycki, who approved of the overthrow of the czarist regime,[59] was appointed to the Senate (Russian Supreme Court) by the Kerensky provisional government.[60] The new regime obviously wished to secure the services of a man who held progressive opinions, advocated equal rights for women, and was a well-known humanist. However, Petrazycki, whose outlook on current events was extremely pessimistic, did not take up these functions. After the Riga Treaty of 1921, he opted for Polish nationality and returned to his home country, which had recovered its independence.

He accepted a chair of sociology in the Law Faculty of Warsaw University; this chair was created for him, as he had refused that of legal theory. His choice reflected the trend of his research at the time. Toward the end of his life, he sought to investigate the causal relationships which, through law, could provide a basis for rational and desirable social change.[61] After he returned to his country of origin, he devoted himself to teaching sociology, without, however, neglecting the fields of social psychology and legal methodology.[62] His lectures in Polish were considered no less brilliant than his previous teaching in Russia[63]; he continued to attract thousands of students; and many admirers remained faithful to him after his death. Comparatively unknown in Poland until then, his scientific school achieved perhaps its greatest development in this last period of his life, although his former students from St. Petersburg continued to play an important part in it.[64] Petrazycki, in spite of illness, took an active part in the work of the Polish Committee for Codification, entrusted with the task of unifying the manifold foreign legal codes in force in Poland at the time.[65] Though he did not publish much,[66] he

minister's orders. It was added that his conviction on account of the Viborg Manifesto justified governmental distrust. The expressions used by Petrazycki in his answer were considered incorrect.

No further sanctions occurred. In 1913 Petrazycki was re-elected dean by ten votes against one. (See Podgorecki, *op. cit.*, pp. 138 ff.)

[59]Meyendorff, *op.cit.*, pp. 521 ff.

[60]See Langrod, *op. cit.*, p. 6; and Timascheff, *op. cit.* (1955), p. xxxi.

[61]Podgorecki, *op. cit.*, pp. 123 ff.

[62]Emke, *op. cit.*, p. 90; Podgorecki, *op. cit.*, p. 143.

[63]Timascheff, *op. cit.* (1955), p. xxxi.

[64]Langrod, *op. cit.*, p. 10.

[65]There were five codes in force: the Napoleonic Code in a modified version, the Austrian Civil Code, the German Legal Code and the Hungarian Code, while Russian law was in effect on Polish eastern territories.

[66]He was vice-chairman of the International Institute of Sociology (Paris). He was elected in 1928 (to replace the late Paul Morland, professor of Geneva University)

completed his manuscripts and prepared his courses in sociology with a view to their publication.[67]

After the October Revolution in Russia, Petrazycki had become increasingly pessimistic about the lowering of ethical standards and the loss of humanistic feelings.[68] He committed suicide on May 15, 1931, in Warsaw, at the age of 64.

His life throws great light upon his work. Its vicissitudes have been considered as in part responsible for his emphasis on the psychological elements of law. Indeed, a number of writers have sought a link between the life and the work of the founder of the psychological theory of law.[69]

HIS WORKS

Petrazycki's basic concepts were outlined in his early writings, which he prepared during his studies in Germany. These concepts were to mature and acquire additional depth throughout his academic career.

The critical analysis, now famous, which Petrazycki undertook in connection with the drafting of the German Civil Code was based mainly on his conception of law and on a philosophical and psychological analysis of the work of Roman jurists. At the time, the first committee for drafting the German Legal Code (1874-88) — chaired by Pape — in which the famous Romanist, Windscheid, played an important part, was preparing its text. A second committee, chaired by O. Gierke and with an extended membership, was established later (1890-95). The first had been truly Romanistic, leaning toward the direct reception of Roman law. The latter was more nationalistic, insomuch as it avoided mere imitation and sought inspiration from Germanic traditions and experience. Opposing Ihering's

as full member of the International Academy of Comparative Law in the Hague, in which he represented all Slavonic countries.

[67]Timascheff, *op. cit.* (1955), p. xxxi; Podgorecki, *op. cit.*, pp. 123 ff.

[68]It seems highly improbable that political considerations prompted Petrazycki's suicide. Timascheff, *op. cit.* (1955), p. xxxi, maintained that he was deeply disturbed by Pilsudski's *coup d'état* in 1926, as well as by his own Russian experiences. The friends who witnessed the last years of his life were sure that his suicide was the result of the fact that his own world had collapsed, from an ethical point of view. He was concerned with political ethics rather than political events.

[69]See Podgorecki, *op. cit.*, pp. 134-5. The hypothesis is that Petrazycki's interest in emotions stemmed from his difficulty in adjusting to the outside world and in fulfilling his social role. He endeavored to rationalize and "legalize" external pressures and to give a depersonalized character to the impact of the outside world on his psyche. Whatever the case may have been, Petrazycki's theories may serve to explain up to a point the causes of his suicide.

ideas, which tended to prevail at the time, Petrazycki refused to base law on the notion of self-interest. Ihering's theory was either "nonsense, a unification and an identification of elements without common measure"[70] or an intuitive generalization rather than a scientific formula. Petrazycki viewed individual interests as social, ethical, and economic elements with a definite mission, characterized by some positive aspects (stimulation of the social sense, work, honesty, economic development, etc.) and some negative aspects (anti-social attitudes, egocentrism, cunning, violence, etc.). The final supra-legal and extra-legal aim of legal evolution was, according to him, altruistic, opposed to selfishness and directed towards a supreme spiritual perfection. Throughout his works, Petrazycki stressed the pre-eminence of *love* and derived many logical conclusions from the kinship between law and ethics. Whilst love "asserts itself, under one aspect, *as reason,* reason also asserts itself, under a certain aspect, as *love."*[71]

According to Petrazycki, Roman law does not reflect the practical sense of the ancient legislator, or a wish to balance the interests at stake. He thought that the legislator acted intuitively, inspired by a naive sense of what was right and fair, rather than from rational motives. The authors of the code unconsciously expressed the experience of society. Roman law fulfilled a pedagogical mission within a differentiated and slowly evolving community. But, said Petrazycki, if the modern legislator, in his admiration for his Roman predecessors, forgets that Roman law, with its provisions geared to the anarchic economy of Rome and to a social organization based on slavery, is ill-adapted to contemporary reality, imitation will lead only to aberrations and mistakes. The legislator's action will then become haphazard, as he will borrow from heterogeneous sources (deducing general norms, adapting provisions from foreign law, weighing the interests at stake, etc.); such provisions could often be purely subjective. Under such conditions, social conflicts would be bound to occur. As no method of analyzing the mechanism of social order and no understanding of the actual role of legal institutions exist, law would be elaborated without any spirit of foresight.

On these premises, Petrazycki proved that the authors of the first draft of the German Civil Code worked unmethodically, and he proceeded to explain the genesis of the various rules suggested by them. These he related to a blind application of the corresponding rules in Roman law.[72] Roman law, as taught in Germany at the time "included a series of modifications

---

[70]Petrazycki, *Teoria prawa i panstwa w zwiazku z teoria moralnosci* ("Theory of Law and State in Connection with a Theory of Morality") (Warsaw, 1959), I, 433.

[71]Petrazycki, *Die Lehre von Einkommen. . . ,* II, 468.

[72]Babb, *Petrazhitskii. . . ,* p. 795.

which occurred during the feudal period, far inferior to the Roman with respect to individual freedom".[73] He proved also that there were obvious mistakes in the interpretation of the Roman texts and complete misunderstandings as to their meaning. The authors of the German draft were not always aware of the social aims of given provisions. Investigating these matters, Petrazycki came to the conclusion that, in spite of its progressive facade, the draft code was often socially harmful. "The draft B.G.B. seems to overlook that after Roman law, there was a Gospel of *love*;. . .it is more Roman than Roman law itself. . ."[74]

This attack of a young foreigner against a work prepared by the most eminent representatives of German legal science unexpectedly met with admiration, in spite of some initial criticisms. The author's masters, including Heinrich Dernburg,[75] accepted his theses, and some of his concrete suggestions were incorporated into the final draft of the code.[76]

In this early period, Petrazycki formulated the general idea of a normative discipline or "legal policy" ("civil policy" at the time of the drafting of the B.G.B.). Each branch of law, as each science, should have its own "policy," he said, based on an empirical analysis of human behavior in relation to legal norms. This policy would make it possible to assess the various influences of legal provisions upon economics and the social structure, because these provisions would be studied in the light of their results. Throughout his later works, Petrazycki returned to the idea that the psychological processes guiding the formulation of laws should be a separate field of study. He envisaged legislation as going beyond mere justice and tending to a "rapprochement between law and love." Without this "legal policy," the dogmatic study of positive law would be doomed *a priori* to utter sterility. Without a thorough analysis of the social order, without a criticism of positive institutions from this point of view, without drawing conclusions *in hypothesi*, the work is only half done, and the

[73]*Ibid*.

[74]Petrazycki, *Die Lehre von Einkommen. . .* , I, 340.

[75]*Die allgemeinen Lehren des Bürgerlichen Rechts des Deutschen Reichs und Preussens* ("The General Scientific Conclusions to Be Derived from the Civil Code of the German Reich and of Prussia") (Halle/Saale, 1902).

[76]Rudolf Sohm, who defended the governmental text before the parliament, was the most severe critic of Petrazycki's ideas, on which see his *Ueber den Entwurf eines B.G.B.* ("On the Draft B.G.B.") (Berlin, 1897). Some other authors, such as Leonhard, *op. cit.*, expressed the fear that Petrazycki's criticism might undermine future codification, since it was directed against *tigna iuncta*. On the other hand, such authors as Oertmann (*op. cit.*), Mayer (in *441 Jahrbücher für Nationaleokonomie,* 1895 and 1897), von Schey, in his study on the honest and dishonest possessor, etc., were in favor of some of Petrazycki's points.

historical evolution of law cannot be truly understood. Petrazycki's aim was to show to his contemporaries the need for devising and justifying scientifically the means of achieving a new planned reality, to which a conscious and consistent policy would be geared. In this teleological conception, the data of a given science would be used in order to obtain socially desirable behavior and to carry out the education of the community in accordance with the ultimate purpose. To each field of life would thus correspond a science, which would exert a lasting and rational educational influence according to preordained rules.

This was considered, in a sense, a rebirth of the old idea of "natural law," no longer connected with *a priori* absolutes. However, Petrazycki did not relinquish his rationalism and his concern for the use of the experimental method. He resisted the call of the metaphysical sirens, differing thereby from Bergson in France or Scheller in Germany, to whom he was akin insofar as he endeavored to extend the empirical from the level of experience to that of metaphysics. (He went beyond the traditional opposition of empiricism and spirituality. In an age of narrow positivism, he launched a return towards *practical* idealism, while remaining attached to evolutionism and to scientific methods of investigation.)

A modern forerunner of the renaissance of legal philosophy, Petrazycki wanted to discover the rules of rational legislation through the applied study of legal policy. Arbitrary and utopian systems, unrelated to experience and unfitted to the "laws of nature," would be replaced by a genuine science, completely different from its predecessors. This is how Babb characterized him:

> In none of these is there to be found anything really comparable to Petrazhitskii's science of legal policy — not in the naive and unconscious wisdom of Roman law, not in the subservient interpretation and adaptation, by commentators and glossators, of texts which they accepted without question or investigation, not in rationalism which deduced systems from *a priori* premises, not in the historical school, which saw in the organic development of law a mystic process taking place in the secret depths of rational consciousness, not in Ihering who conceived law to be the organic process of development of national life whose moving principle was expediency, nor in positivism, which has thus far established merely empirical laws as to social phenomena not susceptible of verification by deduction (since the phenomena of life cannot be reduced to physical and chemical processes, and the necessary starting point for deduction is therefore absent) and so never rising to the rank of scientific laws. Petrazhitskii considered that the closest analogy was the "dualistic division of jurisprudence existing in the epoch of the so-called natural (reasonable, ideal, philosophical) law." He says that

318

"the significance of the science of natural law as an independent systematic discipline on a level with positive-law jurisprudence consisted in the fulfilment of the lofty and important mission which the future science of legal policy should serve." The analogy seems to be merely that after the fall of idealism and the political reaction following the French Revolution, jurisprudence and the other social sciences lost their ideal guidance and principles. As Petrazhitskii himself pointed out, the representatives of the school of natural law knew nothing whatever of any science of legal policy (in his sense of a discipline starting from premises established by scientific investigation) as a basis for solving problems *de lege ferenda* by a consciously scientific method of thinking.[77]

Petrazycki was firmly convinced of the need for a "legal policy" scientifically designed, but with a teleological character which would provide for study of the aim, the essence, and the historical trends of legal evolution, and so could influence further evolution toward the ideal.[78] From the very beginning of his work, he outlined the general program of this legal policy; he was later to study its content and to draw clear demarcation lines between this and neighboring branches of legal study. This differentiation was to prove extremely important.[79]

[77]Babb, *Petrazhitskii. . .* , pp. 805-6.

[78]Petrazycki listed five fields in which preparatory work should necessarily take place, namely: (1) investigation of human psychology (both individual and collective), with a systematic analysis of the psychic forces at work and of the psychological laws regulating the influence of law on the motives of individual and mass behavior (theory of legal psychology); (2) investigation into the educational impact of law both as a product of civilization and as a force shaping civilization; (3) investigation of the laws which rule social education and promote the appropriate objective principles, as well as corresponding institutions; (4) investigation into the ideal of any law — its final aim as a civilizing force connected with other such forces (study of the role of law within the general history of civilization); (5) methodological investigation aimed at devising a two-phase process: (a) the application to law of the principal method of psychological thought, i.e., deduction from psychological premises (problem of conformity between a legislation and the ideal of love as the supreme good; causal connection between this legislation and the experimental facts of individual and social psychology derived from a psychological analysis); and (b) empirical verification *ex post* (if possible) through the use of the inductive method and of experimental observation (including the use of statistics and of the results of neighboring sciences such as economics).

[79]On the one hand, Petrazycki distinguished the *theory of law*, which does not make value judgments (typical for any "legal policy") but studies legal phenomena as elements of psychic reality, analyzing their role as well as their psychological and ethical repercussions. It is a philosophical discipline concerned with the theoretical

319

This contribution to legal science, with its critical and constructive aspects, its characteristic approach to problems (never lacking in realism and practicality), and its growing impact — even on those who adopted initially a critical attitude[80] — assures by itself the lasting value of Petrazycki's work. In his later writings he was to provide clarification. Moreover, he gave additional depth to the purely legal studies of his early days by widening the sphere of his interests and transcended law *stricto*

treatment of the legal *sein* (the "is" as distinguished from the "ought") pertaining to individual and group psychology. This theoretical science corresponds to sociology in the field of human sciences and to biology in natural sciences.

On the other hand, he admitted the existence of a *dogmatic normative science*, concerned with the content of "official" rules, which it describes, interprets, comments upon, and coordinates (whereas the *theory of law* goes beyond the exegesis of texts in force and embraces *all* legal problems, whether normal or exceptional, positive or negative, or sane or criminal, in their capacity as elements of social life). Petrazycki considered this branch as geared to purely practical aims and wrongly underestimated its scientific value.

Finally Petrazycki dealt with "legal policy," which he confronted with the other two branches of legal knowledge. He added that the introduction of "legal policy" would not require any basic reform of the legal science of the time, since it consisted only of a different approach to investigation.

Petrazycki achieved thereby an important threefold classification of legal studies, avoiding duplication and facilitating necessary and logical differentiation in research. He emphasized the possibility of knowing real law through experimental research into motives for acting or for abstaining from action, connected with a study of human nature and its influence in the field of legal devices. At the same time, he sought obstinately to find a balance between good and bad motives interacting constantly.

[80]E.g., Leonhard, in *Das neue Gesetzbuch als Wendepunkt der Privatrechtswissenschaft* ("The New Civil Code as a Turning Point in the Science of Private Law") (1900), pp. 11 ff. Leonhard was the main adversary of the idea of a civil law policy, but came to accept it as "a modernized form of the fundamental idea of the former natural law." See also: Leonhard, *Das Recht der Schuldverhältnisse in seiner allgemeinen Lehre* ("The Law of Obligations, Its General Scientific Concepts") (1899); Offner, *Studien sozialer Jurisprudenz* ("Studies in Social Jurisprudence") (1894); A. Menger, *Ueber die sozialen Aufgaben der Rechtswissenschaft* ("On the Social Tasks of the Science of Law") (1895); Zittelman, *Die Gefahren des B.G.B. für Rechtswissenschaft* ("The Dangers of the Civil Code for Legal Science") (1896); Lobe, *Was verlangen wir von einem B.G.B., ein Wort an den Reichstag* ("What We Require from a Civil Code, a Word to Parliament") (1896), pp. 29 ff.; and Oertmann in *Archiv für burgerliches Recht*, VIII, 366 ff. Eugen Ehrlich, in *Soziologie des Rechts* ("Sociology of Law") (1913), advocated ideas close to those of Petrazycki. In Ehrlich's view, legal sociology (studying law as a social phenomenon and not as a system of norms) should become a dogmatic science, but with the use of methods borrowed from natural sciences.

sensu to enter the field of the philosophy, methodology, and logic of social progress.[81]

Apart from a series of minor writings, all of which appeared in Russian in various Russian scientific reviews and, dealing with several aspects of legal science, showed the author's extensive interest in legal problems,[82] Petrazycki published in 1900 the outline of his psychological theory of law under the title, *Essays on Legal Philosophy*.[83] The first part of the book was constructive and defined the essence of the theory: the need to relate law to reality, which he considered as rooted in psychology (i.e., observable only through the introspective analysis of mental processes). Law is experienced mainly as the awareness that one is bound by duty. In seeking the demarcation line between law and morality (a necessary quest, since those two psychological elements of reality are parallel), one realizes that only the latter includes imperatives (i.e., unilateral requirements which do not result in obligations towards third parties). Law, on the other hand, is characterized by its predominantly attributive nature (to which its imperative function is subordinate, although the opposite is widely believed). In the second part of his book, Petrazycki reviewed and commented critically on the legal theories of his time.[84]

[81]It is essential, in order to grasp Petrazycki's approach and the place of the psychological theory of law in his work, to realize that his thoughts developed *in reverse*. He did not form his theory of a legal policy directly, but indirectly, owing to his understanding of the *psychological* conception of law and legal science. See Petrazycki (in Russian), The Criticism of My Introduction, in *9 Zhur. Min. Yust., 152 ff.*

[82]See,e.g., the following works of Petrazycki, in Russian: on legal philosophy, "What Is Law?" *Viestnik Prava* I (1899); on administrative law, "Administrative Law," *Pravo*, I (1899); on financial law, "Essays on Custom Duties," *Pravo* (1899), 599 ff., 1001 ff., and 1072 ff.; on penal law, "The Exile of Criminals," *Pravo* (1899), 65 ff., 209 ff., 319 ff., 377 ff., 426 ff., 599 ff., and 901 ff.; on civil law, "The Role of Laws in Civil Law," *Pravo* (1899), 809 ff., and "Proceedings Against the Unlawful Acquisition of Wealth," in *Viestnik Prava*, I, No. 1, 1 ff.; No. 2, 131 ff.; No. 3, 192 ff.; and No. 4, 50; on judiciary law and justice, "The Law and the Tribunal," *Pravo* (1901), 1 ff., 117 ff., 311 ff., and others; on natural law, "The Renaissance of Natural Law," *Pravo* (1902), 1793 ff., 1841 ff., and 1915 ff. (written in connection with "Kant and Hegel" by Novgorodtsev; and on international private law, "Essays on International Private Law," *Pravo* (1911), 2609 ff., 2767 ff., 2851 ff., and 2974 ff.

[83]St. Petersburg (1900).

[84]Timascheff, *op. cit.* (1955), p. xxiv.

This work met with strong opposition, particularly from two Russian professors, B. Chicherin[85] and Prince E. N. Trubetskoy.[86] Both represented legal idealism and objected to Petrazycki's positivistic outlook, according to which the substance and the objectives of law were anchored in reality. Chicherin, who held a neo-Hegelian position, denied that law could be situated on the level of the *sein* ("is") rather than of the *sollen* ("ought"), i.e., outside the normative sphere. In his view, law did not consist of an individual psychological experience, but was a compulsory principle, a universal obligation. He rejected Petrazycki's emphasis on the experimental verification of legal processes. As for Trubetskoy, he reproached Petrazycki with introducing fantasies into the field of law. He did not admit that the essence of natural law could be defined in terms of empirical psychology. This would, in his view, create a confusion between the psychological and the ethical approach.[87]

Aware that the psychological theory of law had to be developed and its intellectual foundations strengthened, Petrazycki did not answer any of the criticisms. His main concern was to define the structure of a new psychology.[88] He carried out thorough psychological studies and published a summary of his conclusions under the title *The Motives of Human Conduct, Particularly Ethical Motives and Their Varieties.*[89] He opposed the classical and purely analytical threefold division of psychological elements accepted by the philosophers of his time. In this view, there existed three parallel compartments: intelligence (cognition – perception of ideas), feelings (emotions – pleasure and pain), and will (aspirations and active experiences). Each of the three was by definition either passive (feelings, intellectual elements) or active (will). Petrazycki objected to the lack of a synthesis based on a combination of mental processes both active and passive. To the three categories already mentioned he added a fourth, more complex: the bilateral experiences which are dual in character (passive and active at the same time), and which include hunger,[90] thirst, and the sexual urge, as well as the sense of duty. It is precisely this

---

[85]B. Chicherin (in Russian), "The Philosophical Theory of Law," *Voprosy phil i psikh*, LV (1900), 365 ff.

[86]E. N. Trubetskoy (in Russian), "The Legal Philosophy of Prof. Petrazycki,," *Voprosy phil. i psikh*, LVII (1901), 9.

[87]Babb, *Petrazhitskii. . .* , p. 578.

[88]Timascheff, *op. cit.* (1955), p. xxv.

[89]Published in Russian in St. Petersburg (1904), translated into German in 1907, into Polish by J. Finkelkraut in 1925. An English abridged version, adapted by H. W. Babb, appeared in 1955 under the title *Law and Morality*.

[90]Petrazycki differentiated psychological and physiological hunger, the former being experienced as a need and an incitement to fulfill it, the later being merely a need

. . . discovery of the complex, or bilateral, experiences [which] was a decisive step in the development of Petrazhitsky's theory, since both law and morals or, more exactly, both legal and moral experiences belonged to this class. Bilateral experiences are, however, most diversified; hence a theory of law in terms of mental experience could be formulated only on the basis of a classification of these experiences.[91]

Emotions or emotive impulses, being bilateral in nature − in connection with the dual (both centripetal and centrifugal) structure of the nervous system and its double physiological function − are the prototype of psychic life with its ambivalent passive and active character.

Since he placed law and morality in the same intellectual category, unlike all those who endeavored to differentiate between them, Petrazycki needed to provide additional clarification on this crucial problem. This he did in what has been considered as his *magnum opus*,[92] *The Introduction to the Study of Law and Morality: The Bases of Emotional Psychology*, published in 1905[93] and followed in 1907 by *The Theory of Law and State in Connection with a Theory of Morality*.[94] In these works, Petrazycki expounded his fundamental ideas on the difference between law as an intellectual phenomenon (pertaining to reality, since it is an individual emotional experience) and as a system of compulsory norms (laws, jurisprudence, customs, etc.). Although most jurists identify the latter with the notion of law, it is in fact a mere fantasy; according to Petrazycki, it is the *psychological* phenomenon which is real, in spite of being unnoticed (because it cannot be discovered and analysed without being artificially provoked) and impossible to observe directly from the outside. When a loan is contracted and its term comes, all that occurs is a series of mental pictures formed by the contracting parties and based on an anticipated assessment of their respective acts (duty impulse). This impulse is a bilateral *experience,* both active and passive. "The law is therefore to be found in the minds of those who have the corresponding experiences, and nowhere else."[95]

(which outside circumstances, e.g. the way in which a meal is served, may prevent from having a psychological counterpart).

[91]Timascheff, *op. cit.*, (1955) p. xxv.

[92]*Ibid.*, p. xxvi.

[93]In Russian, 1905; second edition, 1907; third edition, 1908. Polish translation, 1930; second edition, 1959 (translated by J. Lande). German abridged translation, 1933 (covering pp. 11-112). English translation (*Law and Morality*), 1955.

[94]In Russian, 1907; second edition, 1909-10. Polish translation, 1959 (First volume translated by J. Lande; second by W. Lesniewski).

[95]Timascheff, *op. cit.* (1955), p. xxvii.

323

Petrazycki traced a demarcation line between law and morality: between the "bilateral" legal phenomenon (legal obligation and subjective right) — imperative *and* attributive — and the moral phenomenon, characterized by the imperative element alone. He also stressed their common ethical basis — the fact that they belonged to the same category of ethical phenomena — a fact which was also to be pointed out by Duguit. He noted that an imperative (i.e., "thou shall not kill") may have a purely moral meaning at times or a purely legal one at other times. He gave both elements the psychological meaning which underlay the whole of his theory rather than an ethical meaning. In his deep relativism, he denied the objective existence of any ethics — and therefore that of law as well as of morality — outside the sphere of individual experience. Thus, according to Lande, he elaborated "for the first time something which resembled the physics of mores planned for so long."[96] This contribution threw a new light on the role of morality in relation to law and provided legal thought with many original and provocative concepts.

Although he had not done so in 1900, Petrazycki answered the criticisms of his theory in its developed and, in a sense, final form. His *magnum opus* caused a "storm of indignation."[97] Several great Russian specialists, such as V. I. Sergueyevitch[98] (a sociological positivist), P. I. Novgorodtseff[99] (a neo-Kantian idealistic legal philosopher), G. Szerszeniewicz[100] (a legal positivist), and others[101] opposed the psycholog-

---

[96]Lande, *Leon Petrazycki*, p. 25 (quoted from offprint). See also B. Gourevitch, *The Road to Peace and to Moral Democracy. An Encyclopedia of Peace* (New York, 1955), II, 292, 610-1.

[97]Timascheff, *op. cit.* (1955), p. xxix.

[98]In Russian, "The New Doctrine of Law and Morality," *Zhur. Min. Yust.*, II (February 1909), 1-57; and "Answer to Petrazycki," *Zhur. Min. Yust.*, II (February 1910), 101-28.

[99]In Russian, "The Contemporary Problems of Natural Law," *Iur. Viestnik*, I (1913), 18-28; and "The Pyschological Theory of Law and the Philosophy of Natural Law," *Iur. Viestnik*, III (1913), 5 ff.

[100]In Russian, *The General Doctrine of State and Law* (Moscow, 1911) and *The General Theory of Law* (Moscow, 1912). It should be noted that Gabriel Szerszeniewicz (the Russian transcription of his name was Shershenevitch), considered as one of the most eminent specialists of commercial law in Russia and a teacher of great standing, was, like Petrazycki, of Polish descent, a deputy to the first Russian Duma (representing the town of Kazan), and a professor of law (at Moscow University). All his writings were in Russian.

[101]See, e.g., Kistiakovsky (in Russian), "The Reality of Objective Law," *Logos*, II (1910), 193 ff.; "The Crisis of Legal Doctrine," *Iur. Viestnik*, I (1914), 70; and *The Social Sciences and Law* (Moscow, 1916).

ical theory of law in articles, pamphlets, and treatises. Petrazycki took the opportunity, in his answers to Sergueyevitch[102] and Novgorodtseff,[103] to lay down his own doctrine once again. In particular, he explained his position with regard to natural law in his answer to Novgorodtseff and repeated that legal policy was an empirical science in the making, as he had already said in his first works. It was in this sense that he advocated a renaissance of natural law as a psychological conception, but not in its abstract form; he wished to include causes as well as results of practical experience.[104] The supporters of classical natural law refused to recognize in Petrazycki's work a different approach to their theory, while Petrazycki, rejecting all *a priori* absolutes, used a knowledge of the laws of causality as his starting point and, applying these laws to legal policy, endeavored to lay the foundation of a reasonable and rational law. This controversy played a great part in the scientific life of the time and was to have important theoretical repercussions outside Russia.

Always interested in the problems of education, and those of higher education in particular, Petrazycki published in 1907 two volumes in Russian entitled *University and Science*. This great study of the theory of higher education and of educational policy has been compared by Timascheff[105] to *Wissenschaft als Beruf*, which the great German sociologist Max Weber published fourteen years later. Petrazycki dealt with many research and educational problems to which he returned on several subsequent occasions. He studied "the psychology of science."[106] He applied his general psychological theory to the educational field and stressed the causal dependence of scientific phenomena as psychological

[102]Petrazycki (in Russian), "The Critique of My Introduction," *op. cit.*, pp. 152-9 (November 1909); "Reply to Sergueyevitch," *Pravo* (1910), 1927 ff. and 1980 ff.; and *The New Doctrine of Law and Its Critique by Sergueyevitch* (St. Petersburg, 1910).

[103]Petrazycki (in Russian), "Social Ideal and Natural Law," *Iur. Viestnik*, II (1913), 5 ff.

[104]Novgorodtseff answered, in "The Psychological Theory of Law and the Philosophy of Natural Law," *Iur. Viestnik*, I (1913), that according to him legal science could not be considered as a causal science.

[105]Timascheff, *op. cit.* (1955), p. xxxi.

[106]My former student, Prof. G. L. Seidler, now president of the Maria Curie-Skoldowska University at Lublin (Poland), enabled me to consult the Polish translation of a Russian unpublished manuscript by Leon Petrazycki ("Psychology of Science") which was saved during the Warsaw insurrection 1944; it is dated 1912 and is kept now in the archives of the Chair of Theory of State and Law (Law Faculty, Maria Curie-Sklodowska University). I would like to thank Prof. Seidler and his assistants for their help. (G.L.)

processes making up a *class* of notions anchored in reality. He viewed science as a real phenomenon, worthy as such of a thorough study through introspection, both in order to achieve greater knowledge and for practical reasons.[107] The lecture course was advocated as the basis of any university education and the starting point of the "science of scientific

[107]In his courses on the psychology of science, Petrazycki dealt mostly with:

(1) The distinction between "pure" and "applied" sciences (or arts) Petrazycki wanted to separate strictly the two categories of science, between which reigned a traditional confusion. On the one hand, one should take into account the existence of *teleological* sciences with a practical character, based not only on causal relationships but also on a series of rules belonging to given "classes" of knowledge (e.g., mathematical notions). On the other hand, there are normative sciences (moral, legal, esthetic, etc.) which, without covering causal relationships, lay down some principles of behavior *in se*. See J. Kalinowski, *Teoria poznania praktycznego* ("Theory of Practical Knowledge") (Lublin, 1960), p. 105.

(2) The need for providing each field of human life with scientific enlightenment derived from a theoretical basis and rational rules of behavior. Many mistakes could be avoided if science filled existing gaps and oriented human behavior. Whereas the physical sciences provide adequate theoretical enlightenment, the sphere of psychic phenomena (i.e., motives of behavior, character training, psychological inclinations and their formation) remains in the dark, since psychological techniques are insufficiently developed.

(3) The need for a thorough study of the rational technique of scientific knowledge, of methodology, of specific causal relationships, and even of the theory of science, which creates the atmosphere underlying the theoretical approach to the phenomena investigated. Science, viewed from a psychological angle, includes specific psychic phenomena, specific intellectual and emotional processes, and products of human thought similar to those on which religious beliefs are based.

(4) Emotions which play a specific part owing to their intensity and to the important phenomenon of "emotional contamination," a series of biological processes which create "instinctive" and unconscious impulses. In the coexistence of human beings, this "contamination" acquires an increasing importance owing to the atmosphere of university education. Petrazycki studied in detail the influence of the university environment, the direct impact of individual professors, the attraction of scientific circles, the interest created and sustained through lectures, and the "spiritual power" of masters. A psychological disposition is thus created which stimulates future favorable reactions and the reception of scientific theses, helped by a suitable ideological and emotional attitude. The listeners become "psychologically open" to the truths taught and (thanks to this "emotional contamination") to the influence of the milieu, provided that the university (*universitas litterarum*) does not become an institute of professional training for practical ends alone, but remains a source of values independent from their utilization, and provided also that the subdivision into

thought" (*scientis scientiarum*) which, by becoming increasingly democratic, would play an all-important role in civilized countries and perfect the "technique of thought."[108]

In 1911, Petrazycki published a volume on *Shares, the Stock-Exchange and the Theory of Economic Crises* in which he covered again the problems he had dealt with more summarily in 1898.

Legal thinkers have a limited influence on the theory of knowledge or on scientific methodology, because their efforts are mainly devoted to a given branch of the legal sciences. Petrazycki was an exception to this rule. Distrusting ready-made ideas, even if they had been accepted for generations, he tended to rethink all basic notions and to investigate the marginal problems arising in the course of his legal and philosophical studies. He became therefore aware of the lack of any appropriate research method in the social sciences and was led to investigate scientific methodology in general. Realizing that methodological deficiencies prevented the "human sciences," such as biology and psychology from fulfilling their aim, and wishing to achieve the level reached in this respect by the natural sciences, he undertook thorough methodological research beyond the narrow framework of his main studies on law and morality.

Petrazycki's methodological doctrine, which deserves to be better known than it is at present, has the merit. . .of grasping dynamic reality and of coordinating the legal point of view with the sociological and the psychological.[109]

This purely objective scientific methodology is characterized by two main principles:

1. The independent creation of classes (categories of analyzed phenomena) as a starting point for any rational scientific investigation. It is essential to elaborate and formulate general ideas and theories, correctly classified in relation to some common and specific traits (attributes or particular features), either existing in reality or merely imagined.

faculties does not become air-tight and does not prevent – materially and psychologically – the psychological unification and the *convivencia* of all students: the source of community spirit. Thus is developed the sociopsychological process through which new generations accede to previous generations' type and level of thought. A genuine "school of thought" is gradually created, brings about "useful habits" of scientific thought, becomes progressively more and more democratic, and perfects the technique of thought.

[108]Petrazycki developed the same ideas in 1899 in his work on *The Stock Company* (in German).

[109]G. Langrod, "La Science politique en Pologne" ("Political Science in Poland"), *La science politique contemporaine: Contribution á la recherche, la méthode et l'enseignement* (Paris: UNESCO, 1950), p. 197.

Petrazycki rejected the traditional way of making definitions in the abstract (by observing a given class and comparing its components with those of related classes), which amounted, in his view, to a vicious circle. Indeed, each class is unlimited numerically. In order to ensure that they are correctly formed, all objects which can be taken into account should be reviewed, their distinctive traits sought out, and the absence of the same traits in other subjects verified. A class would thus be formed on the basis of logical considerations[110] and would include all phenomena sharing the same trait. The choice of this common trait would rule out all different phenomena, even if they happen to be related to those composing the given class. To be scientifically valid, such a class would be capable of serving as a starting point to an adequate scientific theory.

2. The adequate character of any scientific theory is dependent upon two conditions. Indeed, each theory must state the existence of a logical or causal link given between the characteristic trait (*differentia specifica*) of a given class — which is the logical predicate. The two conditions required for this are: (a) that the given theory be true in relation to the *whole* "class", i.e., in relation to the *differentia specifica* of all the phenomena covered by the class; and (b) that it be true *only* in relation to the *differentia specifica* of these phenomena to the absolute exclusion of all others belonging to other classes.

If the first condition is not fulfilled, the theory is "mobile" (in the words of Petrazycki, "it jumps"), because it is too narrow and does not cover the whole class, but only applies to part of it. If the second condition is not fulfilled, the theory is "lame," because it is too wide and applies, apart from the given class, to other phenomena outside it.

The first mistake, which is particularly frequent, can be illustrated by the example of social theories which endeavor to explain all social problems by reference to a single element. The second can be illustrated by the example of numerous theories built around a central notion accurate as such, but disregarding the exact "breadth" of the given class. This mistake is due either to conventions in terminology or to the use of purely practical criteria, as, for instance, in several traditional theories of legal science.

Petrazycki's scheme was intended to permit a verification of the adequacy of any scientific theory from both points of view. He also demonstrated how a complete system of theories could be established according to the superiority, the inferiority, or the coordination of classes. Indeed, he endeavored to form increasingly wide "superclasses," covering entire species. These were intended to help solve the major problem of

[110]Petrazycki rejected "linguistic" definitions based on characteristic terms or commonly used expressions, which cover heterogenous objects under a purely *external* denomination.

philosophy, since, when two adequate theories were formed (one concerning physical, the other psychological phenomena), a third theory could be elaborated to cover a common "class" of "real phenomena" characterizing the two previous classes.

In order to arrive at a correct class exempt from the mistakes mentioned above, the existence of necessary relationships, either logical or causal, between objects should be established in each case.[111] Generalizations[112] or definitions based on methodological or logical mistakes should definitely be avoided. The identification of a general notion with its external criteria or with classifications founded either upon quantitative and indeterminate or practical and technical criteria is illegitimate. Petrazycki condemned any dogmatic approach, as well as "logical passivity" and a *naive* submission to the notions of everyday language.[113] His was "the highest and perhaps the most ambitious endeavor to raise humanistic thought to the scientific level. . . .Therefore it would not be astonishing if in the future − when his essays are finally assessed − it was thought that, during the first century after positivism postulated the scientific value of human knowledge, Petrazycki achieved the greatest results in that direction."[114]

Toward the end of his life, Petrazycki devoted his work to sociology. As has already been said, he occupied the chair of this subject at the Law Faculty of Warsaw University until his death.[115] "He concentrated his thoughts on sociological problems, and no longer on the methodological problems of legal theory. Indeed, having considered that the question of a legal policy was crucial, he came to see as a capital problem the research. . .on which planned and rational modifications of the social order (to be introduced by means of legislation) could be based."[116] His writings on sociological matters are unfortunately lost, but his opinions are known, thanks to his disciples.[117] His social analyses were based upon the

[111]Lande, *Petrazycki. . .* , p. 11.

[112]This does not mean that existing "inadequate" theories should be rejected, since they can be reinterpreted and thus made accurate.

[113]Balogh, *op. cit.*, p. 76.

[114]*Ibid.*, p. 31.

[115]This chair, created for Petrazycki, had no other holders and was discontinued when he died.

[116]Podgorecki, *op. cit.*, p. 123.

[117]See Szymon Kachan, "Teoria przystosowania i doboru naturalnego" ("The Theory of Adaptation and Natural Selection"); and Jerzy Ossowski, "O przedmiocie socjologii" ("On the Object of Sociology") and "Teoria przysto-

theory that social change is due to the phenomenon of unconscious "intelligent adaptation" to reality. (This related to his theory of the unconscious "genius" of nature itself.)[118] His research was not limited to the philocentric, sociocentric, or egocentric laws of social progress.[119] After analysing and assessing the trends of social change, he defined its aim

sowania i doboru naturalnego" ("The Theory of Adaptation and Natural Selection"). These are in *Prace socjologiczne*, the yearbook of the Leon Petrazycki Sociological Circle of Students of Warsaw University (Warsaw, 1935). See also J. Lande, "Socjologia Petrazyckiego" ("The Sociology of Petrazycki") in *Przeglad Sociologiczny*, XII, 1948, pp. 229-65; Henryk Pietka, *Teoria prawa* ("Theory of Law"), Part I, "Sociology," a mimeographed course (Warsaw, 1947); and Podgorecki, *op. cit.*, pp. 122-35. See finally J. Lande, "O tzw. socjologii naukii" ("On the So-Called Sociology of Science") in the book commemorating Fryderyk Zoll (Cracow, 1935), pp. 511-2.

The only sociological study by Petrazycki published in Polish is *O dopelniajacych pradach kulturalnych i prawach rozwoju handlu* ("On Complementary Cultural Trends and the Laws of Commercial Development") (Warsaw, 1936). The second volume of Petrazycki's *Theory of Law and State* (Polish edition, 1959) ends with the words: "I intend to publish separately a book, *Outline of Sociology and the History of Political Theories. . . . .*which will also contain a more detailed exposition of the theory of the impact of law and of the historical laws of its development." (P. 682.)

Regarding the fate of Petrazycki's sociological manuscripts, Lande stated that two were lost in Russia during the First World War and the third was kept by the author in Warsaw. This last manuscript is reported to have been stolen from Petrazycki's widow in Pruszkow after the Warsaw insurrection of 1944. Attempts to trace it, made in Poland after the war, proved unsuccessful.

[118]Petrazycki, *Introduction.* . . . p. 409 and *passim*.

[119]Podgorecki, *op. cit.*, pp. 124 ff.

The philocentric laws of the species, based on its adaptation, apply to the human, as well as to the animal, world. They go beyond the normal framework of sociology. This is the struggle for life, as defined by Darwin. The mother who saves her child is acting under the influence of emotions (impulses), which are elements of psychic life produced by the adaptation of the species. She risks her own life to save a representative of the future generation of the species. The defense of the species imposes on the individual a motive stronger than the preservation of self.

Egocentric laws result from experience which associates an emotion with some individually favorable elements. Similar to logical induction, this process is not based on reasoning, but only on emotion, either positive (attraction) or negative (revulsion). When a dog is house-trained, it is not the causal relationship between his misbehavior and punishment which he perceives; gradually he comes to associate his own negative emotions (resulting from punishment) not with the accidental and changing elements which may occur, but with the main elements – the same in each case. Human intellectual operations do not progress as rapidly

as being the triumph of universal, rational, and active love: the pure love of one's neighbor, representing the ideal of men freed from legal and moral constraint.[120]

Petrazycki held the optimistic belief that new social values, including solidarity, are formed not through dialectic argument, but through "emotional contamination" within any social group defending its own values, its prestige, or its survival. His ideal was the general benevolence of all men, served by and serving legal reform.[121] He believed that the social character improved[122] in the course of its adaptation to collective life and tended towards the ideal of love already formulated in *Lehre von Einkommen*. This was initially either ignored by writers as mere phraseology deprived of any serious meaning and significance, or attacked with triumphant irony as an unreasonable idea, detrimental to the rest of the program of legal policy;[123] but this ideal of love also had its

as the course of events, which provide a valuable lesson through the repetition of experience.

Sociocentric laws, decisive from the sociological angle, can be observed readily, since any social group is a laboratory. The feeling of solidarity, the assessment of what is good or bad for the group, the exchange of experiences, and the gradual shaping of new collective values belong to this category of laws. Intellect plays a lesser part in this connection than the process of "emotional contamination" within the group, even accidental or temporary. An "emotional climate" is created and the members of the group are compelled to defend it, even at the cost of their own lives. If the group is attacked from the outside, various positive and negative reactions take place and their repetition produces an "average common experience," owing to an adaptation proportioned to the danger faced by the group. Petrazycki considered this phenomenon of adaptation as resulting from a "super-genius," higher than the "genius" shown in the adaptation of the individual. Those three types of process may be in conflict with each other or reinforce each other. The emotional climate includes the heritage of the past – even a remote past. This accounts for psychic reactions which do not seem justified any longer (e.g., emotional reactions to hunting or fishing).

[120]See Petrazycki, *O ideale spolecznym i odrodzeniu prawa naturalnego* ("On the Social Ideal and the Renaissance of Natural Law") (Warsaw, 1925), pp. 73 ff.

[121]Kotarbinski, *op. cit.*, pp. 7 ff.

[122]See Petrazycki, *O ideale. . .* , pp. 7 ff.

[123]R. Sohm, *Ueber den Entwurf eines bürgerl. Gesetzbuches* ("On the Draft of a Civil Code") (1896), pp. 25 ff.

champions and supporters among scientific authors. It was also presented under another form by Stammler,[124] as his doctrine of "just law".[125]

Petrazycki devoted special attention to *legal* sociology and evolved "probably the most developed theory, not on the social genesis of law, but on its social action and function."[126] In his view, law has a particularly wide sphere of influence in society and plays a socially useful part (together with ethics) as a powerful means of coordinating collective behavior, which is ruled by the general principles of social adaptation. Socially, law is more important than ethics, since it entails a series of means of constraint, of rewards and punishments, produced by legal experience reflected in individual psychology and by the trend toward the unification of behavior patterns (far less characteristic of ethics). "Normative facts" are translated as legal projections in the individual's psychological experience. Such projections, on which positive norms are based or through which they are eliminated from collective psychological experience, act as a unifying element.[127] Petrazycki departed from any given

[124]R. Stammler, in *Das Recht der Schuldverhältnisse* ("The Law of Obligations"), writes of the "Gemeinschaft frei wollender Menschen" ("The community of men with a free will"): "Petrazycki, in his plan for a science of the policy of civil law, arrived at similar conclusions and a similar conception of the problem. Such a conception of the formal final aim and absolute criterion is entirely accurate and does not deserve to be attacked as severely as it was by Sohm. Indeed, when this scholar, opposing Petrazycki, maintains that the purpose of law is to provide selfishness with the limits required by equity, the question arises of what is understood by equity as a criterion of the value of law. And since Sohm does not explain this anywhere, his criticisms do not improve on Petrazycki's thought." (P.41.)

See also Stammler, *Wirtschaft und Recht nach der materialistischen Geschichtsauffassung* ("Economics and Law in the Materialistic View of History") (1886); and "Wesen des Rechts und der Rechtwissenschaft" ("The Essence of Law and of Legal Science"), in *Kultur der Gegenwart*, Part II (1902).

[125]Petrazycki, *Introduction. . .* (Polish edition, 1959), p. 19. It should be noted that Tolstoy, who wanted to base all human relationships on purely moral foundations ("a spontaneous fullness of love"), was nevertheless opposed to the legal approach. He attacked Petrazycki's ideas in spite of their emphasis on the ethical element in law and on love as the supreme end. On this, see Tolstoy (in Russian), *On Law; Exchange of Letters with a Jurist* (1910). See also Gustav Radbruch, *Rechtsphilosophie* ("The Philosophy of Law") (4th ed.; Stuttgart, 1950), p. 134; and Babb, *Petrazhitskii. . .*, p. 535, fn. 158.

[126]Podgorecki, *op. cit.*, p. 133.

[127]Petrazycki classified his "normative facts" in 15 categories, on the pattern of history of law: doctrine (*communis opinio doctorum*), the Scriptures (Gospels), collations of customs, *Corpus iuris civilis* in the Middle Ages, experts' opinions

positive system and investigated the very foundations of law. According to him, the binding force of positive law is derived from such normative facts, not from external constraint; and it is owing to them that there is a correspondence between duty and obligation in the minds of individuals.

Law is not limited, in this view, to the rules officially in force in the given community. Since both the state and the law have been psychologically re-interpreted, the latter is no longer exclusively dependent upon the former. Like linguists, moralists, and students of religion, jurists should understand that, apart from official rules (on which assessment is based), the law consists of other heterogeneous phenomena which exist in fact, whatever their source may be.

Petrazycki criticized the tendency to limit the natural domain of law to actual legislation and added to this the rules followed by primitive communities, the rules of sports and games, the customary rules of social behavior, the rules applied by lunatics coexisting in asylums, the moral code enforced by criminals, and the mental processes of children.[128] He

(Roman *responsa*), precedents, legal maxims, etc. Timascheff, *op. cit.* (1955), p. xxxviii, says: "According to Petrazhitsky, normative facts are those elements of legal (eventually moral) experience which point to the very foundations of the experience of being 'bound by duty.' His discussion of normative facts (sections 35-38) is an excellent instance of a theory based on the class concept of law, and not on law as it appears in a concrete legal system. The theory of normative facts could and should be correlated with Petrazhitsky's psychological theory restated in terms of modern psychology. The experience of normative facts operative in a given culture would then appear as a stimulus-situation, the response to which would be the formation of new learned behavior-tendencies with legal (eventually moral) content. This could give new impetus to the theory of the internalization of law, which concerns the relationship between legal norms and individual legal consciousness."

[128]Georges Gurvitch, in "Une philosophie intuitiviste du droit" ("A Philosophy of Law Based on Intuition") in *Archives de Philosophie du Droit* (1931), p. 414, says: "The criticism addressed by Petrazycki to any theory which means to define Law – and particularly positive Law – as a function of the State, and, more widely, of constraint, belongs, owing to its dialectic norm and its depth, to the classical texts of world legal literature." Gurvitch sees in Petrazycki's "emotional intuitivism" a thought close to Max Scheler's phenomenological philosophy and to Franz Brentano's school. See *Encyclopedia of Social Science* XXII (New York: 1934), p. 104.

In his own works, such as *Le temps présent et l'idée du droit* ("The Present Time and the Idea of Social Law") (Paris, 1932), pp. 132-50 and 279-94, and *L'experience juridique* ("The Legal Experience") (Paris, 1935), pp. 153-69, Gurvitch, like Petrazycki, considers that law includes all social norms (characterized by "the ability to embody a positive value by the very fact of their existence" and by "the predominance of an active element, of a task to perform").

extended *ad infinitum* the sources of positive law, though he realized that some of the rules noted above should not set a pattern and though certain of them went against official prescriptions. (Similarly, slang does not respect the rules of grammar.) As legal phenomena were no longer required to have a normative formal coloring, research was extended to all *real facts*. In the conception of "intuitive law," two types of psychological reaction to official rules in a social community were differentiated. On one hand, the fear of sanctions relates to the belief that the official character of such rules justifies in itself the respect due to them. On the other hand, *the consciousness of duty*, regardless of sanction or even of any authority, is operative. This is the sphere of "intuitive law," fully autonomous and unstandardized, produced by imperative as well as attributive emotions, and changing both with individual characteristics and with the process of historical evolution. Intuitive law, to be distinguished from custom, exists within each legal system and adapts itself slowly but regularly to historical development. Without ever being affected by arbitrariness or decay, it always displays a unifying tendency.[129] The content of the vague notion of justice[130] is thus clarified and integrated into an intellectual system parallel to positive law.[131]

This work, insufficiently known at present, proves that "he was aware that sociology is indispensable in order to grasp the change of the social

[129]Petrazycki, *The Theory of Law and State* (Polish edition, I, paragraph 36).

[130]Timascheff, *op. cit.* (1955), p. xxxvii, says: "Petrazhitsky's treatise opens new horizons for the scientific interpretation of justice. In an illuminating section (32), he identifies justice with 'intuitive law.' Instead of the loose and vague terms in which justice is commonly discussed, Petrazhitsky formulates a system of propositions based on 'intuitive law', and couched in terms analogous to those applicable to positive law. For one who does not accept Petrazhitsky's broad concept of law, justice of 'intuitive law' forms a cluster of peripheral phenomena located around the nucleus of the law; they must be interpreted as an area of culture permeated by legal considerations without actually being part of the law. But one has to concede that scientific analysis of this area of culture is a prerequisite to the discovery of uniformities in the process of legal change, prediction of the probable consequences of enactment or repeal of a statute, better understanding of the process through which judicial decisions are arrived at, and the solution of many other important problems. In these regards, Petrazhitsky's work is full of stimulating ideas which merit systematic development."

[131]"Intuitive law" may be in direct or indirect conflict with positive law, because it may go against the "official" rule when its injustice is felt intuitively. Therefore intuitive law may destroy positive law by revolutionary means. Petrazycki sought the main causes of political revolutions in collisions between these two types of law (see Babb, *Petrazhitskii. . .* , p. 569), although they tend towards a balance (see Gurvitch, *Une philosophie intuitiviste. . .* , p. 417).

matter parallel to which consciousness develops."[132] "Petrazycki is probably the most eminent creative theoretician in the field of legal sociology."[133] Indeed, his work opens new prospects on the social functions of law, both organizational and educational.[134]

Both in his *opus magnum* and in several articles... Petrazhitsky exhorted the legislator to be conscious of the educative potentialities of official law and thus prepared a solid foundation for the conception of law as "social engineering."[135]

A thorough analysis of his work shows that the founder of the psychological theory of law went beyond a purely subjective conception resulting from the emphasis on emotions. "Aware of the interaction between psychic... and social, phenomena, he devoted his attention mainly to the action of consciousness on other economic and sociological phenomena, which exposed him to criticism for his 'psychologism'."[136] He met with other criticisms[137] mostly on account of the optimism with which he viewed law as a crystallization of all the values involved and therefore as reflecting the interests of the social group as a whole.[138] This would mean that legal systems always tend towards the general good.[139] Though Petrazycki saw antagonisms between conflicting moral assess-

---

[132]J. Kowalski, "Refleksje nad wydaniem dziel Leona Petrazyckiego" ("Reflections on the Publication of Leon Petrazycki's Works"), *Panstwo i Prawo*, X (1960), 563.

[133]Podgorecki, *op. cit.*, p. 123.

[134]See Petrazycki, *Theory of State and Law* (Polish edition) I, pp. 257 ff.

[135]Timascheff, *op. cit.* (1955), p. xxxviii.

[136]Kowalski, *op. cit.* p. 565.

[137]See the section following, entitled "His School and His Opponents."

[138]Podgorecki, *op. cit.*, pp. 132 ff.

[139]E.g., Kowalski, *op. cit.*, p. 568.

"Whilst Durkheim thought that sociology could only be justified if it were delineated as an autonomous field, Pareto remained an engineer in his perpetual search for mechanical analogies in the field of social sciences. Excessive concentration on the identification of the subject matter or overriding confidence in the interdisciplinary applicability of a scientific methodology, led to different distortions. Unlike Durkheim's sociologism, unlike Pareto's cybernetics, Petrazycki's problem-centered approach avoided both a restrictive definition of the discipline and a limitative methodological commitment." (M. Clifford–Vaughan and M. Scotford-Morton, "Legal Norms and Social Order: Petrazycki, Pareto, Durkheim," *British Journal of Sociology*, XVIII [1967], No. 3, 269 ff.).

ments, he believed that those best adapted to the needs of the community and the commonweal would prevail. He was also reproached with having considered power and economic relationships as derived from psychological phenomena and independent from economic necessity (although this did not prevent him from using the concepts and methodology of materialism). Instead of the antagonism between social and psychological structures, he adopted an ideal of solidarity as his starting point and endeavored to erase the contradiction between materialism and idealism.[140] This is why traditionalists saw him as a socialist, and socialists as a conservative — a "revisionist" who resorted misleadingly to materialist methodology and terminology. As the author of remarkable dogmatic analyses (particularly in his early monographs), Petrazycki passes often for a legal positivist, in the usual sense of this term. His realistic outlook, his firm rejection of all metaphysics, and his methodological views seem to confirm such a classification. However he can also be assessed as a legal "metaphysicist" because of his opposition to the neo-Kantian school of law and to any differentiation between the empirical and the spiritual, because of his endeavors to resurrect a kind of relativistic "natural law" (i.e., a "legal policy")[141] and because all of his postulates are built upon the key notion of *love* as the supreme ideal of each individual and of the whole society. Thus legal idealists could attack him as a positivist, whereas

[140]Kowalski, *op. cit.*, pp. 564 and 568; and Kotarbinski, *op. cit.*, pp. 9 ff.

[141]See Petrazycki's preface to his *Introduction. . .* (Polish edition), pp. 11 ff: "The creation of a science of legal policy as a separate discipline, serving the aims of progress and betterment of the legal order, owing to the scientific, methodical and systematic elaboration of the problems at stake. . .would not represent a new and unprecented conception in the history of the sciences: it would be rather a renewal of the dualistic division of law, a division which existed already at the time of the so-called natural (rational, ideal, philosophical) law school. The meaning of the science of natural law as an autonomous systematic discipline, beside positive law, consisted in fulfilling this important and valuable mission, which will have to be filled by the future science of legal policy and which exceeds the possibilities of practical and dogmatic legal science, limited to the interpretation and systematization of the positive law in force, in order to 'serve the practice'. . . .(But) the school of natural law did not have either a system of premises or a scientific method indispensable to elaborate scientifically founded politico-legal theories and was not even aware what these premises should consist of and what the method of thought in the field of legal policy should be. . . .The creation of such a discipline is a task to be carried out in future by collective work, and to investigate the nature of such premises and of the method of thought in the field of legal policy is the first condition of this achievement. The examination of causal particularities, of the causal action of law in general, and of its various types and components in particular, would be the foundation of a scientific legal policy. . . . "

positivists blamed his theory for containing fantasies in which psychological and ethical aspects are confused, and for ignoring the real existence of legal norms. At the same time, because he viewed the problem of the binding force of law and that of the essence of the state (in its relationship with law) from the sociological angle, Petrazycki was accused of neglecting the purely legal aspect and the specific viewpoint of the person who applies the law, particularly that of the judge.[142] Because of his basic psychological concept (the theory of emotional psychology as extended to the state and the law) and his notion of law as a mainly psychological phenomenon (belonging to the ethical class), he was mainly seen as a radical individualist, unable or unwilling to fully grasp the role of the social factor, and, in general, the meaning of psycho-social elements.[143] Since he considered legal evolution as an unconscious rather than rationally calculated process, he was believed to be a supporter of Savigny's historical school, although he rejected the notion of a "national spirit." As this original thought did not fit any of the traditional compartments and could not be labelled according to current schemes,[144] his ideas were talked of as a "typically Russian ethos" too difficult for Westerners to grasp, or as mysterious work produced by the juxtaposition of a warm heart, an implacable logic, and an extremely wide range of thought.[145] Thus all the critics have assessed mere fragments of a work

[142]Balogh, *op. cit.*, pp. 83-4.

[143]Babb, *Petrazhitskii. . .* , pp. 555-6, says: "There has been so much written as to Petrazhitskii's ignoring the social nature of law, even by writers who recognize and acknowledge his enormous services to legal philosophy, that we should consider with some care his examination of the social functions of law (with a special analysis of property from this point of view) — the distributive function and the organization function, the law of social serving and 'individual-free' law, and law as a factor and product of social-psychological life. Throughout, Petrazhitskii emphasizes the social significance of law, examining its rule of serving the welfare of the masses and not of the individual. Law is the product of the action of unconsciously successful *mass* psychic adaptation of *social* psychic processes. It is an essential psychic *factor of social life* and of the development of spiritual culture. The motivational and educational influence of law corresponds generally to the advancement of social welfare and the triumph of what is socially good. Law, like morality, is a 'complex and mighty school' for socializing the national character and adapting it to reasonable life together, serving spiritual progress and the ideal of active love in mankind."

[144]See M. M. Laserson, "Positive and Natural Law and Their Correlations," in *Interpretations of Modern Legal Philosophy* (published in honor of Roscoe Pound) (1947). Laserson stresses the basically sociological character of Petrazycki's theory and the fact that it shows law to be a product of mass adaptation.

[145]See Balogh, *op. cit.*, p. 84.

which is only accessible in part, and tend to concentrate on one of its aspects without encompassing the full range of Petrazycki's thought.[146]

HIS SCHOOL AND HIS OPPONENTS

It has often been deplored that Leon Petrazycki's work should not have had a wider audience and that his thought should have remained unknown or underestimated by so many.[147] This is all the more paradoxical since its originality cannot be doubted and since, from various points of view, it has been a landmark in the evolution of modern legal thought.[148] The First World War, with the many new practical problems it raised; the communist revolution in Russia, which ended or disrupted a series of works by Petrazycki's students and admirers at St. Petersburg University; the fact that Petrazycki's writings have not been translated into Western languages and thus made accessible to the international scientific world;[149] and the subdivision of scientific thought into national branches, often isolated, and the subsequent decrease in belief that all were contributing to the common intellectual heritage of mankind:[150] all this has prevented his thought from playing its part historically or in the immediate future.

Nevertheless, his ideas did cause much intellectual controversy, in which some supported him warmly while others expressed categorical objections. A school was thus formed and, after a period of stagnation, the times seemed to have become more favorable to the thorough study of all, or nearly all, of Petrazycki's works: not that they could ever become "popular," since they depart from the routine methods of science. "Equally remote from Marxism, from Darwin's sociology and from the theory of dogmatic or analytical law which predominated in Europe,"[151] his theory frightens away those who prefer the easy and the superficial; it requires background preparation and cannot be treated as a series of unrelated ideas.

[146]See Roscoe Pound, *Harvard Law Review*, LI (1938), 809.

[147]See Langrod, *L'oeuvre juridique, passim.*

[148]See Langrod, *Northwestern University Law Review,* VI (1956), 831-3.

[149]Indeed, it was only in 1955 that *Law and Morality* appeared in the United States, and in 1959 that a Polish translation was published.

[150]See Timascheff, *op. cit.* (1955), p. xxxv.

[151]Laserson, "La sociologie russe" ("Russian Sociology"), in *La Sociologie du XXe siècle* (Paris, 1947), p. 677.

Several authors who considered themselves members of this school and asserted that they were continuing Petrazycki's work accepted, however, only some of his theses and objected more or less definitely to others. Such a fragmentary and schismatic reception of a thinker's contribution is comparatively frequent.[152] It is all the more understandable in the case of Petrazycki because of the breadth of his interests, which makes differences of opinion on some aspects almost unavoidable. Nevertheless, all the parts of his work seem logically related. To reject a part of his theses is tantamount to rejecting the whole; thus several of his supporters have proven to be so in name rather than in fact.

During the Russian period of his activity, Petrazycki's students in St. Petersburg were faithful to him in spite of the opposition with which his ideas were received by most of his colleagues at the Law Faculty.[153] Even neo-Kantian philosophers, such as B. Kistiakovsky[154] and V. Taranowsky,[155] adopted the psychological theory in the framework of their pluralistic definition of the nature of law.[156] Several other students from St. Petersburg endeavored to disseminate Petrazycki's ideas in various forms.[157] Attempts made to combine the psychological theory of law

[152]This happened also with Léon Duguit. See Langrod, "L'influence des idées de Léon Duguit sur la théorie générale du droit" ("The Influence of Leon Duguit's Ideas on the General Theory of Law"), *Revue Juridique et Économique du Sud-Ouest (Serie Juridique)*, III-IV (1959), 129 ff.

[153]Thus, e.g., A Kruglevsky, a student of Petrazycki, presented to the Law Faculty of St. Petersburg a thesis for a master's degree on *The Criminal Attempt*, based on his professor's theories. It was to be rejected by the faculty only because of "the negative attitude of the majority of professors toward Petrazhitsky's ideas," as noted by Timascheff, *op. cit.* (1955), p. xxxi.

[154]In Russian, "The Reality of Objective Law," *Logos* II (1910), 193 ff., and "Crisis of Jurisprudence," *Yur. Viestnik*, I (1914), 70 ff. The same author wrote, in Russian, in *Social Sciences and the Law* (1916), pp. 285 ff.: "The idea of looking at the law as a psychological phenomenon has proven to be fruitful. Many of Petrazycki's pages on legal mentality can be considered classic. Very interesting are his statements about the actualization of the prescriptions of law and morals, on the violation of these prescriptions, on the reaction provoked by such violations, and on the tendency of the law to unify the views of parties confronting each other." However, Kistiakovsky denied that Petrazycki's theory explained the reality of law as a universal phenomenon.

[155]In Russian, *The Encyclopedia of Law* (1917). A German translation appeared in Berlin in 1923.

[156]Timascheff, *op. cit.* (1955), pp. xxxi-xxxii.

[157]Concerning Russian authors who accused Petrazycki of ignoring the social nature of law, see Babb, *Petrazhitskii...*, p. 555, fn. 195. Among Russian emigre

with Marxism are particularly noteworthy. Made initially by Petrazycki's disciples,[158] they were to be resumed later on various occasions.[159]

writers, the most important were: (1) G. K. Guins (in Russian), "Characteristics of the Scientific Creativeness of Petrazhitsky," *Isv. Yur. Fac.*, (Kharbin, 1931); *Petrazhitsky* (Kharbin, 1931); and *New Ideas in Law* (Kharbin, 1931-2); p. 654; (2) Gurvitch (in Russian), "Petrazhitsky," *Sovremennyja Zapiski*, XVII (1931), 480 ff.; (3) Laserson, "Russische Rechtsphilosophie" ("Russian Philosophy of Law"), *Archiv für Rechts- und Wirtschafts-philosophie*, VI (1933), 289 ff.; (4) Meyendorff, "The Theory of Petrazhitsky," in *Modern Theories of Law* (Oxford, 1933); (5) Pitirim A. Sorokin, *Contemporary Sociological Theories* (1928); "The Organized Group and Law Norms," in *Interpretations of Modern Legal Philosophy* (1947), pp. 668 ff.; and *Soziologische Theorien im XIX und XX Jahrhundert* ("Sociological Theories of the XIX and XX Centuries") (Munich, 1931); and (6) Timascheff, "Petrazhitsky's Philosophy of Law," in *Interpretations of Modern Legal Philosophy* (1947), pp. 736 ff.

[158]Pre-eminent in this connection was the Marxist, M. A. Reisner, who published in 1908 a study in Russian entitled "The Theory of L. J. Petrazycki, Marxism and Social Ideology," an English translation of which was published in *Soviet Legal Philosophy*, (1951), 71-80. Reisner endeavored to harmonize Petrazycki's and Marx's theories. Like Petrazycki, he considered law as a psychological phenomenon. But, instead of an emotional basis, he sought an ideology viewed realistically from the angle of social classes. Thus each class had its own law. Law was viewed as having no objective existence, but as based upon subjective beliefs which were psychic constructions (a similar outlook was shared by E. Mach). Since Marx classified law as a part of ideology which belonged to the social superstructure (and not to the economic basis), but did not develop this thesis to its logical conclusion, Reisner resorted to Petrazycki's theory in order to clarify this subject.

As a vice-commissar for justice after the October Revolution, Reisner influenced the revolutionary regime to bring about the suppression *uno actu* of the whole czarist legislation and its replacement by "intuitive law." Codes and laws were to be erased and to give way to the social consciousness of the workers and peasants in power, supplemented by a small number of decrees enacted by the new government. Reisner's proposal was an attempt to translate into fact the notion of justice embodied by Petrazycki's emotional theory.

The decree No. 1 on tribunals, dated November 27, 1917 (*Sob. Uzak, RSFR*, I, No. 40, paragraph 50), as well as several other regulations, was a reflection of this trend, about which see Timascheff, *Introduction...* (1955), p. xxxii, and J. N. Hazard and I. Shapiro, *The Soviet Legal System. Post-Stalin Documentation and Historical Commentary* (New York: Parker School of Foreign and Comparative Law, 1962), pp. 3 ff. No code was to be published for five years. Judges were to pass decisions according to "revolutionary consciousness," while the Commissariat for Justice acted as a guide to a certain extent. Legal chaos and generalized uncertainty were to result. Lenin's "strategic retreat" involved the rejection of experiments based on Reisner's theses. Codes appeared gradually and consciousness was no longer the only source of inspiration of the tribunals. See

However, his Polish compatriots and former students in St. Petersburg[160] and those who were in turn taught by them[161] formed the most lasting

M. Mouskhély and Z. Jedryka, *Le Gouvernement de l'U.R.S.S.* ("The Government of the U.S.S.R.") (Paris, 1961), pp. 229 ff.

[159]Later, other writers undertook similar studies in which Petrazycki's theories were analyzed in the light of Marxism. Their purpose was to build a bridge between the psychological theory of law and Marxist materialism. See G. L. Seidler, *Doktryny prawne imperializmu* ("The Legal Doctrines of Imperialism") (Warsaw, 1957), pp. 61 ff., and a study of the psychological trend in legal science, in *Panstwo i Prawo*, VIII-IX (1952); Fritzhand, "Prawo i moralnosc w teorii Petrazyckiego" ("Law and Morality in the Theory of Petrazycki"), *Panstwo i Prawo*, VIII-IX (1952); and Kowalski, *op. cit.,* pp. 562 ff. Authors adopting the official communist viewpoint condemned these essays. See G. L. Seidler, *op. cit.,* pp. 61 ff.; S. Rozmaryn, "Prawo i Panstwo" ("Law and State"), *Demokratyczny Przeglad Prawniczy*, XI (Warsaw, 1949), 17; Kowalski and A. Turska, "Kilka uwag dotyczacych burzuazyjnej socjologii prawa" ("Some Remarks on the Bourgeois Sociology of Law"), *Panstwo i Prawo*, VII (1961), 19; and M. Maneli, "Teoria Panstwa i Prawa Leona Petrazychiego" ("Leon Petrazycki's Theory of State and Law") *Nowe Drogi*, V (Warsaw, 1960).

See also Timascheff, *Introduction. . .* (1955), pp. xxxii-xxxiii: "Later on, Petrazhitsky's name became taboo in the Soviet Union. He was classified among the idealists (which he certainly was not), while Soviet law and jurisprudence turned to legal positivism in its extreme form identifying the law with norms enforced by the state. Of course, the Soviet definition of law goes further and insists that the will of the state is tantamount to the will and interests of the dominant class. This identification is, however, taken for granted, as a kind of *praesumptio juris and de jure.* Nothing could be more removed from Petrazhitsky's views."

It should be noted that, after a period of total rejection, a slight change seems to have taken place. Marxists advocate a more thorough study of this work and assess it more moderately. They reject previous extreme criticisms, in order to adapt to "socialist culture" the valuable elements of Petrazycki's theory. Thus, a Polish communist writer states: "It seems that the creative reception of the results of Petrazycki's research on the appearance of legal phenomena in the psychological sphere will prove useful to the Marxist theory of law. Petrazycki's tremendous work in this field and its value have not been fully appreciated and utilised as yet." (Kowalski, *op. cit.,* pp. 562, 570.) This accounts for the translations recently published in Poland, the studies devoted to him, and the considerable interest stimulated by his work.

[160]Mainly his translators into Polish, Lande and Wiktor Lesniewski. See also Witold Wegedis, *Podstawy polityki prawa miedzynarodowego* ("The Bases of the Policy of International Law") (Warsaw, 1938).

[161]Lande's school (in Wilno and later in Cracow) included, among others: (1) Jerzy Sztykgold (killed in the war in 1939), author of *Luki w prawie a hipoteza*

group of disciples, spreading and interpreting Petrazycki's thought with an enthusiasm that is seldom stimulated by legal studies. It is in this sense that one can refer to Petrazycki's "school," continuing in his lifetime and after his death. Its members are still at work and make a valuable contribution by re-interpreting the Master's writings, by making them more easily accessible to new generations, and by providing them with rectifications and addenda.

The head of this school was Jerzy Lande (1886-1954), professor of legal theory at the Jagellonian University of Cracow, and one of Petrazycki's most talented disciples in St. Petersburg. He acquainted a whole generation of Polish philosophers and jurists with the Master's work,

podstawowa w czystej teorii prawa Kelsena ("The Gaps in the Law and the Main Hypothesis in the Pure Theory of Law by Kelsen") (1938) and *Psychologiczna teoria prawa pozytywnego* ("The Psychological Theory of Positive Law") (unpublished, 1937); (2) Czeslaw Frydman-Nowinski, *Dogmatyka prawa w swietle socjologii*; ("The Dogmatic Approach to Law in the Light of Sociology") (1936), and *Domniemania prawne* ("Legal Presumptions") (1938); (3) Witold Steinberg, *Zagadnienie rzeczywistosci norm prawnych* ("The Problem of the Reality of Legal Norms") (1930); *Prawo sasiedzkie* ("The Law of Neighborhood") (1933); and *Z logiki norm* ("From the Logic of Norms") (1947); (4) Czeslaw Martyniak, *Le fondement objectif du droit d'après St. Thomas d'Aquin* ("The Objective Foundation of Law According to St. Thomas Aquinas") (1931); *Moc obowiazujaca prawa a teoria Kelsena* ("The Binding Force of Law and Kelsen's Theory") (1938); and *Problem filozofii prawa* ("The Problem of Legal Philosophy") (1939); and (5) Jozef Zajkowski (killed in the war in 1939), *Wstep do badan nad pojeciem interesu w prawie i procesie cywilnym* ("Introduction to the Studies on the Notion of Interest in Civil Law and Procedure") (1936) and *Wykladnia ustaw wedlug Petrazyckiego i wedlug jego teorii* ("Interpretation of Laws According to Petrazycki and to His Theory") (1936).

Henryk Pietka, author of *Slusznosc w teorii i praktyce* ("Equity in Theory and in Practice") (1929); *Przedmiot i metoda socjologii prawa* ("Introduction to the Science of Law") (1946); and *Teoria prawa*, did not belong to Lande's school, since he was a student of Eugeniusz Jarra (at Warsaw University), whom he succeeded in his chair. However, in the course of his research, he became increasingly inclined towards Petrazycki's theoretical conceptions. Jerzy Kalinowski, the author of works quoted above, a student of Martyniak and his successor in the chair of philosophy of law at the Catholic University at Lublin, advocated a metaphysical, neo-Thomistic conception of natural law, while investigating Petrazycki's theories and stressing Stammler's dependence on them.

It should be mentioned again that even the Polish authors who did not share the views of the Master were greatly influenced by his thought and contributed to its diffusion. They often used it as a platform from which they started to crystallize their own opinions, often formed *a contrario*. See, e.g., *Ogolna nauka o prawie* ("The General Science of Law"), ed. Bronislaw Wroblewski (a student of Petrazycki) (Wilno, 1936-8).

to which he devoted a major part of his life. Having studied critically the various modern trends in legal theory, he published a series of comments, translations, and biographies of Petrazycki, with whose scientific views he agreed, without, however, imposing them on his own students. Many of these, however, came under the influence of Petrzycki's theories and formed the embryo of a Cracow school. In Warsaw, a group of Petrazycki's Polish students formed, between the two world wars,[162] the Leon Petrazycki Sociological Association of Students of Warsaw University. Its leader at the time was Jerzy Finkelkraut-Licki, later acting professor of labor law at Warsaw University, who translated several of Petrazycki's works into Polish. The Association enabled Kachan and Ossowski to publish their works, which have already been quoted above. In the sixties, a committee was formed in Warsaw under the chairmanship of the famous Polish philosopher, Tadeusz Kotarbinski[163] (then president of the Polish Academy of Sciences); it was under the auspices of this committee that Polish translations of Petrazycki's writings, edited by Leon Kurowski, professor of the Law Faculty of Warsaw, were issued by the State Scientific Publications[164] bureau.

The Polish legal philosopher Eugeniusz Jarra, who held the chair of legal theory at Warsaw University until 1939, is often counted as a supporter of Petrazycki, whose disciple he claimed to have been and some of whose ideas he adhered to in his *General Theory of Law*.[165] In fact, he followed Petrazycki up to a point, but differed in his attempt at conciliation between the conception of law as a psychological phenomenon and an emphasis on legal norms in force. This represented an important concession to legal positivism without implying a categorical rejection of Petrazycki's "psychologism." According to Jarra, legal norms

[162]This association was recreated at the end of the Second World War.

[163]Kotarbinski is the founder of the theory known as "praxeology," according to which the widest possible norms, endowed with the greatest efficiency, should be elaborated on the basis of practical experience, envisaged either as a conglomeration of facts concerning productivity or as a sum of generalizations relating to the secrets of efficiency. See Kotarbinski, *Traktat o dobrej robocie* ("Treatise on the Well-Done Work"), XIII (1958). The praxeologist is interested in utilitarian assessments of human activity viewed from the angle of its output (skill, ability). Kotarbinski takes into account the emotional aspect of the expressions used with reference to this context and, to this extent, he shares the theory of Petrazycki. Cf. T. Pszczolkowski, *Wybrane Zagadnienia prakseologii* ("Selected Problems of Praxeology") (Warsaw: Polish Academy of Sciences, 1962), p. 89.

[164]See final remarks by L. Kurowski, in Petrazycki, *Introduction* . . . (Polish edition, 1959), pp. 477 ff.

[165]*Ogolna Teoria Prawa* (Warsaw, 1922).

are psychological phenomena, but are related to objective sources: namely, the psychological experience of the community rather than that of the individual. Such a view is remote from Petrazycki's theory, in which a compulsory legal norm is the *verbal expression* of psychological phenomena – an expression contained in a legal text – whereas legal phenomena themselves exist *in reality*. Jarra excluded all the psychological consequences of legal norms, which he considered as normative judgments, not as *normative* facts. Interpretation tends therefore to explain the essential meaning of norms on the basis of their texts and their sense, while taking into account the imperatives which they conjure up in the legal mentality of the collective group. Interpretation results, therefore, from a kind of plebiscite of all mature members of the community capable of interpreting a text. In other words, Jarra did not reject the dogmatic conception of law any more than Petrazycki's opponents did (though he did not reject the psychological conception either). He also opposed a basic element of Petrazycki's theory: namely, intuitive law. He thought that it was not "serious" to extend the notion of law as an attributive and imperative phenomenon beyond the limits of "official" law; i.e., the legal rules in force. In his view, neither the rules of sport and games, nor those of social usage, nor those of gangs could be taken "seriously."[166] He considered, therefore, that: (1) if law is a psychic phenomenon, it resorts to collective, and not to individual, psychological experience, as evidenced by mass opinion (at this point, Jarra departed from the psychological theory by recognizing only community phenomena and seeking a uniform legal stereotype); (b) if law is respected intuitively in everyday life, this respect is a form of unconscious obedience to positive law ("norms of equity," constructed like legal norms but autonomous in relation to them); and (c) only the psychological phenomena of normal adults representing the majority in a given society make up the law.[167]

Thus, Jarra's hybrid theory differed from Petrazycki's in so many essential ways that he should not be considered as belonging to this

[166]In his unpublished course of lectures on the theory of law, Lande refuted this thesis with the argument that, in linguistic studies, there are no doubts about the opportunity of studying the slang used by delinquents or the language of children, whether "serious" or not.

[167]In the same lectures, Lande reproached Jarra with not having defined either the notion of "normality" or that of "uniformity." He maintained also that Jarra's definition of law ("bilateral norms organizing from the outside the basic social relationships, under the authority of a community feeling for order") remains imprecise. (What is a "community feeling for order," what are "basic social relations," and are these feelings uniform?). Lande accused Jarra of having thus denied the process of introspection (characteristic for Petrazycki's theory), since he was concerned only with psychic phenomena "from the outside." Moreover,

"school." However, he made such concessions to the psychological approach, in order to reconcile it with pure dogmatism, that any study on the Polish psychological theory of law must take into account his theory as a compromise between opposite views. His contribution is all the more signficant since he influenced his students[168] and played thereby a significant part in educating the generation of Polish jurists of the period between the two world wars.

Petrazycki's nonconformity, together with the fecundity and novelty of his ideas, was bound to meet with adverse reaction. The list of his opponents in Poland would be long. In the first place, one should note Antoni Peretiatkowicz (1884-1956), professor of legal philosophy at Poznań University and chairman of the Polish Institute of Public Law until 1939. In his various works,[169] he thoroughly analyzed the legal phenomenon in its psychic aspect, with special emphasis on the elements of natural law. He reproached Petrazycki with seeking law at the level of *sein* (real existence) and situating it only among individual psychological phenomena. He doubted the validity of this effort, since, he claimed, it did not take into account a whole category of sciences of "normative logic," for which real existence is not a decisive factor, since only the binding force of the given rules matters in this connection, regardless of the psychological basis. This criticism was strongly attacked by Lande, who explained it as the product of a misunderstanding concerning Petrazycki's classification of the sciences. This classification did cover the sciences mentioned by Peretiatkowicz, but was opposed to any normative position in relation to the study of real phenomena.

Another important Polish critic was Czeslaw Znamierowski, professor of the theory of the state and the law at Poznań University and author of many philosophical and legal works.[170] A sociologist who took psychological elements fully into account, he was opposed to the conception in

Jarra would have disagreed with Petrazycki by considering law no longer as a class comprised of certain psychic phenomena, but by identifying it with a system of norms in force, endeavoring thereby to fuse the theoretical and the dogmatic notions within a compulsory system.

[168]Particularly Pietka, who attempted also to free law from all the external elements attached to it by Petrazycki's inventive mind. (See fn. 161.)

[169]See A. Peretiatkowicz, *Wstep do nauk prawnych* ("Introduction to Legal Sciences") (7th ed., 1949) and *Studia prawne* ("Legal Studies") (Warsaw, 1938).

[170]See C. Znamierowski, *O przedmiocie i fakcie spolecznym* ("On the Social Object and the Social Fact") (1921); *Psychologistyczna teoria prawa* ("The Psychological Theory of Law") (1922); *Podstawowe pojecia teorii prawa* ("Basic Concepts of the Theory of Law") (1924); *Realizm w teorii prawa* ("Realism in the Theory of Law") (1925); *Prologomena do nauki o panstwie* ("Introduction to the Science of the State") (1930).

which social reality had a psychological character and considered such reality as the product of society alone. This criticism seems typical of those made by sociologists,[171] who largely viewed Petrazycki's theory as solipsistic, excluding from reality all that is external to individual thought. Znamierowski blamed Petrazycki for transforming legal reality into psychological reality (i.e., individual reality), thus attributing to legal norms the character of temporary norms which exist only as long as an experience is actually lived, whereas in fact they represent a lasting regulation of human relationships. The psychological approach was thus presented as neglecting the continuity of the binding force of legal rules, a continuity admitted both in legal science and in practical life. Znamierowski viewed norms as "things *sui generis*," in accordance with Emile Durkheim's approach to social phenomena as "things." In other words, the conflict revolved around the notion of reality. According to Petrazycki, the binding force of the legal norm, as it is conceived in juridical practice and in the general dogmatic theory of law, is not *reality*, but an *ideal* notion. Reality is the application of the norm (e.g., a judgment imposing an obligation) by the interested parties under the supervision of a judge who, whatever the emotional projection of the facts which they may have formed, pronounces the law by settling the dispute. According to Lande, Petrazycki did not transform legal into psychological reality, whereas Znamierowski confused the theoretical notion with the dogmatic concept, due to the fact that "legal reality" is one and the same thing as the continuity of the binding force of legal rules. Thus Znamierowski would have created reality *ab nihilo*, since norms are not part of reality, as has been demonstrated by Petrazycki and other scholars: for instance, Kelsen.

In fact, Petrazycki's fame suffered most from the "conspiracy of silence" which, in connection with world events and international upheavals, caused his system to be insufficiently known and under-

[171]On Russian pre-revolutionary authors (Orzhenskii, Khvostov, Palienko, Kokoshin, Kistiakovsky, Szerszeniewicz) see Babb, *Petrazhitskii...* p. 555, fn. 195. See Mrs. Eileen Markley Znaniecka, *La Sociologie polonaise* ("Polish Sociology") in *La sociologie du XXe siècle*, p. 705: "Petrazycki's theory leads to the most complete psychological autimization of social systems which can be found in the history of social thought." See also Podgorecki, *op. cit.*, p. 70: "It should be noted that the action of pressure groups opposes up to a point by its very existence the validity of Leon Petrazycki's view, which seems to admit a degree of proportionality between the social needs felt and the law by which these are served..." Likewise, Timascheff (see his *Introduction...*, pp. 22, 59, 69, 80, 97, 136, 286, and 308), who contributed so greatly to a wider and better understanding of Petrazycki's works, opposed his views insomuch as he devoted his research primarily to social psychology. See also Florian Znaniecki, *Wstep do socjologii* ("Introduction to Sociology") (1922), pp. 65, 262.

stood.[172] Even if writers on philosophy, sociology or legal theory did devote some attention to him, it was in the form of brief remarks or of biographical notes[173] without recognizing the true worth of his theory. Language barriers, the often hermetic formulation of his thought, and the very volume of his work[174] (due to an intellectual profligacy, generally unconscious, but nonetheless regrettable) are additional obstacles to his fame. It is only during the second half of this century that an evolution has begun, owing to the publication of increasingly complete and exhaustive translations and comments.[175]

Although it would be difficult to assess to what extent the increasing interest shown in legal psychologism is connected with the impact of Petrazycki's work, there is no doubt that several eminent jurists have

[172]See Langrod, *L'oeuvre juridique . . .*, chapter 1.

[173]See, e.g.: (1) A. Baumgarten, *Die Wissenschaft vom Recht* ("The Science of Law") (1920); (2) Georges Cornil, "A propos d'un livre posthume de Petrazhitsky" ("About a Posthumous Book by Petrazycki"), *Archives de Philosophie du Droit et de Sociologie Juridique* (1931), pp. 403 ff., and "La complexité des sources du droit comparé" ("The Complexity of the Sources of Comparative Law") in *Introduction à l'étude du droit comparé, Recueil d'etudes en l'honneur d'Edouard Lambert*, I (1938), pp. 364-5; (3) H. de la Fontaine Verwey, "Een paladijn der rechtswetenshap, Petrazycki, 1867-1931" ("A Leading Figure of Legal Science, Petrazycki, 1867-1931"), *Rechtsgeleerd Magazijn* (Haarlem), LII (1933), 233 ff.; (4) Haskin, "Leo von Petrazycki," *Revista General de Legislacion y Jurisprudencia* (Valencia), XVI (1934), 799 ff.; (5) Waclaw Komarnicki, *Leon Petrazycki* (Wilno, 1931); (6) V. Kruse, *The Right of Property* (trans. from Danish) (Oxford, 1938) and *The Community of the Future* (London-Copenhagen, 1950); (7) Landau, *Die Voraussetzungen der psychologischen Rechtslehre L.v. Petrazycki's* ("The Premises of the Psychological Theory of Law by L. Petrazycki") (1922); (8) H. Pietka, "Leone Petrazycki," *Revista Internazionale di Filosofia del Diritto* (1932), 109 ff.; (9) M. Rümelin, *Rechtsgefühl und Rechtsbewusstsein* ("The Feeling for Law and the Consciousness of Law") (1925); (10) W. Sauer, *Rechts- und Staatsphilosophie* ("The Philosophy of Law and State") (1936); (11) R. Szydlowski, *Sila a prawo* ("Force and the Law") (Warsaw, 1946); and (12) Wroblewski, *Studia Filozoficzne*, I-II (1960), 267 ff. Cf. "Principal Commentators on Petrazhitsky's Theory of Law," bibliography of Petrazycki, *Law and Morality*, pp. xliv ff.

[174]According to the Leon Petrazycki Association in Warsaw, Petrazycki's literary heritage is assessed to amount to approximately 35 volumes of 400 pages each. His manuscripts were subdivided, before the Second World War, into 58 groups (philosophy, methodology, legal policy, economic policy, evolution of psychology, sociology, theory of crises, classification of sciences, nature of the state and of power, critical analyses, etc.).

[175]The contribution of Hugh W. Babb, professor of law at Boston University, as a translator, commentator, and interpreter of Petrazycki's works, is beyond praise.

envisaged law from a psychological angle, while others have returned to the idea of a scientifically conceived "legal policy." The latter are the representatives of American "functionalism," whose school is headed by Roscoe Pound.[176] Sceptical about dogmatic law, they consider law as a factor of social equilibrium, contributing to a compromise between conflicting interests in a community (social engineering).[177] The functionalist view of law serves some social postulates, such as the protection of the family, general security, the moral sense, economic and cultural progress, and the protection of individual life.[178] The influence of judges, freely applying the functional method, based on experience, and endeavoring to shape social life by harmonizing contradictions, is instrumental in this connection. As concerns the psychological school, the important Scandinavian school of A. Hagerström (Sweden)[179] and Alf Ross (Denmark)[180] should be given special consideration. Among its main contributors are Wilhelm Lundstedt[181] and K. Olivercrona.[182] Regardless of the differences between these authors' views and a subsequent subdivision of the Scandinavian school into two branches,[183] all of them are close to Petrazycki's psychological theory, and particularly the "Uppsala school." In discussing this school, Professor Timasheff said:

> The members of the so-called Uppsala school have posed the same problem as Petrazhitsky, the problem of realistic interpretation of

[176]See R. Pound, *Control Through Law* (New Haven: Yale University Press, 1942).

[177]See, e.g., S. P. Simpson and R. Field, "Social Engineering Through Law," *New York University Law Review*, XXII (1947), 145.

[178]About the psychological theory based on Freud, but adapted to law, see, e.g., R. West, "A Psychological Theory of Law," in *Interpretation of Modern Legal Philosophy*, pp. 767 ff.

[179]See A. Hagerström, *Der römische Obligationsbegriff* ("The Roman Notion of Obligations") and *Inquiries into the Nature of Laws and Morals* (1953).

[180]See A. Ross, *Toward a Realistic Jurisprudence* (1946); *Theorie der Rechtsquellen* ("The Theory of Legal Sources") (1929); and *Kritik der sog. praktischen Erkenntnis zugleich Prolegomena zu einer Kritik der Rechtswissenschaft* ("Criticism of the So-Called Practical Knowledge and Introduction to a Critique of Legal Science") (Copenhagen-Leipzig, 1933).

[181]See W. Lunstedt, *Legal Thinking Revised. My Views on Law* (1958) and *Die Unwissenschaftlichkeit der Rechtswissenschaft* ("The Unscientific Character of the Science of Law") (Berlin, 1932).

[182]See K. Olivercrona, *Law as a Fact* (1939) and "Is a Sociological Explanation of Law Possible? " in *Theoria*, XIV (1948), pp. 167 ff.

[183]See Langrod, *L'influence des idées de Léon Duguit . . .*, pp. 138-9; and Seidler, *op. cit.*, pp. 95 ff.

law on a psychological basis. They try to replace the objective "ought to be" (belonging to the realm of ideas) with the subjective experience of right and duty. This is very close to Petrazhitsky's theory; but, contrary to Petrazhitsky, the Scandinavians are not inclined to expand the concept of law to cover what the latter called intuitive law. The partial coincidence of views is an example of the familiar phenomenon of converging development in science; in any case, the members of the Uppsala school did not have direct access to Petrazhitsky's work. This did not prevent one of them, Karl Olivercrona, from writing a lengthy criticism of the theories of the Russo-Polish master.[184]

Whatever opinion each of these authors may have had about the validity of Petrazycki's ideas, all of them — supporters and opponents alike — felt convinced that they were confronting a rare scientific accomplishment. The "faithful" P. Michailowski commented:

> As Copernicus, the astronomer-monk, introduced the light of truth into astronomy and created the heliocentric conception of the solar system, providing thereby the theoretical foundations for the future development of this science and freeing it from antique optical illusion, i.e., the "axioma" of a geocentric vision of the universe, thus Petrazycki, the new Copernicus, brought to contemporary legal science the new light of a scientific truth, by creating the *psychological theory of law*, which made it possible to understand the error of representing the phenomenon of law as fixed in the outside world, and revealed its existence in the internal: in the very *psyche* of man.[185]

The Doctrine [186]

The psychological theory of law brought to legal science elements which, although they were by no means new, made it possible to understand the essence of law in its various aspects.

The role of psychology in influencing juridical phenomena has been stressed by numerous theoreticians. As examples one could quote on the

[184]See Timascheff, *Introduction . . .* (1955), pp. xxxiv-xxxv. There is no doubt, however, that Scandinavian authors were familiar with German literature and thereby with Petrazycki's German writings.

[185]*Op. cit.*, pp. 140-1.

[186]This part sums up the main points of the previous discussion insofar as the psychological theory of law is concerned, without taking into account the other theories outlined by its founder. The purpose is to stress those aspects which seem, even without considering Petrazycki's work as a whole, to provide a lasting scientific contribution to the science of law.

one hand E. Zitelmann,[187] E.R. Bierling,[188] Georg Jellinek, and A. Hold Ferneck; on the other, N. Korkunoff.[189] These pioneers of the psychological conception of law endeavored to demonstrate the shortcomings of pure positivism in the field of legal knowledge and the unavoidable necessity of establishing closer relationships between legal science and the other social sciences, including psychology and sociology. This view opposed the complete "autonomy" of legal science within the family of

[187]*Irrtum and Rechtsgeschäft. Eine psychologisch-juristische Untersuchung* ("Mistake and Legal Transaction") (1879), a psycho-legal analysis.

[188]*Zur Kritik der juristischen Grundbegriffe* ("A Contribution to the Critique of the Basic Notions of Law") (1877-83) and *Juristische Prinzipienlehre* ("The Science of Legal Principles") (1893-1917). Bierling stated that law, being a product of spiritual life, exists only in the psyche of members of the community and, like Petrazycki, considered it as a bilateral phenomenon. In his course of lectures, quoted above, Lande alluded to the possibility of Bierling's influence over Petrazycki. However, Bierling came to assert that wherever there is a legal phenomenon, a legal norm is at stake, provided that the said phenomenon takes place in the psyche of both parties (debtor and creditor). Thus, on the one hand, Bierling introduced into his theory objective norms (i.e., extra-psychological elements), amalgamating thereby the theoretical and the dogmatic, which Petrazycki separated. On the other hand, by requiring identical psychological phenomena to be experienced simultaneously by both parties engaged in a legal relationship, Bierling formulated a condition which was alien to psychological conceptions. It should be noted that, concerning the psychological reactions of children and lunatics, Bierling solved the dilemma created by his premises by resorting to the psychological phenomena experienced by their guardians or curators. His theory led to fictions transposing the legal conceptions of psychic reality on the normative level. See also Babb, *Petrazhitsky* . . ., pp. 573-4.

As he was familiar with German literature, Petrazycki knew the works of the authors quoted above; he quoted explicitly: e.g., Jodl, *Lehrbuch der Psychologie* ("Handbook of Psychology") (2nd ed., 1888); Höffding, *Psychologie* (1901); and Ebbinghaus, *Psychologie* (1902); He was influenced by the psychological school of W. Wundt, *Grundriss der Psychologie* ("An Outline of Psychology") (5th ed., 1902).

[189]See N. Korkunoff (in Russian) *Lectures on the General Theory of Law* (1888). English trans. by W.S. Hastings (Boston, 1909) and *Russian Constitutional Law* (1883-6). Timascheff, *Introduction* . . . (1955), p. xx, says: "Korkunoff denied the reality of 'the will of the state' which had been a basic assumption by all his German and Russian contemporaries. Instead, he proclaimed the existence of a force engendered by the consciousness of dependency (subordination) on the part of the citizens or subjects. Thus, the state was asserted to be a psychological phenomenon, an important point to be kept in mind when considering the theory of law held by Petrazhitsky." As regards other influences on Petrazycki, especially that of the Austrian psychological school of Franz Brentano, see Babb, *Petrazhitskii* . . ., p. 571.

human sciences, as well as its purely formal and basically logical character. Such a trend of thought was to prove lasting in spite of the repeated successes of "pure" legal doctrine, a concept brilliantly expended in the twentieth century by Hans Kelsen and by his disciples.[190]

It has been said that "allusions to law in terms suggestive of psychology — individual or national intent, or will or consciousness — are to be found as far back as Greek philosophy, and are familiar in such theories as that of the Social Contract."[191] Moreover, as the methodology of the natural sciences was becoming increasingly a pattern for logic itself, the psychological conception of law was developing, particularly after the second half of the nineteenth century. As an example, one could quote Schäffle,[192] who viewed psychology as the substratum of society.

Although this conception is far from new in principle, the contribution of both critical[193] and constructive[194] views of the work Leon Petrazycki seems particularly significant, because these views can be treated as a systematic whole: a conjunction of ideas completing and supplementing each other. Every one of them added to Petrazycki's original views or modified them in accordance with the development of knowledge. Thus, they helped toward a better understanding of the mystery which surrounds the essence of law considered as a specific social

[190]In Petrazycki's lifetime, Kelsen's theory was strongly represented in Polish science: e.g., By W.L. Jaworski (1865-1930) in *Nauka prawa administracyjnego Zagadnienia ogolne* ("The Science of Administrative Law, Its General Problems") (1924) and "Prace z dziedziny teorii prawa" ("Studies on the Theory of Law"), in *Czasopismo prawnicze i ekonomiczne*, XXIII (1925); and by Szymon Rundstein, *Zasady teorii prawa* ("Principles of the Theory of Law") (1924).

[191]Hoppe, *Der psychologische Ursprung des Rechts* ("The Psychological Origin of the Law") (1885), quoted by Babb, *Petrazhitskii . . .*, p. 571, fn. 237.

[192]"Die menschliche oder civile Gesellschaft ist eine reine geistig (psychisch) bewirkte" ("The Human or Civil Community Is Purely Spiritual [Psychological] in Essence"), *Bau und Leben des sozialen Körpers*, III (1881).

[193]See Mikailov (in Russian), "The New Doctrine of Private and Public Law," *Zap. Demidov*, IV (1912), 567 ff. He states that Petrazycki's critique of Ihering's theory and of the draft German Civil Code was at the source of his psychological theory.

[194]Timascheff, *Introduction . . .* (1955), p. xxxvi, says: "Certainly, Petrazhitskii was the first legal philosopher who went beyond programmatic statements about the necessity of treating law as part of reality and beyond merely speculating that this reality was sociological or psychological. His theory, despite its limitations, was a complete, and consistent theory of the reality of law." See also the reviews by Laserson, "The Work of Leon Petrazycki: Inquiry into the Psychological Aspects of the Nature of Law," *Columbia Law Review*, LIX (1951); and by S.I. Shuman, *Journal of Legal Education*, VIII (1955), 112.

phenomenon. If "the sphinx of the essence of law is still a sphinx,"[195] the psychological doctrine succeeded in "emphasizing the empirical character of the theory, based on observation of corresponding real phenomena, as distinguished from earlier theories having to do with unreal objects."[196]

This theory also endeavored, with some measure of success, to take legal science out of the pre-scientific stage in which it found itself under the pressure of dogmatic trends. An important methodological effort was thus initiated, in the spirit of Kant's criticism, which Petrazycki inserted at the beginning of his *magnum opus*.[197] Although it is still impossible to give a satisfactory theoretical definition of law (just as it is impossible to assess the validity of one religion in relation to another), the psychological doctrine introduced a distinction between law as a psychological phenomenon and as a system of compulsory norms, without identifying the two or concentrating exclusively on the latter.

The psychological doctrine launched research on the role of introspection on the actual nature of law as a product of the mind and on the attempt to define the implications of justice. Thus, the problem of natural law, which has always been queried by legal scientists, received the embryo of a logical explanation.[198]

It should also be mentioned that Petrazycki's school, by firmly refusing to see the essence of law in objective reality, external to the observer, is logically bound to reject any outside force such as power or state

[195]Petrazycki, quoted in Babb, *Petrazhitskii* . . ., p. 513.

[196]Petrazycki's letter of April 13, 1931, to Prof. Guins, of the University of Kharbin, quoted in Babb, *Petrazhitskii* . . ., p. 574, fn. 250.

[197]See Petrazycki, *Law and Morality*, p. 1: "The great philosopher Kant poked fun at the jurisprudence of his time as still not knowing how to define law: 'Jurists are still searching for a definition of their concept of law,' he remarked ironically. He himself worked—but without success—to find a solution to the problem, and since his time many outstanding thinkers, philosophers, and jurists have worked in the same field of investigation. Even now, however, 'jurists are still seeking a definition for their concept of law'."

[198]It is worth noting in this connection that, e.g., Bergbohm, in *Jurisprudenz and Rechtsphilosophie* ("Legal Science and Legal Philosophy," I [1892], pp. 79 ff.) denies the validity of natural law theories in general. In the first place, natural law cannot, according to him, fill the gaps in any positive system, since the latter does not have any, by definition (the legislator's silence is either intentional or susceptible to interpretation by analogy). Second, it would be inaccurate to say that natural law contains general principles and positive law (specific rules): since any law is a complete system in itself, if natural law contained general principles, no separate system of positive law would be required in order to deduce specific rules from these general principles. Third, the reality of law results (in this view) from the very fact that it is admitted even by the supporters of natural law.

authority as a decisive element in the creation and the existence of law.[199]

The psychological theory is not misled into deviating from the essence of the object which it studies. As stated by Petrazycki himself:

> The content of traditional legal science is tantamount to an optical illusion: it does not see legal phenomena where they actually occur, but discerns them where there is absolutely nothing of them — where they cannot be found, observed, or known: that is to say, in a world external to the subject who is experiencing the legal phenomena. We shall see that this optical illusion has its natural psychological causes, precisely as the optical illusion (in the literal sense of the word) is perfectly natural, when people ignorant of astronomy suppose (as the science of astronomy itself did down to Copernicus) that the sun rises in the morning and revolves around us.[200]

The authors who represent this trend of thought consider that to locate the legal phenomenon outside the human mind amounts to naive realism. Such realism is viewed as corresponding either to nihilism (since the object of juridical research cannot in fact be found in external reality and therefore is considered nonexistent) or to the creation of fictions (entities which do not exist in fact, but are intended to replace the investigated phenomena in the imagination).

Whatever the validity of the particular thesis supported by this intellectual trend, it plays an important part in juridical thought[201] although its forms change. To underestimate its contribution would impoverish our understanding of legal phenomena.

According to the psychological theory adapted to law,

> The action of law upon the human psyche is of two sorts: (a) ... The first psychological action of law is its *motivational* action. The "experience" of a legal rule produces psychological phenomena in that there is consciousness of the rule and of what is thereby permitted or forbidden, and consequent stimulation or elimination

Consequently, Bergbohm excludes the coexistence of the two parallel systems of law and asserts that only positive law exists in fact.

[199]See Gurvitch, *Une philosophie intuitiviste* ..., p. 414: "The criticism made by Petrazycki of any theory which wants to define law ... as a function of the state and—more widely—of constraint, belongs by its dialectic form and its depth to the classic texts of world legal literature."

[200]Petrazycki, *Law and Morality*, p. 8.

[201]See, e.g., W. A. Tumanov (in Russian), "On Some Psychological Theories in the New Juridical Bourgeois Doctrine," *Sovietskoie Gosudarstvo i Pravo* (Moscow), V (1955), 112 ff.

of motives to act or to abstain. *Fundamental* motivational action is the creation, elimination or modification of (individual or group) motives to act in a certain way. In a normal, healthy psyche, consciousness of legal rights or obligations leads towards corresponding conduct. The operation of this motivation is intensified by the *auxiliary* motivation of various legal norms associating punishment (or other negative consequences) with conduct not conforming to law, and reward (or other positive consequences) with conduct which does so conform, and thus promoting the fulfillment of obligations. The motivational cooperation of these two brings about analogous systems of patterned (individual and social) conduct, leading to a corresponding regime or social order. Moreover *free* legal motivation is also essentially significant in social life — the evocation of motives to (individual or mass) conduct not specifically prescribed by law, but voluntarily practiced by members of society because of existing law, social order and the like, as reasonably necessary and fair in their own interests (or in the interests of their family). ... (b) ... The second psychological action of law is its *educative* action, to reinforce or to destroy, to weaken or otherwise to modify, psychological predispositions and capacities (to act in a certain way) and other elements, propensities or traits of human character. With improvement in the national psyche and the progress of ethics, this educative action changes. The goal of the law in this regard is the gradual education to an ideal condition of the emotional psyche by eradicating anti-social, egoistic, odious and malicious emotional dispositions (and so the very possibility of such conduct) and implanting, developing, and strengthening the opposed, punitive emotional dispositions and thereby creating the psychic inevitability of good, merciful and sympathetic behavior...[202]

The problem of motives for action or abstention, and in particular their impulsive or pedagogical impact, seems basic to the psychological theory.

Although human activity usually appears to be purposive, it is not always possible to trace concrete or even implied reasons as motivation. Indeed, various actions result unconsciously from emotional attraction or revulsion. Besides definite motives (repulsion or attraction, sentimental or purely intellectual motivations, or hedonistic ascetic goals), there exists an "unconscious finality." What is meant thereby is a purely objective, biologically rational motivation, frequently complex, particularly when action is required without enough time for purposive thought.

On the one hand, as Petrazycki stated, it seems an oversimplification to endeavor to connect the whole of collective life with one single criterion,

[202]Babb, *Petrazhitskii* ..., p. 807-8.

whatever it may be.[203] We are dealing, in fact, with the complex result of collective behavior. Since the external behavior of man cannot be dissociated from his psyche, "as the human soul is not an adding machine,"[204] all the elements which affect it should be studied, whatever their form. Therefore, although the psychological doctrine adopts the introspective method as the proper one for observing legal phenomena,[205]

[203]We are dealing here with an opposition to monocausal explanations (e.g., utility, pleasure, pain, etc.). For this reason, Petrazycki objected to the exclusivism of such theories as those of imitation (Gabriel Tarde), conquest (Gumplowicz), race (Gobineau), or economic struggle between classes (Marx). This aspect of Petrazycki's theory has been severely criticized by Marxist-Leninists, as has been already said. They quote in this connection the critique of empirio-criticism by Lenin (in Russian, "Materialism and Empirio-Criticism," in *Works*, XIV, 141 ff.): "Avenarius and Mach consider impressions as the source of our science. Thus, they adopt the position of empiricism (all science comes from experience) or of sensualism (all science comes from impression). But this point of view leads to the difference between the main philosophical trends, idealism and materialism; regardless of the 'new' verbal elements which cover it, it does not suppress the difference between them. Both the supporter of solipsism (subjective idealist) and the materialist can consider impressions as the source of our science. Both Berkeley and Diderot start from Locke. The first premise of the theory of knowledge certainly accepts the fact that impressions are the only source of our knowledge ... [But] by adopting this first premise, Mach is confused about a second important premise: objective reality which is the source of human impressions and which is offered to these. Beginning with impressions as a starting point, one can either follow the direction of subjectivism leading to solipsism ('bodies are entities or combinations of impressions') or that of objectivism leading to materialism ('impressions are pictures of the bodies of the outside world'). See Seidler, *op. cit.*, pp. 69 ff.; W. Reicher (in Russian), "The Psychology Theory of Law in the Light of the Critique of Empirio-Criticism by Lenin," *Sovietskoie Gosudarstvo i Pravo*, VII (1940); and A.I. Denisov (in Russian), *The Theory of the State and the Law* (Moscow, 1948), pp. 338 ff.

Thus, the psychological trend in legal science is often viewed by communist authors as "one of the main trends of bourgeois legal science, opposed to materialistic interpretation. Petrazycki's idealistic theory still corresponds therefore to the interests of capitalism in the period of increasing class antagonisms. It is one of the attempts by bourgeois science to explain law without taking into account the real contradictions of capitalist formation. Consequently, all endeavors to connect the psychological trend with the scientific conception of law are doomed to fail and all attempts made to that effect conceal the danger of introducing idealism into legal theory." (Seidler, *op. cit.*, p. 98.) See also Kowalski, *op. cit.*, pp. 564 ff.

[204]Petrazycki, *Lehre vom Einkommen* . . ., II, p. 544.

[205]Petrazycki, *Law and Morality*, p. 14, says: "The introspective method—simple and experimental 'self-knowledge'—is the sole means of observation, *and of the*

it does not preclude outward observation;[206] moreover, the breadth of this approach to motivation excludes monocausal interpretation of reality. Thus, the description and classification by Petrazycki of the motives involved, as well as the study of the dynamic processes of their action "achieves unprecedented results, by presenting the world of 'motives' in its rich complexity; this is due to an analysis so clear that psychology has never been able to approximate such a result."[207]

On the other hand, the psychological doctrine starts from the premise that there is a trend toward a unification of human attitudes. This trend is due, according to Cornil, to a consciousness

> ... which creates the feeling that some attitudes should be adopted, and others reproved and avoided, i.e., in the sense that social order is necessary.... Common emotions stimulate a general feeling within everyone's consciousness; this general feeling affects in turn the conduct or the behavior of men towards each other. The conjunction of external reactions of the general inward feeling represents what we call mores. Thus understood, mores are therefore the source which reveals the positive social order which is commonly accepted.[208]

The psychological doctrine has been enriched by Petrazycki's reassessment of the classical psychological classification into three categories of elements composing psychological life. This he completed by adding to intelligence (cognition), feeling (pleasure and pain), and will − the first two passive and the last active − a fourth, bilateral, passive and active, category, designated as "impulses" or "emotions." Their bilateral character makes them more complex and variable, in relation to the dualistic structure of the nervous system, and this is why they can be considered as the prototype of psychological life.

---

immediate and reliable cognition and study, of legal and moral phenomena. Without it there is *no possibility whatsoever of any knowledge of them at all.*"

[206]*Ibid.*, p. 17: "The very nature of legal phenomena as psychic processes of a particular class precludes the possibility of employing for their scientific study methods other than: (a) the introspective method (simple or experimental) as the fundamental and indispensable manner of acquiring knowledge of the nature of legal phenomena, and (b) the joint method of inward and outward observation (simple or experimental)."

[207]Lande, *Leon Petrazycki . . .*, pp. 17-8 (quoted from the offprint).

[208]Cornil, *op. cit.*, p. 365.

The scheme[209] established by Petrazycki can be presented as follows:

PSYCHOLOGICAL		REACTIONS	
UNILATERAL		BILATERAL	
ACTIVE	PASSIVE	EMOTIVE IMPULSES	
Will	Feelings, Intelligence	Special	Blanket

Law being a psychological phenomenon (namely, a projection of emotions), the doctrine laid down by Petrazycki shows three kinds of characteristics: first, those relating to specific motives on which human behavior is based; second, those relating to the various processes of adaptation to reality, in connection with the educative mission of law; and third, those relating to the formation of the community, in connection with the unifying tendency of law.

First, it should be stressed that, despite the variety of motives to be taken into account, mutual reinforcement of these does not necessarily occur. Instead, they often tend to conflict, the stronger motives overcoming or offsetting the weaker. As has already been said, some motives can be the product of legal provisions, even if they are not the direct outcome either of the textual content of the law or of the sanctions prescribed. Thus, the interplay of the laws of obligations, succession, and family law may be the source of actions or abstentions on the part of persons other than those directly concerned; the necessity to preserve favorable economic results for oneself or for some other person is at stake.[210] The variety of motives reflects a corresponding variety of emotions and other psychological elements. The process of unconscious evolution of law in connection with this complex motivation causes, on the one hand, the extension of legal requirements affecting human

[209]More detailed explanations of the various aspects of this scheme appear in the first part of this study. (See also Petrazycki, *Law and Morality*, pp. 25 ff.) Lande, *Leon Petrazycki*, pp. 14-5, suggested, in order to eliminate the possibility of a contradiction between the terms "active" and "passive" when linked together, the replacement of those notions by "propulsive" and "submitted to propulsion," respectively.

[210]Thus, one abstains from a commercial transaction in order to avoid a possible material loss (free motive); one pays tax in order to avoid a penalty foreseen by law (auxilliary motive).

behavior (e.g., quantitative increase of the rules, their application to foreign nationals, etc.) and, on the other, the transference of the grounds on which legal prescriptions are based to a higher level of ethics and of efficiency (e.g., transformation of the basis of labor in successive economic regimes, as described by Petrazycki: fear under slavery, interest under free competition, and social service under socialism).[211] One should also consider the phenomenon of the decreasing strength of motives, which tend to cancel each other out in the long run (e.g., penal law is decreasingly severe). The pressure of motive lessens every time there is a qualitatively equal motivation.

However, while Petrazycki utilized the notion of emotions in order to achieve those results in the description and classification of motives, his psychological doctrine went beyond this starting point: even if one no longer admits the predominant role of emotion as the impulse behind every human action, the conception of psychological motives causing human action still stands.

Second, and in connection with the previous point, the psychological doctrine emphasizes the process of social adaptation. This has been covered in the outline of the educative action of law. Thus, law is considered to have a definite social function, in accordance with the theories propounded by Emile Durkheim and Bronislaw Malinowski. The history of mankind is described as a succession of phases of development characterized by evolutionary progress towards increasingly perfect forms. This development should be utilized in order to encourage those processes of social and psychological adaptation. Petrazycki's postulate of "emotional contamination" is relevant here, as social coexistence and solidarity permit the use of individual experiences to the advantage of the community as a whole.

Each psychological force initiated by law implies a lack of adaptation in human nature. The psychological force increases proportionately to the deficiency in adaptation (which results from hereditary emotional impulses of an anti-social character). Such an increase is inversely proportional to the fulfillment of educational programs. The role of law, the cause of which is connected with the deficiency in the education of men, is to educate the community gradually. This implies that law exists only temporarily. It has been said:

> The ultimate problem and task of law is to make itself superfluous and so to be abolished. Its immediate function is to regulate individual activity by influence upon the individual psyche...

[211]Petrazycki viewed the "socialistic order" as "one of centralized or planned organization . . . distinguished from the system . . . of decentralization (wherein a multitude of individuals and economies are separate and independent)." (*Law and Morality*, pp. 310-11).

Eventually the purposes of social education, and the "psyche of love" in the broad sense of Petrazhitskii, will be completely attained. Law will then lose its significance altogether, not in the sense of the Marx-Lenin dogma that Law (like the State) as a purely historical phenomenon and temporary instrument of class struggle or proletariat dictatorship will finally die out, and society operate by purely technical norms of expediency transformed into habit, but because the existence of law will then be psychologically inappropriate. This is not incompatible with the establishment of general plans of action and their voluntary fulfillment by all without any "psychological pressures." The ultimate goal of legal development is the inculation of uncoerced social conduct (established by inner consciousness and will) so that society shall attain a harmonious condition of cooperation in social service.[212] When that goal is reached law will become superfluous and cease to exist.[213]

Third, the psychological doctrine extends to the structure of the social community. Taking into account the average of the psychological motives (ethical, legal, mixed, etc.) which regulate coordinated mass behavior, one should connect the legal system with other systems (e.g., economic)[214] without underestimating the influence of social change on the motives involved. Indeed, the theory of social structure supplements motives with specific criteria: some psychologically identical motives will have a

[212]Petrazycki, *Law and Morality*, pp. 312 ff., distinguishes in the field of law: (1) the law of social-service, which unifies, organizes, and integrates the rights of persons and groups, and which corresponds in its main lines to contemporary public law (although it deals with all social groups, even external to the state, and seems therefore to be wider than the former); and (b) the individual (free) law, allotting rights and obligations to individuals, and so corresponding to private law.

Concerning the first, the more perfect the social structure, the higher the motives of state action are, so that fear is increasingly replaced by a sense of social service. Progress consists in the replacement of means of pressure by the social discipline of every individual. Petrazycki distinguishes dominant authorities, which are free to command, and social ancillary authorities, which act "for the welfare of subjects or of the social group, as distinguished from the rights of the dominant authorities whose objects are commands which influence subjects irrespective of any considerations for their welfare." (p. 313.)

Concerning the second (social structure being a system of coordinated mass behavior, inspired by various motives), legal motivation plays a particularly important part, owing to its capacity to coordinate and unify individual and collective activities.

[213]Babb, *Petrazhitskii . . .*, pp. 809-10.

[214]Economic phenomena, although composing a structural entity separate from political and private law structures, are considered by Petrazycki as conditioned by law, because of the specificity of the social structure.

different social function, depending on the type of social structure in which they exist. The unifying role of law, as emphasized by Petrazycki, is relevant in this context.

The psychological doctrine contains elements which allow a better understanding of the social essence and function of law, considered (in view of its imperative-attributive nature, characterized by bilateral motivation) both as a cause and an effect of socio-psychological life.

The key to this problem is provided by Petrazycki's differentiation, unchallenged by other authors, between two social functions of law: the organizational and the distributive. Both are purely functional, without implying either a metaphysical conception[215] or an emphasis on force.[216] Both correspond to

> ... tendencies of legal mentality and of the development of that mentality. ... to produce a stable and coordinated system of social conduct evoked by law — a firm and precisely defined order — with which individuals and masses can and should conform, and upon which there can be reliance and calculation as regards economic and other plans and enterprises and in the organization of life in general.[217]

Both have an emotional context. The first function reflects the conception of the state as a process[218] and not merely as an organized whole composed of individuals; emotions (feelings of rights and obligations to command or to obey) form a sociological system of coexistence within a community. They are a source of social order.[219] The second function

[215]Thus, the famous historical school of Savigny in German legal science, though it started from psychological premises, stressed the historical element and considered law as the product of national spirit, viewed in a romantic and nationalistic light. According to this conception, based on metaphysics, law develops like language or mores, the starting point of this evolution being a nucleus of unknown origin. In this view, the legal sense is not part of reality, but the source of a dogmatic system. Its evolution resembles a pseudo-biological process.

[216]Petrazycki, *Law and Morality*, p. 129, says: "Like social authority in general, state authority is neither will nor force. Nor is it, in general, anything real. It is an impulsive projection: an impulsive phantasm. It signifies a particular species of rights ascribed to certain persons. . . ."

[217]*Ibid.*, p. 121.

[218]Balogh, *op. cit.*, p. 82.

[219]Petrazycki, *Law and Morality*, p. 121, says: "In the minds of the public and of jurists, the ideas 'law' and 'order' are constantly associated, and it is extremely common to use the expression 'law and order' in place of the word 'law.' What has been set out above indicates the cause of this association and explains the peculiar capacities and functions of legal ethics in general—as compared with

illustrates the attributive character of law, described previously. It consists in granting to individuals and groups various advantages unconnected with their behavior. Thus, for example, the distributive function with reference to means of production or to consumption in economies accounts for the complexity and the psychological nature of law. Property, in particular, seems to be an emotional and intellectual phenomenon which exists only in the psyche of the person who attributes the corresponding right to himself or to another.[220]

As has been said in section I, the psychological theory of law is by no means monolithic. Its supporters represent a wide range of different individual opinions. Nevertheless they can be grouped in one intellectual category, since the basis of their doctrine is common.

This theory cannot be labelled according to traditional patterns, as its critics and supporters alike often do. It is inaccurate to oversimplify the issue by classifying the psychological approach as idealistic[221] or subjective.[222] Indeed, it covers, even according to Petrazycki's views, both realistic and social elements, since it is based on the principle of reciprocal

purely imperative ethics—in the matter of organizing and standardizing social life."

[220]Petrazycki considered current theories on property to be unsatisfactory. According to him, they did not account for the way in which relationships are created between persons and objects. "Here, as in other fields of jurisprudence, the naive-projection point of view is dominant, and this, in general, neither knows, or even takes a cursory glance at, the relevant real phenomena or chains of causation . . . The starting point of a scientific theory of property must be that property is not a phenomenon of the external and objective world. Property is neither a bond between a person and a thing nor the sum total of the prohibitions issued by anyone in respect of anyone. It is a psychic, impulsive-intellectual phenomenon. It exists solely in the mind of one who attributes to himself or to another a right of property." (*Law and Morality*, pp. 123-4.)

Because of the psychic character of the phenomenon, it is the consciousness of the obligations involved which is experienced as imperative and attributive. The use of the object owned and the right of exclusive domination cause a motivation and a behavior which, under the given social circumstances, are considered as typical for any owner.

[221]Gurvitch formulates, in connection with Petrazycki's idea of an intuitive law and with "normative facts" as a starting point, the conception of "ideal-realism." (See, e.g., Claude du Pasquier, *op. cit.*, p. 299.) Laserson, *La sociologie russe*, p. 678, says: "Gurvitch transformed Petrazycki's psychological theory on the multiplicity of 'normative facts' in legal life, into a sociological conception."

[222]Lande, *O tzw. socjologii nauki*, p. 511 ff., says: "According to Petrazycki's theory, social organization appears to be a system of coordinated reciprocal behavior by members of the group, viewed as mass behavior; one can subdivide it into special sectors by starting from the psychic premises which represent the

psychological interpenetration between members of the social community as well as by conditions of material existence.[223]

It seems that this theory is consonant with the trend of progress in scientific thought. Eminent social scientists prove[224] that not only human influence on outside objects, but also human relationships and community institutions can be understood only through the ideas formed about them by human beings. The true elements of social structure are the product of individual opinions formed by men about themselves and about things. Within this structure, different persons may occupy in turn the same positions, not because the people are identical, but because they enter into the same relationship with others and are viewed from the same angle.

It is the merit of the psychological doctrine to have included law, as a social institution, in this intellectual trend necessary for the progress of the social sciences. At the same time, it has gone beyond the dogmatic stereotyped approach which dominated the legal theory scene in its beginnings. Thus, the educative role of the psychological theory is demonstrated, even is one disagrees with some of its postulates. Owing to the efforts made by all the authors of this school, it was among the first to build a bridge between jurists and their neighbors in the social science field. Research on the reality of law was stimulated and firmly based on an inter-disciplinary approach and useful contributions were made towards the development of sociology.

For all these reasons, even critics of this conception as a whole (including supporters of monism as an interpretation of social structure and social change) cannot fail to recognize the lasting value of this approach to law.[225]

average motive of a given action. . . . It is psychology which provides the theory of state organization with data from which the latter deduces its own criteria. . . . Petrazycki is by no means a unilateral psychologist, as his critics often maintain: his social theories are based on psychology, whose results they utilize, but introduce also criteria of their own, which are super-psychological."

[223]See Petrazycki, *Zagadnienie prawa zwyczajowego* ("The Problem of Customary Law") (Warsaw, 1938), p. 47.

[224]See, e.g., F. von Hayek, *Scientism and the Study of Society* (Glencoe, Ill., 1952).

[225]See K. Opalek, ed., "Z zagadnień teorii prawa i teorii nauki Leona Petrazyckiego" ("Problems of the Legal Theory and Scientific Theory of Leon Petrazycki") in *Studia opracowane dla upamietnienia stulecia urodzin* (Warsaw, 1969).

JAROSŁAW A. PIEKAŁKIEWICZ

Polish Administrative Law

In all modern states the body of administrative law is extremely large, and generally it is not codified in the same manner as the other branches of law, but is found in many separate statutes, acts, decrees, and regulations of various government agencies. It brings to mind a tropical jungle with luxuriant vegetation, lianas hanging from tree to tree, new life springing from dead trunks – and all of it barring entrance to a curious intruder. Some old acts are superseded by new ones; others simply die from lack of application; yet still others are revised and amended. This legal jungle is augmented in the communist countries by the state's ownership of the means of production and by its attempt to plan and regulate the whole complex industrial economy.

Contrary to the general opinion held in the West, communist administrative law does not make a clean break with its capitalist past. Even in the U.S.S.R., more than fifty years after the establishment of the Soviet state, some of the laws and principles of the czarist period have survived. In Poland, the communist regime was established in a state which had existed for a thousand years. Although the communist regime introduced many sweeping changes, it was forced at the same time to build on previous tradition and precedent. It is impossible to construct a completely new legal structure in a few years or even a few decades. Some of the laws affecting local government originated as far back as the thirteenth century: e.g., laws relating to planning of village settlements.[1] Many laws and regulations adopted in the nineteenth century are very much in effect: e.g., ten railroad acts, of which the oldest is from 1874.[2]

[1]Piotr Typiak, *Praca w Gromadzie* ("Work in a Commune") (Warsaw: Ludowa Spółdzielnia Wydawnicza, 1960), p. 108.

[2]Jerzy Starościak and Emanuel Iserzon, *Prawo Administracyjne* ("Administrative Law") (Warsaw: Wydawnictwo Prawnicze, 1963) p. 43.

A large amount of prewar Polish law is in use today or has been superseded by new acts only very recently. The most important piece of prewar legislation is the Regulation on Administrative Procedure issued in 1928 by the President of the Polish Republic,[3] which to a large degree forms the theoretical framework of the present administrative law and which, although supplanted in many parts by more recent acts, is constantly referred to by Polish jurists. Also, still important in its theoretical application, even if no longer legally valid, is the Act of the Sejm (Polish parliament) of 1923, concerned with the legal means of appeal from administrative decision.[4] This act in turn was based on the Austrian administrative law and specifically on the Statute of May 12, 1896, of the Austro-Hungarian Empire.[5]

This continuity of the Polish administrative law and its theoretical basis does not mean that the communist government is not constantly revising it in an effort to bring the law into accord with present political and technological conditions. Many changes have been necessitated by the alteration of social, economic, and technological circumstances. Others have resulted from the conscious efforts of the Communist Party to bring Polish administrative law into line with communist ideology.

The development of administrative law in the Polish People's Republic can be divided into three separate periods:[6]

1. The first period extended from 1944 to 1947, when the main framework of communist rule was constructed and embodied in the following legal policies: legislation on land reform,[7] nationalization of some of the forests,[8] nationalization of industry, mining, transportation, banking, insurance, and most of the commerce;[9] and decrees on the organization and functions of local government (*Rady Narodowe*),[10] on the organization of the civic militia,[11] on the appointment of the

[3]*Dziennik Ustaw (Dz.U.)* (The Official Gazette of the Polish Republic), No. 36, Entry 341.

[4]*Ibid.*, No. 91, Entry 712.

[5]Wacław Dawidowicz, *Ogólne Postępowanie Administracyjne* ("The General Administrative Procedure") (Warsaw: Państwowe Wydawnictwo Naukowe, 1962), p. 12.

[6]See Starościak and Iserzon, *op.cit.*, p. 42.

[7]*Dz.U.* (1945), No. 3, Entry 13. The original decree was passed September 6, 1944 and amended January 17, 1945.

[8]*Dz.U.*, (1944), No. 15, Entry 82; amended in 1948, *Dz.U.*, No. 57, Entry 456.

[9]*Dz.U.* (1946), No. 3, Entry 17; amended in 1946, *Dz.U.*, No. 72, Entry 394.

[10]*Dz.U.* (1944), No. 5, Entry 22, amended in 1944, 1945, and 1946.

[11]*Dz.U.* (1944), No. 7, Entry 33.

provisional government,[12] and on the structure and functions of public administration.[13] This first period was crowned by the Constitutional Decree of February 19, 1947, the so-called Little Constitution.[14]

2. The second period, which extended from 1947 to approximately 1955, was characterized by the reorganization of the Polish government on the Soviet model, with complete disregard for Polish historical tradition and differing social and economic conditions. This slavish imitation of Soviet practices resulted in a nearly complete breakdown of efficient administration and economy, and produced unbelievable chaos in administrative law. The present constitution of the Polish People's Republic was enacted in 1952[15] and was a faithful reproduction of the Stalinist constitution of 1936.

3. The last period, which began in 1955, has not yet ended and can be described best as a time of reform, codification of administrative law, and reorganization of the structure of government in the spirit of the "Polish road to socialism," not completely separate from Soviet influence and dominance, yet taking into account specific characteristics of the Polish nation. The most important achievements are the reorganization of local government by the act of 1958,[16] permitting some decentralization in the administrative decision-making, and the code of administrative procedure of 1961.[17]

Communist Theory of Government: Unified State Administration

Before discussion of the specific branches of Polish administrative law, it is necessary to describe briefly the governmental structure of the Polish People's Republic and the communist theory from which this political body originates. The socialist state in theory bears no resemblance to the "bourgeois" state, but is something completely novel in form and function. Marx, in the *Civil War in France*, and Engels, in the introduction to the German edition of the *Communist Manifesto*, categorically state that the working class cannot simply take over the already existing machinery of the bourgeois state, but is compelled to destroy it and on its smoking ruins construct new political organs based on entirely new principles and

[12]*Dz.U.* (1944), No. 19, Entry 99.

[13]*Dz.U.* (1944), No. 2, Entry 8.

[14]*Dz.U.*, No. 18, Entry 71.

[15]*Dz.U.*, No. 33, Entry 232.

[16]*Dz.U.*, No. 5, Entry 16, amended in 1962.

[17]*Dz.U.*, No. 30, Entry 168.

designed for different ends. Following the example of the Paris Commune, the protelarian state is to be based on the structure of communes, called soviets in the U.S.S.R. and the Nation's Councils in Poland.

The Constitution of the Polish People's Republic takes full account of this fundamental role of the Nation's Councils by declaring proudly in its two opening articles:

> The power in the Polish People's Republic belongs to the working people of towns and villages. The working people exercise their political power through their representatives elected to the Legislative Assembly (*Sejm*). . .and to the Nation's Councils. . . .

The Nation's Councils form one indivisible structure with the central government and are an integral part of it. They are not just another type of bourgeois self-government with its limited prerogatives; they belong totally to the *unified state administration*. There is no formal division between the central government and the local self-government. Each Nation's Council is considered to be the fullest political organization representing the local population, but at the same time it is the only state organ in a given territory. In the unified state structure the local officials are both functionaries of the central government and elected by the local population. Theoretically this provides the perfect opportunity for officials' responsiveness to the local electorate and, at the same time, enforcement of the state's general policies. It is a mass grass-roots participation in the administration of the state.

The Nation's Councils in Poland exist on three levels of local government: the Commune Councils, each covering the territory of a few villages or one small town or urban settlement; the County Councils, embracing several communes; and, finally, the Province Councils, which include several counties. The membership of each council is "elected" every four years by the population of the territory under the jurisdiction of the council, from a single list of candidates selected by the ruling Communist Party. Each council in turn elects its presidium – the executive committee, which directs the activities of the council and local administration. The actual day-to-day affairs are in the hands of the departments of the presidium. These are staffed by professional civil servants. The departments, apart from performing the functions of the local government, are the territorial branches of the central ministries.

In Western terminology, the council would be the legislative body; the presidium, the executive branch; and the departments, the administration. This division is violently and emphatically denied by the communist theoreticians, who maintain that the Nation's Councils are both legislative and executive bodies, rather than purely parliamentary. The council proper meets in sessions of one day's duration a few times a year. In practice most decisions are made by the presidium and by the departments, the latter acting on the instructions of the presidium and of the central ministries.

At the top of the pyramid of the Nation's Councils rests the National Assembly (*Sejm*), which may be regarded as the Nation's Council of the whole country. It elects the Council of State, which performs the functions of a collective president and supervises in general terms the activities of the Nation's Councils. The *Sejm* also appoints the government of the Polish People's Republic; that is, the Council of Ministers. The Council of Ministers directs the work of the presidia of the Nation's Councils, and the individual ministers regulate the performance of the departments of local government.

It must be stressed here that the overall decisions in all legislative and executive matters concerning the Polish government are made by the Communist Party. The Party, known as the United Workers' Party (*Polska Zjednoczona Partia Robotnicza*), is officially only one of the three political parties in Poland. The two noncommunist parties, the United Peasant Party (*Zjednoczone Stronnictwo Ludowe*) and the Democratic Party (*Stronnictwo Demokratyczne*), are not in opposition to the dominant Communist Party, but recognize without reservation and fully submit to the communist leadership. All three parties are grouped together in a super-party organization called the Front of National Unity (*Front Jedności Narodu*). The Front, and not the parties separately, presents the program and the list of candidates to the electorate. In fact, the F.N.U. is a front organization of the communist movement not unlike the communist-front organizations formed in democratic societies. It exists for the same reason — to draw maximum support while obscuring its true character. And indeed, in a "socialist democracy" there is theoretically no need for the proliferation of political forces because, after the elimination of the capitalist class, only working people of towns and villages are left, and the state power belongs to them.[18] They are represented and led by the "vanguard of the proletariat": the Communist Party.

> In a. . .People's Democracy where the state power is in the hands of the working people and the leading unit is the party of the working class, the position of this party in relationship to the highest state organ is of a superior character. . . .In principle, in the socialist state, the Marxist-Lenist Party, with regard to its basic function, is the only and exclusive political formation.[19]

[18]Constitution of the Polish People's Republic (from now on referred to as the Constitution), art. 1, para. 2.

[19]Wiesław Skrzydło, "Z Problematyki Genezy i Istoty Partii Politycznych" ("Some Problems of Genesis and Character of Political Parties"), *Annales Universitatis Mariae Curie-Sklodowska* (Lublin), V, Section G, No. 3 (1958), 64.

Such a position assumes complete concord between an individual's private interest and the state's policies, and unity of interest between the local and central government. It leads to a disregard of safeguards for the rights of the individual versus state power and for the independence of local bodies from the all-embracing might of the central authority, both so vital to Western democractic political thought and practice. It leads to a specific theory of administrative law, because:

Today, it is perhaps more just to concentrate, not on the matter of controlling the functions of the administration and safeguarding the citizens against it, but on the matter of securing, by administration, the needs of the citizens.[20]

This statement, in view of the actual political reality, means that the function of administrative law is not to restrain the government in its relationship with individuals, but to promote efficient enforcement of the policies of the central authority which originate with the Communist Party leadership, which after all, determines "the needs of the citizens." The sword of justice can never be directed against the breast of communist dictatorship itself because:

Law is a political phenomenon. This statement forms the base of the Marxist theory of State and Law. To a question — What is a legal act? Lenin answers: "An expression of the will of the classes which have won and kept the state power in their hands."[21]

Legal Foundations and Their Interpretation

Theoretically, the most important source of Polish state law is the Constitution. The legal principles expressed by this fundamental law are superior to any other norms. The Constitution establishes the political character and the structure of the state and determines the prerogatives of various branches of government. It places sovereignty in the hands of the working people and guarantees their power and freedom against their enemies.[22] Furthermore, the Constitution specifies that the laws of the Polish People's Republic are the expression of the will and interest of the

[20]Jerzy Starościak, "Nowe Elementy Systemu Kontroli Administracji" ("New Elements of the Control System of Administration"), *Państwo i Prawo*, No. 1 (Jan. 1961), 20.

[21]Stefan Rozmaryn, *Konstytucja Jako Ustawa Zasadnicza PRL* ("Constitution as the Fundamental Statute of the Polish People's Republic") (Warsaw: Państwowe Wydawnictwo Naukowe, 1961), p. 73.

[22] Constitution, Art. 3, para. 1.

working people.[23] This must be understood in conjunction with the declaration, in the preamble, of the principle of the dictatorship of the proletariat, which in practice leaves the determination of such interests and enemies to the leadership of the Communist Party.

Polish jurists stress the dynamic character of the Constitution and regard it as entrusting the government not only to prevent the enactment of unconstitutional laws but also to lead the Polish nation to its final goal — communism.[24] This assumed dynamism opens the door to a specific interpretation of the letter of the document, which should not be regarded as a description of the existing legal and political pattern, but as a guide to future development.[25] The Constitution itself is composed in a vague manner, leaving many basic questions to be regulated by subsequent parliamentary acts. It can serve equally well different leaderships and the usual Party attempts to equate politically expedient acts with ideological principles of freedom, equality, and social justice. It is important to point out that the Constitution did not prevent the use of extreme terror during the so-called Stalinist period, declared today to be a gross and direct violation of "socialist legality."

The most glaring example of this vagueness is the absence of a lucid definition of the power by which the state organs make law. This has resulted in widely varied interpretations and differences in practical application, causing some embarrassment to Polish legal minds.[26] The omission is vital, since to a large degree it invalidates the constitutional provisions requiring strict observance of the law by all organs of the state[27] and permitting them to act only on the basis of legal norms.[28] The difficulty lies in determining what the law is. Should the administrative branch act only on the basis of the parliamentary statues of the *Sejm*, or also on the decrees of the Council of State and the Council of Ministers? Or should regulations of various ministries and local normative acts of the Nation's Councils be regarded as sufficient ground? This legal dilemma could be resolved by the establishment of independent judicial bodies charged with the duty of binding pronouncement as to the validity of various normative acts. The Council of State is empowered to give

[23]*Ibid.*, Art. 4, para. 1.

[24]Rozmaryn, *op.cit.*, p. 23.

[25]*Ibid.*, p. 41.

[26]Maurycy Jaroszyński, *Zagadnienia Rad Narodowych* ("Problems of the Nation's Councils") (Warsaw: Państwowe Wydawnictwo Naukowe, 1961), p. 170.

[27]Constitution, Art. 4, para. 2.

[28]*Ibid.*, Art. 4, para. 3.

369

interpretation as to the meaning of the parliamentary statutes[29] and, assuming that the Constitution is only a special statute, of the Constitution. Perhaps we can also apply this reasoning to the decrees of the Council of State itself. The Council of State is elected from and by the communist-dominated *Sejm* and as such it cannot, even by a long stretch of imagination, be regarded as a politically independent body. It may only prevent free interpretation of law (i.e., not in accord with the general policies of the communist leadership) by lower organs of administration. Normative acts of the Nation's Councils and their presidia can be invalidated by the higher councils in the structure if they are contrary to law or the general policies of the state. Again we run into the problem of determining what the law is. It appears that the law is what the political forces declare it to be, since the councils are dominated and controlled by the Communist Party.

This constitutional vagueness, which leads to a free interpretation and creation of legal norms, gives rise to a suspicion that the communist lawmakers write all their acts in an obscure and confusing manner in order to make changes without revision of basic statutes. Milovan Djilas, once a communist lawmaker himself, supports this opinion by stating:

> With the passage of time they (the Communist lawmakers) became familiar with this kind of difficulty (of revising the law), so they always left loopholes and exceptions in their laws, in order to make evasion easier. . . .[30]

The Supreme Court of the Polish People's Republic is not empowered to pronounce on the constitutionality of parliamentary or administrative acts. Its powers of legal interpretation are limited to general supervision of the lower courts, and, in addition, result from the court's character as the highest appellate body.[31] The members of the court are appointed by the Council of State — as are all professional judges in Poland[32] — for a period of five years,[33] and in view of this fact it would be unreasonable to assume the courts' independence from administrative pressure. The appointment of the judges of the lower courts is in direct violation of the

[29]Constitution, Art. 25, para. 1.

[30]*The New Class* (New York: Frederick A. Praeger, 1960), p. 110.

[31]Constitution, Art. 51, para. 1 and 2, and the Statute on the Supreme Court (Ustawa o Sądzie Najwyższym), February 15, 1962, *Dz.U.* No. 11, Entry 54.

[32]*Rocznik Polityczny i Gospodarczy 1962* ("Political and Economic Yearbook") (Warsaw: Państwowe Wydawnictwo Ekonomiczne, 1962), p. 78.

[33]Constitution, Art. 51, para. 3, and the Statute on the Supreme Court. (See fn. 31 above.)

Constitution, which specifies that they must be elected.[34] The official explanation of this obvious unconstitutionality is that the introduction of the election of judges would yet be premature,[35] and the lack of independent and effective judicial review leaves the government's position unchallenged.

The outer limits of the administrative law are determined by the civil rights provisions of the Constitution. These provisions impose a restriction on the government and draw the line beyond which the legislative and executive branches are forbidden to advance. They protect a man against the monster of his own creation — a bureaucratic zealot determined to produce human well-being despite individual desire. The declared aim of the Polish People's Republic as specified in the Constitution is to fortify and enlarge the rights and freedoms of citizens;[36] therefore, it guarantees freedom of speech, press, assembly, and parade, and petition.[37] The Constitution lacks completely provisions determining the means by which these guarantees can be enforced.[38] In 1956 a Polish professor of law asked in desperation:

> What practical meaning have these provisions? Literally none! They mean either that these matters will be regulated in future legislation, obviously not bound by anything in the Constitution, or that. . .the previous valid legal state will remain without change.[39]

In any case the enforcement of these vital guarantees is left in the hands of the government. Since the Communist Party has complete control of the legislative and executive branches, its leadership is free to regulate these matters in any way suited to its purpose. The provisions do not impose any limitation in the sphere of administrative law or administrative action. The Constitution also forbids the creation of organizations with purposes or activities directed against the political and social structure of the Polish People's Republic.[40] Again, the determination of organizations subject to this provision is left to the government, which in practice may declare any association illegal.

[34]Constitution, Art. 50, para. 1.

[35]*Rocznik Polityczny i Gospodarczy 1962*, p. 78.

[36]Constitution, Art. 57.

[37]*Ibid.*, Art. 71.

[38]Compare the wording of the U.S. Constitution in the First Amendment, which explicitly forbids Congress to make laws abridging these freedoms.

[39]Kazimierz Biskupski, *Władza i Lud* ("The Rule and the People") (Warsaw: Książka i Wiedza, (1956), p. 21.

[40]Constitution, Art. 72, para. 3.

The administration could be restrained from infringement of civil liberties by independent courts and the procuracy, who enjoy a special position in all communist countries. As mentioned above, the courts are closely welded to the government and are not free or strong enough to oppose the political forces. Judges are appointed and can be recalled at any time by the Council of State. They are charged with the responsibility of protecting the system of the people's democracy and encouraging its development toward socialism.[41]

The procuracy, which forms a separate structure from the courts or other branches of state administration, is empowered by the Constitution to protect the rights of citizens.[42] It also is charged with the supervision of all state organs below the central government level as to the legality of their activity and their normative acts.[43] The Prosecutor General is appointed and recalled by the Council of State;[44] the prosecutors of the provinces are appointed by the chairman of the Council of State; and the county prosecutors by the Prosecutor General.[45] This mode of selection of the prosecutors indicates their dependence on the Communist Party, fully confirmed by practical observation of their activities. They cannot effectively defend the citizen against the administration if the government officials act with the blessing of the Party. They can only curb individual willfulness; they can never oppose the central government. The Party attitude toward the administration of justice in general has been stated brusquely by the First Secretary, Mr. Gomułka, in his speech to the Third Party Congress (March 1959):

> The fight to set the socialist justice and rule of law on solid grounds requires also that excessive liberalism be quickly overcome; it finds its expression in the disrespect shown to the activity of the People's State, in the gradual losing of the class approach to the administration of justice by some judicial bodies, and in a lenient treatment of abuses and embezzlement of public property.
>
> It is necessary to fight against these dangers as much by a proper selection of judicial officials, considering their moral and political

[41]The Law on the Structure of Common Courts (Prawo o Ustroju Sadów Powszechnych), *Dz.U.*, (1950), No. 39, Entry 360.

[42]Constitution, Art. 54, para. 1.

[43]The Statute on the Procuracy of the Polish People's Republic (Ustawa o Prokuraturze Polskiej Rzeczypospolitej Ludowej), July 20, 1950, *Dz.U.*, No. 38, Entry 346, Art. 3, para. 1 and 2.

[44]Constitution, Art. 55, para. 1.

[45]The Statute on the Procuracy. . . , Art. 8.

[46]Władysław Gomułka, *Przemówienia, 1959* ("Speeches") (Warsaw: Książka i Wiedza, 1959), p. 147.

attitude, as by a further adjustment of the existing legislation to the needs of the people's state and cementing the socialist social order.[46]

This approach to law reflects Russian, rather than Western European, legal tradition, according to which the role of law is to protect and support not so much the individual citizen as the state itself.[47]

Delegated Legislation

By "delegated legislation" we mean the ability of the administration to issue legally valid normative acts. It is clear from the above discussion that such legislation is not predetermined or checked effectively by the Constitution or by judicial review. The limitations that exist result from political controls or originate with the governmental hierarchy. Polish legal theory defines a normative act as that which "expresses a principle of action not consuming itself by application; it means applicable to an unspecified number of incidents."[48] In other words it is an act directed toward the general public and not addressed to a specifically named individual. In Poland, such acts are issued, first of all, by the *Sejm*, then by the Council of State and the Nation's Councils of all levels, and by all organs of the state administration – the Council of Ministers, individual ministers, the presidia of the Nation's Councils, and other specialized agencies of the government. The normative acts of the *Sejm* are basic and original legislation. The Council of State issues decrees with the same legal power as the acts of the *Sejm* when the latter body is not in session. These decrees must be approved by the *Sejm* at its next meeting.[49]

The question arising here is whether the decrees of the Council are delegated or original legislation. They are valid on pronouncement, and their validity cannot be challenged on the grounds that the *Sejm* may refuse their approval. In any case the question is theoretical since the communist-controlled *Sejm* never uses its right of invalidation. In fact, the large bulk of Polish legislation is in the form of Decrees of the Council, although the council is not a legislative, but an executive branch: a collective President of the Republic. The practice of legislation by decree

[47]For elaboration, see Harold J. Berman, *Justice in Russia; An Interpretation of Soviet Law* (Cambridge, Mass.: Harvard University Press, 1950); rev. ed. under title, *Justice in the U.S.S.R.* (New York: Vintage Books, 1963).

[48]Henryk Rot, *Akty Normatywne Rad Narodowych i Ich Prezydiów* ("Normative Acts of the Nation's Councils and Their Presidia") (Warsaw: Wydawnictwo Prawnicze, 1962), p. 32.

[49]Constitution, Art. 26, para. 1.

gives the government legal ground for legislation with the virtual omission of the representative body; such legislation, at least in parts, has the character of delegated and not parliamentary legislation. The Council of State, however, cannot enact by decree the National Economic Plan and Budget, as the Constitution specifically delegates enactment in this field to the *Sejm*.[50]

The Council of Ministers, individual ministers, and other heads of central government organs (commissions, committees, etc.) are entitled to issue normative acts, but only on the basis of existing statutes of the *Sejm* or decrees of the Council of State and for their fulfillment and enforcement.[51] The Council of Ministers is responsible to the *Sejm* and, between its sessions, to the Council of State.[52] On the basis of this hierarchical subordination, both the *Sejm* and the Council of State can revoke normative acts of the Council of Ministers or individual ministers.

The practice of delegating the legislative authority of the *Sejm* to the Council of Ministers is quite common. The best example is provided by the important statute on the Nation's Councils.[53] The statute leaves many vital decisions, which should have been settled by legislation (e.g., membership of the presidia and its functions and rights[54] and the principles of publication of the normative acts of the councils[55]) for regulation by the Council of Ministers. Delegation to individual ministers of the right to legislate on fundamental matters is also a common practice. For example, the Statute on the Elections to the Nation's Councils[56] leaves the regulations of the form and the manner of composition of the electoral rolls to the Minister of Internal Affairs. The roll may be used to pressure the electors to participate in elections and to vote for the official candidates. The Minister of Internal Affairs is also in charge of the Security Police (political police), a power which increases the possibility for intimidation of voters.

The Constitution does not empower *expressis verbis* the Nation's Councils to pass normative acts, apart from the regional economic plans

[50]*Ibid.*, Art. 19.

[51]*Ibid.*, Art. 32, para. 8.

[52]*Ibid.*, Art. 30, para. 2.

[53]Statute of January, 1958, on the Nation's Councils (Ustawa z dnia 25 stycznia 1958 r. o Radach Narodowych), *Dz.U.*, No. 5, Entry 16.

[54]*Ibid.,* Art. 52 and Art. 58, para. 2.

[55]*Ibid.*, Art. 36, para. 2.

[56]Ustawa z dnia 31 października 1957 r., Ordynacja Wyborcza Do Rad Narodowych, Art. 34, para. 1, *Dz. U.,* No. 55, Entry 270.

and budgets.[57] This prerogative can be deduced from the role of the Councils as "local parliaments" and is specified in the Statute on the Nation's Councils of 1958.[58] The Statute declares that the councils are entitled to issue legal acts generally applicable in the given territory on the basis of the existing law. The acts may be divided into two groups: acts issued as a result of the higher acts and for their fulfillment, and acts pronounced on a council's own initiative which are legally justified by the general statute of a superior order, such as the Constitution or parliamentary acts. As we progress down the structure of the Nation's Councils we find fewer and fewer acts on a council's own initiative and more acts on orders from above.

Many Polish jurists maintain that the presidia of the Nation's Councils also are empowered by the Statute of 1958 to issue normative acts.[59] This interpretation results from the fact that the provision on the normative acts is included in the general part of the Statute dealing with the Nation's Councils *sensu largo*. Despite the opposition of some Polish lawyers,[60] the presidia do in practice issue normative acts. Furthermore, a chairman of a presidium is permitted to issue normative regulations in emergencies, but these regulations require approval of the presidium at its earliest meeting.[61] If they are not submitted for consideration by the presidium, they automatically lose their validity as of the date of the meeting,[62] just as if their approval had been denied. Generally speaking, local normative acts are issued by the councils in their function as "local parliaments" and by the presidia as "local cabinets"; but the acts of the presidia are not, in practice, of a lower degree than the acts of the Councils, a situation which of course negates the principle of legislation exclusively by the local representatives and limits the representative independent character of the Nation's Councils. Moreover, most normative acts of the presidia are issued on the instructions from the Council of Ministers or individual ministries. This practice enables the government to enact valid normative acts without consultation of the parliament. All the Council of Ministers has to do is to instruct every presidium of every Province Nation's Council to promulgate

[57]Constitution, Art. 41.

[58]*Dz.U.*, No. 5, Entry 16.

[59]Rot, *op. cit.*, p. 16.

[60]A few legal scholars have devoted some attention to this controversy.

[61]Regulation of the Council of Ministers on the Rights and Duties of Members of the Presidia of the Councils (Rozporządzenie Rady Ministrów o Prawach i Obowiązkach Członków Prezydiów Rad), *Dz.U.*, No. 48, Entry 236.

[62]Statute of 1958, Art. 57, para. 3.

the same normative act. In this way the government obtains legislation binding the entire Republic without the formal act of the *Sejm*.

The question of publication of the normative acts of the Nation's Councils and their organs is not clearly settled by the existing law. The Constitution does not mention this problem, and it is felt by some of the Polish jurists that this is yet another important omission related to the issue of delegated legislation.[63] The Constitution requires only publication of the statutes of the *Sejm* and decrees of the Council of State, but even in this case does not make the validity of these acts dependent on publication.[64] The publication of the acts of the central government is regulated by the Statute of 1950 on the publication of *Dziennika Ustaw* and of *Monitor Polski*.[65] The Statute of 1958 on the Nation's Councils leaves the problem of publication for solution by the Council of Ministers.[66] The council issued the appropriate regulation in 1958.[67] It commanded the publication in the official gazettes of the provinces of all "legal regulations" of the Nation's Councils and their presidia.[68] The regulation does not explain what is meant by "legal regulations" and, in practice, many normative acts of the local government are not published at all. As a rule, taxation acts, acts establishing housing density norms,[69] and acts on the commune funds[70] are not included in the official gazettes. Also omitted are the acts on the budget and the economic plan. A close look at the character of these acts may suggest that for political reasons their publication is embarrassing for the government or that the government does not wish to publicize economic plans and budgets too widely.

Still another weakness of the existing law on delegated legislation should be mentioned: the lack of uniform legal nomenclature. As a result, normative acts appear under a great variety of titles (regulations,

[63] Jaroszyński, *op. cit.*, pp. 181-3

[64] Constitution, Art. 20 and Art. 26.

[65] *Dz.U.*, No. 58, Entry 524.

[66] Art. 36, para. 2.

[67] *Dz.U.*, No. 19, Entry 78.

[68] *Ibid.*, para. 3.

[69] How many meters of living space should be allocated to one person.

[70] Commune funds result from the difference between the market price and the price paid to farmers for compulsory deliveries. These sums are returned to the local government for use on special projects: e.g. road-building.

resolutions, acts, laws, decrees, etc.), which makes classification extremely difficult if not altogether impossible.[71]

Administrative Decisions

An administrative decision is the definite and final expression of the will of an administrative organ. It can be prepared by any functionary of the administration, but it is always issued in the name of the organ and over the signature of its director. However, the decision is valid even if the official has overstepped his regulatory power, e.g., issued a decision without the knowledge of the director.[72] In issuing a decision, the organ represents the state and binds not only itself, but also the whole state administration.

In Polish administrative law, administrative decisions are divided into two basic types: one-sided and two-sided. One-sided decisions are valid without the wish of the affected party: e.g., the military draft. Two-sided decisions result from the application of a petitioner (e.g., for a change of name). In both cases the administrative organ must act on the basis of law[73] and cannot refuse to take prescribed action. In addition, the organ "is bound by the directives of the economic plan, political norms (which often do not have the form of a legal norm), and norms of socialist morality."[74] In plain language, the administration is directed in its decisions by the party, which determines the "socialist morality" or extra-legal code of administrative behavior based not on law but on political expediency. As is often pointed out by many communist jurists, this has a special application in the communist state, in which the administration is called upon to participate actively in building the new society. A similar degree of partly illegal flexibility is given to the organs of justice.

Normative acts often allow the administration a certain amount of discretion in its activities. They indicate that an administrative organ acts by its own judgment, they permit several different solutions of the same matter, or they direct the organ to issue an administrative act without specifying the conditions and form of such an act. They also may instruct the organ to decide in accordance with the general policies of the state and public interest, leaving the definition of both to the administration

[71]Rot, *op.cit.*, p. 88.

[72]Starościak and Iserzon, *op.cit.*, pp. 210, 211. The official, of course, is subject to disciplinary or even criminal procedure.

[73]Constitution, Art. 4, para. 3.

[74]Starościak and Iserzon, *op.cit.*, p. 169.

itself.[75] In all these instances the freedom of decision-making is limited by Party control and by the right of reversal granted the higher bodies in the state structure.

A certain amount of discretion is necessary for efficient administration. Officials should not be unduly restricted by the central administration in their everyday activities. In practice, constant interference by the local secretary of the Party is quite common and is criticized even by the Party's top leadership as hindering effective administration. At the same time the Central Committee of the Communist Party holds the local secretaries responsible for the performance of local government, and it is unreasonable to expect any of them to refrain from assuming a role as actual heads of the local administration.

Communist ideology requires the administration to participate actively in "the organization of the toiling masses for labor and improvement of their material conditions."[76] This task requires special "socio-organizational" decisions. These usually result from normative acts commanding certain projects but not specifying a means of execution. For example, the Statute of 1958 on the Nation's Councils requires local government to forest wastelands and protect woods.[77] Decisions in socio-organizational matters do not have binding legal power and cannot be enforced by administrative execution. Administration must use other means at its disposal, such as various types of incentives (bonuses, medals, and agitation). In practice, when socio-organizational persuasion fails, the administration presses the local Nation's Council to pass a normative act and then to enforce it with full use of the state repressive power. In fact, citizens have very little choice; if persuasion fails they must perform the required function under the force of law.

The validity of a given administrative decision is determined by the following conditions:

1. It must be issued by the organ legally competent to act (i.e., competent as to its place in the administrative hierarchy and its geographical location).

2. It must be in accordance with provisions of law which allow settlement of the given matter by the administrative decision and not, for example, by restricting it to a normative act.

3. It must be prepared and delivered in the strictly prescribed manner.[78] Administrative procedure is regulated by the Code of Adminis-

[75]*Ibid.*, p. 171.

[76]*Ibid.*, p. 176.

[77]Art. 24, para. 3.

[78]Starościak and Iserson, *op. cit.*, p. 171.

trative Procedure of 1960.[79] According to the Code's general principles, the organs of administration should: (a) act on the basis of law, interpreted in accordance with the interest and with the goals of the construction of socialism (here the Code repeats the general provisions of the Constitution discussed above); (b) guard socialist legality and, therefore, enforce observance of the law by the subordinate administrative units and by the citizens; (c) act in an objective manner and determine fully all existing facts; (d) act in the interest of society and in the justifiable interest of a citizen; (e) ensure that the parties are not harmed because of ignorance of the law; (f) allow full representation of the parties before arriving at a decision; (g) preferably apply persuasion rather than force and explain fully a negative decision; (h) act directly and speedily (matters which do not require documentation should be dealt with at once; other business must be considered within two months from the date of application); and finally, (i) deliver all decisions in writing.[80]

The provisions of the Code concentrate on two areas: one ensures that the administration protects the interests of the state and the political goals of the ruling Communist Party; the second protects the citizen from undue frustration and abuse in his dealing with the bureaucracy. The first area already is well protected by all existing law, including the Constitution, and its repetition in the Code is simply one more restatement of the obvious. Protection of a citizen's right is grossly neglected, and legislation in this field is very necessary. However, one may suspect that one more statute will not greatly improve the matter unless the general attitude and the relationship between the ruled and the rulers change. As long as the state's interest is accorded unlimited priority and the individual is regarded as a cog in the machinery of the steam-roller smoothly moving toward communism, no formal legislation will ensure protection of the citizen. This is obvious to anyone who has had the unpleasant experience of trying to settle even the simplest matter in a Polish office. The rudeness of lower officials is enough to convince anyone of the obvious fact that not the citizen but the man behind the desk is the king.

> The official is allowed to forget the citizen's grievance; he can lose his petition; he does not have to keep the stated deadline. But let the citizen be late a day. . . then nothing can help him.[81]

The application of the Code is not vigorous partly because many officials are not familiar with this long and complicated document and

[79]Kodeks Postępowania Administracyjnego, *Dz.U.*, No. 30, Entry 168 (henceforth referred to as the Code).

[80]*Rocznik Polityczny i Gospodarczy 1961*, pp. 149-51.

[81]Wiesław Iwanicki, "Pisz na Berdyczów," *Trybuna Ludu* (Warsaw) No. 55 (February 24, 1962).

partly because of inefficient organization of work, which prevents the issuance of decisions in the prescribed period of time.[82] Also, the communist belief that all human ills can be corrected by detailed administrative regulations—which produces a flood of orders, instructions, and directives originating from the top and descending like a plague on the lower organs—does not help matters. Civil servants are busy answering forms and sending out the required regulations to subordinate bodies and do not have time to act on applications of ordinary citizens, who are considered unwelcome intruders.

Polish administrative law adheres to the principle of appeals inside the administrative structure and does not utilize judiciary or special administrative courts. The Code establishes as an appellate body the organ directly above the one which decides in the first instance.[83] Thus the presidium of the County Council serves as the appellate organ for the presidium of the Commune Council, and the presidium of the Province Council works in the same capacity for the presidium of the County. Logically, therefore, no appeal is possible from decisions of the central agencies.

In connection with the appellate system, all decisions are divided in legal terminology into final and temporary decisions. A final decision is one not subject to appeal, and all rulings of central organs and of second-instance organs fall into this category. Temporary decisions can be appealed only once. All decisions become final if they are not challenged within fourteen days from the date of their pronouncement. A temporary decision cannot be enforced by the state during this fourteen-day period, but a citizen is free to carry it out immediately, provided he is the only person affected.[84] In case of appeal, the appellate body is required to pass its judgment within a month, unless special conditions require the extension of this statutory period.[85] A decision of the first instance must be executed immediately if it is so decided by a specific statute[86] or if such a performance is necessary because of specific circumstances resulting from the following: danger to human health and life, prevention of heavy material losses to the national economy, a specially important interest of the affected party, or some other important social consideration. For example, an order to repair a building in danger of collapsing must be executed at once. The party which suffers losses as a result of immediate execution must be paid damages by the deciding organ of administra-

[82]Jadwiga Mikołajczyk, "Przestroga," *Trybuna Ludu*, No. 340 (December 11, 1961).

[83]Art. 110, para. 2.

[84]Code, Art. 113, para. 1 and 2.

[85]*Ibid.*, Art. 32, para. 1 and Art. 116.

[86]*Ibid.*, Art. 113, para. 3.

tion.[87] A temporary decision may be performed before the end of the fourteen days set for appeal if it is acceptable to all parties or if all parties relinquish in writing their right to appeal.[88]

The question arises as to who is competent to rule on the acceptability of a temporary decision. The Code is rather vague in this matter, and there is a danger that, at least in some instances, citizens may be deprived by the administrative organ of their right to appeal if the organ chooses to rule that the decision is to their satisfaction. Some Polish writers argue that such a ruling requires consent in writing by the parties,[89] but this is not explicitly evident in the Code itself. An appeal must be addressed to the organ of the second instance but deposited with the office of original decision.[90] The latter is legally bound to convey the petition to the appellate body and to notify all concerned parties of the appeal.[91] It also is entitled to repeal its own decision within fourteen days on the basis of the appeal of all parties.

A special role is accorded to the procurator who, apart from serving as the prosecutor for the state, is a guardian of the legality of all administrative decisions and a protector of the rights of citizens.[92] The latter function gives him the right to be a party to any administrative procedure and as such to appeal a temporary decision, but only on legal grounds.[93] The procurator may appeal in the interest of the party or against it, depending on his interpretation of law. In addition, social and professional organizations can require to be included in any administrative action in their field of activity as defined by their charter or if inclusion is demanded by social interest.[94] They are considered to represent the whole society, although they might be regarded as specific pressure groups which do or do not represent the public interest. They are often used as spokesmen for the Communist Party, owing to the communist control of their leadership, on occasions when the Party regards its own direct intervention as politically unwise. If they participate in administrative action they automatically obtain the right to appeal a temporary decision.

[87]*Ibid.*, Art. 100, para. 1.

[88]*Ibid.*, Art. 115.

[89]Dawidowicz, *op. cit.*, p. 205.

[90]Code, Art. 112, para. 1.

[91]*Ibid.*, Art. 114.

[92]Statute on Procuracy, *op. cit.*, Art. 3.

[93]Code, Art. 114.

[94]*Ibid.*, Art. 28.

The Code gives the citizen a fair chance to petition for redress of what he considers to be an unjust decision. This safeguards his interest from the illicit actions of minor officials but, as the decisions of the central authorities are not subject to review, it does not protect him against the state itself. The practice of appeal within the structure of the administration, with the higher officers reviewing the activities of their subordinates, protects the bureaucracy from public challenge to their general policies. The interference by the procurator's office and by social and professional organizations is actually a check on the administration to see that it does not violate the general line of the Party, and is not an added protection for the individual.

Criminal-Administrative Colleges

Petty offenses or misdemeanors are dealt with in Poland by special courts called Criminal-Administrative Colleges, which are not to be confused with the French Administrative Courts functioning as appellate bodies from administrative decisions. The colleges are closer in character to Justices of the Peace in the United States, although they are not a part of the judiciary system but are incorporated in the structure of the Nation's Councils and hence are an appendage of the administration. The principles of this system originated in the prewar period,[95] and the colleges are now regulated by the Statute on the Criminal-Administrative Pronouncements of 1951.[96]

The colleges have primary jurisdiction in cases specified explicitly by the law, excluding treasury matters and business which is under the competence of territorial organs operating outside the structure of the Nation's Councils.[97] Among these are the Marine, Mining, and Measurements Offices. The colleges are attached to the presidia of the Province and County Nation's Councils, and to the presidia of cities with province or county status. The Commune Nation's Councils, if they so wish, may constitute the colleges, subject to approval by the county presidium. The province colleges are exclusively organs of appeal. Each college is composed of a chairman, vice-chairman, and ordinary members, all elected

[95]Regulation on the Criminal-Administrative Procedure of 1928 (Rozporządzenie o Postępowaniu Karno-Administracyjnym), *Dz.U.*, No. 38, Entry 365.

[96]Ustawa o Orzecznictwie Karno-Administracyjnym, amended in 1958. Uniform text, *Dz.U.* (1959) No. 15, Entry 79 (henceforth referred to as the Statute on C.A.P.).

[97]Statute on C.A.P., Art. 2, para. 1.

by the parent council for a three-year term. On the average, the membership of the county colleges is about thirty.[98] The chairman and vice-chairman should have law degrees,[99] but regular judges and officials of the procuracy and attorneys-at-law cannot be elected to membership in the colleges.[100] The exclusion determines that, in practice, the leading positions in the colleges will be filled by employees of the administration, because outside the administration, procuracy, advocacy, and judiciary there are few people with legal training. The chairman is usually one of the members of the presidium and the vice-chairman is one of the officials of the presidium's Department of Criminal-Administrative Pronouncements – most likely its head.[101] The inclusion of local administrators in the colleges ensures the uniformity of sentences with the general policy of the state and limits greatly the independence of the criminal-administrative courts. This limitation is strengthened by the prerogative of the chairman, who may request a Nation's Council to recall any member of the college: considering the normal docility of the councils, such a request may be equated with removal. One Polish writer rightly complains that administrators are made judges by the system of criminal-administrative jurisdiction.[102] It is only fair to point out that communist political theory does not recognize the formal division of governmental powers. The normal courts, however, can maintain more independence, at least from local administration, and a citizen is generally better protected by the ordinary judiciary.

The colleges do not sit as one court but are divided into panels, (membership determined by the chairman) which judge individual cases and impose penalties of three kinds: censure, fine, and imprisonment. A censure is the mildest form of punishment and is applied in crimes from which the social damage is minimal.[103] The colleges' fines range from 5 to 4,500 zlotys (about 20 cents to 187 dollars at the official rate of exchange) depending on the gravity of the offense and the limits specified in statutes. In case of nonpayment, a term of imprisonment is imposed in

[98]Starościak and Iserzon, *op. cit.*, p. 252.

[99]Statute on C.A.P., Art. 5, para. 2.

[100]Regulation of the Minister of Internal Affairs (Rozporządzenie Ministra Spraw Wewnętrznych), February 18, 1959, *Dz.U.*, No. 15, Entry 81.

[101]Starościak and Iserzon, *op. cit.*, p. 252.

[102]Jaroszyński, *op. cit.*, p. 228.

[103]Starościak and Iserzon, *op. cit.*, p. 254.

which one day of prison is equal to twenty to forty zlotys.[104] The basic penalty of imprisonment from one day to the maximum of thirty days cannot be combined with a fine unless the crime involves an illegal profit. The colleges transfer the cases to normal courts if they consider that the offense requires a more severe punishment than permitted by the criminal-administrative system.[105]

There are four types of procedure under the criminal-administrative system: normal, command, accelerated, and mandate. Normal procedure is started by an accusation by state organs or institutions, or by social organizations or an individual citizen. The chairman examines the accusation, and if in his opinion it requires a trial, he appoints a panel to hear the case and sets the date. He may order the civic militia (police) to conduct an additional investigation. Only in special circumstances is the accused excused from appearing in person and, if he is absent without permission, the panel may order that he be brought in by force. During the hearing the accused has the right to appoint a counsel; any citizen qualifies. An attorney-at-law may represent a client only in cases involving a prison sentence or in appeals. The role of public prosecutor is played by a member of the militia or another organ of state administration designated for this function by the Council of Ministers. The panel may invite a social organization of which the accused is a member to give evidence as to his character. The case is public and is presided over by the chairman of the panel, who rules on matters of procedure and order. The procedure is much more informal than that of the normal courts. In a case in which the accused pleads guilty, no further hearing is necessary and the panel delivers its decision at once.

In a command procedure the decision is reached by the chairman of the college without the hearing; this method can be employed only in minor offenses in which the fine is no more than 300 zlotys.[106] The accused can appeal the decision and demand a panel hearing.

The accelerated procedure may be of the normal or command type, and it differs from the two only in the shorter period permitted for an appeal (three days instead of seven) and in the provision that the sentence must be executed immediately. The accelerated procedure cannot be employed

[104]Emanuel Iserzon, "Reforma Orzecznictwa Karno-Administracyjnego," *Państwo i Prawo*, No. 8-9 (1959), 261.

[105]The maximum prison term and the maximum fine are the same as provided for by the Law on Violations of 1932, but the value of the maximum penalty of 4,500 zlotys was much higher in 1932 than it is today, when the average monthly net wage is 1,980 zlotys. See *Rocznik Statystyczny, 1968*, ("Statistical Yearbook") (Warsaw: Główny Urząd Statystyczny, 1968), p. 520.

[106]Starościak and Iserzon, *op. cit.*, p. 257.

by the college at will but must be introduced by the chairman of the Council of Ministers for the whole of the Republic or by the presidium of the Province Nation's Council for the territory of the province. It cannot be in force for longer than six months. It is used only when there is an abnormal increase in specific crimes.

The mandate procedure is the simplest method employed, and it applies to minor violations in which the offender is apprehended committing the crime and there is no doubt as to his identity. The maximum penalty is 100 zlotys collected on the spot by the arresting officer of the militia or other organ entitled to do so by the chairman of the Council of Ministers. The offender must express his agreement to the imposition of the penalty in this way or otherwise he must be accused and tried at a proper hearing.

The decision of the college may be appealed within seven days to a normal (county) court if it involves a prison sentence, or to the next higher college in all other cases. The right to appeal is given to the accused as well as to the procurator, the militia, or the organ which prosecuted and the state body which provided the original accusation. The appeal may be tried publicly or in camera if the appellate college so decides.

The general supervision of the activity of the Criminal-Administrative Colleges is exercised by the Ministry of Internal Affairs and by the Nation's Councils and their organs over the colleges in their territory. The presidium of the Province Nation's Council can annul any decision of the college in the province if it decides that it is without legal grounds or obviously unjust; the annulment may be in favor of the sentenced at any time, and against him only within three months from the date of the decision. In annuling a decision, the presidium instructs the college to try the case again, but with a different panel.

The importance of the criminal-administrative jurisdiction is illustrated by the fact that in 1967 the colleges dealt with 505,100 cases, while in the same period the common courts heard 348,000 criminal cases.[107] The following table describes the nature of crimes under the jurisdiction of the Criminal-Administrative Colleges and their frequency between 1961 and 1967.[108]

The special jurisdiction for minor offenses outside the normal court system is perhaps necessary and justified, provided that it guarantees the citizen at least a minimum safeguard against bureaucratic abuses. The Polish system of Criminal-Administrative Colleges is too closely connected with the actual administration to assure this basic protection. Filling of all the leading positions by the administrative officials is unwarranted. Ordinary citizens could perform the judicial functions with more

[107]*Rocznik Statystyczny, 1968*, pp. 586, 589.

[108]*Ibid.*, table 4, p. 586.

ADMINISTRATIVE PENALTIES[a]

	1961	1962	1963	1964	1965	1966	1967
				in thousands			
Cases submitted	463.1	435.6	475.7	453.0[b]	465.6	495.0	505.5
Cases dismissed	55.6	42.6	42.5	27.9	34.1	37.8	35.1
Penalties imposed in this for offenses in the following categories:	357.8	329.8	356.9	295.0	362.0	402.1	413.0
Petty thievery, speculation etc.[c]	–	–	–	–	–	–	19.5
Hooliganism and alcoholism	134.0	128.7	143.7	121.7	134.7	146.7	143.8
Order on public roads	51.0	63.2	76.9	79.5	113.6	136.9	138.6
Public health and sanitary regulations	18.8	17.4	17.2	11.2	13.7	14.0	14.2
Prevention of fire regulations	10.5	10.6	13.6	8.3	8.0	8.5	6.8
Agriculture, animal husbandry and forestry	38.9	32.1	30.0	19.5	26.7	22.6	17.7
Administration and control of population movement	12.6	13.5	16.0	11.7	17.6	15.1	14.3
Others	92.0	64.3	59.5	43.1	47.7	56.3	58.1
Persons found not guilty	70.8	59.3	59.8	47.9	53.7	48.8	41.8

a. Decided by the Criminal–Administrative Colleges attached to the presidia of the Nation's Councils.
b. Together with the cases included in the amnesty – Decree on Amnesty, July 20, 1964 (*Dz. U.*, No. 27, Entry 174). By the power of the amnesty in 86.8 thousand cases the procedure was not originated or it was dismissed.
c. Cases transferred to the competence of the Criminal-Administrative Colleges on January 1, 1967 (The Statute on the Transfer of Some Petty Crimes as Misdemeanors to the Criminal-Administrative Jurisdiction, June 17, 1966, *Dz. U.*, No. 23, Entry 149).

objectivity and general fairness if they were assisted by legally trained clerks. Again one suspects political motivation, which tends to result in the staffing of all branches of the government having quasi-judicial duties with state bureaucrats in order to ensure the protection of the state's interest in all aspects of life. Even with trusted personnel, the leadership has felt it necessary to allocate the power of annulment to the province presidia, doubly ensuring that even one drunkard cannot rock the boat of the communist state.

Conclusion

The jungle of Polish administrative law is thicker than that in most other states. It bars entrance not only to a curious casual intruder but also to a professional hunter. A well-known Polish professor of administrative law used to start his classes by declaring that, if total Polish law is "one hundred," administrative law alone is "ninety-nine."[109] This percentage applies not only to bulk but also to internal complication. The confusion results from the imposition of a new system on the old, and in many respects fine, tradition. It also results from the schizophrenia of the communist mind which, on the one hand, desires to provide more freedom of expression on ideological grounds and more decentralization necessitated by the demands of a modern industrial society and, on the other hand, fears revolution and is addicted to controls. The Polish Constitution, the statutes, and the administrative law itself are full of paragraphs guaranteeing personal freedoms and protection of citizens against the state, only to be nullified by other provisions which take these guarantees away because they stem from the assumption that the citizens and the state are one. The traditional defenders of civil rights — the independent courts — are deprived of their role by the theoretical denial of the division between the judiciary, legislature, and administration. The courts are only an appendage to the state administration, and the role of the law, and especially of administrative law, is to ensure that the state and Party policies are enforced. The protection of the individual occupies a secondary role. Obsession with controls produces many anomalies which create difficulty in determining the law and therefore make enforcement hard, if not, in many cases, impossible. It is not easy to decide on the hierarchical order of statutes, regulations, and orders, many of which are written in a confusing and contradictory manner. Practice shows that in many instances the administrator with the best intentions cannot decide which law to apply and is forced to take short cuts — unfortunately not always legal. Here, the Communist Party, the master of legal simplifica-

[109]Prof. Emanuel Iserzon.

387

tion, plays its role by instructing the administration in the right procedure. In many cases the Party's intervention is necessary to cut through the jungle of legal and administrative confusion. "Socialist legality" is an unwritten law of political expediency as pronounced by the leadership of the Communist Party. It is as if in Poland there were two sets of state law — one on the books and yet another, superior to the first, in the Party's program of the day.

WENCESLAS J. WAGNER

General Features of Polish Contract Law

General Features of Polish Contract Law[1]

Quite naturally, the political upheaval imposed upon the Central European countries after World War II brought about important changes in their legal systems. As far as the area of "public law" is concerned, it could not be otherwise. But what was the impact of the structural developments of these states on their "private law," and particularly, on the law of contracts?

It can readily be seen that the area of matters on which individual citizens may contract is much more restricted in those countries than in countries with traditional legal systems. The so-called "socialist" states which are "on the way to communism" introduced as one of their first economic reforms the principle of state ownership of most means of production and business enterprises.[2] The industrial and commercial life of the country, as well as the relations between the state enterprises or "socialist organizations," are based on economic planning.[3] In such a situation,

---

[1] The author expresses his gratitude to Professor Rudolf B. Schlesinger of Cornell Law School for his valuable suggestions on the original draft of this study. A part of this study is based on the introduction to the Polish law of contracts, prepared by the author for the fall 1961 session of the General Principles Project of Cornell Law School and published, with some changes, in *American Journal of Comparative Law*, XI (1962), p. 348. The term "socialist" is used in this article interchangeably with "communist," and pertains to countries utilizing planned economy.

[2] The most important branches of Poland's economy were nationalized by the law of Jan. 3, 1946, *Dz.U.*, Feb. 5, 1946, No. 4, Item 17, as amended.

[3] Economic planning was introduced by the decree of Oct. 1, 1947, *Dz.U.* No. 64, Item 374 (1947). Art. 3 of the Constitution of 1952 provided that the Republic shall "organize a planned economy on the basis of enterprises in social ownership."

there is not much room for commercial transactions of importance between private individuals or enterprises.[4]

In spite of the fact that all communist countries have a common ideological background, and that the economic system of the Soviet Union exerts a strong influence on all the others, there is no uniform pattern in their economic structure. As a matter of fact, differences between them are pronounced. The situation in Poland and Yugoslavia is more similar to that of the traditional economic systems than that in other communist states. Thus, contrary to many other communist countries, agricultural land in Poland has remained by and large in private hands (though the larger farms have been liquidated), with some degree of freedom left to the farmers.[5] Of course, they are required to sell the major part of their farm products to the state. Although, in theory, such deliveries are made in accordance with contracts concluded between the state and the producers, in fact the system amounts to a kind of tax. What remains may be used by the farmer or sold on the open market, subject – in many instances – to price regulations enacted by the state. Nevertheless, in such situations the contractual relations between the parties involved are more or less similar to those existing between contracting parties in the traditional systems of law. Moreover, handicrafts and some small industrial enterprises, although heavily burdened with taxes, have been left in the hands of private individuals.

In the socialized sector, also, Polish law speaks of contracts, meaning contracts between state enterprises. But are such contracts comparable to consensual obligations in the traditional sense? Of course, "such a problem cannot be determined by labels."[6]

For some problems of such a system, see, e.g., Pounds and Spulber, eds., *Resources and Planning in Eastern Europe* (1957).

[4]In Poland, as early as 1948, 94% of industry was nationalized. See Szwejcer, "Les nationalisations en Pologne," in *14 Travaux et recherches de l'Institut de Droit Compare de l'Universite de Paris; Les nationalisations en France et à l'étranger* (1958), pp. 213, 241.

[5]Siekanowicz, "Land and Peasant in Poland," in Gsovski and Grzybowski, *Government, Law and Courts in the Soviet Union and Eastern Europe* (1959), II, 1809. In 1956, 78.8% of arable land was in the hands of individual farmers, 8.6% belonged to collective farms, and 12.6% constituted government farms. *Ibid.*, p. 1843.

[6]Schlesinger, "The Common Core of Legal Systems – An Emerging Subject of Comparative Study," in *XXth Century Comparative and Conflicts Law – Legal Essays in Honor of Hessel E. Yntema* (1961), pp. 65, 69. The author continues: "The fact that two institutions both are labeled 'contract,' does not make them comparable. Nor is comparability assured by superficial similarities of positive rules or of other institutional elements." He concludes: "In functional terms, the

Contracts in the Poland of today may be concluded between three types of parties: private individuals, cooperatives, and state-owned enterprises. Subject to some important qualifications to be discussed later, consensual obligations among members of the first group do not differ from those concluded in the traditional legal systems. On the other hand, contracts concluded between socialized economic units constitute a new legal institution. Besides these two extremes, there are intermediate situations: contracts concluded between socialist entities on one part, and individuals or co-operatives on the other. Many of those belong to the first category (e.g., a co-operative purchases supplies from a government store). Some, however, are regulated by special rules unknown in the traditional legal systems such as the contract of "contractation," as will be explained below.

In foreign trade, the state or one of its corporations may enter into contracts with "capitalist" parties. In such a case, it is clear that traditional rules of contract law will apply. With reference to foreign trade, General Conditions of Delivery of Goods have been adopted by international agreement among the communist countries. Interestingly, these General Conditions by and large reflect traditional rules of contract law.

In the following observations about consensual obligations in Poland, the traditional contracts will be discussed first. "Contracts" among socialized economic units will then be taken up. This will be followed by a brief discussion of international contracts covered by the General Conditions of Delivery of Goods.

Traditional Contracts

Consensual obligations in the modern Polish state were governed by the Code of Obligations of October 27, 1933, in force as of July 1, 1934,[7] supplemented by the Commercial Code of June 27, 1934, in force as of the same year.[8] These Polish enactments,[9] the result of many years of hard work and careful drafting, were favorably received all over the world. This is what the great French legal scholar Henri Capitant stated in his preface to the French translation of the Code of Obligations:

comparability of a free contract and of a contract between plan-fulfilling state enterprises is highly problematic."

[7]*Dz.U.*, October 28, 1933, No. 82, Item 598.

[8]*Dz.U.* June 30, 1934, No. 57, Item 502, as amended.

[9]For details about the work of codifying Polish law, see Nagorski, "Codification of Civil Law in Poland (1918-1939)," in *Studies in Polish and Comparative Law* (London 1945).

The qualities of method and of formulation are undeniable and striking even at first sight. . . . Because of its precision, its clarity and the shortness of its articles, the Polish Code is much more akin to the Swiss Civil Code than to the German. It has avoided heavy and unpleasant casuistry. . . . We believe the work to be completely successful.[10]

The relationship between the Commercial Code and the Code of Obligations was regulated by the following provisions of the Commercial Code:

Art. 498 § 1. Legal transactions of a merchant, connected with the running of his enterprise, are commercial transactions.

Art. 499. If a transaction is commercial for one of the parties, the rules of commercial law are applicable to both parties, unless the law provides otherwise.

After World War II, both codes remained in force, except for some provisions which were repealed. They had to be applied in the light of a new law on the General Principles of Civil Law, enacted first on November 12, 1946,[11] and in another version on July 18, 1950.[12] This statute repealed and changed many articles in the general part of the Code of Obligations and simply restated some others.

This statute and the Code were the primary source of the law of contracts in Poland until 1965, during the efforts to codify the law.[13] A draft

[10]Nagórski, "Draft of a New Civil Code for Poland," in *Studies of the Association of Polish Lawyers in Exile in the United States,* I (1956) pp. 51, 52-3. The Code has been translated into French by Sieczkowski and Wasilkowski, with cooperation of Henri Mazeaud (*Code des Obligations,* 1935).

[11]*Dz. U.,* 1946, No. 67, Item 369.

[12]*Dz. U.,* July 22, 1950, No. 34, Item 311.

[13]For a presentation of the problem by a judge of the Supreme Court of Poland see Bachrach, "Problems of Legislation and Codification in Poland," *Law in the Service of Peace,* IV (New Series) (1956), p. 85. For him, the problems "directly relevant" to legislation and codification are "the forms of the class struggle." The important considerations for legislative policy were as follows: "After the rout of isolated groups of rebels, we had to cope with the resistance and active opposition of the bourgeois class, more particularly of the big landowners in the countryside and the petty bourgeoisie of the towns, which, undoubtedly less vital, was none the less bitter and dangerous. The attack launched by the class enemy was most keenly felt in those places where the result of our policy had been weakest" (p. 86). "Concern for giving expression through law to the will and to the interests of the working people is shown precisely in the search for suitable juridical methods and in the form that they assume" (p.88). See also Wasilkowska, "Zadania Komisji Kodyfikacyjnej" ("Tasks Confronting the Codifying Commission"), *Państwo i*

civil code prepared by the Ministry of Justice in 1947-8 was inconsequential. In the light of comments by one of the theoreticians of the socialist law, the reason for the failure was the fact that the project attempted to improve the old system of law rather than to establish a new one conforming to the changed conditions of the political and social structure of the state,[14] and using Soviet patterns as a model in order to avoid costly experiments.[15] On September 27, 1950, the presidium of the government decided again to instruct the Minister of Justice to take care of the job, along with the preparation of a new criminal code. A drafting committee was appointed by the minister, the latter reserving the chairmanship for himself. The project was ready in 1954. Discussions followed in legal periodicals and during a special meeting of jurists, organized by the Polish Academy of Sciences and the Ministry of Justice on December 8-10, 1954. The proceedings of this meeting were published.[16]

During the three days of discussions, seven sessions were held. Two were devoted to the law of obligations. One dealt with the problem of performance of contracts and liability for nonperformance; the other with some questions of the law of sales. The third part of the Draft Code covered the law of obligations.

The traditionally fundamental principle of the law of obligations, that of freedom of contracting, has been omitted from the Draft Code of 1954. There was no mention even that a contract is an enforceable agreement between the parties. An obligation, according to the Draft Code, is a right of the creditor to request some performance from the debtor. The traditional principle had been preserved, with some limitations, in the project of 1948, Article 579 of which read as follows:

> Within the limits settled by the law in force, and in particular by provisions on economic planning, the coming into being and the contents of contractual obligations are subject to the free will of the parties.[17]

Prawo, XII (1957), No. 1. The author points out that the main idea of codification of the Polish law is the "socialist democratization" of the law.

[14]Wolter, *Prawo cywilne, częsc ogolna* ("Civil Law, General Part") (1955), pp. 46-7; 2nd ed. (1963) p. 41.

[15]*Ibid.*, p. 48. This observation has been omitted from the second edition.

[16]*Materjaƚy dyskusyjne de projektu kodeksu cywilnego Polskiej Rzeczypospolitej Ludowej* ("Discussion Materials to the Draft of a Civil Code of the Polish People's Republic") (1955).

[17]*Ibid.*, p. 184.

The 1954 project had no similar provision. The omission was pointed out and criticized during the discussion of December 9, 1954. Professor Czachórski[18] said in his paper:

It seems that the project goes too far and avoids even a most careful and general mention of the effect of intention on the creation, contents, and performance of obligations, within the boundaries set by mandatory principles of law (ius cogens), and particularly, by the rules on economic planning. The project only includes various limitations and modifications of the principle of "freedom of contracts" which is not spelled out clearly. The limitations concern primarily intercourse between entities of a socialized economy.

The lack of a general provision laying down the principle of "freedom of contracts" seems particularly unfounded with respect to relations between individuals. In my opinion, this principle should not be given too great importance. However, only this principle can justify the existence. . .of (some) contracts. . . .[19]

The Draft Code of 1954 met with criticism and was not recognized as satisfactory. On many points criticism went in the direction opposite to that of Professor Czachórski. Opinion was expressed that the Draft did not depart substantially enough from the traditional approach and did not take into account the new socialist way of life; and the Supreme Court of Poland refused to attach much importance to the rules laid down by the Draft. It held that the Draft was merely an expression of the opinions of the committee which prepared it as the best method of regulating legal institutions in a way most conforming to the social, economic, and political foundations of the present system of government. The court added that there was no ground for believing that solutions contrary to the Draft, and resting on the presently applicable legal provisions, such as the Code of Obligations, would be repugnant to the principles of the system of government and to the purposes of the People's State.[20]

[18]Vice-President, University of Warsaw, and former Dean of the Law School.

[19]In the 1960-1 issues of some Polish legal periodicals, Professors Buczkowski, Wolter, Jodłowski, and Gwiazdomorski engaged in a discussion about freedom of contracts. The last asserted that freedom in the traditional sense did not exist in Poland any more, in spite of the fact that Art. 55 of the Code of Obligations, proclaiming freedom, had not yet been abrogated.

[20]Supreme Court decision of May 25, 1955 (4 Cr. 516/55) in *O.S.N.* 3/56/70; Swięcicki, ed., *Prawo Cywilne z orzeeznietwem, literatura i przepisami związkowymi* ("Civil Law, with Judicial Decisions, Literature, and Special Legislation"), I (1958), p. 15.

The work on the code continued. It was announced that about three hundred amendments to the draft were submitted.[21] A new draft was made public in 1955. However, it did not become law. A new codification committee was established by a decree of August 23, 1956, composed of practitioners and theoreticians.[22]

In October, 1956, Gomułka took control of the government, and the tide turned against "Stalinism"; this development did not exert much influence on the shaping of the rules of contract law. It is to be noted, however, that Professor Wasilkowski, chairman of the Codification Committee, published an article on "Problems of Codification,"[23] in which he pointed out that changes in the contents of the Polish civil, criminal, and procedural law should be made in so far as the necessities of socialist construction demand, but all formal changes should be made with great caution, in order to retain all benefits of existing statute and case law where they still appear to be valuable.[24] For some fields of law, the developments of 1956 had a marked significance.[25]

A new draft of the code was published in 1960.[26] It was accepted in the first reading by the Codification Committee, but did not represent the final word of its twelve members. In the foreword, it was pointed out that a public discussion on the project was advisable before the drafting of the final text. As in the Draft of 1954, there was no provision in the Draft of 1960 for freedom of contracting. New drafts were published in 1961 and

[21]Bachrach, *op. cit.* (fn. 13), p. 92.

[22]Gross, "Recent Changes in the Law and Judicial Organization of Poland," *Law in Service of Peace,* IV (1957) No. 2, 110, 112.

[23]*Prawo i Życie* ("Law and Life"), No. 19 (1958).

[24]See note, "The Review 'Law and Life' (*Prawo i Życie*) 1958," *Review of Contemporary Law* (1959), 156, 158.

[25]Particularly, on the reorganization of the Bench (Law of May 27, (1957). "... Changes have been imposed by the living developments which have introduced into our judicial system an entirely new climate answering to the progressive content of the changes which occurred in Poland in October, 1956. And this new climate finds expression in the respect paid to the independence of the Bench, and the firm determination in the administration of justice to observe the strict process of law shown." (Gross, *op. cit.* fn. 22, p. 114.) The Bar was reorganized by the Law of November 19, 1956. (*Ibid.,* p. 115.). However, by a new law (*Dz.U.,* Dec. 21, 1963, No. 57, Item 309), far-reaching restrictions were imposed on the members of the Bar, who were forced to practice in teams in accordance with the Soviet pattern.

[26]Certain Polish efforts aiming at codification were favorably appraised by some *emigre* legal scholars. Thus, it was pointed out that there was a trend in the direction of making courts "the chief guardians of legality and of private rights."

1962; at last the new code was enacted on April 23, 1964,[27] and came into force on January 1, 1965. The Code of Obligations and the Commercial Code were abrogated.

Many rules of contract law, laid down by the Code, do not depart from well-established patterns of the civil law world and from the prewar Polish law. Following the frequent approach, a "General Part" precedes other parts of the Code. In the field of contracts, the methodology followed by the Code does not seem to be the best. Thus, most of the provisions on contracts (and in particular, those on formation of contracts — Articles 68-81) are found in Chapter IV (On "Legal Transactions") of the "General Part," but some others are located in Part Three: "Obligations" (and in particular, in Chapter III: "General Principles of Consensual Obligations," Articles 384-96).

The Code does not give a definition of a contract. However, it affirms the pre-existing law by emphasizing the intention of the parties. Thus, when the parties negotiate with each other, the contract comes into being only when agreement is reached on all points which were being discussed.[28] In interpreting contracts, the "common intention of the parties and the purpose of the contract" should be given effect, rather than their literal wording.[29] The Supreme Court of Poland held (while Article 108 of the Code of Obligations, predecessor of the above provision of the Civil Code, was in force) that the same rule is applicable to unilateral declarations of will; therefore, the intention of the party making the declaration and his purpose should be investigated.[30]

The Code does not lay down a general principle of freedom of contracting. Wolter stated that the bourgeois principle of the freedom of

Grzybowski, "Reform and Codification of Polish Laws, *Am. J. Comp. L.*, VII (1958), 393, 398. In the field of criminal law, because of unhappy experiences in the Soviet Union, "Polish legal thought turned to the Polish tradition." (*Ibid.*) "The legislative techniques, the return to liberal institutions, and a realistic appraisal of the economic and social conditions of the country indicate that [the Commission's] approach will be cautious and free from doctrinal anticipation of the future in terms of legal provisions designed for some still nonexistent social structure. Hence, the emphasis on professional qualifications for members of the legal profession, whether on the bench or at the bar." (*Ibid.*, p. 401.) Unfortunately, the final product was a disappointment. The Criminal Code of April 28, 1969 (in force as of January 1, 1970) shows Soviet influence and has some vague provisions.

[27]*Dz.U.*, May 18, 1964, No. 16, Item 93.

[28]Art. 72.

[29]Art. 65 § 2.

[30]Supreme Court, decision of Aug. 31, 1948, K. C. 315/48. Święcicki, *op. cit.* (fn. 20), I, 130.

contracts serves as a tool for the interests of "big capital," and must give way in the system of organized economy where the anarchistic idea of free competition is replaced by socialist planning. In relations between individuals, it must be seriously limited, particularly so as not to permit any exploitation of men by men on the capitalist pattern.[31]

Of course, the usual rule, that contracts contrary to the law are void, has been accepted by the Code; the relevant provision extends the application of the rule to instances in which a party sought to bypass the law. Article 58 § 1 of the Code reads as follows:

> A legal transaction contrary to the law or which aims at bypassing the law is invalid, unless a relevant provision admits another result, and in particular, that invalid clauses of the legal transaction are replaced by relevant provisions of the law.

The next section of the Code is more unorthodox. Modeled after similar provisions of the Soviet law, and rephrasing a rule laid down in Article 41 § 1 of the General Principles of Civil Law of 1950, Article 58 § 2 of the Code provides that "a legal transaction which is contrary to the principles of community life is invalid." This brings the Polish contract law into line with the theoretical foundations of the "People's Democracies." The same term (used in Articles 76 of the Constitution of 1952) is found in a number of other provisions of the Code. Thus, Art. 94 of the Code reads as follows:

> An impossible condition and a condition contrary to the law or principles of community life nullifies the legal transaction if it is a condition precedent, and is considered as non-existing if it is a condition subsequent.

A provision on the construction of declarations of intention is to the same effect. Article 107 of the Code of Obligations read as follows:

> A declaration of intention should be interpreted in accordance with the requirements of good faith and customs of honest dealing, due account being taken of the circumstances in which it was expressed.

It has been repealed, and in its place Article 65 § 1 of the Code provides:

> A declaration of intention should be interpreted in accordance. . .with the principles of community life and established customs.[32]

[31]Wolter, *op. cit.* (fn. 14), 1st ed., pp. 301-2.

[32]Similarly, Art. 56 lays down the rule that "a legal transaction brings about not only those consequences which are provided for in it, but also those which result from the law, principles of community life, and established customs."

Again, Article 5 of the Code provides that "one is not permitted to make use of a right which would be contrary to the social-economic purpose of this right or to the principles of community life in the Polish People's Republic." Another general principle, expressed in Article 4, repeats the provision of Article 1 of the General Principles of Civil Law and reads as follows: "Provisions of civil law should be interpreted and applied in conformity with the principles of the system of government and purposes of the Polish People's Republic." The same idea is expressed in some detailed provisions of the Code, such as Article 354 § 1:

> "The debtor should carry out the obligation in conformity with its essence and in a way corresponding with its social-economic purpose and the principles of community life. . . .

The new approach has been commented on in the following way: "In spite of the fact that the principle of freedom of contracts was substantially curtailed in the socialist system of government, the parties can still *freely* determine the contents of obligations to a certain extent."[33]

These broad provisions make it possible for the courts to interpret statutes as well as contracts in the way they think proper. The courts make frequent use of them,[34] and thus there is always the possibility that the intention of the parties may be defeated, or that a specific statutory provision may be deprived of its effect.

As an example of the application of Article 1 of the General Principles of Civil Law, analogous to Article 4 of the Code, a case of 1950 may be cited. Contrary to common law, in cases of unlawful impairment of health and earning capacity, the Polish Code of Obligations provided for recurrent payments (like an annuity) rather than a lump sum as standard damages,[35] but permitted granting of a lump sum by the court "for important reasons."[36] Invoking Article 1 of the General Principles, the Supreme Court refused to recognize the desire to establish a business enterprize as an "important reason" for granting a lump sum. The court pointed out that the plaintiff's intention was to establish an enterprise based on capitalist principles, and, referring to his contention that this was an "important reason," continued:

[33]Ohanowicz and Górski, *Zobowiazania – Cześć szczegółowa* ("Obligations – Detailed Part") (1959), p. 4.

[34]A summary of decisions applying these general provisions is given in Świecicki, *op. cit.* (fn. 20) and in Litwin, "Zasady spolecznego wspólzycia w orzecznictwie Sadu Najwyzszego" ("The Principles of Community Life in the Decisions of the Supreme Court"), *Nowe Prawo*, No. 12 (1953), p. 4.

[35]Art. 161. The same rule was applicable to damages owed to survivors for causing a wrongful death (Art. 162). The corresponding articles of the new code are 444 § 2 and 446 § 2.

[36]Art. 164 § 1 of the former Code of Obligations; Art. 447 of the Civil Code.

This position is reminiscent of ideas which grew on the background on the old economic system, the capitalist system, in the light of which ownership of one's own "economic outpost," or enterprise run on the principles of the capitalist economic system, was considered the best assurance of the financial situation of an individual. In the new conditions of the governmental system, in the social and economic system of the People's State, such a position cannot be, of course, recognized as right, and the interpretation of Article 164 § 1 of the Code of Obligations, based on ideas connected with the previous system, is untenable.... The purpose of the institution of compensation for unhappy accidents cannot be the creation of new capitalists.

In interpreting Articles 161-166 of the Code of Obligations, and in particular, in connection with Article 196 of the statute on social insurances, i.e., when the problem is compensation for accidents which happened at work, it should be kept in mind, first, that in the system of a people's democracy the basic source of livelihood for everyone should be the work done within the limits of the possibilities and physical and intellectual capacities of the given individual, and then, it should be taken into account that the People's State extends its protection to individuals unable to work, and in particular, to those who are disabled because of accidents at work, and grants them help.[37]

There are numerous cases in which the broad provision of Article 3 of the General Principles[38] (or Article 5 of the earlier version) has been applied by the Supreme Court and lower tribunals. Thus, recognizing that the employer dismissing an employee from his job does not have to give any reasons, the Supreme Court indicated that such a dismissal nevertheless will not be treated as valid if the dissolution of the employer-employee relationship does not satisfy the social purposes of the law which protects the employee, or the requirements of good faith.[39]

In effect, the employer may be forced to continue the employment of a person he does not want.[40] But Article 3 may work against the interests of the employee. Thus, even though an employment contract, by oversight of the employer, has not been formally terminated, the principles of com-

[37] Supreme Court, decision of Nov. 14, 1950, C. 299/50 – Zb. O. 1/52/11, P.iP. 8-9/51, 436, N.P. 11/51/39, P.Z.S. 8-9/51/93. Świecicki, op. cit., I, 16, 369.

[38] This article was analogous to Art. 5 of the Civil Code, but was narrower, as it did not have any reference to the "social-economic purpose."

[39] Supreme Court, decision of June 21, 1948, C. Prez. 114/48, Zb. O. 3/48/61, P.iP. 9-10/48/147, P.N. 9-10/48/305, Świecicki, op. cit., I, 22-3.

[40] In this respect, American labor law may be in agreement with Polish law.

munity life will not permit the employee to recover his accumulated salary if he has neglected to clear up the situation.[41]

In another case involving a labor situation, an employee's working duties and hours were changed. The Supreme Court pointed out that the employee was "a member of the team, responsible for the fulfillment of duties, assigned to a state industrial enterprise," and continued:

> Therefore, it is contrary to the principles of community life, on the part of the employee, to insist on the wording of the contract and disregarding the vital needs of the enterprise in which he works, to refuse to perform during a short, temporary period of time, duties which are fully adequate to his professional qualifications, only because those duties are not identical to the ones provided for in the contract, and in particular, because they lack the character of executive work, which was connected with the job contracted for.[42]

Some other cases involved the problem of eviction. Thus, it was held that Article 3 of the General Principles made the validity of a notice of eviction from an apartment dependent on consideration of the effect of the eviction on the life of the tenant and his family, taking into account its size, the age of its members, etc., even if the statutory requisites for terminating the contract of tenancy had been met.[43] The termination of tenancy of premises used for a pharmacy and a request for eviction, at a time when in the locality involved there were no other premises adequate for a pharmacy, was considered contrary to the principles of community life and detrimental to society, and was not given effect.[44]

Again, the Supreme Court indicated that a suit to evict a person who had been in possession of and tilled the land for many years, necessarily raised, at the very outset, a problem of conformance of the plaintiff's request with the principles of community life. In such a case, the mere statement that plaintiff had the right he was seeking to enforce was insufficient; it was necessary to establish that, contrary to first impressions, in this particular case the owner did not abuse his right.[45]

[41]Supreme Court, decision of Oct. 3, 1953, I C. 3031/52, *P.U.G.* 3/54/112. Święcicki, *op. cit.*, I, 32.

[42]Supreme Court, decision of Oct. 16, 1952, C. 1906/52, *N.P.* 7/53/67, *P.U.G.* 3/53/104, Święcicki, *op. cit.*, I, 33.

[43]Supreme Court, decision of Mar. 13, 1956, 1 Cr. 197/56, *O.S.N.* 4/56/111. Święcicki, *op. cit.*, I, 26-7.

[44]Supreme Court, decision of Dec. 7, 1949, C. 1675/49, *Zb. O.* 1/50/22, *P.iP.* 1/51/145. Święcicki, *op. cit.*, I, 37-8.

[45]Supreme Court, decision of June 18, 1954, 1 Cr. 730/54, *N.P.* 12/54/90. Święcicki *op. cit.*, I, 34.

400

Among other instances of invoking Article 3, there was a case in which the Supreme Court asserted that the social interest in not demolishing buildings once they are erected was so great that it took precedence over the interest of the person requesting abatement, even if the structure had been built in bad faith.[46]

According to the comments of one of the foremost legal writers of present Poland, the formula of "good morals," used in the traditional systems of law, is much more objectionable than the new general provisions of the communist enactments:

> In bourgeois theory, the above ideas are treated as mandates of morality. But there, they amount to mere phraseology, as the characteristic feature of the exploiting class is its moral downfall. And it could not be otherwise, as the decisive goal of the bourgeoisie was and is the striving to profit, and money is the only yardstick of the value of an individual. The bourgeoisie "did not leave between men any other tie than a bare business, than a 'cash payment,' devoid of any sentiment."[47]

The same author contends that ideas of good faith, good customs, and principles of honest dealing

> make it possible for the court, because of the abstract character of those concepts, to bypass the provisions of its own bourgeois statute when its application is disadvantageous to the capitalist. The application of the above-mentioned criteria takes place above all in the evaluation of the means of performing contractual obligations.[48]

These criteria

> are a mask for the direct goal and the moving spirit of capitalist intercourse, particularly in the period of monopolistic capitalism, which goal is the striving towards the attainment of the highest possible profit by way of exploitation, destroying and ruining the major part of the country's population.[49]

In contrast to such "abstract formulas," the author asserts that the Soviet idea of "principles of the socialist common life" is "a concrete concept."[50] It is

[46]Supreme Court, decision of June 30, 1951, C. 704/50, *Zb. O.* 2/52/45. Święcicki, *op. cit.*, I, 36.

[47]Szer, *Prawo Cywilne, część ogólna* ("Civil Law, General Part") (1955), p. 26, citing Marx and Engels. In the third edition, of 1962, the author's comments have been rephrased.

[48]*Ibid.* See also Wolter, *op. cit.* (fn. 14), 1st ed., pp. 61-2.

[49]Szer, *op. cit.* (fn. 47), p. 173.

[50]*Ibid.*, p. 26.

based on the premises of socialist morality....As categories of morals appear the concept of good and evil, duty and justice, conscience and honor, which have general character. The application of those general principles of behavior finds its expression in the so-called principles of socialist common life, which means in socialist customs.[51]

The counterpart of this idea in Polish law is that of the "principles of community life."[52] There is no difference between those principles and the moral norms. Their reflection is, e.g., the "priority of the social interest or equalization of social with personal interests."[53] According to the author, the new approach "introduced an objective evaluation of care required in socialist intercourse."[54]

And discussing the present Polish rule on the invalidity of some legal transactions, he points out that by virtue of Article 41 of the General Principles, the following principal categories of transactions should be considered as unlawful:

(1) Transactions contrary to the principles of the system of government and the social and economic structure of the State, such as those which are directed against the rights of state or co-operative property; repugnant to the principles of economic planning, to the economic system of accounting, to "financial discipline," or to laws regulating prices.

(2) Transactions which violate mandatory legal norms, like those which regulate the form of contracts, legal capacity of the parties, prohibiting some transactions, etc.

(3) Transactions which transgress the purposes of planned economy entities stated by the law.[55]

As transactions contrary to the principles of community life in the People's State, he further enumerates those which support or enable conduct contrary to "socialist morality," and those which aim at bypassing the law.

Another theoretician of the present system observes that the sources of those principles are

rules of morality which are the expression of the convictions of the majority of the society, or of the working people of the towns and

[51]*Ibid.*, p. 27.

[52]*Ibid.*, p. 28.

[53]*Ibid.*, p. 29.

[54]*Ibid.*, p. 30.

[55]*Ibid.*, pp. 206-8.

402

villages in their striving to build socialism and wind up the remnants of the capitalist structure.[56]

However, the principles of community life should not be identified with the rules of morality, "which have a general character, while the principles. . . are characterized by concreteness and their association with separate forms of social relations."[57] In the establishment of the principles, "the leading role is played by the consciousness of the workers' class, having hegemony in the society, and being led by its *avant-garde* — the party."[58] The "most progressive part of society" is chiefly responsible for their coming into being; they then acquire a mandatory force "irrespective of the passive attitude or even resistance of those elements which continue to represent retrogressive or clearly inimical ideas (remnants of the capitalist class)."[59]

However, even some high authorities in Poland recognize that there is danger in those general provisions. Opening the discussions on the Draft Civil Code of 1954, the Minister of Justice Swiątkowski expressed the opinion that Articles 1 and 3 of the General Principles enable the courts to avoid the application of statutory provisions which have become obsolete, and stated that as a result some statutes become dead even if they are not repealed. He acknowledged that judicial decisions of this kind often are not uniform, which leads to the violation of the rule of law, prevents the citizens from claiming their justified rights, and causes injustice.[60]

In an article which appeared in a Polish legal periodical, the author criticized the attitude of some courts and complained of some decisions which showed a danger of "legal nihilism" by a careless and mistaken application of Article 3 of the General Principles. This attitude is reflected in judicial references to the "principles of community life," without making clear what principle is at stake, and without any analysis of the factual situation from the viewpoint of applicable provisions of law. The author pointed out a dangerous tendency of inexperienced judges[61] to supplant all law with Article 3, and appealed for an effort to make the idea of "the principles of community life" more concrete.[62]

[56]Wolter, *op. cit.* (fn. 14), 1st ed., p. 63.

[57]*Ibid.*

[58]*Ibid.*, p. 64.

[59]*Ibid.*

[60]*Materjały*. . .(fn. 16), p. 7.

[61]Many judges, appointed after World War II, did not have adequate legal preparation.

[62]Różański, "O błędach w orzecznictwie niektórych sądów powiatowych przy stosowaniu art. 3 p.o.p.c." ("On Errors in Some Decisions of County Courts in the

403

Another author admitted:

Unfortunately, it is necessary to state that also in the socialist doctrine there is, up to now, a lack of a satisfactory analysis of the form of social norms which is made up by the principles of community life, in spite of the fact that their role . . . is tremendous. . . . The lack of theoretical studies resulted in that the courts themselves had to look from case to case for solutions, which sometimes — fortunately, infrequently — were erroneous, actually leading to the undermining of the obligatory force of legal norms on the ground of their pretended repugnancy to the principles of community life.[63]

Polish legal scholars living in the Free World are quite trenchant in their criticism. Citing some articles of the General Principles and of the Constitution of 1952, one of them states:

Thus both the law . . . and the Constitution call for a political interpretation of the law. A law should be interpreted and applied. . .in the light of the policies of the government in pursuit of the general 'purpose of the People's State.'

This brings the class war approach into the operation of law, substituting bias for objectivity. Great uncertainty is thereby created and the door is open to an arbitrary interpretation and application of legal rules.[64]

As to the concept of "community life in the People's State," which replaced that of good faith and good morals but has a broader connotation, the author states that it "opened the door for . . . arbitrariness," and that "this new method of construction of contracts may always be used to the detriment of the true intentions of the contracting parties."

Another author comments:

These principles opened the way to a "free legal interpretation" of [these] general notions. . . . New judges duly indoctrinated, as well as the old ones forced to follow the communist party line, were thus armed with wide powers of interpretation enabling them to give a new meaning to such basic institutions and notions as property, contract, discharge of obligations, good faith and to remold them in accordance with the requirements of the so-called "socialist legality" or "socialist rule of law."[65]

Application of Art. 3 of the General Principles of Civil Law"), *Nowe Prawo,* XI-XII (1956), 138. Święcicki, *op. cit.*, (fn. 20) I, 24.

[63]Wolter, *op. cit.* (fn. 14), 2nd ed., p. 61.

[64]Siekanowicz, "Contracts in Postwar Poland," 5 Highlights (Mimeographed, Library of Congress, 1957), pp. 493, 494-5; and Gsovski and Grzybowski, *op. cit.* (fn. 5), II, 1307, 1313.

[65]Nagórski, *op. cit.* (fn. 10), p. 57.

It is interesting to note that, due to the above criticism, there were no provisions parallel to Articles 1 and 3 of the General Principles in the draft of 1960. However, the concept of "principles of community life" was referred to in some detailed articles of the draft. The idea reappeared, in its full scope, in the draft of 1962.

The study of the present Polish law of contracts, just as that of the law of other communist countries, should be undertaken with the effect of those general principles in mind. Their application may have a bearing, in a concrete factual situation, on the effect of specific, seemingly neutral rules such as those dealing with offer and acceptance.

Another point should be made. An ever-decreasing amount of prewar statutes are still in force. The Supreme Court of Poland has made clear[66] that they were retained by the will of "the people's legislator," are a part of the legal system of the "People's Poland," and must be abided by, unless they are repugnant to the principles of the system of government or to the purposes of the People's State.[67]

The question arises whether, and to what extent, judicial decisions from the prewar period are good authority in Poland today. This problem was discussed by the Supreme Court of Poland in 1948, and the following resolution was carried at a plenary session of the Court:

Whereas. . .a distinction should be made, from the viewpoint of the present system of government, between those judicial decisions and legal principles, laid down in the period between the two wars, which are still applicable, and those which are inapplicable, because of the fundamental revamping of the Polish State, as authorities for current judicial decisions of Polish courts,
The Plenary Session of the Supreme Court resolves:

1) To recognize. . .that the decisions of the Supreme Court and the legal principles from the period between the wars (1918-1939), which are repugnant to the present system of government and the statutes which are in force, have today only a historical meaning.

2) To state that only those judicial decisions and legal principles from the above period between the wars are still good law which do not contain this repugnancy.

3) To entrust the evaluation of a given judicial decision or legal principle and its classification under the first or second point of the present resolution, to the several judges sitting in the case, the ques-

[66]Supreme Court, decision of Dec. 5, 1950, C. 323/50, *Państwo i Prawo* (1951), No. 8-9, 420; and of June 30, 1951, C. 649/50, *Zb. O.* 2/52/44, *Państwo i Prawo* (1952), No. 2, 312. Święcicki, *op. cit.* in (fn. 20), I, 12.

[67]See Art. 1 of the General Principles of Civil Law and Art. 4 of the present Civil Code.

405

tion whether this evaluation is well founded being subject to the normal control by higher courts.[68]

In spite of this resolution, the courts and authors are rather reluctant to cite any prewar Polish judicial decisions.

With the above reservations, the legal rules concerning contracts between individuals, in force in Poland, are comparable to the corresponding rules in the traditional legal systems. Even though the principle of freedom of contract is not expressly recognized, the parties are permitted to regulate relations between them substantially according to their will so long as the state is not interested in the subject matter of the agreement.

Contracts Between Socialized Economic Units

It is conceivable to regulate the whole economic life of a country and the relations between its industrial and commercial enterprises by a set of governmental decrees and ordinances, without any room for negotiations between the entities involved. As a matter of fact, such a system once was tried in Russia, but it did not work. Even the planned economy theoreticians admit that it was never carried out in a pure form, as "it fails in the light of the impossibility of eliminating the influence of the law of values."[69] On the other hand, the economic system of Yugoslavia is based on a fairly free market; the difference between a "capitalist" system and this type of a socialist regime lies mainly in the nature of the ownership of enterprises.[70] The most common type of socialist system is the one in which the enonomic life of a country is based on a curious set of rules — a blend of administrative and contract law, the first prevailing in relations between the socialized enterprises and the superimposed co-ordinating agencies of the state, while the second governs the relations of the entities *inter sese.*[71] However, as will be seen, this contract law has a special flavor unknown in the traditional legal systems.

The application of all general rules of contract law to the contracts of government-owned enterprises is hardly conceivable. True, even before the

[68]Plenary Session of the Supreme Court of Nov. 25, 1948 — *Państwo i Prawo* (1949), No. 3, 120, *Demokratyczny Przegląd Prawniczy*, XII (1948), p. 58; *Przegląd Notarjalny*, III-IV (1949), p. 184; *Przegląd Ustawodawstwa Gospodarczego*, IV (1949), p. 84. Święcicki, *op. cit.* (fn. 20), I, 11-2.

[69]Buczkowski, "Zagadnienia prawne 'modelu' gospodarki socjalistycznej" ("Legal Problems of a 'Model' Socialist Economy"), *Państwo i Prawo* (1958), I, No. 13, 786, 790.

[70]*Ibid.*

[71]*Ibid.*

whole Code of Obligations had been repealed, the applicability of its provisions to "contracts which are the creation of socialist economy" had to be viewed in the light of Article 1 of the General Principles of Civil Law, and before they could be relied upon, an inquiry had to be made in each instance as to whether they should be given effect.[72]

In Poland, as in other communist countries, special rules have been enacted as to contracts between socialized economic units and as to the method of settling disputes which may arise between them. In seeking to draw conclusions as to the similarity or dissimilarity between this set of rules and the contract law of noncommunist countries, we must proceed with caution. Comparison limited to some detailed rules may reveal that some of them are similar; a civil-law relation may be said to exist between "socialist organizations" or enterprises, "even if one of them did not want to conclude a contract with the other and was compelled to do so by a decision of an arbitration commission";[73] but it does not follow that the institutions under consideration are comparable. In the traditional legal systems there is no planned economy; the business life of the nation rests, by and large, on private initiative. Of course, there may be contracts with the state; but then the general principles of contract law will be applicable.[74] "The law of contracts, as the West knows it, is an instrument of a liberal society and a free market economy."[75]

The very fact that in the communist countries there is a special branch of the law dealing with planned economy contracts (even if it may be embodied in a general civil code), while other rules are applicable to transactions between individuals, furnishes some evidence that this branch is a new one, having no counterpart in the law of other countries; it comprises situations which may arise only in the communist systems. Of course, sometimes the rules in force in both situations may be the same. Thus, the Czechoslovak Civil Code of 1950 (replaced by a new code in 1964), speaking of "liabilities arising from the exercise of the unified economic plan" provided in Article 212, section 2, that "in the absence of any other provision the legal relations which come into being in this manner shall be ruled by this law." Even so, the application of the rules may be different. The most important object of planned economy contracts will be to carry out the plan, not to give effect to the intention and expectation of the

[72]Supreme Court, decision of May 25, 1955, Cr. 516/55, *O.S.N.* 3/56/70. Święcicki, *op. cit.* (fn. 20), I, 14.

[73]Mihaly, "The Role of Civil Law Institutions in the Management of Communist Economies; The Hungarian Experience," *Am. J. Comp. L.,* VIII, (1959), 310, 311.

[74]However, some specific rules applicable to the details of the transaction may be different from those prevailing in other contracts.

[75]Mihaly, *op. cit.* (fn. 73), p. 310.

contracting parties,[76] which usually will be instrumentalities of the state.[77]

In recent years, in the Soviet Union and other communist countries there have been frequent discussions whether the general civil code should regulate only relations between private individuals, leaving all problems relating to state enterprises to be dealt with by special enactments, or whether some provisions of the civil code should be applicable in all kinds of transactions. By now, the trend is settled in the latter direction.

In July, 1960, projects concerned with the General Principles of Civil Law and Civil Procedure were published in Moscow. After discussion, they were adopted as law (on December 8, 1961) — in amended form — by the Supreme Soviet. The principles serve as the starting point for civil codes and other legislation in the several republics of the Soviet Union, and exert a strong influence on the law of other communist countries. Article 2 of the General Principles of Civil Law and Article 2 of the Russian Civil Code of June 11, 1964, provide that by civil legislation are regulated relations

> between state, co-operative and public organizations with each other; between the citizens and state, co-operative and public organizations; between the citizens with each other.[78]

The Polish Code follows the same pattern, and attempts to merge the "economic law" into the general civil law. The very first provision of the Code[79] proclaims that the Code "regulates civil law relations between units of socialized economy, between individuals, and between units of socialized economy and individuals." However, on many points the Code makes exceptions from the general provisions and lays down special rules applicable to these units. Such are, in particular, provisions on the "Duty

[76]"Even when there is a superficial similarity of rules, it is clear that the social function of a contract between two plan-fulfilling state enterprises, operating without reference to a market, is quite different from that of a contract in a society in which the bargaining of individuals and groups provides the principal mechanism for giving effect to their own wishes and preferences.... In functional terms, the comparability of a free contract and of a contract between plan-fulfilling state enterprises is highly problematic." Schlesinger, *op. cit.* (fn. 6), p. 69.

[77]"The director of an enterprise, its leaders, and the 'work-collectives' are actually not the enterprise's master; they are executors of mandatory plans." Mihaly, *op. cit.* (fn. 73), p. 327.

[78]Similar provisions are found in the new civil codes (effective 1964) of the following Soviet republics: Ukrainian, Uzbek, Latvian, Kazakh, Turkmen, and Tajik.

[79]Art. 1 § 1.

408

to Conclude Contracts Between Units of Socialized Economy."[80] The Code makes it clear that these special rules are applicable to "state institutions and social organizations of the toilers, the duty of which consists in the carrying out of economic activity,"[81] while – in case there is no specific statutory rule to the contrary – provisions of the Code referring to individuals are applicable to legal entities which are not units of socialized economy.[82] Right after stating these rules, the Code provides that in case of need, the government may regulate intercourse between economic units "in a way contrary to the provisions of this Code."[83] Thus, previously enacted and future statutes and decrees in this field have been sanctioned, and the rules of the Code have only a "subsidiary" character.

The author of a leading recent treatise on obligations commented:

> The most important [problems] concern obligations of planned economy units. Principles in accordance with which regulations of these legal relationships must take place are essentially different from principles of obligations in the approach of the Code of Obligations as a statutory enactment dating back to the prewar period, because the foundations of statutory enactments of the socialist type which regulate transactions between the entities of planned economy are different from the traditional premises of the law of obligations in the capitalist period.[84]

[80]Art. 397 through 404.

[81]Art. 1 § 2.

[82]Art. 1 § 3.

[83]Art. 2.

[84]Ohanowicz, *Zobowiązania – Część ogólna* ("Obligations – General Part"), (1958), p. 4. Prof. Katzarov, in his article on "La planification comme problème juridique," *Rev. Int. Dr. Comp.*, X (1958), 298, pointed out that economic planning established some "new legal institutions," and in particular, a "super-source" of the law of obligations, which is the economic plan. The aim of this "super-source" is "improvement and limiting of the rule of nullity of classical law in order to obtain a change, and not a nullity of all rights and obligations which hinder the carrying out of the plan"(p. 309). He states that the new system could bring about "the replacement of contract law by administrative law, and of the contract by the administrative order." However, this approach was not adopted. Along with the nationalization and socialization measures, some private law activity was reserved for the state enterprises which have a personality separate from that of the state. Therefore, the economic plan as a "super-source" of the law of obligations "can modify or annul legal or contractual relations, but only under the condition (1) that these relations are repugnant to the carrying out of the plan, and. . .only during the time (2) and to the extent (3) that it will appear necessary

The Polish Minister of Justice stated in 1954 that the socialist legal institution called "contractation" is one of the principal forms of carrying out the economic union between town and country, although it is unknown in the traditional legal systems.[85] The same observation is applicable to other types of planned economy contracts.

The basic law relating to these contracts was the Statute of April 19, 1950, on planned contracts in a socialized economy.[86] The statute was supplemented by an executive order of the Chairman of the State Commission for Economic Planning of May 15, 1953.[87]

Contrary to the principles of the traditional law of contracts which do not impose upon anyone a duty to enter into contractual relations except in rare situations, Article 2 of the above statute required the state enterprises and those controlled by the state to conclude planned agreements in order to fulfill their duties in the carrying out of the economic plan. This provision, understandable in the system of law in which it was enacted, illustrates well the main difference between the two fields of contract law. The Chairman of the State Commission for Economic Planning established a list of superior economic institutions which enter into general agreements,[88] while lower units concluded detailed agreements between themselves (Article 7). Direct contracts, without general agreements, were possible in some cases (Article 10).

The statute expressly required planned economy contracts to conform to the economic plan of the state and to the interests of the national economy (Article 18). If these considerations were violated, the State Arbitration Commission might modify the contracts, or even declare them altogether invalid (Article 20). No disputes relating to planned economy

for the carrying out of the plan.... It follows that the elevation of the economic plan of the State to the level of a source of obligations is a new phase of the penetration of public law into the field of contractual law, especially in relations between state enterprises ..." (p. 310). It also follows that "the economic plan...becomes a source of contractual law to which the real contractual law, created by the contracting parties, is subordinated. All that, in a contract, is out of harmony with the economic plan...must be rectified or declared null" (P. 311). For a recent, thorough discussion of some aspects of planned economy contracts, see Loeber, "Plan and Contract Performance in Soviet Law," *Ill. L. Forum* (1964), p. 128.

[85]*Materjaly*...(fn. 16), p. 6. For provisions on contractation in the Civil Code, see Art. 613 through 626.

[86]*Dz.U.*, No. 21, Item 180 (1950).

[87]*Mon. Pol.*, Order 28/1953, Item 109.

[88]Such general agreements or contracts are favored in the Soviet Union and most other planned economy states. However, "the introduction of the general contract did not meet with much success in Hungary." Mihaly, *op. cit.* (fn. 73), p. 317.

contracts were adjudicated by the courts. They were to be submitted to arbitration, in accordance with statutory procedure.

Some of the provisions of the statute were incorporated, with or without changes, in the Draft Code of 1954. Many provisions of the statute itself have been criticized, and it was replaced by the decree of May 16, 1956, on Delivery Contracts Between Socialist Economic Units.[89] The new law, of course, had the same objectives as the old one, and did not introduce any departure from the general approach to contracts in a planned economy system. Article 1 of the decree laid down the rule that relations between socialist economic units are based on contracts, but, naturally, obligations to enter into agreements and other implements of planned economy had to be retained.[90] It seems, however, that under the decree, the rules of the Code of Obligations are more readily applicable than under the former statute.[91] The decree has been supplemented by an executive order of the Chairman of the State Commission for Economic Planning of October 15, 1956.[92] This law contained no provisions constituting a direct counterpart of Articles 7 and 10 of the old one. One of the articles provided for the possibility of making contracts by administrative orders:

> In exceptional cases, warranted by economic necessity, the Council of Ministers may authorize the head organs of the state administration to issue orders directing the subordinate socialist economic units to make deliveries to other socialist economic units without a contract having been concluded between them. These orders create rights and duties for the recipient and the purveyor in the same way as if a contract were entered into between them.[93]

As an interesting example of the ways in which transactions between private individuals differ from those between socialist organizations, the question of sellers' and buyers' obligations in sales transactions may be cited.

One of the papers read during the 1954 discussion on the Draft Code dealt with the provisions on sales, and a lively exchange of views followed. According to the traditional approach, "a contract to sell goods is a contract whereby the seller agrees to transfer the property in goods to the

[89]*Dz.U.*, May 30, 1956, No. 16, Item 87.

[90]Art. 2.1 reads as follows: "The Socialist Economic Units have the obligation to enter into delivery contracts having as purpose the fulfillment of planned purposes."

[91]Siekanowicz, *op. cit.* (fn. 64), p. 501.

[92]*Mon. Pol.*, Nov. 2, 1956, No. 89, Item 1016.

[93]Art. 7.

buyer for a consideration called the price,"[94] while a sale is an agreement whereby the seller presently transfers the property to the buyer.[95]

In communist countries all important enterprises are state-owned, and their property belongs to the state. This makes it difficult to speak of a transfer of title. How can there be a sale, in the traditional sense, if both parties are agents of the same principal, if sales transactions are not subject to the free will of the parties, but are mandatory, and if their subject matter is not the transfer of ownership from the seller to the buyer? This is the answer given by one commentator:

> This type of sale. . .is just a public or social function having for its sole purpose to implement the economic plan. These "contracts" are the typical planned ones and the parties who are in duty bound to make them and to abide by them have practically no possibility of deciding on their contents. They are dictated by the economic plan, by numerous administrative regulations and, finally, fixed in full details by "model contracts" prepared and issued by the proper authorities.[96]

In connection with this, provisions concerning the sale price are interesting:

(1) The settled prices on the day of the delivery will be applicable.
(2) The parties cannot fix the prices in a contractual way, except in cases where they were authorized to do so in regulations concerning the prices.[97]

The Draft Code of 1954 drew a distinction between sales in the traditional sense and those between planned economy units. In the first situation, the Draft Code substantially repeated Article 294 of the Code of Obligations by providing that by a sales contract "the seller obligates himself *to transfer to the buyer the ownership of the goods,* and the buyer obligates himself to pay the price"[98] (italics added). Article 294 of the Code of Obligations included in the definition the sale of a property right, while in the Draft Code there was a separate article on that point,[99] making rules on the sale of goods applicable to the "sale of rights," the word "property" being omitted.

[94]Uniform Sales Act, section 1, para. 1. However, the moment of the passing of the title may be different in various legal systems.

[95]*Ibid.*, section 1, para. 2.

[96]Nagórski, *op. cit.* (fn. 10), p. 75.

[97]Executive Order of Oct. 15, 1956, Enclosure 2, § 54.

[98]Art. 456 § 1.

[99]Art. 468.

412

On the other hand, Article 456 § 2 of the Draft Code of 1954 provided that "by a sales contract between state enterprises the seller obligates himself *to deliver the goods to the buyer* and the buyer obligates himself to pay the price" (italics added).

The duality of the definitions of sale was criticized[100] on the ground that the latter definition unduly restricted the duties of the seller and that the old approach of the Code of Obligations was flexible enough "to be fully applied in different types of sales which take place in socialist transactions."[101] It was pointed out that not only goods, but also various rights, such as those pertaining to literary property or patents, may be the subject matter of a sale. Even if this is so, and even if transactions between socialized enterprises should be called sales, they certainly are sales of a peculiar kind, having no counterpart in the traditional legal systems. In spite of their peculiarities, however, these transactions are called sales in the communist countries, and some incidents of the traditional sales law are applicable to them.

The Draft Code of 1960 retained the duality of the definition of a sale set in the Draft of 1954. Article 456 of the Draft Code of 1960 read as follows:

§ 1. By a contract of sale the seller obligates himself to transfer to the buyer the ownership of the goods and to deliver the goods to the buyer, and the buyer obligates himself to take delivery of the goods and to pay the price to the seller.

§ 2. In sales between state organizations the seller obligates himself to deliver the goods to the buyer and to leave them to his exclusive disposition, and the buyer obligates himself to take delivery of the goods and to pay the price to the seller.

However, not all planned-economy contracts are concluded between state-owned enterprises. Some of them have as parties socialized economy units on one side and private individuals on the other. A typical contract of this kind is called, strictly following the Russian pattern,[102] "contractation." The subject matter of this kind of contract is the compulsory sale of farm products to the state. The producer is not permitted to place all his products on the open market. The producer may be either an individual or a socialized economic unit.[103]

[100]*Materjaɫy...*(fn. 16), p. 289.

[101]*Ibid.*, p. 288.

[102]Nagórski, *op. cit.* (fn. 10), p. 73.

[103]For a discussion in English of this type of contract, see Siekanowicz, *op. cit.* (fn. 64), pp. 502-5.

The final text of the Civil Code did not introduce substantial changes. The text of Article 456 of the Draft of 1960, renumbered as Article 479 in the Draft of 1962, finds its place in Article 535 of the Code, with only one change: the words "in sales between state organizations" have been replaced by "in sales between state organizational units." Again, the chapter on planned-economy contracts[104] confirms the pre-existing rules. The Code permits the Council of Ministers or a leading organ of the state administration, acting under its authority, "to settle general conditions or patterns of contracts for a definite kind of contract between units of socialized economy or between these units and other persons."[105]

Detailed analysis of planned economy contracts in Poland would require a special study. Only a small part of such a study would cover points which can be stated in the language of traditional contract law. A system of these contracts exists in all communist countries, with variations. There is no counterpart in the traditional legal systems.

Disputes involving planned economy contracts escape jurisdiction of the general courts and are submitted to arbitration, following the pattern of the Soviet Union and accepted in other communist countries.[106]

General Conditions of Delivery of Goods

An additional source of Polish, and more generally, of communist contract law, particularly in the field of sales, is a document drafted in 1957 (signed on December 13) and applicable to contracts of sale concluded on or after January 1, 1958, between the foreign trade organizations of the member states of the Council for Mutual Economic Aid. Eight planned-economy countries were parties to this agreement, called General Conditions of Delivery of Goods: Albania, Bulgaria, Czechoslovakia, the

[104] Art. 397 through 404.

[105] Art. 384 § 1.

[106] See Grodecki, "State Economic Arbitration in Poland," *Int. and Comp. L.Q.*,IX (1960), p. 177. For the distinction between judicial and arbitral procedure, see Tyczka, "Droga postępowania arbitrażowego" ("The Way of Arbitration"), *Państwo i Prawo* (1955), 588. In general, the most important function of arbitration in socialist countries is the enforcement of the economic plan. By arbitration it is possible "to modify or annul existing contractual relations, or else to provide for the creation of such relations: in other words, the conclusion of contracts between the various enterprises, or between them and the state itself." Katzarov, *op. cit.* (fn. 84), p. 313. See also Kufel and Tyczka, *Postępowanie arbitrażowe* ("Procedure in Arbitration") (1963). Some commentators have pointed out that this arbitration is very different from arbitration as understood in the West, that it amounts merely to a special form of judicial proceedings.

German Democratic Republic, Hungary, Poland, Rumania, and the U.S.S.R. Mongolia was added in 1962.[107]

The General Conditions constitute a unification of the law of sales in transactions between the above-mentioned countries. They are based on experience gained in previous bilateral agreements between the communist states,[108] and are applicable unless the parties should agree that "because of the specific nature of the goods and/or special characteristics of its delivery a departure from particular provisions. . .is required."[109]

Like similar projects prepared by the Rome Institute for the Unification of Private Law and by the Hague Conference, the General Conditions do not purport to replace the municipal law of the participating states, and are applicable only in foreign trade. The legal nature of the General Conditions is not quite clear. Some legal writers consider them as an international multilateral treaty,[110] but others consider them mere recommendations,[111] as they were not agreed upon and duly ratified according to procedures followed in international conventions.

Following the usual communist pattern, the General Conditions provide that

all disputes which may arise out of or in connection with the contract shall be subject to consideration by arbitration, the jurisdiction of general courts being excluded, in an arbitral tribunal established for such disputes in the country of the defendant.

However, if the parties agree, the dispute may be submitted to an arbitral tribunal of a "third Member-Country of the Council for Mutual Economic Aid."[112]

It is to be noted "that each of the countries of planned economy has a permanent foreign trade arbitration tribunal which is in many respects like a court."[113] Substantive provisions of the General Conditions could easily

[107]Grzybowski, *The Socialist Commonwealth of Nations* (1964), pp. 57, 59.

[108]Berman, "Unification of the Contract Clauses in Trade Between Member-Countries of the Council for Mutual Economic Aid," *Int. and Comp. L.Q.,* VII (1958), p. 659. The text of the General Conditions is taken from this article. See also Bystricky and Landa, "The Unification of Laws on International Sale," *Rev. Contemp. L.,* VI (1959), p. 67.

[109]Preamble to the General Conditions.

[110]E.g., Jakubowski, "A jednak ius cogens," *Handel Zagraniczny* (1960), p. 28, cited bv Grzybowski, *op. cit.* (fn. 107).

[111]Bystricky and Landa, *op. cit.* (fn. 108), p. 73.

[112]§ 65.

[113]Berman, *op. cit.* (fn. 108), p. 664.

be applied to transactions between "capitalist" countries. True, economic planning and specialization prevail among the entire group of the signatories; but this is not reflected in the General Conditions. The situation is hardly comparable to that in the internal systems of these countries, where the ministries, various commissions, and other agencies of a well-developed bureaucracy are directing and controlling the whole economic life at every stage and at all times.

Conclusion

It should be pointed out that in the private sector the rules of the Polish law of contracts do not essentially differ from the law of other traditional systems of law, with the exception of some general clauses which, if abused by the courts, can thwart the principles of other statutory provisions. However, in the sector of transactions between the socialist enterprises, a special set of rules has been developed. Even though some of them may in terms be similar to or the same as those in the private sector (and may, indeed, be incorporated by reference), the whole set constitutes a separate branch of the law which lies outside of the law of consensual obligations. It must be doubted whether such a set of rules can fruitfully be compared with rules and principles traditionally governing agreements among individuals which are the result of bargaining in a free market. On the other hand, it might be interesting and useful to compare the law of contracts between socialist enterprises with Western institutions in which the elements of freedom and of bargaining are limited or nonexistent, such as contracts resulting from *Kontrahierungszwang,* or perhaps government contracts in some of the Western countries.

Finally, the new Czechoslovak Civil Code of February 26, 1964,[114] which replaced the Code of 1950, did not follow the prevailing contemporary pattern in the communist countries. While it regulates the relations between private individuals with each other and with socialist economic units, it leaves out the whole field of economic contracts concluded in the performance of the economic plan, departing from the approach of the Code of 1950. Thus, in Czechoslovakia, such contracts are no longer considered a part of the civil law.[115]

[114]*Sb.,* No. 19, Item 40 (1964).

[115]The new Czechoslovak Civil Code has been described as "truly revolutionary," as it "rejects traditional Western civil law doctrine" and introduces "a new spirit, a new application of law"; compared to it, the Polish Code is "certainly *not* revolutionary." Rudziński, "New Communist Civil Codes of Czechoslovakia and Poland: A General Appraisal," *Ind. L. J.,* 41 (1965), 33, 46, 68.

Prominent Polish Legal Scholars of the Last One Hundred Years

The editor originally planned to include in this chapter biographies of prominent Polish jurists. Surely the administration of justice as demonstrated by the coordinated work of judges, attorneys, and law enforcement officers is no less important than the activity of law professors. But the selection of a handful of jurists as the outstanding representatives of the Polish bench and bar raised insurmountable difficulties. Because a different legal system prevails in Poland and other civil-law countries, judges do not have the opportunity to leave permanent records of their achievements similar to those of their common-law colleagues. Only a fraction of Polish court decisions finds the way into law reports, and the names of the judges who have written the decisions are not revealed. In such a system there is hardly any possibility for the judge of a court of last resort to build up a reputation such as Marshall's, Holmes's, or Frankfurter's. The prestigious positions of presidents of the Polish Supreme Court and of the Supreme Administrative Tribunal, of ministers of justice or solicitors general might have narrowed the number of eligible names to a score or less, if the bearers of such positions could be considered as preferred candidates for inclusion in this chapter. However, appointment to high administrative position does not necessarily reflect the highest qualifications of a candidate as a lawyer. The selection of a few of the most prominent Polish attorneys at law, whose names have survived world wars and the political upheavals of the last generation was still more difficult. In addition, published biographical data on the great Polish lawyers of the past are so scarce outside Poland that such a selection did not appear feasible.

In consequence, after consultation with the editor, it was decided to limit this chapter to biographies of some Polish law professors. Their scholarly production, published, accessible, and reviewed and appraised by area specialists, offered more objective guidelines for selection.

The following biographical sketches are not the result of the independent research work of the compiler. Heavy borrowing from Polish sources listed at the end of each sketch was unavoidable. The purpose of this chapter is to give the English-speaking world brief information on the lives and activities of selected Polish law professors. There are many great law professors living now, but it was decided to include here only those whose books have been closed. The reader may be surprised in not finding among the biographies some truly great names. The surprise may be justified, and the compiler offers the following explanation.

Between the birth of the earliest professor included in this chapter (Balzer, born 1858) and the death of the latest (Makowski, died 1959), one century passed. The history of Poland showed more significant changes during this past century than the history of many other countries. Every professor whose life is presented on these pages was born in the second half of the nineteenth century, at a time when there was no independent Polish state and no truly native Polish law in force. Rather than to devote their lives to teaching and researching the foreign law then in force, quite a few young Polish lawyers preferred to study the history of Polish law or to make careers in Roman law. Thus the preponderance of legal historians in this study is explained. Due to differing political conditions prevailing in the Polish territories under Russia, Prussia, and Austria, young Polish legal scholars of the time were attracted by the universities which enjoyed the greatest academic freedom — those under Austrian control. Thus the preponderance of Cracow and Lwów professors in this study is explained.

To include here biographies of all the Polish law professors who deserve inclusion would require three times the allotted space. In addition, published material on many persons who died during or prior to World War II is unavailable in the United States. Nevertheless, it is hoped that these pages will give the reader an insight into the life, work, and achievements of some of the great Polish law professors of the recent past.

OSWALD BALZER (1858-1933)

The life of this great Polish legal historian was closely connected with the city of Lwów. Born the son of a county administrator on January 23, 1858 in Chodorów, Oswald Balzer moved in 1871 to Lwów, forty-five miles north, and remained there for the next sixty-two years. Balzer's activity was confined to an area of a few blocks not far from the center of the city. His apartment was not more than ten minutes' walk to the

Provincial Archives in St. Bernard's Monastery, where he worked for more than forty years. In between was the building of the "old" university, where Balzer taught for forty-eight years. Even when, after World War I, the School of Law was moved to the magnificent building of the former Provincial Legislature, Balzer remained in the same classroom on the second floor of the centuries' old university building on St. Nicholas Street where he had started his teaching career in 1884. The classroom was named the Balzer Room after his death, and the street where he lived was renamed Oswald Balzer Street.

Balzer was an unusual man. His working capacity was unlimited. Holding a full-time job as the director of Provincial Archives, he taught his classes daily at lunch time between noon and one o'clock. He conducted his famous seminar in Polish constitutional history on Saturdays between four and six in the evening. At the same time he published more books and articles than some entire faculties. This pace of life and work was steadily maintained for more than forty years.

Oswald Balzer graduated with high honors from the secondary school in Lwów in 1878, and entered the School of Law of Lwów University. Interested in historical problems, he attended at the same time classes in the history department. He spent one year at the Jagiellonian University in Cracow, where he studied under the legal historian Michał Bobrzyński and graduated in 1883. The next year he moved to Berlin and conducted research under the well-known German legal historian Heinrich Brunner, as well as under Bresslau, Hinschius, and Schmoller. After returning to Lwów, he submitted to the Law Faculty his study, "The Genesis of the Crown Tribunal," a history of the judiciary in sixteenth-century Poland.[1] He drew ably on the 347 pages of the study a picture of the supreme royal judicial court in the last period of the Jagiellons, the attempted reforms, and finally the evolution of the law of 1578 by which the Supreme Tribunal was introduced in the Crown. A favorable review of this work was prepared by Balzer's former teacher in Cracow, Bobrzyński, since Lwów did not have at that time specialists on the history of Polish law. On the basis of this review, Balzer was granted permission to teach as a docent by the Lwów Law Faculty.

Balzer was promoted in 1887 to associate and in 1890 to full professor of Polish legal history. A special chair for this subject was created for him. Polish constitutional history had been taught at the Lwów University before, but only as a part of other subjects more historical than legal in emphasis. Balzer also taught the history of Polish civil procedure, and for many years (1894-1918) Austrian constitutional history as well. He used to admit twenty students (ten law students and ten history students)

[1] *Geneza Trybunału Koronnego, studjum z dziejów sądownictwa polskiego XVI wieku* (Warsaw, 1886).

yearly to his seminar in Polish constitutional history. He paid special attention to the selection of seminar members and was very demanding as to the quality of papers presented during the academic year. Eventually a remarkable number of his seminar members became scholars of distinction, and not only in the field of legal history.

As a teacher, Balzer had the rare ability to talk in a clear and fascinating manner even on such apparently dry and lifeless subjects as medieval law sources. Nobody ever referred to his classes as boring. As a great master of Polish language, he spoke in accomplished literary form. Unfortunately posterity cannot enjoy Balzer's lectures in his own voice. Mimeographed outlines for the use of students were reissued eight times. Balzer expressly forbade in his will the publication of these materials in a book form; he believed that they were incomplete and could not serve as the replacement for a full course in Polish constitutional history. Such a course was planned by Balzer for decades but was not finished.

Balzer was Dean of the Law Faculty twice: in 1892-3 and in 1913-4. He was elected Rector Magnificus (President of the University) in 1895-6.

A list of Balzer's publications fills many pages. It has been compiled and published by Z. Wojciechowski in the first volume of the book published in Lwów in Balzer's honor in 1925,[2] and supplemented by the same author in the *Historical Quarterly* in 1933.[3]

The best known work of Balzer, published in several editions, was a book on social and political reforms brought about by the Constitution of May 3, 1791.[4] Well aware of the successful beginning made a hundred years earlier in the study of the comparative legal history of Slavic peoples by Czacki, Rakowiecki, and Maciejowski, Balzer tried to revive this specific approach to the study of legal history by publishing a clearly organized booklet on this subject in 1906.[5] His dream of an independent chair of comparative Slavic legal history at one of the Polish universities has never been fulfilled, but works by Władysław Namysłowski (stimulated by Balzer) between the two world wars filled the need for further study at least partially.

The principal field of Balzer's research activity was the medieval period of Polish constitutional history. He stated repeatedly that the seventeenth

[2]Przemysław Dąbkowski, ed., *Księga pamiątkowa ku czci Oswalda Balzera* (Lwów, 1925).

[3]*Kwartalnik historyczny*, XLVII (1933), 440-4.

[4]*Reformy społeczne i polityczne Konstytucji Trzeciego Maja,* published originally in *Przegląd Polski*, XXV (1891), 221-60, 461-96, and, as a separate reprint, published in Cracow. The second edition appeared under a slightly different title. The third and last edition was published in Warsaw in 1920.

[5]*Historja porównawcza praw słowiańskich* (Lwów, 1900).

and eighteenth centuries had been researched reasonably well, but that the medieval beginnings of Polish legal institutions had been badly neglected. In his work on capitals of Poland (1916)[6] he expressed the opinion that Gniezno was Poland's capital until 1037 and Cracow afterwards. A work more historical than legal and acclaimed as one of his best, is the *Genealogy of Piasts* (1895).[7] To the same category of historical works may be added his multi-volume work on the *Polish Kingdom, 1295-1370,* published in 1919-20.[8] Relatively early in his career, he published valuable monographs on the history of financial administration[9] and on history of criminal law in Poland.[10] Several works on the old Polish criminal procedure, along with the outline of a university course on the history of Polish civil procedure,[11] published posthumously, should be mentioned. He devoted several separate studies to the judicial history of Armenian colonists, governed by their own special laws, in medieval Lwów.[12] After his death his voluminous study on the Polish chronicle writer Wincenty Kadłubek was published, as well as his critical edition of the Statutes of King Casimir the Great.[13]

As a research scholar, Balzer was in a better position than his predecessors in other Polish universities, who worked at the time when primary legal sources were not yet available. Though busy for decades with evaluation and interpretation of published sources, which he knew perfectly well, he was also a great master in editorial work. His ambitious plan to publish a complete, critical collection of Polish medieval law could not be realized, but he was at least successful in publishing one volume of the *Corpus Juris Polonici,* covering the years 1506-22, as well as the first

[6]"Stolice Polski," in *Studia nad historią prawa polskiego,* IV, pt. 7, 963-1138.

[7]*Genealogia Piastów* (Cracow, 1895).

[8]*Królewstwo Polskie, 1295-1370* (Lwów, 1919-20).

[9]*Skartabelat w ustroju szlachectwa polskiego* (Cracow, 1911), and *Narzaz w systemie danin książęcych pierwotnej Polski* (Lwów, 1928).

[10]*O prawnej i bezprawnej ucieczce zbrodniarzów według statutów Kazimierza Wielkiego* (Cracow, 1882). *O księdze kryminalnej sanockiej z lat 1551-1638* (Lwów, 1890).

[11]*Przewód sądowy polski w zarysie* (Lwów, 1935).

[12]*Sądownictwo ormiańskie w średniowiecznym Lwowie,* in *Studia nad historią prawa polskiego,* IV, pt. 1 (1909); *Statut ormiański w zatwierdzeniu Zygmunta I z r.1519,* in *Studia nad historią prawa polskiego,* IV, pt. 2 (1910); and *Porządek sądów i spraw prawa ormiańskiego z r.1604,* in *Studia nad historią prawa polskiego,* V, pt. 1 (1912).

[13]"Stadium o Kadłubku," in his *Pisma pośmiertne* (Lwów, 1934); and "Statuty Kazimierza Wielkiego, in *Studia nad historią prawa polskiego,* XIX (1947).

installment of the next volume, covering 1523-6. World War I prevented the continuation of this great project. According to unanimous opinion of specialists, the published volume of the *Corpus Juris Polonici* is on the highest level of editorial art, and a noted advance over the *Volumina Legum*, published in the eighteenth century.

As director of Provincial Archives, Balzer was responsible for the collection of valuable administrative and judicial files from the past, scattered through numerous county offices in Galicia. On his initiative thousands of volumes of old land titles were brought to the Archives, where they served as invaluable primary source material for Balzer and other scholars.

Balzer was not only a great scholar but also an excellent organizer of scholarly work. In 1900, he founded the Polish Society for the Advancement of Arts and Sciences in Lwów,[14] reorganized twenty years later into the Learned Society of Lwów.[15] The founder was the president of the society until his death. Members of the Polish Academy of Arts and Sciences who lived in Lwów became the nucleus of the Learned Society. Later more members were admitted, until, in the mid-thirties, the total number exceeded 200. The many activities of the society in all fields of knowledge, and in providing for lectures and serial publications, give testimony to the vitality of the society and its president.

A special series, *Studies in the History of Polish Law,*[16] was begun by Balzer in 1899 and remained under his editorship until 1933. Balzer edited thirteen volumes, containing forty-three contributions by twenty-seven authors.

In the earlier period of his activity, Balzer wrote almost one hundred book reviews; in the year 1887 alone, he published twenty-six. Some of them are of monograph length.

Balzer was a Polish legal historian. He wrote almost exclusively in Polish. Once in his long life, however, he gained fame in an international field. During a controversy between Hungary and the Crown Land Galicia over the part of Tatra mountains including the well-known lake Sea Eye (*Morskie Oko*), Balzer defended Galicia's rights before an international arbitration commission in Graz. His historical study on the subject, prepared with meticulous care, contributed to Galicia's victory over the Hungarian claim. A special book on this subject was published in Lwów in 1906. Very unusual international aspects of this litigation were the subject

[14]Towarzystwo dla popierania nauki polskiej.

[15]Towarzystwo Naukowe we Lwowie.

[16]*Studia nad historią prawa polskiego.*

of an article by J. Błociszewski in *Revue générale de droit international public*.[17]

It is to be added that Balzer accomplished what he did despite physical handicaps: he was crippled by scarlet fever in childhood, and his hearing was severely impaired during the latter half of his life. He was a kind, patient, and modest man, and extremely industrious. He never tolerated student cheating. Teaching at a time when class attendance by students was not mandatory, and in a classroom adequate for only a fraction of the students registered for his course, he demanded, nevertheless, the personal appearance of each student at least at the time he signed the student's study book. Professor Balzer, a kind old man, was seen indignantly throwing away those study books of absent students submitted for his signature by their colleagues.

Although they were not solicited and not wanted, many honors were bestowed on him. He was an active member of a dozen of Polish learned societies, including the Polish Academy of Arts and Sciences, as well as a member of five national academies of other Slavic countries. He had five honorary Doctor's degrees. He was an honorary citizen of four different cities, and gained the highest Polish government distinctions after 1918. A special memorial book in his honor was published in two volumes in 1925, containing seventy-five contributions by Polish and foreign scholars.[18]

Oswald Balzer died in Lwów in January 11, 1933.

Writings on Balzer include:
Przenysław Dąbkowski, *Oswald Balzer, życie i dzieła, 1858-1933* (Lwów, 1934).

"Balzer Oswald Marjan," *Polski słownik biograficzny*, I (Cracow, 1935), 245-8 (containing a full bibliography up to 1935).

Leon Halban, "Oswald Balzer, człowiek i dzieło," *Roczniki Humanistyczne* (1960) No. 4, pp. 109-17.

WŁADYSŁAW ABRAHAM (1860-1941)

The seminar in canon law conducted by Abraham for some forty years at the University of Lwów demonstrated some unusual features. One of them was the large number of professors of legal history, Church history, and canon law of the local university and of other universities as well who attended regularly. Even the rector of the University Gerstmann was a member of Abraham's seminar during his tenure of office. For university

[17]"L'Oeil de mer, un conflit de frontières entre l'Autriche et la Hongrie réglé par jugement arbitral," X (1903), 419-35,

[18]Dąbkowski, *op. cit.*

assistants and a handful of selected senior students, the seminar served as the school for an academic career. Despite its limited practical significance and lack of excitement, Church history and canon law became, under Abraham's direction, a scholarly attraction in Lwów. Reading and exegesis of old Latin documents was an unforgettable experience for seminar members, who learned from the venerable professor what to look for behind and beyond the written texts and what life was like in past centuries when the court records had been written. Abraham's profound erudition, combined with his liberal attitude toward human weaknesses and his sense of humor, made him an ideal moderator for scholarly meetings. His seminar took place on Fridays between four and six and was a spiritual banquet.

Abraham was born on October 10, 1860 in Sambor, where he finished his primary and secondary education. He studied law and history at the Jagiellonian University in Cracow, under professors Heyzmann and Bobrzyński. Early recognized as a promising young scholar, Abraham worked during his student years with the Provincial Archives in Cracow, supported by a scholarship of the Polish Academy of Arts and Sciences. After graduation in 1883, he practiced for two years in a law office and in a court. Abraham undertook early in 1885 a study trip to Berlin, where he studied under the German canonist Hinschius. After Berlin came Rome. Abraham was attracted by the wealth of the Vatican Archives, by that time already opened for research. He returned to Cracow in 1886 and submitted to the Law Faculty of the Jagiellonian University a study on the inquisitional canonical process in the statutes of Innocentius III and in contemporary doctrine.[19] The study was accepted, and Abraham became a docent of canon law in 1886. He taught in this capacity for two years. In 1888, vacancies occurred simultaneously in Cracow, where Professor Heyzmann had retired, and in Lwów, where Professor Kasznica had died. Both universities asked for Abraham's appointment as an associate professor. The Ministry of Education in Vienna decided for Lwów, and Abraham's entire subsequent career was closely tied with the University there. Promoted to full professorship at the age of 30, Abraham published in the same year (1890) one of his most important books on Church organization in Poland up to the middle of the twelfth century.[20] A second edition of this great book was published in 1893 in Lwów, and a third edition in Poznań in 1962.

The years spent in Cracow as well as the first decade in Lwów witnessed an impressive number of Abraham's publications, such as a study on the

[19] *O procesie inkwizycyjnym w ustawach Innocentego III i w nauce współczesnej* (1887).

[20] *Organizacja Kościoła w Polsce do połowy wieku XII.*

424

beginnings of the right of patronate in Poland,[21] an article on the establishment of the bishopric and the cathedral chapter in Cracow,[22] an article on the convention in Łęczyca in 1180,[23] and a study on the case of Muskata[24] (dealing with the genesis and history of a controversy between the German bishop in Cracow and King Władysław Łokietek). His study on the first clash between church and state in Poland[25] dealt with the times and activities of Archbishop Henryk Kietlicz. In 1893, Abraham edited and published the synodal statutes of the delegate Gentilis of 1309.[26]

Abraham's activity also included field work as deputy director (1896-1902), and later as director of the so-called Roman Expedition, financed by the Polish Academy. He conducted an unusually fruitful research in Roman and especially in Vatican archives and libraries, where he looked for documents pertaining to the history of Poland and particularly to the Polish church-state relations. He repeatedly published extensive reports of his work and findings in Rome.[27]

A bibliography of Abraham's writings published up to 1930 is to be found in a two-volume memorial book issued to commemorate fifty years of his scholarly activity.[28] A full bibliography, compiled by Jakub Sawicki, is included as an appendix to the third edition of his *Church Organization in Poland* (Poznań, 1962) (pp. 331-59). It contains well over 200 items.

Abraham's reputation as the leading Church historian was established by his three fundamental books. They are the above-mentioned work on Church organization in Poland up to middle of the twelfth century, and

[21]*Początki prawa patronatu w Polsce* (1889).

[22]"Początki biskupstwa i kapituły katedralnej w Krakowie" (1900).

[23]"Zjazd Łęczycki w roku 1180" (1889).

[24]*Sprawa Muskaty* (Cracow, 1894).

[25]*Pierwszy spór kościelno-polityczny w Polsce* (Cracow, 1895).

[26]*Statuty legata Gentilisa wydane dla Polski na synodzie w Preszburgu, 10 listopada r. 1309* (Cracow, 1897).

[27]*Sprawozdania z poszukiwań w archiwach i bibliotekach rzymskich o materiałach dla dziejów polskich w wiekach średnich* (Cracow, 1899 and later).

[28]Przemysław Dąbkowski, ed., *Księga pamiątkowa ku czci Władysława Abrahama* (Lwów, 1930-1).

works on the beginnings of the organized Latin church in Ruthenia[29] and the conclusion of marriage under the old Polish law.[30] Abraham was active mainly in the area of the history of the Church in Poland and adjoining countries, and also in dogmatic study of old and new canon law. Canon law was an obligatory subject for second-year students. It was a major subject taught five hours weekly for the whole year. The amount of material required for examination was formidable. The sources of canon law alone, an examination area especially liked by Abraham, although less so by students, filled a sizable volume. Despite this rather heavy teaching load, Abraham enriched Polish legal literature by many valuable works. At the beginning of the century he wrote some shorter historical contributions, based on materials discovered in Roman archives, including *The Attitude of the Roman Curia to the Crowning of King Łokietek*,[31] *Jacob Strepa, the Archbishop of Halicz*,[32] *The Beginnings of the Latin Archbishopric in Lwów*,[33] and *Latin Bishoprics in Moldavia in the Fourteenth and Fifteenth Centuries*.[34]

World War I, despite the temporary occupation of Lwów by Russian troops in 1914-5, had little impact on Abraham's scholarly productivity. Besides a contribution to a collective work on historical relations between Poland and Lithuania,[35] Abraham wrote about seignioral permission as the marriage requirement for subjects and about marriage fees,[36] and published a book entitled *Critical Studies on the Medieval History of Provincial Synods in the Polish Church*.[37]

After the promulgation of the Code of Canon Law in 1917, Abraham presented an analysis of it in an article published the next year.[38] After

[29] *Powstanie kościoła łacińskiego na Rusi.* The first and only volume was published in Lwów in 1904.

[30] *Zawarcie małżeństwa w pierwotnem prawie polskiem,* in *Studia nad historią prawa polskiego,* IX (1925).

[31] *Stanowisko Kuryi Papieskiej wobec koronacji Łokietka* (Lwów, 1900).

[32] *Jakób Strepa, arcybiskup halicki, 1391-1409* (Cracow, 1908).

[33] *Początki arcybiskupstwa łacińskiego we Lwowie* (Lwów, 1909).

[34] *Biskupstwa łacińskie w Mołdawji w wieku XIV i XV* (Lwów, 1902).

[35] *Polska i Litwa w dziejowym stosunku* (Warsaw, 1914).

[36] "Z dziejów prawa małżeńskiego w Polsce: zezwolenie panującego lub panów na małżeństwa poddanych i świeckie opłaty małżeńskie," in *Księga pamiątkowa ku czci B. Orzechowicza* (Lwów, 1916), I, 1-70.

[37] *Studja krytyczne do dziejów średniowiecznych synodów prowincjonalnych Kościoła Polskiego* (Cracow, 1917).

[38] *Nowy kodeks prawa kanonicznego* (1918).

the adoption of the Polish Constitution of 1921, Abraham gave a penetrating study of its provisions dealing with religion, the Church, and church-state relations.[39] Always keenly interested in Polish ecclesiastical law, he spent considerable time in studying old sources in various parts of Poland. As partial result of these studies, he published a monograph on the oldest synodal statutes of the Archdiocese of Gniezno.[40] A few years later he wrote a similar study covering the diocese of Płock.[41] Abraham planned to organize a publication of all sources of Polish ecclesiastical law in a collection, *Concilia Poloniae*. This plan has not been realized as yet. At this time he also wrote a preparatory study to his later great monograph on marriage in Polish law – an interesting work on pre-marriage negotiations by special emissaries of the bridegroom.[42]

In the last years of his life Abraham took part in the International Congress held in Rome in 1934 in commemoration of *Decretalia* of Pope Gregory IX, promulgated 700 years earlier. His paper, under the title "Jus canonicum particulare in Polonia tempore Decretalium Gregori IX," was published in the *Proceedings of the Congress* (Rome, 1936), III, 407-14. After retirement in 1935, Abraham published an article on the benefit of clergy in the Polish Church legislation of the thirteenth century.[43] He contributed also to *Piniński Festschrift* an article on the legal personality of a bishopric and the Statute of Łęczyca of 1180.[44] His last published work was a study on legal foundations of royal appointment of bishops in old Poland.[45]

As an outstanding scholar and professor, Abraham could not avoid numerous honors and recognitions. He was Dean of the Law Faculty in Lwów in 1894-95, in 1914-15 (during the Russian occupation of Lwów), and in 1915-16. He served as Rector Magnificus in 1899-1900. The Polish Academy of Arts and Sciences elected him a corresponding member in 1893, and an active member in 1903. No fewer than four Polish universities bestowed honorary Doctor's degrees on him. He was elected an

[39]*Konstytucja a stosunki wyznaniowe i Kościół* (1922).

[40]*Najdawniejsze statuty synodalne archidiecezji Gnieźnieńskiej* (Cracow, 1920).

[41]*Z dziejów ustawodawstwa synodalnego diecezji Płockiej* (1925).

[42]*Dziewosłęb, studyum z diejów pierwotnego prawa małżeńskiego w Polsce* in *Studia nad historyą prawa polskiego*, VIII (1922), pt. 2.

[43]"Privilegium fori duchowieństwa w ustawodawstwie Kościoła Polskiego w wieku XIII," *Collectanea Theologica*, XVI (1936), 1-16.

[44]"Osobowość prawna biskupstwa a statut Łęczycki z roku 1180," in *Księga pamiątkowa ku czci Leona Pinińskiego* (Lwów, 1936), I, 1-22.

[45]"Prawne podstawy królewskiego mianowania biskupów w dawnej Polsce," in *Studia historyczne ku czci Stanisława Kutrzeby* (Cracow, 1938), I, 1-12.

honorory member of the Polish Historical Society. With his retirement from the Law Faculty in 1935 he was named an honorary professor.

A rather short, heavy-set man with a benevolent look, a good lecturer, and deeply religious, Abraham was liked by his colleagues and revered by the students, who approached him as youngsters approach a good and wise grandfather. He died in Lwów under German occupation on October 15, 1941.

Writings on Abraham:
T. Silnicki, "Władysław Abraham, 1860-1941," Życie i Myśl (Poznań), 1950, No. 1-4.

Jakub Sawicki, "Władysław Abraham," Kwartalnik Historyczny, LIII (1946), 407-13.

– – – "Władysław Abraham," Rocznik Towarzystwa Naukowego Warszawskiego, XXXI-XXXVIII (1938-45), 163-6.

Michał Patkaniowski, Dzieje Wydziału Prawa Uniwersytetu Jagiellońskiego (Cracow, 1964), pp. 334-6.

IGNACY KOSCHEMBAHR-ŁYSKOWSKI (1864-1945)

The lives and careers of legal scholars born in the second half of the nineteenth century and presented in this chapter generally follow a pattern: a young man attends the university closest to his home, undertakes a study trip to Germany for one year, submits a few years later a study to his alma mater, is admitted as a docent, and later advances through associate professorship to professorship, which he keeps for decades as a member of the same faculty.

The career of Koschembahr-Łyskowski was completely different. He was closely connected with not less than four universities. He studied at and graduated from the University of Berlin. He was admitted as docent and he taught as an associate professor at Fribourg University, Switzerland. As a full professor he taught at the Lwów University, then under Austria, and at the Warsaw University, in independent Poland. Born February 3, 1864, in Żelichowo, near Gdańsk (Danzig), he lived in Prussia until his late twenties, and then lived in Switzerland for almost ten years, followed by a period of fifteen years within the Austro-Hungarian monarchy and thirty years in Warsaw. He lectured with equal fluency in Polish, French, and German.

Koschembahr-Łyskowski specialized in Roman law. He studied in Berlin under Pernice, Mommsen, Brunner, and Hinschius. The title of his doctoral thesis was Die Collegia Tenuiorum der Römer. This dissertation, published in 1888, was repeatedly cited by Mommsen, Godschmidt, and others as a true contribution to the knowledge of Roman law. Recognizing the advantages of working with a different law faculty, he settled for a while in Fribourg, where he wrote a fundamental study in the field of Roman civil procedure, under the title, *Die Theorie der Exceptionen nach klassischem römischen Recht.*[46] This study was accepted as a partial requirement for habilitation, and the next year Koschembahr-Łyskowski began his classes in Roman law. In 1895 he became an associate professor in Fribourg. During his stay in Switzerland he published several studies, one of which was *Die deutsche Schule des klassischen römischen Rechts, zugleich ein Beitrag zur Beurteilung der Bedeutung des römischen Rechts für die modernen Rechte.* In connection with the progressing codification of the Swiss civil law, Koschembahr-Łyskowski wrote an article, *Zur Vereinheitlichung des schweizerischen Privatrechts.* As professor of Roman law, he could not ignore the sensational discoveries of legal papyri in Egypt. He wrote an article about the scrolls of papyri unearthed in Fayum, but he never concentrated on this new specialty, as did Mitteis and later Taubenschlag.

The great event in his life came when he received an invitation to take over the chair of Roman law at the University of Lwów. Koschembahr-Łyskowski gladly accepted, and for the first time in his life started to teach in his native Polish. As professor in Lwów, he had the opportunity to combine teaching with research and to continue his scholarly activity, which was crowned by the publication of his best work, *Die condictio als Bereicherungsklage im klassichen römischen Recht.*[47] Although based on Roman law, this study had a significant impact on Austrian and German judicature and aroused an animated debate in legal periodicals of that time. His other publications during the first decade of the twentieth century included *Prolegomena to the History of Roman Law,*[48] *On the Concept of Property,*[49] *On the Place of Roman Law in the Austrian Civil Code,*[50] and *Significance of Law.*[51]

After the retreat of the Russian troops from Warsaw in World War I, Koschembahr-Łyskowski received a call from the Warsaw University, and in 1915 became professor of Roman law in the capital of Poland. A demanding examiner, he taught West European legal history in addition to Roman law until his retirement. These twenty years spent at Warsaw

[46]Berlin, 1893.

[47]Weimar, 1903-07; 2 vols.

[48]*Prolegomena do historii prawa rzymskiego* (1900).

[49]*O pojęciu własności, zarazem jako przyczynek do nauki o żródłach prawa* (1902).

[50]*O stanowisku prawa rzymskiego w austriackiej ustawie cywilnej* (1910).

[51]*Znaczenie prawa* (1911).

University were the best in his life. Koschembahr-Łyskowski occupied various positions with the University administration, and in 1923-4 served as the Rector of the University.[52] He was active as a member of the Polish Academy of Arts and Sciences, as well as of the Warsaw Learned Society. As early as 1919 he was appointed a member of the Polish Codification Commission. In 1927 he served as a vice-president of this commission. For many years, he was chairman of the subcommittee which prepared a draft Polish marriage law (with Lutostański as reporter).

Koschembahr-Łyskowski also lectured at the universities of Paris and Nancy in 1928 and took part in several international congresses. At the Second International Congress of Comparative Law in The Hague, in 1923, he presented a report on "La réparation morale dans la législation polonaise la plus recente.[53] The *Proceedings* of this congress include his address during the reception offered by the mayor of Leyden for the members of the congress.[54] The entry of his name on the list of members of the congress is followed by numerous titles and offices he held at that time.[55] For some years he also acted as Polish representative to the International Labor Office in Geneva.

As a professor in Warsaw he wrote in Polish and French, gradually expanding from the field of Roman law to that of civil law. His writings on Roman law are as follows: "Social and State Elements in Roman Private Law,"[56] "Conventiones contra bonos mores dans le droit Romain,"[57] "Naturalis ratio en droit classique Romain,"[58] "Quid veniat in bonae fidei iudicium en droit classique Romain,"[59] *Les facteurs intérieurs de*

[52]His traditional speech at the ceremony of installation as Rector Magnificus, on October 28, 1923, was about Roman law and present times ("Prawo rzymskie a czasy dzisiejsze"), and was published in Warsaw in 1925.

[53]Published in *Themis Polska*, series 3, VII (1932).

[54]II, 629.

[55]"Koschembahr-Łyskowski, I. de, Professeur de droit romain à l'Université de Varsovie; Vice-President de la Commission de Codification; Représentant de la Société Polonaise de Législation Civile, de la Commission Polonaise de coopération juridique internationale, Varsovie." (II, 525.)

[56]"Czynnik społeczny a czynnik państwowy w prywatnym prawie rzymskim," published with a French summary in *Themis Polska*, series 3, I.

[57]In *Mélanges de droit romain dédié a Georges Cornil* (Paris, 1926).

[58]In *Studi Bonfante*, III (Pavia, 1929).

[59]A report on the Seventh International Congress of Historical Sciences in Warsaw in 1933.

l'évolution du droit Romain privé,[60] and *Judicial Notice of Commercial Usages in Classic Roman Law.*[61]

As member of the Codification Commission, Koschembahr-Łyskowski often reported on the progress of the preparation of a draft civil code. His reports were published mostly in French: "La codification du droit civil en Pologne et les transformations modernes du droit civil,"[62] "Quelques dispositions générales d'un projet de code civil polonais,"[63] and *Projet de code civil de la République de Pologne, Livre I, Dispositons générales.* His last work, *Le code civil et la coutume,* was published in 1939.

Koschembahr-Łyskowski received an honorary degree from the University of Nancy in 1928. At the end of his career, the Law Faculty of the Warsaw University bestowed on him the title of Honorary Professor. He spent the years of World War II in Milanówek (near Warsaw), where he died on January 11, 1945, a few months before the end of the war.

Writings on Koschembahr-Łyskowski:

Jerzy Falenciak, "Ignacy Koschembahr-Łyskowski, 1864-1945," in *Rocznik Towarzystwa Naukowego Warszawskiego,* XXXI-XXXVIII (1938-45), 201-2.

FRYDERYK ZOLL, JR. (1865-1948)

Fryderyk Zoll, Jr., was born on February 1, 1865, the son of the great professor of Roman law (1834-1917). His early years were hardly different from those of many middle and upper class youths in the Austro-Hungarian monarchy in the second half of the nineteenth century. He finished secondary school in Cracow and became a law student at the Jagiellonian University. After early graduation with a Doctor's degree, he undertook the traditional one-year study trip to Western Europe (1889-90). He went first to Leipzig, where he attended classes of Professor Regelsberger, and then to Göttingen, where he studied under the aged but still active Rudolf von Ihering. He also spent several months in Paris.

---

[60]*Uwzględnienie przez sędziego zwyczajów obrotu w prawie klasycznym rzymskim* (1936).

[61]Published in 1924.

[62]In *Revue Trimestrielle de Droit Civil,* XXVII (1928), 551-78, and as a separate reprint by Sirey in Paris.

[63]In *Revue Polonaise de Législation Civile et Criminelle,* I-III (1928-31); translated into German in *Zeitschrift für Polnisches Recht- und Wirtschaftswesen* (Warsaw), 1928-31; and into Italian in *Rivista di Diritto Privato* (Padua), I-II, (1931-2).

431

Zoll was employed for the next seven years with the Department of Commerce in Vienna. This experience formed the basis for his later interest in problems of unfair competition and industrial law. Work with the Commerce Department did not deter his legal research; during this period he prepared the study on patent law[64] which opened the way to his academic career. As a docent on Austrian civil law he began to teach at the University of Vienna. When a vacancy occurred at the Jagiellonian University, Zoll accepted a call from Cracow. He was appointed associate professor in 1897, and full professor in 1900. He occupied the chair of civil law at the Jagiellonian University for fifty years.

Under the influence of his father, Zoll was a lifelong admirer of Roman law. He tried to apply to modern legal problems many basic concepts of Roman law well settled many centuries ago. Influenced by the towering personality of Ihering and attracted by his incomparable writings, Zoll chose the teleological legal method as his own, seeking the purpose of law and its adaptability to human needs as the criteria for its application.

With this approach, Zoll attempted to undermine the practice prevailing in Austria and founded on specific statutory provisions that interests in land could be transferred only by title registration in the registry of deeds. Under conditions in rural Galicia, where a significant part of the population was still illiterate at the beginning of the century, vending and purchasing of land was common to peasants without title registration. Rigid application of statutory provisions caused a great deal of injustice. Zoll wrote as many as seven articles on this subject in the decade 1907-16,[65] trying to prove that transfer of land based on valid title did pass property rights even before or without registration. He had the great satisfaction of seeing such a case won, when the Polish Supreme Court found for the first time in 1921 that Zoll's reasoning was right.

With his first study of patent law, in which he proved that patent rights may be possessed in a way similar to the possession of physical things, Zoll entered the field known for some time as rights on intangible assets: i.e., copyright, patent, and trademark law. He emphasized the personal rights of the author, for example, and concentrated on the study of such rights in general. His long article on personal rights as viewed by Austrian private law[66] is to be noted. A number of later contributions in this field prompted higher authorities to appoint Zoll the chief reporter on copyright law on the Polish Codification Commission. He may surely be

[64]*Privatrechtliche Studien aus dem Patentrechte* (Vienna, 1895).

[65]The best known is *Tradycja jako sposób nabycia własności na rzeczach nieruchomych* (Cracow, 1907).

[66]"Prawa osobiste w zarysie ze stanowiska prawa prywatnego austryackiego," *Czasopismo prawnicze i ekonomiczne,* 1903.

named the author of the Polish copyright law of 1926; he also wrote the best commentary on this law.[67] The same may be said for the Polish law of 1928 on the protection of inventions, industrial designs, and trademarks.

Another field in which he specialized was the law on unfair competition. As early as 1897, Zoll published an article on unfair competition and its forms as seen by private law.[68] He was opposed to the notion of combatting unfair competition by the methods of criminal law, which enumerated forbidden activities. He advocated instead the construction of subjective rights of the businessman to be protected against infringement. A quarter of a century later Zoll was working as chief reporter on a Codification Commission subcommittee on unfair competition. His law against unfair competition was promulgated in 1928. His commentary, written together with A. Kraus, followed.[69]

As an unusually skilled draftsman, Zoll deserves credit for two more pieces of outstanding legislation in the mid-twenties (1926): on international private law, and on the conflict of laws in internal relations.[70] As is well known, Poland inherited at least four different legal systems in 1918. Uniform regulation of conflict cases was a necessity. Both laws of 1926 were internationally acclaimed as statutory masterpieces. They were replaced only recently by a new Polish law on conflicts. Zoll's outline of the international private law was published in several editions as part of his multivolume civil law textbook, as well as separately.[71]

The first decade of the interwar period saw Zoll's most intense activity. He was an extremely active participant in the deliberations of the Codification Commission. The stabilization of Polish currency came in 1924 when the Polish złoty replaced 1,800,000 of the old Polish marks. Inflation had made havoc of the relations between debtors and creditors. Directed by his deep feeling of justice, Zoll drafted a bill aiming at more balanced sharing of losses caused by the collapse of the Polish monetary system in the postwar years. His endeavors were crowned with success. The so-called Valorization Law, generally known as Lex Zoll, was promulgated in 1924. Zoll wrote on the subject both prior to the

[67] *Polska ustawa o prawie autorskiem* (1926).

[68] "Nieuczciwa konkurencja i jej objawy ze stanowiska prawa prywatnego," *Przegląd prawa i administracji,* 1897.

[69] *Polska ustawa o zwalczaniu nieuczciwej konkurencji* (1929).

[70] *Międzynarodowe prawo prywatne i międzydzielnicowe prawo prywatne* (1926).

[71] *Międzynarodowe prawo prywatne w zarysie* (1931). Fourth edition, 1947.

enactment of this law and after.[72] The statute was used as a pattern for similar legislation in some other countries.

Zoll's interests and activities expanded beyond the fields mentioned above. He was a professor of civil law, and within the civil law it was the law of property which he chose as his specialty. His very valuable study on possession dates back to 1903.[73] It is not surprising that the Codification Commission entrusted him with one more tremendous job: to prepare a draft of the Polish law of property. Zoll wrote a draft which was debated vigorously within the commission in the last years before World War II. This draft was accepted as a basis for the first Polish decree on property of 1946.

A mention should be made of Zoll's publishing activity connected with teaching. He wrote several good textbooks on civil law. Prior to 1914 his textbook on the law of obligations appeared,[74] followed in 1909 by a work on the general part of civil law. His first concise outline of Austrian civil law was put on the market in 1910.[75] This book was expanded in its second edition, published in 1921. Another civil law textbook, covering Western Poland where the Prussian legal system prevailed, was published in early twenties in cooperation with Professor Ohanowicz.

At about the same time an introduction to the law of property was published by Zoll.[76] It contains chapters on the law of things, on possession, and on registers of titles, including mortgages.

A team of legal scholars headed by Zoll succeeded in publishing between 1931 and 1937 a four-volume textbook on Austrian civil law, then still in force. It included studies of the general part, the law of things, the law of domestic relations and wills, and the law of mortgages.[77] After

[72]"Projekt ustawy o waloryzacji należności pieniężnych opartych na tytułach prywatno-prawnych," *Czasopismo prawnicze* (Warsaw, 1923, and separately); *Rosporządzenie Prezydenta Rzeczypospolitej z dnia 14. maja 1924 o przerachowaniu zobowiązań prywatnoprawnych z motywami o objasnieniami oraz dodatkami dla nieprawników opracowanemi przez Prof. Fryderyka Zolla i Dra Bronisława Hełczyńskiego* (Warsaw, 1924).

[73]"Posiadanie według prawa austryackiego," *Przegląd prawa i administracji* (Lwów) 1903.

[74]*Zobowiązania* (Cracow, 1907).

[75]*Prawo prywatne w zarysie przedstawione na podstawie ustaw austryackich* (Cracow, 1910).

[76]*Prawa rzeczowe na ziemiach polskich* (Warsaw, 1921).

[77]*Prawo cywilne opracowane głównie na podstawie przepisów obowiązujących w Małopolsce, przy współudziale Jana Gwiazdomorskiego, Leona Oberlendera i Tomasza Sołtysika* (Poznań, 1931-7).

434

World War II another four-volume edition of his textbook was published in Cracow in cooperation with Adam Szpunar.[78] This edition also includes the law of obligations. Three volumes were republished in 1948. His textbooks served thousands of Polish law students.

Zoll was elected Dean of the Law Faculty three times: 1907-8, 1925-6, and 1933-4. He served as Rector of the Jagiellonian University in 1912-3. Members of the Polish Academy of Arts and Sciences elected him a corresponding member in 1914 and an active member in 1928. In addition, he was a member of several other Polish and foreign learned societies. He received honorary Doctor's degrees from three Polish universities.

As a professor, Zoll had the good luck to prepare at least eight students for their later professorial careers.

Between the wars he often took active part in international congresses on the law of copyright and industrial property, as well as on unfair competition. He represented Poland five times: at Geneva, The Hague, Warsaw, Lugano, and Rome. In this way he became personally acquainted with many leading Western European legal scholars, particularly the French ones. He was a member of a special committee of the congress in Rome (1928) which established personal rights of authors regarding their writings.

It may be mentioned that Zoll served for three difficult years (1916-9) as superintendent of the Cracow school system, acknowledging in this way his feeling that top priority was due to the task of youth education. He was a noted authority on school legislation. His lectures on this topic were published in 1932.[79]

Zoll died in Cracow on March 23, 1948. French professor Marcel Plaisant, a colleague who worked with him at international congresses, summarized admirably Zoll's achievements, with special stress on his authorship of five major Polish statutes. He paid tribute to this "jurisconsult of high competence who insisted on essential valuable principles, evaluated by his keen analytic mind, rarely encountered elsewhere, and who explained legal concepts by able comparisons drawn from the profound depths of his knowledge."[80]

Writings on Zoll:

Jan Gwiazdomorski, "Szkoła teleologiczna: Fryderyk Zoll Młodszy," in M. Patkaniowski, ed., *Studia z dziejów Wydziału Prawa Uniwersytetu*

[78]*Prawo cywilne w zarysie* (Cracow, 1946-8). The volume dealing with the law of conflicts was written in cooperation with Professor Przybyłowski.

[79]*Prawodawstwo szkolne* (Cracow, 1932).

[80]*Le Droit d'Auteur* (Geneva), LXI (1948), 104.

Jagiellońskiego (Cracow, 1964) pp. 287-96.
Adam Vetulani, "Śp. Fryderyk Zoll," *Państwo i Prawo,* III (1948), No. 5-6, 86-9.
Adam Szpunar, *Nauka prawa prywatnego i procesowego w Polsce* (Cracow, 1948), pp. 12-3.
Marcel Plaisant, "Frédéric Zoll, nécrologie," *Le Droit d'Auteur,* LXI (1948), 104.

WŁADYSŁAW JAWORSKI (1865-1939)

Władysław Leopold Jaworski was born on April 5, 1865 in Kaski, the Sandomierz district, in the part of Poland then under Russian rule. His parents sent him to schools in Cracow, where the relatively more enlightened Austrians offered the best opportunities for the Polish population. This was not unusual; the list of Polish lawyers born in Russian Poland who became later prominent members of the Law Faculty in Cracow also includes Roszkowski, Oczapowski, Krzymuski, Ulanowski, Rostworowski, and Górski. Jaworski attended secondary schools in Cracow and graduated from the Jagiellonian University with a Juris Doctor degree in 1888. He supplemented his legal education by a study trip to Berlin and Paris. After his return, he worked for a number of years with the Solicitor General's Office[81] in Cracow, the best apprenticeship possible for an academic career in civil law. A university professorship had been Jaworski's dream since his early years.

His start in this direction was not auspicious. As a young lawyer he disliked the dogmatic method of law teaching then prevalent in Austrian law schools. Interested in the economic aspects of the law, he was not satisfied with a system that did not extend beyond the dry letter of the statute. He submitted a study on easements in Austrian law[82] to the Law Faculty in Cracow, exposing in a lengthy preface his critical attitude toward the dogmatic method. At that time Jaworski was the author of two published works, one on the theory of remedies for damages,[83] and the other on damage caused by the exercise of one's own rights in real property.[84] The faculty answered Jaworski's application for the position of docent with a firm "No." The reason given was that Jaworski had failed

[81]Prokuratoria Skarbu.

[82]*Nauka o służebnościach według prawa austryackiego* (Cracow, 1892).

[83]*Zarys teorii wynagrodzenia szkody* (Cracow, 1891).

[84]*Szkoda zrządzona wykonywaniem swego prawa na nieruchomościach* (Cracow, 1892).

436

to prove that he could cope properly with legal problems in the selected branch of law.

Jaworski did not give up. He wrote another study, this time on legal problems connected with second mortgages in Austrian law.[85] This dogmatic study, written in accordance with traditional requirements, was accepted by the faculty, and Jaworski was admitted as a docent of Austrian civil law at the Jagiellonian University. As it will be seen, Jaworski had really changed his attitude: his later writings reveal the typical dogmatist.

He devoted the next several years to a detailed study of Austrian and provincial Galician statutes concerned with land title registration and the law of mortgages.[86] In his translation of the Austrian statute (enacted originally in German), Jaworski used for the first time legal terms prevalent in the legislation of the Polish kingdom. His commentary was used extensively by law practitioners for more than forty years. Along with his work on the law of mortgages, Jaworski wrote, in cooperation with Wróblewski, a commentary on the Austrian civil code.[87]

Jaworski was appointed professor in 1899. He taught civil law at the Jagiellonian University along with Professor Fruderyk Zoll, Jr. Endowed with a keen analytical mind, Jaworski soon became a leading representative of positivism in teaching and research.

At the same time, Jaworski's studies on the law of real property gave rise to his later interest in social aspects of land ownership in Galicia, especially in the relationship between landlords and peasants. He became deeply involved in politics. Closely connected with the conservative newspaper *Czas* ("Time") in Cracow, he was active in the so-called neo-conservative movement. Jaworski was a member of the Galician legislature for thirteen years (1901-14) and a member of the Austrian parliament in Vienna for seven years (1911-8). An ardent Polish patriot, he represented the group which hoped to restore Poland's independence with Austria's help. Polish legions organized by Józef Piłsudski at the start of World War I had a strong supporter in Jaworski, who wanted to have the legions maintained to the very end of the war. After 1918 Jaworski retired from political life for good to devote his remaining years to teaching and research. For many years he edited the legal periodical *Czasopismo Prawnicze i Ekonomiczne* ("Review of Law and Economics").

As early as 1910, Jaworski expanded his activity into the field of administrative law. He taught administrative law and prepared a temporary

[85]*Prawo nadzastawu wedle ustawodawstwa austryackiego* (Cracow, 1894).

[86]*Ustawa o księgach publicznych* (Cracow, 1897).

[87]*Komentarz do kodeksu cywilnego.* (Cracow, 1900-4).

edition of Austrian administrative law for student use.[88] This edition was supplanted by a permanent text on Polish administrative law in 1924.[89]

In independent Poland he returned once more to civil law with the publication of a two-volume work on civil law in Polish territories.[90] It included, however, only the marriage law and the law regarding relations between parent and child.

As a former politician, Jaworski could not remain silent when the foundations of the new Polish state were laid. He compiled the constitutional laws in force and wrote a commentary to the Polish Constitution of March 1921.[91] Several years later he wrote his own private draft constitution with an extensive commentary.[92] His draft constitution provided widely expanded protection of human rights and reflected his attempt to institute a proper balance of state rulings and controls. However, his draft was not taken into consideration when the March Constitution was amended in 1935.

After 1919, Jaworski was appointed chairman of the Civil Law Section of the Polish Codification Commission. He concentrated mainly on the law of property, but also worked in the area of agrarian law. He headed the Committee on Agrarian Law of the Codification Commission, and he prepared a draft agrarian code.[93]

In 1929 he published a book on the reform of the Polish system of notaries public.[94] In March 1924 the Philosophical Society in Cracow organized a symposium on the theory of law. Jaworski edited the papers of this symposium.[95] Near the end of his life, Jaworski became deeply interested in legal philosophy. A positivist in his earlier years, indifferent in religious matters and a rationalist in dealing with social and political issues, he now adopted a viewpoint of Christian universalism bordering on mysticism. In the philosophical concepts of St. Thomas Aquinas he divined the solution to many of the problems he had dealt with in his own writings.

Jaworski died in Milanówek on July 14, 1930. One year later a book was published about his life and work, with contributions by Estreicher,

[88]*Prawo administracyjne austryackie* (Cracow, 1914-5).

[89]*Nauka prawa administracyjnego* (Warsaw, 1924).

[90]*Prawo cywilne na ziemiach polskich*, 2 vols. (Cracow, 1919-20).

[91]*Prawa Państwa Polskiego* (Cracow, 1919-21).

[92]*Projekt Konstytucji* (Cracow, 1928), pp. 715 ff.

[93]*Projekt kodeksu agrarnego* (1928).

[94]*Reforma notariatu.* (Cracow, 1929).

[95]*Prace z dziedziny teorii prawa* (Cracow, 1925).

438

Zoll, and others.[96] It included a full bibliography of his writings, compiled by his son, Iwo Jaworski.

Writings about Jaworski:
Józef Buszko, "Jaworski Władysław Leopold," in *Polski słownik biograficzny*, XI. (Wrocław, 1964-5), pp. 115-8.
Konstanty Grzybowski, *Normatywizm w filozofii prawa: Władysław Leopold Jaworski*, in *Studia z dziejów Wydziału Prawa Uniwersytete Jagiellońskiego*, ed. M. Patkaniowski (Cracow, 1964) pp. 103-16.
Władysława Leopolda Jaworskiego życie i działalność, z wykazem bibliograficznym prac, zestawionym przez Dra I. Jaworskiego (Cracow, 1931).

STANISŁAW WRÓBLEWSKI (1868-1938)

Wróblewski was a man who combined the deepest knowledge of Roman law with the highest competence in the modern civil law, including commercial law, the law of negotiable instruments, and insurance law. For two decades Wroblewski used his profound knowledge as a member of the Polish Codification Commission.

Stanisław Wróblewski was born on May 5, 1868, in Tenczynek, in the district of Chrzanów. After graduation from a secondary school in Cracow, he studied law at the Jagiellonian University. Among his professors was the great Romanist, Fryderyk Zoll, Sr. Wróblewski earned the doctorate in law with highest distinction (*sub auspiciis Imperatoris*) in 1891. He continued his studies, as was customary at that time, for one more year in Berlin under Pernice, Goldschmidt, and Eck. After returning from Germany he entered the judicial career in which he was active for several years.

At the same time he submitted to the Law Faculty of the Jagiellonian University the product of his studies in Germany, a study published in Vienna under the title *Zur Lehre von der Collision der Privatrechte*.[97] This study, devoted to the analysis of most fundamental concepts of subjective law, was accepted by the Law Faculty as his habilitation thesis, after being reviewed favorably by Zoll and F. K. Fierich. Wróblewski was admitted as docent of the history and dogma of Roman law. He remained for some time in his judicial position, teaching Roman law part-time and working on

[96] *Władysława Leopolda Jaworskiego życie i działalność, z wykazem bibliograficznym prac, zestawionym przez Dra I. Jaworskiego* (Cracow, 1931).

[97] Vienna, 1894.

his next book, on the Roman law of possession.[98] This book brought about his promotion to associate professorship in 1901. He became a full professor in 1906.

In dealing with Roman law on the university level, some professors put emphasis on pure Roman law as codified by Emperor Justinian. Others have preferred to emphasize the so-called *Usus Modernus Pandectarum*, i.e., Roman law after its reception in Western Europe, and with the addition of rules of canon law, Germanic laws, and German judicial practice. Wróblewski started his scholarly career in the last decade of the nineteenth century, at the time when the so-called *Pandekten* were still in force in many German states. He found it more reasonable to teach Roman law in modern form than to spend time and effort tracing "pure" Roman law. In the course program presented to the faculty at the start of his teaching activity he included the well-known statement that "Windscheid is not inferior to Paulus, but he is much more valuable to us, just as it is easier and more expedient to teach reading today using an alphabet prevailing today than medieval Gothic."

Wróblewski's best work on Roman law is his outline of lectures on Roman law,[99] published in two volumes in 1916-9. It contains a general part and a section on property law. In this work Wróblewski presented his conception of the proper method in dealing with Roman law. Previously this subject had been treated sometimes historically, sometimes dogmatically. Wróblewski combined both methods. In the first volume of the outline he dealt with the history of internal conditions of Rome, the sources of Roman law, and the history of Roman law after Justinian's death. In presenting the history of sources, Wróblewski described concisely a number of well-known Roman jurists, not hiding his well-founded conviction that some of them (e.g., Gaius) did not deserve their fame. In the second volume, Wróblewski dealt dogmatically with the basic institutions of Roman private law. The whole work was entirely original, full of bold new conceptions, and written in an accomplished literary style. It was, however, too difficult for beginning students. It was written for legal scholars.

Well before World War I, Wróblewski extended his scholarly interest to the Austrian private law then in force in Galicia. His annotated edition of the Austrian Commercial Code,[100] published initially with Professor Rosenblatt, was expanded to two volumes in its third edition (1906-17). The second volume included supplementary legislation, such as the law of

[98]*Posiadanie na tle prawa rzymskiego* (Adademia Umiejętności, *Rozprawy Wydziału historyczno-filozoficznego*, Series 2, XII (Cracow, 1899).

[99]*Zarys wykładu prawa rzymskiego.*

[100]*Powszechna austryacka ustawa handlowa* (Cracow).

440

corporations and the law of bank checks. Wróblewski also published an annotated edition of the Austrian law of bank drafts.

His annotated edition to the Austrian law of inheritance,[101] published in Cracow in 1904, was planned as a practical commentary. But in reality it is a scholarly work containing solid theoretical studies on basic concepts of the law of inheritance, as well as on legal institutions characteristic of the Austrian law of decedents' estates only, as for example, the probate procedure and the meaning of the certificate of inheritance. This bulky volume (950 pages) served for a long time as a learned monograph (or, rather, a series of monographs). It ceased to serve as a practical commentary after amendments to the Austrian Civil Code were enacted in 1914-6. Wróblewski's interest in the law of inheritance later served him when he was chief reporter of this branch of law for the Polish Codification Commission. His work contributed greatly to the law of inheritance in force in present-day Poland.

A two-volume edition of the Austrian Civil Code, annotated by Wróblewski, was published in 1914-6.[102] The decisions of the Austrian Supreme Court in Vienna were utilized extensively, supplementing the explanations of the annotator.

Wróblewski was not an easy and fast writer. He considered each word, corrected his own drafts many times, and approved publication only after he felt a manuscript could not be improved in any way. His style is not easy to read. In his endeavor to be concise, he often uses long and complex sentences so as to cover within one breath a complex definition or statement. He tried to say much with few words, encompassing an entire concept in a single sentence without missing anything.

As an accomplished lawyer who believed in the fundamentals of Roman private law, he was opposed to those who paid exaggerated attention to utilitarian and economic considerations in the interpretation and construction of statutes.

Following World War I, Wróblewski was finally able to turn his attention to Polish legislation after working so long and so well on Roman and Austrian law. He wrote commentaries on the Polish laws of negotiable instruments of 1924,[103] and 1936, a commentary to the law of cooperative societies (1921),[104] and the beginning to a great commentary

[101]*Komentarz do par. 531-824 Ausryackiego kodeksu cywilnego, prawo spadkowe.*

[102]*Powszechny Austryacki kodeks cywilny z uzupełniającymi ustawami i rozporządzeniami, objaśniony orzeczeniami Sądu Najwyższego,* 2 vols. (Cracow, 1914-8).

[103]*Polskie prawo wekslowe i czekowe* (Cracow, 1924). Second edition, 1930.

[104]*Polska ustawa o spółdzielniach* (Cracow, 1921).

on the Polish Commercial Code of 1934. Unfortunately, only 240 pages were published before World War II, covering the first forty-three articles of the code.

Wróblewski was twice elected Dean of the Faculty of Law (1910-1 and 1917-8). He declined election as Rector of the Jagiellonian University in 1919.

He was a scholar of the highest caliber, but not an outstanding teacher. He did not consider the Faculty of Law as a school; students used other materials to prepare for examinations. Wróblewski's classes were simply too difficult. He did not take into account the level of students' preparation in his classes. He spoke in exquisite form, but the response was usually poor, because average students could hardly follow. The same was true with his seminars. Only the toughest members survived, among then Wróblewski's ardent admirer — later a great professor and scholar — Rafał Taubenschlag.

Wróblewski was elected a corresponding member of the Polish Academy of Arts and Sciences in 1910. Relatively few legal scholars were honored by membership in the Academy. Those who were often reached the top. Soon after being elected an active member, Wróblewski became the secretary general of the Academy, and in 1929 vice-president. In 1934 he reached the highest position possible for a Polish scholar — the presidency of the Academy. He remained in this position until his death.

In 1926 Wróblewski was appointed president of the Supreme Audit Chamber of the Polish Republic. He spent several years serving in this capacity. The President of the Polish Republic appointed him to membership in the Polish Senate in 1935.

Wróblewski did not live to see the horrors of the new war. He died in Warsaw on December 18, 1938.

Professor Gwiazdomorski concludes a study on Wróblewski's scholarly activity by saying: "He was not an ordinary man. He was a scholar of the highest stature, most eminent among eminent lawyers, pride and jewel of the Jagiellonian University."[105]

Writings on Wróblewski:
Jan Gwiazdomorski, *"Konstrukcja w nauce prawa cywilnego i prawa rzymskiego; Stanisław Wróblewski,"* in *Studia z dziejow Wydziału Prawa Uniwersytetu Jagiellońskiego*, Michał Patkaniowski, ed. (Cracow, 1964) pp. 269-86.

[105] Jan Gwiazdomorski, *Konstrukcja w nauce prawa cywilnego i prawa rzymskiego; Stanisław Wróblewski.* In *Studia z dżiejów Wydziału Prawa Uniwersytetu Jagiellońskiego,* ed. M. Patkaniowski (Cracow, 1964), p. 286.

Michał Patkaniowski, *Dzieje Wydziału Prawa Uniwersytetu Jagiellońskiego od Reformy Kołłatajowskiej do końca XIX stulecia* (Cracow, 1964), pp. 331-3.

Adam Szpunar, *Nauka prawa prywatnego i procesowego w Polsce* (Cracow, 1948), pp. 11-2.

JULIUSZ MAKAREWICZ (1872-1955)

Juliusz Makarewicz conducted his classes in criminal law at the University of Lwów in its largest auditorium, the *Collegium Maximum*. In spite of the fact that class attendance was not compulsory for law students, there were rarely empty seats when Makarewicz spoke. To say that he was a good lecturer would be a gross understatement. He was a vigorous orator whose words stimulated, attracted, and incited. Students who attended reluctantly the classes of some older professors flocked to the *Collegium Maximum* by hundreds to listen to him.

Makarewicz was born on May 5, 1872 in Sambor. After attending secondary schools in Tarnów and Cracow, he studied law at the Jagiellonian University. He practiced for some time in courts after graduation in 1894. For law study abroad he chose Halle and Berlin. Of all the great German legal scholars of that time, it was Kohler who made the deepest impression on him.

The fact that in a mere three years after graduation he had produced no less than five solid monographs, some of them in book form, may serve as proof of his amazing working capacity and his early ability to write quickly. The titles of these early works are: *Neurosis and Crime: A Criminal Psychological Study;*[106] *Classicismus and Positivismus in the Science of Criminal Law*[107] (also translated into German); *The Nature of Crime: A Criminal, Psychological, and Legal Study on a Comparative and Historical Basis;*[108] *Ideal Concurrence of Crimes in Austrian Criminal Law;*[109] and *The Evolution of Punishment.*[110] With such impressive credentials for a 25-year-old man, Makarewicz encountered no difficulties in habilitation proceedings at his alma mater or in securing the title of a

[106]*Neuroza i przestępstwo, studium kryminalno-psychologiczne* (1895).

[107]*Klasycyzm i pozytywizm w nauce prawa karnego.* (1896), German translation, 1897.

[108]*Das Wesen des Verbrechens, eine kriminalpsychologische Abhandlung auf vergleichender und rechtsgeschichtlicher Grundlage* (Vienna, 1896).

[109]*Idealny zbieg przestępstw w austriackim prawie karnym.* (1897).

[110]*Ewolucja kary. (1897).*

docent in criminal law. He was appointed associate professor in 1904. Serious differences of opinion on scholarly problems with senior criminal law professor (and his own former teacher) Krzymuski caused Makarewicz's resignation from the chair in Cracow. After he had declined a call from the university in Sofia, Bulgaria, Makarewicz accepted an offer from the University in Lwów, where he was active as a professor of criminal law from 1907 to 1939, and where he lived till death. For many years he also taught philosophy of law. It should be added that the decade of his teaching activity in Cracow was marked by numerous publications on various problems of criminal law and criminal procedure, as well as press law. They were eventually published in German as a collection of essays under the title *Juristische Abhandlungen.*[111]

Before a discussion of Makarewicz's activity in Lwów, some characteristic features of his scholarly works should be pointed out. His approach was completely antithetical to that of Krzymuski, who never deviated from the theory of classicism. Makarewicz, to the contrary, was an ardent promoter of the new sociological school, headed at that time by Liszt. He attempted to discover the sociological character of crime by digging deeply into historical, ethnological, and comparative legal sources. His book on the nature of crime was particularly well received by reviewers. Makarewicz worked on a second, updated edition but, facing a flood of new publications in this field, he soon abandoned the plan and wrote an entirely new work instead. This was the book which made him internationally famous.

His *Introduction to the Philosophy of Criminal Law* was published in German in 1906.[112] Any reader of this book will immediately recognize it as one of the fundamental treatises on the subject in world literature. It is not limited to a discussion of the philosophy of criminal law, but deals with basic concepts of criminal law on broad sociological, historical, and comparative foundations. The amount of digested literature and other sources is overwhelming. The book starts with a critical review of prevailing trends in the philosophy of law and proceeds to a detailed presentation of differences between the concepts of immorality and criminality in various times and places. The chapter on the evolution of crime traces the progress from ancient crimes against the stronger, through crimes against the modern concept of the deity, to crimes against society. Another chapter deals with the evolution of punishment, and gives an amazingly clear picture of the evolution of the concept of guilt. Two paths are considered: the development from collective to individual guilt, and

[111](Leipzig-Vienna, 1907).

[112]*Einführung in die Philosophie des Strafrechts auf entwicklungsgeschichlicher Grundlage.* (Stuttgart, 1906).

444

from objective to subjective guilt. Behind this simple scheme a solid treatise is to be found of such a permanent value that exactly sixty years after its publication a new photographic edition was put on the market in Western Europe in response to continuing demand.

Makarewicz maintained his scholarly production record after moving to Lwów. He returned to the problem of crime concurrence by writing a study: *Verbrechenskonkurrenz oder Gesetzeskonkurrenz.*[113] Shortly thereafter, he prepared a textbook on Austrian criminal procedure.[114] Two years later he finished a monograph on causes of criminality.[115] Always interested also in non-legal aspects of criminal law and procedure, he wrote an original article on the psychological foundations of a sensational trial.[116] By the end of World War I, he had readied a textbook on criminal procedure for the Polish kingdom.[117] His provocative essay on crime and punishment[118] followed.

Among several textbooks authored by Makarewicz, his *General Criminal Law,*[119] first published in 1914, deserves to be singled out. This is not a textbook on the general part of criminal law; it covers the entire field of criminal law. It was one of the first textbooks on comparative criminal law, since it was not limited in subject to a single legal system. Ten years later a second, significantly enlarged, edition of this book was published.[120]

Makarewicz never neglected the field of legal history. He conducted serious independent research on some old Polish legal institutions[121] and even wrote an entire treatise on Polish criminal law of the eighteenth century.[122]

During the entire interwar period Makarewicz was active with the Criminal Law Committee of the Polish Codification Commission. In this

[113] In *Österreichisehe Richterzeitung* (1907).

[114] *Zarys postępowania karnego austriackiego* (1909).

[115] *Źródla przestępczości* (1911).

[116] "Psychologiczny podkład sensacyjnego procesu," in *Gazeta Sądowa Warszawska* (1913).

[117] *Procedura karna dla Królestwa Polskiego* (1918).

[118] *Zbrodnia i kara* (Warsaw, 1922).

[119] *Prawo karne ogólne* (Lwów, 1914).

[120] *Prawo karne, wyklad porównawczy z uwzględnieniem prawa obowiązującego w Rzeczypospolitej Polskiej* (Lwów, 1924).

[121] E.g., "Instygator w dawnem prawie polskiem," *Archiwum Towarzystwa Naukowego,* I, pt. 2, No. 4.

[122] *Polskie prawo karne Polski przedrozbiorowej* (1919).

capacity he was responsible for a draft of the Polish Criminal Code, which eventually became law in 1932. This is not the place for an analysis of this new and original criminal code, which still remains in force in Poland with some postwar amendments. It must be said that this code bears the indelible imprint of Makarewicz's intellect, his profound knowledge of comparative criminal law, and his philosophy.

In Makarewicz were brought together a philosophical mind, the skill of a codifier, and the talents of an outstanding commentator. As the "father" of the Polish Criminal Code he was eminently qualified to prepare its annotated edition; and he wrote five editions in the same number of years.[123] His annotations are preceded by an introduction on the fundamental characteristics of the code. He finds them in subjectivism and individualism (as opposed to objectivism and collectivism), in an humanitarian approach in meting out punishment, and in the protection of the community against certain types of criminals. Makarewicz's commentary on the criminal code served as the textbook for law students in Lwów, along with his course in comparative criminal law, published earlier.

Makarewicz was also politically active. For a number of years he served as a member of the Polish Senate from the Christian-Democratic Party. He was Rector of the University of Lwów in 1923-4.

During the Soviet occupation of Lwów in 1939-41, Makarewicz was not permitted to teach. During the subsequent German occupation in 1941-44, the Law School in Lwów was closed. Makarewicz remained in Lwów to the end of his days. In the last decade of his life he worked on problems of criminal attempts, of habitual criminals, and of guilt according to English law.

Makarewicz died on April 20, 1955, in Lwów. Ten years later, at a special session of the Polish Group of the International Association of Criminal Law held in Warsaw, Polish scholars delivered a number of papers on various aspects of Makarewicz's philosophy.

Writings on Makarewicz:
Stanisław Pławski, "Juliusz Makarewicz," *Państwo i prawo*, X (1955), 252-5.

– – – "Walka Makarewicza o praworządnosc," *Państwo i prawo*, XXI (1966), 239-46.

Władysław Wolter, *Nauka prawa karnego od drugiej połowy XIX wieku* in *Studia z dziejów Wydziału Prawa Uniwersytetu Jagiellońskiego*, ed. M. Patkaniowski (Cracow, 1964), pp. 332-4.

– – – "O założeniach filozoficznych poglądów Juliusza Makarewicza," *Państwo i prawo*, XXI (1966), 231-8.

[123]*Komentarz do Polskiego kodeksu karnego* (1st ed., Lwów, 1932; 5th ed., Lwów, 1938).

JULIAN MAKOWSKI (1875-1959)

Most of the great jurists presented in this chapter excelled in teaching and legal research. Julian Makowski also managed to perform simultaneously the duties of a high official in the Polish Ministry of Foreign Affairs. This was not a temporary assignment; it lasted for more than twenty years.

Makowski was born in Warsaw on February 6, 1875. He studied law at the Universities of Cracow and Warsaw, spent some time in Paris and Antwerp, and earned his Doctor's degree at the University of Poznań relatively late, in 1919. He began to teach in Warsaw at a private commercial school before World War I. After serving for two years (1917-9) with the commercial court in Warsaw, he was associated, for the whole of his remaining career, with the Higher Commercial School in Warsaw, which in time became a state institution of higher learning as the Main Commercial School.[124] Makowski taught international law as an associate professor after 1919, and as a professor after 1936. In 1937 he was elected Rector of the Main Commercial School, and remained its leader even at the time of clandestine activity during the German occupation. After World War II, Makowski taught at the Academy of Political Sciences in Warsaw, an institution later renamed the Main School of Foreign Service.[125] In the last years of his teaching activity he narrowed the scope of his lectures to the law of diplomacy.

In 1919, shortly after the re-establishment of independent Poland, Makowski was appointed Director of the Treaties Division in the Ministry of Foreign Affairs, a position which he occupied until the mid-thirties and again in the forties. In the last decade of his life, he was active as a legal counsel for the Minister of Foreign Affairs, with the rank of a Minister Plenipotentiary.

His work in the Treaties Division was pioneering. Regaining independence lost in the eighteenth century when international intercourse was not so highly developed, Poland faced considerable difficulty in establishing new treaty-making rules, drafting basic treaty clauses and ratification documents, and interpreting correctly constitutional provisions concerning foreign relations. Makowski's accomplishment was to direct the activities of the Treaties Division in the most difficult initial period, as well as later during most of the interwar period. He took part in several international conferences and negotiated some international agreements as a representative of the Polish Republic. He played a significant role in the International Conference for the Unification of International Law at the

[124] Szkoła Główna Handlowa.

[125] Szkoła Główna Służby Zagranicznej.

Hague in 1930. As an outstanding expert in the law of treaties, Makowski was invited to deliver a series of lectures at the Academy of International Law at the Hague in 1931.

His writings are varied. As a long-time teacher of international law, Makowski offered several editions of his own textbook to his numerous students. As a practical worker in the Ministry of Foreign Affairs he had a specific feeling for issues dominant in international relations at a given time, and he wrote articles and papers dealing with legal aspects of these issues. Finally, as a man who had to deal constantly with international treaties, Makowski made a number of valuable contributions in this area, in which he combined theoretical considerations with practical experience. He was also the initiator of important collections of international documents — collections being enlarged to this day.

Prompted by the absence of Polish textbooks on international law at the outbreak of World War I, Makowski published in 1915 his *Foundations of International Law*.[126] Planned originally as a textbook for the use of students only, the book grew in size and learned contents in subsequent editions. Published in the second, third, and fourth edition under the title *International Law*,[127] the book appeared for the last time in 1948 in its fifth edition under the title *Textbook of International Law*.[128] The last edition was a bulky volume of 772 pages, a far cry from the *Foundations* of 1915. Consideration of the international developments of thirty years, together with the knowledge and skill of the author, made this treatise a worthy competitor to the famous works on international law written by two other Polish professors, Ehrlich and Cybichowski.

Makowski's monographs had always a touch of actuality. Almost as if he were a legal counsel of the Ministry of Foreign Affairs, Makowski wrote books and articles aimed at strengthening Poland's position in international relations whenever he felt that the Polish interests were in need of solid legal arguments. Makowski wrote three works on the international legal status of the Free City of Gdańsk (Danzig): *The Free City of Gdańsk from the Standpoint of Constitutional Law*,[129] *La situation juridique du territoire de la Ville Libre de Dantzig*,[130] and *The Problem of the Statehood of the Free City of Gdańsk*.[131] Well aware of the tremendous significance of Polish access to the sea, Makowski foresaw well in advance

[126] *Zasady prawa międzynarodowego* (Warsaw, 1915).

[127] *Prawo międzynarodowe* (Warsaw, 1918, 1922, 1930).

[128] *Podręcznik prawa międzynarodowego* (Warsaw, 1948).

[129] *Prawno-państwowe położenie Wolnego Miasta Gdańska* (Warsaw, 1923).

[130] Paris, 1925.

[131] *Zagadnienie państwowości Wolnego Miasta Gdańska* (Warsaw, 1931).

all the future tragic complications leading to World War II. Like many foreign scholars attracted by the peculiar international status of Gdańsk, Makowski argued that this Free City was not a sovereign state, that it lacked the traditional attributes of a state, and that Polish prerogatives in the territory of Gdańsk should be expanded. His publications dealing with Gdańsk were often criticized by German legal scholars who represented contrary views.

In opposition to the German revisionist movement based partly on the Article 19 of the Covenant of the League of Nations, Makowski wrote his own interpretation of the meaning of this article, *Article 19 of the League of Nations Covenant,*[132] published in both Polish and French.[133] Disturbed by lack of diplomatic relations with Lithuania caused by the Vilna controversy, Makowski wrote about the Lithuanian problem.[134]

Several of his studies were devoted to problems of international organization, collective security, and peaceful settlement of international disputes. Two of them are *Modern Forms of International Judiciary,*[135] and *Modern Forms of Collective Security.*[136] Like any international law writer, Makowski wanted to have at least one of his contributions included in the prestigious *Recueil des cours de l'Académie de droit international.* He achieved this goal in 1931, when his long article, "L'organisation actuelle de l'arbitrage international," was included in Volume 36 (pages 267-384). After World War II Makowski wrote on the new international organization, the United Nations.[137]

Makowski was active even in the last years of his long life. He wrote in his eighties a book on state organs in international relations[138] and an article on the breach of diplomatic relations and its legal consequences.[139]

[132]*Artykuł 19 paktu Ligi Narodów* (Warsaw, 1933).

[133]*L'Article 19 du Pacte de la Société des Nations* (Warsaw, 1933).

[134]*Kwestia litewska, studium prawne* (Warsaw, 1929). It was published also in French (*La question lithuanienne:* Paris, 1930) and in Italian (*La questione lituana:* Rome, 1930).

[135]*Współczesne formy sądownictwa międzynarodowego,* (Warsaw, 1926).

[136]*Współczesne formy bezpieczeństwa zbiorowego* (Warsaw, 1935).

[137]*Organizcja Narodów Zjednocznonych* (Warsaw, 1946). A second and enlarged edition was published in 1947.

[138]*Organa państwa w stosunkach międzynarodowych, zjazdy międzynarodowe, umowa międzynarodowa* (Warsaw, 1957).

[139]"Zerwanie stosunków dyplomatycznych i jego skutki prawne," *Sprawy międzynarodowe,* 1959, No. 2.

His interest in constitutional law was rather marginal. He wrote on the United States Constitution[140] and published a collection of foreign constitutions in Polish translation.[141] His most valuable contributions, however, were in the area of the law of treaties. Here belongs his *Theory and Techniques of the Conclusion of International Treaties*,[142] later expanded into a fundamental treatise, *On the Conclusion of International Treaties*.[143] Makowski put all his vast practical experience into this latter work.

The old question of whether an author gains more reputation and fame by publishing monographs or source material collections could be asked in Makowski's case also. In 1929, he published a collection under the title *Poland's International Commitments, 1919-1929*,[144] containing data and summaries of 495 treaties. Five years later he published a similar collection under the title, *Poland's International Agreements, 1919-1934*,[145] containing data on 988 treaties and other international agreements. With access to the files of the Ministry of Foreign Affairs, Makowski included in his collection not only formal treaties published with official statutory materials, but also various protocols, notes, and unpublished executive agreements. Makowski had brought his work up to date by 1939, when World War II began.

As a high official with the Ministry of Foreign Affairs, Makowski was well aware of the necessity for the systematic publication of other important documents related to international affairs. In 1933 he initiated the publication of a collection of such documents[146] in Polish, French, and other languages. The collection is continued now by the Polish Institute of Foreign Affairs. As a tribute to its founder, the collection is known as the Makowski collection.

In 1957 Makowski was honored by his colleagues and students by a special commemorative book issued to celebrate half a century of his scholarly work.[147] He died in Warsaw on October 25, 1959.

[140]*Konstytucja Stanów Zjednoczonych* (Warsaw, 1918).

[141]*Nowe konstytucje* (Warsaw, 1925).

[142]*Teoria i technika zawierania umów międzynarodowych* (Warsaw, 1931).

[143]*O zawieraniu umów międzynarodowych* (Warsaw, 1937).

[144]*Zobowiązania międzynarodowe Polski, 1919-1929* (Warsaw, 1929).

[145]*Umowy międzynarodowe Polski, 1919-1934* (Warsaw, 1935).

[146] *Zbiór dokumentów.*

[147]*Księga pamiątkowa ku czci Juliana Makowskiego z okazji 50-lecia pracy naukowej* (Warsaw, 1957).

Writings about Makowski:
Alfons Klafkowski, "Julian Makowski, Nekrolog," *Ruch Prawniczy i Ekonomiczny,* XXII (1960), 315-22.
– – – "Z okazji 50-lecia pracy naukowej Juliana Makowskiego," *Przegląd Zachodni,* XII (1956), No. 9-10, pp. 150-2.
Stanisław Nahlik, "Julian Makowski," *Państwo i Prawo,* XV (1960), 113-6.
– – – "Julian Makowski," *Sprawy Międzynarodowe,* XII (1959), No. 11-12.

STANISŁAW KUTRZEBA (1876-1946)

There was a widespread opinion among law students of southwestern Poland between two world wars that the most difficult year of law studies at the Jagiellonian University in Cracow was the first one. Historical subjects, including the history of Polish law, were taught in the first year, and the examiner most feared was Professor Kutrzeba.

Stanisław Kutrzeba was born in Cracow in November 15, 1876, the son of a businessman. He attended primary and secondary schools in Cracow and gained his doctorate from the Jagiellonian University Law School in 1898. During his law studies he also attended classes and seminars in medieval history. As an outstanding student who worked primarily in the seminar of Professor Bolesław Ulanowski, he had no difficulty in securing a postgraduate fellowship from the Polish Academy of Arts and Sciences for study abroad. He did research work for one year in the Vatican archives, looking for documents pertaining to the history of Poland, as well as in Paris, mainly in the École des Haute Études and in the Bibliothèque Nationale. After his return to Poland, he began to work in the Provincial Archives in Cracow. This work continued for seven years. Close connection with a wealth of unpublished materials encouraged him to specialize in the economic history of Poland with special emphasis on his native city, Cracow.

Under the influence of Ulanowski, Kutrzeba conducted pioneering research in a number of Polish archives and wrote a fundamental study on land and city courts in medieval Poland.[148] As a by-product of his research, he published eight articles on the history of the judiciary in Poland.[149] The study on land and city courts was accepted by the Law

[148]*Sądy ziemskie i grodzkie w wiekach średnich* (Cracow, 1901).

[149]"Studia do historii sądownictwa w Polsce," *Przegląd Prawa i Administracji,* XXVI-XXVII (1901-3).

Faculty of the Jagiellonian University as partial requirement for habilitation, and Kutrzeba became a docent of the history of Polish law.

Serving as a docent and working full time in the archives, Kutrzeba wrote the first volume of his well-known *Outline of the Polish Constitutional Law,*[150] published in 1905. This work, which made Kutrzeba famous, was limited initially to the territory of Poland proper. As the cut-off date, the year of the third partition of Poland (1795) was selected. Based partially on older monographic coverage and partially on his own research, Kutrzeba's work presented for the first time a complete historical outline of Poland's public law prior to the loss of independence. The first volume of the work was an immediate success. Written in a smooth style readily accessible to laymen, the work became not only an established textbook for law students in Cracow for the next fifty years; it also found many readers in the part of Poland under Russian rule. It was published in as many as eight editions. The last one, revised by Adam Vetulani, was published in 1949. For unexplained reasons, not one but two Russian translations were published in Petersburg in 1907.[151] A little later the third edition of the book was translated into German and published in Berlin in 1912.[152]

But Kutrzeba was still a docent; even his *Outline* did not bring about his promotion to associate professorship. To fulfill the faculty's requirement, he wrote a special study on *Murder of a Husband in Polish Law of the Fourteenth and Fifteenth Centuries.*[153] Only then was he appointed to associate professorship, in 1908. He terminated his employment with Provincial Archives and concentrated on teaching and research. In 1912 came the full professorship.

Some years before World War I Kutrzeba had seriously considered the idea of writing a second volume of the *Outline,* this time about the constitutional history of Lithuania. After a prolonged study of Polish and Russian sources and the publication of several shorter studies, he published the *Lithuania* volume in 1914.[154] Two years later a Lithuanian translation appeared in Vilna.[155] And again, as a by-product of his research on Polish-Lithuanian relations, a special collection of documents relevant to

[150]*Historia ustroju Polski w zarysie. Vol. 1: Korona* (Lwów, 1905).

[151]*Ocherk istorii obshchestvenno-gosudarstvennago stroia Polshi* (St. Peterburg, 1907). One edition was translated by Jadwiga Paszkowicz, the second one by J.W. Jastrebow.

[152]*Grundriss der polnischen Verfassungsgeschichte,* (W. Christiani: Berlin, 1912).

[153]*Mężobójstwo w prawie polskim XIV i XV wieku* (Cracow, 1907).

[154]*Historia ustroju Polski w zarysie. Vol. 2: Litwa* (Lwów, 1914).

[155]*Lietuvos visuomenes ir teises istorija* (Vilna, 1916).

452

the Polish-Lithuanian Union was compiled and later published under joint editorship with W. Semkowicz.[156]
During the war years, 1914-18, Kutrzeba was active in two fields. He finished his *Outline* by adding two more volumes dealing with nineteenth-century legal developments on territories belonging to Poland before the partitions.[157] At the same time, well aware of the significance of World War I in Poland's future, he followed current events with keen interest and switched temporarily to journalism. He wrote, at that time, a great number of articles, notes and remarks in the Polish daily press. His political acumen and deep knowledge of Polish constitutional history made him invaluable as a member of the Polish delegation to the peace conference in Versailles. Later, in 1925, he headed the Polish delegation which concluded a treaty with Czechoslovakia on a number of controversial issues.

Polish legal history as a subject in the law curriculum was expanded in the independent Polish Republic after 1918, and the need for new textbooks arose. Kutrzeba published such a textbook on the history of Polish judicial law in 1921.[158]

Between the two world wars, Kutrzeba also published a two-volume work of utmost importance: *Sources of the Polish Legal History*. This work, of permanent value to researchers, has not yet been superseded. Kutrzeba was eminently qualified as an editor of source materials by his long experience with archives.

In 1926 occurred an event of decisive influence on the direction of Kutrzeba's scholarly work: he was elected Secretary General of the Polish Academy of Arts and Sciences. This was a full-time position which left little time for the continuation of scholarly work. However, Kutrzeba continued to teach at the Jagiellonian University. In addition to his regular classes, he conducted a seminar on the history of Polish law. Topics assigned to seminar members were often in fields lacking any monographic coverage. Students were required to work on primary sources. A good knowledge of Latin was indispensable. Not many students could fulfill these requirements; those who did profited enormously.

During his tenure as Secretary of the academy, Kutrzeba compiled and published collections of legislative materials of the Province of Cracow for

[156]*Akta unii Polski z Litwą, 1385-1791* (Cracow, 1932).

[157]*Historia ustroju Polski w zarysie. Vol. 3: Po rozbiorach. Pt. 1. Rządy pruskie. Księstwo Warszawskie. Królestwo Polskie. Litwa i Ruś. Wolne Miasto Kraków* (Lwów, 1917). *Historia ustroju Polski w zarysie. Vol. 3: Po rozbiorach. Pt. 2. Wielkie Księstwo Poznańskie. Galicja* (Lwów, 1917). A second edition of these volumes was published in 1920.

[158]*Dawne polskie prawo sądowe. 1. Prawo karne. 2. Postępek sądowy* (Lwów, 1921).

the years 1572-1620,[159] of Polish military laws and regulations of the fifteenth through eighteenth centuries,[160] and of Polish rural laws for the same period.[161]

To the list of his books two more titles should be added: *The Resurrected Poland* (1914-21),[162] published in four editions between 1921 and 1935, and, for West-European readers the French-language *La question polonaise pendant la guerre mondiale.*[163]

Between the two world wars the Polish Academy of Arts and Sciences became the beneficiary of several large estates whose proper administration was a major job requiring skill and perseverance. As Secretary General, Kutrzeba enjoyed the steady growth of the academy's assets and the vast expansion of its activities. His secretaryship coincided with the best period in the long history of the academy. In the ominous year 1939, Kutrzeba was elected President of the academy after the death of Stanisław Wróblewski. The time of his presidency brought its greatest sorrow; with the German occupation of Cracow in September of 1939, the activity of the academy was suspended. Shortly thereafter Kutrzeba was arrested. He spent several months in the concentration camp in Sachsenhausen, together with many other professors of the Jagiellonian University. He returned to Cracow in broken health and soon became engaged in the dangerous activity of heading a clandestine law school; the Jagiellonian University, along with all others, was officially closed during the German occupation. After the reopening of the university in March 1945, Kutrzeba had the great satisfaction of delivering the first lecture at the Law School. He also prepared for publication a short introduction to *The Theory of the State and Law,*[164] published shortly after his death in Cracow on January 7, 1946.

Owing to his tremendous research and publishing activity, Kutrzeba had advanced rapidly in his academic career. He was Dean of the Law School in the years 1913-4 and again in 1920-1. He served as Rector of the Jagiellonian University in 1932-3. In 1914 he was elected a corresponding member, and in 1918 an active member, of the Polish Academy of Arts and Sciences — the same academy he later headed as Secretary General and

[159] *Akta sejmikowe województwa krakowskiego. Vol. 1, 1572-1620* (Cracow, 1932).

[160] *Polskie ustawy i artykuły wojskowe* (Cracow, 1937).

[161] "Polskie ustawy wiejskie XV-XVIII wieku" (with Alfons Mańkowski), *Archiwum Komisji Prawniczej,* XI (1938).

[162] *Polska odrodzona* (Cracow, 1921). A fourth edition was published in Warsaw and Cracow in 1935.

[163] Paris, 1933.

[164] *Wstęp do nauki państwa i prawa* (Cracow, 1946).

President. A member of many domestic and foreign learned societies, he was honored by election to membership in the Académie des Sciences Morales et Politiques in Paris, of the Czech Academy of Sciences in Prague, and the Hungarian Academy of Sciences in Budapest. He took an active part in national and international congresses of jurists and historians in France, Belgium, Czechoslovakia, Switzerland, Latvia and other countries. In 1938 he was honored by a two-volume work dedicated to him and commemorating forty years of his scholarly work.[165] Fifty authors contributed the same number of valuable articles.

Kutrzeba left behind a rich legacy. A list of his published contributions up to 1937 contains 424 titles.[166] An additional list covering the last decade of his life indicates forty more.[167] The amount of information on Polish legal history available today would be far smaller without his great contribution.

Writings on Kutrzeba:
Special issue of *Kwartalnik Historyczny*, LIV (1947), No. 1, with contributions by Adam Vetulani, Tadeusz Kowalski, and Jan Dąbrowski.

Bogusław Leśnodorski, "Śp. Stanisław Kutrzeba," *Państwo i Prawo*, I (1946), 78-83.

Adam Vetulani, "Stanisław Kutrzeba," in *Studia z dziejów Wydziału Prawa Uniwersytetu Jagiellońskiego*, ed. Michal Patkaniowski (Cracow, 1964), pp. 204-22.

– – – "Stanislas Kutrzeba" (In French), *Czasopismo Prawno-Historyczne*, I (1948), 197-205.

PRAZEMYSŁAW DĄBKOWSKI (1877-1950)

Balzer's best and most devoted student, and later his colleague at the same faculty, Przemysław Dąbkowski was born in Lwów on February 23, 1877. His parents had come from Warsaw. The young Dąbkowski attended secondary schools in Stryj and Lwów. The first seminar he attended as a second-year law student in Lwów was Balzer's, on the history of Polish law. His first seminar paper, prepared from original documents, on vendetta and ransom in Halicz Ruś in the fifteenth century was so

[165]*Studia historyczne ku czci Stanisława Kutrzeby*, 2 vols. (Cracow, 1938).

[166]*Ibid.*, I, ix-xxxiii.

[167]*Kwartalnik Historyczny*, LIV (1947), 55-7.

outstanding that it was published in 1897.[168] Balzer, who was at that time also Director of Provincial Archives in Lwów, secured a part-time job with the archives for his talented student. This event determined Dąbkowski's later career. Affected by the peculiar charm of medieval manuscripts stored within the thick walls of the St. Bernard's monastery in Lwów, he early found his field of study and research: legal history in general, and, more specifically, the history of Polish private law. He spent almost twenty years with these archives, and admitted later that these were the happiest years of his life.

Dąbkowski graduated in 1900 with a Doctor's degree and started full-time work in the archives. This work was interrupted twice by study trips abroad. He studied for one year in Berlin (1903-04) under Karl Zeumer, Josef Kohler (it is amazing how many Polish legal scholars were attracted by Kohler's magnetic personality), and Martin Wolff, as well as under Alexander Brückner, a professor of Slavic literatures. Dąbkowski's second trip abroad took place in 1907-8. During this later trip he visited a number of libraries and archives in Polish territory as well as abroad. His longest stay was in Paris. He wrote a book about his study trips, in which he elaborated his theory that a scholar's activity usually covers the broadest areas when he is in his twenties; studies in depth are not possible, he said, before the thirties.

With Balzer's encouragement Dąbkowski specialized in a field almost untouched before: the history of Polish private law. In the first decade of the century he published a series of monographs dealing with the history of various legal institutions. Titles of some of them are difficult to translate into English, since they present ancient and generally extinct institutions known in Polish law only. These works deal with the prevention of the breach of contract in medieval Polish law;[169] the history of suretyship and guaranty in Poland;[170] the history of creditors' rights and imprisonment for debt;[171] and forms of contracts, with a special excursus on oaths.[172]

[168]"Zemsta, okup i pokora na Rusi halickiej w wieku XV i w pierwszej połowie XVI wieku," *Przegląd Prawa i Administracyi,*" XXII (1897). Reprinted separately in Lwów, 1898.

[169]"O utwierdzaniu umów pod grozą łajania w prawie polskiem średniowiecznem" (Lwów, 1903), in *Archiwum Naukowe,* section 1, I, pt. 1. All monographs cited below were also published separately.

[170]"Rękojemstwo w prawie polskiem średniowiecznem" (Lwów, 1904), in *Archiwum Naukowe,* section 1, I, pt. 1.

[171]"Załoga w prawie polskiem średniowiecznem" (1905), in *Archiwum Naukowe,* section 1, II, pt. 4.

[172]"Litkup" (1906), in *Archiwum Naukowe,* section 1, III, pt. 2.

His study on suretyship and guaranty[173] was accepted by the Law Faculty in Lwów as a part of the habilitation requirement, and Dąbkowski began to teach in 1906 as a docent. This did not disturb his work at the archives. On the contrary, Dąbkowski found that after ten years of work he had accumulated enough material to write a fundamental textbook on history of Polish private law. In three years the work was finished. A two-volume treatise under the simple title of *Polish Private Law*[174] contained in 1300 pages the fruits of his long research. The work was dedicated to Balzer. The dedication itself, simple and brief as it is and written in beautiful old Polish language, may serve as an example of the grateful student who gives to his venerated master his best.

This great treatise marked the peak of Dąbkowski's scholarly activity. He was at that time only thirty-three years old. No one since has written a better treatise on this subject. Dąbkowski became an associate professor in 1910. He continued the steady production of valuable monographs at the average rate of one volume per year. His treatise on the history of legal institutions of deposit and trust[175] was published in 1909. Dąbkowski also wrote several works on Lithuanian law, of which *Status of Aliens in Lithuanian Law, 1447-1588,*[176] and *Inheritance of Various Kinds of Real Estate in Lithuanian Law*[177] are but two examples.

Dąbkowski expanded the scope of his teaching in 1913 to include the history of German law, after his monograph on pledge in Saxenspiegel, Schwabenspiegel, und Deutschenspiegel was published.[178] He was appointed Professor of the History of German Law in 1916.

After the collapse of Austria in 1918 and the emergence of an independent Poland, Dąbkowski received calls to join law faculties in Warsaw, Poznań, and Lublin. He even taught Polish constitutional history and the history of Polish private law in Warsaw during the academic year 1919-20, but ultimately he decided to stay in Lwów.

A second chair of Polish legal history was established for him. For the next fourteen years, the University of Lwów was fortunate to have two

---

[173]See fn. 3.

[174]*Polskie prawo prywatne* (Lwów, 1910-1).

[175]"Wierna ręka czyli pokład. Lwów, 1909," *Studya nad historyą prawa polskiego,* III, pt. 2.

[176]"Stanowisko cudzoziemców w prawie litewskiem w drugiej połowie XV i w XVI wieku, 1912," *Studya nad historyą prawa polskiego,* V, pt. 2.

[177]"Dobra rodowe i nabyte w prawie litewskiem od XIV do XVI wieku" (1916), in *Studya nad historyą prawa polskiego,* VI, pt. 3.

[178]*Prawo zastawu w Zwierciadłach saskim, szwabskim i niemieckim* (Lwów, 1913).

outstanding Polish legal historians: Balzer for public law and Dąbkowski for private law.

Dąbkowski's great treatise on Polish private law was not well suited to students' use. He wrote, therefore, a shorter outline of Polish private law, first published in 1920 and later republished several times.[179]

After the death of Professor Alfred Halban, Dąbkowski also took over the chair of the history of law in Western Europe (Germany and France). His teaching load was heavy; he taught the history of Polish private law five hours weekly, and the history of law in Western Europe an additional five hours weekly. In addition, he conducted two two-hour seminars.

His publishing activity decreased slightly in the twenties and thirties. He wrote at that time more on the holdings of Provincial Archives, concentrating on such subjects as judicial records and the organization of the judiciary, the bar, and law clerks in the eastern provinces of Poland in the eighteenth century and earlier. The list of his publications in this field is too long to be included here, but two titles should be cited as examples: *Old Court Records of Lwów*,[180] and the *Catalogue of Old Polish Court Records of the Ruthenian and Belz Provinces Held by the State Archives in Lwów*.[181]

Dąbkowski also published a number of contributions to the history of social and economic conditions, such as *Economic Conditions of the Territory of Halicz in the Fifteenth Century*,[182] and *National Conditions in the Area of Sanok in the Fifteenth Century*.[183] His interest in the research on the past of the territory in which he lived, was very broad. He contributed also an article on the Wallachian law in old Poland.[184]

The number of Dąbkowski's publications was impressive. In 1927 the Historico-Legal Students' Society in Lwów published a Festschrift to commemorate thirty years of scholastic activity of the beloved profes-

---

[179] *Zarys polskiego prawa prywatnego.*

[180] "Księgi sądowe Lwowskie w dawnej Polsce" (1937), in *Studia nad historią prawa polskiego*, XVI, pt. 1.

[181] "Katalog dawnych aktów sądowych polskich województwa ruskiego i bełzkiego przechowywanych w Archiwum Państwowym we Lwowie" (1937), in *Studia nad historią prawa polskiego*, XXII, pt. 1.

[182] *Stosunki gospodarcze ziemi halickiej w XV wieku.*

[183] *Stosunki narodowóściowe ziemi sanockiej w XV wieku.*

[184] "Wołosi i prawo wołoskie w dawnej Polsce," in *Studia historyczne ku czci Stanisława Kutrzeby*, I (1938), pp. 105-8.

sor.[185] A list of titles of Dąbkowski's publications to 1927 fills pages 519-81 of the Festschrift. At that time Dąbkowski was only fifty years old.

Dąbkowski was not only a prolific writer himself; he was responsible for the interest in research of a number of younger legal historians. In 1925 he founded a special series, *Pamiętnik historyczno-prawny* ("Historico-Legal Memoirs") for publication of the works of younger scholars. Thirteen volumes of contributions by seventeen authors were published prior to 1939.

Dąbkowski also founded and edited a historico-legal periodical under the title *Przewodnik historyczno-prawny* ("Historico-Legal Guide"). Between 1930 and 1939 five volumes were published, with contributions not only in Polish but also in other Slavic languages, as well as in French and German. Two of his brilliant former students, Karol Koranyi and Jan Adamus, served as co-editors.

Dąbkowski was a long-time Secretary General of the Learned Society in Lwów.[186] Balzer was the President of this society. After Balzer's death, Dąbkowski wrote a book about his life and activity.[187]

The seminars conducted by Dąbkowski were crowded. Both the subjects he taught were first-year subjects, and Dąbkowski was too kind and too polite to deny admission to anybody. As the result, the seminars had the appearance of large classes. But a natural selection worked well in this case. Only the best students continued as seminar members in the next year. Some of them (at least nine) later became noted scholars, such as Koranyi (who died recently as a professor in Warsaw), Adamus, Hejnosz, and Sreniowski.

Dąbkowski was Dean of the Law Faculty in Lwów in the twenties. He was an active member of the Czech Academy of Arts and Sciences in Prague and a corresponding member of the Polish Academy of Arts and Sciences and the Bulgarian Academy in Sofia. He had an honorary Doctor's degree from the University of Bratislava. The Ukrainian Shevchenko Scientific Society in Lwów made him an active member for his valuable contributions to the history of Galicia; he was one of only two Polish legal scholars distinguished in this way.[188]

Dąbkowski was a quiet scholar — very serious and modest, and almost shy. He was not such an outstanding lecturer as Makarewicz. In his

---

[185]*Pamiętnik trzydziestolecia pracy naukowej prof. Dr. Przemysława Dąbkowskiego, 1897-1927, wydany staraniem Kółka Historyczno-Prawnego Słuchaczów Uniwersytetu Jana Kazimierza* (Lwów, 1927).

[186]Towarzystwo Naukowe we Lwowie.

[187]*Oswald Balzer; Życie i dzieła* (Lwów, 1934).

[188]The other was Balzer.

speaking engagements he preferred to have the text before his eyes, carefully prepared ahead of time, even when it was only a very brief address.

Under this unsmiling and not colorful facade a warm heart was hidden. He liked students, and students liked him, not only for his leniency during examinations, but for his tact, helpfulness, and absolute fairness. He had never any personal enemies. When the Soviets came to Lwów in September 1939, Dąbkowski remained, and soon was appointed Professor of History of State and Law. He taught during the years 1939-41 and again after 1944.

He died in Lwów on December 18, 1950, the greatest authority on the history of Polish private law. Due to his modesty, Dąbkowski was not known outside the group of legal historians. He wrote almost exclusively in Polish,[189] and this fact is also responsible for his limited reputation in the Western world.

Writings on Dąbkowski:
Karol Koranyi, "Przemysław Dąbkowski, 1877-1950; wspomnienie pośmiertne," *Czasopismo Prawno-Historyczne,* III (1951), 474-6.

Pamiętnik trzydziestolecia pracy naukowej prof. Dr. Przemysława Dąbkowskięgo, 1897-1927 (Lwów, 1927).

KAROL LUTOSTAŃSKI (1880-1939)

Karol Lutostański was born in Radom, near Warsaw, on January 13, 1880. At the end of the nineteenth century Warsaw had more lawyers than any other city in Czarist Russia, including the capital, St. Petersburg. Lutostański followed the prevailing trend and chose law as his profession. While a student in Warsaw, he participated in the compilation of the Polish legal bibliography later published by Suligowski. After graduation in 1904, Lutostański undertook a study trip to Leipzig, Berlin, and Paris. He concentrated mainly on the law of domestic relations, a specialty to which he remained faithful for life.

Back in Warsaw he practiced law, at the same time doing legal research and contributing to legal periodicals. He began his close association with the *Gazeta Sadowa Warszawska* ("Warsaw Judicial Journal") by writing articles, notes, and reviews; later he became a member of the editorial board. Newly returned from the stimulating trip abroad and not yet overburdened by professional and civic duties, Lutostański published a

---

[189]As one of few exceptions an informative note in French may be cited: "Les codes Napoléon en Pologne," *Revue des Études Napoléoniennes,* XXXV (1935), 362-5.

series of longer articles of permanent value on such subjects as the nature of woman's rights[190] and the nature of a husband's authority,[191] and on inheritance by a surviving spouse.[192] This last contribution triggered considerable debate because of the ambiguous construction of pertinent provisions of the Polish Civil Code of 1825 and the Napoleonic Code.

One of his first independent research contributions was a study of private and public elements in civil procedure.[193] Lutostański's best known work is, however, a book on betrothal – a study in the field of marriage law – published in Warsaw in 1907.[194] Three years later came a study on the influence of wedding form on the validity of marriage according to Catholic canon law.[195]

Shortly before the outbreak of the World War I, Lutostański founded, in cooperation with Rundstein and Nagórski, a quarterly publication, *Themis Polska* ("Polish Themis"). This was the revival of an old Warsaw periodical defunct since 1830. Eight volumes of the new series were published before 1918. Nine more bulky volumes, edited by Lutostański before World War II, contained many valuable contributions.

During World War I, Lutostański stayed mainly in Switzerland. Anticipating great historical events, he worked feverishly on a collection of basic documents and sources of information about Poland. As the result of his work, two volumes of documents were published: *Les partages de la Pologne et la lutte pour l'indépendance*[196] and *Régime politique et administratif dans la Pologne prussienne.*[197] These two volumes of documents were very useful to the members of the Polish delegation to the Peace Conference. Lutostański translated both the Treaty of Versailles and the Treaty of St. Germain-en-Laye into Polish. Well aware of scarcity of good legal textbooks in the Polish language during the first years of independence, he translated the well-known treatise by Esmein, *Eléments de droit constitutionnel français et comparé.* This treatise was used as a textbook on constitutional law by students in Poland.

[190]"Charakter praw kobiety."

[191]"Charakter władzy mężowskiej."

[192]"O spadku po współmałżonku."

[193]*Z badań nad pierwiastkiem prywatnym i publicznym w procesie cywilnym* (Warsaw, 1907).

[194]*Zaręczyny, studium z zakresu prawa małżeńskiego* (Warsaw, 1907).

[195]*O wpływie formy na ważność małżeństwa w katolickiem prawie kanonicznem* (Warsaw, 1910).

[196]Lausanne, 1918.

[197]Paris, 1918.

Following the organization of the University of Warsaw, Lutostański became a member of its faculty in 1919. He taught civil law, first as an associate and soon thereafter as a full professor. His lectures, published in several editions,[198] were used by students as examination summaries. Lutostański three times was elected Dean of the Warsaw Law Faculty, and served in this capacity in 1929-30, 1932-3, and 1934-5. Only one who realizes the enormous number of law students (more than a thousand) at the Warsaw University between the two world wars can properly appreciate the amount of work required for running such a school.

But Lutostański was not only a professor and dean. He had the rare capability to work well in several time-consuming and responsible positions at the same time. For two decades he was President of the Mianowski Foundation for the Advancement of Learning — an unpaid position in which Lutostański helped to publish books on various branches of science and to distribute grants for research.

Living and working in the capital city, he was more fully exposed to responsible assignments of national prominence than his colleagues at other universities. Lutostański was vice president of the Society for the Protection of Authors' Rights, a member of the *Trybunał Kompetencyjny* (Polish Jurisdictional Tribunal), president of the Lawyers' Association in Warsaw, and a member of the Warsaw Learned Society.

During years spent abroad, mainly in Switzerland, Lutostański established many friendly contacts with foreign personalities. His election to the presidency of the Polish Committee of the International Institute of Intellectual Cooperation in Paris enabled him to continue his previous activity as an unofficial ambassador of Polish culture. He was able to utilize his fluency in foreign languages as well as his personal charm when he played host to a convention of the International Institute in Warsaw. Shortly before World War II, Lutostański received an honorary Doctor's degree of the University of Lille, in France.

He was appointed director of the Legislative Department in the Ministry of Justice in 1935. Without giving up his professorship, Lutostański accepted the appointment because he was at that time also deeply involved in legislative work, especially the drafting of bills,which he liked. He gained considerable experience in legislating as a member of the Polish Codification Commission, of which he was later vice-president. As an expert in the law of domestic relations, Lutostański acted as reporter of the Subcommittee on Marriage Law. After years of work, a draft marriage law was prepared, mainly as the result of Lutostański's efforts. He

[198]*Prawo cywilne obowiązujące w b. Królestwie Polskiem, repetytorium egzaminacyjne* (4th ed.: Warsaw, 1935).

published the reasons for the draft of marriage law passed by the Codification Commission in 1929.[199]

The draft marriage law was submitted to the government, but it was never discussed during legislative debates because of the strong opposition by the hierarchy of the Catholic church. As the reporter of the Subcommittee on Marriage Law, Lutostański had to deal with three fundamental problems: (1) whether marriage law in independent Poland was to be civil or religious; (2) if marriage law was to be civil in principle, how far the denominational element should be admitted; and (3) to what degree, if any, divorce might be permitted.

It should be remembered that Poland inherited in 1918 no fewer than four different sets of marriage laws. One was of completely lay in character, without any religious elements (German); however, the three others were denominational. Marriage cases were under the jurisdiction of ecclesiastical courts in the formerly Russian section of Poland, while state courts had exclusive jurisdiction in the formerly Austrian and German sections. The procedure of moving from one part of the country to the other, or formally changing religions to avoid the harsh limitations to which members of certain denominations were subjected, created chaotic and highly undesirable conditions.

Lutostański maintained that only the state could bring uniformity and order into this highly complicated issue. He proposed a state marriage law in Poland, uniform for members of all religions. Marriage before a civil official was to be introduced as the rule, but a religious ceremony was also to be permitted. Even the religious form alone was to be accepted as legally valid, provided that a civil official issued a marriage certificate on the basis of a statement by the priest that the parties had been married in a religious ceremony. The subcommittee also proposed the introduction of divorces in specific and rather exceptional circumstances, with obligatory conciliation proceedings before the granting of a divorce, and with full protection of children's rights. Because of clerical opposition, this draft did not become law during Lutostański's lifetime. Another member of the Subcommittee on Marriage Law, Zygmunt Nagórski, reported the meetings of the subcommittee as a most pleasant and stimulating experience. Lutostański, as the reporter, was always perfectly prepared for the meetings, with materials on corresponding legal institutions in foreign legal systems and statistical data and judicial decisions ready at hand. He defended his conclusions, and most of the decisions of the subcommittee were made unanimously.[200]

[199]*Zasady projektu prawa małżeńskiego uchwalonego przez Komisję Kodyfikacyjną w dniu 28. maja 1929* (Warsaw, 1931).

[200]Zygmunt Nagórski, "Karol Lutostański," in *Ludzie mego czasu* (Paris, 1964), p. 152.

World War II terminated abruptly Lutostański's fruitful and many-sided activity. He fell as one of its first victims. He was killed during the bombardment of Warsaw by the Germans in September 1939.

Writings about Lutostański:
W. Czachórski, and J. Wasilkowski, "Wspomnienie o profesorze UW Karolu Lutostańskim," in *Państwo i Prawo*, II (1947) No. 12, pp. 57-59.
Zygmunt Nagórski, "Karol Lutostański," in *Ludzie mego czasu* (Paris, 1964), pp. 145-61.

RAFAŁ TAUBENSCHLAG (1881-1958)

Rafal Taubenschlag, an "internationally recognized scholar in the field of ancient legal history and in particular a pioneer in the domain of juristic papyrology,"[201] owes his remarkable popularity in the Western scholarly world to the fact that his writings are mainly in English, French, German, or Italian, rather than in his native Polish.

He was born in Przemyśl on May 6, 1881 and studied law at the Jagiellonian University in Cracow in the years 1899-1904. There he was encouraged by Professors Zoll, Sr., and Wróblewski to concentrate on the history of ancient law as his field of specialization. After earning his doctorate, he continued his studies in Leipzig under Professor Mitteis, one of the few scholars in the world specializing in the law of juristic papyri. Taubenschlag's seminar paper of Ptolemaic arbitrators, written in Leipzig, was published in 1907.[202] In the same year an article written before his trip to Leipzig was also published by a leading legal periodical. Its subject was the history of the contract of deposit in Roman law.[203]

Taubenschlag tried unsuccessfully to join the law Faculty in Cracow, submitting his published study on the courts of Laocrits.[204] He applied again, presenting this time a study on the history of earnest money in Roman law,[205] but again without success. Not discouraged, Taubenschlag

[201] Adolf Berger, "Rafał Taubenschlag," *Polish Review*, III (1958), No. 3, p. 3.

[202] "Die Ptolemäischen Schiedsrichter und ihre Bedeutung für die Rezeption des griechischen Privatrechts in Aegypten," *Archiv für Papyrusforschung*, IV, 1-46.

[203] "Zur Geschichte des Hinterlegungsvertrages im römischen Recht," *Zeitschrift für das Privat- und öffentliche Recht der Gegenwart*, XXXV (1907).

[204] "Sądy Laokrytów", *Przegląd prawa i administracji*, XXXI (1906), 845-904.

[205] "Historya zadatku w prawie rzymskiem," *Rozprawy Akademii Umiejętności*, Wydział historyczno-filozoficzny, XXIX (1910), 1-59.

wrote a book on the Roman and Greek law of guardian and ward.[206] This time his teacher and sponsor, Professor Wróblewski, declared at a meeting of the Law Faculty that if Taubenschlag were rejected once more, he — Wróblewski — would immediately quit the faculty and open an attorney's office in Cracow with Taubenschlag as his partner. The threat worked.[207] Taubenschlag was admitted as docent of Roman law in 1913.

World War I began the following year, and Taubenschlag served for some time with military courts but eventually managed to resume his research activity during the war. His book on criminal law in Greek-Egyptian law appeared in 1916.[208] In the same year he also published his first article in the *Zeitschrift der Savigny-Stiftung für Rechtsgeschichte*, about *patria potestas* in the law of papyri.[209] At this early time Taubenschlag also became interested in Polish legal history. His first study in this field was on Jakób Przyłuski, a Polish Romanist of the sixteenth century.[210] Appointment to associate professorship came in 1918. After presentation of his next study on Roman law at the time of Diocletian,[211] Taubenschlag became a Professor of Roman Law in 1921.

The two decades between the world wars were his happiest. In connection with his teaching, he translated, in co-operation with W. Kozubski, the well-known German textbook on Roman law written by Sohm.[212] A few years later Taubenschlag published his own textbook of Roman law.[213] He also compiled a source book of Roman private law for the use of his seminar members.[214]

[206] *Vormundschaftliche Studien, Beiträge zur Geschichte des römischen und griechischen Vormundschaftsrechts* (Leipzig-Berlin, 1913).

[207] Adolf Berger, *ibid.*, p. 4.

[208] *Das Strafrecht im Rechte der Papyri* (Leipzig, 1913).

[209] "Patria potestas im Rechte der Papyri," XXXVII (1916) 177-230.

[210] "Jakób Przyłuski, polski romanista XVI w.," *Rozprawy Akademii Umiejętności*, Wydział Historyczno-filozoficzny, XXXVI (1918), 232-76.

[211] "Das römische Privatrecht zur Zeit Diokletians," *Bulletin de l'Académie Polonaise des Sciences et Lettres* (Cracow, 1919-20) pp. 141-281.

[212] Rudolf Sohm, *Instytucje, historia i system rzymskiego prawa prywatnego* (Warsaw, 1925).

[213] *Instytucje i historia rzymskiego prawa prywatnego* (Cracow, 1934). Later editions were published in Warsaw under the title, *Historia i instytucje rzymskiego prawa prywatnego* (2nd ed., 1938; 3rd ed., 1945: 4th ed., 1948).

[214] *Wybór źródeł do rzymskiego prawa prywatnego* (Cracow, 1931); 2nd ed., Warsaw, 1946.

One of his more remarkable studies is "The History of the Reception of Roman Law in Egypt."[215] Based on extensive papyrological documentation, this study was acclaimed as a new and significant contribution to the history of Roman law in imperial provinces. A similar study on the reception of Greek private law in Egypt followed.[216] Taubenschlag prepared during the reviewed period no fewer than fifteen articles for the *Pauly-Wissowa Realenzyklopädie der Klassischen Altertumswissenschaften* ("Pauly-Wissowa Encyclopedia of Classical Antiquities").

During this period he wrote further studies on the history of Polish law, among them works on Polish civil procedure in the eighteenth and nineteenth centuries,[217] Polish medieval criminal law,[218] and Roman-Byzantine influences on the Second Lithuanian Statute.[219]

Even before 1939, Taubenschlag showed his keen interest in the law of Graeco-Roman Egypt, as evidenced by his numerous publications in this field. As the result of events connected with World War II, he concentrated on this area during the last fifteen years of his life. Taubenschlag was fortunate to escape to France before the German invasion of Poland. A scholar of international renown, he was appointed Professor of Roman Law at the University of Aix-en-Provence on the very day of his arrival. One year later, however, he was compelled to seek refuge beyond the ocean. He went to New York, where he found employment first with the New School for Social Research and later with Columbia University as a Research Professor of Ancient Civilizations. With the assistance of Professor William Westermann, Taubenschlag found favorable research conditions which allowed him to concentrate all his time and effort on an English version of his great book on the law of Graeco-Roman Egypt in the light of papyri, 332 B.C. to 640 A.D.[220] This was only the first part of a planned treatise dealing with private law. A second volume, devoted to constitutional and administrative law, was published four years

[215] "Die Geschichte der Rezeption des römischen Privatrechts in Aegypten," in *Studi Bonfante*, I (Milan, 1930), 367-440.

[216] "Die Geschichte der Rezeption des griechischen Privatrechts in Aegypten," in *Atti del IV Congresso internazionale di papirologia* (Florence, 1935), pp. 259-81.

[217] "Proces polski XIII i XIV wieku do Statutów Kazimierza Wielkiego," in *Studia nad historią prawa polskiego*, X (Lwów, 1927) pt. 3, pp. 367-469.

[218] "Prawo karne polskiego średniowiecza," in *Studia nad historią prawa polskiego*, XIV, (Lwów, 1934), pt. 3, pp. 245-340.

[219] "Wpływy rzymsko-bizantyńskie w drugim Statucie Litewskim," in *Studia nad historią prawa polskiego*, XIV, (Lwów, 1933), pt. 2, pp. 210-44; translated into Italian in 1937.

[220] New York, 1944.

later.[221] A revised and enlarged edition of both appeared in one sizable volume in Warsaw in 1955. This is a fundamental work, well known all around the world.

During his stay in the United States, Taubenschlag did not limit himself exclusively to scholarly work. He was also a skillful organizer, and as such he strongly supported the idea of creating in America the Polish Institute of Arts and Sciences, which was established in New York.

Taubenschlag returned to Poland in 1947 and took over the Chair of Roman and Ancient Laws at the University of Warsaw. A Papyrological Institute was created in Warsaw soon thereafter, and Taubenschlag was entrusted with the direction of its legal research department.

He wrote scores of publications in the last decade of his life. They covered not only Roman and Hellenistic, but also Greek, Babylonian, and Syrian law. By that time an eminent expert in the field, he published an introduction to the law of papyri[222] and prepared an entirely new Roman law textbook.[223] He did not live to see his chapter on the influence of Roman law in Poland published in *Ius Romanum medii aevi* in 1962.[224]

Taubenschlag contributed a great many writings to domestic and foreign legal and historical periodicals, as well as to collections of essays published in honor of prominent legal scholars: Cornil (1926), Abraham (1930), Bonfante (1930), Jaworski (1931), Riccobono (1932), Wilcken (1933), Albertoni (1935), Zoll (1935), Piniński (1935), Stoicescu (1940), de Visscher (1949), Sinko (1951), Schultz (1951), Arangio-Ruiz (1952), Koschaker (1953), Paoli (1955), and Calderini (1957).

It is no surprise that a Festschrift in commemoration of his seventy-fifth birthday and fifty years of work in the academic field, published in Wrocław in 1956,[225] consisted of three volumes, with contributions by some ninety scholars. The first volume includes articles by thirty-two leading foreign legal historians, written in English, French, Russian, German, and Italian. Few other Polish scholars have attained such great international acclaim. A bibliography of Taubenschlag's publications (1904-55) was printed in the first volume of this Festschrift.

During his stay in New York, Taubenschlag began to publish a new periodical with the title *Journal of Juristic Papyrology*. After his return to Poland he transferred the periodical to Warsaw and continued as

[221]Warsaw, 1948.

[222]*Archives d'histoire du droit oriental,* 1952, pp. 279-376.

[223]*Rzymskie prawo prywatne na tle praw antycznych* (Warsaw, 1955; 2nd ed. 1969).

[224]"Einflüsse des römischen Rechts in Polen," in *Ius Romanum medii aevi* (Milan), V (1962), pt. 8, pp. 1-26.

[225]*Symbolae Raphaeli Taubenschlag dedicatae* (*Eos*, XLVIII).

editor-in-chief. Warsaw, which never before had been a noted center of papyrological studies, now became world capital of juristic papyrology. The *Journal* is published in English under the sponsorship of the Polish Academy — an impressive example of what the talent and administrative ability of one great man can accomplish. Taubenschlag was also for years a co-editor of *Archives d'Histoire du Droit Oriental* (Brussels).

He liked to attend international congresses and to deliver papers. Sometimes he presided at section or even plenary meetings. His contributions may be found in the *Proceedings of the International Juridical Congress* (Rome, 1934); the *Proceedings of the Fourth International Congress of Papyrology* (Florence, 1935); the proceedings of the fifth such congress at Oxford, 1937; and the *Proceedings of the International Congress of Roman Law and Legal History* (Verona, 1948).

Many honors were bestowed on this outstanding scholar. He was Dean of the Law Faculty of Jagiellonian University in 1929-30 and again in 1935-6. The Polish Academy of Arts and Sciences in Cracow elected him a corresponding member in 1927. He became a titular and ultimately an active member of the Polish Academy in Warsaw in the fifties. He was also a member of foreign academies in Bologna (following 1935) and in Turin (following 1937). In 1938 he became a member of the *Société Jean Bodin pour l'histoire Comparative des Institutions* in Brussels. He received an honorary Doctor of Laws degree at Warsaw University in 1950.

In order to preserve for posterity the great number of Taubenschlag's minor but nonetheless valuable contributions scattered through dozens of serial publications and collective works written during the fifty years of his scholarly activity, the Polish Academy in Warsaw arranged for a re-issue of his sixty-six studies originally published in languages other than Polish. Two volumes, numbering almost 1500 pages, were published under the title *Opera minora* in Warsaw in 1959. The great Romanist Arangio-Ruiz wrote the preface in Italian.[226]

Taubenschlag, who carefully scrutinized tens of thousands of ancient documents during his lifetime, suffered a serious eye disease toward the end of his days and was almost blind in the last years. His assistants and others read for him what he needed and what interested him. He died in Warsaw in June 25, 1958, and was buried in Cracow.

Writings on Taubenschlag:

Adolf Berger, "Rafał Taubenschlag," *Polish Review,* III (1958) No. 3, 3-11.

Józef Modrzejewski, "Rafał Taubenschlag," *Nauka Polska,* 1956, No. 4, pp. 132-7.

[226]This preface was later reprinted as an obituary in *IVRA, Rivista internazionale di diritto Romano e antico* (Naples), X (1959), 146-8.

Waclaw Osuchowski, "In memoriam Raphael Taubenschlag, 1881-1958" (in English), *Journal of Juristic Papyrology*, XIII (1961), 7-15.

− − − "Prawo rzymskie na tle prawa antycznego: Rafał Taubenschlag," in *Studia z dziejów Wydziału Prawa Uniwersytetu Jagiellońskiego,* ed. Michal Patkaniowski, (Cracow, 1964) pp. 297-308. Taubenschlag's writings, 1904-1955, compiled by J. Modrzejewski, are listed in *Symbolae Raphaeli Taubenschlag dedicatae*, pp. 1-16.

ROMAN LONGCHAMPS DE BERIER (1883-1941)

"This coming year I will present to you the Polish law of obligations, just enacted. After more than one hundred years the first major piece of Polish civil legislation has become the law of the land. Please keep this in mind when attending classes and later preparing for examinations." These were the words of Professor of Civil Law Roman Longchamps de Berier in the last days of September 1933, as he started his classes at the School of Law, University of Lwów. The first major pièce of Polish civil legislation in more than one hundred years was the *Kodeks zobowiązań* (Code of Obligations) of September 30, 1933. Professor Longchamps was the chief reporter of the law of obligations on the Polish Codification Commission.

Roman Longchamps was born in Lwów on August 9, 1883, the son of a physician. He attended schools in his native city and earned a Doctor's degree in law at the University of Lwów in 1906. Immediately after graduation, he started his legal career in the Lwów branch of the Office of the Solicitor General. A position with this office was coveted by many lawyers at that time. It gave an opportunity for the best civil law training imaginable. In addition, it was a distinct honor to serve as a government attorney. A number of future professors of civil law and high judges had such positions as a starting point. Daily contact with complex legal cases stimulated research and writing activity. Longchamps published his first legal article in 1907.[227] A few years later appeared his valuable monographic study on juristic persons.[228] After a critical review of prevailing theories, he chose the so-called real construction and leaned toward a somewhat modified version of Ihering's definition of subjective rights.

[227]"Zaufanie w zewnętrzny stan rzeczy," *Przegląd Prawa i Administracji*, 1907.

[228]"Studia nad istotą osoby prawniczej," *Przegląd Prawa i Administracji*, 1911, 1912, 1913, and as a reprint in 1911.

Bibliographical work was not difficult for Longchamps. He compiled a Polish legal bibliography for the years 1911 and 1912,[229] continuing and supplementing in this way the well-known bibliography of Suligowski. In connection with the enactment of the first two amendments to the one-hundred-year-old Austrian Civil Code, Longchamps published critical remarks. But the field particularly close to his interests dealt with the problem of warranty, and his habilitation study (1916)[230] was devoted to this problem. During his tenure with the Solicitor General's Office, Longchamps spent one year in Berlin, where he studied with Josef Kohler and Theodor Kipp.

After habilitation, Longchamps taught civil law in Lwów, first as a part-time docent only. Appointed an associate professor of civil law in 1920, Longchamps relinquished his duties at the Solicitor General's Office and devoted full time to teaching and research. Two years later he became a full professor.

There were two professors on the Lwów faculty for the subject of civil law. During the first years after his appointment, Longchamps was the junior professor, Ernest Till (1846-1926) being the senior. After 1926, Longchamps became the senior professor. As junior professor of civil law came Kazimierz Przybyłowski, who moved after 1944 to the Jagiellonian University in Cracow. Longchamps maintained the most cordial relations with both colleagues, in spite of the significant differences in age.

The period between 1922 and 1939 was the most prolific in his life. He taught Austrian civil law, then still in force in Galicia. From 1933 on, he taught the Polish law of contracts and torts, and for many years he also taught French civil law, along with labor law and mining law in the thirties. Between the two world wars Longchamps also served on the Law Faculty of the Catholic University in Lublin. He commuted, mainly in the spring at the time of yearly examinations. Volumes of duplicated materials, traditional study tools at the Lwów and Lublin Law Schools, were by-products of his teaching activity. His classes often required advance preparation on the part of students, since his precise but highly technical language was not always easy to follow. Especially during seminar meetings for advanced students, he seemed to take such a high level of knowledge for granted that some participants had a hard time properly comprehending some passages. But Longchamps never tried to convince anybody that law, and particularly civil law, was an easy subject.

In 1922 Longchamps published an introduction to the study of civil

[229]*Polska bibliografia prawnicza za lata 1911-1912* (Lwów, 1913).

[230]*Rękojmia z powodu wad i braków a obowiązek świadczenia* (Lwów, 1916).

law.[231] This book is a treatise on a comparative basis, since it deals with legal systems prevailing in different territories of resurrected Poland. In this way an attempt was made to lay foundations for the unification of Polish law. To the same period belong outlines of Austrian civil law and French civil law in force in different parts of Poland, published in the *Polish Legal Encyclopedia* in 1925. A little later, his work on the conclusion and dissolution of marriage according to laws in force in Poland was published.[232]

After 1922 Longchamps participated actively in the codification of the Polish law of contracts and torts. Working first under the direction of Ernest Till, he became the chief reporter of this branch of civil law on the Polish Codification Commission after Till's death in 1926. He contributed a number of articles on the law of contracts and torts to Polish and foreign legal periodicals, as well as to *mélanges* published in honor of Władysław Abraham, Leon Piniński, and Edouard Lambert.[233] He presented papers at several congresses and conferences. His *magnum opus*, however, was the annotated draft of the Polish law of obligations.[234] He also wrote a voluminous textbook on the law of obligations, finished in 1938[235] and reissued in a second edition in 1939. Its distinctions are its clear organization and precise language. This great book is used even now, despite the fact that the Code of Obligations of 1933 has not been in force as a separate statute since the enactment of the Polish Civil Code of 1964.

Few professors attended so many conferences and congresses with such success. After 1912 no Polish conference of legal scholars took place without his active participation. Longchamps also attended such congresses abroad as the International Congresses of Comparative Law in the Hague in 1932 and 1937. In 1932 he was the general reporter of a section of the law of contracts, at which time he presented a report on the general rules on the formation and non-performance of contracts. In 1937 he presented a report on liability for damages caused without intent in Polish law. He was the general reporter on this problem and the chairman of

[231] *Wstęp do nauki prawa cywilnego ze szczególnym uwzględnieniem kodeksów obowiązujących w b. Królestwie Kongresowym, Małopolsce i W. Ks. Poznańskim* (Lublin, 1922).

[232] *Zawarcie i rozwiązanie małżeństwa podług prawa obowiązującego w Polsce* (Lublin, 1928).

[233] "L'influence du droit public sur le contrat de travail dans le droit civil polonais," in *Introduction a l'étude de droit comparé; Recueil d'études en l'honneur d'Edouard Lambert* (Paris, 1938), III, 544-58.

[234] *Uzasadnienie do kodeksu zobowiązań.*

[235] *Zobowiązania* (Lwów, 1938).

another session. He took also part in the International Legal Week (*Semaine International de Droit*) in Paris in 1937, where he presented a paper.[236] In 1935 he lectured in Paris and Lyon on the new Polish law of obligations. He was instrumental in the organization of a Polish-French alliance in 1937, and served as the chairman of the Polish group of this alliance.

Longchamps was also interested in closer legal cooperation among Slavic peoples. He took an active part in the first congress of lawyers of Slavic countries in Bratislava in 1933. During the congress he delivered the key paper on the unification of the law of obligations of Slavic countries.

Longchamps was an active member of the Polish Learned Society in Lwów, and a corresponding member of the Polish Academy of Arts and Sciences from 1931 on. He worked for three decades in the Lawyers' Society in Lwów, first as an ordinary member, and from 1938 on as its president. For twenty years he edited the periodical *Przegląd Prawa i Administracji* ("Legal and Administrative Review"), first as co-editor and later as editor-in-chief. He wrote some of the articles and many of the book reviews published in this periodical.

The Law Faculty of Lwów University elected him four times to the deanship (1923-4 and 1929-32). He was Prorector of the University from 1934 to 1938. On September 1, 1939 — the very day of the beginning of World War II — he became the Rector of the Lwów University under the most difficult conditions. He decided to stay in Lwów. During the first Soviet occupation of Lwów, Longchamps taught in 1940 and 1941 selected problems of the Soviet law of contracts and torts, as well as the law of contracts and torts of the Western European legal systems. In March of 1941 he presented a paper on liability for damages caused by dangerous activities according to Western European laws. The occasion was a conference organized by the Lwów Law Faculty.

As in September of 1939, Longchamps stayed in Lwów in the last days of June 1941, when the Germans invaded the Soviet Union. But this time disaster struck. He was arrested by the German police in the night of July 3, 1941, and murdered, together with his three sons, shortly thereafter.

Professor Longchamps was a man of high personal culture. Slim, of middle stature, elegant, with handsome face and graying hair, as I remember him he was the ideal university representative to an international congress. As Dean, Prorector, and later Rector of the University, he fulfilled his duties with great dignity. He was well liked by both colleagues and students for his quiet and friendly character. Tactful and helpful in his behavior, he served more than once as a trouble-shooter

---

[236]"La revision des contrats par le juge dans le droit civil polonais," *Travaux*, II, 105-20.

among less well balanced colleagues. His profound knowledge of the law of contracts and torts has been fully utilized: it has been transformed into living Polish law — a code of obligations which is still alive, albeit under a different name.

Writings about Longchamps de Berier:
Kazimierz Przybyłowski, "Ś.p. Roman Longchamps," *Państwo i Prawo*, II (1947), 64-8.
Adam Szpunar, *Nauka prawa prywatnego i procesowego w Polsce* (Cracow, 1948), p. 14.

ANTONI PERETIATKOWICZ (1884-1956)

Antoni Peretiatkowicz was born on June 13, 1884, in Boruchov, Volhynia, at that time a province within the Russian Empire. After graduation from a secondary school in Kamieniec, Podolia, he began law study at the Warsaw University, but soon moved to Lwów, and finally earned his doctorate from the Jagiellonian University in Cracow in 1909. He had the good fortune to be able to pursue his studies in Paris, Geneva, and Heidelberg. He studied under Georg Jellinek, whose fundamental work, *Allgemeine Staatslehre,* he later translated into Polish.[237] Under the impact of Jellinek's personality, Peretiatkowicz chose constitutional law and political doctrines as the main area of his specialization.

Even before his study trip Peretiatkowicz had some works published. He was recipient of a special award of the *Gazeta Sądowa Warszawska* ("Warsaw Judicial Journal") in 1908 for his work on legal philosophy and comparative method.[238] In 1908 his article on Polish philosophy of the twentieth century was published in *Archiv für Rechts — und Wirtschafts-philosophie.* The next year brought a work on the Turkish constitution.[239] During his stay abroad he prepared a short study on new trends in jurisprudence, with special emphasis on the new approach of the judge to statutory law.[240]

[237]*Ogólna nauka o państwie* ("General Doctrine of the State," originally published in 1900).

[238]*Filozofia prawa a metoda porównawcza.*

[239]*Konstytucja Turecka na tle porównawczym* (Warsaw, 1909).

[240]*Prąd nowy w prawoznawstwie, ustawa a sędzia* (1912). It was also published in German in *Zeitschrift für Privat- und öffentliches Recht der Gegenwart,* Vienna, 1913. A third edition was published in Poznań in 1922.

At an early date (1913) he wrote his penetrating study on the legal philosophy of Jean-Jacques Rousseau.[241] Since Peretiatkowicz's book concentrated on Rousseau's legal philosophy, it was a valuable addition to an enormous literature which until then had been limited mainly to the political influence of Rousseau's theory, and to its practical consequences. This book was accepted by the Law Faculty of the Jagiellonian University in the habilitation procedure, the Peretiatkowicz became a docent of legal philosophy in Cracow in 1914. During the First World War, he published an extensive review of the recent literature of legal philosophy.[242]

New universities founded in the postwar independent Polish Republic created a high demand for qualified professors. Peretiatkowicz received an invitation from the Catholic University in Lublin, where he taught as an associate professor for a few months in 1919. In April of the same year he answered a call from the new University of Poznań to organize, as a professor and dean, an entirely new legal-economic faculty. After two years of successful deanship, Peretiatkowicz became the Vice-Rector of the University in 1920-1. He combined rare abilities as an administrator, teacher, and writer. It should be added that he directed not one but two schools at the same time; he taught also at the private Higher Commercial School in Poznań from 1926 on, and was director of this school from 1930 until 1938, when the school became the State Commercial Academy. Peretiatkowicz then became the Rector of the Academy and remained in this position until September of 1939. For three years prior to World War II, Peretiatkowicz was also Rector of the University of Poznań, and in addition taught classes, wrote books, and edited the quarterly *Ruch Prawniczy i Ekonomiczny*, ("Legal and Economic Trends") – an incredible record. The quarterly had been founded by Peretiatkowicz in 1920 and was published regularly for almost twenty years. As editor-in-chief, Peretiatkowicz was responsible for twenty volumes consisting of eighty issues. A great many of his own articles, notes, and reviews were included. Suspended in 1939, this periodical resumed publication long after the end of World War II, and is now known as *Ruch Prawniczy, Ekonomiczny i Socjologiczny* ("Legal, Economic, and Sociological Trends").

Peretiatkowicz reached the peak of his activity during the decades 1919-39. He was the founder, vice-president and, from 1922 on, president of the Legal-Economic Society in Poznań.[243] In 1922 he became chairman of the Organizing Committee of the Seventh Convention of

[241]*Filozofia prawa Jana Jakóba Rousseau* (Cracow, 1913).

[242]"Literatura encyklopedii i filozofii prawa w latach ostatnich," in *Czasopismo Prawnicze i Ekonomiczne* (Cracow, 1916).

[243]Towarzystwo Prawnicze i Ekonomiczne w Poznaniu.

Polish Lawyers and Economists in Poznań. He invited to this convention, for the first time, several French legal scholars, taking advantage of foreign contacts he had made during his stay in France before World War I. Later a year rarely passed without prominent French jurists taking part in joint Polish-French conferences. The French government bestowed on Peretiatkowicz honors for fostering Polish-French intellectual cooperation.

Early in 1920 Peretiatkowicz initiated a collective work under the title *Encyclopedia of Law Prevailing in Poland.*[244] He acted as editor-in-chief of this project from 1923 to 1926, in which time five parts were published. His own contribution was a chapter on Polish constitutional law.[245] Fully aware of the significance of good reference literature in foreign languages, he wrote a booklet, *Rechts und Staatskunde des modernen Polens* in 1924. Shortly thereafter he returned to the subject he liked most: political doctrines. He wrote the *History of Political Doctrines of the Nineteenth and Twentieth Centuries*[246] and works on Kelsen's theory of law and state,[247] on the Fascist state,[248] and also on the Polish author Andrzej Frycz-Modrzewski.[249] His five minor works, scattered in various periodicals, were republished in a collective work under the title *Studia prawnicze* ("Legal Studies") in 1938.

Besides the scholarly work described above, Peretiatkowicz was the author of several legal textbooks. The numerous editions of these textbooks serve as the best evidence that he was particularly successful in this kind of writing, His *Wstęp do nauk prawnych* ("Introduction to Legal Science"), first published in 1932, had seven editions, the last one in 1949. His *Państwo współczesne* ("Modern State") had not less than nine editions between 1916 and 1948. Well known and very popular were his excellent annotated editions of the Polish Constitution of 1921.[250] Some of his textbooks were also used by departments of education for classes in the introduction to political science. Particularly popular among students was his *Outline of Administrative Law.*[251] His *Modern Encyclopedia of*

---

[244]*Encyklopedia prawa obowiązującego w Polsce* (Cracow, 1923-6).

[245]*Ustrój konstytucyjny,* in pt.1, pp. 1-37.

[246]*Historia doktryn politycznych 19 i 20 w.*

[247]*Teoria prawa i państwa Hansa Kelsena* (1938).

[248]*Państwo faszystowskie* (Poznań, 1927).

[249]In *Życie i myśl.*

[250]*Konstytucja Rzeczypospolitej Polskiej i ważniejsze ustawy polityczne i administracyjne.*

[251]*Podstawowe pojęcia prawa administracyjnego* (2nd ed.: Poznań, 1947).

Political Life[252] was designed as a reference book for Polish readers. Under Peretiatkowicz's editorship, a reference book on modern Polish culture was published in 1932.[253]

After World War II Peretiatkowicz compiled the Constitution and more important public laws into a collection under the title, *Political Code.*[254] His last scholarly contribution, written shortly before his death, was *The General Principles of Law as a Source of International Law.*[255] The author was compelled to rewrite this work several times and condense it in order to pass the state censorship. His activity after World War II was merely a remote reflection of the glorious interwar period.

Peretiatkowicz died in Poznań on December 18, 1956. Two months later, the University arranged a solemn meeting in memory of the man who served the university so well for thirty-seven years. The Dean of the Law Faculty, Kolańczyk, as well as Professors Rosiński, Górski, and Pospieszalski delivered speeches. The broad scope of the Peretiatkowicz's activity was outlined, and his personal traits – tact, understanding and ability to cooperate in a team effort – were stressed.

Writings about Peretiatkowicz:
"Akademia żałobna dla uczczenia pamięci prof. dra Antoniego Peretiatkowicza," *Ruch Prawniczy i Ekonomiczny*, 1958, pp. 325-34.

Marian Pospieszalski, "Antoni Peretiatkowicz," *Sprawozdanie Poznańskiego Towarzystwa Przyjaciół Nauk,* 1956, pp. 112-4.

[252]*Współczesna encyklopedia życia politycznego z uwzflędnieniem życia gospodarczego. Podręczny informator dla czytelników gazet.* Published in three editions.

[253]*Współczesna kultura polska: nauka, literatura, sztuka, życiorysy uczonych, literatów i artystow* (Poznań, 1932).

[254]*Kodeks polityczny: Konstytucja marcowa i ważniejsze ustawy polityczne* (Warsaw, 1946).

[255]*Ogólne zasady prawa jako źródło prawa międzynarodowego, a tendencje kosmopolityczne* (Poznań, 1956).

476